VALERII PERELESHIN

Life of a Silkworm

Valerii Pereleshin, portrait by Humberto Marques Passos, Rio de Janeiro, 10.6.1982. Used with the kind permission of the artist.

OLGA BAKICH

Valerii Pereleshin

Life of a Silkworm

UNIVERSITY OF TORONTO PRESS
Toronto Buffalo London

Toronto Buffalo London
www.utppublishing.com

ISBN 978-1-4426-4892-0 (cloth)

Library and Archives Canada Cataloguing in Publication

Bakich, Ol'ga Mikhaĭlovna, author
Valerii Pereleshin : life of a silkworm / Olga Bakich.

Includes bibliographical references and index.
ISBN 978-1-4426-4892-0 (bound)

1. Pereleshin, Valeriĭ. 2. Authors, Exiled – China – Biography. 3. Authors, Exiled – Brazil – Biography. 4. Poets, Russian – 20th century – Biography. I. Title.

PG3476.P4145Z385 2015   891.71'4   C2014-908441-2

University of Toronto Press acknowledges the financial assistance to its publishing program of the Canada Council for the Arts and the Ontario Arts Council, an agency of the Government of Ontario.

University of Toronto Press acknowledges the financial support of the Government of Canada through the Canada Book Fund for its publishing activities.

Contents

Acknowledgments

I have loved Valerii Pereleshin's poetry since the days of my Harbin youth. Many years later in Toronto I learned that he was alive and living in Brazil and wrote to him, and we corresponded for the last six years of his life. I greatly appreciated his letters and the many poems, typescripts, photographs, books, and various materials and mementoes which he sent me. Regrettably, at the time I had no plans to write his biography; that idea came much later. I hope that he would have liked this book.

A large debt of gratitude goes to all those who generously entrusted me with Pereleshin's letters, poems, photographs, and materials. Olga Tourkoff let me acquire a large collection of Pereleshin's letters to her mother, Mary Custis Vezey, to Iu.V. Kruzenshtern, and to several other people, as well as materials from their archives. Nina Fouchier (Mokrinskaia) kindly sent me Pereleshin's letters to her, as well as other relevant materials, and the same kindness and trust were shown by my parents M.A. and T.P. Bakich, my aunt V.V. Bakich, the Chernishev family and their daughter Elena, V.A. Leonard (Leont'ev), V.A. Sinkevich, M.S. Struve, Nora and Efim Krouk, Ingrid Drizul', Lidiia Iastrebova, and Nataliia Gracheva-Mel'nikova. Professor Simon Karlinsky and Peter Carleton generously sent me photocopies of Pereleshin's letters and materials from Professor Karlinsky's archive and encouraged me in my work. V.V. Shkurkin let me photocopy and publish Pereleshin's letters to his uncle, P.P. Lapiken. V.A. Slobodchikov sent me photocopies of Pereleshin's letters to him and other materials and shared his impressions and thoughts in his correspondence with me. Dr Richard Davies at the Brotherton Collection, Special Collections, Leeds University Library, sent me photocopies of Pereleshin's letters. E. Vitkovskii and

V. Rezvyi emailed Pereleshin's letters of 1971 to Vitkovskii, as retyped by Rezvyi.

Victor Salatko, Pereleshin's brother, answered only two of my letters, but after his death I was fortunate to acquire the few remains of his family archive, where I found his lengthy unfinished and unmailed letters to me. I am grateful to Arlee Geary, his trustee, for her invaluable help and for sharing her memories of Victor Salatko. Many thanks go to Natasha Carrol-Page, Lidiia Salatko's daughter from her first marriage, for many materials of the Salatko family.

I am especially grateful to researcher Steve Upton for his absolutely indispensable and generous help in obtaining official documents on Pereleshin's detention and deportation from the United States. I also thank officials at the US Department of Homeland Security for releasing and sending me copies of the relevant files.

V.V. Mouhanoff and Z.P. Popova shared their recollections of the poet as their classmate in the YMCA Gymnasium and V.A. Leonard his memories of knowing him in Harbin and Tianjin. So did Otto Schmidt, Venusto Castro Francisco Lopez, A.B. Kirilloff, M. Dobrinina, and Winston Leyland, all of whom kindly recalled their contacts with Pereleshin. Professor John Barnstead of the Department of Russian Studies, Dalhousie University, sent me some of Pereleshin's poems with kind words of encouragement. I am grateful to Marjolijn Abel, who sent me materials on Pereleshin's participation at the Poetry International Festival in Rotterdam in June 1989, and to the poet Hannie Groen for generously sharing her memories of Pereleshin at the festival.

I am grateful to Dr J.P. Hinrichs for his assistance in my research in the Valerij Perelešin Archive in Bibliotheca Publica Latina (BPL) in the Department of Western Manuscripts at Leiden University Library. Thanks to Dr Hinrichs's foresight, this archive is preserved and available to scholars. I am grateful to the Scaliger Institute, which awarded me a fellowship in 2003, and to the most helpful archivists at the Leiden University Library. I also thank Dr Hinrichs for our conversations about his contacts with the poet and his permission to read Pereleshin's letters to him.

I worked in several other archives and am grateful for the kind assistance of Professor Stanley Rabinowitz at the Amherst Center for Russian Culture at Amherst College, Massachusetts; Tat'iana Chebotareva at the Bakhmeteff Archive, the Rare Book and Manuscript Library, Butler Library, Columbia University; archivists at Beinecke Rare Books and Manuscript Library, Yale University; Anatolii Shmelev and Ronald Bulatov of the Hoover Institution; and archivists at the Bancroft Library, University of California, Berkeley.

I am most grateful to Dr Mark Gamsa for his great and invaluable help. I am also thankful to Professor Emeritus Boris Thomson, University of Toronto, and to Professor Norman Smith, University of Guelph, for their support, encouragement, and advice.

I would also like to thank the many people who helped me in various ways: Veronica Ahrens-Pulawska of Globus Slavic Bookstore in San Francisco, Victor Andrei Bakich, Thomas Keenan, Ella Kuznets, Jeanny Lam, Patricia Polansky, N. Razzhigaeva, Professor Emeritus Emmet Robbins of University of Toronto, Dr Harry Simmons, the poet Fraser Sutherland, Roland Vonk, and Philippa Wallace Matheson.

My sincere thanks go to the anonymous readers of the manuscript. Very special gratitude goes to Richard Ratzlaff, Humanities Editor at University of Toronto Press, for all his encouragement and support, and to Barbara Porter and Catherine Frost.

The portrait of Valerii Pereleshin which is used in the frontispiece is by Humberto Marques Passos.

Preface

Паутину нежную, клейкую,
матерьял отличный,
извиваясь невидной змейкою,
производит червь шелковичный
   из себя самого
   (Больше нет ничего).
Те же клейкие строки, поводы
для чужих раздумий,
создаю, на тризну, на проводы
с каждым годом идя угрюмей,
   из себя самого
   (Больше нет ничего).
"Шелковичный червь," 29.12.1967

A tender, sticky web,
a fine material,
is produced by a silkworm
twisting like an invisible snake
   from its own self
   (There is nothing else).
The same sticky lines
for other people's reflections,
for funeral feasts, for partings, I create
every year walking in deeper gloom,
   from my own self
   (There is nothing else).
"Silkworm"

The Russian émigré gay poet Valerii Pereleshin once wrote: "In my opinion, a poet needs no biography (what biography could a silkworm possibly have?)."[1] As the poem says, both spin beautiful creations "from my own self, / (There is nothing else)." He also noted: "It is best not to know anything about poets, no biography. […] Even the most beautiful flower becomes ugly under a microscope."[2]

But we want to know, for a love of poetry draws us to its creators. Pereleshin acknowledged this in an autobiographical sketch: "I will not omit dark aspects and 'dirty linen,' because this carefully concealed real state of things might be useful to future biographers, critics, and historians of Russian émigré poetry. […] Is mine a complex and difficult life? But who has it simple and without dark clouds?"[3]

Valerii Frantsevich Salatko-Petrishche (1913–92; pseudonym Valerii Pereleshin) left Russia at the age of seven during the Civil War and lived in China, in the cities of Harbin, Beijing, and Shanghai, for the next thirty-two years (1920–52) marked by strife among Chinese warlords, the Japanese occupation, the Sino-Japanese War, the Second World War, and the post-war changes. In the course of these turbulent years, he became a poet, not simply a Russian poet, but a Russian émigré poet, a most significant distinction. His language and culture originated in the pre-revolutionary Russian life defiantly and proudly treasured by émigrés. He was educated in Russian institutions in Harbin, a major centre of emigration in China, and published four books of poetry and a translation from English and became a monk in the hope of escaping from his homosexuality. In 1953, after a failed immigration to the United States and deportation back to China, he and his mother managed to settle in Rio de Janeiro. In his Brazilian period (1953–92), he gradually returned to poetry and, in time, became an openly gay poet. In this biography the words "gay" and "homosexual" are used interchangeably, although each has its own history, connotations, and context. He published another nine books of poems in Russian, a book of poems in Portuguese, as well as four books of translations: two of Chinese classical poetry into Russian, one of Brazilian poetry into Russian, and one of Russian poetry into Portuguese. Many poems and translations remain unpublished.

Pereleshin was a major poet of the twentieth century. His poetry of the Chinese period belongs to the Russian literature of the first-wave émigrés, while the Brazilian period places him among the post-war survivals and the second-wave poets, who had left the USSR during and after the Second World War. Unlike many émigrés, who tended to be indifferent to the countries that sheltered them, he deeply loved China and Brazil and enriched his life and poetry by mastering their languages.

The present book is a duet: the poet is the soloist, and the biographer the accompanist who complements the poet's solo with data from other sources. The wealth of biographical materials required a careful selection, as impartial as possible, for both the solo and the accompaniment. At times, the voices in this duet fall silent: his for reasons known only to him (and silence speaks), and the biographer's because of a lack of knowledge.

Valerii Pereleshin speaks to us with his poems, memoirs, letters, articles, and various writings. No diaries survived; in the early 1940s he burned his Beijing diary and asked his mother to destroy the volumes left in Harbin. He later claimed that he had never kept them. After his death, his brother thought that there had been a diary, but it seems to be missing.[4] Pereleshin, however, was a most prolific and eloquent correspondent, and his letters resemble diary entries.

His poems – over 2,000 in Russian, some 150 in Portuguese, a few in English, and one in Chinese – form a poetic diary. In this biography, Pereleshin's poems and quotes from them are reduced to English prose translations, and here lies the major difficulty: Russian and English poetry are so different in their rhythms, rhymes, word stresses, and connotations that translation, no matter how skilful, fails to convey fully the magic and mastery of the originals. As a small compensation, the two parts and all sections within the thirteen chapters begin with epigraphs of his poems or of excerpts from them in Russian. Throughout the book translations of all excerpts and poems, unless otherwise indicated, are the biographer's. The limits of this biography do not allow a detailed textual analysis, but it is hoped that the book will draw scholars and readers to explore his great poetic legacy.

What you will hear is a tale, both simple and complex, and full of anguish, passion, and poetry.

Figure 1 Valerii Pereleshin in Irkutsk (ca. 1915) Bibliotheca Universitatis Leidensis BPL 3266 1, f. 6. Used with permission.

Figure 2 Valerii Pereleshin as a student at the YMCA Gymnasium, Harbin, first on the right in the front row, ca. 1928. Author's personal archive.

Figure 3 Valerii Pereleshin as a graduate of the Harbin Law Faculty, 1930. Author's personal archive.

Figure 4 E.A. Sentianina and her sons, Victor and Valerii Salatko-Petrishche, ca. 1936. Bibliotheca Universitatis Leidensis BPL 3266 2 [6]. Used with permission.

Figure 5 As Monk Herman, Beijing, 1940. Bibliotheca Universitatis Leidensis BPL 3266 2 [9]. Used with permission.

Figure 6 In his room at Casa dos Artistas, Jacarepaguá, 1989. Courtesy of Roland Vonk, Rotterdam.

Figure 7 Grave of the mother and son at the English Cemetery, Gamboa, Rio de Janeiro. Courtesy of E. Chernishev and A. Bakich.

Figure 8 Pereleshin's books.

VALERII PERELESHIN

Life of a Silkworm

PART ONE

CHINA, 1920–1952

Это небо – как синий киворий,
Осенявший утраченный рай,
Это милое желтое море –
Золотой и голодный Китай.
Я люблю эти пестрые стены
Эти дворики, сосны, цветы.
Ах, не всем же, не всем же измены:
Сердце, верным останься хоть ты!
Сердце мудрое, где ни случится,
Как святыню, ты станешь беречь
Этих девушек кроткие лица,
Этих юношей мирную речь.
И родные озера, озера!
Словно на материнскую грудь,
К ним я, данник беды и позора,
Приходил тишины зачерпнуть.
Словно дом после долгих блужданий,
В этом странном и шумном раю
Через несколько существований,
Мой Китай, я тебя узнаю!
"Китай," 11.12.1942

This sky is like a deep blue cupola,
Spread over the lost paradise,
This dear yellow sea is
Golden and hungry China.
I love these motley walls,
These small courtyards, pines, flowers.
Ah, betrayals are not for everyone:
Heart, at least you remain faithful!
Wise heart, no matter where you will end,
You will treasure, like sacred objects,
The gentle faces of these girls,
The peaceful talk of these young men.
And the native lakes, the lakes!
As if to my mother's bosom,
I, the vassal of misfortune and disgrace,
Came to them for a scoopful of silence.
As if my home after long wanderings
In this strange and noisy paradise,
After several existences,
My China, I recognize you!
"China," 11.12.1942

1 Russian Childhood

The Salatko-Petrishche Clan

Но соблюду прием условный,
не обойдусь без родословной
и поищу в семье моей
хотя б ногайцев, но князей.
Почту заветы постоянства:
таков издревле был девиз
катившегося вниз дворянства:
упрямый Лепельский уезд
держал за Польшу меч и крест.

But I will follow a conventional device,
and will not leave genealogy out
and search in my family
for princes, even if from Nogai Tartars.
I will honour precepts of loyalty:
since the olden days, such was the motto
of the gentry clan going downhill:
the stubborn Lepel' District
for Poland held a sword and cross.

Poem without a Subject
(Poema bez predmeta),
Canto One, X, 40

"'Grandpa, I'd like to learn something about the history of our clan,' – I said, eighteen at the time, to the civil engineer Erazm Frantsevich Salatko-Petrishche, a holder of several decorations of the Russian Empire and a Full Councillor of the State, who worked then (in the 1930s) as a math teacher at a Russian Non-Classical Secondary School in Harbin. – 'I don't have anything. But on top of the wardrobe there are some papers on who was suing whom.' My father, Frants Erazmovich, gave me my grandfather's papers after he died in 1938."[1] In this bundle, the future poet Valerii Pereleshin found an Imperial Decree of 1860, which traced nobility of the clan to Mikhailo Salatko-Petrishche, who in 1621 had owned Zhuravna, Gorodtsa, and a few other estates in the Lepel' District of the old Polotsk Princedom in Belorussia; Pereleshin could not find "any of these godforsaken holes on the map."[2] The area had been ruled by the Grand Duchy of Lithuania, then by Poland, and from the end of the eighteenth century by the Russian Empire.

One of Mikhailo's descendants, Pereleshin's great-grandfather Frants Salatko-Petrishche (Sałatko-Petruszcze in Polish), received a medical degree from Kiev University in 1850; he and his wife, Elizaveta Adal'bertovna (née Shepers) from Hanover, had two children, Erazm and Teofilia. In 1862, when "a mine collapsed and the miners were buried alive, the doctor Frants Gerasimovich and several others went down to rescue them, but another collapse followed and everyone perished. [...] The possibility of enrolling the two semi-orphans in privileged educational institutions depended on proof of nobility. Thanks to the persistence of my great-grandmother, the document confirming the status of the Salatko-Petrishche clan as ancient nobility exists in several certified copies."[3]

Pereleshin's paternal grandfather, civil engineer Erazm Ioann Kazimir (with the Russian-style patronymic Frantsevich) Salatko-Petrishche (1861–1938), spoke Polish, Russian, German, and French, and worked throughout Russia. He and his wife, Maria Rozalia (née Shumovska), had seven children, one of whom, Frants Erazm Kazimir Ioann, born on 3 June 1889 in Lava Village in St Petersburg Region, was Pereleshin's father. Frants Erazmovich earned an engineering degree from Tomsk Imperial Technological Institute in 1912 and worked on the construction of Route II of the Trans-Baikal Railway and on the Trans-Siberian Railway.[4]

In his fifties Pereleshin became interested in his ethnicity, conceding that it mattered largely as "a theme (intelligent and necessary) for poems."[5] In 1921 his grandparents registered with a Polish representative in Chita, and his mother held that her in-laws were "Poles by blood and citizens of independent Poland," pointing out that the inscription on the grandfather's grave in Harbin said that he was a Pole. Pereleshin's father, however, declared himself to be Russian in one document and Belorussian in another, and in 1942 he converted to the Russian Orthodox faith.[6] Pereleshin thought that his ancestors were "Belorussian converts to Catholicism": "the first mention of the clan appeared in a document of 1620, when Belorussia was a part of Poland." The surname was "Polish-Belorussian, or rather Belorussian": Salatko from *salo* (lard) with a common ending of Belorussian surnames *-tko*, while Petrishche, with its suffix *-shche*, meant "Big Peter," probably referring to someone in the clan.[7]

Although in his autobiographical *Poem without a Subject* (*Poema bez predmeta*) he stated that "Belorussia is my fatherland," he had an "inborn attraction to Poland" and learned some Polish: "Can it be the call of blood?"[8] When Harbin émigré poets were planning a collection of poems dedicated to Poland, which had been invaded by Nazi Germany, Pereleshin, "commiserating with all my heart," wrote "To Poland" (*K Pol'she*, 22.2.1940), which lamented the occupation of "the beautiful ancestral country" and called upon young Poles to fight for freedom: "The grandson cannot participate, / but will not grow tired of praying / for the friendship of the Russian eagle / and the free Polish bird." The Japanese authorities in Manchukuo did not permit this publication, and Harbin Russian periodicals did not dare to publish his poem.[9]

The Polish theme kept appearing in his poetry. "Shame" (*Styd*, 27.9.1978) speaks of Russified Poles such as the explorer N.M. Przheval'skii (Przewalski), painters Kazimir Malevich (Kazimierz Malewicz) and Mikhail Vrubel' (Wróbel), and émigré poet Vladislav Khodasevich (Władisław Hodasewicz): "And what of my Polish gentry clan? Court pages and cavalry captains, / doctors and chamberlains stand in a row: / I see betrayal in their service records / and unflattering examples of Russification. // And I myself, alas, far away from Poland, / swear my fond feelings – in Russian!" The 1980 visit of Pope John Paul II to Rio de Janeiro prompted several poems; "Prayer for Poland" (*Molitva za Pol'shu*, 9.2.1982) wished "for the unbroken spirit of Poland to rise / and never know white or red Tsars ever again."

Like some émigrés, he prided himself on belonging to hereditary gentry, claiming that "all Russian culture was created by the gentry," and he yearned for heirlooms, but in hard times in Harbin his father had sold a family silver goblet of 1797 and his own father's ring with the coat of arms had been lost.[10] In "Signet Ring" (*Persten'*, 27.7.1969), the poet turns his grandfather's vague description of the coat of arms into "an artillery gun with a stubborn forehead / on a dark red background." In 1977, when a distant relative sent him a sketch of the coat of arms depicting a cross, a sword, cannons, banners, and a key, he toyed with the idea of having a signet ring made.[11]

The Burakov Family

Она, как символ благородный, Евгенией наречена.	She, like a noble symbol, Was named Evgeniia.

Poem without a Subject
(*Poema bez predmeta*),
Canto Two, XLVIII, 103

Pereleshin subtitled the story of his mother's family "With a Shoulder Bag and Staff." His maternal great-grandfather, Feodor Kirillovich Burakov, head of a civil service department in the city of Perm', on retirement "wandered all over Russia on foot. In Siberia he usually travelled by train: train crews knew him, and it was enough to say that he was going to visit his son Aleksandr, a railway employee in Omsk, for a seat to be found for him. We don't know whether the Russian Empire of that time had pensions, but even if Feodor Kirillovich had none, he made some money from making 'models' of churches, monasteries, kremlins, and towers from gold and silver foil and coloured paper and selling them by church and monastery fences. He led the life of a 'wandering minstrel,' though Mum does not know whether he sang any songs, spiritual or those 'bemoaning his fate.' [...] On the last visit to his favourite son Aleksandr [Sashen'ka], the old man was already quite ill: 'I've come to you, Sashen'ka, to die.' And he died quietly at his son's place."[12]

This favourite son and his wife, Elizaveta Zakhar'evna Nasilevich (Nasilewicz), whose father was a Pole, had two daughters, Evgeniia, born on 21 January 1892 in Samara, and Zinaida, who died of scarlet fever at the age of five. Evgeniia, Pereleshin's mother, recalled that "wherever we lived (we were railway builders and constantly travelled to new construction sites), our apartment had a joiner's bench with sparkling piles of metal shavings under it. [...] My father made very fine things, such as pharmaceutical scales, candleholders, and jacks. He also did carpentry. How we needed all this when we would arrive at some remote Siberian place where nothing was available! Of course, things could have been made by workers at his disposal, but it was his charming *hobby*."[13]

During the suppression of the 1905 Revolution, Evgeniia's father was transferred from Kurgan in Tobol'sk Province to Omsk, but she was left with an uncle and aunt to graduate from Aleksandrovskaia Girls' Gymnasium and Mariinskaia Middle School. In the spring of 1910, she went to St Petersburg to study philology and history at the Women's Higher Education Courses, known as Bestuzhev Courses, founded by the historian K.N. Bestuzhev-Riumin at a time when women were not admitted to universities in Russia. By 1910 its diplomas were recognized as equal to those of a university. Pereleshin's mother left no recollections, but from accounts of others one can imagine her excitement, the first sight of St Petersburg, life in rented rooms, lectures, famous professors, libraries, occasional trips to operas and concerts, grief over

Tolstoy's death in November 1910, and political activities, which she found annoying.[14]

Birth of a Poet, 1913

Ангара, снегопад, рекостав. Люди, сухо плечами пожав, говорили: – Безрадостный вид! Даже солнце его не живит. Правда: зябнут осины в саду, да ворона чернеет на льду. От окна отошел я давно и плотнее завесил окно. Если ж ветер кайму теребит занавески – изгоя знобит, и мелькают, и пляшут с утра рекостав, снегопад, Ангара.	The Angara, snowfall, frozen river. People, with a cold shrug of shoulders, said: – A cheerless view! Even the sun does not brighten it. It is true: aspens shiver in the garden, and a crow looks so black on the ice. I stepped away from the window long ago and drew the curtains tighter. If the wind shakes the fringe of a curtain, the exile shivers, and from the morning on, the frozen river, snowfall, the Angara keep flashing and dancing.

"The Angara, snowfall, frozen river"
(*Angara, snegopad, rekostav*), 20.7.1972

In the summer of 1912 Evgeniia Burakova went to visit her parents in Omsk. Vladimir Vasil'evich Koloshin, who later played a role in her life, courted her, but she "preferred my father (a man with a terrible character), and Vladimir Vasil'evich, a priest's son, gentle and devoted, was defeated by hereditary gentry." That summer she married F.E. Salatko-Petrishche and abandoned her studies. The newly-weds settled in Irkutsk, where he worked on the Trans-Siberian Railway.[15]

Their first son, Valerii, was born there on 7(Old Russian style)/20(New style) July 1913, and the second, Victor, on 10/23 October 1915, also in Irkutsk. By the Russian law of the dominant religion (if one parent was Orthodox, the children had to be Orthodox), both brothers were christened in the Russian Orthodox Church.[16] As the poem "Pope John Paul II in Rio de Janeiro" (*Papa Ioann Pavel II v Rio-de-Zhaneiro*, 11.6.1980) says, "by a whim of the Russian law, / which had been oppressing my Lepel' District, / the eight-point cross of Kiev, Constantinople, and Holy Mt Athos / became my fate."

Pereleshin attributed a mystical significance to the date of his birthday on 7/20 July and his name day on 7/20 November. Seven became "my favourite, and, moreover, simply MINE": "Did you notice that Valerii, Salatko, and Petrishche [in its Russian spelling] all have seven letters? Add the fact that by the old calendar I was born on the seventh day of the seventh month in the year (1913) with the sum of the numerals divisible by seven. My ordination as a monk took place on 7 May, and I was given the name Herman (*German*) [with a hard sign at the end of the word in the old Russian spelling], which has seven letters."[17] It was a very special number: "There are seven days of creation, seven days of the week, seven circles of ancient cosmography, seven archangels, seven mysteries, seven ecumenical councils (before the division in the Church), seven primary colours, seven stars of the Great Bear, seven music notes (though Chinese has only five), seven fat and thin cows, and seven full and empty ears of wheat in Pharaoh's dreams. Mystics state that seven is the number of the completeness of being (three faces of divinity and four corners of the world, that is, the entire invisible and visible world). In the Bible and in the Apocalypse, the number seven is definitely mystical: seven archangels, seven pipes, seven churches, and so on. In many illnesses, the crisis occurs on the seventh day, the human body renews itself every seven years, including even a person's character, and so on."[18] He once commented that "it would be 'piquant,' if I were to die on the seventh, though I cannot guarantee that." The "piquancy" nearly came true: he died at 23:50 p.m. on 6 November 1992,[19] and the date of his death is generally considered to be 7 November.

His father's work briefly took the family to Verkhneudinsk, now Ulan-Ude, and then to Chita, where he became head of the Chita-I Section of the Trans-Siberian Railway. They lived in "one of the best apartments in the railway settlement," and Pereleshin fondly recalled "mother's grand piano, dining room, a large lampshade with a beaded fringe (when wind shook it, whimsical shadows dashed around on the walls), the garden where I befriended a larch and a bird-cherry tree, the yard where shiny black anthracite coal was delivered in winters, and walks with my grandfather along the railway line, cloudberries, blueberries, snowdrops, mushrooms, and wild strawberries."[20] As he commented in a third-person autobiographical sketch, "the first conscious years in the life of the future poet are inseparably connected with railways [...], with walks along the rails and sleepers and his father's inspection trips to other stations. A love of railways stayed with him all his life."[21] In "Return" (*Vozvrashchenie*, 12.12.1971) the poet imagines a visit to Chita: "I have found the unforgettable house. / [...] // So that's my hearth and home: / the house is degraded, the garden dug over ... / Homeless is the returned pauper / with his violent, child-like sobs."

Leaving Russia, 1920

Младенцем ты покинул свой Байкал, но, странствуя, все родины искал,	You left your Lake Baikal as a small child, but in your wanderings kept searching for a homeland,
как будто там, где сердце ты забыл, не только снег и ветер между скал.	as if the place where you have left your heart is not just snow and wind among the rocks. "Homeland" (*Rodina*), 1.4.1971

In 1913, the year of Pereleshin's birth, Russia celebrated the 300th anniversary of the Romanov dynasty; he wrote, "complex fates awaited almost everyone who was born on the eve of the First World War."[22] Pereleshin was four when the 1917 Revolution destroyed Tsarist Russia. The ensuing Civil War of 1918–22 spread to Siberia and the Russian Far East, and Chita as an important railway junction became one of the crucial fighting grounds between the Red and the White forces.

At this time, the growing incompatibility between Pereleshin's parents deepened, especially when his mother wanted to leave Russia and his father resisted, believing in the ultimate victory of the Whites. She started planning her escape from the failing marriage and the horrors of the Civil War and visited Harbin, the major station on the Chinese Eastern Railway (CER), in October 1918 and March 1919.[23] This railway was built in 1898–1903 in Northeast China by Tsarist Russia, and its large easement zone was considered to be a Russian colonial extension of Siberia. Over half of Harbin's 70,000 residents were subjects of the Russian Empire who worked on the CER or in commerce and business; the rest were Chinese. The city was soon swamped with émigrés from Russia.

The Salatko-Petrishche family survived the Civil War thanks to Japanese officers stationed in their Chita apartment: Japan was one of several countries which sent troops to save the doomed Empire. Captains Sakita and Yagi told Pereleshin's mother, "while we are here, you have nothing to fear, but when we leave, you had better get away." She and her sons left for Harbin on the last train of Japanese troops pulling out of Siberia, and the Red Army took Chita on 22 October 1920. In her passport, next to the stamp dated 6 October 1920, she jotted: "The date of the final arrival in Harbin."[24] Pereleshin, a frail, sickly child prone to attacks of uremia, was deeply affected by "the lash of hunger and devastation" of the Civil War.[25] "From Childhood Recollections" (*Iz vospominanii detstva*, 14.2.1969) offers glimpses of that time: "'Was killed,' Chita was filled with whispers, / 'Engineer Aleksandrov ...' / – 'Because of some deductions ...' / – 'For stolen government firewood ...' // And tomorrow in clean underclothes / they will honour St Walpurgis / and perform a demonic / Liturgy at drunken May Day celebrations."

The family discord was equally traumatic. Unlike some émigré writers, he left no reminiscences of his early years, except for terse comments: "Memories of an unhappy childhood are quite capable of poisoning an entire life. Many things in my life go back to such recollections (and it is impossible to make the distant past cease to exist)"; "I had no childhood. I became sober minded and put on a mask of irony too early."[26] More was revealed to his friend, Harbin poet Lidiia Khaindrova, when her marriage broke down: "Mum left my father when I was about six and my brother three and a half. I believe (and I often said this to her) that, on her part, it was in fact the most sensible step in her life. In any case, it was much more sensible than her marriage, based only on the argument that 'after all, one has to marry someone at some point.' This basic untruth caused a lot of falseness, much suffering, disappointment, and fights. When she left, Mum did what you are doing now and let the children stay in her husband's family. She immediately went to Harbin. A year later she returned to Chita, not to her husband, but to get her children. In those terrible revolutionary years, she walked on railway ties and across broken bridges. I remember how she appeared in our garden, loaded with toys for us. After a fierce struggle, with threats and the support of good friends, she won us back and took us to Harbin."[27]

In 1920 the seven-year-old boy became one of many émigré children for whom Russia remained a patchwork of childhood memories, adults' recollections, and depictions in books. Everything was taken away from his generation, except for one treasure: their language.

2 Harbin: On the Way to Becoming a Poet

Harbin Émigrés

[…]	
Пусть мы бедны и несчастливы	Though we are poor and miserable
И выбиваемся едва,	And are barely coping,
Но мы выносливы и живы	We are resilient and alive,
И в нашем образе жива –	And though foreign stars are cold,
Пусть звезды холодны чужие –	The severed head
Отрубленная голова	Of the undying Russia
Неумирающей России.	Is alive in our image.

"We" (*My*), 10.2.1934

"Platforms of Chita Station, / depot and the quiet sobs of locomotives, / and then – a fairy-tale Harbin," Pereleshin recalled in "Falling Asleep" (*Pered snom*, 10.12.1971]). On arrival, he saw for the first time the art nouveau curves of the Harbin Central Railway Station with its candlelit icon of St Nicholas of Myra in Lycia, the protector of travellers. The Station Square narrowed into Railway Station Avenue going uphill, past the grand buildings of the Russo-Asian Bank, the former Garrison Club, and private mansions, to the wooden St Nicholas Cathedral, a symbol of Russian Harbin. Manchurian autumn lingered in all its splendour; it would slowly give way to severe winter.

The Chinese Eastern Railway (CER) had transformed the fishing and trading port on the Songhua (Sungari) River into an administrative and commercial centre of Russian interests in China, a remnant of Tsarist dreams of Yellow Russia. In 1918–22, of 2 million people who left Russia, over 200,000 came to China, and in the 1920s some 165,000 former subjects of the Russian Empire lived in Harbin. The city with its still-functioning former Russian administrative organs, churches, schools, clubs, and other institutions lulled many émigrés into seeing it as a Russian semi-colony which would shelter them until the restoration of the old order in Russia. Feeling no need to adjust to China and learn its language, they gave their children a Russian education. Pereleshin spoke for many when he wrote: "It was in the 'Russian' Harbin that I learned Russian literature, came to love it, and became a Russian poet. I pine not so much for the city of Chita, where I spent my early years (frozen, hungry, under artillery fire), but for that Russian presence which I found in Harbin: schools, libraries, university, and the church."[1]

Mother's Second Marriage, 1922

Заморышем, голодным сиротой Я русские перешагнул границы – Ножонками, похожими на спицы, Ступил в Китай пшенично-золотой. [...]	A hungry, starving orphan, I stepped over the Russian border And, on legs thin like knitting needles, Entered the golden-wheat China.

"Tale of Life"
(*Povest' zhizni*), 27.8.1975

Pereleshin enjoyed his new life with his beloved mother by his side, plenty of food, and pleasures such as his first ride in an automobile. It was much later that he wondered how his life might have turned out had they emigrated to Paris, the centre of Russian emigration: "A most glorious city, a heavenly paradise, / why didn't you open your doors to me? / Alas, I grew up in Harbin."[2]

Two years later, his mother, an "attractive, very sensitive, intelligent woman, unforgettable and desirable," a "splendid beauty" shining at Harbin balls and "driving men crazy," married Vasilii Evgrafovich Sentianin, head of the Pension Department and creator of social security in the CER. Pereleshin maintained that the marriage of his thirty-year-old mother and "sixty-four-year-old" Sentianin (he was, in fact, sixty) was in name only, but actually there were strong feelings, if not love.[3] They met in the Railway Club, where she briefly worked as a hostess, and Sentianin started sending her flowers, treats, homemade wines, and even a box of 100 eggs for her boys, with apologies for the "modest gifts." In the accompanying notes he rejoiced at "extremely desirable" meetings with the "darling *kapriza*," his blend of *kapriz* (caprice) and *markiza* (marquise) after the costume she once wore at a fancy dress ball: "I would have said '*my* darling *kapriza*,' but, I'm afraid, it's unlikely that such a beautiful woman could belong to anyone but herself."[4] Rumours of another suitor forced him to confess: "I am ill, and *my grave illness is you.*" Soon she became his "dear, precious Zhenichka," a diminutive of Evgeniia, and on 16/29 October 1922 Sentianin married his "darling *kapriza.*"[5]

The new life was "heavenly: a huge railway apartment with a garden and a yard, horses and carriage." Like other CER senior officials, Sentianin led a comfortable life, and he and his new wife entertained railway administrators, émigré scholars, writers, and cultural figures.[6] Victor remembered him as "a man of great heart and exceptional culture," and Pereleshin saw him as "a member of the Russian liberal gentry, somewhat a follower of Voltaire," and "a wonderful stepfather." He took his stepsons with him on some official trips to the beautiful Greater Xing'an Mountain Range, introduced them to the Harbin Museum of the Society for the Study of the Manchurian Region, and advised them to study Chinese.[7]

The good life did not last long. In 1924 the USSR and the Chinese Republic signed an agreement to operate the CER as a joint enterprise on a principle of parity, and the USSR demanded that all employees be Soviet or Chinese citizens. Many took Soviet citizenship, some for patriotic and political reasons and others, the so-called Harbin radishes (Red on the outside, White on the inside), to keep their jobs. The rest became Chinese citizens or were fired.

Sentianin resigned on 1 February 1925 "owing to illness," and the family moved to his house in the Majiagou suburb of Harbin. Although the state of his health was an excuse not to take a Soviet passport, his severe uremia soon stopped responding to treatments, and he died on 3 October 1927; "literally all Harbin walked to the cemetery."[8] When Pereleshin became a priest-monk, he conducted memorial services on the anniversary of his death. He kept his stepfather's few volumes of the *Brockhaus and Efron Encyclopedic Dictionary*, jokingly calling himself "a rather cultured person, but only to the letter D," and his 100-year-old Swiss clock, "its sonorous voice memorable from childhood."[9]

Father and Other Relatives

[...]
Был мир таким. И как я не хотел
Перерастать отмеренный предел!
Пусть маленьким остался бы поныне –
Не в пиджаке, не в узком пальтеце,

В задумчивом туберкулезном сыне,
А не в сухом, насмешливом отце.

Such was the world. How I did not want
To grow out of the measured limit!
I wish I could have remained a child,
Not in a man's suit, not in a cheap tight overcoat,
Not in a dry derisive father,
But in a pensive tubercular son.

"Recollection" (*Vospominanie*), 16.2.1974

In 1921, his father, with his parents and other relatives, also emigrated to Harbin. He found work on the CER until 1930, when his application for the obligatory Soviet citizenship was rejected and he was fired, after which he supported himself by contracts and expert opinions in court cases.[10]

The divorce left "much bitterness," and "the roots, which determined my inner world and thus my entire future fate came from the estrangement between my parents and within the family." His father "was right in thinking that E.A. (our Mum) was always embittered towards him and that Victor and I were influenced by her," but Pereleshin "would not have forgiven Mum if she had left me with the father. The divorce of his parents is a painful event for a child, but tyranny cripples his soul forever." The father and son were incompatible, and "my childhood was, of course, dark: I feared my father and hated him" – "a tyrant," "a cold man" with "a terrible character."[11] In the early 1930s Pereleshin's first visiting card read: "Valerii Aleksandrovich Salatko-Petrishche." The patronymic spurned his father and honoured his mother: she was Evgeniia Aleksandrovna and one of her pen names was E. Aleksandrova.[12]

It was only "with the passing of years" that "my shortage of love for my grandparents and my father torments me with a belated remorse. All I can do now, when they are long gone, is to pray for them." He felt particularly guilty about his paternal grandmother: "only once, before the end, / I visited you, already ill, / with my cold father. / Did you know that you were dying? / You were selecting for me / a larger, juicier pear from a tray, / as if this was what I came for. // […] // Sometimes I come across / your prayer book *dla kobiet* [for women]. And / remorse is devouring me, / and the slap of shame is burning."[13]

Sentianina's mother, along with her new family and relatives, also came to Harbin, thanks to Sentianin's work in the Hunger Aid to Russia campaign, where prominent participants were permitted to bring out relatives. In 1913, her mother had left her husband for a German colonist, M.F. Naam (Naham), who had eight or nine daughters and a son from his first marriage. She had two daughters with him, and Sentianina now met her half-sisters, so close in age to her own sons that the four children played together.[14]

School Years, 1920–1930

Слабее всех, почти слепой калека В гимназии страдал я от задир, И утешал меня запретный мир	The weakest of all, almost a blind cripple, In the Gymnasium I suffered from bullies, And the forbidden world of the teachers' office
Учительской: надежная опека! Опять синяк. Изгладит ли аптека Мне со скулы кулачный сувенир?	Consoled me: a reliable protection! Another black eye. Would a pharmacy Blot out a souvenir from a fist to my cheekbone?
Сойду ли я в чистилище-надир С отметиной?	Or would I go down with this mark To the nadir of purgatory?

"Going Back" (*Nazad*), 8.4.1980

Pereleshin first attended D.L. Khorvat Gymnasium, but after his mother's remarriage Sentianin enrolled his stepsons in the prestigious CER Commercial Schools. In 1924, after the Sino-Soviet agreement, the Soviets took over many railway institutions, including the Commercial Schools, and soon fired its director and several teachers for taking a line "clearly hostile to the interests of the USSR and the establishment of Sino-Russian friendship."[15] Many parents transferred their children to non-Sovietized schools, one of them being the YMCA Gymnasium, and Sentianin "without hesitation" did the same.[16]

The YMCA had relocated its Siberian branch to Harbin in 1918 after the departure of the American Expedition Troops from Russia. In September 1925, the Harbin YMCA opened a gymnasium, which followed the pre-revolutionary Russian curriculum with the addition of English language studies. The change was not unsettling for Pereleshin: in his grade 4 class thirty-eight pupils out of forty-four came from the Commercial Schools, and many teachers moved to the YMCA Gymnasium as well.[17] He fondly recalled YMCA director Howard Lee Haag for his fairness, foresight, and imperfect Russian, and enjoyed his wife's classes in English; "we never felt the Haags to be Baptist missionaries and did not even suspect it. The Gymnasium was 'a private Russian' school and the overwhelming majority of pupils were Russian and Orthodox. We had classes in scripture and fasted every Great Lent, and the Gymnasium was closed on all twelve major Orthodox holidays. The Haags were quite worldly. The missionary side of Mr Haag revealed itself rather unexpectedly in moralizing plays; in one, the somewhat plump Haag acted the part of Christ."[18]

Pereleshin was a top student in almost all subjects. Near-sighted and timid, he shunned sports, games, pranks, and school parties. Some classmates remember him as a puny and slovenly loner, with pimples and damp hands, looking older than his age. Boys bullied "the eleven-year-old gnome," and girls thought that he despised them and avoided him. One teacher recalled him as "quite fragile ('don't touch me')," and Pereleshin agreed, adding that he "hated crowds."[19] He sought refuge in the YMCA library, in the novels of Jules Verne, and in Russian poetry, "a lot of real nonsense, / but also *Stone* [Osip Mandelstam's *Kamen'*] and *Gardens* [Georgii Ivanov's *Sady*]."[20] Another form of escape was stamp collecting, which he started in 1923 with Italian stamps of 1917–22 with attached labels advertising "Singer" sewing machines and "Columbia" record players. All his life he remained "a passionate stamp collector, even though it is an obvious vanity."[21]

He also tried his hand at poetry. As he later noted, rhyme in his "Ludwig VII Had a Son Philip" (*Liudvik VII imel Filippa syna*, ca. 1924) was weak or absent. His first translation, "King Hilarius and the Pauper" (*Korol' Gilarii i nishchii*, ca. 1926), was of a poem found in the *Illustrated London News*, where the king fires the disobedient Councillor Willoughby and appoints a pauper as a new councillor.[22] Both attempts reflect his fascination with royalty, which led to another refuge, a "delightful" game of kings. Inheriting his great-grandfather Burakov's skill in crafts, he cut 12-centimetre figures out of paper, drew their faces in profile, and dressed them in foil from chocolate bonbons to represent kings, queens, senators, ministers, and other political figures, with names and dates of birth written on the back. He played France, his brother played Germany, and the boy next door, Aleksei Shchelokov, played England; "before my invention we were given tin soldiers, but it was unbearably boring: soldiers had no individuality and could only fight. But here was life in its entirety, with love, women, ambition, greed, treachery, heroism, governments, and struggles for power or wealth."[23]

Events in the game were recorded in a chronicle, and it gradually "grew more complex: we created entire states, each with an emperor and court, senate, parliament, generals, admirals, officers of all ranks, the Pope and cardinals, nuns, theatre, wars, chronicles, gold reserves (that same foil), banknotes, political parties, ministries, and most complex geographical maps," a World Bank, an International Club with roulette, newspapers, writers, and poets. He was in full control of this world of wars, *coups d'état*, revolutions, murders, and executions.[24] As he recalled in "Games" (*Igry*, 25.9.1987): "Ah, my God! Away from dolls, / how freely and easily we lived / within this game, with Alesha and my brother!"

At the age of fifteen he decided to stay with the pre-revolutionary Russian orthography. A language reform for dropping some redundant letters and the hard sign after a final consonant had been debated in Russia for some time, and in 1918 the Soviet government decreed the proposed reforms. Many émigrés defiantly kept the old orthography. Some Harbin schools, including the YMCA Gymnasium, introduced the new orthography, but Pereleshin presented his teachers with "the *fait accompli*: I am writing according to the old orthography, without any mistakes, and I do not foresee any objections!"[25] His decision had no political motivations; he genuinely believed that the old orthography best conveyed the sounds of the Russian language, and he was "totally devastated" when, during Manchukuo times, "exactly on 30 November 1943," Harbin printing presses switched to the new orthography: "My mother, a witness of this 'minor coup,' said that it was unlikely that the Japanese, indifferent to the matter, had ordered this change. It would be more correct to guess that it was done by leaders of the Bureau for the Affairs of Russian Émigrés in Manchukuo who were not sparkling with culture." Like some other émigré writers, I.A. Bunin and B.K. Zaitsev among them, Pereleshin wrote in the old orthography all his life and used the new style only on his typewriter, since he could not obtain keys in the old style. He always regretted that only his first three books were published in the old orthography.[26]

Law Faculty Student, 1930–1937

Живешь в глуши страны чернильной	You live in the backwoods of an ink country
Записок, выписок и книг	Of notes, excerpts, and books,
И дышишь летописью пыльной	And inhale dusty chronicles
Забытых лавров и квадриг.	Of forgotten laurels and Roman carriages.
Ты в этот мир бежишь от мира	You are escaping into this world
Суровых стихотворных нег,	From the world of austere poetic bliss,
Так от прохладного зефира	Like a snowdrop wrapping itself in snow
Подснежник кутается в снег –	Against a chilly Zephyr –
Чтоб вдруг из-под снегов латыни,	So that unexpectedly from under the snows of Latin,
Подтаивающих весной,	Thawing a little in spring,
Вдохнуть внезапно воздух синий,	You can suddenly inhale the blue air,

Веселый, легкий и сквозной,
Чтоб после двух ночей бессонных
Среди тысячелетних строк –
Вдруг разглядеть вверху бездонный
Сквозной и синий потолок ...
И грудь ты открываешь жадно
Ритмическим ветрам родным,
Ветрам веселым и отрадным,
Парнасским бурям ледяным.
И мнится: ямбом пятистопным
Гремит военная труба,
Анапестом нерасторопным
Вдоль окон тащится арба ...

Cheerful, light, and draughty,
So that after two sleepless nights
Among the thousand-year-old lines –
You suddenly see the bottomless,
Transparent, and blue ceiling above ...
And you greedily open your chest
To beloved rhythmical winds,
Cheerful and joyful winds,
To Parnassian icy storms.
And it seems: a military horn
Is singing in iambic pentameter,
And a Chinese cart is dragging outside
In sluggish anapest ...

"You live in the backwoods of an ink country" (*Zhivesh' v glushi strany chernil'noi*), 20.5.1935

In 1930, Pereleshin graduated with the distinction *magna cum laude*. His choice of further Russian education in Harbin was limited to the Law Faculty, Polytechnic Institute, Pedagogical Institute, and Oriental and Commercial Institute, while he dreamt of philology, Sanskrit, or eighteenth-century Russian literature in the pre-revolutionary Moscow University. When he settled on law, his mother, "without the slightest hesitation" supported him, and his father agreed to help with the tuition.[27] The curriculum of the Law Faculty, opened in 1920, followed that of the Russian law faculties, and the Faculty survived both the Sovietization of 1924, the takeover by the Chinese authorities in 1929, and modifications in its programs. The professors consisted of a "renowned Pléiad" of émigré scholars and a few sent from the USSR.

In his first year Pereleshin did not miss a single lecture: "Roman Law attracted me with its common sense, International Law threw a new light on the history of Western Europe, and State Law called for a re-evaluation of my semi-childish 'political convictions.'" Like others, he was mesmerized by Professor N.V. Ustrialov, "our pet and demigod, / who resourcefully changed landmarks / and immediately became a success, / had met Trotskii, / had become a National-Bolshevik. / Like Chicherin and Bukharin, / he trustingly played with fire, / until he was burned by it." In subsequent years, Pereleshin "went only to lectures given by the most talented speakers or simply fascinating people."[28]

His four years at the Law Faculty took place during a crucial time in China. In September 1931 Japan began its occupation of the Northeast, and in early February 1932 Harbin fell to the Japanese. In March of that year Japan established the puppet state of Manchukuo, installing the former heir to the Manchu Qing dynasty, Pu Yi, as the Supreme Leader; in March 1934 the state was transformed into the Manchu Empire with Pu Yi as the emperor. Some Harbin Russians started leaving for other Chinese cities, particularly Shanghai, and further, to the United States or Europe. In 1935 the USSR sold its share of the CER ostensibly to Manchukuo, but actually to Japan, and some 20,000 railway employees with Soviet passports were repatriated, most to perish in Stalinist purges.

In December 1934, the Japanese, as one Harbin Russian put it, "playing on Russian patriotism and hatred of Communism, established the Bureau for the Affairs of Russian Émigrés in Manchukuo with a network of various branches, organizations, semi-military cells, and clubs. *Agents provocateurs* squeezed in among the true patriots. Detachments of Russian youths were sent to the USSR as saboteurs, often to a certain death."[29] The Harbin Russian Fascist Party played a major role in this Bureau, but "the Russian emigration mostly found the Fascist guardianship oppressive: the Fascists were supported only by the Japanese and committed outrages under their protection."[30]

On graduating in 1935, Pereleshin ordered a new visiting card: "Valerii Frantsevich Salatko-Petrishche. Candidate of Law." His thesis analysed the division of goods between a landowner and a renter-producer in Roman law. On 20 August 1935, on the recommendation of his supervisor, Professor G.K. Gins, Sentianin's old friend and "Uncle George" to Pereleshin, he was retained to write a master's thesis on Chinese civil law, with the stipulation that he would learn Chinese. It was then that Pereleshin truly "discovered the Chinese world."[31] The key word is "discovered": like the vast majority of Harbin Russians, he had been ignorant of the Chinese language, culture, and history. Some Chinese was inefficiently taught in a few Russian schools, though not in the YMCA Gymnasium. Russian contacts with the Chinese were limited to workers, shopkeepers, peddlers, and servants, who were expected to know some Russian or converse in Sino-Russian pidgin.

Pereleshin was interested primarily in the theoretical aspects of law. In retrospect, he believed he should have studied not law, but Chinese; in his undergraduate years he had already felt a surge of interest when he happened to attend an open oral examination in Chinese. Now he became a first-year student in the Oriental Department of the Law Faculty, which aimed to produce translators and interpreters for the CER; Russian professors were assisted by Chinese teachers from Beijing. The course was tough: twenty of the 120 first-year students of 1927–8 had proceeded to the second year, but only eight graduated after four years. As one of them recalled, Professor S.N. Usov's response to complaints was: "Transfer to the Law Faculty: there you can graduate after eighteen exams and don't have to attend lectures."[32] Pereleshin fell in love with Chinese and "studied it almost in defiance: the fashion then was for Japanese." If he found Professor Usov "fault-finding and often sarcastic," Professor I.P. Baranov "instilled in me love for this rich culture for the rest of my life." [33]

Youth of a Poet

Оправдана двуспальная кровать,
Которая сынами плодовита,
И велено законами Левита
Ослушников камнями побивать.
  Один из них, я не хочу скрывать
  Ни от судьи, ни от архимандрита,
 	
  Что с детских лет судьба моя надбита,
 	
  А с трещиной – куда себя девать?
Глава и стих ... Сам Бог ветхозаветный
 	
Ни миловал ни женщины бездетной,
Ни бунтаря, ни труса, ни скопца.
  Берется врач лечит меня гипнозом:
 	
  Мои шипы сведутся до конца,
  Но не цвести без них стихам и розам!
	A double bed, fertile
	With sons, is justified,
	And stoning of those who disobey
	Is ordered by the laws of Leviticus.
	  One of them, I do not want to conceal
	  Either from a judge, or from an
	    archimandrite
	  That my fate has been fractured from
	    the childhood,
	  And with the crack where am I to go?
	Chapter and verse ... The God of the Old
	  Testament
	Had no mercy for a childless woman,
	For a rebel, for a coward, for a castrate.
	  A doctor is offering to cure me by
	    hypnosis:
	  My thorns will be removed completely,
	  But poems and roses will not bloom
	    without them!

"Fate" (*Sud'ba*), 7.5.1978

Pereleshin was a bright and serious student, but poetry, not scholarship formed the core of his life. As he commented on a poem written at the age of five and saved by his doting mother, the rhymes were bad, but "the metre was instinctively retained. Indeed, I've never had to learn the basics of versification: the elementary knowledge came to me ready-made from somewhere." Skipping children's books, he immersed himself in poetry, and notably it was not Alexander Pushkin, but Mikhail Lermontov, a romantic poet of exceptional musicality and sadness, who captured the child's heart.[34]

In 1927, *Megaphone* (*Rupor*), one of many Harbin Russian newspapers, launched a weekly "Young Reader" (*Iunyi chitatel'*) page, and fifteen-year-old Pereleshin "summoned the courage" to send his "Three-Horse Cart" (*Troika*, ca. 1928), under a pseudonym, René, after his step-aunt, Renée Naam. The poem was published on 11 February 1928 and, half in jest, he later considered "celebrating my fiftieth anniversary on 11 February 1978." Six more poems were published in that year.[35] In 1929 he engaged in his first polemics in "Young Reader." His poetic response "To Papin the Siberian" (*Papinu-Sibiriaku*, 1929) spoke of preferring "the poets of dear antiquity," Torquato Tasso, Ludovico Ariosto, and Dante, and of "being captivated from an early age" by Lermontov and his "inspirer" Byron, because "not everything is accessible to people" in Nikolai Gumilev and Sergei Esenin. At the time he had not read any of them, except Lermontov.[36]

In the early 1930s, he assembled his unpublished juvenile poems into several thematic cycles in handwritten booklets with titles and page numbers. The most significant thing about these poems is their open expression of a major theme of his entire oeuvre: love of a man for a man, condemned by religion and society. Russian émigrés, including those in Harbin, brought with them the scathing homophobia of their native land. Traumatized, homeless, they clung to religion, and the Russian Orthodox Church Abroad zealously guarded its precepts on all varieties of sin. Pereleshin attended Russian Orthodox church with his mother, scripture was taught by Russian priests in the YMCA Gymnasium, and homophobia was strongly instilled in his sensitive and religious soul.

He early "sensed being different. [...] From the age of fifteen, without any outside temptations, I discovered in myself an inborn inability for a 'normal' love for a woman"; "you can very well imagine the morals of the 1920s in Harbin: no one even dreamed of *such things*. A fifteen-year old adolescent was not and could not have been 'dissolute'; he simply caught himself being *in love* with his classmate." His heart was "immediately given to the exceptionally bright Iura [Georgii] Volkoff, who soon became my only friend and to whom I wrote many immature, but passionate poems. The desire was naturally there, but I could never overcome my shyness: there were never any *words*."[37]

In these early poems the beloved is openly male. "Blue Bird" (*Siniaia ptitsa*), the earliest cycle of July 1930 – March 1931, reads like romantic letters, where the poet confesses his "secret" and "deep sorrow," hides a red flower in a bouquet of white lilies, and yearns to give himself to his "dear, the only one," "the incomparable," "the radiant" young man. The following two cycles were written in the summer of 1930, when, after graduation, his "luminous blue bird," Georgii Volkoff, left Harbin to study physics at the University of British Columbia, and heartbroken Pereleshin turned to poetry: "many of my youthful poems, which now seem devastatingly bad, are about him."[38] The epigraph to the cycle, "Sinful Thoughts" (*Greshnye dumy*) of September 1930 – September 1931, says: "These songs are evoked / by spring waters, / they are born and fostered / by sinful thoughts." The poet weeps over his love, realizes the futility of praying for mercy, and rebels against God, who preaches love and forgiveness, but condemns his love. The cycle, "Acceptance of Mystery" (*Priniatie tainy*), March 1931 – March 1932, yearns for "news from a distant land," sadly foresees Volkoff's marriage, and speaks of resignation: "as long as I can write poems, / I do not need anything in the entire world." In the published version of this poem as "Happiness" (*Schast'e*, 25.8.1931), these lines are diluted to "as long as I believe in freedom and peace, / I do not need anything in the entire world," echoing Pushkin's famous "There is no happiness in the world, / only peace and freedom."

The next cycle, "Two Queens," August 1931 and March 1932, was "stealing from [Alexander] Blok, but only the trappings: snows, fogs, wind. At that time, I understood zilch in Blok as Blok." The poems describe snowstorms and plead with Madonna, Fiancée, Tsarina, or Queen to save him, but, as the poem "I'll recall our first meeting" (*Nashu pervuiu vspomniu vstrechu*, ca. 1931) says: "the Mortal One conquers the Eternal One, / semidarkness conquers Light." The poems were weak, but "metre (iambic pentameter, dactylic trimeter, anapestic trimeter, trochaic pentameter) was quite varied. The two longer poems, 'Snow Death' (*Snezhnaia smert'*, 1931) and 'The Last Snowstorm' (*Posledniaia v'iuga*, 1931), were written, as I discovered later, in logaedic verse or *pauznik*," popular in the Silver Age of Russian poetry. His few reviews in the "Young Reader," signed as an anagrammatic Avrelii, criticized young poets for stale or "completely unacceptable" rhymes.[39] Some poems from "Two Queens" appeared in "Young Reader" under a new pseudonym, The Distant One (*Dalekii*). The editor, Arsenii Nesmelov, a prominent Harbin poet, "one day became sick of my most monotonous 'creations' and decided, on my behalf, that it was time to stop. I don't recall the title of my next 'snowstorm' poem, but Nesmelov changed it to 'The Last Snowstorm' (*Posledniaia v'iuga*, 1931). I took the hint. It was my last contribution to the 'Young Reader' page."[40]

Then, "one evening at the end of May 1932, Mum decided that it was time for me to grow up and publish in a real literary and artistic journal, *Border* (*Rubezh*). [...] I categorically refused to see the editor (it was scary). Mum then almost forced me to give her some 'simpler' poems and on the reception day (Thursday) went to the editorial office on Commerce St, no. 17. I waited at home in a total emotional upheaval."[41] The editor Mikhail Rokotov (M.S. Bibinov) recalled how "an elegant, very attractive lady came into the office and, handing me a small stack of papers, modestly asked me to look at the poems of her 'younger brother.'" Rokotov found the poems "youthful, but already fully mature and faultless in form," and "seized" the young poet "as a new and great discovery of *Border*." His mother and Rokotov selected Pereleshin as his pseudonym. His first poem in *Border*, "With every meeting you are better and closer" (*S kazhdoi vstrechei luchshe Vy i blizhe*, 21.4.1932), published on 11 June 1932, refutes recollections by others that the pseudonym was invented later in a literary studio, when someone called him a wood-goblin (*leshii*) and he became Pereleshin.[42]

He dismissed this first poem in *Border* as "devastatingly bad, but the editor knew best; submissions of other beginners were, probably, even worse." The poem admires someone's "clear eyes" and "wise words" and rejoices that "I know, I know, I will see You tomorrow." One could not tell that "You" was a man, a Law Faculty graduate, B.I. Abramov.[43] Gender camouflage is easy in Russian: the formal "you" (*vy*) requires plural verb agreement in all tenses, and the informal "you" (*ty*) reveals gender only in the past tense. These ambiguities made it possible for his poems to appear in the Russian émigré press, and they never revealed the sex of the beloved.

The journal *Border* had been launched in 1926 by M.S. Lembich, the owner of a popular newspaper *Dawn* (*Zaria*), and both were later taken over by another publishing magnate, E.S. Kaufman. Unlike many other periodicals, *Border* lasted until the arrival of the Soviet Army in August 1945: its longevity was due to its appeal to a wide audience as well as compliance with Manchukuo policies and propaganda. Each issue of some twenty-four pages carried poems and short stories; translations from English, French, or German; reviews; news and photographs; advice on fashion; beauty tips; recipes; a crossword; a cartoon; and so on. Many young people began their poetic lives in its pages. The editorial office was located in the apartment of a barrister, S.Ia. Reznikov, whose wife, E.S. Kaufman's sister, was the manager of the journal; their daughter, Nataliia Reznikova, a Law Faculty graduate and a poet, contributed poems and other writings. She invited Pereleshin to her literary salon and introduced him to Harbin literary circles.[44]

By this time over 100 books of poetry in small editions had been published in Harbin. In the early 1920s, several young poets had startled readers with poetic and verbal experimentation in books such as Venedikt Mart's *Emerald Worms* (*Izumrudnye chervi*, 1921) and *Stolen Death* (*Ukradennaia smert'*, 1921); Fedor Kamyshniuk's *Music of Pain* (*Muzyka boli*, 1918) and *Petals: A Tablet* (*Lepestki. Skrizhal'*, 1919); and Sergei Alymov's *Kiosk of Tenderness* (*Kiosk nezhnosti*, 1920), *Call of the World* (*Oklik mira*, 1921), *Harp without Lightning* (*Arfa bez molnii*, 1922), and *Drunken Heart* (*P'ianoe serdtse*, 1926).[45]

In the late 1920s and the 1930s older poets who wrote in more traditional styles emerged. "The master of Harbin Parnassus" was Arsenii Nesmelov (A.I. Mitropol'skii), a veteran of the First World War and the Civil War, who had already published several books in Russia. In Harbin, his collections *Reflection of Blood* (*Krovavyi otblesk*, 1929), *Without Russia* (*Bez Rossii*, 1931), *Siding* (*Polustanok*, 1938), *White Flotilla* (*Belaia flotiliia*, 1942), and poems in Harbin periodicals show a remarkable and tragic talent. Unemployed, Nesmelov also wrote many poems, satirical verses, and short stories on request, saying that a poet, like a shoemaker, worked for a living and produced to order. In the 1930s he became a member and a bard of the Russian Fascist Party under the pseudonym N. Dozorov, but never showed his long poem *Georgii Semena* (1936) and a book of poetry *Only Such!* (*Tol'ko takie!* 1936) "to Mum and me and was ashamed of [...] this Fascist self-humiliation."[46]

Another prominent older poet was Aleksei Achair (A.A. Gryzov), who also fought in the White Army, "never fully recovered from shell shock, and suffered incredible headaches and tics."[47] His books *The First* (*Pervaia*, 1925), *Laconisms* (*Lakonizmy*, 1937), *Wormwood and the Sun* (*Polyn' i solntse*, 1938), *Paths* (*Tropy*, 1939), and *Under the Golden Sky* (*Pod zolotym nebom*, 1943) often spoke of love for his native Siberia and for Cossacks. He penned the oft-quoted lines about émigrés: "Fate did not break or bend us, / even though it pushed us flat to the ground, / and because our homeland kicked us out, / we spread it all over the world." He worked as a senior secretary of the YMCA and a secretary of its Education Department, where he tended to give "long-winded homilies on the virtue of goodness. He had the same persona in his poetry: long-winded, tiresome, but most pure. His poems gained a lot in recitals": "on a grand piano, he searched / for melodies and played. / The music pleasantly conveyed / the 'clattering of hooves,' / the virgin might of the Urals, / and the grandfathers' thrust to the east. / The bewitching piano drew us into unknown distances, / we advanced with a military regiment, we drowned with Ermak. / The music also took us / to Tatar crescents, / as 'la-illa-il-alla' burst out / to intercept Tsarist armed forces, / and to psalms of schismatic dissenters, / as we climbed the Himalayas."[48]

Other prominent older poets were Leonid Eshchin, who, traumatized by the Civil War, drank himself to death in 1930; Vsevolod Ivanov (of the same first name and surname as the Soviet writer), a poet, prose writer, and journalist; Marianna Kolosova, whose poems called for a bullet for every drop of White blood shed in the struggle to save Holy Russia; Aleksandra Parkau, another nostalgic fighter for the beloved homeland; Irina Lesnaia and her gentle poems about nature; and a few others. They were soon joined by Pereleshin's generation of those who came to China as children or who were born there.

Churaevka Literary Circle, 1932–1934

Под шляпы – от света, В подушки – от шума, От ветра и ночи – Под воротники. Уходим, как в Лету, Уходим угрюмо, Чудим и бормочем И пишем стихи.	Under the hats – away from the light, Under the pillows – away from noise, Under the collars – away From the wind and the night. We are leaving, as if into Lethe, We are leaving gloomily, Act oddly and mumble, And write poems.

"Under the hats – away from light"
(*Pod shliapy – ot sveta*), 1.12.1934

In his memoirs, Pereleshin entitled the chapter on young poets "The Circle Widens," and, indeed, his circle widened rapidly when, in October 1932, someone took him to a meeting of the literary and artistic circle, Churaevka. The circle had evolved from literary evenings at the home of an older poet, Aleksandra Parkau. After one such evening, Achair had invited young people, still discussing poetry on the sidewalk, to the YMCA, and some "young men and women, timid, shy, started coming to see Achair … Stricken with fear, they showed him their first poetic attempts."[49]

In 1926 Achair had formed a literary and artistic circle, initially called Young Churaevka (*Molodaia Churaevka*), later simply Churaevka, at the YMCA. The name came from the novel *The Churaev Family* (*Churaevy*,

1925–6) by émigré writer G. Grebenshchikov, who had set up a Churaevka farm and a publishing house, Alatas, in the United States. He wrote to his fellow Siberian Achair: "Go ahead and form a branch of Churaevka in Harbin, have your plot of land, your house, your initiative, your creativity, and turn theory and words directly into action, into merry play."[50] Achair's goals were more modest: to help young people develop their talents. The YMCA became a Russian cultural centre, which housed Churaevka's evenings, at times attracting 500–600 people to lectures and discussions on historical and political topics, spiritual crises of the times, life in the USSR, literature, and art, followed by poetry recitals, concerts, plays, and exhibitions.[51]

The poetry circle became quite active. As one participant recalled, "explanation for this suddenly flared thirst for poetry among young people is possible only by Dostoevsky's belief that in order to write, one has to suffer. In the mass of Russian people flooding Harbin, there was not a single family that did not suffer in one way or the other from the war, revolution, and then the second, the Civil War. Almost everyone's life was broken, and if not broken, then dislocated, and young people were no exception: they bore their share of common grief. The tragic note of those years is felt in the poetry of every Churaevka poet, even if he was fourteen."[52]

Poetry recitals were called "By the Green Lamp," after the St Petersburg circle attended by Alexander Pushkin, and on the YMCA stage the light from under a green lampshade softly illuminated the faces of poets as they read their poems. In 1929, they published their first collection *Staircase to the Clouds* (*Lestnitsa v oblaka*); in the opening poem by T.A. (T. Andreeva), Gumilev welcomes a young poet ascending a staircase to a garden of poetry in the clouds. In 1931, a second, more accomplished collection, *Seven* (*Semero*), introduced Larissa Andersen, Nina Il'nek, Nataliia Reznikova, Lidiia Khaindrova, Nikolai Shchegolev, Nikolai Svetlov (Nikolai Svin'in), and Mikhail Shmeisser.

By the autumn of 1932, when Pereleshin, a law student at the time, joined Churaevka, some poets had left Harbin, but there remained a vibrant core, though, as one recollection emphasized, "it was hard to imagine a group more heterogeneous in character, tastes, and views." Most, like Pereleshin, were in their late teens or early twenties. This "nursery of saplings" met on Fridays when "every poet read his new work, first for a general impression, and then for an assessment. After that the text was distributed for a visual perception." The studio was far from a "mutual admiration society": the criticism was sharp and to the point.[53]

At first, Pereleshin "did not dare to read his poems," dreading critiques from sarcastic members such as Nikolai Peterets and Petr Lapiken. Finally, as one member recalled, "a small narrow-chested youth with the wrinkled face of a clever dwarf, expecting recognition, read a poem with the lines 'A white nun is wandering, / wandering in a withering garden,' which seemed so credible to him." This poem, as well as "Snowy Death" (*Snezhnaia smert'*, 1931), were "torn to pieces. Peterets was particularly bloodthirsty. 'This is a total imitation of Blok,' he hissed. 'And your poems in *Border*, including the notorious 'White Nun' [the poem "In the Autumn" (*Osen'iu,* 24.12.1931)], reprinted in newspapers, are, indeed, an obvious rehashing of Apukhtin!" He was attacked "for generalities, for impersonal nature combined with external smoothness, and for the influence of doubtful examples, such as Ratgauz, Fofanov, and others," though he had not even heard of these minor nineteenth-century poets, who were prone to pessimism and melodrama.[54]

This "baptism by fire" was devastating: "For some time, not only did I not read anything in the studio, but also, as I remember, I stopped writing. In general, I did not want to live."[55] Only in early 1933 did he ask another member, Georgii Granin (Georgii Saprykin), to recite his "At Sunset" (*Na zakate*, 29.1.1933) as an anonymous submission, and "something unforeseeable took place. All the poets and poetry fans were delighted. In my entire life I have not heard again so many joyful exclamations." "At Sunset" was written in response to Peterets's suggestion for everyone to write about Nordic sagas, Solveig, and similar topics as a tribute to Larissa Andersen, with whom he was in love. Pereleshin's poem had "no Solveig, but there were sagas, northern maidens, ancient boats, Valkyries, and Norman swords."[56]

At first, as one member recalled, Pereleshin "was not liked and no one suspected a poet in him,"[57] but it did not take him long to blossom. He enjoyed studying theoretical works by Andrei Belyi, Valerii Briusov, Boris Tomashevskii, Viktor Zhirmunskii, and others and discussing favourite poets. He valued Gumilev and "for almost the rest of my life adopted the Acmeist method of constructing poems," while for Granin "the five big ships" of poetry were Blok, Gumilev, Briusov, Maiakovsky, and "perhaps, Esenin." Sergei Sergin (Sergei Petrov) admired Maksimilian Voloshin and his "Fiery Parisians" (*Plamenniki Parizha*), "because events of the French Revolution in these sonnets astonishingly reminded one of what was taking place in Russia." They all disliked Boris Pasternak, and traces of his influence led to ironic accusations of "Pasternscum" (*pasternakip'*).[58] They avidly read émigré poets in Europe such as Georgii Adamovich, Aleksei Eisner, Georgii Ivanov, Dovid Knut, Vladislav Khodasevich, Antonin Ladinskii, Boris Poplavskii, Anatolii Shteiger, Vladimir Smolenskii, and Marina Tsvetaeva. Pereleshin admired Khodasevich and Ivanov, but "no one could be better than 'my' Ladinskii." When he wrote to his favourite, Ladinskii sent him his collections *Black and Blue* [*Chernoe i goluboe*] and *Northern Heart* [*Severnoe serdtse*].[59]

Pereleshin lived poetry. The YMCA closed at midnight, and discussions moved to the streets of Harbin: "Almost every Tuesday and Friday I walked either Slobodchikov and Lapiken home to their Docklands suburb, or Peterets and/or Granin to Majiagou, or Shchegolev to Corps Town. Then they walked me back. Then I walked them home again. On some cold nights, at the end of these walks, we would come to my place and continue talking with Mum for another two–three hours by the samovar. In the course of these long evenings, we would discuss the latest political news (Japanese occupation of Manchuria, Hitler's rise to power, Italian invasion of Abyssinia) and new books. We mentioned dozens of names, commented on the works of Ivan Bunin, Mark Aldanov, Ivan Shmelev, Mikhail Osorgin, Boris Zaitsev, on almost all poems and articles in *Contemporary Notes* (*Sovremennye zapiski*, Paris), and planned new ways of work in Churaevka. [...] Meetings, meetings ... Entire life consisted of meetings, of 'long talks over wine,' or of playing mahjong."[60]

In 1932–4, they published an irregular newspaper, *Young Churaevka* (*Molodaia Churaevka*), later *Churaevka*. In an editorial, Granin declared in telegraphic style: "So far the emigration has not produced its own poet. It is hard to be a true poet in exile. He will not come from the older generation: it is coming to its end. It buries itself in the past. It cherishes an idyllic homeland. He will come from the younger generation. From the second generation. For them emigration is a fact to fight against or to accept: one of the two. We must confess: émigré poetry is dying. [...] Young people are young. They have not become strong yet, have not acquired a foothold. There are no masters of poetry. But there will be. [...] Russian poetry is dying. Because before the resurrection one must first die."[61] Most issues included Pereleshin's poems, articles, and reviews, the latter signed V.P., Sigma, or Avrelii.

The older generation of poets criticized the newspaper. Antistigmat (Nesmelov) wrote that "the hot-house nature of Churaevka only harms its members" and their poems had no connection with historical time and place. Pereleshin disagreed: "'modifiers of time and place' only lessen a poem's chance of, if not immortality, then at least of a long life. It is great that it is not important to know where and when Pushkin's 'Prophet' [*Prorok*] and Lermontov's 'Branch from Palestine' [*Vetka Palestiny*] were written."[62] The poet Vasilii Loginov stated that "Churaevka's members have been forever infected by pessimism, very harmful and dangerous" and quoted Pereleshin's "unbearable ugliness of early wrinkles" from "Concerns about Daily Bread" (*Zaboty o nasushchnom khlebe*, 16.4.1934). He ominously attributed Pereleshin's "Parisian" pessimism to his "real nature, which does not merit approval" and further censured Pereleshin for saying in the article "Closer to the West!" (*Blizhe k Zapadu!*): "our cultural capital (we have no political capital) is Paris, while here we have, sad as it is, distant boondocks of the Russian emigration."[63]

In Paris, the émigré poet and critic Georgii Adamovich found *Churaevka* "not bad at all," and "we were encouraged by these words. Not only were we noticed in the 'capital of the world,' but Adamovich *himself* spoke of us with approval."[64] But then, the Parisian *Numbers* (*Chisla*), which had already published a poem by Nikolai Shchegolev and accepted one of Pereleshin's poems, had *Churaevka* reviewed by Iu.T., who garbled surnames and dismissed its poetry as unoriginal and influenced by "poets of twentieth-century Petersburg, as well as some contemporary poets." Pereleshin angrily retorted in *Churaevka*: "Brilliant *Numbers* finally condescended to our provincial immaturity, condescended and thought: how glad the province would be, with what reverential delight it would shine! [...] Really! Paris – and Harbin! *Numbers* – and *Churaevka*! Harbin poets deserved 'at least politeness.'"[65]

In the autumn of 1933, Peterets and Shchegolev decided to break away from Achair's tutelage and with the support of some members formed a "Poet's Circle" or "Poet's Workshop" with Gumilev as "a suitable figure for canonization: Acmeism, Adamism, selfless bravery, and a martyr's death from a Bolshevik bullet."[66] This challenge to their mentor was marred by nasty anonymous epigrams aimed at Achair in a Churaevka album, where members and guests were free to jot down comments and impressions. Achair stepped down and graciously wrote in his farewell article: "I am literally happy that now, in the eighth year of existence, your firmly established nucleus acknowledged it to be its duty to bear the entire responsibility for the life and activities of the circle."[67]

What destroyed Churaevka was not this rebellion, but a heady mix of young loves and rivalry and the political situation in Manchukuo.

Peterets and Granin fell in love with Andersen, described as "an airy, 'apple-blossom' girl," but she was not interested in either. Peterets "showered his love with fairy-tale names – Solveig, Valkyrie, Giaconda – and wrote poems, not too openly confessing his love. At the same time, he, clever and sensible, knew that his love was not likely to be reciprocated."[68] Granin, unlike Peterets, was attractive, and his pseudonym implied strength and polish; he "imagined himself to be Pechorin [the disenchanted hero of Lermontov's *Hero of Our Times*], hating himself for rosy cheeks, youth, and lack of success with women, who treated him as a child and who was, indeed, a child."[69] Peterets resorted to "painfully offensive epigrams," which mocked Granin's surname Saprykin and his peasant origins; it was "cruel, but we all were cruel then in the typical way of youth."[70] Granin took the unrequited love and mockery badly. In cheap basement restaurants, where the poets would order vodka and "two pickled cucumbers for eight people," Granin "would get drunk faster and uglier than anyone. [...] He once got drunk and kept shouting in English: 'Come back!' He probably noticed that when the Chinese drink, they shout *ganbei*! [Bottoms up!]. Innocent *ganbei* became 'come back,' and the drinks would sometimes 'come back.'"[71]

Granin hinted that he would commit suicide on Churaevka's seventh anniversary on 28 March 1933. Everyone got "emotional and concerned. We visited each other and kept suggesting ways of preventing this great disaster and subsequent scandal. [...] Peterets alone was completely calm. 'Why are you so tense, Valerii?' he asked. 'I know Granin well. I can tell you with total confidence, I can promise you, his Mum, and his stepfather that he will not kill himself, but get drunk.'"[72] At the well-attended celebration, Pereleshin stood by the door to the main hall and suddenly heard swearing, blows, and crashes from a nearby classroom. Slobodchikov rushed to separate Granin and Shchegolev, and the two fighters ended on the street, where Shchegolev shouted: "You ... you ... you ... are Granin!" and Granin shouted back: "And you ... you ... you are also Granin!"[73] Granin then started coming to the studio drunk and a couple of times vomited in a drawer of a school desk at the YMCA. At Achair's request Churaevka expelled him. A few days later, in a cheap hotel Granin took an overdose of veronal. His life was saved, and newspaper reports hinted at unrequited love.[74]

Pereleshin faced his share of heartbreak. He fell in love with Granin and went to taverns with him. In his poems, dismissed later as "repulsive," "Dragged out the limp, the heavy" (*Vyvolok bezvol'nogo, tiazhelogo*, ca. 28.12.1932) and "At the hunched doorstep of a tavern" (*Na kabatskom sgorblennom poroge*, ca. 28.12.1932), a drunk companion tenderly calls the poet his only, his best friend, but the poet's aching heart warns him that "sober people never repeat their drunken tenderness."[75] Granin was soon replaced in his affections by Vladimir Slobodchikov, but their relations "consisted of mutual respect, frequent meetings in Churaevka, or at his and my homes, where we played Preferans or mahjong."[76] Slobodchikov's eyes, "blue as Lake Baikal," were sung in several poems; "More guarded talks" (*Nastorozhennei rechi*, 19.9.1933) says that "as in the delirium of an illness / or in a crazy dream / I will throw myself into the abyss, / into their deep blue depths." The unpublished "Letter" (*Pis'mo*, 10.4.1934) declared that, "hiding in the darkness, / but coming to love the light with you, / I will take the torch out of the amphora / and call you my brother!" His infatuations were limited to veiled poems, whereas Petr Lapiken, nicknamed "Murochka," reacted to Nikolai Shchegolev's rejection of his love with a petty revenge: at one meeting he read a poem allegedly by Andrei Belyi and, when Shchegolev greatly admired it, confessed that he wrote it himself.[77]

Tragedy, 1934

Не плакать о сердце своем,	Not to weep over one's heart,
Не плакать о горе чужом	Not to weep over another's grief,
И над неприкрытыми ранами,	Or over open wounds,
И даже над целыми странами,	Or even over entire countries
Что гибнут во зле мировом, –	That perish in the world's evil, –
Не плакать уже ни о чем.	No longer weep over anything.

"Not to weep over one's heart"
(*Ne plakat' o serdtse svoem*), 1.4.1935

Life in the Japanese puppet state of Manchukuo was "so gloomy that extraordinary willpower was required to avoid seeking oblivion in drugs or vodka."[78] Émigrés were leaving, and Churaevka lost Andersen, Lapiken, and Peterets to Shanghai, and Lidiia Khaindrova to Dairen. In mid-1934 Pereleshin chaired the poetic studio, and the remaining members met informally "to read poems, discuss new books, and wonder about the future, our own and that of Churaevka, literature, and Russia."[79]

The expelled Granin joined the Harbin Russian Fascist Party and in its newspaper *Our Way* (*Nash put'*) and journal *Nation* (*Natsiia*) "smeared not only the YMCA (he saw the Baptist missionaries as Masons and subversives), but also his former Churaevka friends," thinly disguised as insulting "Akhsatir" (Oh, the Satyr!) for Achair, "Zavodchikov" (Factory Owner) for Slobodchikov, or "Pupiken" (Belly Button) for Lapiken. Pereleshin was not mentioned; on the contrary, Granin, in his dark Fascist uniform with a holstered gun, visited his former friend, who "had stopped trusting him a long time ago."[80] When Granin started having long secret talks with Sergin, who was involved in the pro-Soviet organization "Perfect Youth" (*Otmol*), the Churaevka poets tried to talk to him, but Granin was, as one recalled later, "abrupt and aggressive, giving a strange impression of a person who was losing his balance. It looked as if he was under the influence of narcotics. He reproached us: allegedly we were slighting him, and this freed him to write anything about Churaevka. Sergin was his closest, perhaps his only friend, and he did not have to report their conversations."[81]

In the early morning of 7 December 1934, Sergin's mother ran over to Pereleshin's place, as they lived nearby: her son had not come home the preceding night. From a neighbour's phone Pereleshin called his mother at work at the Russian-language Japanese newspaper *Harbin Times* (*Kharbinskoe vremia*), but she had not heard anything. On returning home late that night, she told him that Granin and Sergin had committed suicide in the seedy Nanking Hotel. The mother and son rushed to Sergin's place to prevent his parents from learning of the tragedy from the morning papers. The gates were locked, and Pereleshin helped his mother climb over the fence and followed. The door was opened immediately. Sentianina told them that Sergin was very ill, and Pereleshin whispered the truth to his father.[82]

Sergin's suicide note, published in Harbin newspapers, said: "I am shooting myself. Would Iura [Granin] be able to take the revolver from me and shoot himself? My dear ones, forgive and forget. The funeral should be civic. Long live the USSR! I do not hold anyone responsible for my death. S. Petrov." Granin's note read in part: "I am asking crime reporters not to invent sensational and touching versions of a tragic love. It's not worth it, and I will be grateful. Moreover, there was no love at all. The funeral, naturally, should be according to religious rites. Glory to Russia! Georgii Granin. 5.12.1934."[83] Slobodchikov claimed that the original notes "were immediately removed and replaced by others, written in a desirable way. This could have been done only by Fascist followers." Harbin writer Boris Iul'skii later told Pereleshin that both notes ended up "in the ominous collection of crime reporter Kannenberg, who 'collected death notes.'" The Japanese *Harbin Times* and the Fascist *Our Way* alleged that Sergin was ordered to kill Granin, "an active Fascist and fighter against Bolshevism, Judo-Masons, and decadent tendencies in literature, and then, afraid of punishment, shot himself."[84]

Pereleshin, deeply distraught, recalled how, on his last visit, Sergin had recited his poem "Maria of Egypt" (*Mariia Egipetskaia*), which depicted the struggle between heaven and hell, salvation and destruction, the abyss of sin and saintliness. Pereleshin walked him home and, "with 'the second sight,' sensing the shadow of approaching terrible events," instead of "see you later" said "farewell."[85] The day after the suicides, Pereleshin wrote "Poet: In Memory of Sergei Sergin" (*Poet. Pamiati Sergeia Sergina*, 7.12.1934), recalling how his friend worked during the day and wrote poetry at night, when "the eternal Russia, / without adjectives and badges, / came to him during golden nights / through the lines of unfinished poems."

Pereleshin saw Sergin as "a typical martyr of those terrible times, a weak and nervous person, even overly sensitive," "much more complex than the image of 'a Soviet *agent provocateur*' created by the Fascists in *Our Way*."[86] Granin, on the other hand, was "by no means an 'innocent victim' and had nurtured the idea of suicide for a few years before the catastrophe." Larissa Andersen was not answering his desperate letters, and Pereleshin's mother recalled a vial of poison, hidden by him in their buffet; others talked of how one night Granin had banged on the door of a coffin-maker to order a coffin and asked to be accompanied to the cemetery. One of his poems said that at his own funeral "I will be laughing so much: / after all, it is so funny!"[87]

Pereleshin "never stopped thinking about the tragedy with its last act in a disreputable Japanese hotel." At the time, Harbin newspapers were reporting many suicides by people of all ages and classes, defeated by poverty, despair, unemployment, unrequited love, or drugs, made easily available by the Japanese. Churaevka poets admired poems with suicidal themes, especially Anatolii Shteiger's "Ballad about a Gymnasium Pupil" (*Ballada o gimnaziste*) and Boris Zakovich's "Isn't It Better to Fall Asleep" (*Ne luchshe li usnut'*), and "simply raved" about Georgii Ivanov's "Bluish Cloud" (*Sinevatoe oblako*), where lines describing the clouds over a forest alternated with thoughts of a person holding a gun to his temple. A poet, Mikhail Volin (Mikhail Volodchenko), claimed that Granin wanted this poem to be inscribed on his gravestone.[88]

At the same time, in 1934–5, the YMCA became a target of orchestrated attacks by the Russian Orthodox Church and White Russian and Fascist circles with the encouragement, if not the instigation, of the

Japanese rulers of Manchukuo. When the émigré scholar, painter, and theosophist N.K. Roerich visited Harbin on the way to his second trans-Himalayan expedition, the YMCA held an exhibition of his paintings and invited him to be a guest speaker at an Evening of Russian Culture. Lapiken, who was to speak on behalf of Churaevka, came directly from a tennis court in an open-neck shirt and canvas shoes and in his welcome speech recited a satirical poem by émigré poet Don Aminado, where Hindus spun like corkscrews to prevent a cholera epidemic. The young audience "was roaring with delight: Tibetan paintings, exotic Hindu-like guests, and, the main thing, 'style.' That's how our Murochka excelled! Applause lasted for a long time, and someone even shouted: 'Encore!' The only person who did not applaud and in general looked disapproving was Roerich."[89]

Lapiken's prank, however, was nothing compared with the anti-Masonic witch-hunt that was launched in the pro-Japanese and Fascist press. Achair and Roerich were rumoured to be members of a Masonic organization, and Roerich was pressured to praise publicly Japan and its policies. Although most classes in the YMCA Gymnasium were in Russian and scripture was taught by Russian Orthodox priests, it was accused of denationalizing Russian youth. The leader of the Russian Fascist Party, K.V. Rodzaevskii, barrister V.F. Ivanov, and others regularly attacked "Judo-Masons" in the press, and the Fascist *Our Way* declared: "The struggle against the YMCA is a holy duty of every person, because the Synod of Bishops of the Russian Orthodox Church Abroad in its general message on Masons has warned Russian people not to have contacts with the YMCA and condemned it as a Masonic organization, hostile to Christianity and of revolutionary nature, directed towards destroying the principles of national statehood."[90] In vain did Achair defend the YMCA as a Russian Cultural Centre under the banner of "God, Homeland, and Integrity," listing its achievements in cultural work and pointing out that young Russians were taught to be loyal to their homeland and Christian faith, to preserve national dignity, and to be honest and decent people.[91]

In such an atmosphere, the YMCA and Churaevka were blamed for Granin's and Sergin's suicides, and rumours were spread about a "Parisian-style" suicide club, "a vile invention of 'Fascists' to undermine the YMCA."[92] *Our Way* called upon Harbin poets and writers to form a new literary association. The Fascist Party would announce, without any prior consultation, that such and such poets would recite poetry at the Fascist-controlled Russian Club, and the "general political atmosphere was such that it was dangerous to refuse."[93]

Churaevka no longer met, but "in the memory of several years of joint work" Pereleshin, Reznikova, Khaindrova, Slobodchikov, Shchegolev, Volin , and Victor Vetlugin (Pereleshin's brother who occasionally wrote poems) compiled an anthology, which came out on 22 April 1935 in a print run of 200 copies. The title, *Convolutions* (*Izluchiny*), echoing Blok's lines "bitter wine pierced / all convolutions of my soul," was "not very successful, but in some senses it was the right choice: the anthology contained a terse, still youthfully confused, at times naïve record of changeable times and equally changeable souls." It was "a transitional step from poetry within a circle, expressed so vividly by *Seven*, towards diversity. At first, everyone wrote more or less the same (*Seven*), and the difference was not in principles, but in dimensions (of talent and mastery). By the time of *Convolutions*, the monotony of a circle had disintegrated and independent leanings of poets had emerged." Each poet was given five pages, and "it was unanimously decided to have five for Sergei Sergin."[94] Pereleshin contributed "Under the hats – away from light" (*Pod shliapy – ot sveta*, 1.12.1934), "Concerns about Daily Bread" (*Zaboty o nasushchnom khlebe*, 16.4.1934), "Honey" (*Med*, 16.12.1934), "In the Theatre" (*V teatre*, 1.7.1934), and "Summer" (*Leto*, 12.6.1934).

The anthology was praised by *Border*'s editor, Rokotov: "Although young, the poets are already fully formed, fully independent poets. All have mastered the form, know how to shine with bright and apt images, fresh rhyme, and musicality, and successfully avoid banalities." Vsevolod Ivanov responded with "a good-natured, even tender piece of satire," Nikolai Svetlov in Shanghai wrote that "interesting poems by Nikolai Shchegolev and Valerii Pereleshin draw special attention [...] V. Pereleshin accepts life with radiance, creating a beautiful halo over it with his rich fantasy. He is sentimental and thoughtful within reason. One can believe in his poetic strength."[95]

Other reviewers slammed it. A writer, Mikhail Shcherbakov, grumbled that most poems showed "deliberate exhaustion, almost decrepitude of the soul." The poet Vasilli Loginov entitled his review "Act Oddly and Mumble," using a line from Pereleshin's "Under the hats," which he then quoted in full (see the epigraph to the section "Churaevka Literary Circle" in this chapter). His verdict was: "The book is grim, the poems are grim, and for some reason, alongside the grimness, they are full of totally unjustified self-conceit." Two-thirds of this review then praised V.A. Popov's book *Notes of a Fisherman* (*Zapiski rybolova*) and its advice on fishing on the Songhua River. It was, according to the title of Nesmelov's rebuttal, "Malicious Spitting at Young Poets."[96]

The Fascist journal *Nation* launched a predictable attack: "They are not with us. They have become connected with the YMCA, an institution deeply hostile to National Russia. [...] Let's read this little book, let's think about it, and express our opinion: 'Like a monk, I renounce life and your eyes,' 'My youth is going away with unnoticeable steps,' 'Youth is leaving, like a boat sailing away into the sea,' 'The whole life is already in the past,' 'We are leaving, as if into Lethe, we are leaving gloomily,' 'And reticence of a semi-orphan (alone always, alone everywhere),'" the last two quotes coming from Pereleshin's poems. The reviewer added: "it would have been vulgar [...] to demand good spirits, fire, and sabre-rattling from these young people, corrupted and deprived of free will by Messrs Haags, Achairs, and Churaevka. [...] It is not accidental that the collection includes poems of Sergin, who committed suicide and wrote in his note: 'Glory to the USSR.'"[97]

In Paris Khodasevich noted that "V. Pereleshin is undoubtedly talented," and Ladinskii agreed: "By the culture of verse and the skill in treating material, V. Pereleshin and S. Sergin draw greater attention than others," and he quoted in full Pereleshin's "Under the hats – away from the light" (*Pod shliapy – ot sveta*, 1.12.1934). Critic Mikhail Tsetlin noted that "*Convolutions* reveals the seriousness of the participants. The editor Valerii Pereleshin is the most distinctive. The bitterly ironic tone of his poems is unique and memorable."[98] Pereleshin was invited to select some poems for the Paris anthology *Anchor* (*Iakor'*, 1936) and he sent poems by Achair, Nesmelov, and Shchegolev and two of his own, "Under the hats – away from the light" and "The Chosen" (*Izbrannik*, 11.8.1934), which he later condemned as "absolutely awful, in the spirit and style of the poet Mariia Shkapskaia."[99]

Convolutions was the last act of Churaevka. For Pereleshin, this poetic circle was "a piece of my life at the very start of the poetic road, a capsule of Harbin air at the beginning of the 1930s."[100] There he studied poetic theory, apprenticed as a critic and editor, formed life-long friendships, experienced infatuations and tragic loss, and developed his poetic style and his key themes of unrequited love, sin, religious anguish, and the essence of being a poet. Churaevka was his apprenticeship, and he considered 1935 to be the start of his poetic life.[101] Many Churaevka poets continued to write sporadically, but poetry did not consume their lives in the way it did Pereleshin's.

3 Harbin: The Poet as a Monk

Love Affair, 1935–1936

О, для чего ты так улыбнулась, –
Разве улыбок нет других?
Слабое сердце еще не проснулось,
Милая, спящего побереги!
  Милая, пусть никогда друг другу
  Мы не протянем зовущих рук,
  Только бы в эту не падать вьюгу,
  В это безумье, мой грозный друг!
[...]
Страшно мне, страшно! Ты снегом веешь,
О, не зови меня, не зови ...
Нет, ты ведь тоже щадить не смеешь,
Пленница требовательной любви.

Oh, why did you smile like that,
Aren't there any other smiles?
A weak heart has not yet woken up,
Darling, take care of the sleeping one!
  Darling, though we would never extend
  Summoning arms to each other,
  Let's avoid falling into this snowstorm,
  Into this madness, my threatening friend!
[…]
I am afraid, afraid! You are bringing snow,
Oh, don't call me, don't call …
No, you too do not dare to be merciful,
A prisoner of demanding love!

"Before Love"
(*Pered liubov'iu*), 3.7.1936

In the summer of 1935, Pereleshin's aunt Emiliia Naam introduced him to the mother of a girl she was tutoring. Elena Aleksandrovna Genkel', fourteen years older, married, with a daughter from her first marriage, befriended the young poet. His "Cinderella" (*Sandril'ona*, 28.8.1935), dedicated to her, empathized with "my golden Cinderella," whose prince had tried her crystal slipper on the feet of many girls, had dropped and smashed it, and would now never find her.

Genkel's husband was soon transferred to Dairen, the Japanese name for Dalian in Chinese and Dal'nii in Russian. She "wanted me to write to her; we corresponded and decided that we had fallen in love."[1]

She invited him to spend the summer of 1936 with them. Pereleshin's mother, aware of his gay infatuations, thought that he "was mistaken (!)" and an affair with an older woman would help, while he, afraid of brutal religious censure and social derision, imagined that he might "get straight" and "become like everyone else."[2] The sin of having an affair, and with a married woman at that, paled in comparison with what was seen as a much greater sin.

It was his first sight of the sea, a break from studies, and relief for his weak lungs and the rheumatic aches in his feet from walking in old and often wet shoes.[3] Lelia, as he now called her, and her young lover read poetry, swam, sunbathed, went for walks, and played with her teenage daughter. Genkel' scribbled at the end of his letter to his mother: "Valerii is with us, and I am happy, what else can I say? I am glad for him … and for myself, and I have more fun; I have someone to take care of, and I love him dearly."[4] When her husband, ignorant or indifferent, returned from work, they all went for a swim: "In the cold foamy surf / the blue sea was splashing, / and stars in the depth of the sea / seemed to have fallen down / from the fiery night sky. / Then a lighthouse would start blinking. / Back to the beach! Coffee and cognac, / a toasted piece of bread / and, a Poseidon of Japanese blessings, / a seaweed soup *udon*."[5]

It was in Genkel's house that he read Nina Berberova's *Chaikovskii*, heard the *Pathétique*, and "understood everything once and for all": "Nadir of anguish, the zenith of symphonies, / the *Pathétique* is thundering, / and my denigrated life / burns my eyes with the fire from my palms. / Mocked and doomed, / exposed to the very end, / to the most shameful nakedness, / I start openly talking to myself. // […] My ears are filled again with / the mocking scherzo – and an adolescent's scream: / a humiliating spring is spurting / out of the restless heart. / Crushed by the first half / of the symphony, I sneaked out / from the drawing room, like a crafty thief. / I ran down the stairs. Turned round the corner / once, twice, three times. The sobbing of loud laughter / rushed after me: stop! / There, on an empty square, / boys were playing soccer, / – was it a prediction of more bitter evils, / created by my delirium?"[6]

After he returned to Harbin, the lovers kept in touch, and in the following spring Genkel' invited him again, but, unable to tell her the truth, he vaguely spoke of leaving "for the above": "If I could truly love you with my 'entire' being, I would not dream of leaving, but I am powerless, and my spirit is split. […] I suffer unbearably, and I am fated to suffer all my life from this accursed duality, which, it means, is *necessary for some purpose*. […] I sin, and already repent, regret, and mock myself. […] It seems that God clearly leads me along a difficult path and demands new and yet new renunciations. He wants me to free my heart from all worldly attachments to people and things."[7] His "Rebuff" (*Otpoved'*, 6.6.1937) was a further duplicity: "So, do you regret that I have not become totally / happy, like a faithful dog, in a cramped doghouse, / where, instead of the sky, I would have / caresses of your hands and your wonderful voice? // No, I cannot live without muses and writing; / for the sweet paradise of the southern nature, / for your most fascinating captivity / I will not give up my sufferer's freedom."

Genkel' was puzzled and hurt. When her bitter comments reached him, he wrote to a common friend, nastily commenting that it was time for "the amorous Dairen lady," "the old woman, to console herself" and that she "understands absolutely nothing in poetry and […] and sees everything as a reference to herself." Her brief visit to Harbin in 1939 turned her into "a most evil enemy. […] She openly said to Mum that 'she saw and heard so much at our place' that now she knew us quite well, especially me. Moreover, in the city (at the Achairs', by the way), she started some very dirty gossip about me, involving Mura Lapiken."[8] In retrospect, he saw her as a Circe, whose "overly tender shoulder" had briefly captivated him: "This was my first and last experience of intimate relations with a woman. The result was pathetic: I finally understood that 'normal' life was not for me." Although his mother kept "advising me to marry ('there are devoted and loving women') and 'to raise a good boy,' I did not succumb. I cannot think of my affair with a married wench (a society lady) without shuddering: how repulsive all that was!"[9]

Illness and Decisions, 1937

Лирный напев забыт –
Ныне на зов иной
Сердце твое спешит:
Сердцу пора домой.
[...]
  Ты говоришь: "Нигде
  В мире не отдохну,
  Только в святом труде,
  В том восковом плену.
В годы, когда я пел
И ликовал во грехах,
Там обо мне скорбел
	The lyre tunes are forgotten –
	Now to a different call
	Your heart is rushing,
	It's time for the heart to go home.
	[…]
	  You say: "Nowhere
	  In the world will I find rest,
	  Only in holy work,
	  In that captivity of beeswax.
	During the years when I was singing
	And rejoicing in sins,
	A monk in his cell

В келье своей монах.
  И когда по меже
  Худшего зла я шел,
  Ждали меня уже
  В улье печальных пчел."
Ну, так входи, входи:
Здесь, прилетев домой,
Сердце умрет в груди
И оживет – пчелой!
	Was grieving for me.
	  And when I was walking along
	  The border path of the worst evil,
	  They were already waiting for me,
	  In the beehive of sad bees."
	So, come in, come in:
	Here, having flown home,
	The heart will die in your chest
	And will be reborn as a bee!

"On the Threshold"
(*U poroga*), 13.10.1936

By the mid-1930s, Sentianina and her sons had become "catastrophically impoverished." Sentianin's assistants in the Hunger Aid to Russia campaign had "included embezzlers and thieves, and Vasilii Evgrafovich was constantly covering up the sins of others and thus contributed to his financial ruin."[10] Sentianina, an impractical and gullible widow, was left with "a mortgaged house and several relatives as advisers, who speeded our downfall." She tried to cope by taking in tenants, but by January 1931 had to take a loan for 7,000 silver dollars at 20 per cent with the house as collateral. Three years later, sued for non-payment, she sold the house, and "after that, our financial ruin was swift." She bought another "heavily mortgaged house," unkempt, cold, and bleak, but by 1939 was forced to sell it as well and rent an apartment.[11]

She earned very little from freelancing for Russian émigré newspapers *Dawn*, *Gun-bao*, and *Harbin Times*, and for the journal *Border*, and at times she pawned her gold bracelet and jewellery to survive. Pereleshin studied at the Law Faculty and Victor at Harbin Polytechnic; neither worked.[12] Their father himself often had to borrow money and complained to Pereleshin that "no matter how great my financial difficulties are, they do not depress me as much as Victor's repulsive attitude to me and to Grandfather, and E.A.'s sulking and defending Victor. Both are sowing wind and will reap a storm."[13]

The family became so impoverished that in the spring of 1937, a month before the examinations, Pereleshin dropped out from the Oriental Department and, even though he had a law degree, got a job as a daily reporter at *Gun-bao*: "I lost two years of zealous study, and another beloved thing was ripped out of my heart." After a few weeks of this "vile job" he moaned that he had to run around and work so hard that "I crawl home totally wrecked, half-asleep by nine, quickly eat my portion of rice porridge, and fall into bed. [...] Poems are a distant past."[14] In October 1937 the Japanese closed the Law Faculty and its departments: "one aspect of the Japanese occupation policy in Manchuria was destruction of the Russian educational system. Japanese 'consultants' with unlimited powers appeared at all institutions of higher learning, and before long our faculties were closed one after another. My dream of a professorship died with it."[15] What did not die was his love for the Chinese language and culture.

In the summer of 1937 an outbreak of dysentery, rumoured to have been caused by Japanese experiments in bacteriological warfare, swept Harbin. Sentianina and Victor recovered quickly, but Pereleshin spent "a grim month" at the Kazem-bek Memorial Monastery Hospital and at one time his father was told that his condition was hopeless.[16] During his convalescence, Pereleshin met another patient, Vasilii (Vasia) Nesterenko, who was dying of tuberculosis, and grew "tenderly attached" to his meekness, "cornflower-blue eyes," and tearful pleas for visits after Pereleshin's discharge. At home Pereleshin prayed for his life to be exchanged for Vasia's and came down with severe laryngitis, which he took as acceptance of his prayers. Two days later, barely recovered, he rushed to the hospital, where he learned that Vasia had died: "Ah, had I been more enlightened and pure, / the Lord would have helped dear Vasia. / [...] / Even now in a golden iconostasis / I look for his thin body and the cloak, / awkwardly thrown / on the dying body: / through the decay of hospital blankets / a saint was shining to me."[17]

It was then, at the age of twenty-four, that he made two crucial decisions: to publish a book of poems and to become a monk. From his hospital bed he heard the bells of the nearby Kazansko-Bogoroditskii Monastery and watched monks going to prayers and working on its grounds. He keenly felt "the futility of my attempts to set myself into a routine life of the overwhelming majority. This discovery shook and frightened me: society of that time did not permit any variations from 'man – woman.' I had to run away from myself into higher regions, where gender loses any meaning, that is, to a monastery."[18] Images of monastic life appeared in his poems well before "the blessed beehive of black bees / entered my heart as a symbol."[19] In "Monk" (*Monakh*, 13.1.1934), a monk looks at "human beehive" where young faces "long for sinful happiness," subdues his flesh, and returns to his cell to declare his love to God. In "Dream" (*Son*, 27.9.1936), church doors, funereal bells, and black cassocks call to the poet: "Look how blessed / are the hearts and lips / that day and night / are searching for Christ. / The entire cheerful, / triumphant swarm, / like black bees, / is flying to fetch you!"

On the Way: The First Book of Poetry, 1937

Мать, первенца в Китай счастливый с собою взяв издалека, моею стала терпеливой учительницей языка. Как впечатлительная пленка, хранила, полная любви, солдатиков и медвежонка и рифмы первые мои. Ей, благодарный бесконечно, за каждый навык трудовой, я сердце посвятил навечно и самый ранний сборник свой.	My mother brought her first-born from afar to fortunate China and became my patient language teacher. As a sensitive photo film, she saved, full of love, toy soldiers and teddy bear and my first rhymes. Eternally grateful to her for every work habit, I have forever dedicated my heart and my earliest collection to her.

"Dedication 2"
(*Posviashchenie* 2), 14.1.1972

Following the booklets containing his early cycles, in 1933–4 he proceeded to more ambitious rehearsals for a future book by creating several mock-ups with title pages, tables of contents, and pagination.[20] The first, "MCMXXXIII," dedicated "To Dear Mum, a keepsake from Valerii. 8.12.1933," comprised six parts. The first was "Eternal Rome" (*Vechnyi Rim*, 21.4.1932), an expansion of the earlier "Orthodox Russia drowned" (*Pravoslavnaia Rus' utonula*, ca. 1932), where three sections in different metres portrayed the destroyed Orthodox Russia and the eternal triumph of the First Rome. The theme barred it from Russian émigré periodicals, but not from the Japanese-controlled *Harbin Times* (*Kharbinskoe vremia*) and Shanghai journal *Phoenix* (*Feniks*).[21] On reading it, a Harbin poet, patriotic Marianna Kolosova, angrily shouted at Pereleshin: "I hate you! You are my enemy, because you are an enemy of Russia!" His reply was that the poem "echoed my origins in a Polish Catholic family" and that "a Russian can be Orthodox, Catholic, Lutheran, Jewish, Muslim, or even an atheist."[22]

The second part, "Bracteates" (*Brakteaty*), contained poems on Scandinavian themes written in Churaevka and filled with images from Icelandic sagas – Adelgunda, Valhalla, Valkyries, and "a torn horizon / with a herd of storm clouds driven into a lather." The third, "Firebird" (*Zhar-ptitsa*), consisted of love poems, where "bird," a feminine noun in Russian, concealed the sex of the beloved. In the fourth, "Addenda," the apocalyptic "End of the World" (*Gibel' mira*, 1933) was followed by more love poems with genderless or feminine addressees. The fifth,

"Renunciation" (*Otrechenie*), presented poems on painful non-gender-specific love and ended with its renunciation. "In front of me again, again" (*Peredo mnoi opiat', opiat'*, 30.10.1933) speaks of temptations, which force the poet to abandon "shards of angelic childhood / and youthful purity," and of "the exciting power" of "dark, suppressed, / persistent, earthly, / and undisguised passion." If he was frank in his early booklets, now he was getting quite adept at camouflage.

The second booklet of two parts, "MCMXXXIV" and "MCMXXXIV-II," also was dedicated "To Dear Mum." The poems grew more mature in their treatment of unfulfilled love and the joys and sorrows of being a poet. A few had feminine pseudonyms. "April Evening Is Fresh and Silent" (*Aprel'skii vecher svezh i tikh*, 31.1.1934), written at his mother's request for her "Women's Page" in *Gun-bao*, was signed Anna Perovskaia. Anna was taken from Akhmatova, whom he called "an ailing genius" in his "To a Poetess" (*Poetesse*, 22.4.1932), and Perovskaia after "*pero*," a pen. In this poem, a woman wanders on a spring evening, evading "unhurried embraces" and "dark blue eyes / (more blue than this blue night)." Then, he and his aunt Emiliia Naam invented a poet called Mariia Kareeva; Emiliia "prompted" topics, and he wrote sentimental, mediocre poems for *Churaevka* and *Border* on the joys, hopes, and disappointments of a woman in love. One of them, "Oath" (*Kliatva*, 14.1.1935), was, he admitted, "all Tsvetaeva." Emiliia Naam as Mariia Kareeva even came to several meetings of Churaevka, though not everyone was taken in by the hoax.[23]

He later judged many of these poems to be "an utter horror," "imitating" and "simply stealing" from Blok and using "*merde*" rhymes. In the early 1940s, he asked his mother "to throw those stupid notebooks into the stove: there is nothing good in them" and became furious when she arranged for some to be published: "I do not consider this shit in *Border* under my signature as mine, and I definitely forbid you to publish anything from the old garbage."[24] His mother saved every one of these booklets.

In the life-changing summer of 1937, he initially entitled his first book *Wings* (*Kryl'ia*), a title "very suitable thematically; I imagined an artist designing a cover with this motif." At that time he had only heard about the gay poet Mikhail Kuzmin's *Wings* (1905), which he later described as "a lace-like, charmingly depraved novel [...]; its theme clearly sounds in my 'To Lucien Létinois' [*K Lus'enu Letinua*, 4.9.1934]." Lapiken and Reznikova talked him out of *Wings*, "and, no matter how bitter it was to give up the idea already so dear to me, I nevertheless agreed with their arguments, precisely because some threads from the yet unknown to me Kuzmin might be traced in my poems."[25]

The final choice, *On the Way* (*V puti*), had many echoes. One was Lermontov's famous "I am coming out alone on the road, / a rocky way lies ahead of me. / The night is quiet, the desert heeds to God, / and a star is talking to a star." Another echo came from Gumilev's "On the Way" in *Pearls* (*Zhemchuga*, 1910, 1918), which says that the time for games is over and one should forge ahead on "the way" to an eternally flowering garden. The choice also might have been influenced by J.K. Huysman's *En route* (1895), which Pereleshin had read in translation during his summer in Dairen.[26] The novel traces the spiritual development of the hero, who, after searching for his way in life, retreats to a Trappist monastery. In Pereleshin's poetry, the phrase "on the way" first appeared in "Calm eyes are with me on the way" (*So mnoi v puti glaza spokoinye*, ca. mid-1931), where the poet follows "the way" towards "a promised land / prepared for me by a Queen."

Like all books of poetry in Harbin, *On the Way* had to be self-financed, but he had no money. Lidiia Khaindrova, now in Dairen, tried to help. In the Churaevka years he was "immediately and forever captivated by [...] this beautiful and charming lady with the Caucasus-type face (wonderful large velvet eyes, very white skin). [...] Her entire appearance, noble, gentle, full of goodwill, won favour once and for all."[27] They corresponded, and she in vain appealed to a former Harbin Russian, Petr Balakshin, editor of the literary journal *Land of Columbus* (*Zemlia Kolumba*) in San Francisco, hoping that he might publish it: "Pereleshin's life has lately become very harsh; he and his entire family are in a bad financial state, at times nearly starving. These circumstances apparently led, I would say, to a mental confusion, because the role, or rather the monastic vocation, does not fit Valerii, as I used to know him in Harbin; it could have been expected of the late Sergei Sergin. Valerii Pereleshin will soon be ordained a monk, and his mother is in despair. This choice does not seem horrible for people who are older and know life, but, as far as I know, Valerii is not yet twenty-six [he was twenty-four], and his great talent will be doomed to decay. To distract him a little from this thought, his mother is now looking for any means to publish a collection of his poetry."[28]

In the end, Sentianina borrowed money for the deposit to Dawn Printers, and *On the Way: Poems 1932–1937* (*V puti: Stikhi 1932–1937*), in a run of 300 copies, came out on 16 October 1937, dedicated "To my mother Evgeniia Aleksandrovna Sentianina." The back cover listed E.A.

Sentianina as the publisher and V. Pereleshin as the author. One can imagine the excitement they felt on holding the slim paperback with its wonderful smell of fresh ink. Even a minor mistake in the table of contents could not mar their joy.[29] Friends in Harbin, Dairen, and Shanghai, and Volkoff in Canada sold copies to friends and acquaintances, and eventually the book paid for itself and even made a little money.

All forty-four poems, in chronological order by year, had appeared in Harbin periodicals. The book opened with "Eternal Rome" (1932), "my first significant poem, written at the age of nineteen,"[30] followed by two 1933 poems on Scandinavian themes; twelve poems represented 1934, eight 1935, seventeen 1936, and four 1937. The title said it all: a young poet is searching for his way in life. In "Rebuff" (*Otpoved'*, 6.6.1937), it is a "thorny path, / and narrow gates are at its end"; monks in "Instruction" (*Nastavlenie*, 31.10.1936) advise him to get "away from the beaten path" and seek "a narrow borderline path [*mezha*]." This constriction is reinforced in "Fate" (*Rok*, 31.10.1935), where the poet feels like a "small boat, squeezed into locks," and "Enlightenment" (*Prozrenie*, 22.5.1934) celebrates clarity, no matter how painful.

One way in life is to follow the wings of poetic inspiration. He longs for nightly visits of his "bright and winged Muse" in "Barely up from the bed" (*Edva podniavshiisia s posteli*, 20.5.1934) and for "rhythmic winds" and "icy storms of Parnassus," and he fears becoming a bookworm swallowed by academic libraries in "You live in the backwoods of ink country" (*Zhivesh' v glushi strany chernil'noi*, 20.5.1935). Another way leads to the "narrow gates" of the highly idealized monastic world, where he could become free of sinful desires and passions. In "Instruction" (*Nastavlenie*, 31.10.1936) the "black, meek ones" beg "the boy" to avoid temptation of "tender hands," because "love is the start of decay / and the voice of the flesh is the voice of lies." The poet appeals to God in "At Night" (*Nochnoe*, 14.11.1936): "Your unfaithful slave [...] / is weak in body and spirit" and asks to be accepted as a prodigal son.

The notion of an unnamed "sin" appeared in several poems. In "Calling" (*Izbranie*, 9.1.1936), the poet wishes to forget "the sinful burden, / with a love note burning in the stove"; in "On the crossroads by shop windows" (*Na perekrestkakh u vitrin*, 6.11.1933), "a gloomy and puny boy" watches people flirting on the streets and weeps with shame at home. Most significantly, the book included "To Lucien Létinois" (*K Lius'enu Letinua*, 4.9.1934), "the first open declaration of the poet's concealed nature." The poem, addressed to Lucien, admires his likeness to a girl, his golden hands "worthy of sin or ailment, / and tears, and kisses, and rings," and his last tubercular breaths, captured by "the sacred and sinful" lips of Verlaine and "sounding more beautiful / and higher than any pure and sinful / earthly love." When this poem first appeared in *Border*, very few readers got its meaning, but it caused "a storm" in the editorial office, and the publisher angrily reprimanded the editor for the oversight.[31] In "Concerns about Daily Bread" (*Zaboty o nasushchnom khlebe*, 25.2.1934), the poet mourns his love in yet another "camouflage, because the poem is about Iura Volkoff [...], my most ardent youthful love." "In the Theatre" (*V teatre*, 1.7.1934) and "Jeune Premier" (*Pervyi liubovnik*, 1.7.1934) stem from his brief infatuation with a young tenor, Nikolai Sliusar', whose stage name was Nezhin.[32] Notably, he did not include his early poem "In the Morning" (*Utrom*, 21.1.1933) with its direct question: "Do those who love have sins?"

Pereleshin liked his first "child": "it has a thematic and spiritual unity: the book is truly 'The Way,' which, in many of its directions, led to an internal desert: from sovereign Catholicism, from simple impulses of friendship and heart, through the fiery baptism of creative work, to humble, downtrodden Orthodoxy, strong only in its truth, to tired sonnets, to an indignant misogyny of 'Instruction' or 'Temptation.'"[33]

The "indignant misogyny" came from religion. In "Monk" (*Monakh*, 13.1.1934), it is a monk who sees girls with "destructive / passions in the shadows of their eyelashes, / and their single sigh holds harm no less impure, / than in the eyes of loose and sinful women." In "Woman" (*Zhenshchina*, 9.2.1934) a woman entices a man not by love, fragrances, rustle of silks, and pale skin, but by coming in the night, like a "biblical sinner," with loosened hair, white shoulders, and sultry lips. In "The End of Wandering" (*Konets stranstviia*, 27.4.1938), in a quatrain omitted from the book, a monk would welcome a novice only if he forgot "the one who conquered / your strict shame and unawareness of your accumulated strength, / if you forever forgot that image and that voice, / if you forgot the daughters of humankind." On the other hand, "Seamstress" (*Beloshveika*, 14.4.1935) and "Dragonflies" (*Strekozy*, 10.10.1935) empathize with hardships of women's lives, and "Misogynist" (*Zhenonenavistnik*, 28.3.1938) tells a man that if he has never kissed hands of a beautiful woman, he "is not worthy / of believing, crying, and singing as humans do."

In 1968, inscribing a copy of *On the Way* for a friend, he wrote: "Many poems 'resonate' in me even today." Another retrospective comment, in 1975, emphasized that "one of my first 'adult' themes was the refusal to accept the world. I was probably given the soul of a Manichean. In my world view, there is a sharp separation between light and darkness, good and evil, spirit and flesh, striving for purity and attraction to 'the very boiling' of sin. The key word of my entire life is duality. I rush between two poles. In my first book I was already guessing my path in life: towards overcoming the temptations of 'Maya' and moving to refinement of spiritual capabilities. I have already formed the ideal of monastic life, of asceticism."[34]

Reviews were favourable, though brief and superficial. N. K-ov (Karypov) in *Gun-bao*, O. Shtern (D.G. Satovskii-Rzhevskii) in *Dawn* (*Zaria*), M. Tal (Talyzin) in *Harbin Times*, and N.R. (Natalia Reznikova) in *Border* paid compliments and cited some stanzas. Achair described Pereleshin as "going the neoclassicist way" and hoped that "his Muse would manage to combine the calling of the heart with the calling of human spirit." Georgii Adamovich wrote in *Latest News* (*Poslednie novosti*, Paris) that Pereleshin was "clever and inventive. While being a 'singer,' he always remains a 'writer' as well, as Goethe taught."[35]

Some forty years later, Aleksis Rannit wrote that in his first book Pereleshin was a "skillful craftsman" of poems aiming at "chamber-music lyricism," distinct from the "Paris Note" of Georgii Ivanov, Georgii Adamovich, and others, and closer to the "cold" line of Baratynskii, Gippius, Gumilev, Khodasevich, and Bunin.[36]

Monk Herman, 1938

Лишь бедный черноризец новый
украдкой сядет за стихи,
его игумен шлет суровый
идти замаливать грехи.
  Но что? Лицом угрюм, как туча,
  игумену на стыд и страх,
  клобук на брови нахлобуча,
  он благохульствует в стихах!

As soon as a poor new monk in his black cassock
furtively starts writing poetry,
a severe Hegumen sends him
to go and pray for forgiveness of sins.
  But what of it? With a face grim like a storm cloud,
  to the Hegumen's shame and fear,
  the monk pulls his black cap to his eyebrows
  and blasphemes in his poems!

"Impromptu"
(*Ekspromt*), 14.10.1939

As Pereleshin later recalled in the third person,

> Verlaine and Lucien, Lord Henry and Dorian Gray, Shakespeare and Willy Hughes, and, more distantly, Hadrian and Antinous, and, in reverse, Alcibiades and Socrates, that's how one way of thought was projected. At

> the time, this way seemed capable of overcoming the terrible law of life, which enslaved the spirit of the flesh and turned a proud individual personality into one of the zeroes in millions, an ordinary procreator. The poet had never conquered that adolescent fear of a full-blooded life, inevitable and therefore repulsive. He ran away to the romantic cult of friendship, to a library, to an academy, to monastic life, back to a hypocritical 'acceptance of the inevitable,' but he did not conquer it. The personality, like his life, became split forever.[37]

Sensitive and deeply religious, Pereleshin wanted not only to become a monk, but also to get a theological education and rise in the monastic hierarchy. By the early 1930s, the Harbin Russian Orthodox Eparchy, established in 1922, looked after some forty churches and two monasteries in Harbin and in settlements at CER stations. The eparchy jealously controlled its flock, fought against missions and sects, and set up Higher Theological Courses to train future priests. In 1934, these courses were absorbed into the St Vladimir Institute with Theological, Polytechnic, and Oriental-Economic faculties, founded by the Japanese authorities of Manchukuo as a part of their plan to take over all Russian education. At the opening ceremony, Archbishop Meletii's speech on the Russian emigration's losing its culture in foreign lands was followed by a speech in Japanese by the notorious "Konstantin Ivanovich" Nakamura of the Japanese gendarmerie. In 1935, its first dean, Professor M.P. Golovachev, was arrested and expelled from Manchukuo for speaking against the Japanese control.[38]

In the autumn of 1937, Pereleshin enrolled in the Theological Faculty, ambitiously recalling how "Larissa Andersen saw my photograph on graduation from the Law Faculty and said: 'What a passionate face! And the eyes are strict, like those of an Archimandrite.'"[39] The Theological Faculty, proud of being the heir of theological academies of old Russia, had some fifty students in two programs, one for Harbin residents and another for those who studied by correspondence and came for examinations. Students faced a four-year program of courses such as Old Testament, New Testament, History of Fundamental Theology, Church Archaeology, Logic, Psychology, Philosophy, Pedagogy, General and Russian Church History, and Liturgy. Teaching the "Manchurian Language," as Chinese was called in Manchukuo, and the "State Language," that is, Japanese, was soon abandoned.[40] Now he "carried home, like fetters, / the soul-saving books: / *Comparison of Ancient Liturgies*, / canons, lives of saints. / I wanted to reach biblical / sources,

I was learning / that the decrepit world was saved by Christ, / promised through the prophets / a long time ago." He particularly enjoyed studying Latin, Church Slavonic, and Greek, and took some private lessons in Hebrew.[41]

At the same time, he entered the Kazansko-Bogoroditskii Monastery as a novice, hoping to become an industrious bee in a beehive buzzing with good deeds. The monastery, founded in 1922, was a large compound comprising the church, bell tower, residence for monks, printing press, workshops, cattle barns, and the Kazem-bek Memorial Monastery Hospital, all located in the outlying Gondatti Suburb of Harbin.[42] As "Repayment" (*Otplata*, 6.10.1939) says: "in this world you have chosen not peace / and not the warmth of a settled home, / but a hard bed and a lectern, / and ancient renowned volumes."

Everyone had tried to talk him out of entering the monastery. His mother "responded to my departure with great suffering," making him feel even more apprehensive and guilty:

> On the whole, I enter this world timidly and cautiously: I am leaving Mum behind with her incredible loneliness (except for me, she does not have a single friend in the whole world) and her total helplessness and tiredness of life. Her financial situation is unenviable: there is a thousand and a half left from the sale of the house. One cannot do anything with such amount; it would be enough for a year or two of a very frugal life. I have never been, it's true, much help in this respect, but still, tying myself with this step, I am forever cutting off a future possibility of at least compensating for the losses and helping Mum in some way. I am afraid and ashamed that her poverty and things worse than poverty will be an eternal reproach for me, and the realization of my uselessness and impotence deprives me of the last energy and strength on this difficult road. With these thoughts I have arrived at the monastery, and they never leave me.[43]

At that time, as if to still his heart and draw a line, he had his first sexual experience with a man, a Chinese house painter.[44]

In the monastery he took part in services, baked communion bread, studied typesetting, and went to evening lectures at the Theological Institute. On 7 May 1938, he was ordained Monk Herman (*German*), in honour of St Herman of Kazan' and Sviiaga; the name days were close, St Herman on 6/19 November, and Valerii on 7/20 November. The ordination was gruelling: "I spent three days and three nights in the church, with 'Lord, have mercy upon me!' sung in a funereal tune."

On the assigned day, after lengthy prayers and questioning, the novice crawled on his knees three times to the hegumen and handed him scissors; the first two times he was rejected and humbly kissed the hegumen's hand. On the third approach, the hegumen took the scissors, cut out a cross in the novice's hair, and gave him a new name as a sign of total abandonment of the world. The new Monk Herman was then dressed in a tunic, with a *paramand* (a square cloth depicting the eight-point cross on the instruments of the Passion and the Adam's skull) tied to his body as a sign of following the Saviour; a cassock, belt, and mantle were put on over the tunic. A *kamelaukion*, a tall black hat, was placed on his head, his feet were encased in sandals, and he was handed a prayer rope. Elated, he "immediately felt as if I was born in a cassock and had never been Valerii."[45]

His new life was full of deprivations, work, and hardships. Some monks were ignorant and envious; others drank heavily. He saw that

> personal freedom is curtailed by statutes and conscience (for those who feel; others eat meat, drink vodka, and keep friendships with women). Thus, a romantic youthful daydream […] crumbles to dust at the first Lent or after a month or two of monastic life. Monks face this inner, invisible tragedy (some run away later, even when endowed with high rank: I know one defrocked hegumen; others 'lose it' and turn from idealistic 'sons of light' into career-minded officials). Monastic life was not a departure, but an entrance to a new, constrained world of serving one's neighbours and God (the other way round, God and one's neighbours). In the monastery I see some excellent people, true Christians (mostly simple, uneducated people), and I hope that the Lord will also give me wisdom and strength to bear this cross.[46]

A change in superiors brought more difficulties. Monastery Head Archimandrite Vasilii, the dean of the Theological Faculty, was forced to leave Manchukuo for criticizing the subservience of the Harbin Eparchy to the Japanese and to their stooge, the Bureau for the Affairs of Russian Émigrés in Manchukuo. Before long "the entire brotherhood, one and all, grumbled and railed" against the new father superior, Priest-Monk Innokentii, "a bitter, two-faced, and simply mentally ill person." Life "became intolerable": this "real madman introduced switching lights off at 9:30 in the evening and planned locking up the entrance gates, to be unlocked only during services." Pereleshin clung to his "safety valves" – the Theological Faculty and teaching scripture at the Harbin

Ecclesiastical Seminary – "otherwise, it would have been completely impossible to bear the cross of obedience to a person such as Priest-Monk Innokentii." In vain did he hope for Archimandrite Vasilii, now a bishop in Potsdam, to invite him to Germany or for Bishop Iuvenalii to return as the head of the monastery.[47]

He formed "exceptionally warm" relations with Father Varsonofii, whose "tragedy was vodka. He usually drank a little, but sometimes went on a binge. In such cases this mighty man covered himself with shame, because no one dared to restrain him from an all-night service, when, at the end, each of the believers approached to be anointed with oil and breathed in the smell of raw vodka. I did not dare to ask him to miss the service and stay in his cell, but envious people and enemies among the monks even rejoiced at his humiliation."[48]

Father Varsonofii used to say to Pereleshin:

> "Many call me a drunk. But what kind of a drunk am I? A drunk is the one who is lying around on the ground, and I've never done that." This distinction, however, did not save Father Varsonofii from a reckoning. One early morning, Dimitrii Voznesenskii, bishop of Hailar and the First Vicar of Archbishop of Harbin Eparchy [...] a lecturer at the Law Faculty and at the Theological Faculty, [...] came to the monastery. After Liturgy, the Right Reverend announced the decree of the eparchy head, which listed in detail all the evil deeds and sins of Father Varsonofii, down to the fact that he had ordered the locking up of the walk-through yard of the monastery, thus making access of local residents to their houses difficult, because local streets were drowning in mud. Much was said about Father Varsonofii's weakness for vodka. Listening to this, Father Varsonofii was shedding large tears.[49]

The censure was instigated by the "possessed" Priest-Monk Innokentii, "who inflicted many humiliations on Father Varsonofii with his denunciations and later forced me to leave the monastery." Only after Father Varsonofii was transferred to Beijing Eparchy, "did it become known how many good deeds he had done and how many needy people he had been helping. Practically every day, some poor woman would come to the monastery to see the kind monk who had regularly supported her."[50]

Pereleshin coped with "two repulsive sides of monastic life: vodka and bedbugs, but religious control over my literary activities was worse." As he confided to Khaindrova,

> your reflection that I am first a poet and then a monk brings bitter thoughts. Alas, others also notice: I am constantly having frictions with the higher spheres. The other day, Bishop Dimitrii suggested that I become my own spiritual censor and no longer publish in *Border.* He did not dare to appoint a guardian: it would have strongly suggested medieval morals. [...] I have no intention of publishing my poems in *Heavenly Bread* (*Khleb nebesnyi*) [a religious journal published by the monastery] next to humorous verses of degenerate scribblers. I might have temporarily submitted to a ban on writing poems (i.e., not on writing, but on publishing), but the bishop does not demand this, and rightly so, because I am too noticeable a figure for such a measure to pass unnoticed by society.[51]

Although in "Farewell to Muse" (*Proshchanie s muzoi,* 30.5.1937) the poet begged his "deceived Muse, my beautiful pagan," not to weep over his betrayal, he continued to write poems. He could not see "anything unorthodox" in "Death of a Poet" (*Smert' poeta,* 14.8.1938), which offended his superiors: "it is simply a discussion of the old theme of the compatibility of being a monk and of having spiritual freedom. I am convinced that half the bishops in our Church will not demand presentation of only dogmas and religious discussions from a monk-poet."[52] Even when he published as Vl. Nezhdanov, Bishop Dimitrii, "a suppressor of spirit, a merciless arch formalist," "kept attacking me precisely on this matter, the most sensitive one, picking not on individual poems, but on the creative work in general." Pereleshin stood his ground: "Of course, I have no intention of giving up poetry even for a golden cap, even for a bishop's staff. I shall fall silent if I 'dry up,' but as long as I have this voice, I must write and I will": "for Mum and for the Muse I remain Valerii as before."[53]

To the displeasure of his superiors, Pereleshin participated in a Poetry Evening on 26 May 1939. Achair's recital of poems to music was followed by readings from Arsenii Nesmelov, Loginov, Elizaveta Rachinskaia, Vasilii Obukhov, Mikhail Shmeisser, Faina Dmitrieva, Reznikova, and Andersen (on a visit from Shanghai). Khaindrova's and Pereleshin's poems were read by others: she was in Dairen, and Pereleshin, as a monk, could not perform publicly.[54] Another source of conflict was his interest in Catholicism: "I often spoke freely, for example, of my admiration for St Francis of Assisi and St Thérèse of Lisieux." He did not present *On the Way* to the archbishop, because "'Eternal Rome' will not be to his liking." Some priests in Harbin came to call him "Perechertov" (*Pere-devil*).[55]

The main problem, however, was that on "entering a world, where questions of sex did not have the slightest significance, I did not know that monastic life in itself does not create miracles and that in moving from a soft bed to a hard one I would take my illness with me. At the time I saw my indifference to women and attraction to my own sex as an illness."[56] As he confided to Khaindrova, "would a black veil covering my monk's headgear and a cassock save me from that cruel inner discord which poisoned my entire youth? You know my poems well, and you'll understand what I want to say: this is my only and constant theme."[57]

Grateful for Khaindrova's friendship and support, he helped her with her first book, *Steps: Poems of 1931–1938* (*Stupeni: Stikhi 1931–1938*), "in fact, edited it" and "rejoiced, as if it were mine," emphasizing that he had always liked "the inner aspect of your poetry."[58] The title showed a thematic bond with *On the Way*. Two poems were dedicated to Pereleshin. "People's talk brought to you" (*Molva zemnaia prinesla k tebe*, 1937) says: "And the world with its hostility and anguish / have disappeared into darkness. And you, the wise one, have arrived, / blessing the carefree world / and tender morning with your gracious hand." In "Muse" (*Muza*, 1938), Muse is weeping, like a broken-hearted mother, because a man's soul refuses to understand her. Several other poems presented an image of a monk, "a wanderer and a poet," who left earthly joys for "the wisdom of books" and prayers and who alone was given wings of patience and healing light.

Before long, Priest-Monk Innokentii, "one of the evil spirits in my life," created such "an unbearable atmosphere of hatred and distrust" that one day Pereleshin simply walked out of "the place which had seemed a 'good beehive'" and moved home to his mother.[59] It was a mutiny. Khaindrova then appealed to Archbishop Victor, the head of the Russian Ecclesiastical Mission in Beijing, who suggested that Monk Herman apply for a half-year's transfer to Beijing or Shanghai. The mission head also wished him to continue his theological education "at all costs" and was ready to let him go to Harbin for examinations. The Harbin Eparchial Council granted him a three-month leave, and Khaindrova lent money for travel expenses.[60]

His departure was delayed by the disastrous flood in Tianjin, which stopped all trains, and he was unable to leave until 24 September, sad to part with his mother, but relieved at going: "Not a single one of my enemies has left such bitter and unpleasant memories on leaving Harbin as Bishop Dimitrii."[61] He later tended to gloss over the harsh reality of the monastery and the censorship, claiming that he had left on doctor's orders and transferred to Beijing "drawn by the desire to master the Chinese language under the guidance of famous Beijing *xiansheng* [Chinese teachers] and to work in the splendid library of the Ecclesiastical Mission."[62] In fact, the good beehive turned out to be a hornet's nest, where Monk Herman was an alien irritant.

Good Beehive: The Second Book of Poetry, 1939

[…]
На той скале, что вытянулась плоско, –
Твой монастырь, откуда ты ушел,
Обитель звонов, ладана и воска.
Жилище черных простодушных пчел!
Зачем ты преступил его ворота
И вышел в мир превратностей и зол?
Забудь же снова зов водоворота,
Вернись туда, где были для тебя
Почтенье младших и вождей забота!
Ты спишь, старик, едва не погубя
Блуждающую душу, ты безумен,
Свободы жалкий призрак возлюбя.

Но хор монахов, радостен и шумен,
Уже тебя заметил и спешит
Тебе навстречу сам седой игумен.

И вот ты снова в добрый улей влит;

Но ты молчишь, смущенный и суровый,
И только взор незрячий говорит
О том, что ты созрел для жизни новой.

[…]
Your monastery, which you have left,
The abode of bells, incense, and beeswax,
Is on that flat long rock.
A dwelling of simple-hearted black bees!
Why did you step out of its gates
Into the world of vicissitudes and evil?
Forget again the call of the vortex,
Return to the place where you had
Respect from juniors and care of the leaders!
You are sleeping, old man, nearly ruining
Your wandering soul, you are mad,
Having fallen in love with the pathetic phantom of freedom.
But the choir of monks, joyful and noisy,
Have already noticed you, and
The gray-haired Hegumen hurries to meet you.
And now again you are merged into the good beehive;
But you are silent, uncomfortable, and stern,
And only the unseeing eyes reveal
That you have matured for a new life.

"A Runaway" (*Beglets*), 14.12.1937

Delayed by the flood, Pereleshin was still in Harbin when his second book of poetry, *Good Beehive* (*Dobryi ulei*), came out on 5 September 1939.[63] The name on the cover said "Valerii Pereleshin (Monk Herman)." The book, he knew, would get his superiors "mad with anger. Archimandrite Filaret finds my poems *totally secular*, and that's Archimandrite Filaret, a progressive in the clerical world! I can imagine what will happen to Bishop Dimitrii, priests, and my 'abbot,' Priest-Monk Innokentii!"[64]

The title came to him in the hospital. As he described it in a third-person account, "it was a terribly slow return to life. Strictly speaking, there was no flesh left, but precisely then the flesh saw the most rudely sensual dream in its entire existence. Years later, this theme of ineradicable evil, rooted in the subconscious world, appeared in the poem "Le mal invincible" (15.3.1943). All around him, August leaves were turning gold, monastery bells were ringing, and bees kept flying into his room. He saw the image of a 'good beehive,' of a working community of sexless bees, of self-sacrificing monks seeking a different way in life. It seemed that monastic life was the end of the process presented in the poet's first book [...], and the title for the second book was born: *Good Beehive*,"[65] where "good" (*dobro*) contrasted with evil (*zlo*).

Twenty-two poems of *Good Beehive*, arranged in chronological order by year, overlap with the first book: one each from 1934, 1935, and 1936; seven from 1937; eight from 1938; four from 1939; plus a translation of a Chinese poem. He worked hard to put them together: "old poems are quite different in spirit and do not coexist with the new."[66] If in his first book images of a monastic life in poems such as "Good Beehive" (*Dobryi ulei*, 8.10.1937) suggest the way, in the second the poet has found his destination. "The End of Wandering" (*Konets stranstviia*, 27.4.1938) emphasizes that there is no place for his Muse even by the outer gates. This particular poem "caused, according to my archimandrite, 'a whole storm': how could I write that a schema monk looked like a wood demon?"[67] In "Death of a Poet" (*Smert' poeta*, 14.8.1938) the poet's arm is "encircled, as if chained, by the sleeve of black clothes," and now he, "a timid and inexpert psalm singer," picks up "an alien reed pipe."

The poems present "'a year in a monastery.' In this small collection I predicted (in "Runaway" [*Beglets*, 14.12.1937]) leaving the monastic life. I understood very soon that it was impossible to run away from myself, from my own duality. No matter in what bed you put a patient, the illness will remain. In *Good Beehive* I had already foreseen that psalms would lose out to songs of pagan Muse."[68] Discordant notes sound in the enmity between his wise right hand and the revengeful left in "Two Hands" (*Dve ruki*, 24.8.1937); in the question "Why have you, in the midst of your way, / started thinking, and not at all about God?" in "Deliberations" (*Razdum'e*, 1.5.1939); and in begging God to turn him into clay for an amphora in "Prayer" (*Molitva*, 9.5.1939). Two poems stand apart thematically. "We" (*My*, 10.2.1934) is a defiant statement of the mission of the first-wave émigrés to preserve "the undying Russia," and "Not to cry about someone else's heart" (*Ne plakat' o serdtse chuzhom*, 1.4.1935) echoes the Parisian note of despair over the state of the world. His translation of a Chinese poem showed his growing interest in Chinese poetry.

In his review "Poems of One Theme" Nesmelov described the poems as "superb" and "heavy," like precious metals; their echoes of sadness and bitterness "accompany even the most voluntary renunciation in every living soul." He noted conflicting notes in "The End of Wandering" and "Death of a Poet" and concluded that the poet "is almost blind to the world beyond himself." Pereleshin agreed: "He is right in saying that I write only about myself and do not see the world because of my own self."[69]

Although Pereleshin was to return twice for examinations at the Theological Faculty, his Harbin childhood and youth were over. His lonely and desperate struggle to suppress his homosexuality plunged him into the celibate world of service to God, the world which condemned his very core of being a gay poet.

4 Beijing: "Wonderful, Beloved City"

Beijing Ecclesiastical Mission

[…] Стою, как путник давний и бездомный, У мраморного белого столба, И город предо мной лежит огромный, Как целый мир, как море, как судьба. Так высоко стою, так величаво Вознесся храм Лазурных Облаков, Так высоко, что умолкает слава И только ветра слышен вечный зов. О, если бы, прервав полет невольный, Сюда прийти, как голубь, в свой ковчег, Впервые под сосною белоствольной Вздохнуть и упокоиться навек! […]	I am standing like a homeless traveller of long ago By a white marble column, And the huge city stretches in front of me, Like an entire world, like the sea, like fate. So high I stand, and so majestically The Temple of Azure Clouds rises, So high that glory falls silent And one can hear only the eternal call of the wind. Oh if only, breaking an involuntary flight, I could come here, like a dove, to my arc, And under the white-trunk pine For the first time to sigh and find eternal peace!

"View of Beijing from Biyunsi"
(*Vid na Pekin iz Bi-iun'-sy*), 27.6.1943

On 25 September 1939, a day of "golden Beijing autumn," bespectacled Monk Herman in his black cassock and monk's tall hat got off the train at Qianmeng Railway Square, hired a cab ("a hefty rickshaw" in a later poetic account) and set out for the Beijing Ecclesiastical Mission. On the way, he marvelled at the beauty of ancient towers and gates, multitude of colours and sounds, kaleidoscope of shop signs, and bustle and vitality of the crowds. Harbin with its semi-Russian life was a young provincial hybrid; it was the ancient Beijing that captured Pereleshin's poetic heart with its unforgettable beauty and the air of history and traditions. It became the "wonderful, beloved city," "sweeter than home," forever remembered "with keen love."[1]

The Russian Ecclesiastical Mission traced its beginnings to the middle of the seventeenth century, when the Qing government destroyed the unauthorized Russian settlement of Albazin on the Amur and captured some Cossacks, who then accepted service in the Manchu Eight Banners troops. An old temple in a northwest area of Beijing, known as Beiguan, was converted into an Orthodox chapel for them, and from 1715 Russia continued to send missions to maintain the faith among the Albazin descendants, who had intermarried with the Chinese. By the time of Pereleshin's arrival, Beiguan had a cathedral, two churches, a monastery, nunnery, library, school, printing press, mill, candle factory, and dairy.[2] The mission, as the head of the Beijing Eparchy, looked after five churches in Shanghai, three in Tianjin, and one each in Harbin, Kalgan, Hankou, Dairen, Port Arthur, Liaoshan near Qingdao, Changchun, and Mukden. It repelled Soviet attempts to seize its property, looked after Russian émigrés, and published dictionaries; studies focused on China, Manchuria, Mongolia, and Tibet; religious texts in Chinese; and a monthly journal, *Chinese Evangelist* (*Kitaiskii blagovestnik*).[3]

Beiguan struck Pereleshin as "a real Chinese town with tiled roofs, brick walls, numerous stairs, back alleys, and large parks":

> its heart was St Innokentii of Irkutsk Church with an adjacent apartment for the mission head. This building had been, it seems, the temple of the fourth prince of the Manchu dynasty, and its architectural style was untouched. Golden dragons intertwined on the ceiling, and the multicoloured ornamentation of its columns and pilasters poignantly merged with cherub heads on the walls, austere icons, and the ancient icon of St. Nicholas of Mozhaisk. [...] In the choir behind a lattice most choristers were Chinese, singing in Church Slavonic. [...] At the Lunar New Year, it was the Mission's tradition to hold the liturgy entirely in Chinese, and some psalms, "Cherub," for example, acquired a harmony inaccessible in inflectional languages. Chinese touches were present every Saturday, when one *cathisma* was read in Chinese. Sometimes, when a chorister read the six psalms, Chinese priests uttered many holy exclamations in Chinese. All this was very touching: truly, no Hellene, no Israelite! The roof of the church was covered with coloured tiles, predominantly green, and figures of legendary animals to frighten the evil spirits were lined along the finials. A symmetrical Greek cross towered above the entrance.

North of St Innokentii Church stood All Holy Martyrs Church with its monument to 222 Orthodox Chinese, Manchus, and Mongols who were massacred during the Boxer Rebellion. Close by, the Assumption Cathedral with its blue cupola and cross looked "quite 'Russian,' but here, too, icons of many Christ's disciples had Chinese faces, an endearing, though imprecise detail, which reminded one that the Saviour belonged to the whole world and that each nation was right in accepting him in its own way."[4]

At that time, the head of the Twentieth and, as it turned out, the last, Mission was Archbishop Victor (Sviatin), a Russian Civil War veteran. Under the Japanese occupation, Victor became a spiritual leader of the Tianjin-based Anti-Comintern Committee of North China and preached that the glory of Holy Russia would shine with the victory of "imperial Japan, national-socialist Germany of Hitler, and fascist Italy of Benito Mussolini." The Japanese awarded him an Order of the Rising Sun, and, as Pereleshin said later (verbatim from English), "he very often invited the people to pray for a Japanese victory and the restoration of 'National Russia.' That was his chief idea at that time. Archbishop Victor published an Easter address to the Orthodox Christians, even at the time when Germany was defeated, inviting everybody to hope for restoration of Russia and a Japanese and German victory."[5]

Life in Beiguan, 1939

В колеснице моей лечу
над землей на четыре "чи,"
и закутан я не в парчу,
а в одежду из чесучи.
Вновь Наньчицза передо мной:
это улица или лес?
Столько вязов над головой
в непроглядный срослось навес!
Ночь, весна. От земли тепло.
Эта улица – "чжи жу фа":
выпевается набело
поэтическая строфа.
Чесучи своей не помни,
возвращенец издалека:
помни – крылья только одни
на бесчисленные века.
А теперь колесницу сна
задержи, ночной пилигрим:
это свет из того окна,
что когда-то было твоим.

I am flying in my chariot
four "*chi*" above the earth,
wrapped not in brocade,
but in Chinese cotton clothes.
Nanchijie is again in front of me:
is it a street or a forest?
So many elms intertwined overhead
into an impenetrable canopy!
Night, spring. Warmth rises from the earth.
This street is "*zhi ru fa*" [straight as a hair]:
the poetic line
is singing naturally.
Forget your cotton clothes,
as you are returning from afar:
remember that only one pair of wings
is granted for countless ages.
And now hold still the chariot of dreams,
nocturnal pilgrim:
this light is from the window
that once used to be yours.

"Beijing" (*Pekin*), 3.7.1972

Father Varsonofii welcomed Pereleshin "as a relative," and the mission head turned out to be "exceptionally charming, courteous, cultured, and kind. I presented him with my book; he thanked me and a few days later said that he liked my poems. So I can continue my literary work: a poet and a monk are compatible."[6] At first it seemed that "Beijing had no intrigues. [...] The archbishop's attitude to my poems in *Border* was calm, though he later gently asked that 'Beijing' not be put [under Pereleshin's name] in publications. He reads *Border* regularly and frequently comments on my poems. In particular, he renamed my "Miserly Heart" (*Skupoe serdtse*, 29.10.1939) "Blind Heart" (*Slepoe serdtse*), saying that a person withdrawn into himself loses more than he gains and that one should love the world in spite of its ugliness and cruelty."[7]

The Beijing years became "a most important stage" in his life. The order of his priorities is revealing: "Here I will study Chinese language and literature, read, help in the publishing house, teach, and serve in the church." The monks, however, were "fed a bare minimum and given a roof; as for the rest, everyone has to take care of himself. [...] As a result, Beiguan old-timers walk around like ragamuffins, ignore various illnesses, and so on."[8] To earn some money, he took on the "hard and thankless task" of teaching in a Church school in the Legation Quarter: Russian émigré children attended English or French schools and went to Sunday classes for Russian and scripture. At one meeting, Pereleshin "soundly criticized the parents of these unbearable little Russian foreigners."[9] In contrast, he loved teaching at the mission's Russo-Chinese school, which had over 100 Chinese pupils. At first, he taught not only Russian and scriptures, but also Japanese, as demanded by the Japanese authorities, and took some Japanese lessons to keep a step ahead of his pupils. In April 1940, he participated in "a great joyous occasion: sixteen pupils of the mission school, their young teacher Wu, four adults (the most interesting were a son and his elderly mother), and three babies of Orthodox Chinese couples were christened. At the school's request, I was godfather for most of them."[10]

In Beijing winters, the weather fluctuated between freezing winds and warm sunny days; "yesterday we had an unexpected snowfall, but towards the evening it got warm again. It snowed all day and clung beautifully to branches of evergreen pines and thujas. I kept recalling Ladinskii: 'As in a Scandinavian drama, / in the last act, suddenly, / snow is falling in scoops / from someone's tender hands.'"[11] Although he wrote later that "we endured the cold relatively easily," at the time his letters were full of complaints. His room was so cold that he wore a housecoat over his cassock; although he had a small heating stove, no coal was issued until November. He continually contracted colds and lost weight, but a request by another monk to give him extra milk, butter, eggs, and a double portion of bread was rejected.[12]

Much was expected of the educated Monk Herman. In December 1939 he also worked as a librarian and "found a multitude of wonderful books, in spite of the fact that the mission's ancient library had been burned down to the last book during the Boxer Uprising." Another duty was that of office clerk: "the entire correspondence of the mission head passes through my hands, eyes, and memory. [...] The mission head has already written in very warm tones about me to Metropolitan Meletii, Bishop Ioann, and Archimandrite Nafanail. By the way, he wrote to the latter: 'I thank the Lord for this monk.'" At one time he even represented the mission at the Cultural and Educational Commission of the Anti-Comintern Committee.[13] Some monks distrusted and envied this graduate of the Law Faculty, student at the Theological Faculty, and poet, and they argued that no important duties should be assigned to him and he should be forbidden to leave Beiguan even for the Japanese lessons. The director of the mission school, A.S. Ostroumov, "a slanderer and intriguer of the most petty and vile kind," fearing for his job, gave the mission head a fifty-point denunciation of Monk Herman, which the head dismissed after listening to the first fifteen points.[14]

When Archimandrite Nafanail, a former White Army officer, returned from a trip to Yugoslavia, Pereleshin was delighted to find him "amazingly sophisticated, clever, brilliant, and warm-hearted," "without a shade of hypocrisy, but only with simplicity, calmness, humility, and exceptional charm"; "he has an inspired, clever face and beautiful fingers. He is educated and loves music and photography. We have acquired a major cultural force."[15] The liking was mutual. When Pereleshin blundered in a liturgy, on return to his cell he found "a wonderful branch of white lilac, stuck in the door handle. I immediately guessed: it was a greeting from Father Nafanail." Although Pereleshin sometimes grumbled about Father Nafanail's strict rules and assignments, the friendship was much appreciated. The two spent some evenings "talking about my poems, which left a deep impression on Father Nafanail, and he made many apt and subtle comments." In the father's cell, Pereleshin for the first time heard a recording of Wagner's *Parsifal*, "which forever shook me and acquired the same standing as *The Pathétique*."[16]

The small Russian community in the Legation Quarter noticed the young poet-monk. The family of the late Lieutenant-General D.L. Khorvat, the former CER manager and *de facto* governor of the CER zone, still lived in the former Austrian Embassy; on meeting Pereleshin, his widow, K.A. Khorvat, a minor musician and writer, bought his books of poetry. The widow of Baron von A. Stael-Holstein, a sinologist and specialist in the philology of Central Asia, hired him to tutor her children.[17] The former Austrian Embassy also housed Professor Ia.Ia. Brandt, "the sweetest old man who welcomed me exceptionally warmly, as all Beijing residents tend to do." Brandt presented Pereleshin with his *Teach Yourself Chinese Conversational Language*, published by the mission and promised him a forthcoming textbook.[18]

Another new acquaintance was D.P. Panteleev, the mission's secretary and editor of *Chinese Evangelist*. Panteleev, "erudite, partial to slight mockery," did not know Chinese, but, like many old-timers, knew the city and showed Pereleshin the old Beijing. Pereleshin became "totally and forever captivated" by the Imperial Winter Palace, even though "everything shows the sadness of neglect. Some marble beast statues, which chase away evil spirits but are powerless against people, were stolen, and many of the porticos were turned into sheds and lost colour, while the ceilings were taken apart for firewood. Nearby [...] there is a Chinese university, and students built a toilet near the Wall of Nine Dragons. Now the wall is repaired and cordoned off with wire, but will the wire save it? I saw a marble crocodile with the head and half of its body broken off and carted away, and banisters of a marble bridge over a small ravine overgrown with planted grass, now dry, were stolen."[19]

In Panteleev's company he visited Meishan, the hill where the last Ming emperor hanged himself from a tree: "for a long time this tree had been kept in irons, and only the revolution freed it. We sailed across the lake on a scow, pretty and very clean, and went up the labyrinth inside the hill to its top. [...] The sun had just set beyond the Western Hills, and one could see the grey-blue fog thickening among the hills." After sightseeing, Panteleev would invite him to a Chinese restaurant for soup with mutton, cabbage, garlic, and fish-bone noodles, accompanied by wheat buns, sprinkled with sesame seeds, which became one of Pereleshin's favourite meals.[20] Another new friend, S.M. Syrova-Vakhromova, showed him more ancient sites and took care of him, giving him useful gifts such as cod liver oil and arranging for his cassock and clothes to be laundered and garments of departed monks altered for him.[21]

The most important new friends were the Korostovets family, who also lived in a wing of the Austrian Embassy. Pereleshin loved the story of how F.I. Korostovets, son of former Russian envoy to China I.Ia. Korostovets, was awarded the Order of the Resurrection of Asia by the Japanese "for his quietness and irresponsibility" in some Russian collaborationist organization and promptly tied it to the tail of their dog Fil'ka. Just at that time one Russian, who, "it was said, did not shun ties with the Japanese gendarmerie, came over, and the order-bearing Fil'ka was hurriedly dragged away to a distant corridor."[22] Korostovets's wife, Mariia Pavlovna, was one of the five daughters of the late sinologist and diplomat, P.S. Popov, and, "as one Beijing wit said, the five sisters had one husband and one son." The mission head called them "the prophetic sisters" for their knowledge of astrology, philosophy, and the occult.[23] The Korostovets family hired Pereleshin to tutor their son Mark, and on Sundays he usually dined at their place, which "truly became my home." They gave him treats, clothes, and shoes that Mark had outgrown, and the father and son layered the cement floor of his freezing cell with newspapers, mats, and a carpet, sealed the windows with paper strips, and installed a heating stove.[24]

Mariia Korostovets became his closest friend. Some fourteen years older, she believed that their meeting was predestined:

> I knew that I would meet you, that is, not you precisely, but a close friend from a very distant past. For many weeks before, I felt 'someone' approaching me, and one day, when I went to Beiguan, the Voice in my head said: "you will meet this friend today in the church." I was at the liturgy and looked around, but there were no new faces. The service ended, and I was leaving, disappointed and surprised. The Voice deceived me, but the Voice could not deceive ... And suddenly, between the two exit doors, still inside the church, I bumped into a swiftly entering slim monk, a stranger to me, in glasses, with a beautiful curve of the lips. My first thought was: is he really the one? But one does not argue with the Voice. I immediately struck up a conversation with you and invited you to our place. That's how our friendship started.[25]

She was convinced that he was in Beijing "for her sake, because she was passionately praying to God for a brother, who would support her (and I always thought that it was she who was supporting me! It turns out that in dark days, which she has as well, she consoles herself with the thought that Father Herman exists, and it means that all is well). Mariia Pavlovna is a mystic, and a genuine mystic."[26] She made their meetings "joyful and memorable" and showered him with gifts. Together they visited "many wonderful nooks of this huge, ancient city" and strolled in parks as he recited his new poems to her. The beauty of Beijing gave him "an endless amount of thoughts and sources for poetic work."[27] He had originally "believed in astrology no less than in alchemy, until she offered to compile my horoscope and, after talking about important and significant matters, added pensively: 'In two weeks you'll have an abscess on your right hand.'" Ten days later he caught his hand on a prickly branch, and the scratch became infected. He then studied astrology with her and for many years afterwards compiled a horoscope on his birthday "to know opportunities and dangers awaiting me (though I do not believe in unconditional predetermination or fate; such belief is somehow immoral)."[28]

On 30 March 1940, a significant step in his advancement in the monastic hierarchy took place, and he wrote to his mother: "I am rushing to bring you joy. Your prayers are answered, and today the mission head, Victor, bestowed the rank of deacon-monk upon me. Thus, I am facing a difficult service for forty days and, in general, service for life. [...] Now life has acquired meaning, deep content, and goals, minor and immediate, major and distant."[29] It could have been done earlier, but the Harbin Eparchy dragged its feet, and when it finally agreed to his permanent transfer to Beijing, Metropolitan Meletii pointed out that Monk Herman had not been promoted in Harbin because of his "strong sympathy towards Catholicism."[30]

His first duty as a deacon-monk was to go to Tianjin and assist the ailing Archpriest Feofan Zhui, a descendant of Albazin Russians, with lengthy Easter services. Pereleshin rejoiced at this opportunity "to absorb more new impressions, thoughts, and people." Father Feofan was "a model priest, and his wife and children are also ideal. I received payment for services and a gift from Father Feofan to a total of $100.00. The work was difficult, but I was fed and well paid. The ninth day after Easter was particularly hard: all the trees in Tianjin had died after the flood, and it was unbearably hot at the cemetery. We conducted no less than thirty memorial services in three or four hours."[31] It was flattering "to be greeted by strangers in the street and respond, because they are welcoming a monk, not Valerii Pereleshin. The latter, however, is also known here," and A.P. Shnapshtis, a one-time chairman of Churaevka, organized an evening of Pereleshin's poetry.[32]

He had "a good look at Tianjin and saw not only palaces, but also slums." The city, with its foreign concessions, was "a stone mass," "a corner of

Europe," so unlike his beloved Beijing, which was "China, ancient, real China."[33] In Tianjin he marked the second anniversary of his becoming a monk: "such dates are somewhat frightening: you look back and suddenly think that so little has been accomplished and such big responsibility has been assumed. The day after tomorrow is another 'stage': the end of my forty-days' service. I did not even notice this rather long period: I flew as if on wings. If I ever were a monk, it was precisely during this period." However, he declined a permanent posting to Tianjin: "in Beiguan I am in the capital of Beijing Eparchy, at its pulse, while here is a province; here the emphasis is on the Church and request services, while there it is on prestige, scholarship, and teaching."[34]

On his return on 10 May 1940, he felt "very happy, as I have never been before. Even outsiders notice my 'radiance,' not very bright, but very obvious."[35] He found time to write poems and translate Coleridge's *The Rime of the Ancient Mariner*, which he had studied in his final years at the YMCA Gymnasium. He had already worked on this "almost untranslatable" poem in the monastery in Harbin, "taking advantage of the lack of inspiration" for his own poems.[36] Now he enjoyed the challenge: "the content is fantastic and gloomy, but with an excellent and enlightening central thought." His text lacked marginal notes, but once he had the complete edition, he left them out because they "distracted the reader." He strove to convey the metre, rhyme, and stanzas of the original, but in places resorted to a rather liberal translation and improvisation. Years later, he conceded that his translation had many shortcomings.[37]

The translation was published in *Border* in August 1940 and as a book on 4 September 1940. He could not afford a special cover and illustrations, "artistic, with the sea, romanticism, and salty wind," but was "on the whole pleased, though, of course, many things still have to be polished and improved." In 1944, in Shanghai, he learned that it had been translated by Gumilev in 1919 and felt that his "audacious attempt" was "in vain, because one cannot write better than Gumilev." In the early 1970s, he acquired Gumilev's translation and was "very intrigued" and apprehensive that it might subconsciously influence him were he ever to rework his own edition.[38] His translations from English extended to a few poems by a theosophist, Ella Wilcox (1850–1919), popular in her day for mediocre, but passionate poems. He "did not pursue precise translations, but rather wrote on borrowed themes," as indicated by the subtitles "After Ella Wheeler Wilcox."[39]

At the end of May 1940, Pereleshin went to Harbin for examinations at the Theological Faculty and, as he already knew, found a big change at home. His brother Victor had left for the United States; their plan to meet in Dairen on Victor's way to Shanghai fell through.[40] The brothers did not get on. Pereleshin considered Victor "neurasthenic" and depressive and felt that Victor's "attitude to Mum leaves much to be desired. He believes that our difficult circumstances are her fault, and I think that this false opinion (how could there be any fault, apart from gullibility, inexperience, naiveté, and an unfortunate combination of circumstances?) will determine his future behaviour."[41] Victor, in turn, saw his brother as "egocentric," a person who, "though not lazy, felt burdened by any paying job; he would spend nights writing poetry or letters, reading, sorting his stamps, but used all means to avoid routine work." Pereleshin became a theological student and monk to avoid working, and "Mum and I were deeply hurt that during our difficult times Valerii continued his studies and did not help us."[42]

Victor's life developed differently from his older brother's. He was expelled from the YMCA Gymnasium "for an insignificant offence" and enrolled at the A.S. Pushkin Gymnasium.[43] He also wrote poems, but stopped because "one poet is enough in any family." He studied electromechanical engineering at Harbin Polytechnic, and although he and his classmates had to accelerate their studies to graduate before the Polytechnic was closed by the Japanese in 1938, his diploma project won a prize for excellence. He could not find work, lived at home, took odd jobs, tutored, and taught evening classes at the YMCA. In winter he and his mother "often had to choose between heating the apartment and eating."[44]

Like many Harbin Russians, Victor felt that it was "necessary to get out of Harbin; there will never be a good life here" and applied for a visa to the United States; it was planned that he would then sponsor his mother and brother.[45] The US visa arrived in March 1940, but the Japanese, taking a dim view of the departures of professionals, would not issue an exit permit. Victor appealed to their neighbour, Colonel Martynov, known for his involvement in shady assassinations and kidnappings, and the colonel arranged for a visa to Shanghai.[46] Victor's mother gave him most of her emergency fund, and Victor hid the money and the American visa in the false bottom of his suitcase. As he recalled, "the day of my departure was sad. I said good-bye to Mum and petted our old bulldog Jimmy, knowing that I would never see him again. All my relatives and friends came to the railway station to see me off."[47]

Pereleshin was glad that "the miracle we were praying for had happened" and chided his mother for seeing Victor off "with tears: it would have been better to postpone the 'hysterics.' [...] Don't worry and don't feel sad: everything is turning out for the best and will continue to do so. Your sons are on good paths in life, and it is entirely your accomplishment." When his father complained that Victor had forgotten about him before leaving, Pereleshin defended his brother, and his father "was forced to make a belated discovery: suddenly, Victor has turned out to be 'intelligent, kind-hearted, and noble.'"[48] In San Francisco Victor could not find work, and his "painful and nervous" letters stopped. Only in May 1941 did they learn via friends that Victor, now Victor Frank Salatko, had joined the US Army. No correspondence was possible during the war; as Pereleshin wrote to his mother, "I often think about Victor and always remember him. Now I love him almost as much as I love you."[49]

"After the storms caused by Victor's departure," his mother was happy to welcome Pereleshin home, and he managed to stay not in the mission's residence, but with her. After sleepless nights over books, he passed twenty examinations and left in September 1940, briefly stopping in Mukden to see "the old city with all its beauty."[50]

Priest-Monk Herman, 1941

Так много раз сближались наши руки,	Our hands got close so many times,
Глаза с глазами стали так дружны,	Our eyes became so friendly,
Что нам уже ни сроки, ни разлуки,	That we no longer fear time constraints,
Ни глаз чужих обеты не страшны.	Separations, and promises of other eyes.
Ах, пусть любовь горами двигать может,	Ah, although love can move mountains,
Но одного не победит любовь:	It cannot conquer one thing:
Что у меня твоей белее кожа,	My skin is whiter than yours,
А у тебя медлительнее кровь!	And your blood is slower!
[...]	[...]
Смолою почек пахнет прелый воздух,	Musty air smells of resin from buds,
Белеет поздний парус вдалеке.	White sail moves tardily in the distance,
Но не сумею рассказать о звездах	But I will not manage to tell you about stars
Я на твоем чудесном языке.	In your wonderful language.
А ты, когда гуляешь по аллее	And when you stroll along an alley
С высоким юношей твоей страны,	With a tall youth of your country,
То у тебя лицо еще смуглее	Your face looks even duskier
И бездны глаз особенно темны.	And abysses of eyes especially dark.
	"Limit" (*Predel*), 22.2.1941

After the Harbin trip, Pereleshin continued teaching in the mission school and working in the library, as well as tutoring four Chinese teenagers, "possible future priests." His workload increased in February 1941 after he was appointed mission treasurer, but he felt good: "monastery life is more beautiful and joyous than any other, and very nourishing for the imagination: owing to a total absence of impressions from real life, they have to be invented or sought among old memories. That's why, no matter how paradoxical it sounds, the monk's lyre does not stop sounding in a major key."[51]

On 9 March 1941 he was ordained a priest-monk. The mission head presented him with a silver cross, and the new priest-monk proudly pinned on his badge of the Theological Faculty and the badge of the Ecclesiastical Academy, which had belonged to Metropolitan Innokentii (Figurovskii), head of the Eighteenth Mission. Mariia Korostovets brought him a pot containing a lilac hyacinth, lilac being the bishop's colour. On the next day, all 100-odd pupils of the Mission School with their Chinese teachers came to congratulate him, followed by his older Chinese students. It was a triumphant day, but deep down he was more and more aware that he was "in the monastery by chance."[52]

He was also getting "fed up" with theological studies: "I wish I could live as a free man, to read and to think. The main thing is the Chinese language. How impatiently am I waiting for that joyful day when I can submerge myself in it!"[53] In January 1940, when some Americans visited the mission, Reverend George D. Wilder invited him to see their College of Chinese Studies. Pereleshin wanted to enrol, but the mission head baulked at the cost, offered to pay for a Chinese tutor, and advised him to study Japanese. He continued to study Chinese "with a passion," on his own and with Chinese friends, and to use the mission's "ample Chinese library."[54]

This passion rekindled his interest in translation. In 1938, on a November evening, walking home along Harbin streets to the monastery after classes at the Theological Faculty, he suddenly remembered a poem, "Song of Yichuan" (*Yichuange*) by Gai Jiayun, from his Chinese textbook at the Oriental Department, where it was wrongly ascribed to the famous poet Li Bai. He started translating it in his head, continued at the monastery, and immediately faced one of the major difficulties, that of connotations. The first three lines gave him no trouble, but the fourth line, referring to Liaoxi in the Northeast, where the woman's husband was sent, "would not come for a long time, and I kept changing it." In his translation in *Border* and in *Good Beehive* the woman is dreaming "about the skies of my native land." In his 1970 anthology, *Poems on a Fan* (*Stikhi na veere*), where the poem is entitled "After Parting" (*V razluke*) and the author correctly given as Gai Jiayun, this line was changed to the still inadequate "about the dear guest from a distant land."[55]

When he was in Tianjin in 1940, the husband and wife A.N. and I.I. Serebrennikov presented him with their *Flowers of Chinese Poetry* (*Tsvety kitaiskoi poezii*, 1938), claiming in the introduction that it was the first anthology of Russian translations of Chinese poetry. The book had 187 classical poems, a few written after 1917 in colloquial language, and religious hymns from Léon Wieger's *A History of the Religious Beliefs and Philosophical Opinions in China* (New York: Paragon Book Reprint, 1927). The Serebrennikovs knew no Chinese and relied on translations by Legge, Giles, Obata, Fletcher, Acton and Chen Shih Hsiang, Hundhausen, and de Morant, with the help of a friend who knew European languages. Their free, unrhymed renderings were greatly embellished in places they considered to be too prosaic. Among the poems by anonymous authors Pereleshin found a mistranslation of Gai Jiayun's poem, entitled "Awakening."[56]

He knew he could do much better: his knowledge of Chinese was growing, he was a poet, and he had translating experience with *The Rime of the Ancient Mariner*. By November 1943 he had translated thirty-six poems from *Poetry of a Thousand Masters* (*Qianjiashi*) and *Three Hundred Poems of the Tang Dynasty* (*Tangshi sanbaishou*) and had published some of them in *Border*.[57] In 1942, with the help of his tutor, G.M. Tang, he translated the anonymous ballad *Mulan* about a devoted daughter who, disguised as a man, fought against invaders of her homeland; it was published in the 1943 New Year issue of *Border*. Pereleshin loved the ballad: "One day, walking in a quiet Beijing lane, I heard a young Chinese singing the first line: *Jiji fu jiji*. I responded spontaneously in the same loud shrill falsetto: *Mulan danghu zhi!* The singer did not expect this at all. Every Chinese person knows the ballad, but a *yangguizi* (foreign devil) knowing it was the greatest surprise. [...] I was rewarded with a smile of sincere admiration."[58] His interest in the ballad might have come from *Mulan congjun* (*Hua Mulan Joins the Army*), "a landmark Occupation film," which premiered in 1939 in Shanghai and was shown in other cities. Oddly enough, he later claimed that he had translated the ballad after the war in Shanghai from a text given to him by his colleague, the translator Ge Baoquan.[59]

Life was going well but for "the matters of the heart [...]. I alone am to blame here." He found himself briefly attracted to one of his senior students: "Thank God, it's over. If it does not come back, life will be easy again." Before long, however, "I, to my most wretched trouble, / became infatuated with young Petia Du."[60] In the spring of 1941, he fell in love with another student, Pavel Bai Jizhang, a nephew of his former

Chinese teacher at the Oriental Department in Harbin. On 22 May 1941, "fate joined me very closely with Pavel," or, fondly, Pavlusha, and "this adolescent unselfishly fell in love with me." "To a Pupil" (*Ucheniku*, 25.11.1942) speaks of a youth who would "laughing, follow me / right through darkness and storm / and appear before the crowds / as the beloved pupil." For the first time in his life, his love was reciprocated, and "we lived in utmost closeness for two and a half years […]. Whose fault is it that I am what I am, that I fall in love where it is forbidden? No one's, if not my own, but even then the fault lies somewhere else, in another, former life. After all, it is almost a law of nature for each talent to be accompanied by something like this, something odd, a constant source of pain."[61] He and Pavel were so careful that people gossiped about his friendships with Syrova and Korostovets: "both women draw attention away from the more dangerous circumstances." The mission head even "forbade Mariia Pavlovna to be seen with me alone in the parks," and they had to meet secretly in distant places.[62]

Stay in Harbin, 1941–1942

Посланник памятного края, Холодный ветер, ты спешишь, Как черный демон пробегая По склонам черепичных крыш. Но мне твои ожоги любы И дух мой весел на ветру: Родные, северные губы Ласкал ты нынче поутру!	An envoy from a memorable place, Cold wind, you rush on, Running like a black demon Over the slopes of tiled roofs. But I love your scorching touches And my spirit rejoices in the wind: This morning you were caressing Those beloved northern lips!

"Wind" (*Veter*), 20.8.1940

On 24 June 1941, two days after Nazi Germany's invasion of the USSR, Pereleshin went to Harbin for the final examinations. Mindful of Japanese censorship, he wrote to Khaindrova: "I have been in a terrible mood; now we all are ailing in our hearts."[63] He had passed all the examinations by December, but could not get a permit to return to Beijing; on 7 December 1941, Japan attacked Pearl Harbour, the USA entered the Second World War, and travelling restrictions were imposed.[64] A "new, glorious life" in Manchukuo was dominated by terror and atrocities by the Japanese; people were arrested and disappeared, and residents fearfully whispered about bacteriological warfare laboratories on the outskirts of Harbin. The war led to severe shortages of basic goods and food, and people grimly joked that shops sold only two kinds of sausages: one was "Marusia poisoned herself" and another "We'll all be there."[65]

During this enforced stay, Pereleshin participated in the East Asian Competition of Russian Poets and Writers, held by the Bureau for the Affairs of Russian Émigrés in Manchukuo. The first such competition in 1940 had attracted sixty-two poets; Pereleshin's "Reckoning" (*Rasplata*, 4.12.1940) had won the Lyrical Poetry prize, but had been disqualified because he lived in Beijing, not in Manchukuo.[66] Submissions for the second competition in 1941 with a first prize of 100 Manchukuo *gobi* came from sixty-nine poets and thirty-three short-story writers. The jury included the head of the Japanese Military Mission, General Yanagita; the head of the Bureau for the Affairs of Russian Émigrés in Manchukuo, General V.A. Kislitsyn; the leader of the Russian Fascist Party, K.V. Rodzaevskii; and senior Japanese officials. Pereleshin's "Return" (*Vozvrashchenie*, 9.12.1941) won in the Lyrical Poetry category.[67] As one jury member confided, it was not considered his best, but the jury, except for Achair, voted for it because of the previous disqualification. Pereleshin, in full monastic attire, received the award: "I have a foggy recollection of the banquet (not very grand, because of the war), but remember a somewhat drunk poet, Vasilii Obukhov, shouting 'Banzai!' in a shrill tenor, the rather embarrassed figure of Arsenii Nesmelov (who was awarded the third prize), and the proud and happy face of my Mum."[68]

Some submissions were published in a two-volume edition, *By the Native Borders* (*U rodnykh rubezhei*). The introduction declared that émigré literature was dead in Europe and had "an incidental character" in the United States, while this competition "emphasized the successful life of generations of Russian émigrés and showed deep interest in Russian enlightenment by the leading circles of Japan and Manchukuo."[69] Pereleshin's "Choice" (*Vybor*, 20.1.1942) and Khaindrova's "Ancestor" (*Predok*) sharply differed from servile offerings such as Rachinskaia's panegyric "Samurai Country" (*Strana samuraev*), dedicated to the memory of General Nogi, and S.A. Poperek's (Nedolin) "Victory in Hawaii" (*Pobeda na Gavaiakh*), dedicated to the "valiant Nippon Army."

Pereleshin's poetic standing was reinforced by yet another competition in late 1942, when *Border* published poems by Achair, Andersen, Bibikova, Darem, Dmitrieva, Iankovskaia, Karamzina, Alla Kondratovich, Vera Kondratovich, Napolova, Nedel'skaia, Nesmelov, Pereleshin, Rachinskaia, Reznikova, Satovskii Junior, Serebrennikova, Shmeisser, Skopichenko, Sofonova, Spurgot, Tel'toft, Zavadskaia, as well as Liudmila

Brouer from Istambul and Iurii Miroliubov from Brussels; readers were asked to vote for the best by sending in a coupon from the journal. The prize was 50 *gobi*. Pereleshin grumbled that winning depended on the number of copies bought in order to get voting coupons, and when his "To the Winged One" (*K toi, chto krylata*, 16.10.1942) won, he wrote to his mother in jest: "I doubt that you alone could have bought 113 issues of *Border*."[70]

In the early spring of 1942, still in Harbin, Pereleshin was asked by Protopresbyter Father Mikhail Filologov, vice-chairman of the Eparchial Council, to conduct Easter services in the Chol River settlements on the CER west line. Cossacks who had fled there after the Civil War had lost touch with their wives in the USSR and now lived with other women. When the local priest refused them communion for this sin, they stopped supplying him with food, and he was forced to leave. Pereleshin agreed, more out of curiosity than a sense of duty.[71]

He travelled by train to Bukhedu station, where he switched to a branch line "across Xing'an Mountain Range (endless track loops and vistas of mind-boggling beauty)." Getting off the train, he heard "a loud scream: 'That's him!' As it turned out, I was recognized by a young woman [...] from my photo in a newspaper's report of the poetry competition in Harbin." "The torture by hospitality" started: he had to visit every house, eat large meals, and drink lots of tea, as he refused vodka. Priest-Monk Herman travelled from one small settlement to another with a local psalm reader, who lugged his heavy suitcase containing vestments, church plate, and prayer books. At the Easter liturgy, he enjoyed "a stupendous success" by reading the Gospel in Hebrew, Greek, Latin, English, French, Spanish, Polish, Chinese, and Russian, as well as a sermon of St John Chrysostom in his own translation from Church Slavonic into Russian. Even the priestless sect *bespopovtsy* and local Tatars were impressed. He christened a baby in the family of a Russian woman and Chinese man, where the wife told him that her husband, unlike Russian men, who were largely lazy drunks, was hardworking and kind. A Russian policeman, dying of tuberculosis, noticed Pereleshin's shoes drenched in snow and said: "Take my boots, Father," adding without bitterness, "After all, I will no longer need them."[72]

During his Harbin stay he saw his father for the last time, at his conversion to Russian Orthodoxy. Archpriest Nikolai Mukhin and Pereleshin "conducted the Liturgy, and my father received communion from the goblet brought by me from the altar. He was given the name Erazm, one of his Catholic names and his father's name, because Frants was not Orthodox." In 1944 Pereleshin asked his mother to pass on his fourth book of poetry to his father, adding, "I fear that he might die this year or the next." Although Pereleshin later claimed that he had "felt rather close to my father," who was "quite proud of my poems," neither he nor Victor had had much contact with him. He died in Harbin in 1953, when both his sons were no longer in China. Victor thought it was "approximately in 1952" and Pereleshin "in about 1955."[73]

He finally received his exit permit in late April 1942. The parting was hard on his mother: "I was sure that after my departure you would first of all lie down and sleep for some two weeks, and that's what you did." Although they did not see each other again until 1950, in their years apart they exchanged frequent and fond letters in which he shared most of his joys and sorrows with her. Never again did he see "my little Russian Harbin."[74]

Star above the Sea: The Third Book of Poetry, 1941

Из дверей открытых	From the open doors
Пенье льется ровно:	Singing is flowing evenly;
Во дворе на плитах	Flagstones in the yard
Бархатистый мох.	Are covered with velvety moss.
Мимо скал и мелей	Past rocks and shallows
Правь, корабль церковный!	Navigate, the ship of the church!
Ave, maris stella –	*Ave, maris stella* –
Как вечерний вздох.	Like an evening sigh.
В полумрак базилик,	Into semidarkness of basilicas,
Где бессильны шквалы,	Where squalls are powerless,
Где недолги штили,	Where the sea is calm for a while,
Убежим навек!	Let's run away forever!
Felix coeli porta!	*Felix coeli porta!*
Дверь овцам отсталым	For lambs who lag behind
Ты рукой простертой	Open the door to the ark
Отвори в ковчег.	With your outstretched hand.
Solve vincla reis!	*Solve vincla reis!*
Дева, к нашим путам	Maiden, condescend
Снизойди скорее,	Quickly to our fetters,
Путы разреши!	Absolve us of them!
Путь открой нам ясный –	Reveal a clear way for us –
Iter para tutum –	*Iter para tutum* –
Стань звездой прекрасной	Become a beautiful star
Гибнущей души!	For the perishing soul!

"Mukden Cathedral"
(*Mukdenskii sobor*), 14.10.1940

Publication of his third book was delayed by the cost and the feeling that his latest poems had no harmonious connections. He also feared it would distract him from "the immediate goal of my life: to get rid of textbooks forever and become a free man, to read what I want, to study what my heart desires, deeply, to the very roots, and not jump from course to course, from one scholarly field to another, like a flighty moth. I hate textbooks with a dark hatred: creativity begins above them."[75] Nevertheless, by the end of January 1941, "thanks to the latest inspirations," he put together his third book, "the greatest event of recent times and most pleasant." Still in Harbin, he submitted the book to Dawn Printers and was "pleasantly surprised" that his debt for *The Rime of the Ancient Mariner* was overlooked.[76]

The initial titles of *Vesper mundi* or *Wings* were abandoned, especially when Khaindrova took the latter for her second collection. It annoyed him: "I will always find my own titles; let's leave Kuzmin with his *Wings* alone. Khaindrova will trip up on this: everyone will involuntarily be looking for the explanation for duplicating the title."[77] He settled on *Star above the Sea* (*Zvezda nad morem*), a "central" image from "Mukden Cathedral" (*Mukdenskii sobor*, 14.10.1940), where, as the poet strolls past the Catholic cathedral, the words of "Ave Maris Stella" hauntingly enter the poem: "perhaps it is a recollection of a Latin hymn read a long time ago, or an echo of someone's poem which I had totally forgotten." *Maris stella* symbolized "faith in the final triumph of spirit over flesh (and of truth over evil in the external world) and in the curative power of suffering." *Border* refused to publish this poem, because, like "Eternal Rome," it showed a spiritual connection with Catholicism, which was deemed inappropriate for a Russian Orthodox believer, let alone a monk.[78]

Star above the Sea came out on 8 September 1941, with "Valerii Pereleshin" on the cover and "Valerii Pereleshin (Priest-Monk Herman)" in the publication data at the back. The striking cover displayed the title from the cut-out of a seven-point star on the dark blue front: "the star could not be five-point or six-point (Communist or Star of David), but being seven-point by default acquired a mystic depth. Seven is the numeral of the total wholeness of being (the sum of three and four: three is Trinity, totality of invisible and immortal worlds; four is four corners of the world, symbolizing the entirety of the visible world)." The design and cost of the cover were a gift from Korostovets.[79] Like *Good Beehive,* it comprised twenty-two poems in chronological order, three from 1938 and 1939 each, nine from 1940, and seven from 1941: "it is best, though not obligatory, to arrange poems by years. I hold to it to benefit from all its advantages: the poems in *On the Way* and *Good Beehive* were internally connected and had a certain dialectic, and one poem responded to another. In *Star above the Sea*, the connection is considerably weaker."[80]

The main theme of the book was an appeal to save the poet's perishing soul by showing him the way: the "good beehive" of monastic life was no longer the answer. The opening "Despair" (*Otchaianie*, 24.8.1938) sets a somber tone: the poet's wings as "two arms of a cross" raise him high, but the world above is deaf and indifferent to his "fragile lyrics." He gets caught in "destructive nets" and betrays God by desiring "the unforgivable happiness of meetings, / touches, looks, and exclamations." In "Reckoning" (*Rasplata*, 4.12.1940) the poet rejects Ariadne's guiding thread and loses his way in a labyrinth; in "Day of Judgment" (*Strashnyi sud*, 11.1.1941), crushed by "forbidden storm," "crimson with shame," he awaits a severe verdict; in "Teacher" (*Uchitel'*, 20.6.1941), the God-given teacher comes to punish him; and in "Languor" (*Tomlenie*, 9.1.1941), he is asking God: "Why did Your star shine to me / and guide me, like a mother, for so many days? / Return the lost grace / to the rejected soul, the soul of Saul!"

Torn by the conflict between his faith and his desires, in "Homunculus" (*Gomunkul*, 17.7.1940) the poet wishes to have been created in retorts of medieval alchemists, to know no lust or pain and stand above humans, who are but "worms in the decaying swamp, / whose life is pitiful, but dreams are daring, / whose spirit is winged, but does not rise above the flesh!" "My Horoscope" (*Moi goroskop*, 22.6.1941) concludes the book: "My soul, bleeding like a wound, / where are we to run from the blade? / But there is a balsam, a joint gift / of Venus and Uranus, – my poetry." The poem circles back to the opening "Despair," but ends on an optimistic note: "O harpy, known as fate, / answer, what else would you have taken away? / My life lies like the ruins of Troy, / but the spirit is growing and wings are spreading."[81]

The secondary theme of "unforgivable happiness of meetings," eases the darker notes. In prophetic "Happiness" (*Schast'e*, 24.9.1940), his "little happiness" is a gift of memory, and, "setting on his way" to "his southern home," the poet takes nothing but memories of winds, evenings, grass, a pensive September sky, dusk, the smell of pines, a cemetery garden, a volume of Gumilev's poetry, and joy in a glance of dark eyes. His brief infatuation with Petia Du is expressed in tantalizing "Wild Apple Tree" (*Dikaia iablonia*, 22.2.1941), where the feminine gender of "apple tree" camouflages the tale of seducing a young innocent sapling with "improper dreams."

Star above the Sea is significant for the first appearance of the Chinese theme. In "Trip to Dongling" (*Poezdka v Dun-lin*, 14.10.1940), two foreigners view Chinese relics and scratch their "barbaric names" on a hunchbacked wall. "Painting" (*Kartina*, 15.1.1941), dedicated to Korostovets, describes a traditional landscape, painted with "the lightest and most perfect brush," of steep rocks with a green valley below, and a path up to the mountain top, where a tall pine stands, "triumphantly, calmly, indifferently": "As soon as death, sonorous and good, / will catch up with me with its unhurried step, / I know, my soul would truly / come to wander in these fanciful mountains." The last quatrain would echo in a much later poem, " From Afar" (*Izdaleka*, 9.5.1953): "I know calmly and simply: / on the day I die I will certainly return to China."

In her review, N.R. (Reznikova) wrote that his poetry "attracts by its spare, concise, and interconnected nature, by internal unity of content and rhythm. [...] All Pereleshin's poems speak of overcoming temptations and hardships, and that is why they have strength and optimism." G. Savskii (Satovskii-Rzhevskii) described him as "a poet of thought, and his Muse is, first of all, a wise Muse, not that light-headed and fickle goddess which inspires young poets." Boris Iul'skii placed him in the forefront of several serious poets in the East Asia and wrote that his "poetic work steadily follows the path of perfection. No influences are detectable in this collection, or in the preceding one: they are Valerii Pereleshin himself. He stands close to classical poetry."[82]

"Philosophy of Suffering," 1942–1943

Я – веселый из самых веселых,
И ко мне не касается зло:
Я пишу о деревьях и пчелах,
Прославляю Господне тепло.
Но, о чем бы ни начал беседу,
Непременно сорвусь, упаду:
Говорю про венок и победу,
Проговариваюсь про беду.
Я читаю ненужные книги,
Я волнуюсь, томлюсь и грешу,
Но, излюбленную, как вериги,
Как стигматы, я муку ношу.
Ты желанна мне, боль, и приятна,
Как пустыннику ветер пустынь.
О, звезда моя, будь незакатна
И меня никогда не покинь.
Я люблю тебя, тайное пламя,
Умудренная, добрая боль:
Для меня ты – высокое знамя
И у райского входа пароль.

I am cheerful of the most cheerful,
And evil does not touch me:
I write about trees and bees,
Glorify the Lord's warmth.
But, no matter what I start talking about,
I unfailingly fail and fall:
When I talk about a wreath and a victory,
I let my misfortune slip out.
I read unnecessary books,
I get emotional, pine, and sin,
But like fetters, like stigmata,
I carry the beloved torment.
You are desirable, pain, and pleasant,
Like desert winds for a hermit.
Oh, my star, do not set down
And never abandon me!
I love you, the secret fire,
The wise and good pain:
You are a high banner for me
And a password into paradise.

"Justification"
(*Opravdanie*), 22.2.1941

Stranded in Harbin for over nine months, Pereleshin worked on his thesis, "Philosophy of Suffering, " for the degree of what was called "Candidate of Theology" under the supervision of his favourite professor, I.I. Kostiuchik. Impressed by Pavel Florenskii's *The Pillar and the Ground of Truth* (*Stolp i utverzhdenie istiny*), Pereleshin decided "to devote myself not to theology, but to philosophy" and planned to continue with "Philosophy of Mercy" or "Philosophy of Freedom" for his master's degree thesis.[83] Kostiuchik began to see in him a future colleague and arranged for several of Pereleshin's sermons to be published in *Heavenly Bread* to promote his theological scholarship. By mid-September 1942, in Beijing, he had complied with Kostiuchik's revisions and submitted the thesis.[84]

"Philosophy of Suffering" developed one of the major themes in his poetry. His main argument was that the Church declined to look deeply at suffering, when in fact everything stemmed from it. Suffering did not come from the devil and could not be equated with evil; one should not avoid it, but turn it into a resurrecting and nourishing force, into a source of spiritual and creative growth. It was a substantial work, which examined how suffering was viewed in the Old and New Testaments and by western philosophers (Bentham, Plethon, Swedenborg, Schopenhauer, Schelling, Hartmann, Kierkegaard, Leibniz, Pascal, Fedotov, Shestov, Florenskii), Chinese philosophers (Mengzi), Catholic mystics (Ruysbroeck, St Francis of Assisi, St Thérèse of Lisieux), poets (Leopardi, Heine, Lenau, Lamartine, Shelley, Wilde, Pushkin, Lermontov, Blok, Gumilev, Khodasevich, Kuzmin), writers (Dostoevsky, Rozanov, Merezhkovskii), and Buddhists.

Each of the twenty-three chapters began with an epigraph, the first one, remarkably, in Chinese with a Russian translation: "Having reached the limit, everything becomes its opposite." Other Chinese quotes included an inscription in the Jilesi monastery in Harbin: "The wheel of law constantly turns." The epigraph for chapter 15 was Pereleshin's translation of Wang Zhihuan's poem "Ascent to a Tower." Other epigraphs were taken from the Bible and Buddhist writings; from Russian poets in Russian; from Ralph Waldo Emerson in English; from Racine, Malebranche, and St Thérèse of Lisieux in French; and from Pope Leo in Latin. He often quoted Russian poets, including his favourites, Lermontov, Kuzmin, Georgii Ivanov, and Ladinskii. Poetry, he wrote, was pessimistic by nature and sought an escape from this world; suffering and creativity were interconnected. He compared poets to Queen Niobe, who, in her pride and defiance of the gods, rejected the world for its perishable nature and cruelty, and he concluded one chapter with his poem "Niobe" (*Niobeia*, 20.12.1941), first begging Niobe to pray and submit and then identifying with her defiance: "And when, having lost the most precious dreams, / our hearts, all alone, will dissolve in tears and blood, / we will receive the innermost inspirations / and tell about our imprudent eagle-like flight."

He later admitted that "at the time, 'Philosophy of Suffering' seemed to me a significant work, but now my opinion is totally different. I have changed, it's true, from a believer to an agnostic, but I also see shortcomings in the work itself. Some most useful books were entirely unknown and inaccessible to me. Had I read them, there could have been no 'philosophy.'"[85]

On 20 April 1943 the Academic Council awarded him the degree of Candidate of Theology and retained him to work on a master's degree thesis. Kostiuchik's evaluation praised the wealth of sources and suggested a better coordination of some chapters. The decision was announced in *Heavenly Bread*, which published chapters 10, 11, and 15.[86] Pereleshin was jubilant: "yet another important stage in my life is completed." He spent Saturday, 8 May 1943, strolling in Taimiao Park and on Sunday celebrated with the Korostovets family: "we had wine *Flot-d'Or*, presented to me by Père Emilien, from whom I buy wine for the church; I was saving it for this happy occasion. In the restaurant, instead of the usual dumplings, we had dishes of fish, meat, and shrimp."[87]

Unfortunately, "Philosophy of Suffering" led to suffering for its author, inflicted by two "heresy seekers," who "stole" his thesis from the faculty's archive and launched an attack. One was that same Bishop Dimitrii Voznesenskii, "one of the evil forces in my life," who had been upbraiding him for writing poetry, and another "evil force" was Professor K.I. Zaitsev. It was rumoured that Zaitsev came to Harbin from Paris in 1935 after disagreements with émigré philosophers N.A. Berdiaev and Father Bulgakov, that his real name was Zalkind, and that he was a nephew of the Jewish poet and translator Peter Weinberg. In Harbin, Zaitsev taught in the Law Faculty and the Theological Faculty, and Pereleshin had talked with him about Ladinskii, whom Zaitsev had known in Paris.[88]

In December 1943 Professor Zaitsev submitted a lengthy report on the thesis, asking for annulment of the degree, and Bishop Dimitrii proposed granting a master's degree to Zaitsev for this report. Zaitsev wrote that "Philosophy of Suffering" "flabbergasted, stupefied," and "took him aback" by its profane and un-Orthodox attitude. Priest-Monk

Herman "deviated from the normal path of a Church thinker, who should have established the Church's teachings, then widened the framework of the research, and evaluated some other materials." Zaitsev castigated him for the implied equivalence of Orthodox, Catholic, and Protestant mystics, for writing names of Orthodox saints on the same line of the text as those of heretics, and so on. He found fault with the style, language, and some expressions and individual words; with the way the letter "t" was formed in handwritten insertions; and with the "frivolous tone" and the "revolting" grouping of words "sweetness" and "passion." Priest-Monk Herman was an impressionistic essay writer, "striving for a low literary effect." The report ended with a sinister warning of unspecified temptations and the ruinous road on which this priest-monk had embarked, becoming a victim of certain evil directions of thought.[89]

Professor Kostiuchik was "enraged, threatened to resign from the faculty, and stated that if my work was declassified, he would demand the disqualification of all previously approved works, because mine was the best in all the years of the faculty." On 1 October 1944, Kostiuchik submitted a rebuttal, refusing to change a single word in his evaluation of this "independent, original, not theological or psychological, but philosophical study."[90] Pereleshin, most upset, asked his mother to get copies of Zaitsev's report and Kostiuchik's rebuttal: "how wretched is the milieu that I depend on. Such absurdity is impossible in any other field." He even thought of publishing "Philosophy of Suffering" together with these reports: "it will be a famous book."[91] The unresolved controversy would later contribute to his departure from the monastic order.

Hardships in Beiguan

[...]	
Силой вражьей, силой скрытною	Everything is crushed and taken away
Смято все и отнято:	By a hostile force, a concealed force:
Волчью стаю ненасытную	Who can manage to tame
Приручить сумеет кто?	This insatiable pack of wolves?
Слишком дорого обходится	This tyranny of the stars
Этот звездный произвол.	Is costing too much.
Помогай нам, Богородица,	Help us, Mother of God,
Защити от стольких зол!	Protect against so much evil!

"Stars" (*Zvezdy*), 5.11.1943

When he returned to Beiguan on 23 April 1942, lilacs were blooming in the first warm rains, and acacias were about to burst into flower. May brought "a regular Beijing dust and sand storm," and "sand crunched everywhere, the wind was moaning outside and doors were rattling on their hinges."[92] It was hard to settle down, as he confided to his mother in the third person: "It is nerves and the wish to write poems. This is his third letter 'home.' But where is home, where is his real home now? […] The priest-monk is very upset and uneasy. He has almost stopped studying Chinese, although he continues to copy liturgy in Chinese. He has almost ceased reading and tries to fill inner emptiness by exchanging stamps with others. And, of course, Pavlusha comes often."[93]

He missed his mother. She lived alone and did not get along with her mother and half-sisters, abandoned by the philandering M.F. Naam. By the 1940s the Japanese had shut down most Russian periodicals, and the new editor of *Border*, writer K. Saburov, often reduced her small earnings by replacing some of her lines with his own and paying himself for it. The mother and son nicknamed him "Horror" after he inserted this word into one of her stories and claimed payment for it. In winter, unable to buy firewood, she "lived in her winter coat," and Pereleshin persuaded the mission to grant her a small monthly subsidy.[94] He sent her money and parcels of wartime necessities such as stockings, thread, soap, and tea by people going to Harbin, bypassing the unreliable mail. Korostovets and he arranged for royalties for their poems, short stories, and articles in *Border* to be paid to her.[95]

He kept urging her to join him in Beiguan, where she could work as a journalist and proofreader and could freelance for Harbin periodicals, but she hesitated to leave Harbin with its larger Russian population, acquaintances, and occasional male friends, one of whom Pereleshin sarcastically called "your knight."[96] In the autumn of 1943, she renewed her acquaintance with V.V. Koloshin, an "admirer" from her youth, now a widower and professor at the Japanese Polytechnic, and soon moved in with him. Pereleshin later claimed, as he did about her second marriage, that it "was not a 'marriage,' but a partnership," but at the time, he was "endlessly glad to hear of your happiness, though I also feel a little sad that now you basically no longer need my care. […] May God protect you and your friend."[97]

In the autumn of 1942, Priest-Monk Herman participated in a memorable event. Since the early 1920s, the bodies of Great Prince Sergei Mikhailovich, Great Princess Elizaveta Feodorovna (sister of the late empress), Princes Gavriil, Igor', and Ioann (sons of Great Prince

Konstantin Konstantinovich), Fedor Semenovich Remez (Court Manager of Great Prince Sergei Mikhailovich), and nun Varvara (Iakovleva), all murdered in Alapaevsk by the Red forces on 5 July 1918, had been kept at the mission cemetery outside the North Gates (Andingmen). The remains of Great Princess Elizaveta Feodorovna and nun Varvara had later been sent to Jerusalem. In 1938, the Japanese permitted Mission Head Victor to move the bodies to Beiguan, where they were placed in zinc coffins at the All Holy Martyrs Church, but those of Prince Igor' Konstantinovich and F.S. Remez were still in wooden coffins, owing to the lack of funds.

The latter remains were now to be sealed in zinc coffins as well, and the ceremony was held on the day when the USSR celebrated the thirty-fifth anniversary of the October Revolution. Principal religious and political émigré leaders attended a public prayer for the tsar and his family, the White military, and all Russians killed during the Revolution and the Civil War. The evening service at St Innokentii's Church was followed by a solemn procession: "Dark figures carrying torches under the arches of the windowless, low-ceilinged temple and mournful singing gave the impression of an ancient Christian service in the catacombs. After the lity for the dead, the two coffins were carefully carried out of the church. Accompanied by funereal ringing of the ancient bells of Beiguan, the procession proceeded to the Assumption Cathedral. Crosses were carried first, followed by the choir continuously singing 'Holy God' and by torchbearers, Deacon Nikolai with a censor and a candle, Archimandrite Nafanail, and Priest-Monk Herman, all in robes and holding burning candles." The next morning, in the presence of the mission head, Father Nafanail, and Priest-Monk Herman, representatives from the Bureau for the Affairs of Russian Émigrés and the Anti-Comintern Committee, officials, journalists, and photographers, the remains were transferred into zinc coffins, encased in wood and bound with iron, with the tsarist crown depicted on the handles. The decomposed body of Prince Igor' still had a paper wreath on his head, and his hands held a small scrap of paper: when the coffins had been sealed in Alapaevsk, there had not been enough absolution papers and some had been torn in strips to be shared. After the ceremony, some people asked permission to take boards of the old Alapaevsk coffins as mementoes.[98]

The year 1942 ended on a tragic note. On 20 December, Father Nafanail returned from a trip to Tianjin, went to bed late, and missed the morning Liturgy. Monks banged on his door and windows, broke the double lock, and found him dead. The mission head, suspecting carbon monoxide poisoning from the heating stove, ordered resuscitation, but it was too late. Pereleshin, on learning of "the death of my father and brother, served the entire Liturgy through sobs." On 23 December Father Nafanail was buried in a crypt under All Holy Martyrs church. In the obituary Priest-Monk Herman wrote: "He was a talented preacher, brilliant orator, thoughtful clergyman, true spiritual father of Beijing monks and of many dozens of parishioners, a tireless administrator who invested his entire soul in complex and difficult matters of the mission, a kind monk, an ascetic and zealot." Many years later, retyping his recollections of Father Nafanail, he added by hand: "Finishing this, I sobbed inconsolably."[99]

Pereleshin was not alone in thinking that "there were many mysteries in the death of Father Nafanail," who on the eve of his Tianjin trip said to Pereleshin: "Father, pray for me, I suffer greatly!" On discovering his death, the mission head immediately took away Father Nafanail's diary and told Pereleshin that autopsy must be avoided at all costs. Pereleshin, interpreting for the Office of the Public Prosecutor, heard the mission head insisting on carbon monoxide poisoning. However, rumours held that Father Nafanail took some "berries" to end his life. He had unsuccessfully opposed the mission head in leasing land to the Japanese for their powdered milk factory, prison, and execution grounds; he had had strong disagreements with Japanese stooges at the Anti-Comintern Committee, and "all unseemly methods, including the most powerful – cynical slander – were unleashed to break his resistance." He faced "merciless persecution," especially when L.N. Gorchakova, allegedly a princess and in the employ of the Japanese Military Mission, spread rumours that Father Nafanail had fathered a child by a woman who lived in the mission while her husband was working in another city.[100]

Distressed by the general situation at the mission, Pereleshin hoped to get a position in the Legation Quarter church, and he and Mariia Korostovets "planned every step and action to attract people and money."[101] In May 1943, its priest failed to get parishioners to sign a petition against Pereleshin, and Pereleshin redoubled his efforts. The mission head, however, was not supportive, and their "relations became cool and more distant, though it is often impossible for him to manage without me (especially with languages, as no one knows any), and then I become fashionable."[102]

His life in Beiguan was becoming difficult: "a real attack of all the dark forces in Beijing was organized against me." His service and work were criticized by a certain Uspenskii, and the mission head seemed to side with this "greatest evil for the mission." His stand against the Japanese encroachments put him "in the way of a group of Russians and Japanese who were striving to seize the mission property."[103] Furthermore, some monks were indignant at poems in *Border* such as "Elegy" (*Elegiia*, 11.12.1942), which spoke of sacrificing a forbidden love. His friendships with Syrova and Korostovets, who could "bite people's heads off for my interests," were considered inappropriate. Korostovets made things worse by becoming possessive and quarrelling with him "to the point of tears and blows," and he was relieved when, in May 1943, she went to Shanghai on learning that her son was planning to marry.[104]

His affair with Pavel and his casual infatuations did not stay secret for long, and he was well aware that he "played into their hands (by adventures with boys)" and was "a very bad monk."[105] It was getting clear that he would be forced "to move (perhaps temporarily) to Shanghai, though not by the will of the mission head and not in the mission's interests, but owing to the force of external circumstances, completely insurmountable at present. I hope that I can return soon, or that some changes for the best will take place. Beijing is dear to me as a homeland, but I myself was not cautious."[106] He was right. In the autumn of 1943, when the Shanghai Diocese needed a scriptures teacher, "the mission head grabbed the chance to defuse tensions, and I, giving in to his cowardice, consented. No one could touch me personally, but when he asked me to help him out, I agreed to leave, although I do not share his fears and hopes."[107]

On 31 October 1943, he wrote to his mother: "Tomorrow, at 11:50 a.m., I am leaving for Shanghai, almost with joy. Another page of my life is turning over, and I hope that the next one will be better, much better. [...] Don't think that there are only grounds to be displeased with me; a lot of bitterness has accumulated on my side as well. Beijing is my most beloved city, but I do not want to return too soon, and the mission head guessed this, saying during our last conversation: 'when I call you, I don't know if you would want to return to me.'"[108]

Parting with Pavel was heart-breaking, but he was left with "grateful memories. I will be clutching this feeling, even its shadow; Pavel is a part of all my plans for the future. There is no connection between my departure from Beijing and Pavel. One of the reasons was my insatiability; it is other people, not Pavel, that harmed me. But there also was a deliberate intrigue, an entire party strongly disturbed by Father Nafanail, then by Father Avraamii (also deceased now), and then by me.

Once we three were removed one after another, the archbishop became a prisoner and pawn in the hands of this party."[109]

Sacrifice: The Fourth Book of Poetry, 1944

Нет, не торжественной осанной	No, not a triumphant hosanna
Перед величьем бытия, –	In the face of the grandeur of existence,
Смиренной, но благоуханной	Let my life be a sacrifice,
Да станет жертвой жизнь моя!	Modest, but filled with fragrance!
	Epigraph to *Sacrifice*, 1943

Pereleshin was already in Shanghai when *Sacrifice* (*Zhertva*) was published in Harbin. The war was draining Japan and Manchukuo, and shortages and austerity measures had escalated to a punishing level. At first he wondered whether to postpone the book "until better times, because it will cost a lot and there is no one to sell books to," but he went ahead, because "the money is so valueless now, that the best thing is to spend it usefully right away." He mailed the manuscript and some money to his devoted mother, and the book came out in April 1944.[110] It was one of only three poetry books published that year in Harbin; the other two were *Luminous Ring* (*Svetloe kol'tso*), a posthumous collection by Nina Zavadskaia, who died at age fifteen of typhoid, and *Great Eastern Asia* (*Velikaia Vostochnaia Azia*), a lengthy poem by G. Satovskii-Rzhevskii slavishly extolling Japan and its designs in Asia.

Sacrifice turned out to be his last book for the next twenty-five years. The back cover listed 300 copies, but his mother had 500 printed. He was "eternally" grateful: "How many trials you went through, how much time and effort you sacrificed for my *Sacrifice*!" It was "a heroic deed on her part: Manchuria was starving and freezing, there was no paper for the cover, except yellow, and no paint, except green: so the cover looked like 'fried eggs with green onions.'" The only upsetting feature was that the book was printed in the new orthography. She was selling the book in Harbin, and he was selling it in Shanghai, for "the cost of two pounds of bread."[111]

Pereleshin had replaced the book's initial title *Vesper – Evening of the World* with *Sacrifice*: "life sacrificed to God, sacrificial love, as in "Elegy" (*Elegiia*, 11.12.1942), and its other aspects."[112] It was so much a book of Beijing poems that he removed "Stars" (*Zvezdy*, 5.11.1943) and "Fog" (*Tuman*, 3.12.1943), written in Shanghai, from the final draft. Of its thirty-eight poems in the usual chronological order, only one was written in Harbin in 1938; the rest were composed in Beijing or on trips to Harbin: one in 1939, two in 1940, four in 1941, eleven in 1942, and nineteen in 1943.

He later dismissed *Sacrifice* as "light," "not a daughter, / but a trifle of a book,"[113] but most poems showed him at his best at the time. The only lapse was the opening poem, "Radonezh Tale" (*Radonezhskaia skazka*, 28.7.1938), earlier published in *Border* as "Tale of the Christianization of Russia" (*Skazka o kreshchenii Rusi*). It was a sixteen-stanza morality tale of a holy hermit treating the frozen paw of a bear, who then tells all beasts and forest demons that they too belong to God. The poem might be attributed to the sentiments of a newly ordained monk or to appeasement of religious mentors.

In his first three books the poet had searched for his way in life, imagined it to be in the good beehive of monastic life, and then appealed to *stella maris*, who alone "could help the perishing world, not against human will, but in response to a plea to Her and to a common sacrifice. The latter word evolved into the new book, *Sacrifice*."[114] The quest for the way remained one of his main themes. Torn between being a monk and a poet, in "Morning" (*Utro*, 4.11.1942) he begs God for a sign in the form of "a bird, butterfly, or star" and asks: "Why have I been abandoned by You, / like a refugee from a blessed land?" In "Choice" (*Vybor*, 20.1.1942), the poet chooses "the pure way, honourable and free," and regards evil as "all kinds of whirlpools, / and children's laughter, and women's warmth, / and petty prickly cares." The "unbearable pain" of God amputating his arms in "Another Way" (*Inoi put'*, 7.2.1943) turns him into "a beloved son of God, / a free spirit and a pure man. // [...] What is an irrevocable inaccessible sin / to me, an impotent cripple?" In "Mal invincible" (14.3.1943) the poet, "a sinner," cuts off his hand "which had tempted him from childhood," but at night the amputated hand creeps towards his throat with a dagger.

The painful quest nourishes his poetry. In "Alchemy" (*Alkhimiia*, 14.3.1943) the poet-alchemist and his trainee Muse toil at turning pain into "the gold of purest inspirations." In "To the Winged One" (*K toi, chto krylata*, 16.10.1942) it is not *stella maris*, but his abandoned pagan Muse who is "my star, my salvation," whom he begs "with the flame of love to send to my soul / your blessing or inspiration, that seed of spirit however it is named!"

China became a powerful presence, quite different from its role as an abstract exotic background in the work of other Russian poets in China.

"China" (*Kitai*, 11.12.1942), which forms the epigraph to Part One of this biography, expresses the poet's love for the country and its people. Lakes, lotuses, and pines, with their special places in the Chinese poetic imagination, live in his poems. "The Last Lotus" (*Poslednii lotus*, 10.9.1943), however, was removed at his mother's insistence, although it is not clear whether because identifying with a lotus as "the last bard of freedom" meant freedom from monastic restrictions or opposition to the Japanese rulers.[115] The poem appeared only in his fifth book *Southern Home* (*Iuzhnyi dom*, 1969).

His growing love for China led to the tug of war between Russia and China in his heart and in poetry. Only one poem, "Nostalgia" (*Nostal'giia*, 19.9.1943), speaks of Russia: "Russia, Russia, my golden homeland: / with my generous heart I love all countries of the world, / But only you, Russia, do I love more than China." It was written when, swept by patriotic feelings during the war, Pereleshin hung a map of Russia over his bed, but the poem also professes his love for his "tender stepmother" China, where "gentle yellow people have become my brothers."[116] In her review Khaindrova picked on this "almost total absence of poems about Russia": "If the first generation of émigrés loves its homeland with certain reservations, why can we not imagine that the next generation would come to love China first and then Russia?"[117]

The book contained seeds of themes fully developed later. "Sin, you are my amazing swing, / my blessing and damnation" in "Abyss" (*Bezdna*, 15.3.1943) expanded into his sixth book *Swing* (*Kachel'*, 1971). Poems such as "Repayment" (*Otplata*, 6.10.1939), "Precipice" (*Propast'*, 16.10.1942), and "Return" (*Vozvrashchenie*, 9.12.1941), expressing yearning for an escape and a sanctuary, led to his seventh book, *Sanctuary* (*Zapovednik*, 1972).

One reviewer, N. Klimov, attested that Pereleshin was "one of the most gifted and interesting Russian poets in the East" and that his latest book had "the same high level of mastery, as the preceding one." The book was "tragic in its basis" and escapist in its daydreaming, as if written at the turn of the century in its formal and thematic discord with the time. Mariia Shapiro spoke of him as "one of the most gifted poets in East Asia." A pseudonymous "Compass" described the poems as "conversations with himself, alone, in silence," striving to test temptations and sacrifice his soul. The critic noted poems about China, "the home of his inherited exile." Nesmelov's review was "intelligent and fair. I feel sick of overly excessive praises. A little coldness is even better: it is more serious and reliable."[118]

In 1944, Syrova enclosed a dried flower from Zhonghai in her letter to him, and it "excited me with a sweet torment. There is no city better than Beijing, my native one, the real one, the only city in the world! I would have flown there without a backward glance!" In the 1970s, on rereading his Beijing poems, he "felt such desire to see all those places and parks, temples and towers … A large part of my heart is left there!"[119] He missed Beijing all his life.

When Pereleshin left Beijing, he was thirty years old. He had advanced in the monastic hierarchy, finished his theological education, studied Chinese, become recognized as one of the best Russian poets in China, and published two more books. As in Harbin, he led a dual life of external compliance and painfully growing internal freedom. In his poetry he still resorted to camouflage, but now he had gay affairs and his first gay relationship. His liberation was decades in the future, but life in Beijing was the beginning.

5 Shanghai: Fogs and Chimeras

Shanghai Diocese, 1943

По утрам белесоватые туманы
и в тумане, словно айсберги, дома,
и безликие химеры и обманы,
равнодушием сводящие с ума.
  Лучше б огненное зарево позора,
  где, как мученик, на крест я вознесен,

  чем слепые волокнистые озера,
  завлекающие в тусклый полусон!
Но, когда уже мы радости не ждали,
вдруг, покорны мановенью с высоты,
расцветали изумительные дали,
голубели небывалые цветы.
  И когда изнемогали мы под гнетом

  невесомых и кочующих морей,
  вырастали за нежданным поворотом
  осиянные пролеты галлерей.
И в просветы заколдованного круга
ты меня с собой на небо позвала:
побежим туда, посмотрим друг на друга
в переполненные солнцем зеркала!

In the mornings, there are whitish fogs
and houses emerging like icebergs,
and faceless chimeras and deceptions
driving one crazy with their indifference.
  I'd rather accept a fiery glow of disgrace,
  where, like a martyr, I've been raised on
    the cross,
  than these blind fibrous lakes,
  enticing into a lackluster semi-slumber!
But when we no longer expected joy,
suddenly, obedient to a call from above,
amazing vistas blossomed
and fantastic flowers bloomed blue.
  And when we were exhausted under
    pressure
  of weightless and wandering seas,
  illumined spans of galleries
  appeared behind unexpected turns.
And through breaks in the vicious circle
you called me to join you in the sky:
let's run there, let's look at each other
in the mirrors overflown with sunlight!

"Fog" (*Tuman*), 5.12.1943

Pereleshin's trip turned into "the most horrible nightmare." The train was overcrowded with "long-suffering" Chinese, some travelling even in the toilets. After crossing the Yangzi by ferry, they waited for the delayed train and, as people pushed at the barriers, Japanese guards, "drunk with power" and "with impassive and almost cheerful faces," took off their belts and lashed out at the crowd. Pereleshin, caught like "a dumb woodchip," barely escaped the lashes and nearly lost his travel bag.[1] On 3 November 1943 he finally arrived in Shanghai. The city was "starving and freezing, a curfew was imposed from 11:00 at night to the morning, and every day someone was seized and imprisoned."[2]

Pereleshin disliked Shanghai from the start and "hated it more and more every day." The people seemed "unkind and unattractive" and their dialect "barbarian and very crude"; in winter "the sky is always grey, there are frequent rains and fogs, which leave the same slush as rain"; summers were hot and humid and the air was "totally motionless, stifling, so that there is simply no energy to get up."[3] The only thing that charmed him was the fog, which in his first months "came daily, spreading fibrous wings over the streets and making everything seem unreal and enchanted, and streetcars were running with the lights on in the daytime. It was beautiful!"[4]

He was angry with the mission head and heartbroken at parting with Pavel and his beloved city. In his first Shanghai poem, "Stars" (*Zvezdy*, 5.11.1943), his horoscope shows "rusted Mars" leading "evil avengers" to menace his dreams, "deceitful Mercury" denouncing him, Venus putting on a mask of languor and dreams, and Uranus threatening fatal upheavals. "To Judges" (*Sud'iam*, 7.12.1943) attacked his enemies, not directly naming Bishop Dimitrii Voznesenskii and others, who "are declared to be heralds of Spirit, / but in truth are nothing but slaves," who chain the human spirit and dictate what should and should not be written: "in the future, I believe, there will be / a just trial for the judges: / the descendants will condemn those who condemned / and extol the condemned."[5]

Pereleshin was assigned a room in the Cathedral House on rue Paul Henri, next to the grand Cathedral of the Most Holy Mother of God. His new superior, Bishop Ioann, formerly of the White Army and a graduate of the Belgrade Theological Faculty, was "always smiling, gentle with children, but demanding and merciless to subordinates," though "one cannot deny one thing: he does not spare himself. He serves every day, does not miss a single evening service, eats once a day, does not sleep at night, and constantly visits hospitals, orphanages, prisons, and sick people. But he has no love."[6]

Pereleshin's duties were to serve in the cathedral and attend the bishop's services, public prayers, and weekly meetings of priests. Monks were not paid, and the money he earned for teaching scripture at a Russian high school and at the Girls' Gymnasium of the League of Russian Women barely covered a daily meal and necessities. The "burdensome" necessity of teaching left little time for "studying Chinese and working on my master's dissertation." He soon started "finding loopholes under the strictest discipline and adroitly escaping into them, as everyone does," and serving "in a compact way: a night service takes only one hour, and Liturgy a little more."[7]

He refused to see that in some ways he had brought this transfer upon himself: "I still don't know why it was necessary for me to be in this grey and uninteresting city under the rule of the crazy bishop and in a very uncertain financial situation."[8] When the mission head visited the Shanghai Diocese in March 1944, Pereleshin hoped to accompany him to Qingdao and be transferred, but the head, "a two-faced and exceptionally cowardly person," kept "actively hiding from me: he knows that the conversation will be sour."[9]

He desperately yearned for Beijing and for Pavel: "my heart is longing for joy, especially in spring, when there is such a high and light sky, when the sun shines above the tidy park seen from my window, when at every step I meet hundreds and thousands of beautiful faces and bodies. I want to wander by a sleepy lake, breathe the aroma of pines, admire outlines of the far-away Western Hills, and listen to peaceful melodic speech and distant sounds of *huqin* [a Chinese musical instrument]."[10] However, he had no money to visit and heard enough horror stories of exorbitant bribes and overcrowded carriages with no food or water. He missed his mother: "I pray for our deepest wishes to come true: to see Victor (or at least know that he is fine), see each other, and survive to the end of the war, to the happy end. [...] You are my greatest consolation, if not simply the only one. Otherwise, I would not know what to live for."[11]

What helped him to cope were old and new friends; half of Shanghai's 50,000 Europeans were Russian émigrés, mostly from Harbin.[12] Mariia Korostovets happily resumed their friendship and her care of him. She, her son Mark, and Pereleshin started selling on the black market scarce goods, such as coffee, honey, wool, bicycle tires, bean oil, and paint, sent from Beijing by her husband and sisters. He soon had some money to send to his mother through the popular arrangement of paying a Russian in Shanghai, whose relatives in Harbin would then repay his mother; he also regularly sent parcels of buckwheat, soap, clothes, or jewellery with trusted travellers. At one time he "made more money than I could spend" and, with the windfall from selling powdered milk, was able to have daily meals at Princess A.S. Ukhtomskaia's diner.[13]

His dear friend Lidiia Khaindrova rushed to greet him on his first day in Shanghai. She worked as a cashier in a café after being fired by the Japanese from her job as a Dairen correspondent for the Harbin *Dawn* for "liberalism [...] incompatible with the principles of the New Order" and forbidden to publish in Manchukuo. Her lover, M.P. Grigor'ev, a translator from the Japanese, who had a Japanese wife and children, died in Dairen on 16 July 1943, allegedly of a heart attack, though rumours held that he was murdered by the Japanese.[14] Another Churaevka friend, Vladimir Slobodchikov, and his wife, Harbin poet Ol'ga Tel'toft, came to the cathedral to welcome him, and he became a frequent guest of "the Gumilev couple," as the two poets were called after Gumilev and Akhmatova. In the summer of 1944, Tel'toft left her husband for Iaroslav Semenov, a son of the notorious Ataman Semenov, and Slobodchikov attempted suicide. Tel'toft and Semenov moved to Harbin, where she "behaved like a crown princess of the future 'Sibchukuo' (it was expected that Japan would win the war and make Siberia a buffer state, a Japanese colony, with Ataman Semenov as the head of the 'state')." In August 1945, after the Red Army allegedly shot her husband in front of her, Tel'toft committed suicide.[15]

Pereleshin also met people at the Russian Social Club, where he was invited to give lectures on philosophy, which were attended by some forty people. One of them was a former ballet dancer, A.N. Sal'nikov, now a yoga healer and publisher of an occult journal. Little did Pereleshin know that much later, in Brazil, he would "devoutly pray for the peace of his soul and make a sign of the cross" over Sal'nikov's body when he collapsed while dancing at a party.[16] Another was a pianist, Duchess N.N. Leikhtenbergskaia, who years later came to his defence in the United States. His poems, "Music" (*Muzyka*, 16.6.1944), dedicated to her, and "The Bell" (*Kolokol*, 11.8.1944) conveyed impressions from her performance of Debussy's "La cathédrale engloutie."[17] A former Harbin poet, Izida Orlova, invited him to her artistic evenings and meetings of mystics, and her place "soon became almost like a home to me."[18] An émigré painter, Taisia Jaspar, asked Pereleshin to sit for her in his monastic garments, but without glasses. He liked the portrait: "the expression of my eyes is captured well. It is precisely the portrait of a poet, who is, by the way, also a priest," "a monk, but even more a poet." His mother wanted to buy it, but he wrote back that it was an expensive and "cumbersome thing in need of a frame." Jaspar left for France after the war and then for the USSR, and the fate of the portrait is not known.[19] One day in October 1944 he received an unsigned letter from Harbin: "I don't know the woman you are grieving about, but I cried bitterly, horribly, stupidly at your 'Morning' (*Utro*, 4.11.1942). [...] When I read your 'Conversation on the Way' (*Beseda v doroge*, 29.3.1939), I thought: I will never, never write to him ... But no matter how far I move away from you, my angel always brings me back ... My kind one, my luminous and relentless one, you know how painful and frightening life is for me, but you are leading me and will protect me ..." He sensed "a great heart and exceptional sensitivity" behind "the melodramatic tone," and they began to correspond.[20] The young woman, Anita Gincenberg, was ecstatic: "I have found you, my eternally unforgettable one," and, like Korostovets, she felt that she "immediately recognized him." She did not suspect that he was gay: "I have always thought and believed that a great love (I've learned much from your poems) will come to a person like you. I want to know everything, everything: who she is, what her name is, how she looks (beautiful, of course)."[21] His "Answer" (*Otvet*, 26.10.1944), dedicated to her, said: "I will not coo like a tender dove, / I will not submit to ancient caresses. / How, how am I to respond / to such love, without loving?"

His heart pined for Pavel: "Previously I loved only my joy in him; now I love the person and see in him a haven of faithfulness and peace. This angel did not need anything for himself."[22] When his mother objected to his plans for living together with her and Pavel after the war, he tried to explain: "for some reason, every woman sees marriage and the production of babies as the ideal of life. But, after all, I made my choice a long time ago, preferring freedom to this 'chicken coop.' Freedom gave me education, developed my modest poetic talent, permitted me to travel (and will in the future), and enriched me with many emotions and pleasures. [...] Now I see that I have to take into consideration your disapproval. You are absolutely right that life is given for joy and even for 'having silly fun,' but I want to enjoy life and 'have fun' in my own way."[23] His new infatuations ruined his relationship with Pavel: "I did not know what an insatiable appetite for enjoyment I had. Pavel was not enough, and that's why I lost my little blue tit-bird. Now I have another little blue tit, an untamed surrogate, but I would have exchanged him and all others, even the beautiful and the depraved, for Pavel. I have learned this lesson well: love for one person is more valuable than pleasures from many. Pavel is my fate, or rather a gift from fate. I was not sufficiently grateful, and now I am deprived of it. I gnash my teeth."[24] He became briefly involved with a young Russian, and when the man left Shanghai "another little part of my heart broke off, no, not broke off, but was crudely severed." He fell in love again and so powerfully that he nearly fainted after a Liturgy and recalled the Song of Songs: "Strengthen me with wine, refresh me with apples," afraid to add, "I am exhausted from love."[25] There were other "unfortunate infatuations," but "the pain is always rewarded. [...] In general, I have never and nowhere written so much as here, as if to refute the general view that it is impossible to write in Shanghai." In April 1945, "a fine adventure brought me a lot of joy. It is hanging by a thread and, it seems, will not last beyond a few meetings, but I am calm and cheerful."[26] He shared some of these "sinful joys" with his dismayed mother: "you are right, my love adventures are repulsive, but, after all, I did not invent this situation, and it is necessary for something as well. Is this torment a payment for my talent? I have been given much; do I pay from this credit by walking on the razor's edge? [...] I have simply fallen too low, and therefore priesthood burdens me."[27]

Friday Poetry Circle, 1943–1945

[...]
Колесницы Божьей крылатой
Два безжалостных колеса,
И в груди живой, разъятой
Боль живет – слепая оса.
  Но и эту кровь искупленья
  Я стерпел и больше стерплю –
  Оттого, что слаще спасенья
  Золотое слово "люблю."
Не прошу ни сна, ни покоя,
Только силы, силы терпеть,
Оттого, что счастье большое
Даже раненым сердцем петь.

Two merciless wheels
Of God's winged chariot
Left the pain, a blind wasp,
In the slashed open living bosom.
  But I have endured this blood
  Of atonement and will endure more,
  Because the golden words "I love"
  Are sweeter than salvation.
I am not asking for sleep or rest,
But only for strength, for strength to endure,
Because it is a great happiness
To sing even with a wounded heart.

"Angels" (*Angely*), 1944

The influx of Harbin Russians to Shanghai in the 1930s led to the publication of a few books of poetry and short-lived journals and the formation of several literary circles such as a briefly revived Churaevka, Parkau's literary salon, and the Tuesday Circle. The pro-Soviet Union of Returnees (*Soiuz vozvrashchentsev*) was formed in 1937, and the Soviet consulate sometimes invited its members to receptions and films. When Pereleshin heard in Harbin that former Churaevka members Peterets, Shchegolev, and Svetlov supported this "return to homeland," he commented: "they are not going there, but singing praises from afar."[28]

The Nazi invasion in June 1941 split émigré communities into "defeatists" (*porazhentsy*), who wished for Nazi victory as leading to the liberation of Russia, and "defenders" (*oborontsy*), who hoped for a Soviet victory. If the support was covert in Harbin, in Shanghai some émigrés applied for Soviet citizenship and wanted to enlist in the Soviet Army, but no passports were issued during the war.[29] The poets Lev Grosse, Vsevolod Ivanov, Nora Kulesh [Krouk], Valerii Odintsov, Val'demar Perli, Peterets, Svetlov, Levan Khaindrava, and Shchegolev published a patriotic collection, *Poems about Homeland* (*Stikhi o rodine*, 1941). As one Shanghai poet wrote, "it was 'our war' [...]. No matter what you thought about Soviet propaganda, an announcer's voice telling of new defeats tugged at the heartstrings." In her literary salon Parkau recited: "Our Russia is fighting, / our cities are burning," and, as Pereleshin recalled, "these lines chilled us"; at the time "the choice was between the Allies and Russia (the USSR then tried to seem to be Russia) on one side and the Japanese and Hitler's Germans on the other."[30]

During the Pacific War, the Telegraph Agency of the Soviet Union (TASS) represented the closed Soviet consulate. Its vice-director, M.F. Iakshamin, frequently appeared at émigré cultural events, including Parkau's salon, which drew Khaindrova, Slobodchikov, Tel'toft, Andersen, Shcherbakov, Volin, Peterets, Shchegolev, Pereleshin, and a few others. The Union of Returnees became the Club of the USSR Citizens, set up with Soviet backing in the French Concession, almost next door to the branches of the Harbin Bureau for the Affairs of Russian Émigrés and the Harbin Fascist Party.[31] The club's membership grew with the news of Soviet victories. On 31 January 1943, many saw a documentary film on the surrender of General von Paulus at Stalingrad, and money was raised to send gold cigarette cases to Stalin and to General K.K. Rokosovskii. Club members studied the USSR constitution, attended political lectures, held concerts and plays, ran chess and sports competitions, and formed subsidiary groups such as the Society of Soviet Engineers and Technicians, the Society of the Red Cross Friends, and the Association of Soviet Women; the latter collected money and supplies for the Soviet front line, hospitals, and orphanages.[32]

Pereleshin avoided politics, but went to some meetings of émigré literary circles, giving a talk on Russian symbolism and reciting his poems in the Tuesday Circle.[33] His main affiliation was a new Friday Circle, which evolved from a pro-Soviet journal, *Today* (*Segodnia*). Launched in June 1941, this weekly combined pro-Soviet articles and reprints from the Soviet press with advice on summer resorts near Shanghai, photographs of girls in swimsuits, and similar material. It was not doing well, and in 1943 its editor, Iu.A. Shtraus, a former correspondent of St Petersburg's *New Times* (*Novoe vremia*), passed his hard-to-get publication permit to Shchegolev, Peterets, and his wife, journalist and poet Iustina (Mary) Kruzenshtern-Peterets, while remaining the editor-publisher of the journal.[34]

The three new editors produced fifteen fortnightly issues from the end of March to 1 November 1943, the articles written largely by Peterets or Shchegolev under a variety of pseudonyms. The range of topics was extensive: the war in Europe and in Russia; religion, philosophy, and the occult; Russian, Soviet, and foreign writers, poets, musicians, and philosophers; literary criticism; poetic theory; and memoirs. The journal was openly pro-Soviet: "we, as if suddenly, through the fog of lies and slander, saw the mighty silhouette of the advanced country, of the defender of human freedom and the highest cultural achievements."[35] The Soviet Union was engaged in "an intense war of intellect, a clash of souls, and a battleground of ideas." "Roads of Smolensk Region" (*Dorogi Smolenshchiny*), a popular wartime poem by the Soviet poet Konstantin Simonov, in which the words "Russia" or "Russian" occurred nine times, was quoted as an example of Russian patriotism, and the journal proclaimed that the Soviet Union was Russia, and therefore anti-Soviet statements were anti-Russian. The articles glorified all Soviet policies, the 1936 constitution, the unity of the Communist Party and the people, and Soviet literature and culture. Lenin was proclaimed to be "the will and brain of the world proletarian movement," and Stalin, with his definition of writers as "engineers of human souls," Gorky, and Maiakovsky were often quoted. The editors professed a "deep connection between dialectical materialism and Christian thought," because both advocated life not for oneself or for others, but with everyone and for everyone.[36]

One significant theme in the journal was Peterets's slogan of "fighting for quality": poets were workers of the pen and had to improve their production through hard work, study, and criticism.[37] He had severely criticized Shanghai poets in "Stables of Shanghai Parnassus" (*Koniushni shankhaiskogo Parnasa*), published in a Shanghai newspaper, and now in *Today* he attacked the Shanghai monthly *Thought and Creativity* (*Mysl' i tvorchestvo*, 1942–1943) as "a receptacle of all kinds of filth," that is, extremely poor poems. An angry debate followed this rude, but frank criticism.[38] "Fighting for quality" was put into practice with articles on poetry, rhyme, alliteration, metre, and genres, emphasizing that how to say was just as important as what to say. The journal published poems by Khaindrova, her brother Levan, Vladimir Pomerantsev, and Grosse, and short novels by Kruzenshtern-Peterets and Shchegolev. The prose was very weak, the poetry somewhat better, but not outstanding.[39] Then Shtraus transferred his publication permit to the Epoch Publishing House and dumped the Peterets-Shchegolev-Kruzenshtern team. *Today* continued under new editorship until 1948 as a dull pro-Soviet journal, which advocated "repatriation." The last issue of the trio came out on 1 November 1943, two days before Pereleshin's arrival in Shanghai.

"God himself has sent you, Valerii!" exclaimed Peterets, when he bumped into Pereleshin on a Shanghai street; he then invited him to join a new Friday Circle intended to continue the "fight for quality" of *Today*.[40] Pereleshin was happy to join his old Churaevka friends, now in their thirties; Andersen and Khaindrova were divorced and Peterets and Shchegolev were married. He became acquainted with Peterets's wife and with Varvara Ievleva, an announcer on a French radio station. The membership was by invitation: Korostovets was invited on Pereleshin's recommendation, but Volin was voted down. Slobodchikov, who worked for the French police and had heard of possible TASS subsidies, declined, but Peterets and Shchegolev made him promise not to tell Pereleshin, who might have also refused. The eight members were later joined by Pomerantsev, a former Churaevka "green youth, usually silent."[41]

The Friday Circle included a TASS informer, the jazz musician Vitalii Serebriakov, a Soviet citizen since Harbin. He offered his room in a converted garage for weekly meetings and, though not a poet, was "unfailingly and silently" present.[42] He secretly assessed Peterets and Shchegolev as Marxists; liked Kruzenshtern's satirical pieces, but found her "cool" to their views; fell in love with Andersen, imagining them to be "two lonely young people, who discovered many points of contact: music, bicycles, horses, nature, silence. [...] He tried to draw her into the Marxist-Soviet faith, but Larissa remained 'a cat who walks alone.'" Pereleshin, he reported, "wrote the gloomiest poems and had the greatest fun at the Friday meetings. Everything Soviet was organically alien to him."[43]

The poetry circle was "not 'a mutual admiration society,' and no one took criticism as a personal insult. The banner which Peterets and Shchegolev raised before my arrival to Shanghai and I unconditionally supported was: 'To Fight for Quality!'" Pereleshin believed in "merciless criticism. From 1932 on, we have stuck to it, keeping in mind that a strong poet would endure and a weak one who would not deserved no pity."[44] The members invented an inspiring game. Each week, everyone jotted down a theme on a piece of paper, rolled it up, and placed it in a glass. One roll would then be pulled out to reveal a theme, and the following week they read their poems on this theme, which would be analysed by everyone.[45] The suggested themes reflected their lives. Kruzenshtern-Peterets recalled: "As the war went on, it was harder and harder to get together, but we did. Air raids were, of course, the hardest obstacle; the street lights were out, and it was quite difficult to make one's way. At first, people could keep the light on in their houses, provided they had thick and solid drapes. [...] Then electricity was rationed, and we would sit around the table in the light of a little oil lamp, rather like an icon-lamp. That gave the theme 'Lamp.'"[46] "Smoke" was suggested by Shchegolev, who had earlier written a poem with this title, and "Cat" by Andersen, who loved and kept cats, or by Kruzenshtern-Peterets, the owner of splendid cats Darling and Toutou. Pereleshin provided "Home," "Mirror," and "Angels" and Korostovets "We Are Weaving Lace."[47] "Gioconda" echoed Churaevka and also Granin's tragic infatuation with Andersen; an epigraph to his "To Your Cold Name" (*Za Vashe kholodnoe imia*) was Maiakovsky's line "Gioconda, who should be stolen and was." Notably absent were themes such as emigration, China, and war.

They "escaped into this 'game' from the ocean of hatred, cruelty, injustice, and suffering around us." The "inspiration pulled out of a glass" worked well: "writing poems on set topics does not seem very serious, but I was pleased with my poems and included many in my later books ... The same is true of other poets: their poems [...] were major successes. After all, no one has to take a 'theme' literally: 'Ring' symbolizes reserve, and hopelessness, and eternity, and 'Home' a man's purpose here on earth and in the other world. [...] A given theme only looks given, but in fact a poet remains completely free and writes how he wants and what resonates in him. [...] I personally never wrote a single line 'by obligation' and not once 'forced' myself to write."[48] Pereleshin was the most productive participant, writing on nineteen topics out of twenty, leaving out only "Dostoevsky"; he took critical analysis seriously, evaluated poems in great detail, and admitted that "my poems were far from always the best of what was written on each theme."[49]

They took turns giving talks. Khaindrova spoke on Vladislav Khodasevich and on Arsenii Nesmelov, Pereleshin on Blok's "Nightingale Garden" (*Solov'inyi sad*) and on Russian poetry in China, Schegolev analysed contemporary Russian poets in China, and Peterets presented a critical overview of Pereleshin's poetry. Only one talk, by Shchegolev, was political and pro-Soviet.[50] In the spring of 1944, they discussed publishing a book of Sergin's poems, and Pereleshin asked his mother in

Harbin to approach Sergin's mother, but nothing came of the idea. In 1969 he unsuccessfully tried again "to find a trace of Serezha's manuscripts."[51] The members shared meagre meals, problems, and celebrations. Pereleshin's thirty-first birthday on 20 July 1944 was marked with an "émigré cocktail" (much lemonade and little vodka) and a modest supper. Pereleshin loved the meetings and resented having to leave before ten o'clock: Bishop Ioann, the "maniac, [...] raised hell" if he was late in returning to the "wolf pit," as he called the Cathedral House.[52]

At the end of 1944 "a wing of death wounded us." Peterets became gravely ill and was diagnosed first with typhoid, then with pleurisy. A Catholic priest gave him communion, and friends gathered at his bedside in a hospital. On 11 December 1944 he asked Andersen to get him some wax; thinking that he wanted honey, she rushed out, but by the time she got back, he had died in his wife's arms: "Everyone was ready for this, but nevertheless the news endlessly saddened us. [...] I decided to conduct a memorial service for him (he was, as you remember, a Catholic, but always loved the Orthodox faith)."[53] Pereleshin mourned this "most enlightened man," "full of tolerance and gentleness," "a very good poet and one of the best critics that I have ever known, a rare friend," and "one of the most important formative influences in my life, especially as a critic." The members continued to meet, but "more gloomily than before"; there were arguments, and not everyone showed up.[54] Many years later, Korostovets wrote to Pereleshin: "The most vivid memory of our meetings – do you remember? – was the first Friday after Nikolai Peterets's death, when we three, Larissa, you, and I, were setting the table for supper and, without any agreement, set a place for him. At that moment we heard nails tapping on the window (remember, he had long well-groomed nails). Larissa said: 'That's he!' You went and 'opened the door for him.' And I, I recall, loudly said: 'Kolia, if this is you, give us a sign!' The electric bulb went off and on, off and on."[55]

Pereleshin took the Friday theme of "Angels" for his first long poem "Angels" (*Angely*, January–May 1944), "a cosmogonic poem about competition among the seven archangels in creating the world; I thought of it a long time ago. It is turning out very beautifully and harmoniously, but smacks of Gumilev's 'Dragon.'" In May 1944, after one "very sweet person" left Shanghai, Pereleshin "simply howled" with "a piercing pain which, like a wasp, settled in my heart," and used this comparison both in a letter to his mother and in the poem.[56] It was "an example of my alchemy": "I have stocked up on incurable sadness, which gives such ease to writing poetry. I am ready to pay with even greater suffering to finish the poem. It is amazing how precise and unshakeable this law of compensation is. One must give up joy of love for happiness of creativity, and, once it is given up, it is as if the skies of another world open, and one can write as long as there is time. From this latest 'amputation' I have acquired the sixth and seventh parts of the poem and nearly finished the conclusion."[57]

Pereleshin was pleased with this "singing, silvery" work: "I have never written anything so elevated and resonant. There is nothing erotic in it, not even images: everything is pure, clear, and holy. […] 'Angels' are Beijing colours, pines, and lakes, free from the tinge of sensual attractions." It was "a work as unearthly and pure as the air over the Western Hills of Beijing, as the sky over Lake Xihu which I fell in love with, and day and night I keep hearing the lapping of its waters (before that, for years I would hear the rustling of birch trees by the Temple of Heaven)."[58]

"Angels" had a dedication, introduction, and seven chapters, one each for the archangels, to a total of 140 quatrains. It was well received in the Friday Circle and published in September 1944 in *Ray of Asia* (*Luch Azii*) in Harbin. He and Korostovets dreamed of "a book in an almost square shape (16 by 12 cm) with five stanzas per page." Peterets privately "subjected it to a severe, but in many respects sensible criticism," which initially angered Pereleshin, but "some ten years later I reread his comments and got angry again, but less so, and twenty years later I rewrote the entire poem, accepting many of his suggestions. Not all, of course, but many."[59] It was published as "Poem about Creation of the Universe" (*Poema o mirozdanii*) in his sixth book, *Swing* (*Kachel'*, 1971).

End of the War, 1945

[…]	
Но в день, когда весь мир низринется	But on the day when the entire world
В безумие войны последней,	Will plunge into madness of the last war,
Утешится душа-пустынница,	The hermit-soul will be consoled,
Заулыбается победней:	Will smile more victoriously:
Отрадно быть ни с кем не связанной,	It is a joy not to be tied to anyone
Ни перед кем не виноватой	And not guilty in front of anyone
В час, ею же самой предсказанный –	In the hour predicted by the soul –
На красном празднике Гекаты!	Of Hecate's red celebration!
Ей будет некого и нечего	The soul will have no one and nothing
Терять в смерчах атомной бомбы:	To lose in the tornados of an atom bomb:
Ни фунта мяса человечья	A poet did not donate a single pound
Поэт не внес для гекатомбы!	Of human flesh for hecatomb!

"Consolation" (*Uteshenie*), ca. 1.6.1948

In the last year of the war, Pereleshin often got up early and went to a park with a Chinese textbook; he studied "in snatches, everywhere: I pull a piece of paper from the pocket and try to recall characters that I know according to a certain system." Electricity being off in the evenings, he "burned all the candles and little stubs left from confessions" to study and write.[60] He kept working on *Poems on a Fan* (*Stikhi na veere*), announced in *Sacrifice* as "a collection of poems by ancient Chinese poets, in preparation for publication." He taught in Russian schools and gave private Russian lessons to a group of Chinese youths, who bought him Chinese treats after the class and walked him home "merrily, with jokes and laughter."[61]

The winter of 1944–5 was "unheard of in its severity": "There is nothing more horrible than cold with no hope of getting warm. [...] I dropped by the bishop's yesterday: he is freezing, as we all are. His admirers wanted to put in a heating stove, but he refused: if there is heat, it should be in all rooms. This is very noble. I am sure that our archbishop [Victor] would have come to a different decision."[62] Wartime life in this "repulsive cold city, an evil city" made him miss his mother even more: "You are absolutely necessary for me: otherwise, for whom would I get a grip on myself and not succumb to the terrible temptation of a different, totally final departure? [...] Believe me in one thing: everything that I will ever have will be only for you. In spite of my rather difficult character, my dream is to give you true warmth. Let some of it go to Mariia Pavlovna (Korostovets) and to Pavel, both of whom were kind to me when I had nothing and truly gave me everything they had (each in her or his way). I often dream of a quiet, peaceful, leisurely life somewhere in Qingdao or Manila, definitely by the sea. I dream of easy and inspiring work, many fresh flowers in vases, poems, and strolls on the seashore along an alley of acacia trees. It will not be possible to gather everyone around me (Mariia Pavlovna hates Pavel), but at least some people will be close by. It would be so great, but for that it is necessary to endure cold, dirt, hopeless boredom, and uncertainty in tomorrow."[63]

In mid-January 1945, he asked for leave to visit Beijing, not so much to see the mission with its "treacherous and cowardly head," but the beloved city: "I often see Beijing not only in dreams, but for real [...]. I see a most ordinary small street with some stranger walking along, and I am hounded by remorse for so many lost opportunities." He wondered about "my joy" Pavel: "so much time has passed that there might be nothing left of my love."[64] At the back of his mind he nourished the hope of staying in Beijing. Bishop Ioann "almost agreed," provided he had a medical certificate, and he got his visa on 17 February 1945. Two days later, on a crowded street, a pickpocket stole his wallet with the visa, and Pereleshin wondered whether "the Lord saved me from something a lot worse" and whether "it was necessary for me and Pavel to get more distant from each other. But for whom and why is this necessary? If it was such an evil thing, why was it permitted from the start?" He became convinced that "fate had acted. In Beijing I would have wrung my neck (the thief's hand restrained me, but in this case it was a different will, the higher one), while here, in the shadows, I will survive till the end of this difficult time."[65]

At this time, his close friendship with Korostovets turned ugly. Initially she was "a comfort in bitter days, / a sister and simply a human being / with limitless generosity of warmth, / although at times her care / was getting too much / and I ran away from frequent meetings, / as a devil from frankincense."[66] Already jealous of Pavel in Beijing, she now tried to forbid him to see men: "With all her good qualities, she is a terrible tyrant and wants to control my life at all costs. I don't understand why I should have this boa round my neck."[67] They argued, quarrelled, "divorced," and reconciled: "she loves me like crazy, jealously, possessively; she demands that I give her my 'entire heart.' As a result of her attacks, she is losing her place in my heart. She burdens me, she simply makes me sick by coming every day for five to six hours." The more he tried to free himself, the more she "adopted an unbearably accusatory and prophetic tone, eternally reminding me of my shortcomings, telling me what to do, and threatening me with divine punishment. It all makes me nauseous."[68]

In the small Russian community people started referring to her as his "patron," "lady-love," "nanny," and "the priest's wife" and needling him: "Mrs Korostovets, it seems, considers you her property."[69] Appalled, Pereleshin began to "decisively and openly hate her": "I got all the thorns of family life and not a single joy of it." This "vampire" insisted that "in the depths of my heart I allegedly worship her, love only her, and just force myself to deny my 'tenderness.'" She told him that the problems with his theological thesis were caused by his "breaking the agreement," when, to lessen her worries about his second trip to Harbin in 1941, he had given her his black notebook of poems, inscribing it: "To my only sister Mariia I am leaving not a part, but my entire heart." When her "persecution became unbearable, I removed this inscription with a special liquid. She became highly enraged: it was foretold in

God's name that my [theological] diploma would be annulled and my badge removed. This is total nonsense. The entire theory is built on the premise that I am some kind of 'mystical' husband of Mariia Pavlovna, that we are created for each other, that my horoscope *clearly* indicates that I cannot have any other wife except Mariia Pavlovna. How can one take this seriously?"[70]

His "nasty character," "irritable and venomous," was getting out of hand, and she "started turning quarrels into shouting, swearing, and even physical fights." When she made a derogatory remark about his mother, he "hit her several times. In spite of this, she clutched me in a death grip. She turned up again today, although I was very sick."[71] If he left his room, she would run after him, grab him by the cassock, tearing it, and continuing to swear outside and even inside the cathedral: "Everyone is convinced that a person behaving like this has a right to forget boundaries between a lay person and a priest, and a monk on top of that: in a word, act as only a lover does." After one fight he locked his door, but she broke it down, and when he ran out to hide at the altar in the cathedral, she waited in his room. Her son Mark had to come and fix the door.[72]

This painful entanglement soon made him homeless. On 11 April 1945, after yet another quarrel, they were drinking tea in his room, when a cathedral guard, Pakhomii Wang, burst in and accused him and his "*madamka*" of removing his kettle from the common stove. Pereleshin pushed him out and locked the door, but the drunk Pakhomii smashed it and attacked him. When Pereleshin pinned Pakhomii down, Priest Nikolai Li, "another repulsive brute," came to Pakhomii's aid and shoved Pereleshin down the stairwell to the second floor, with Korostovets running after him. Pereleshin staggered to his feet and rushed outside, calling for help. Russian passers-by accompanied him to his room, and he packed his things and took them to Serebriakov's room in a coverted garage where the Friday Circle held their weekly meetings. A Shanghai Russian policeman went with him to Bishop Ioann, where his two attackers tried to shout him down. Pereleshin said that he would return only when his safety was assured, but, to his anger and dismay, the bishop did not stand up for him. Some Russians were incensed, while others believed Pakhomii's story of finding Pereleshin and Korostovets in bed together.[73]

From then on, Pereleshin stayed in Serebriakov's room during the day and at night slept on a table in the Girls' Gymnasium, hoping to move there during the summer vacation. He had no regrets about leaving the "stinking cesspool" of the Cathedral House, and whenever he saw "in the distance people from the Cathedral House, I felt repugnance and, in contrast, satisfaction that I had left."[74] In June 1945, when "that lunatic" Bishop Ioann ordered him to attend clergy meetings, Pereleshin refused because he "was astonished to learn that the guard, the instigator of the scandal, was fired, went to confession, and received communion, although by the Church rules he could not do so for three years after such an incident. Now this skunk is planning to go to Beijing, where, of course, he will be kindly accepted by the Most Holy Fat Man [the mission head] into service, even though he had stolen several books from the mission library, for which he had been sent to Shanghai."[75]

His friendship with Korostovets was over. When his new crush, Chen Sixing, the hero of "Little Star" (*Zvezdochka*, 19.3.1946), dropped by the Friday Circle with a friend who was looking for a teacher of Russian, Korostovets, who happened to be there, slammed the door in their faces. Pereleshin pacified the infuriated young men and, after they had left, firmly told her that he "would not allow any guardians over me" and that her good care had disappeared in the harm she had inflicted on his soul. He was greatly relieved when she left for Beijing in June 1945. As he wrote to his mother, "I no longer believe in mysticism or astrology. I firmly believe in joy, in the quiet tenderness of 'Little Star,' in Pavel's faithfulness, and in your unfailing heart."[76] He later found a room "almost three times bigger than in the Cathedral House. [...] I am glad that I left, and I know that I will never return."[77]

These upheavals did not stop him from working on his next book, and he considered 1944 to be "most fruitful." He abandoned plans for a book entitled *Rosa Mystica*, when Orlova "liked the title so much that she took it for her *Mystical Roses* (*Misticheskie rozy*, 1946)."[78] Pereleshin's *Southern Home* (*Iuzhnyi dom*), including his portrait by Jaspar, was soon ready, but "the price of paper has gone up ferociously, and I have to be patient and wait for the end of the war." His hopes revived after the war, especially when Orlova made him a gift of enough paper for 300 copies and suggested designs for the cover and the first letters of poems. The printing costs, however, were prohibitive,[79] and *Southern Home* had to wait another twenty years for publication.

In May 1945 he wrote to his mother: "The end of the war in Europe brings us closer to our goal: peace in the entire world. Then we'll start creating again. If only everyone would survive! Where is our Victor now?" He dreamed of settling with her in a parish in Shanghai, Hong

Kong, Indo-China, Singapore, or the South Sea islands and continuing his literary work. Harbin, "a pathetic provincial town," was no longer an option.[80]

On 13 August he heard newspaper boys shouting in the streets: "Harbin, Hailar, Jilin, and other Manchukuo cities under the hail of bombs! Special telegrams!" He rejoiced that "the war will end any day now, and it will be truly appropriate to think (cheerfully) about plans, tasks, and the means of achieving all I want."[81] Everything seemed possible: "I take my notebook with Chinese characters, and I see a Beijing *hutong* [lane] or nook in a park, or you in front of the typewriter. Pavel's beautiful dark hands appear before my eyes, and I hear Victor greeting me."[82] Shanghai was liberated by the US Army, and the Victory Day was celebrated on 3 September 1945. Streetcars started to run and restrictions on electricity and water were lifted, but some rationing remained and inflation ran rampant. In early 1946 he learned that Victor, being colourblind, had served as a military engineer in Alaska and was now demobilized and living in San Francisco.[83]

In these post-war months, Pereleshin wrote his major work, a crown of sonnets entitled "The Way of the Cross" (*Krestnyi put'*, November 1945), a genre he much admired for its "exceptional elegance: sonnets are woven like garlands of flowers."[84] Peterets had written a crown, "Heart is a Phoenix" (*Serdtse feniks*), presented in the Friday Circle, and Kruzenshtern-Peterets had grieved his death in a crown, "Desert" (*Pustynia*). In August 1945 Pereleshin, while looking through a Polish prayer book, noted that "except for the fourteen stops of the Saviour on the way to Golgotha, this number does not appear in the entire treasure house of world culture. [...]. I am sure that my 'The Way of the Cross' for a long time will remain the crown of this most refined form."[85]

The title echoed *On the Way*, as the poet addresses Jesus in "The Way of the Cross": "Lead me on Your steep way, / so that I will be neither happy, nor loved: / entrust the treasure of sufferings to me. // One day, happy and ailing, / lifting my pliant arms, / I will ascend the black cross with You!" He saw it as "a religious work, though not conventional (Orthodoxy is combined with Catholicism according to Vladimir Solov'ev's recipe: if it is impossible to unite them in the collective life, nothing prevents us from individual unification)." If some Russian Orthodox readers would see it as "a Latin heresy," "in my heart I am more Catholic than 'Orthodox,' and the main thing is that the fourteen stations on the Way of the Cross were not noticed by the Orthodox Church."[86]

All his life he was very proud of "The Way of the Cross": "it is written according to the strictest form and has an organic concept: fourteen stations on the Road to Calvary and fourteen sonnets." The work "hints at justifying death on the cross with subsequent resurrection. But somehow I do not want to be too hopeful: after all, the horror of the black cross of despair, of terminal darkness precedes the justification of Golgotha. I am not sure if my words are convincing, but I see the cross as precisely *black*." In the last years of his life he reiterated that it was "the highest achievement of my entire life; *no one* can equal it."[87]

Fatal Step, 1946

Так растекаться ли по древу?
Пожалуй, расскажу прямей,
что и меня опутал змей,
как зазевавшуюся Еву,
и, чтоб не прозябать, а жить,
пошел я к палачам служить!

Shall I wax eloquent about it?
I'd rather be more direct:
I too was ensnared by a serpent,
Like the inattentive Eve,
And in order not to scrimp, but live,
I've gone to serve the executioners!

"Poem without a Subject"
(*Poema bez predmeta*),
Canto Six, XLI, 283

After the war, the Soviet consulates pressured émigrés to take Soviet passports. In the former Manchukuo, many émigrés, isolated from the rest of the world and traumatized by arbitrary mass arrests by the Soviet secret service, SMERSH, applied out of fear, expedience, or misguided patriotism. They were issued surrogate passports of "war-trophy citizens," as consulate officials brazenly called them. Pereleshin's mother was among some who did not apply.

In Shanghai, about 10,000 émigrés, some quite eagerly, took Soviet passports.[88] Pereleshin, never a Soviet sympathizer, initially did not do so; his ensnarement was gradual. In 1944 he was commissioned by Shchegolev to write on Lermontov and E.A. Baratynskii for the pro-Soviet publication *New Life* (*Novaia zhizn'*), and in May 1945 he cryptically mentioned to his mother that he would "probably join Shchegolev." His translations of short stories by Luo Huasheng (1893–1941) appeared in the Shanghai Soviet periodicals *Windows onto China* (*Okna v Kitai*) and *Epoch* (*Epokha*), and he was "paid so much better than for pathetic lessons" that "life has become more cheerful."[89]

He did some freelance translating for TASS and was hired full time as of 1 July 1946. The job required that he take a Soviet passport, and this "'fatal step' was taken entirely under pressure from people for whom I was working and under circumstances which did not permit me to risk losing the job at that moment."[90] As he defended himself to the US immigration officials (verbatim from English), "I remained a Russian emigrant until 1945, when I was compelled by the Tass News Agency, where I had my job at that time, to take out a Soviet passport. [...] I applied for it in March 1946 and I received my passport in July of the same year. Since that time I was considered in Shanghai, China, as a Soviet citizen. The reason I took that Soviet passport, I will explain. It was under the compulsion of the Tass News Agency where I had my work. If I did not take the passport, I would lose my job immediately and at that time I had already stopped Officiating as a Priest, and moreover, I was sick at that time." He did so (verbatim from English) "very reluctantly on the last day of the term set for the USSR consular authorities for this purpose and not before I was lectured by Yakshamin, who mingled flattery with veiled threats in his harangue. When I confessed that my intention was to go the U.S.A., he said that it would be as easy to go there as a USSR citizen as to go there as a refugee."[91]

He received his passport on 12 July 1946: "in vain I lied and procrastinated: / I did not dare to decline / the 'red-skinned passport.'" In August, the Communist Party secretary, A. Zhdanov, attacked the journals *Star* (*Zvezda*) and *Leningrad* for ideologically harmful works, in particular pieces by Anna Akhmatova and Mikhail Zoshchenko. Both were expelled from the Union of Soviet Writers in the course of a campaign against apolitical literature and western culture. At a meeting in Shanghai Kolosova, in tears, said that Zhdanov's speech "horrified her as a statement of inexpressible cruelty and revengefulness. How could one talk of a mythical forgetting of offences when Zhdanov has accused Akhmatova for her religious and monarchist statements of 1911 and 1914?" Kolosova renounced her Soviet passport, and several people, including Kruzenshtern-Peterets, did the same. As Kruzenshtern wrote, "the Zhdanov declaration smashed all my illusions."[92]

Pereleshin kept the Soviet citizenship, naively seeing it not as a proof of political allegiance, but as a great opportunity to use his Chinese language skills and participate in "a vast publishing activity of translations of famous works by contemporary Chinese writers." His work in TASS involved translating Mao Zedong's monographs and "a humongous amount of newspaper editorials and articles on politics, law, and economy."[93] He loved it: "The TASS office ... Rows of typewriters. / Clacking, chatter. In a dense smoke / a bearded monk can be seen / in a cheap cassock and with a cross, / the only one without a cigarette. / Just look at him: what a sight! / He needs no drafts: / he goes through a fanciful sentence, / thinks deeply once or twice, / corrects a few words, / and keeps translating and translating / with fewer words, faster, / and without huge dictionaries!" He believed himself to be "the best TASS translator," proven by "privileged conditions: I don't work for seven hours, but only five, because I translate more (and much better) than others do over the whole day."[94]

Working for TASS greatly improved his proficiency in Chinese and made him critical of Soviet specialists. Fedorenko, "a 'sinologist' as I am a pilot," worked on translating the classical poem *Li Sao* by Qu Yuan and "walked around with a large crowd of Chinese assistants, who racked their brains for Latin names of countless native plants, plentiful in *Li Sao*, but non-existent in Russian."[95] The TASS director, V.N. Rogov, another "hopelessly weak translator, who got Chinese employees of TASS to do all the work for him," allegedly could not even write his name in Chinese. In the Soviet edition of *Lu Xun's Collection* (*Sbornik Lu Xiunia*), originally published in Shanghai in 1949, Rogov put his name under Pereleshin's translations.[96]

Pereleshin helped the Chinese scholar and translator Ge Baoquan "in a friendly manner and passionately," in translating Blok's poem "Twelve" into Chinese, while Ge Baoquan introduced him to works of contemporary writers such as Ba Jin and Lu Xun.[97] Now earning a decent salary, in the summer of 1947 he visited Moganshan, a mountain resort "of astonishing beauty: clouds (under our feet), fogs, pines, bamboo." He was "almost happy, the work is good, and I am appreciated."[98]

Lucien, 1946

Те дни, когда приходишь ты ко мне,	I mark the days when you come to see me
Я отмечаю в книжке календарной	In my calendar diary
И в памяти, навеки благодарной:	And in my eternally grateful memory:
Пускай живут, отражены вдвойне	Let them live, doubly reflected
В бумажной и в сердечной глубине!	In the depth of paper and of heart!
[…]	[…]
О, нам бы плыть неведомо куда,	Oh, if only we could sail into the unknown,
В какое бездорожье голубое,	Into some blue expanse without roads,
Под дальний гул растущего прибоя –	To the distant sound of the growing surf,
Но только так бы плыть, чтобы всегда	But sail only in such a way that we two would
И в море нас, и в мире было двое!	Always be together in the sea and in the world!

"To a Friend" (*Drugu*), 17.9.1946, dedicated to Liu Tiansheng

After the war Pereleshin contacted Pavel and received a photograph of "now adult, but on the whole the same beloved, unforgettable face," fondly recalling "the best times" with him. He continued to seek "joy" in affairs with young Chinese men: "yesterday this joy, very pure and very sweet, visited me. Would he come again? Today, in any case, I feel full of strength and very happy."[99] "Answer" (*Otvet*, 4.3.1946) speaks of the ever-present conflict between "love, the miracle-creator of life," and the dark corner where "icons are silent in their answer," when "again, I choked with happiness, / looking into intoxicated eyes / and inhaling, in the delirium of sweet passion, / the aroma of the warm and dark hand. // The body was flowing and singing, / it bewitched, tormented, and burned, / and with songs I glorified the body, / a fragrant and tender evil."

In the summer of 1946, in a Chinese kiosk near the Cathedral, Pereleshin met a textile factory worker and book seller, Liu Xin, whose childhood name was Tiansheng. They "fell in love easily and immediately: / a warm stove summoned us / to undress completely and lie down, / and he would willingly do so." Liu Xin, or his Lucien, as Pereleshin called him, became "a significant part of my heart": "how can I break away from China after this?"[100] They spent Saturday nights together, and in the mornings Pereleshin went "to serve Liturgy. Almost for the first such time, I said to myself: 'Valerii, you will soon lose the right to celebrate Liturgy.'" "Drunk with happiness," he imagined God saying to him: "You are coming to My pedestal, / all eaten up by a sinful lie: / through the mystery of the cross / you see different lips, you dream of a different satiety, / not with God's, but with earthly flesh, / not with God's blood, but with saliva."[101]

The lovers went to Hangzhou, "visited the small island of Huxinting (Pavilion of the Heart of Xihu Lake), saw ancient houses on the distant shore, took in the romantic atmosphere of Fanhuo Pavilion, where cranes used to be set free, and viewed the Qiyuandong underground caves, Lin'yin Monastery, the Needle-Shaped Pagoda, the half-rotten thousand-year-old pagoda Liuheta, the Thunder and Wind Tower." Liu Xin's presence is felt in "Night on Xihu" (*Noch' na Sikhu*, 3.7.1946), "Huxinting" (*Khusintin*, 26.11.1951), dedicated in one copy to him, and, years later, "In the Caves of Ziyundong" (*V peshcherakh Tsy-iun'-dun*, 20.4.1973).[102] Their acquaintance with a young man Shuanghong ("Red Frost") was captured in "Red Leaves under the Frost" (*Krasnye list'ia pod ineem*, 15.5.1947), which Pereleshin rewrote in Chinese; Liu Xin liked his first and only attempt at Chinese poetry.[103]

Liu Xin, "a most honest and pure idealist, who sincerely believed in revolution," was a member of the Chinese Communist Party. In June 1947, he was arrested by the Kuomintang, and Pereleshin burned "pernicious books" hidden in his room. Liu Xin's father rushed over to say that his son could be freed for a bribe, but even with money from all relatives, he was $15 short. Pereleshin gladly gave him all he had.[104] His lover was released in a few months: "I remember the day in the midst of vacation: / a motionless heavy heat. / Sluggish, the alarm clock gloatingly / ticked above me. / What anguish! Suddenly Liu Xin appeared, / and the day immediately turned luminous, / liberated from heat and spleen ... / Green tea, lotus paste *oufen*, / smoke of a fragrant cigarette / of the Chinese brand 'Barking Dog,' / and inexhaustible dialogue – / answers and more questions." Liu Xin repaid the money and presented Pereleshin with the three-volume *Ciyuan* dictionary, which he kept all his life.[105] They drifted apart when Liu Xin became fully involved in political work.

"And This Treacherous Radiance!" 1946

Не лги мне, бессмертная книга,
Прекрасным обманом не льсти,
Что легкое, доброе иго
Легко и приятно нести.
  Когда-то, ребенок доверчивый,
  Влюбившийся в голубизну,
  Себе приказал я: очерчивай
  Необщую всем кривизну!
Забредив о сладком покое,
О празднике после труда,
Я легкое бремя благое
На плечи взвалил навсегда.
  Но в мире – и музы, и грации,
  И утренних снов кружева,
  Когда зацветают акации
  И кругом идет голова.
И стала любимая книга
Солгавшей мечтой о святом,
И стало желанное иго
Угластым и острым крестом.
  Над бедной моей биографией
  Слова золотые легли
  Эпиграфом – нет, эпитафией
  И глыбой могильной земли.

Don't lie to me, immortal book,
Don't flatter with a beautiful deceit
That it is easy and pleasant
To bear a light and good yoke.
  Some time ago, a trusting child
  Who fell in love with the blue,
  I ordered myself: draw
  An exceptional curvature!
Dreaming about sweet peace,
A holiday after the labour,
I loaded the light and blessed yoke
Forever upon my shoulders.
  But the world has Muses and Graces,
  And lace of morning dreams,
  When acacias start to bloom
  And the head is spinning.
And the beloved book became
A deceitful dream about holiness,
And the desired yoke became
A many-cornered and sharp cross.
  Over my poor biography
  The golden words have formed
  An epigraph, no, an epitaph
  And a mound of earth over the grave.

"Good Yoke"
(*Igo blagoe*), ca. July 1945

Pereleshin knew that his church superiors were incensed with him, but he too grew disillusioned and cynical: "belonging to this caste of liars and intriguers offers some advantages, that's all. Serving Liturgy gives me a purely æsthetic pleasure, next to good poems, Chinese characters, and beautiful flowers, but as soon as the garments stand in the way of joy, I will free myself from them."[106] Moving out of the Cathedral House was "a step towards liberation from fetters": "I am a passionate and weak person, and joy is everything for me." And yet, "during Lent, I have become more sensitive and several times thought that I was unlikely to have the strength to reject all this beauty."[107]

In March 1945 he got an "alarming telegram" from his mother: in view of Professor Zaitsev's damning report, the Theological Faculty was reconsidering his candidate's degree, but "the secret nature of the entire intrigue made an open intervention impossible. Officially, I know nothing about it." From 28 March 1945, in this time "of great contempt," he stopped signing his letters "Priest-Monk Herman."[108] At his request, Bishop Ioann asked the Theological Faculty for a prompt and favourable resolution, but when Pereleshin also appealed to the mission head, the latter's "cowardice again turned out to be stronger than all the given promises." It was the mission head, after all, who had forced him to leave Beiguan: "Most of all I fear the kindest people. If at some point I should decide, let's say, to hang myself, I cannot think of a better accusatory note than 'I ask NOT to blame Archbishop Victor for my death.'"[109]

He sent a letter to the dean of the Theological Faculty, Father Gur'ev, to be read at the Eparchial Council meeting. He pointed out that he had studied Christian philosophy for five years and had been awarded the degree of Candidate of Theology with the metropolitan's sanction. Zaitsev's reassessment violated a basic principle of justice: if it was determined to ban philosophical topics, the decision could not be retroactive. Furthermore, no court would try a person without his knowledge, but neither he nor his superior, Bishop Ioann, were informed. He threatened to defend himself against such arbitrary actions by appealing to higher authorities.[110] Getting no answer infuriated him: "If some lever does not suddenly turn this whole matter around, I will leave, I will definitely leave. But first, I will let them fully expose themselves. [...] Meanwhile, let him be malicious, let the vile syphilitic stink, let him engage in sanctimony and hypocrisy."[111]

He was furious with this "vile syphilitic": "my poems are the main reason for the anger of 'Archscum' Dimitrii Voznesenskii and his followers. [...] But let my Muse live and flourish to spite the spiteful.

Her consolations are dearest to me; if I have to choose, I know what to choose."[112] He was always "pecked for almost all my poems precisely by that group. Fortunately, rank-and-file priests did not read poetry, but some bishops did. And there were always volunteers, who drew bishops' attention to every 'incautious' word."[113] In early August 1945, in one last desperate attempt, he wrote to his mother: "I have a copy of 'Philosophy of Suffering.' Let them inform me precisely which twenty-two paragraphs, in the opinion of these cretins, are 'not suitable,' and I will reduce them to their level. It's unthinkable to rewrite the whole thing."[114] By mid-August, however, Manchukuo was occupied by the Soviet Army, all émigré organizations and institutions, including the Theological Faculty, were closed, and the matter was never resolved.

Another factor in his great disillusionment with the Church was the post-war political fight over émigré churches. During the war, eparchies in China lost contact with the Russian Holy Synod Abroad, and the USSR schemed to bring them over to its side. In the spring of 1945, when patriotic feelings ran high and Soviet propaganda proliferated, the Harbin Eparchy asked the Moscow Patriarchate to be accepted into its jurisdiction. The mission head, Archbishop Victor, secretly did the same, fearing retribution for collaborating with the Japanese and now claiming that he wanted "to preserve the Beijing mission for its legal owner (i.e., the Patriarchal Church in Moscow)." Bishop Ioann in Shanghai initially agreed with his superior in Beijing, but when contact with the Russian Holy Synod Abroad was established in September 1945, he chose to remain loyal to it.[115]

The ensuing struggle between the two archbishops (Bishop Ioann was promoted in 1945) dragged on for two years. Victor, controlled by the Soviet consulate, took Soviet citizenship in February 1946, dismissed Ioann from his position, and in the company of Soviet officials paid a visit to Nanjing to establish himself as the head of the Beijing Eparchy and thus of the Shanghai Diocese. Soviet Vice-Consul N.S. Anan'ev threatened Ioann with the seizure of the cathedral. Ioann, armed with Chinese citizenship (since July 1946) and the resolution of the Holy Synod Abroad's granting him independence from the Beijing Eparchy, told Anan'ev that this was not the USSR and that he, Ioann, was the head of the new Shanghai Eparchy. He asked the Chinese police for protection against a possible seizure. When pro-Soviet Shanghai newspapers called Ioann a fascist and a Japanese collaborator, his supporters distributed leaflets with the texts of Victor's pro-Japanese and anti-Soviet speeches.

On 19 October 1946, Archbishop Victor was arrested by the Chinese authorities for collaborating with the Japanese, being a leader of the Anti-Comintern Committee, and leasing a part of Beiguan to the Japanese for a concentration camp. He was kept in the infamous Bridge House, where the Japanese had tortured and murdered their prisoners. His arrest was like "a bomb explosion": collaborators among émigrés saw that their new Soviet passports could not protect them. Four days later, under pressure from the Soviet authorities, Victor was released on US$5,000 bail, paid by the Soviet consulate, but he was forbidden to leave Shanghai. In November, two days before his trial, Victor was admitted to a hospital, allegedly with a minor stroke. Some suspected that it was faked on the order of Soviet Consul Khalin, while others maintained that Khalin, "a rude and intolerant man, who disliked priests, especially of Victor's type," drove him to it, angered by his failure to transfer smoothly all Church properties to the USSR. The Soviet embassy appealed to the Chinese government, and the latter, burdened with larger problems, let him go. His release was celebrated with a banquet at the Soviet consulate. In April 1947, he returned to Beiguan.[116]

The struggle ended with two decrees. On 22 October 1947 Moscow Patriarch Aleksii confirmed Archbishop Victor as head of the Russian Ecclesiastical Mission in China, and on 26 November 1947 the Holy Synod of the Russian Orthodox Church Abroad appointed Archbishop Ioann as head of the Shanghai Mission.[117] In 1949, with the establishment of the People's Republic of China, Victor was appointed patriarchal exarch of Eastern Asia, and the Harbin, Beijing, and Shanghai eparchies came under the jurisdiction of the Moscow Patriarchate. By that time Ioann was already in the United States. The Beijing Mission was closed in 1954, the East-Asian exarchate in 1955, and Archbishop Victor left for the USSR in 1956. The USSR handed Beiguan over to the Chinese authorities, and part of it was allocated to the Soviet embassy.[118]

Pereleshin was one of the six Shanghai priests who took Victor's side: "Both [Victor and Ioann] were dear to me, each in his own way: I sincerely loved one and revered the other as a righteous man. When the Father [Victor] was confined in the Chinese prison with thieves and murderers on the say-so of the righteous person, I finally went over to the Father's side."[119] The director of the Girls' Gymnasium sided with Ioann, and Pereleshin, who served in its in-house church, "left a letter in the altar, saying that I forbade anyone to officiate in the Gymnasium Chapel of Holy Sophia without direct permission from Archbishop Victor, and I took the *antimension* [a consecrated square of linen or silk with religious symbols] home." He was dismissed from the gymnasium at the end of the school year allegedly for saying that at the Russian orphanage the abbess had fresh milk given to the nuns and sour milk to the orphans.[120]

The complex tangle of all these events contributed to Pereleshin's growing decision to leave the monastic order, but at its core was the realization: "I attempted to enter monastic life to get away *from homosexuality*, which I did not choose, but was given. When, after seven years, I became convinced that 'no matter what bed you chose for a patient, his illness would remain on that bed' and that monastic life did not help, I returned to civilian life."[121] The last straw was a chance meeting with the attacker of his thesis: "One day, on Avenue Joffre, I met the notorious Kirill Iosifovich Zaitsev, a white priest [not a monk], who for some reason was masquerading as a monk (in a skull cap and with a rosary). I swore almost aloud and went straight to a barbershop to cut my hair and shave. My 'departure' was not decided by this encounter alone; the infamy of Zaitsev was, of course, an external reason."[122] His hopes to settle old scores with this "utmost black-hundred type" came to nothing. Zaitsev immigrated to the United States and became Archimandrite Konstantin in Jordanville Monastery; his other enemy, Archbishop Dimitrii Voznesenskii, was arrested by the Red Army in August 1945 and disappeared into the Soviet camps.[123]

Leaving the monastic order was a most painful decision. "Mosaic" (*Mozaika*, 3.8.1945) speaks of the Good Shepherd abandoning a lone sheep to its peril, and "To the Teacher" (*Uchiteliu*, 23.9.1947) echoes it: "You left me, as you did Saul, / alone in the desert." The most telling is "Conversation with God" (*Beseda s Bogom*, 13.11.1947): "Now You should know that I will never push anyone towards You, / You should know that I will not bring You down on anyone's shoulders, / and will not throw into Your depth / an ailing and beggarly human soul!" As he commented many years later on a typescript of "To Oscar Wilde" (*Oskaru Uail'du*, 7.5.1981): "a funny coincidence: on that very date of 7 May I was ordained a monk. And it changed nothing."

He often stressed, "formally I am not a 'defrocked monk'" and not on "canonical leave," but he simply stopped wearing monastic clothes and serving in church. He freed himself to start a new life (verbatim from English): "In the street I wear a Chinese robe (it's light and comfortable). Yesterday I asked one of my pupils [...] to pick a Chinese name for me. My fate is, on the whole, remarkable. I have lived in China for the better part of my life and have come to love the Chinese more than 'my own' Russians (in general, I don't speak of exceptions). If only I were born Chinese." His Chinese name, Xia Qingyun, had actually been given to him much earlier, in January 1944, by his private Chinese students.[124]

Years later, he recalled the 1920s visit by Metropolitan Sergii of Japan to Harbin. When the metropolitan listened to welcoming speeches in the YMCA Gymnasium, he "stood in the central passage, then suddenly took several steps to the side, came up to me, and, placing his hand on my shoulder (quite heavily), stood like that until the end of the speech. I remember that this 'choice' greatly impressed me. I wondered what made the metropolitan chose me among some 150 schoolchildren" and whether "some sixth sense foresaw a future priest in me." Pereleshin entitled this recollection "And This Treacherous Radiance!"[125] As "Conversation with God" (*Beseda s Bogom*, 13.11.1947) says: "I had believed You. I had loved You, / I had run in the footsteps of the treacherous light."

Post-war Years, 1945–1949

Я говорю: простая ностальгия,
Упадок нервов, близкая весна,
И грусть от недосмотренного сна –
И это все. Но, верно, есть другие
Причины веские, чтоб, сам не свой,
В такие дни я плакал над собой.
Бездомности не выплакать стихами,
Усталости верней поможет сон,
Влюбленности … но каждый, кто влюблен,
Живет надежды ласковыми снами,
И лишь поэт отрады ждать готов
От колдовства безрадостных стихов.

I say: it's a simple nostalgia,
A nervous collapse, the coming spring,
And sadness from an interrupted dream –
And that is all. But certainly there are other
Weighty reasons for me, not quite myself,
On such days to weep over my life.
You cannot sob the homelessness out,
Fatigue is better aided by sleep,
Infatuation by … but everyone who is in love
Lives by tender dreams of hope,
And only the poet is ready to wait for joy
From the magic of joyless poems.

"Sextets" (*Sekstiny*), 18.11.1947

Russian émigré life in Harbin ended overnight with the Soviet occupation of the northeast in August 1945, but in Shanghai the demise was gradual. Some books of poetry were still being published, including Kruzenshtern-Peterets's *Poems* (*Stikhi*, 1946), Orlova's *Mystic Roses* (*Misticheskie rozy*, 1946), E.E. Iashnov's posthumous *Poems* (*Stikhi*, 1947) and a few issues of the literary journal *Antigone* (*Antigona*) edited by Kruzenshtern-Peterets.

In May 1946, the Friday Circle published an anthology entitled *Island* (*Ostrov*), in memory of their "island" in the raging ocean of the war.

The two editors, Shchegolev and Pereleshin, arranged poems "not by authors, but by themes in a fan-like structure," with poems on each of the twenty themes in alphabetical order by author. The selected 140 poems formed "the best collection of poems by different authors" in China, though it was somewhat like "an incubator."[126] The anthology was later shunned as pro-Soviet because of Shchegolev's foreword, which spoke of "an unquestionable loyalty to the new spiritual culture, which is being created in the new socialist state" and of striving for quality because "new Soviet culture assumes the need for a constant fight for quality, which in turn ensures deep understanding of the new Soviet culture." This statement was "unacceptable to some members even in the year it was published. However, the wartime patriotic enthusiasm smoothed some sharp corners, at least *until* the infamous Zhdanov's speech against Akhmatova and Zoshchenko. *Island* was published *before* Zhdanovism; it was Zhdanovism that made us quarrel and split into two camps. At the time, we all had no hope of going abroad, so that the most anti-Soviet of us had to be cunning and adaptable. [...] The foreword remains on its author's conscience. Shchegolev's statements were apparently necessary for those in the group that were close to the Soviet embassy. It went 'against the grain' with me, but I was alone. We would not have been able to publish *Island* if this issue had split us."[127]

The fund-raising evening was attended by the Soviet cultural attaché, N.T. Fedorenko, and other officials, and Fedorenko bought all four of Pereleshin's books. The latter, in a tiny gesture of defiance, autographed them in the old orthography. Fundraising and prepublication sales were not enough, however, and the Soviet consulate subsidized the anthology. Nonetheless, it was apparently not deemed pro-Soviet enough, and at the launching party Fedorenko shouted at the poets and clashed with the outspoken and indignant Kruzenshtern-Peterets.[128]

For Pereleshin, 1946–7 "were the vortex years: / poems, talks, hundreds of books." He joined the Society of Soviet Citizens, which held meetings, lectures, and performances, ran a free diner for unemployed Russians, and set up various clubs.[129] The society campaigned to restore a monument to Alexander Pushkin, built by émigrés in 1937 and taken down for metal scrap by the Japanese, and *New Life* held a competition for the best cantata about Pushkin. Pereleshin's mediocre "Pushkin Cantata" (*Pushkinskaia kantata*, ca. 1.6.1946) lost to Slobodchikov's equally mediocre work. In 1947 Pereleshin became vice-president of the Association of Soviet Journalists and Literary Workers, where he lectured on versification and composed interesting examples of gloss, Spenserian stanza, elegy, rondel, blank verse, triolet, five-line stanza, and sestina.[130]

Repatriation of Shanghai Soviet citizens began in the summer of 1946. First, the children from some poor families were shipped to Soviet orphanages ahead of their parents; then, in June 1947, repatriation was offered to 3,000 young Soviet citizens and 150 orphans, with free travel, unlimited luggage, jobs, apartments, and no import duties. The offer was soon expanded to mass repatriation: the Soviets feared that delays would lead to more people giving up their Soviet passports. The Chinese government was pressured to refuse resident permits to those who had renounced Soviet citizenship and it agreed to do so for six months. Some 8,000 people applied for repatriation, and those who had served in the Japanese and foreign intelligence were repatriated first, to be used for detecting enemy "agents."[131] Serebriakov, the Friday Circle informer, headed the Aid to Repatriates Committee. Free repatriation was soon withdrawn, and, on the instigation of the Soviet consulate, the Society of Soviet Citizens set up a donation fund and organized fund-raising concerts. At a banquet for some 300 well-off Shanghai Soviet citizens, Military Attaché General N.V. Roshchin spoke of the people's sacrifices during the war and post-war hardships, and many people pledged donations and were later heavily pressured into paying large sums to the Repatriation Fund.[132]

In August 1947, a Soviet ship arrived to pick up the repatriates, and a huge poster on its side declared: "We are happy that the Homeland has accepted us as equal members of the family!" Archbishop Ioann came to bless the repatriates, many of whom he knew personally. Some 4,300 people left Shanghai in the autumn, and more followed in the summer of 1948. Nine people in the first group left the ship during a stop in a Chinese port, two more jumped overboard and swam to the shore; eleven in the second group did not show up. The grim joke was that the ship "Gogol'" came for "dead souls," a pun on Gogol's *Dead Souls.* Some 5,000 Soviet citizens did not go.[133] Pereleshin bade farewell to his friends Khaindrova, Shchegolev, Pomerantsev, and Grosse; Slobodchikov left a little later. None fared well in the Soviet Union, except the notorious journalist Natalia Il'ina, who had first worked for the Japanese and then for the Soviets in Shanghai and had prospered in the USSR after publication of her novel *Return* (*Vozvrashchenie*, 1957–66), which heavily smeared Russian émigrés and foreigners in China and gained her a membership in the Union of Soviet Writers.[134]

Pereleshin did not even think of repatriation. In August 1947, armed with an affidavit from his brother, he applied for an immigration visa to the United States and was interviewed at the US consulate-general on 15 November 1948. His old friend Georgii Volkoff, now a professor at the University of British Columbia, suggested he write to the Department of Slavonic Studies at the same university. In his letter, Pereleshin called his Soviet citizenship a necessity for survival, and in the supporting letter to Ottawa Volkoff repeated that it was done "entirely under economic pressure," "capitulating to the demands of hunger." The Canadian response was that the political situation in Shanghai made it impossible to assess the applicant.[135] Pereleshin hoped that once he got a visa to the United States, he would (verbatim from English) "liquidate my passport, which now makes my position very vulnerable in the event of international complications. [...] If China now were peaceful and happy, I would not leave here. Too many deep roots tie me to this lovely land with its kind and gentle people. But the threads of fate are not woven by us, and one always has to sacrifice something in order to realize something else. Let my heart be still."[136]

He continued to work for TASS. In 1948 he went to Beijing for a couple of weeks on a trip that was likely connected with his work, though he later claimed that it was "a mere coincidence" that he flew together with the Soviet official Iakshamin and stayed in the same hotel. He visited his favourite places and strolled along the streets of the beloved city, saw his former lover Pavel, and met with Archbishop Victor, whom he found "very lonely and very unpopular."[137] In 1967, on learning of the archbishop's death in 1961 in the USSR, Pereleshin's obituary for Victor largely reflected his own feelings: "the late metropolitan had never forgotten his years in China. He had not forgotten the archbishop's church in Beijing [...], his semi-Chinese residence, strolls along the long, pine-lined alley to the slim pinkish-blue bell-tower, talks during these strolls (the archbishop often called himself 'peripatetic'), inspections of Beiguan, trips to Beijing parks, musical compositions of his closest colleague and friend Archimandrite Nafanail (Porshnev), Chinese priests, choir singers, and schoolchildren at the mission's Russo-Chinese school, as well as us, his Russian colleagues and assistants. In the poem 'From Afar' (*Izdaleka*, 19.5.1953), written in Brazil, the present author wrote: 'On the day that I die I will for sure return to China.' There is not the slightest doubt that Metropolitan Victor also felt the same nostalgia and always missed the country where he had spent the larger part of his enlightened life."[138]

Pereleshin resigned from TASS only in December 1948. As he stated later, he was (verbatim from English) "underpaid, because they never could fix my salary. They always paid in Chinese money and Chinese money went down and down, and sometimes I received $45 a month. It was much below what was necessary. That was one reason. The other reason, as I mentioned before, was that I preferred not to be connected with any Soviet official institutions, because at that time already I was hoping to get an American visa, and for receiving this visa I thought it was better not to be connected with them, and the other side of it was that I was not sure that they would allow me to leave China if I were employed by Tass, and the third reason was a personal one. There was one case when Mr Rogov stole an article which I translated." Nevertheless, Pereleshin continued to freelance for TASS and found other translating jobs through TASS.[139] In 1948, the USA had pulled out of China, the Chinese People's Army was advancing, and the remaining Russians with papers from the International Refugee Organization (IRO) formed a committee to plead with other countries, preferably the United States, to take them in. The only offer of a temporary refuge came from The Philippines, and in January–May 1949 the IRO evacuated some 5,000–6,000 émigrés to Tubabao, on Samar Island, from where they eventually dispersed to other countries. Archbishop Ioann went with them and soon left Tubabao for Washington, DC, where, in his black monastic robes, a staff in his hand, he begged the Senate, allegedly on his knees, and succeeded in getting the Displaced Persons Act of 1948 amended to include Russians from China.[140]

By this time Pereleshin had finally decided "to get rid of the Red stigma," but "the devil made me" entrust the vitally important matter of exchanging his Soviet passport for the IRO émigré papers to Mikhail Volin. For some reason Volin failed to do it, but kept the application fee: his "dishonest actions were indicative of the morals of the Russian emigration in China. After all, he played with my life and death. [...] I could have become an émigré, gone to Samar [Tubabao] and from there to the United States or Australia. But human fates often depend on trifles and worthless people."[141] A different version was offered to the US authorities (verbatim from English): "Why did I not renounce my Soviet passport before the Chinese reds occupied Shanghai? There were several reasons. If I chose to become a 'stateless' person and go to the camp in Samar Island, I might be sure of a 'premature death' within no long time, because I had several pneumonias and a T.B. in the past, and the conditions of living in the camp were leaving much to desire. Another reason: after having applied for my American visa any substantial change (such as of nationality) might afflict my quota with eventually losing one year of expectation. And the last, but not least, was that having a mother in Harbin, Manchuria,

I could not risk inflicting on her certain undesirable consequences of such a renouncement."[142] In order to leave Shanghai, he applied for a visa to India, planning to wait there for the US visa, but could not find a permanent resident to vouch for him; he was willing to try Brazil, but did not have the required US$3,000 as guarantee.[143] The civil war in China impeded contact with his mother. In February 1949, he wrote to Koloshin in Harbin that he had had no letters from her for over two years and many of his to her were returned. He was greatly relieved when she wrote back that she had not heard from him for quite a while and was greatly concerned, and they happily resumed corresponding and making plans for the future.[144]

In mid-March 1949, he received the necessary papers from Victor, passed medical tests, and waited for the visa (verbatim from English): "Everybody, in one way or another, tries to run away from here – not because of fear of the Chinese communists, but more out of fear that following them will come 'our' brave youth in leather jackets. That's one thing, and another – in the event of non-recognition by the US of a possible new government in China, diplomatic connections will no doubt be interrupted for a more or less long period, and then my leaving will either be postponed or will not be realized at all." He wanted to give up his Soviet citizenship, but (verbatim from English) "not in Shanghai, because then my situation will simply become dangerous." He was still waiting for a visa in September, writing to his mother that Victor's "friends are very inhospitable."[145]

In May 1949, the Chinese communists took Shanghai, and the People's Republic of China was proclaimed on 1 October 1949. At first "some illusions remained: it seemed that journals and newspapers in Russian would still be issued and it would be possible to be published in them and remain an apolitical lyrical poet and sinologist."[146] By 1950 Shanghai had become "unbelievably empty. Almost all my friends have left. Sometimes, there is nowhere to go to cheer up." The main problem was that "there is no one to write poems for. There are no places to publish."[147] Only four poems were written in 1949; as his poem "To the Teacher" (*Uchiteliu*, 23.9.1947) says: "there is nothing more tragic, / than the sea drying out, / the poet falling silent, / grief becoming forgettable." He was "descending into infernal regions of despair, but did not take this suffering into the depths of my heart and it did not give me anything creatively. Otherwise, a long poem would have been written, but the author would have been dead. Or, is a song, perhaps, dearer than life?"[148]

6 The Long Farewell

"Soviet Agent" in the USA, 1950

При свече с единственным другом,	In the candlelight with my only friend
Алфавит и цифры кругом.	We face the circle of the alphabet and numbers.
Быстрый уж нешироким лугом,	Little saucer, crawling fast
Ползай, блюдечко, по бумаге,	On the small meadow of the paper,
Разгадать судьбу помоги!	Help to guess my fate!
Я глаза нарочно зажмурю	I will close my eyes on purpose
(Буквы складывать будет друг)	(My friend will put the letters together)
И не вслух запрошу про бурю	And I will ask in my heart about the storm
И про то, широк ли мой луг:	And whether my meadow is wide:
Разомкнется ли черный круг?	Would the black circle break open?
Вот почти догорел огарок,	The candle has almost burned down,
И, под грохот незримых льдин,	When, with the rumble of invisible ice floes,
Был объявлен горький подарок:	A bitter gift was announced:
"Ты вернешься в Китай 1 [один]."	"You'll return to China 1 [alone]."

"Fortune-telling"
(*Gadan'e*), 3.3.1969

The US visa arrived on 16 January 1950 and Pereleshin renewed his Soviet passport on the same day (verbatim from English), "because some applicants told me that a visa could only be stamped in a valid passport." He received the exit visa on 19 March and the Hong Kong transit visa on 12 April 1950, and Victor sent money for travelling expenses.[1] Chang Kai-shek's blockade of Shanghai forced him to leave China via Tianjin, and, as they had arranged, his mother moved there to see him off and wait for her sons' sponsorship. She parted with heartbroken Koloshin, her mother, and half-sisters, jotting in her notebook: "And so, on 16 April 1950, at 10:40 in the evening, I left Harbin, where I had emigrated from Chita and lived for thirty years."[2]

Pereleshin arrived in Tianjin by train with his new lover, Tang Dongtian, a sixteen-year-old schoolboy, whom he had met in 1949. His Tanchik, as Pereleshin called him, was "exceptionally faithful," and although "I have a difficult character, this boy and I live together in peace and friendship."[3] On 22 April 1950, the mother and son had a joyful reunion, and then, with "deathly anguish,"[4] he learned how the Soviet Army had arrested not only leaders and members of the Bureau for the Affairs of Russian Émigrés in Manchukuo, the Russian Fascist Party, and willing and unwilling collaborators, but also masses of innocent people. Some 20,000 were taken to the USSR to be executed or sentenced for lengthy terms in camps. In Harbin, Soviet soldiers robbed, assaulted, and killed Russians and Chinese in the streets and in their homes, went on drunken sprees, and raped women.

On 28 April 1950, bidding sad farewells to his mother and to Tang Dongtian, he sailed off to San Francisco on the SS *General Gordon* of American President Lines. He was eagerly looking forward to a new life, where he hoped to write, publish, translate, and teach. He relished his first ocean voyage, sightseeing in Japan, playing table tennis on board, flirting with young men, and lusting after a beautiful Indian prince.[5] Then, in Honolulu, a US official boarded the ship, questioned everyone, and urged passengers to inform on communists. A few days before they reached San Francisco, the ship authorities confiscated his Soviet passport and travel documents.[6]

When the ship docked on 23 May 1950, 150 passengers of various nationalities, including Pereleshin, were taken in buses "with barred windows" to the Immigration Service Detention Center, "known to its inmates as 'Witch-Hunt Tower.'" As another Shanghai Russian with a Soviet passport, A. Saranin, described, they were first crammed "into two barred and meshed cages with standing room only, men in one, women in the other. I felt as if I was back in my prison cell in Russia twenty years ago." They had to strip naked and were searched; their luggage was closely inspected, and Saranin's family bible and icon were seized. Then "the aliens" were locked up in barrack-like cells holding about fifty people each, men and women separately.[7]

The case against Pereleshin had originated in Shanghai. On 20 July 1948, a police officer reported to the US Naval Intelligence that in the early 1930s Pereleshin had worked for the Japanese South Manchurian Railway, taken a trip to Mongolia, and been trained in espionage by a Soviet General Galin (Bliukher), and that in Shanghai he worked as a TASS political correspondent and translator and organized strikes by Chinese workers. Another report branded him a Japanese spy. On 1 November 1948, an informer related that "V. Pergeshin" worked for TASS throughout the war and trained the Chinese for the Soviet intelligence service. These reports "didn't come to the attention of the consular office," which issued his visa.[8] Moreover, he had a variety of names: Salatko-Petryshche, Salatko-Petryshcae, Salatke-Petristche, Pereleshin, Pereteshin, Pergeshin, Father Germaine, Reverend Herman, V. Nejdanov, Aurelius, Sigma, Kayurin, Anna Perovskaia, as well as Sa-la-te-ko and Hsia-Shing-Yun.[9]

On 26 and 29 May and 1 June 1950, an officer of the Immigration and Naturalization Service, John H. McGowan, asked Pereleshin "hundreds of most boring questions," all "focusing on one thing: my connection with TASS and the Soviets in general. I replied that I had been translating from Chinese for any person or institution willing to pay […]. I said, by the way, that other TASS employees were permitted to enter the USA, but was told that now the US government has often regretted it."[10]

When questioned why, not being a Soviet sympathizer, he worked for TASS, he replied (verbatim from English): "A translator's work is just the same as a doctor or a priest's work. I did not ask about politics. I always considered it as being private work, although they invited me to work there. I had to have an earning so I consented to join them, but I never wrote a single line of my own in support of communism or Russia. Everything I wrote for them was translated. Everything I wrote of my own was just tolerated, not liked, because it was classical and lyrical poetry. A translator is the same as a public notary."[11] Some of his answers sounded naive, flippant, and full of immaterial details, while others might have been funny in other circumstances. Asked about his contacts with Mrs Il'ina, the mother of the sinister Natal'ia Il'ina, he said that he had only seen her on the street. The investigator then asked whether it was recently, and Pereleshin answered (verbatim from English): "Yes. She is a very fat woman." His explanation of how he was "compelled" to take the Soviet passport was (verbatim from English): "at that time Yakshamin was a kind of boss. He asked me, 'Did you apply for a Soviet passport?' I said, 'No, not yet.' He said, 'will you please do it today.' It was the last day so I had to do it."[12]

It gradually began to dawn on him: "my answers did not matter: my fate had already been decided. I *could have been* a Soviet agent: I had previously worked in TASS, quit the job perhaps just for the sake of appearances, and continued to translate from Chinese for TASS. It's true that I also did translations for right-wing customers, […] but this *could have been so*, and consequently *was*."[13] As he wrote later, "once you become a victim of denunciations, / there is no escape from the net / of dozens of tricky questions / and non-existent articles of law. / – In what newspapers did you work? / What were you thinking and who were you friendly with? / Why did you go to Beijing? / Why did you spend time with 'Miss Il'in'? / Whose side did you take / in the conflict of the two hierarchs? / […] / Did you go to the club on Route Grouchy / to save your soul? // […] // When we were locked up, / I felt understandably depressed: / did not wash for weeks at a time, / starved myself, / and instead of a morning coffee / cast a 'detainee's' solitaire, / asking the same question: / 'When will I be destined to get out of here?' / And the sky again was close / to our tall building, / being more welcoming and closer / than the earthly city of San Francisco / in the bloom of mournful beauty, / closer than Yerba Buena and the bridges."[14]

The investigators questioned several Russians from China, some summoned and others coming forward on their own; the names of most are later blacked out in the files. On 30 May 1950, a former officer of the Shanghai Municipal Police stated that Pereleshin, whom he had known in Harbin (verbatim from English), "became a Priest because he believed that he would be appointed a Bishop and when such appointment did not materialize he probably lost interest in the Church and gave up his religious duties." He had "either worked for the Japanese at one time or at least had been pro-Japanese." In Shanghai, he had sided with Archbishop Victor in the Church conflict, had a scandalous relationship with an older woman, earned good money in TASS, served as vice-president of the Shanghai Association of Soviet Journalists and Literary Workers, and was "definitely sympathetic to the Soviet government." His poems had no political context, but revealed "homosexual tendencies," and "the subject may have been a homosexual."[15]

On 6 June 1950, another informer said that he had met Pereleshin in 1926 at the YMCA Gymnasium, where he (verbatim from English) "showed a very unbalanced state of mind, being a brilliant student sometimes, and quite rebellious at other times," had no friends, and avoided sport and social activities. He had "read too early certain books by Engels and Karl Marx." This informer left Harbin in 1931 and met Pereleshin in Shanghai, where the latter supported Archbishop Victor, left the priesthood, and kept his Soviet passport for fear of reprisals against his uncle in the USSR. This informer added (verbatim from English): "very easily following strong-willed persons, Salatko-Petryshcheff would be a poor security risk in every way."[16]

Yet another informer, a former citizen of Yugoslavia, said that he had never met Pereleshin, but knew all about him. Pereleshin's mother had deserted his father, lived with an elderly cashier at the railway, and then squandered her inheritance with an artist, Kachalov, from the Moscow Theatre. Pereleshin always gathered young people around him, became a monk and (verbatim from English) "quickly learned all of the Eastern languages." In Shanghai he "was thrown out of the rectory," because "a prostitute," "Larissa Anders," not a communist, but "just filthy," kept visiting him. In 1946 he stopped wearing monastic clothes and worked for TASS under the pseudonym Pereleshin. This informer (verbatim from English) "was sure that he came here upon approval of the Russian government" and was willing to go and testify in court, "even to Mars, I would go, because he is no good."[17]

The identity of two informers is known. On 1 June 1950, Father Petr Triodin of the Russian Orthodox monastery in San Francisco told the investigators that he had known Pereleshin since 1944 and that Pereleshin had left the Church, had worked for TASS, and in the Church conflict had sided with "the Soviet Church leader." In June 1950, immigration officials questioned Archbishop Ioann in New York. At first the archbishop said (verbatim from English): "if I cannot say something good about a man, I will not say anything," but then added to that damning statement: "when he came to the United States, and called himself a priest, he made a grave mistake. Such action is impossible to explain, and I cannot understand him. I am positive that nobody will recognize him as a priest here, and that not a single bishop will accept him as a priest in the United States." Another priest added that Pereleshin was "an extremely intelligent man who was undoubtedly a communist agent."[18]

Pereleshin "never found out, even a quarter of a century later, to whom I owe the acquaintance with the American lock-up," but suspected that it was "probably an act of revenge by the Shanghai priests who supported Archbishop Ioann," because the denunciations "smelled of / the dear vodka and bedbugs" of the Kazansko-Bogoroditskii monastery.[19] Some names were later suggested to him: a pharmacist Fedulenko; Storozhev, a son of Archpriest Ioann Storozhev; Petelin, a son of another Harbin archpriest; and his Churaevka friend Lapiken. Pereleshin barely knew others, but "when Lapiken was named as my 'destroyer,' I only laughed," because Lapiken had left China in 1941, served in the US

Army during the war, and could not have known names of TASS officials and Soviet sympathizers in Shanghai.[20]

Detention showed who his true friends were. He received no help and no visits from N.V. Borzov, the former director of Harbin Commercial Schools, or from Professor G.K. Gins, "Uncle George," who allegedly said that poets tended to have spiritual breakdowns. His friend Oleg Chernyshev disappeared when an investigator sought him out. In Shanghai Archbishop Ioann had "rushed to visit murderers and thieves, / but I, profaned and imprisoned, / bore the anguish and shame alone. / Neither he, nor Borzov / sent a word: / once you, little thing, got caught, then stay / and wait obediently for the deportation / back to the Red desert! / The bishop was no hero, / but on some holiday, muttering, / he sent communion bread via the duchess, / and this stale bread / was to be a reminder of goodness!"[21]

This duchess, N.N. Leikhtenbergskaia, an inspiration for his "Music" (*Muzyka*, 16.6.1944), "tried to convince someone that I had come not 'on communist instructions,' but to escape from them." She was not taken seriously, as "her main argument in my favour was that I had an 'unusual horoscope,' and, as Victor told me, she was considered not quite normal." She was allegedly threatened that she would have problems in getting US citizenship if she continued to defend Pereleshin.[22] Victor kept visiting, alone or with his fiancée Lidiia Il'vitskaia, and "in vain rushed everywhere, / pleading and vouching for me." Victor wrote to the investigators that he was willing to make a sworn statement that his brother was (verbatim from English) "neither communist, nor communist sympathizer," and vowed to "guarantee that he will not commit any act that will be detrimental or objectionable to the United States in any respect."[23]

His first love, Georgii Volkoff, visited, volunteered to be questioned, and wrote to the US Immigration and Naturalization Service, enclosing several 1948–9 letters from Pereleshin, a few copies of Shanghai's *Today* containing Pereleshin's work, and an earlier letter to the Immigration Service in Canada. He unsuccessfully tried to get the *San Francisco Chronicle* to write about the case.[24] On 29 August 1950 another person, whose name was blacked out in the files, wrote to US Senator Sheridan Downey that many people out of personal animosity, show of loyalty, egos, and misunderstandings denounced (verbatim from English) "a person possessing a much higher brain and higher spiritual qualities than they possess himself. [...] again and again I testify that Valeri S.P. (Father Gherman) *never* was and *never* will be a communist spy." He further stated that, on visiting Pereleshin, he found his views unchanged and was now ready "to fight alone against several people (it seems a miniature of Korea, where a few Yanks have to beat a hundredfold of enemies) ... I want to fight to the end."[25]

Pereleshin spent over three months in detention; it was the height of McCarthyism, and the Korean War started on 25 June 1950. The Immigration Service Detention Center had "all kinds of prison guards: scoundrels worked alongside gentlemen. The latter made life easier, while the former ... made one want to throw oneself out of the window, even though it was difficult: all the windows were barred with thick wire. Apart from prison guards, we had visits from a 'deaconess,' a biddy of uncertain age with restless eyes and a huge cross hanging on her chest. She took our requests to mail a letter or a postcard (and immediately passed them all to the bosses)." Illegal Mexican immigrants were kept on the floor below and amused themselves by pushing a stick through a connecting pipe. Saranin's wife, who was finally allowed to visit her husband, screamed when she saw it, and the stick came up again impaled with an indecent drawing. Pereleshin stepped on it so she would not see it. She told her husband that two women in her cell had tried to kill themselves. Some prisoners became desperate: one person, who claimed to be the son of Kaiser Wilhelm II, attempted to hang himself in the toilet.[26]

Pereleshin was, as Duchess Leikhtenbergskaia put it, like "a lion in captivity": angry, distressed, and plagued by severe headaches. His "best consolation" was the Saranin family, who tried to cheer him up, shared food sent by a relative in San Francisco, and taught him to play bridge, which they did for hours every day. One evening they made a primitive Ouija board and asked the spirits about their future. An answer for Pereleshin was "You will go to China 1," that is, alone, and for him "this replacement of a word with a number proved *the authenticity* of this experiment."[27]

In August 1950 Pereleshin submitted a thirteen-page document titled "A Sworn Statement," where he explained his views and the circumstances of his taking a Soviet passport and lashed out at the injustice of being investigated on the basis of "some unfavourable 'confidential information'" and at the impossibility of proving his innocence "not knowing what you are accused of." It did not help. On 24 August 1950, the US Department of Justice in Washington, DC, permanently excluded him from the United States with the injunction that he would "never and under no circumstances be allowed to enter the United States." He was to be deported to China, to Tianjin, and mercifully not to the USSR, because, as he later sarcastically commented, "their upbringing would not allow it."[28]

On 8 September 1950, Pereleshin was "woken up early. One of the rudest guards (known as 'the Bear') forced me to carry all my suitcases and trunks, saying that it was not his duty to carry my luggage, which was true. He drove me along the endless bridge to Oakland, where I was put on SS *President Pierce*. I immediately fell asleep from exhaustion and did not see the 'deportation comedy' (I discovered later that it was quite a ceremony)." Captain Larsen "at every port locked me up in a tiny room next to the boiler; there was no air and I simply suffocated from heat. With unconcealed pleasure he informed me that he was to deliver me to Tianjin *dead or alive* and that at the slightest attempt to escape he would handcuff me."[29] His luggage was left in San Francisco, and it took Victor considerable time and effort to get it shipped to Tianjin.

In Hong Kong he begged a British official to let him stay, but was told that "a prisoner has no right to ask for political refuge."[30] He arrived in Tianjin in October 1950, "with the unjust brand of disgrace, / humiliated, barely alive, / the head hung low." Years later, he wrote: "how I hate them *all* for this!"[31]

The injustice of Pereleshin's deportation is incomprehensible, especially when some China Russians, who had collaborated with the Japanese, been members of the Russian Fascist Party, or taken Soviet passports and worked in Soviet organizations in China, settled in the United States, just as Nazi collaborators and war criminals from Europe had been able to do.

Tianjin, 1950–1952

[...]	
Последняя – в твоих слегка раскосых –	There's the last – in your slightly almond-shaped –
Любовь – глазах и верность и печаль.	Love – eyes, and fidelity, and sorrow.
Я их возьму с собой – любовь – как посох –	I'll take them with me – the love – as a staff –
Последняя – в светающую даль.	The last one – to the dawn of distant places.
Последняя со мной в могилу ляжет,	The last one will lie down with me in the grave,
Со мной воскреснет и придет на суд.	Will be resurrected with me and come to Judgment,
И ангел нас еще теснее свяжет	And angel will bind us even closer,
И ясно улыбнется, и прикажет:	And smile brightly, and order:
"Как там любили, так любите тут."	"Love each other here, as you have loved there."

"The Last" (*Posledniaia*), 10.1.1952

No letters sent from the Detention Center or entrusted to his cabin mate, a Catholic priest, reached his mother, and she learned of his fate from Victor's letter. Her heart ached for her son, "who had had nothing but trouble" in his life, and "now everything is in the past, ruined, destroyed, broken."[32]

Pereleshin hoped to settle in Shanghai, teach, and translate for TASS, but the Chinese authorities refused his request: they "suspected that the deportation was staged and I might turn out to be a US agent." Tang Dongtian came to Tianjin in December 1950, welcomed the new year with Pereleshin, and in the spring of 1951 moved to Tianjin. The lovers soon got into trouble: "the police and female neighbours of the young man, who was renting a room from some old witch, spied on us. They caught us in a bathhouse. We stayed in prison from 5 July to 20 August [1951]. [...] It was with him and 'for that very thing' that I was imprisoned." His mother was mortified: "What a disgrace! What a disgrace!" and rushed to their friends for help, and former Harbin Russian Vadim Leont'ev went with her to the police to plead for him. When they were released, Tang Dongtian was ordered to return to Shanghai.[33]

No poems were written during the traumatic year, 1950, and only seven in 1951. "Two Hearts" (*Dva serdtsa*, 11.10.1951) spoke about losing his lover: "Two ardent hearts grew into one, / became one living tissue. / ... // How long did their union last? / A moment, a year, a century? / There are no unbreakable ties in this world, / and much too soon they were broken apart." But, having sworn to end his life on a "roughhewn rope," the poet smokes, yawns, sweats, and undresses young people with his "lecherous looks": "this wound / has healed so prematurely, so soon." In "With the art of creative game" (*Iskusstvom tvorcheskoi igry*, 11.10.1951) the poet's life was "at times a paradise, at times hell! But this struggle / swayed me like a swing: / although the spirit was strong and the flesh weak, / pure songs were ringing." The poet, "passionate, virginal, and idle," used to create magic worlds of poems, prayers, and the bliss of infatuation, but "now my beggar-soul / meekly asks for alms."

Pining for Tang Dongtian, Pereleshin wrote his second crown of sonnets, "Blue Tit and Cedar" (*Sinitsa i kedr*), later entitled "Cedar and Bird" (*Kedr i ptitsa*, 1.4.1952). The image came from one of Tang's letters, where he compared Pereleshin to a tree and himself to a bird on its branches; blown away by the wind, the bird wanted to return and would not consider any other perches. The lines reiterated: "You are a powerful cedar, and I a small bird: / the same forest raised us."

Pereleshin wrote later that "Cedar and Bird" spoke of the "affinity of souls, and precisely between a Chinese and a Russian, [...] but at the time I was almost Victorian (in words, not in deeds) and sublimated even this. Now I would have spoken *openly*." He judged it to be below "The Way of the Cross," because it had "no dynamics, which is a huge and unforgivable deficiency in a long work." Moreover, cedar was a masculine noun in Russian and bird feminine, which failed to reflect the true nature of their love. It had "so many shortcomings that I still consider it to be of illegitimate birth. I have never submitted it for publication or included in my collections."[34]

In September 1952, when Pereleshin was leaving China, Tang asked for help in getting to Hong Kong, but Pereleshin was powerless to respond. In his first years in Brazil they kept in touch, and Pereleshin sent him some money via Larissa Andersen, who was still in Shanghai. Tang's life was hard; one letter spoke of the bird, whose wings were broken in the storm, and another asked him not to mention freedom or love in letters. Tang was soon arrested, released, and rearrested. Pereleshin never heard from him again. Only at the end of his life did he realize that, apart from his mother, only Liu Xin and Tang Dongtian had loved him "truly" and "unselfishly," and he wondered whether the two, especially Tang, "whom I loved like my soul, are alive. If they are, both are now elderly people, but they have given me (for my creativity) so much, that age does not matter."[35]

Immigration to Brazil, 1952

[...]	
Ни рас, ни каст, ни вер ... Широк как море,	No races, no castes, no faiths ... Wide as a sea,
Как море, я останусь одинок –	Like a sea I will remain lonely,
Устало отражать чужие зори,	Tiredly reflecting foreign dawns,
Роптать и порываться на восток.	Grumbling and striving to go east.
Свобода, одиночество ... ну, что же:	Freedom, loneliness ... Well, fine:
Сказать по правде, я вполне готов,	To tell the truth, I am quite ready,
Как никому неведомый прохожий,	Like a totally unknown passer-by,
Последним греться у чужих костров.	To be the last to warm myself at foreign fires.
	"Inevitable" (*Neizbezhnoe*), ca. 1.7.1947

Much as he loved China and "tried to adapt to Chinese reality," that reality was now communist: "Mum and I saw it all: moralizing plays, processions, and endless 'meetings' in every courtyard." They "firmly decided to leave the unrecognizable (and quite repulsive) China at any cost."[36] In autumn 1951 Sentianina, who had already obtained a "stateless refugee" certificate from the IRO, applied for immigration to the United States and to Australia, listing her professions as "seamstress, typist" and giving Victor's name in "Additional Affidavit of Support."[37]

In the uncertainty and loneliness of their Tianjin life, Pereleshin and his mother valued the friendship with the Leont'ev family in their "dear home on Dublin Road; apart from that, there is really nothing to remember Tianjin for."[38] He had known Vadim Leont'ev since Harbin, when their common interest in stamps had led to Pereleshin's rejected advances. Waiting for a visa to Australia or Brazil, Leont'ev and his wife taught Russian, very popular in China at that time, and they helped Pereleshin to get teaching jobs in Chinese schools, a conservatory, and the Mining Institute. In 1952, Pereleshin even went on a brief excursion to Beijing with his students at the Mining Institute and saw the beloved city for the last time.[39]

In 1952, Victor managed to get them immigration visas to Brazil by buying a fictitious guarantee of a mechanic's job for his brother. By the summer of 1952, they had all the necessary permissions: from the Shanghai IRO Office to leave China, from the Brazilian consulate in Hong Kong to immigrate to Brazil, and from the British authorities in Hong Kong to travel via that city. They had been vaccinated and issued good health certificates.[40] They received clearances from the Chinese police, and Pereleshin, as a Soviet citizen, had to have his name removed from the Soviet Consulate Register and the register of the Shanghai Journalist Association; for both deletions the consulate extorted money, a standard Soviet treatment of China Russians who were leaving for abroad. The Chinese authorities required departing Russians to surrender their gold and silver objects for assessment, and Sentianina's tsarist gold coins were confiscated. The consulate also spread rumours that the Chinese required all written and printed material to be submitted for close inspection, which would considerably delay departures. Pereleshin and his mother decided to burn many of their papers. He kept only his notebooks, copies of his poems, and reviews of his books. His mother, however, "sending me away on some pretext, did not burn my and my brother's letters, but tied them into a pile and hid them among her clothes and underwear."[41]

They left Tianjin on 18 September 1952 on the Dutch ship *Henrik Yessen* for Hong Kong, where, by a happy coincidence, they met one of Sentianina's half-sisters and her family on their way to Australia. While the mother and son waited for six weeks for a ship to Rio de Janeiro, Pereleshin studied Portuguese, gave a few English lessons, and had a brief affair with a young Chinese man. They witnessed the suicide of a Chinese person who was unwilling to return to the People's Republic of China: "such things happen constantly: either death, or return to the 'homeland.'"[42] This event resonated in his heart and in his poem "Hong Kong" (*Gonkong*, 5.4.1970).

On 10 November 1952 they sailed from Hong Kong on the Dutch ship MS *Tjisadane*.[43] At the first stops, in Belavan-Deli in Sumatra, Singapore, and Batavia, they were not permitted ashore, but after that the restriction was lifted. They visited Mauritius Island, where they were welcomed by a nun, Sister Lelia Macra, a former missionary in China and a traveller on the deportation voyage, and "spent a wonderful day as guests of the Maryknoll Order sisters."[44] In Buenos Aires they were joyfully met by Izida Orlova and her husband, who had settled there, and with them celebrated the Russian Christmas Eve and Sentianina's name day, both on 6 January.[45]

It was on this long ocean voyage that he "threw the Soviet passport overboard (I travelled with IRO documents) somewhere between Montevideo and Buenos Aires. I remember that other passengers carefully hid their Soviet passports from the South American customs … This served as an impetus: I did not want a Soviet passport. Let sharks eat it."[46]

Poetry of the Chinese Life

Чтоб накопить истому грустную,
Я выхожу в ночную синь,
Вдали заслышав неискусную
И безутешную хуцинь.
  Простая скрипка деревянная
  И варварский ее смычок –
  Но это боль и нежность странная,
  Свисток разлуки и дымок.
И больше: грусть начальной осени,
Сверчки и кудри хризантем,
И листопад, и в смутной просини –
Холма сиреневатый шлем.
  Кто дальний, на плечо округлое
  Хуцинь послушную склоня,
  Рукою хрупкою и смуглою
  Волнует скрипку и меня?
Так сердце легкое изменится:
Я слез невидимых напьюсь
И с музой, благодарной пленницей,
Чужой печалью поделюсь.

To stock up on a sad languor,
I go out into a dark blue night,
As soon as I hear a plain
And inconsolable *huqin*.
  A simple wooden violin
  With its barbaric bow,
  But it is pain and a strange tenderness,
  A train whistle and the smoke of parting.
And more: sadness of an early autumn,
Crickets and curls of chrysanthemums,
And fall of leaves, and the pale lilac helmet
Of a hill in dim bluish tint.
  Who far away placed the obedient *huqin*
  On his rounded shoulder
  And with his fragile and dark hand
  Touches the violin's heart and mine?
Thus the light heart will be moved:
I will drink my fill of invisible tears
And share someone else's sadness
With muse, a grateful captive.

"Huqin" (Khutsin'), 10.8.1943

The 1989 collection, *A Russian Poet as a Guest in China, 1920–1952* (*Russkii poet v gostiakh u Kitaia, 1920–1952*), presents 193 of Pereleshin's poems, including two long poems. As the editor, J.P. Hinrichs, explains, they "constitute all the poetry written in China that has ever been included by Pereleshin in a book edition [in China and later in Brazil]. It is essentially a collection of poetry that Pereleshin himself considers to be mature, not a presentation of all the poetry written during the period in question."[47] The collection did not include poems published in various periodicals or which were unpublished. From his first poetic efforts in 1927 to his departure in November 1952, Pereleshin wrote a little over 440 poems, two crowns of sonnets, and two long poems, which constituted a fifth of his poetic legacy. Except for the traumatic 1950, not a year had passed without poems. Well over half were published in his four books of poetry, in periodicals, and in collections in Harbin and Shanghai, and he included many in his later books.[48] Juvenilia and openly gay and anti-clerical poems largely remain unpublished.

Pereleshin disagreed with Hinrichs's assessment that "in his Chinese years Pereleshin wrote many good poems but was unable to develop his own style and create his own themes." On the contrary, "my *themes* were already solely mine: I left behind the youthful period of imitating Blok, Ladinskii, and Gumilev (I liked the latter as a master, but I was not and did not try to be a 'seeker of the unknown'). I can say, not without pride, that I did not imitate anyone from the age of eighteen, though, it's true, at times there were 'echoes' of a poem by one or another poet."[49] In 1940 in China Pereleshin described his poems as "somewhat academic and dry. The poet's heart has less authority than the weight of intellect, mastery, and taste. He leans towards bookishness, caution, and reticence. He is attracted by ancient images and classical versification and composes sonnets, hexameters, and elegiac two-liners." In 1945, he reiterated that his poetry had "perfect harmony, but is governed by reason, and this is its 'ceiling,' the limit of its possibilities."[50]

In terms of genre and formal aspects, the poems of his Chinese period had their roots in Lermontov and in the Acmeist and Modernist poetry of Gumilev, Georgii Ivanov, Ladinskii, and Khodasevich. Guided by Gumilev's emphasis on mastery and clarity, he followed the neoclassical path in his adherence to traditional poetic genres, metre, and rhyme and worked hard to move from many approximate, imprecise rhymes in earlier poems towards greater precision and rich rhymes, an effort which continued throughout his poetic life. Experimentations of the time did not tempt him; his poetics, as Aleksis Rannit wrote later, is "a ship running against the wind."[51]

The thematic cluster in his poetry is unique in the Russian poetry of China and in the Russian émigré poetry in general. He barely touched upon topics popular with most poets of older and younger generations: the Russian Revolution and the fall of the Romanov dynasty, the tragedy of the Civil War, love and deep nostalgia for the lost homeland, the trauma of emigration, and joys and sorrows of "normal" love. He had no interest in history and politics and felt only a vague, abstract love for Russia. His poetry spoke of the irreconcilability of religion and human lives and of his personal quest to overcome it and live a pure and sinless life. At a glance, it might seem egocentric, but it raised, however mutely, the need to question and challenge God, to be free of religion and social bigotry, and to have the right to be what one was. The camouflage, obliqueness, and subtlety of his poems create a tantalizing depth and intensity.

His unnamed "sin" was revealed only in his juvenilia and a few unpublished poems such as "Adolescent" (*Otrok*, 16.10.1934), of the same title as Pushkin's poem of gay love, where the poet's ardent desire for "the slanting curves / of shoulders being bared" is transferred to a luminously beautiful male youth, his young neighbour. "More guarded talks" (*Nastorozhennei rechi*, 19.9.1933), "Letter" (*Pis'mo*, 10.4.1934), and "To a Friend" (*Drugu*, 23.6.1937) long for a destined "brother." His "Alcibiades" (*Alkiviad*, 1.5.1939) "could not have been published in Harbin."[52]

In published poems the sex of the beloved is so skilfully disguised that many readers saw them as expressions of heterosexual love. In 1972 the scholar and critic Aleksis Rannit misread Pereleshin's "Limit" (*Predel*, 22.2.1941) as raising a possibility of a union between a European man and a Chinese woman.[53] Even "To Lucien Létinnois" (*K Lius'enu Letinua*, 4.9.1934) does not speak of his own feelings. When his openly gay book *Ariel* (*Ariel'*) came out in 1976, some devoted Russian readers claimed that it was living in a foreign country, outside the Russian milieu, that had turned him into a homosexual.

His poetry of the Chinese period spoke of seeking a deeply personal salvation in the world, which made him see himself as a sinner. His quest begins in *On the Way*, leads to monastic life in *Good Beehive*, to praying for his perishing soul in *Star above the Sea*, and to painful doubts in *Sacrifice*. His poems reflect the conflict between his faith and his homosexuality, speaking of sin, the Fall, prodigal son, temptation, unconquered flesh, sweet poison of passions, destructive nets, punishment, and the earthly burden of pain and disgrace. His view of this unnamed sin begins to change over time, and in "Abyss" (*Bezdna*, 15.3.1943) the poet proclaims: "Sin, you are my amazing swing, / my blessing and my damnation!" By the late 1940s, a different encoding emerges, that of a cripple, and "Silence" (*Molchan'e*, 8.7.1949) asks: "What are earthly joys / and a golden ray of sun / for those who are forever cast off from the flock / by their humps, blindness, muteness? // … // Perhaps in His Liturgy, / in Heaven, there is some need / for grunting deaf mutes / and for stooping hunchbacks?" Deeply religious, in vain does he beg God to save him, but what saves him is the Muse, who is not permitted to follow him on his chosen path. If in "Hesitation" (*Kolebanie*, 16.12.1943) the poet wonders whether he could let his Muse to be burned, like Joan of Arc, his poetic creativity shows where his loyalties are. The poems towards the end of the 1940s, such as "Rebuke" (*Otpoved'*, 1.7.1945), defend his "severe, majestic, / triumphant fate. […] // Let the enemies, in wild anger, / shout about execution and cross, / I have grown wings, my face is luminous, / and my shield displays an anchor."

As he wrote many years later, "if it were possible at that time (in the 1930s) to live not according to norms, but to one's inclinations, my fate would have been different. But, most likely, there would have been no poet Valerii Pereleshin in this world. […] He would never have had the primary requirement for poetry, pain."[54] In "Pain" (*Bol'*, 28.3.1934) "every step is like walking on the blade of a knife," and in "Enlightenment" (*Prozrenie*, 22.5.1934) unnamed insights bring suffering and torment. With time, as "Justification" (*Opravdanie*, 22.2.1941) says, "you are desirable, pain, and pleasant, // … // I love you, secret flame, / wiser, kind pain," and in "Heaven" (*Nebo*, 7.2.1943), "pain nourishes us instead of bread." In "Alchemy" (*Alkhimiia*, 14.3.1943) the poet acquires "the gold of the purest inspirations" from painful work with his apprentice Muse. In "Pelican" (*Pelikan*, 3.8.1945), "one of my favourite mystical" poems, a pelican feeds all those in need: "I am growing weak, but don't pity me, / cut my flesh, drink my blood; / I am treating everyone to a life-giving drink, / I, a dying Pelican." He saw Pelican as "a symbol of Christ,"[55] but it can also be taken as a symbol of a poet writing his poems with blood.

Another major theme which distinguishes him from other poets is China. He was justifiably "proud that I am one of the pioneers in this field (although Nesmelov and others also wrote poems about China, or rather about Russians in China)."[56] Indeed, other Harbin and Shanghai poets occasionally mention China as a background, a detail, or a stylized concoction; ingrained chauvinism and insularity imposed their limits. Pereleshin's poems in Harbin could have been written in any city of Russian emigration, but in Beijing China conquered his heart and became, as "Nostalgia" (*Nostal'giia*, 19.9.1943) says, "a tender step-mother." Images of the beloved country are captured in hump-backed bridges in "In the Middle of a Bridge" [*Na seredine mosta*, 27.4.1943], in slanted tiled roofs in "Wind" (*Veter*, 20.8.1943), in beloved lotuses of several poems, and in the occasional use of Chinese words ("*Huqin*" [10.8.1943]). A Chinese love of lakes as images of beauty, silence, and peace is shared in "Night on Xihu" (*Noch' na Sihu*, 3.7.1946), which mentions the great poets Qu Yuan and Li Bai and borrows the Chinese poetic image of "a window full of moon" (*okno polno lunoi*).

The poems inspired by his Chinese lovers sing the beauty of their honey-coloured skin, dark abysses of almondine eyes, black forest of hair, and "wonderful language." Translating Chinese poetry began to leave muted, tantalizing traces in his poetry. As has been said earlier, he wrote a rendering of his "Red Leaves under the Frost" (*Krasnye list'ia pod ineem*, 15.5.1947) in Chinese. In the 1940s, when longing for a peaceful sanctuary from the harsh world of suffering appeared in several poems, especially "Xiangtancheng" (*Siantan'chen*, 11.10.1948), "a shelter for my dreams, like an epicentre of all beauty. [...] Almost everyone has his own Xiangtancheng,"[57] and his was his poetry.

"On the Day That I Die"

Это будет простое, туманное утро в Китае.
Прокричат петухи. Загрохочет далекий трамвай.
Как вчера и как завтра. Но птица отстанет от стаи,
Чтоб уже никогда не увидеть летящих стай.

This will be an ordinary, hazy morning in China.
Roosters will cry out. A distant streetcar will begin to rumble.
It is as it was and as it will be. But a bird will fall behind the flock,
Never again to see the flocks that move through the air.

Босоногое солнце, зачем-то вскочившее рано,
Побежит на неряшливый берег и на острова,
И откинутся прочь длиннокосые девы тумана,
Над рекою брезгливо подняв свои рукава.

The barefoot sun, which got up early for some reason,
Will run to the unkempt shore and islands,
And the long-braided maidens of the haze will recoil,
Fastidiously picking up their sleeves above the river.

Ты проснешься и встанешь. И, моясь холодной водою,
Недосмотренный сон отряхнешь с полусонных ресниц.

You will wake up and get out of bed. And, washing with cold water,
You will shake off an unfinished dream from drowsy eyelashes.

И пойдешь переулком, не видя, что над головою Распласталась прилетная стая усталых птиц.	And you will walk down an alleyway, not seeing that, above your head, A returning flock of weary birds has spread out.
Это сердце мое возвращается к милым пределам, Чтобы там умереть, где так жадно любило оно, Где умело оно быть свободным, и чистым, и смелым, Где пылало оно... И сгорело давным-давно.	That's my heart going back to the dear places, To die there, where it loved so intensely, Where it could be free, and pure, and daring, Where it blazed… And burned out long, long ago.
Но живет и сгоревшее – в серой золе или пепле. Так я жил эти годы, не вспыхивая, не дыша.	But even burned out, it lives on – in the grey cinders or ashes. I lived those years like that, not blazing, not breathing.
Я, должно быть, оглох, и глаза мои рано ослепли, Или это оглохла, ослепла моя душа?	I must have gone deaf and my eyes gone blind early, Or was it my soul that went deaf and blind?
Ты пойдешь переулками до кривобокого моста, Где мы часто прощались до завтра. Навеки прощай, Невозвратное счастье! Я знаю спокойно и просто: В день, когда я умру, непременно вернусь в Китай.	You will walk down the alleyways to the lopsided bridge, Where we often said good-bye till tomorrow. Forever goodbye, Irretrievable happiness! I know calmly and simply: On the day that I die, I will for sure return to China.

"From Afar"
(*Izdaleka*), 19.5.1953

The final foot in the last line of each anapestic quatrain in this poem misses a syllable, creating an impression of a suppressed sob, a sigh, a poignant sense of painful closure. This powerful reiteration of the wish, expressed earlier in "Painting" (*Kartina*, 15.1.1941), was written in Pereleshin's first year in Rio de Janeiro, with the Huangpu River in Shanghai and the Hai River in Tianjin flowing before his eyes, though "there was no 'lopsided bridge' and no parting with anyone 'till tomorrow.' That's not the point; it is totally irrelevant whether it happened or not."[58]

Pereleshin was thirty-nine when he left China, where most of his life had been spent surviving in the émigré milieu which rejected the validity of his nature and feelings. Poetry was his escape and his salvation. The pain of leaving never left him: "Even now, in a dream, or a semi-dream, I wander along the streets of Harbin, Beijing, or Shanghai, recall people and meetings of those days, and long-gone stores, boulevards, and benches. [...] My heart has remained broken, but that's what is expected of a poet and the Poet." He was "completely indifferent to Harbin, which is terribly untypical for China, but I will never forget the bare Western Hills of Beijing, brightened in places by scanty pines, the bamboo groves of Hangzhou, the heights of Moganshan stretching beyond the clouds, the lotus leaves on Xihu Lake, the architectural landscape of Beijing and Hangzhou, and even tiny Jiaxing. What is most dear to me in China is the Chinese, the lively, feminine people, so many of whom understood me and reciprocated my love."[59]

PART TWO

BRAZIL, 1953–1992

Родился я у быстроводной
неукротимой Ангары
в июле, – месяц нехолодный,
но не запомнил я жары.
Со мной недолго дочь Байкала
резвилась, будто со щенком:
сначала грубо приласкала,
потом отбросила пинком.
И я, долгот не различая,
но зоркий к яркости обнов,
упал в страну шелков и чая,
и лотосов, и вееров.
Плененный речью односложной
(Не так ли ангелы в раю?)
любовью полюбил несложной
вторую родину мою.
Казалось бы, судьба простая:
то упоенье, то беда,
но был я прогнан из Китая,
как из России – навсегда.
Опять изгой, опять опальный,
я отдаю остаток дней
Бразилии провинциальной,
последней родине моей.
Здесь воздух густ, почти телесен,
и в нем, врастая в колдовство,
замрут обрывки давних песен,
не значащие ничего.

"Три родины," 27.9.1971

I was born by the fast-flowing
untameable Angara
in July, not a cold month,
but I do not remember the heat.
The Baikal's daughter for a while
toyed with me, as with a puppy:
at first roughly petted me,
then kicked me away.
And I, not distinguishing longitudes,
but with eyes alert to colourful novelties,
fell into the land of silk and tea,
and lotuses and fans.
Captivated by the monosyllabic speech
(Isn't this how angels speak in paradise?),
I came to feel a simple love
for my second homeland.
It looks like a simple fate:
at times a rapture, at times a disaster,
but I was driven out of China,
as from Russia – forever.
Again an exile, again in disgrace,
I am giving the remainder of my days
to provincial Brazil,
my last homeland.
The air here is thick, almost corporeal,
and in it, growing into magic,
the scraps of bygone songs,
signifying nothing, will die away.

"Three Homelands," 27.9.1971

7 *Cidade maravilhosa*

Love at First Sight, 1953

Дожди скуповатые
становятся летними,
а травни лохматые
пахучими цветнями.
  Звана запевалами –
  пичужками малыми,
  вся разноголосица
  ворвется – не спросится.
Бразилия звонкая,
свирель первозданная,
жалейка ты тонкая,
возня барабанная.
  Дай Бог тебе здравия,
  Страна моя Травия,
  на тысячелетия,
  земля моя Цветия!
	Stingy rains
	turn into summer ones,
	and unkempt grasses
	into fragrant blossoms.
	  Little birds
	  summoned by leading singers,
	  in their entire discordance
	  are bursting in, uninvited.
	Sonorous Brazil,
	a primeval reed,
	you are a slender pipe,
	you are a rumble of drums.
	  May God grant you well-being,
	  my Country of Grasses,
	  for thousands of years,
	  my Land of Flowers!

"Brazil" (*Braziliia*), 7.1.1972

On 19 January 1953, Pereleshin and his mother stepped ashore, "out of all possible places on earth, almost on the moon, in Brazil," in *cidade maravilhosa*, as the natives call Rio de Janeiro, with Christ the Redeemer on Corcovado spreading his arms in blessing. Pereleshin had never stopped loving war-ravaged and long-suffering China, but his heart instantly embraced this "paradise" of sunshine and freedom: "I love, love, love Brazil and will not leave it for any other place."[1]

The annual Carnival a few weeks after their arrival captured his imagination:

> Drunk with samba, crowds are dancing in a solid mass [...]. Masked processions walk all over the city, and drums do not fall silent all night. Three quarters of all young men put on skirts and make-up, attach false breasts, and walk around, swinging hips and making indecent gestures. A hidden femininity of the Latin race, concealed under obligatory moustaches, comes out. And another thing: this is a revenge on women for their power over men, a distorting mirror of their charms. It is 'I can't live without you, but I despise you in the depth of my soul.' Everything is permitted during the carnival: getting to know anyone on the street, any proposals, pouring cheap perfumes mixed with ether, all kinds and degrees of necking, all for free. Many babies are born in September and October. [...] Carnival is most interesting and beautiful, but also frightening and repulsive."[2]

In 1958, as soon as the law permitted, he and his mother became Brazilian citizens: "I like almost everything here: the carefree people, wonderful climate, beautiful nature, constellations, holidays, and faces. [...] This country has quite large minuses: corruption, inflation, and chauvinism, but they are displayed only in big questions of politics and economy and are not felt in everyday life."[3] What he sorely missed was Russian émigré cultural life, as it had flourished on a small scale in Harbin and Shanghai and still existed in a few European and American cities. From 1947 to the mid-1950s, Brazil had accepted some 20,000 Russian immigrants, including 1,500 from China, but most soon left for the United States, Australia, or Canada. Rio de Janeiro did not have "a single Russian organization, club, circle, or library," other than a small mobile library of "mainly terrible novels, hopelessly outdated, and some classics." A couple of bookstores stocked mostly Soviet books. One family subscribed to émigré newspapers from the United States, and the issues made the rounds among a dozen readers and ended in a residence for the elderly in São Paulo. Two small Orthodox churches served a dwindling number of Russian parishioners.[4] In this respect, the city was a "terrible backwoods," "a cultural backyard," "a real Dead-End City (*Propadinsk*)": "here I am, in the full sense, *omnia mea mecum porto*."[5]

Pereleshin had arrived with US$1.20 in his pocket, but an IRO settlement subsidy and money from Victor helped. The mother and son found an apartment in the suburb of Santa Teresa, where steep streets of stone steps were lined with historical landmarks.[6] They lugged their suitcases uphill by the effort of "stomach muscles," as his mother described, and were "dead beat. We slept like stones: Valerii on the floor on my mattress brought from Harbin (against Valerii's grumbling and Victor's instructions of no luggage), and I on a 'coach,' a wooden trunk just as soft and comfortable as the floor."[7] They managed on Victor's monthly US$60.00 (Cr2,400) while Pereleshin looked for work, but his Russian legal and theological education and knowledge of Russian, English, and Chinese were of no use in Brazil, and his Portuguese was inadequate. He never went to the place which had provided the fictitious job offer: "it is enough to take one look at me to know that I am no mechanic."[8]

A promising opportunity came up in July 1953. The US-based Tolstoy Fund decided to launch a Russian weekly newspaper, *Herald of Brazil* (*Vestnik Brazilii*), in São Paulo, which had had a patchy history of Russian press. The newly appointed publisher, a former Shanghai Russian V.E. Kanel', invited Pereleshin to be the editor and his mother to run a "Women's Page": "All my education, even the Chinese language, has come in handy."[9]

They moved to São Paulo on 21 September, and the first issues of *Herald of Brazil* were issued on 11 and 18 October 1953, with items by Pereleshin, initialled or unsigned, such as "Rio de Janeiro (First Impressions)" and "Sculpture Exhibition in the Museum of Art in Rio de Janeiro." Unfortunately, "on the day of the first issue, a rift arose between us and the newspaper, leading to a complete break." According to his mother, "Kanel' does not understand anything in the newspaper business and ruins everything in an autocratic and insolent manner. In general, he is a swindler and, the main thing, a fool. All others in the Tolstoy Fund in São Paulo are pleasant, and it would have been possible to work there, if it were not for this upstart and dimwit as the boss."[10] They quit, though the next few issues still carried Pereleshin's unsigned contributions. Kanel' was "fired and left huge debts," and the weekly closed at issue no. 8. The experience left them bitter: Pereleshin was owed over Cr5,300, and Sentianina was paid only Cr2,500 of the promised Cr6,000.[11]

On 14 October 1953, at their own expense, they returned to "our beloved city, deciding that if we were to be unemployed, it would be more pleasant in Rio de Janeiro than in an alien, cold, and unpleasant São Paulo. We nearly cried at the sight of Pão de Açucar and Corcovado, which have become dear to us. [...] For two days we lived nowhere: Mum stayed with a female acquaintance, and I slept on the floor at a friend's place (the fifth in one room)."[12] Eventually, they found an affordable two-bedroom apartment in Santa Teresa, on the same street as their first, in "a six-storey house on a mountain," which required "climbing up 128 steps from the square to our street and then going down two floors inside the building." For a while, they lived with the previous tenants, who moved out on 24 April 1954, "a wonderful day in all respects," which brought "a long lost and almost forgotten happiness. It was late in the evening, but we celebrated Easter. We cooked a light supper, bought a bouquet of red roses, and opened a bottle of Martini Vermouth, which I had presented to Mum on her name day. Rejoicing, Mum even made a biscuit torte."[13]

After the São Paulo fiasco, Pereleshin desperately looked for work, but demand was for engineers, draftsmen, technicians, accountants, stenographers, and similar skilled professionals, or labourers. He "hated office work," but took jobs in a jewellery and curio store and then in the office of a small factory; he taught English in a Berlitz School and wrote small items for an English magazine. In 1957, he taught part time in an American school, but was dismissed after the American consul allegedly came to the school with Pereleshin's photograph. He and his mother depended on Victor's regular help, which Pereleshin took for granted and blamed any delays on "his wife's influence." They lived "very frugally (coffee and bread, occasionally some meat)" and from time to time had to rent out one bedroom and a storeroom to various Russians.[14] By the end of 1957 he felt defeated: "no work, money is short, the ailing mother is fretting, and there is always a hopeless loneliness, Mum's and mine. […] All I feel is anguish. My entire life did not work out."[15]

In spite of personal hardships, he tried to get Anita Gincenberg and her sister out of Harbin. She wrote: "I never forget you in my miseries and joys (always more miseries). […] Recently, before a major Church holiday, I went to the monastery, where you used to live, and stood alone at a service all evening. I was absolutely happy. I love walking along Montenegro St, where you lived with Evgeniia Aleksandrovna."[16] Pereleshin initially wanted to sponsor them as his "cousins," then wrote to her: "I personally would be less unhappy if you were by my side as a comrade, a friend, a companion, a friend in misfortune. […] I was not totally dishonest in sponsoring you as my fiancée (although, of course, it would not impose any obligations on you)."[17] The timid sisters succumbed to Soviet propaganda and left for the USSR in 1959; her last letter from Harbin said: "Farewell, my dearest. […] I adored you alone of all people. Farewell. I am not giving my address, as it is obvious that you no longer need it."[18] A year later, she wrote from the Latvian Socialist Republic, and he resumed contact with the woman whom he saw as his Nadezhda Filaretovna von Mekk, Tchaikovsky's patron. Their correspondence stopped in 1977, when he became openly gay and she strongly pro-Soviet.[19]

Poems before the Ten-Year Silence, 1953–1957

Всегда в цвету терновник мой чудесный:	My wonderful blackthorn is always blooming,
Растут в обнимку боль и торжество,	And pain and triumph are growing in embrace,
Но я – то червь, то лебедь поднебесный,	But I, at times a worm, at times a swan of the skies,
Не понял в этой жизни ничего.	Have not understood anything in this life.
Затем ли я пошел тропинкой узкой	Did I follow a narrow path
И разлюбил свой маленький покой.	And stopped loving my small peaceful life
Чтоб стать в истории культуры русской	Just to become an unnoticeable footnote
Невидным примечаньем под строкой?	In the history of Russian culture?
Не лучше ль было сразу отстраниться	Would it not have been better to keep away,
Или хотя бы знать наверняка,	Or at least to know for sure,
Что стоит даже целая страница	That even a whole page is worth
Ползучего уюта червяка?	The crawling comfort of a worm?
	"Doubt" (*Somnenie*), 4.8.1968

Pereleshin's first poems in Brazil stemmed from an infatuation on the ocean voyage. Eighteen-year-old Iura B. reciprocated, but he insisted on secrecy, kept changing his mind, and dated women. In April 1954, to Pereleshin's misery, he broke off the affair: "I have always sought and loved *one* love, with a full and mutual immersion. It is not my fault that people deceive me. It is even less my fault that fate took away Tang Dongtian, the only one who truly loved me and learned to live my life, not only his own."[20]

In his first Brazilian poem, "You, with your sad lunar tenderness" (*Ty s pechal'noi nezhnost'iu lunnoi*, 30.1.1953), a woman is the moon's "round silk fan / raised above the dusky yellow night," a Medea, a witch, and a skilful liar, but the poet, like a sunflower, yearns only for the fiery rays of the sun. In "Sonnet" (*Sonet*, 19.3.1953) "in vain / a sunflower passionately rushes after the sun / to complete its magnificent round." In "Fantasy" (*Fantaziia*, 11.3.1953) the poet wishes to don a magic hat and always be invisibly present in his beloved's life. In these poems the gender is camouflaged, but "Yellow earth of southern bodies and black forests of hair" (*Iuzhnykh tel zheltozem i volos chernoles'e*, 30.1.1953) forms an acrostic of his lover's name and confesses being "seized with a hellish storm of desire / and turning into an accursed bonfire of unquenchable love," of loving many "people of other faiths" with "a forbidden passion," but dreaming of "one's own," used with the masculine ending. "Immortality" (*Bessmertie*, 5.1.1954), dedicated to "Iura B.," expands the Shanghai theme of anti-procreation: a person is not a duplicate of his ancestors, but should discover immortality within himself, and, while his lover might be "right" in wanting children, "the soul ascends to the highest level of being, only when its thirst for life and reproduction extinguishes. If so, then a freak becomes the chosen one, an arhat, a bodhisattva."[21] His vicious parting shot at Iura B. was "Your joyful choice is known" (*Tvoi radostnyi vybor izvesten*, 5.5.1954), which predicts that he will be "chained / by pale-white boring children, / their tummies, running noses, and pee-pee."

After the break with Iura B., Pereleshin's "small joys of life," such as books and stamps, included "dark-skinned eighteen-year-olds, loving and giving affectionate, very affectionate warmth." "Night was casting spells over you" (*Noch' koldovala nad toboiu*, 15.4.1954) was written after meeting a nineteen-year-old Brazilian on the street: "I lost my love, / where happiness was impossible, / but was it just to be tormented again / by a hopeless love?" Sentences in Portuguese started to appear in his poems, and he even tried to write in Portuguese "for planned conquests, but conquests turned out to be possible and even easy without poems."[22] He kept falling in love and heard "many astonishing, most interesting, and incredible stories from these young men over a cup of coffee, in a streetcar, or face to face, when the door is locked!" But they all were "Chinese shadows, appearing and disappearing!"[23] "Li Bai" (*Li Bo*, ca. 1.5.1957), where the drunken poet Li Bai tries to reach the moon's reflection at the bottom of a well, concludes: "He drowned there. But would the end / of a passionate hangover be a lesson to me / and to a moth, which burns itself in a fire?"

Brazil first appeared in "I know you will leave me" (*Ia znaiu, ty menia ostavish'*, 30.1.1953), where the poet begs a genderless "you," most likely Iura B., who soon left for the United States, to stay: "Here, the January heat / has stretched over the incomparable city, / and the sea splashes the foam / of boiling silver. // Here the heart rejoices at the coolness / and swift thunderstorms, when / the phlegmatic flocks of clouds / pass over the distant Corcovado. // [...] // Having seen this earthly paradise, / stay with the palm trees and the sea, / with my love and with me!"

The religious theme of his poetry was continued in "Corcovado" (*Korkovado*, 1.7.1953): "Alone, in the midst of the fading azure of the sky, / I will stay pure, like clouds. // Watching the sun going beyond / the horizon, like a falling discus, / I, the one near, will pray to Christ / for the small world below." "Pyramid" (*Piramida*, 24.2.1955) echoes Shanghai's "Extasis" (29.12.1944): "its theme is truly huge. The standard way of the Church is to learn about God. A searching spirit, becoming pure and gradually leaving material things beneath, looks at God from the purest, highest point, from the top of the pyramid. But in getting to know God, the spirit remains 'an outside observer.' What's needed is not knowledge, but confluence, saturation of the seeker with what is being sought. God, like air and light, will fill the pyramid if, instead of one point, its top, it will turn its wide base to God. Then 'I' will become God, and God will be 'I' in me. And this path is mystic."[24]

He also tried a genre new to him, *ghazals* or Persian quatrains. The four written in 1953 on a bus to São Paulo were expanded into a cycle "*Ghazals* on the Road" (*Dorozhnye gazelly*). He wrote more quatrains later, in 1967–71, to a total of twenty-eight, finding them "best for philosophical sketches." His *ghazals* spoke of one's way in life, the sorrows of love, and the inevitability of death. He even thought of publishing a book of *ghazals*, "With Your Happiness" (*Tvoim schast'em*), the title coming from the *ghazal*: "I am happy with your happiness, as if it were mine, / I languish with your sorrow, as if it were mine. / I have shared my happiness with you, / but the burden of my sorrow cannot be divided." He later changed the title to "Footprints in the Sand" (*Sledy na peske*),[25] but never published it.

In January 1954, he mailed the hundred-odd-page manuscript of *Southern Home*, adding a Brazilian poem "Immortality" (*Bessmertie*, 5.1.1954), to the Chekhov Publishing House in New York. A polite rejection left him dejected: it "will never be published. There is no need for it whatsoever." A year later, in January 1955, he sent a few poems and translations from the Chinese and Portuguese to the New York émigré journal *The New Review* (*Novyi zhurnal*), but the editor replied that the poems were "not suitable" and asked for articles on contemporary Chinese literature.[26]

Pereleshin lost confidence and did not look for other publishers or, once he had a steady job, did not consider self-financing *Southern Home*, as he had done with his other books in Harbin. He felt that "my cross has finally squashed me (it would have happened sooner or later). It is impossible to suffer too much. The living tissues of the heart have burned out." His poems now seemed as if they were "written by someone else. Poetry has totally disappeared from my life. The cost of poems is sleepless nights, nervous excitement, almost hallucinations, and a terrible longing for happiness."[27] Moreover, a succession of Russian tenants in their apartment gossipped about his meetings with young Brazilian men: "my intimate life is discussed by the entire 'Russian colony.' It is impossible to estimate how many lies are added. So, there is no more poetry and will not be. To write for this swine? Or for myself, and put it into a drawer? I simply hate 'Russian people.'" If Victor was "ashamed that he had once written poetry, for me the fact that I can no longer write is a tragedy."[28]

He wrote nineteen poems in 1953, ten in 1954, one in 1955, none in 1956, and six in the first half of 1957, for a paltry total of thirty-six. In one of the last, "Morning of Death" (*Utro smerti*, 1.5.1957), the poet tells his skeleton, "a comrade of the sunless years," that it is free to dig itself into a black hole, while the poet will embark on "a distant flight, with no sorrows, joyful and luminous, / past rusty chains and no longer weighty fetters, / above prisons and toy towers and clouds."

For the next ten years he did not write a single poem.

Librarian at the British Council, 1958–1967

Упоенно и безмятежно
над цветами вьется оса.
Я смотрю со скалы прибрежной
на далекие паруса.
  Это зависть? Сердце очистив,
  огляжусь. Небосвод высок.
  Изумруды травы и листьев.
  Под ногой – золотой песок.
Я не нищий. Так пусть в далеком
обаянии широты
пробегают робким упреком
чьи-то мачты. Мои мечты.

Rapturously and serenely
a wasp hovers above the flowers.
I am looking from a coastal rock
at distant sails.
  Is it envy? Cleansing my heart,
  I glance around. The sky dome is high.
  The grass and leaves are emerald.
  Golden sand is under my feet.
I am no pauper. Then let in the distant
charm of the expanse,
like a timid reproach,
someone's sails go by. My dreams.

"Sails" (*Parusa*), 28.10.1968

By early 1958, Pereleshin's unemployment had led to "distress and utter despair": "I have only one and the same thought: about the end. Obviously,

I am a 100 per cent failure and there is no point in loitering here."[29] Then he had a break. The mother and son became friends with the Kirilloff family, former China Russians. Pereleshin liked the grandmother, M.A. Sapelkina, so much that he dedicated his "Pyramid" (*Piramida*, 24.2.1955) to her. In 1957, A.B. Kirilloff, who worked at the British Council, told Pereleshin of a vacancy. His first application was turned down, but the second led to his being hired first on probation and as of 2 June 1958 as a librarian in the Council's collection of books, films, and records.[30]

The nine years spent at the British Council were a secure and a "very monotonous" time of his life. He and his mother lived comfortably on his salary, supplemented with occasional private lessons in English, Russian, and Portuguese and translations for "World News in Brief" in the periodical *Machinery Lloyd*. He indulged his lifelong passion for stamp-collecting, "the only thing which never betrays me," and his albums, occupying one and a half shelves of a large bookcase, included a splendid Chinese collection.[31] He took his mother to films at the British Council, among them a documentary on Ceri Richards's paintings prompted by Debussy's *La cathédrale engloutie*, which Duchess Leikhtenbergskaia had played in Shanghai. When he bought a record player, the Debussy piano prelude was one of his first records, followed by other nostalgic purchases such as Tchaikovsky's *Symphonie Pathétique* and Wagner's *Parsifal*, "the only musical work which resonates in me in its entirety from the beginning to the end."[32]

He and his mother took trips to Petrópolis, Teresópolis, Lambari, and a few other nearby cities. During Christmas vacation in December 1959, he spent three days in Vale das Videiras in the Araras region and bought a piece of land; he put Cr4,000 down and the remaining Cr70,000 were to be paid in instalments.[33] In 1960, when Faculdade Nacional de Filosofia in Rio de Janeiro and Universidade de São Paulo jointly planned extra-curricular courses of Russian language, he eagerly applied, but was not considered because he did not have a university degree in the subject. In 1962–3 he briefly taught Russian part time at the Santa Ursula University, but the job did not lead to a regular appointment.[34]

In 1959, his brother Victor got a well-paid engineering job in the US International Construction Company, which was building hydroelectrical stations in Brazil, and moved to Rio de Janeiro with his wife, Lidiia. For the first time since the late 1930s they all lived in the same city, but time had "estranged us; on the whole, we have no family." Pereleshin selfishly resented Victor's wife, convinced that "the psychology of a married man changes radically."[35]

This comfortable and peaceful life was severely disrupted, when, on 28 May 1963, while crossing Praia do Botafogo, Pereleshin was knocked down by a car and left unconscious on the street for three hours. His mother, frantic with worry, waited up all night and, on finding his name in the morning newspaper, rushed with Lidiia to the hospital. After three operations he returned to work on 22 July, "in spite of limping, loss of balance, burning in the left leg," loss of flexibility in the broken left arm, and constant fatigue; for some time he staggered and bumped into things. The worst damage was diplopia (double vision), which forced him to wear two pairs of "Cyclops' glasses," one with a clouded left lens and the other with the right lens clouded.[36] Victor paid all the expenses, including Cr500,000 (at that time the US dollar traded at Cr2,500) for the hospital stay and Cr250,000 for a bone surgeon.[37]

A new disaster befell him in 1967. Under Brazilian law, a person dismissed after ten years was entitled to two-months' salary for each year worked, but if the dismissal was earlier, only one month's salary for each year worked was paid: "one does not have to be an orthodox Marxist to agree with an employer that people should be fired before the ten-year limit."[38] In June 1966, after eight years, Pereleshin was informed that his employment might end in September or October. It was rumoured that his pursuit of a young man, either an employee or a library visitor, had partly contributed to this decision.[39] After a year of "agony," in the summer of 1967 he was told that his position would be abolished, but he overheard that someone from England might be hired in his place. He felt suicidal, "but when I imagine Mum AFTER this, the sense of responsibility takes over. It would have been a murder as well. […] Now my mood is almost funereal."[40]

His employment ended on 31 July 1967; he was given a lump sum comprising July's salary, ten monthly payments for nine years of service and for twenty days of unused vacation, and seven-twelfths of the Christmas bonus. There was no pension: the British Council, as an extraterritorial establishment, did not deduct contributions. The money, he figured, would permit him and his mother to cope for about a year.[41] He knew that "Victor, after all, would help us," and, indeed, Victor let them live rent free in his smaller condominium; he and his wife lived in a larger one a few blocks away.[42] Sentianina greatly appreciated his generosity, but Pereleshin was resentful: "I have no job and, consequently, no salary and, consequently, no say; my brother decided that we should move there, and that's that." They had a dining room, two bedrooms, a kitchen, and a storage room, but he grumbled that it was too small and the view depressing and blamed his mother for complaining that in Santa Teresa she had had to carry shopping bags up 128 steps.[43]

The condominium was near Copacabana, which delighted his mother: "What beauty surrounds us! And the shore is half a block from us!" Pereleshin echoed: "It is half past nine in the morning. Gold and deep blue colours. The day is fantastically beautiful. Walking to the post office (some five blocks), I kept looking into all the side streets at the Atlantic Ocean […]. I was catching sight of the islands, and the surf was rolling and throwing up white foam … All this beauty sets the poetic mood (although I know that poems are not written like that)."[44]

They moved in December 1967 and lived at the condominium for thirteen years in their usual disorder: "it is easy to lose things at our place: books and papers cover all wardrobe shelves, tables, and even the floor. Sometimes, one 'Pisa tower' on the table falls down, and 'Valerius Rex' crawls on the floor and picks up scattered volumes (we will not mention what he mutters then)."[45] In "Miscalculation" (*Proschet*, 21.11.1973), the poet imagines how "a future archeologist / would dig down to surviving shelves: / not opening books, he would pull out // strips of paper from dusty spines / and gather scraps of diaries / and a draft, chewed by termites." The mother and son usually stayed up well past midnight, as they used to do in Harbin, Sentianina out of a long habit and Pereleshin from frequent insomnia. He tended to get up very late or very early, in which case he would heat up yesterday's coffee, waiting for his mother to get up and make a fresh pot. They did not cook much and often ate soup for days at a time or lived on coffee and bread. One acquaintance described their place as "a total mess, his mother saying: why bother to clean, when it would get dusty tomorrow?"[46]

Return to Poetry, 1967

Не пленница и не куплена.	Not a captive and not bought.
В плену? Не бежит из плена!	Captured? She does not escape captivity!
Таких, говоришь ты, дюжина:	There are, you say, dozens like her:
Гадалка, воровка, странница –	A fortune-teller, a thief, a wanderer –
Для каждой своя страница	For each one a page
Исписана до конца ...	Is written all to the end …
Но эта – одна – останется,	But this one – the only one – will stay,
Как рост – как горб – как жена.	Like one's height – like a hump – like a wife.

"Muse" (*Muza*), 28.1.1969

In welcoming the New Year of 1967, Pereleshin had no inkling of the great change that was to take place in his life. Still working, he splurged on champagne and white wine, olives and anchovies, cheese and fresh fruit, nuts and bitter chocolate, but very few visitors dropped by, and he and his mother celebrated alone.[47]

In 1949, as Pereleshin recalled in his autobiographical *Poem without a Subject* (*Poema bez predmeta*), on the eve of the Chinese communist takeover of Shanghai, he had been walking on a street and "suddenly saw a woman: 'Oh, I'm so glad! / Valerii, you must help me: / before the siege has locked us in, / I'll escape tonight / by the still open roads.' / – 'Run, Mary, my friend, God be with you. / Farewell, till we meet again.' / – 'But I've so little money. / Help, at least a bit: / perhaps, a penny might save me, / and I won't forget the debt. / But if you can't, go on your way!' / Though a pauper myself, / I gave her five dollars."[48] That woman was Peterets's widow, Mary Kruzenshtern-Peterets. She had not managed to leave Shanghai at that time and had immigrated to Brazil in the same year as Pereleshin. In Rio de Janeiro she occasionally visited him and his mother, but had "an ardent temper and could make a stormy scene, leave without saying good-bye, and slam the door." In 1960, during one such rift, she had left for the United States and they had lost touch.[49]

In April 1967, Pereleshin learned that she was trying to find him and repay that old Shanghai debt. He wrote back that she could, but only if she did not want "to burden her karma" and added: "I am glad not because of this, but because, thanks to this trifle, I can renew my contact with you. Or at least try."[50] He learned that in the United States she took manual jobs, freelanced for the San Francisco newspapers *New Dawn* and *Russian Life*, which did not pay her for her series of memoirs "In Red Shanghai" (*V krasnom Shankhae*). She then moved to Washington, DC, and worked for Victor Kamkin Publishing House and Bookstore, but quit on learning of its subsidies from the USSR and found a job as a writer-translator for Voice of America.[51]

The start of their correspondence coincided with the impending loss of Pereleshin's job at the British Council: "Your letters now are Ariadne's thread for me. Without them, I would have been going to work as if to Golgotha. Any day now I could receive a 'notice.'"[52] She awakened him from the life where he spent money on stamps, records, trips to the countryside, a plot of land in the provinces, but did not subscribe to a single Russian émigré periodical and "grew mouldy in my muddy backwater." He was deeply grateful for her "endless attention. You approached the matter as if I had to be saved from dying of starvation.

[…] You cannot possibly imagine in what vacuum I live. It is almost that same 'drowned submarine' Arsenii Nesmelov was talking about in one of the best poems of his last book."[53] As "In a Drowned Submarine" (*V zatonuvshei submarine*, ca. 1940) says, "try to be a poet / in a drowned submarine, / suffocating / from the palm held to your lips"; overcoming suffocation leads to "a birth of a poet, / which is always miraculous / in sunshine and in the darkness / of drowned submarines."

Kruzenshtern rejoiced: "I am glad, Valerii, that you feel nostalgic about poetry. This is good. This means that there will be poems. Good ones. Actually, you do not have bad ones; they are either powerfully dramatic, like "Yawn" (*Zevota*, 24.5.1945), which I love madly, or peacefully lyrical and soft." She urged him to submit poems to émigré periodicals and work on a book, and she shared her dreams of publishing a book of Nikolai Peterets's poems and one of hers.[54] She introduced him to the émigré journals *Resurrection* (*Vozrozhdenie*, Paris), *The New Review* (*Novyi zhurnal*, New York), and *Edges* (*Grani*, Germany), and the newspapers *Russian Thought* (*Russkaia mysl'*, Paris), *New Russian Word* (*Novoe russkoe slovo*, New York), *Russian Life* (*Russkaia zhizn'*, San Francisco), and *New Dawn* (*Novaia zaria*, San Francisco). When she sent him the 1966 anthology *Concord: From the Contemporary Poetry of Russia Abroad* (*Sodruzhestvo. Iz sovremennoi poezii Russkogo Zarubezh'ia*), he "did not go to the usual Sunday stamp market: stamps can wait!" and read all day "with great interest." The anthology presented seventy-five still living émigré poets, of whom only Mary Vezey and Viktoria Iankovskaia were from China. Kruzenshtern had refused to participate, believing that it was "inspired by the Moscow KGB" via the Kamkin Publishing House.[55]

Her letters became "life itself," and he often ended his with "Write often, very often." As he confessed, "without you I would have remained 'on vacation' and would not have all these exciting impressions, write letters, wait for cuttings and journals, and dream of publishing a book. I am eternally grateful to you."[56] In May 1967, on her advice and with great apprehension, he sent his crown of sonnets "The Way of the Cross" to *Resurrection* in Paris. Had the journal rejected it, "I would probably have lost faith in myself again," but one of the editors, Ia.N. Gorbov, replied: "Your sonnets are excellent," and the crown written in Shanghai in 1945 was published in issue no. 188 (1967) in Paris.[57]

This publication in *Resurrection* brought about his resurrection as a poet. He sent Gorbov his *Sacrifice*, and, twenty-three years after its publication, Gorbov in a "very warm" review heard "notes, unusual to the European ear," because "the author had lived in China since childhood, became acquainted, as very few others did, with its culture, absorbed the sources of its antiquity, and valued and loved the country, which from afar always seemed and seems mysterious, inscrutable, separate. [...] This small book devoted just enough space and attention to lyrical themes, fantasy, mythology, sculptors, and love – what collection omits love? – and the result is rich and diverse."[58] Pereleshin was in high heaven: "It became a real spiritual feast. [...] For the first time in my life, there appears *such* a review: in a thick journal, signed by a famous writer, on five and a half pages!"[59]

In September 1967, Kruzenshtern visited them, unfazed by their "bohemian lifestyle." It was a joyous time, spent in endless recollections and discussions, and, when she left, he returned from the airport "in a state called *emocionado*."[60] His mother wrote to her: "Now Valerii lives only for your letters. How can it be explained, Mary, that now, after many years of total disappearance, you have suddenly appeared on our horizon? And at such a difficult time for us. [...] You have woken Valerii from his hibernation, and all his time has become filled with interests and hopes, with healthy, and this is the main thing, beloved work, creation, enthusiasm, and belief in some good possibilities for himself."[61]

He started to write, and his poems, old and new, began to appear in émigré periodicals. He regretted the years of silence, but sensed that this "abstention" was "a Great Lent of its own kind, when some shifts were taking place within and a spiritual experience was acquired. When the dam broke, the streams burst out, and it is impossible to plug them."[62] Even the loss of the British Council job looked like a blessing in disguise: "without this blow I probably might have remained 'on vacation' in Brazil and never returned to poetry and journalism."[63]

Two poems written in December 1967, the month of Peterets's death, were about his dear "mascot," Kruzenshtern. The first, "Mother, then brother, then the most trusted friend" (*To mat', to brat, to samyi vernyi drug*, 19.12.1967), initially entitled "Sacrifices" (*Zhertvy*), spoke of her life: "A merciless chain of recollections / is closing the circle tighter and tighter. // There is no end to losses, and now again / you will be giving away the last lamb to the wolf. / You will pray. You will lock the door more securely / and quietly [*vstikhomolku*] cry till the morning." The prefix "*vs*" in this neologism from "*vtikhomolku*" (quietly) movingly echoed verbs such as "*vskhlipyvat'*" (to sob from time to time) and "*vsplaknut'*" (to shed a few tears). The second poem, "Silkworm" (*Shelkovichnyi cherv'*, 29.12.1967), dedicated to Kruzenshtern, opens this biography and forms its title. It was, as he rightly believed, "most successful" and "on the same level" as his early, often quoted "Under the hats – away from the light" (*Pod shliapy – ot sveta*, 1.12.1934).

Another venture, "King Saul" (*Tsar' Saul*), "a dramatic poem in four acts," had begun as a sketch in 1952 in Tianjin. In early 1966 he suddenly spent "two almost sleepless nights rewriting the first act," and a year later insomnia produced the second act and "a compilation of all sketches with much reworking. I have some ideas and drafts for the fifth act, but nothing in between."[64] "King Saul," in unrhymed iambic pentameter, was completed in May 1968 with minor revisions in 1970. It was "a very lyrical work, masked as an epic genre ('as if about someone else, but actually about different aspects of my own I')."[65] As Professor Simon Karlinsky later commented, it was "quite archaic," "in the theatrical technique of Aleksei Tolstoi," and Pereleshin agreed: "Now I would have written this tragedy quite differently."[66] Saul was always dear to his heart: his "Languor" (*Tomlenie*, 9.1.1941) asks: "Why had Your star been shining to me / and leading me for so many days, like a mother? / Return lost grace / to the rejected soul, to the soul of Saul!" The theme was picked up in "Teacher" ([*Uchitel'*, 23.9.1947): "But suddenly, in a desert, alone, / You abandoned me, as You did Saul. // From that time on, I belong to the world: / like everyone, I am greedy and passionate, / I am loved with an earthly love, / I am privy to earthly happiness."

Poetic Developments of 1968–1971

За свечой – в тени – Засвечье,	Beyond the candle – in the shadow – Trans-Candle Land,
за шестком – в углу – Запечье,	beyond the hearth – in the corner – Trans-Stove Land,
за спиной – ничком – Заплечье,	beyond one's back – face down – Trans-Shoulder Land,
за рекой – свистком – Заречье,	beyond the river – in a train whistle – Trans-River Land,
Заболотье, Задубровье,	Trans-Swamp, Trans-Oak-Grove,
Заозерье, Заостровье,	Trans-Lake, Trans-Island,
Забайкалье, Заангарье,	Trans-Baikal, Trans-Angara,
Забурунье, Заполярье,	Trans-Waves, Trans-Arctic,
Заамурье, Заонежье,	Trans-Amur, Trans-Onega,
Заграничье, Зарубежье,	Trans-Border, Trans-Abroad,
Забездомье, Заизгнанье,	Trans-Homelessness, Trans-Exile,
Завеликоокеанье,	Trans-Great-Ocean,
Забразилье, Запланетье	Trans-Brazil, Trans-Planet,
За-двадцатое-столетье.	Trans-Twentieth-Century.

"Beyond a candle – in the shadow"
(*Za spinoi – v teni*), 27.5.1972

In his first years in Brazil he had looked to *ghazals* for new directions, and now he followed that with experimental poems of four to twelve lines. This brevity was "the influence of Chinese poets, though I am not quite sure."[67] His unpublished *Southern Home* now seemed "terribly outdated and uninteresting," and acquaintance with post-war émigré poetry provided "a subconscious contribution to writing poems that are not too old-fashioned."[68]

He called these new short poems "little dogs" (*sobachki*), a term borrowed from Shchegolev in Shanghai. It reminded him of their Harbin bulldog, Jimmy, or Dmitrii Evgen'evich (with Sentianina's name as patronymic), and sheepdog, Speedy. An in-joke between the mother and son was calling Pereleshin a "Good Dog" or "Bom Cachorro": "this mythical beast is my double," "one of my extra-literary heteronyms," and "my projection."[69] As "Bom Cachorro" (25.4.1969) says, "Bom Cachorro was useless, / but, on the whole, not that bad. [...] // He howled at the moon in anguish / and wrote poems in Russian / and in his own language."

In these new "little dogs" he "was shifting away from (or rather overcoming) Acmeism and searching for something different." Partly influenced by his new correspondent Iurii Ivask, he "moved forward by groping in the dark," though "with all my present modernism I still stand for greater refinement."[70] He believed, as stated in his article "Decline of Form in Poetry" (*Upadok formy v poezii*, 1969), that metre, rhyme, stanzaic form, caesura, and alliteration were essential, and in his unpublished "Poetry and Verses" and "Russian Rhyme" he severely criticized approximate rhymes and *vers libre*, citing the Soviet poet Evtushenko as a particularly abysmal example.[71]

His experiments stayed firmly within the confines of metre and rhyme. As he commented on "Book" (*Kniga*, 9.1.1970), "today there have appeared lines in an unknown metre: two anapests plus two dactyls in each line. It is not an 'anapaktyl,' but one of the variants of a logaoedic verse. With caesura in the middle."[72] The anapest in "Mirrors" (*Zerkala*, 8.1.1969) had hypometric stress in the last line. As for rhyme, some of his captivating experiments had a variable-stress (*raznoudarnaia*) or, as he called it, "visual" (*zritel'naia*) rhyme,[73] where words with the same or very similar spelling but different stress rhymed in startling patterns, gripping attention and giving depth by unexpected stress shifts, a technique possible in Russian. He rhymed *póvesti* (novella) with *povestí* (to lead), *ovrági* (ravines) with *vragí* (enemies), *béregu* (to the shore) with *beregú* (protect), and so on in a remarkable poem "In the forest" (*V lesu*,

19.1.1969). Other poems were built on two rhymes or homonyms. He briefly experimented with Chinese-style poems in "After the Deluge: Imitating Chinese" (*Posle potopa. Podrazhanie kitaiskomu*, 8.11.1971) and "Imitating Chinese" (*Podrazhanie kitaiskomu*, 16.10.1972) in columns of rhymed monosyllabic Russian words.

Another new direction was the use of thought-provoking neologisms, such as the above-mentioned *vstikhomolku*, and *voroginia* (female enemy) and *vorozhda* (enmity) in what he called a "particularly modernist" poem, "In Misfortune" (*V bede*, 2.7.1969).[74] The poem "Beyond a candle – in the shadow," an epigraph to this section, is built on neologisms, all nouns and not a single verb. He did not like trans-rational language (*zaum'*), but was willing "to let thoughts go to the limits of the incomprehensible and unutterable."[75] As "Over the Abyss" (*Nad bezdnoi*, 30.11.1969) says: "*Zaum'*, nonsense, and absurdity, / reverse sides of the soul, / and reviewers will nag: / write differently! // What am I to do, my men? / Stepping away from the gate, / can one really dance gavotte / over the gaping abyss?"

These poems, largely unpublished, pursued his themes of rejecting the world and seeking an escape and were filled with persistent images of night, darkness, insomnia, fragility, dreams, and mirrors. In the early 1980s he dismissed these beguiling poems as "worse than failures," but felt that "through these futile attempts I found my true style."[76] He soon returned to the strictness of traditional rhymes and metres, but these experiments left many traces in his poetry.

8 Resurrection of the Poet

Searching for Work

Я вечеру рад, как другу, но больше, чем другу, рад безмолвию и досугу: свет, покой, халат. Мой замкнутый мир безгрешный под лампой на столе из ночи вырван кромешной, тонущей во зле. Кичится моя постройка: расхвастался маяк, что печь у него и койка, кофе и коньяк. Но запер ли я калитку? Ведь ураган крылат, и сшит на живую нитку теплый мой халат.	I rejoice in an evening, as in a friend, but, more than in friend, I rejoice in silence and leisure: light, peace, housecoat. My secluded sinless world under the lamp on my desk is torn out of pitch black night, which is drowning in evil. My construction is boasting: the lighthouse brags on that it has a stove and a bunk, coffee and cognac. But have I locked the gate? The hurricane has wings, and my warm housecoat is only loosely threaded.

"Housecoat" (*Khalat*), 29.5.1970

Pereleshin turned fifty-four in 1967. His colleagues at the British Council and local Russians called him "a walking encyclopedia," but he could not find a job. He looked into translating, but the age limit at the United Nations was fifty, and passing a Portuguese-English test at the Indian embassy did not get him a job.[1] He thought of the priesthood, but feared being "obligated to the Church"; "it will be difficult to teach what I am far from sure about and absolutely disgusting to do christenings and weddings." Moreover, his mother was "rather old to be left alone and *desamparada* (helpless). Serving Liturgy is one of the highest imaginable joys, but my return to the active service of the Church will simply be a murder, and a murder of the dearest person."[2]

In mid-1967, on Kruzenshtern's advice, he petitioned the US Immigration Office (verbatim from English) "to reverse my case and revert the sentence, whatever it might have been," arguing that he "had worked for TASS when the USA and USSR were allies" and was "an outspoken, militant anti-communist." Kruzenshtern provided an affidavit of his reliability, and Victor agreed to affirm that "he knows me not only from youthful recollections, but also from the experience of the past years."[3] The application had to be accompanied by a work contract, "a vicious circle, because one has to have a work offer to enter the United States, but to find work one first has to come to the United States!" His enquiries into teaching Russian at Columbia University, American University in Washington, the Russian Center at Fordham University, and Dallas University were unsuccessful. In vain did he appeal to Professor Helen Jacobson, his former colleague at the Harbin Law Faculty, now at George Washington University, and to his new correspondents, Iurii Ivask at the University of Massachusetts, G.P. Struve in California, and Archbishop Ioann Shakhovskoi in San Francisco. He approached Canadian institutions, but York University and the University of Alberta did not reply, the response from McGill University was negative, and the University of British Columbia vaguely mentioned a possibility in the future.[4] In 1968 he was accepted into an intensive ten-week MA program at the Summer Russian School at Norwich University, but he did not apply for a student visa, fearing that it might affect his application for immigration.[5]

In February 1969, Pereleshin was informed by the US Immigration authorities that he had to wait his turn, which Victor saw as a delaying tactic for further investigation. He came to hate the United States "*almost* as much as I hate communists, whom I *know* from my work in TASS and my four years in Red China. The counter-intelligence knows perfectly well who I really am (a translator of Coleridge and of Chinese classical poetry, and to some extent a poet in my own right). [...] Had I sat down on a Soviet chair, I would have died long ago somewhere in Kolyma. Now, another chair has been jerked from under me at the last moment."[6]

He offered his services as a regular correspondent for émigré newspapers, but *New Russian Word* in New York and *New Dawn* in San Francisco declined, because they had almost no subscribers in Brazil.

Pressured by Kruzenshtern, the editor of *New Russian Word*, M.E. Weinbaum, took him on as a freelancer, but payments were so meagre that once, after being paid US$8 for an article on eight Chinese immortals, Pereleshin commented: "a dollar per immortal! What a pity that I did not write about the 500 Buddhas."[7] *Russian Thought* in Paris hired him at US$30 per month, but by French law the money had to be deposited in a French bank. In any case, it was not a solution to his financial straits: "I can work ecstatically for seven to eight hours on articles or news items for *Russian Thought* and on poems, but cannot find a paying job."[8]

When Weinbaum of *New Russian Word* complained about inexperienced editorial assistants, Pereleshin promptly wrote that such work was "a dream of my many years in Brazilian exile." His old and new contacts in the United States, led by Kruzenshtern, persuaded Weinbaum to offer him a job. In May 1968, when he went to the American consulate, he was informed that he had to start a new application and have all his documents, officially translated in Shanghai, to be retranslated by consulate-approved translators. He became so flustered that he worried about his misspelled patronymic, "Frazevich" instead of "Frantsevich," on the *Carteira de identidade de estrajeiro*, issued on his arrival in Brazil.[9] He pleaded with Archbishop Ioann in San Francisco: "Your word (that I am an outspoken anti-communist, as can be proved by my many articles in *New Russian Word* and *Russian Thought*) could be the magic lever." The archbishop's silence was upsetting, especially when "all kinds of Brodsky and Allilueva types arrive without waiting their turn. One word from him would have been enough to speed all this. But would he say it? From his point of view, I am, probably, a 'semi-defrocked priest.'" His hopes expired with Weinbaum's death in 1973.[10]

The odd thing was that his detention and deportation took place in the summer of 1950, but in his petition to the US Immigration in July 1967 he wrote (verbatim from English): "I must refer to some events of 1951. A few years before that time I applied for a U.S.A. immigration visa, and arrived at San Francisco in April or May 1951. At once I was arrested and […] at last deported to Red China in September 1951." In 1968, in another petition, he stated (verbatim from English): "Early in 1951, I was summoned by the US consulate in Shanghai and granted [a] visa to enter the US." He further stated that later he left China in September 1954. The same misinformation appeared in his appeal to Archbishop Ioann, where he dated his deportation 1951 in one letter and 1950 in another. In letters to Aleksis Rannit it was some time in 1950 and probably in April 1950. In his memoirs, *Two Sidings* (*Dva polustanka*), it was, again, "probably" in 1950 in one place and in 1951 in another.[11] This lapse of memory, dangerous in official petitions, might have been caused by a traumatic obliteration, where the exact date is irrelevant, but nevertheless it remains puzzling.

In February 1968, his sister-in-law, Lidiia, got him a proofreader's job in an American newspaper, *Brazil Herald*. He had to commute by bus for two hours for his shift of 6:00 p.m. to midnight. One evening a heavy rain flooded the streets, no buses came, and he sat all night on a box; on another night, he and a co-worker saw men stabbing each other. He sprained his ankle on poorly lit stairs; his reading glasses were stolen and he was reprimanded for missing typos.[12] He hated this "atrocious exploitation. I lose eight to eleven hours a day including the commute, and am paid miserably. Unread and half-read books (I promised to review some) are piling up; there are unanswered letters, drafts of poems, and plans for longer articles (on dualism, reincarnation, the eight immortals, the phoenix, and form in Chinese poetry). [...] I want this penal servitude to end. Then I will be myself again: a professor, a poet, and a journalist."[13] He gave notice on 5 July, much to the indignation of Victor, Lidiia, and his mother. His relations with Victor were already strained by his continuing unemployment. In response to his defence that he was a poet, Victor told him that he "should write not poetry, but prose, not in Russian, but in English, and as well as Hemingway and Steinbeck." However, his mother soon relented, commenting that "poets never have money."[14]

In mid-July 1968, he had some luck: he was hired to teach Russian two hours a week at Escola Naval, the Brazilian Naval Academy, and was paid nearly as much as he had been for proofreading. This work had the prestige which he craved: the academy was "one of the pillars of conservatism, and its coat of arms (with a crown, because it was founded by Emperor Pedro II) is displayed everywhere." He supplemented a Soviet textbook with exercises, tapes, and poems, and once invited his class of seventeen cadets and four officers to his place to read Lermontov. The job lasted on and off until December 1971.[15]

Although his articles brought in very little money and the poems none, he kept contributing to émigré periodicals, using several pseudonyms. Reproached for using them in polemics, he responded with an unpublished article, "Rebuff of the Five,"[16] and poems "Hypostases" (*Ipostasi*, 5.11.1969) and "Images" (*Liki*, 5.11.1969). As the poems describe, there were the "sinologist and law expert," V.F. Salatko-Petrishche; "the inveterate Christian" theologist, V. Kaiurin (an aunt on his mother's side had married a Kaiurin); the fighter for truth, V. Nezhdanov; the anti-Bolshevik fighter, Bogdan Strel'tzov; and the poet, Valerii Pereleshin, "calm, / even-tempered, / as if not of this world." He also used "Sigma," "S-a," or "S." for his "News from Brazil," "Mail from Brazil," and "Brazilian Oddities" and occasionally Boris Pravdin or his Chinese name Xia Qingyun. As Strel'tsov or Kaiurin, he published political poems such as "Red Propaganda" (*Krasnaia propaganda*, 19.4.1969) and "Boomerang" (*Bumerang*, 7.5.1969), and Bogdan Strel'tsov became a character in his *Poem without a Subject*. Pereleshin's views were very conservative: "I am not a democrat; I call my political views 'aristocratism,' and I very much welcome Brazilian 'military dictatorship,' which, in fact, is a clean, honest system, with disdain for the demagogy, promises, and lies of politicians."[17]

Southern Home: The Fifth Book of Poetry, 1968

Взамен побед и бурь и сладострастья,

И мужественной битвы до конца
Ты, Боже, дал мне маленькое счастье,
Какому не завидуют сердца.
Дар памяти! Ни громоносной славы,
Ни жгучих сновидений не влача,
Я только ветры, вечера и травы,

Пускаясь в путь, подъемлю на плеча.
Прощальный день, обманчиво спокойный,
Задумчивое небо сентября,
И сумерки, и сосен запах хвойный
В мой южный дом возьму с собою я.
И память мне не раз покажет снова

Кладбищенский многоречивый сад,
И на скамейке томик Гумилева,
И темных глаз обрадованный взгляд.

Instead of victories and storms, and sensuality,
And a courageous battle to the end,
You, God, gave me a small happiness
Not envied by other hearts.
The gift of memory! Setting on my way,
I will haul over my shoulder
Neither thunderous fame, nor fervent dreams,
But only winds, evenings, and grasses.
The day of parting, deceptively calm,
And pensive September sky,
And dusk, and the smell of pine needles
I will take with me to my southern home.
And many times the memory would show me
The talkative cemetery garden,
And a Gumilev volume on a bench,
And the joyful look of dark eyes.

"Happiness" (*Schast'e*), 24.9.1940

Pereleshin knew "what an enormous sacrifice each new book of Russian poems, read by a few and never paying for itself, represents,"[18] but he resumed the work interrupted almost twenty-five years before. His plans were grandiose: new books of poetry (*Southern Home*

[*Iuzhnyi dom*], *Swing* [*Kachel'*], and *Sanctuary* [*Zapovednik*]), long poems, and drama (*King Saul*); translations from Chinese (*Poems on a Fan* and *Li Sao*); translation of the *Cántico espiritual* by St John of the Cross; translations of Brazilian poetry; and a reprint of the first three books.[19] He was propelled by "an inner conviction that IT IS NECESSARY TO DO SO." When Victor said that nothing would change if he did not, he replied: "Perhaps that's true, but then the question is: is it worth living in this world?" Victor told him to get a job, and the conversation, as usual, escalated to a heated argument, upsetting their mother.[20]

Pereleshin decided to begin with *Southern Home*, although he no longer liked it for its closeness to the Friday Circle themes.[21] He pruned the Shanghai draft and, with Kruzenshtern's help, settled on a most inexpensive publisher, I. Baschkirzew Buchdruskerei in Germany, which quoted US$400 for 1,000 copies. However, Kruzenshtern, as his unofficial agent, ordered 500 copies to save money. In early January 1968 the typescript was mailed: "day and night I keep seeing *Southern Home*, I dream of it, like a fifth-grader in love."[22] When the first copies arrived in July, close to his fifty-fifth birthday, "I immediately ascended to the seventh heaven. [...] Happiness has made me totally crazy, and only today did I come to my senses." His mother rejoiced, and Victor and Lidiia were "enraptured" by Kruzenshtern's help.[23] The book was sold largely via friends and acquaintances in the United States, Canada, Australia, and Europe.

Southern Home comprised twelve poems from the Shanghai draft, an additional seventeen from his Chinese period, a translation of Lu Xun's "From Things Heard" (*Iz slyshannogo*, translated ca. 1947), and only one Brazilian poem, "From Afar" (*Izdaleka*, 19.5.1953): a total of thirty pieces. The poems, except for "The Last Lotus" (*Poslednii lotos*, 10.9.1943), marked "Beijing, 1943," were undated. For the few readers who knew him, the "southern home" from "Happiness" (*Schast'e*, 24.9.1940) referred to Beijing, which lay south of Harbin, but for new readers, as Ia. Gorbov's review shows, it spoke of a new Brazilian home for the "lost Argonaut."[24]

The poems presented themes fully developed in the next two books, *Swing* and *Sanctuary*. In "Agreement" (*Ugovor*, ca. 1.6.1945) the poet reproaches his soul for swinging up to heaven and plunging into earthly sins, and in "Two Conjunctions" (*Dva soiuza*, 19.3.1946) he refuses to choose "between a moment's joy at the cost of hell / or paradise at the cost of grief": he wants both. In "The Searcher" (*Iskatel'*, 5.11.1944) he longs to sail into darkness, to be free, to be "rejoicing in sharp steepness, / drunk with daring, proud of disgrace." In "About One Heart" (*Ob odnom serdtse*, ca. 20.5.1945) the heart wishes "to rest from life" and "shut itself and sleep," and in "Xiangtancheng" (*Siantan'chen*, 11.10.1948), his imaginary sanctuary with a Chinese name, the poet "on the wings of dreams / is hurrying to Xiangtancheng from his prison."

Southern Home continues the contest between China and Russia in his heart. In "Russia" (*Rossiia*, 19.11.1944) the poet says to the land of his birth: "Oh yes, you are a forgotten word, / so many words are more necessary, more resonant, / such as the sounds of a foreign language / and of violins on windy nights." He queries his almost erotic love for it: "Have I truly desired / only the blue-eyed blond Russia / in the almond-eyed beauty / and promises of golden dark bodies?" In "Lost Argonaut" (*Zabludivshiisia argonavt*, 29.6.1947), oft-quoted by some China Russians, the poet, "betrothed to China / from childhood," imagines being born into a large ancient Chinese clan, "into the fanciful net / of characters and poems," but realizes that he is "to the bone marrow a lost Russian Argonaut." His beloved China is tantalizingly present in "The Last Lotus," in a Chinese girl in "Southern Wind" (*Iuzhnyi veter*, 24.1.1948), in beautiful Lake Xihu in "Night on Lake Xihu" (*Noch' na Sikhu*, 3.7.1946), in the tremulous lotus-like girl Yuse in "Music" (*Muzyka*, 15.12.1947), in a Chinese name "Red Leaves under the Frost" (*Krasnye list'ia pod ineem*, 15.5.1947), in "my Oriental friend" in "Cigarette" (*Sigareta*, ca. 1.6.1949), and in the only Brazilian poem, the heartbreaking "From Afar" (*Izdaleka*, 19.5.1953), which is quoted in full above, in the last section of chapter 6.

Love poems continue the camouflage, and even though "To a Friend" (*Drugu*, 17.9.1946) is dedicated to Liu Tiansheng, the name is genderless to a Russian reader. Some poems speak of a growing inner freedom. In "Lost Argonaut," "I am as broad as the vastness of the sea: / embracing and loving everything, / I take in all precepts / and all banners, the entire world." The "Inevitable" (*Neizbezhnoe*, ca. 1.6.1947) echoes it: "Long ago have I outgrown barriers, / outgrown language, and blood, and race, / and all other ancient barriers, / which humans installed around their houses," where "other ancient barriers" might suggest homophobia to a perceptive reader. This poem speaks of the inevitable parting from his genderless lover, who wants children, while the poet's life is "freedom, loneliness … Well, what can I say: / to tell the truth, I am quite ready / to be the last one warming myself by other people's bonfires, / a totally unknown passer-by." For him, it was "a sin and a crime to involve yet another living soul, thinking and feeling as I do, in this hell on earth."[25]

Several poems address his vocation. The "Poet" (*Poet*, 19.11.1944) declares that "there is no mercy for poets"; in "Spring" (*Vesna*, ca. 1.6.1947) "God's poets" are like ephemeral snowflakes "shining with the whitest whiteness"; in "Last Lotus" (*Poslednii lotos*, 10.9.1943) a poet is "the last bard of freedom"; and in "Anthill" (*Muraveinik*, 26.3.1947) he "walks like a Gulliver / above the world of dwarf souls."

The former editor of *Border*, Mikhail Rokotov, complimented him: "you have grown a lot over these years, and not only as a master of poetry, but inwardly as well. [...] Previously, it seemed to me that the only thing not fully satisfactory in your poetry was a certain dryness. I would have preferred more feelings than intellect and more heart with all its trembling, even at the cost of crystal purity and lofty thoughts. [...] Now I feel that in the last quarter-century, when I had not seen your poetic work, the poems new to me have become wonderfully alive and warm, and they not only shine but also give warmth."[26]

Almost all reviews were good. V. Z-n (V. Zavalishin) praised the "originality and charm" of the poet who "inherited the raging thirst for rediscovering the world from Gumilev and has no time to be bored and complain of the cruel fate of an émigré." The Paris poet Ol'ga Mozhaiskaia noted "an influence of ancient China," "great knowledge, taste, and serious work on poetry," tragic loneliness, and the slowly dying soul of a poet. Ia. Gorbov paid tribute to "the perfection of versification, ingenuity and freedom in rhymes, clear sophistication of metrics," and general "mysteriousness."[27] Harbin-born Professor Simon Karlinsky saw Pereleshin as a pupil of Kuzmin, late Gumilev, and early Mandelstam: "His great poetic culture allows Pereleshin to develop the eternal themes of Russian poetry in his own way and within limits of self-imposed restrictions: Pushkin's theme of a poet's loneliness, Tiutchev's themes of spring floods and the dissolution of human personality. [...] The core theme is China, a rare and poorly developed theme in Russian poetry. [...] In Pereleshin's poetry it is the eternal, huge, wise China of ancient traditions and elegant art, China of sophisticated, merciful goddesses and misty mountain landscapes."[28]

One review, however, led to a heated polemic beyond the book. The Paris poet Iurii Terapiano described Pereleshin as "a follower of Acmeism" with "clear and healthy feelings," reminiscent of early Gumilev, "though, of course, 'in a proper proportion'"; his poems were "well composed, but topically not very original." The poet "had apparently lived in China for a long time and possibly knows its language and poetry [...]; the combination of Russian and Chinese in his poetry is not external or forced, but organic and spontaneous, which is new and interesting for us."[29] Pereleshin objected to being labelled "an imitator of early Gumilev (or anyone's imitator in general)" in this "terribly sloppy and arrogant" review and called the critic a "*burro*" (ass): "What is this, in the final analysis? Stupidity or – oh, blasphemy! – some envy?"[30]

Terapiano's review pitted Harbin and Parisian Russian literary figures against one another; the former accused the latter of snobbery towards Russian poets in China and protested against Terapiano's verdict that Pereleshin lacked originality. The Parisians rejected these charges and Georgii Adamovich praised Pereleshin's "freshness and spontaneity."[31] When Terapiano, reviewing the September 1969 issue of *Resurrection*, called Pereleshin's poems old-fashioned, Pereleshin responded with "Two Parises," the Paris of Adamovich, Khodasevich, and Ladinski, and "the somewhat lower Paris of Terapiano and other cynics." He recalled the 1934 review of *Churaevka* by Iu.T., who had scorned China's poets and *Churaevka*.[32] Terapiano denied being Iu.T. and attributed the polemic to "a psychological complex" and "persecution mania" of poets outside France: "in the eyes of these 'maniacs' the 'Parisians' had become envious persons, intriguers."[33]

Although Pereleshin called the polemic "boring" and "nauseous," he was on the warpath, seeing Terapiano's hand in the rejection of his poems by the Toronto journal *Contemporary* (*Sovremennik*) and in being omitted from *Resurrection*'s "The Day of Poetry," a selection of poems by contemporary émigré poets, in 1971.[34] He found another angle of attack in his review of Terapiano's study *Mazdeism, Contemporary Followers of Zoroastra* (*Mazdeizm – sovremennye posledovateli Zoroastra*, 1968), signed Vl. Kaiurin from Tangier, where he criticized what he called the anti-Christian theosophy of Roerich, Terapiano, Boris Nartsissov, and E.P. Blavatskaia, whom he called in his letters "Blevotskaia-Bledovskaia-Blefskaia" (Vomiting-Whoring-Lying).[35] *Russian Thought* refused to publish it, but his letter on this topic appeared in *New Russian Word*, and the review, which "startled the snake-pit of Anti-Christ followers," was published in 1969 in the journal *Edges* (*Grani*).[36]

Kruzenshtern advised him to calm down, but he vowed "to defend not only myself, but also Christianity" against the "spiritual leprosy" of Mazdeism and theosophy.[37] He stopped capitalizing the names of the "gutter dwellers" Terapiano, Roerich, Annie Besant, and Blavatskaia in his letters, nicknamed Terapiano a "teraleech" (*terapiavka*), and circulated his malicious poems, rejected by the émigré press, among his correspondents. He sent Terapiano an unsigned Christmas card with the note,

"Do not touch Christ, and I will not touch you" and the poem "Polemic" (*Polemika*, 10.12.1969): "sadness about him, grey-haired, elderly, / who crunched, like a brittle crystal, / like pocked-out crystalline lens, / is slowing polemic down." The powerful effect of diminutive suffixes in "grey-haired" (*seden'kom*) and "elderly" (*staren'kom*) and of the initial cluster "*khr*," like a sound of cracking, in "*khrustnul khrupkim khrustalem*," is wasted on this poem.[38]

In 1970 another reviewer, Denis Mickiewicz, placed him among the imitators of the Russian Silver Age, and Pereleshin reacted: "I snarled, because it is technically impossible to imitate Briusov, Belyi, Bal'mont, Viacheslav the Splendid [Ivanov], Blok, Gumilev, Akhmatova, Mandelstam and others." Mickiewicz responded with "Towards a Definition of Imitation," which ended with "to be continued," but never was.[39] Pereleshin's earlier "Imitators" (*Epigony*, 19.5.1953) was now followed with "An Order of Imitators" (*Orden epigonov*, 27.6.1971): "Yesterday, when, not hearing doorbells, / horns, or shouting, I fell asleep, / I dreamt that I, the daring one, / formed an Order of Imitators."

These characterizations of Pereleshin as an imitator display an inability to recognize his originality and individuality in poems which structurally remain loyal to the Acmeist striving for perfection of form and clarity of content. Rannit perceptively called him both "an absolutist of classical forms" and "a visionary," aiming at both "precision of form" and "philosophical intensification of content."[40]

Contacts and Conflicts

– Что доброго от Назарета? –
апостол будущий вздохнул –
о нем во всех томах Завета
никто и не упомянул.
  В сужденьи более поспешен
  начетчик в наши времена:
  – Поэт – какой-то Перелешин?
  Что доброго от Харбина?

– What good is coming from Nazareth? –
a future apostle sighed –
in all the volumes of the Testament
nobody ever mentioned him.
  In our times a dogmatic is
  more rush in his judgment:
  – A poet – some Pereleshin?
  What good is coming from Harbin?

"Slow to Convince" (*Tugovery*),
11.2.1975

For the "Brazilian hermit/recluse," letters "substituted for a missing 'milieu,'" and he eagerly awaited a "*cameleiro*," his nickname for a postman borrowed from old stamps with pictures of camels carrying mail in

Africa.[41] He corresponded with well over 200 people, briefly with some and until their or his death with others.

The most treasured correspondent was his "mascot," Iustina (Mary) Kruzenshtern; until her death they supported each other, exchanged poems, and engaged in heated polemics, largely about his gay poetry. Another old friend was Petr "Murochka" Lapiken, who had served in the US Army, earned a doctorate at the University of California, and taught Russian at Monterey. Though not a poet, Lapiken was quite erudite, and they discussed poetry, old orthography, and, obliquely, homosexuality. Pereleshin enjoyed letters from Mary Custis Vezey, a bilingual Harbin and Shanghai poet, now in San Francisco, and from Nina Fouchier, née Mokrinskaia, former Queen of Young Harbin Poets in *Mouthpiece* and Victor's youthful infatuation, who lived in France with her French husband. Lidiia Khaindrova was another resumed friendship: after repatriation to the USSR she had stopped writing poetry and was now starting again, "as before, that is, rather helplessly, but with such flashes of insight that one can only admire them [poems]."[42] As "Across thousands of kilometres and for thousands of years" (*Cherez tysiachi verst i na tysiachi let*, 2.7.1969) says: "there seemed to be no distance and no time, / [...] / perhaps, in none too distant reincarnation / we will hold hands tighter."

A new and "*most trusted friend*" was poet Iurii Ivask, a professor at the University of Massachusetts, who was capable of "looking very deeply into my soul, as no one had done before."[43] What Pereleshin "truly borrowed from him was euphony"; he also greatly valued "a spiritual impregnation," where "some word in passing quickly forms an embryo of poetic ideas which matures into a full poem, even though we are mutually incompatible. I have pain, and Ivask a luminous world view. I have movement of thought, while Ivask is static and sketches with 'coloured pencils.'"[44] "About Iurii Ivask and About Myself" (*O Iurii Ivaske i o sebe*, 27.10.1979) plays on the Estonian *iva* (grain): "Ivask, a large grain, with his wise soul is greater than me," while "I am fated to be / a victim of evil chimeras."

Ivask, aware of Pereleshin's financial difficulties, sometimes enclosed money "for the next book" and hired him to proofread and compile an index for his own book, *Konstantin Leont'ev*. Pereleshin responded with "Narcissus" (*Nartsiss*, 4.2.1973) and "Reading Konstantin Leont'ev" (*Chitaia Konstantina Leont'eva*, 4.2.1973), dedicated to Ivask, who included it at the end of the book.[45] Ivask "interviewed" him for *New Russian Word*, writing to the new editor, Andrei Sedykh: "Pereleshin has a hard life. [...] This 'interview,' by the way, might help him." He also ensured that Pereleshin was included in *Outside Russia: An Anthology of Poetry Written by Russian Poets in Emigration, 1917–1975* (*Vne Rossii. Antologiia emigrantskoi poezii, 1917–1975*) and was hired to proofread this anthology.[46]

Correspondence with Gleb Struve, a poet and professor at the University of California, Berkeley, began when someone sent Pereleshin a photocopy of some pages from Struve's *Russian Literature in Exile* (*Russkaia literatura v izgnanii*, 1956). So little had then been known about Russian poetry in China that Struve mentioned only Arsenii Nesmelov, Aleksei Achair, Nikolai Shchegolev, and Pereleshin, writing about the latter: "In his one and only book (*On the Way*, 1937) some poems were not bad at all, but he too lacked Parisian culture and often plunged into tastelessness. His fate is not known."[47] Pereleshin thanked Struve for this "not quite flattering opinion, although, to tell the truth, in the Far East I was never reproached for lacking taste; on the contrary, I was made an *arbiter elegantiarum* of its own kind. [...] The accusation of tastelessness did not bother me (*de gustibus non disputandum*), but I confess to being amused." He offered to compile a "who is who" of Russian literary figures in China if Struve ever wanted to update the book,[48] and their correspondence, at times acrimonious over Brodsky and other issues, continued until Struve's death.

Another significant correspondent was Aleksis Rannit, an Estonian poet and the curator of Slavic and East European Collections at Yale University Library. When Rannit ordered Pereleshin's books for the library and expressed an interest in some materials from his archive, Pereleshin was delighted with this "appearance of a major star": "in your hands, my poetic heritage will not perish." Rannit wrote back: "what particularly charms me is that you are a *growing* poet. Your beginning was good, but you, thank God, did not rest on your laurels, but, on the contrary, went along the road of ascetic formalism, the only correct way."[49] Pereleshin's letters to Rannit began with salutations such as "Dear Poet, Inexhaustibly Magnanimous," "Dear Poet, the Most Radiant, Fantastically Beautiful, and Unique in General," or "Your Highness."[50] In 1971, on Rannit's suggestion, Pereleshin reworked parts of Rannit's article "China of the Poet Pereleshin," and its publication in *Russian Thought* made Pereleshin's "head spin for several days." He was "endlessly grateful" for Rannit's "splendid, brilliant" follow-up, "Brazil of V. Pereleshin."[51] Rannit's study, "On the Poetry and Poetics of Valerii Pereleshin" in *Russian Language Journal* was "the best gift in the world": "No one has ever written such articles about me: there were reviews, there were articles on various aspects, but not such comprehensive analysis and evaluation." In 1978, Rannit followed up with "Valerii Pereleshin after *Swing*"; as before, its draft was amplified by Pereleshin, who revelled in its publication: "For the first time in my life, my name appears on the cover of the journal together with the names of Dostoevsky, A. Belyi, Pasternak, and two prose writers unknown to me."[52]

Pereleshin's friendships by correspondence were at times sorely tested by his self-appointed guardianship of what he believed to be true poetry. Living far away, "face-to-face with God and conscience," he wanted to continue Peterets's "fighting for quality" and to "speak totally frankly, without favouritism and non-literary considerations."[53] In vain did Ivask warn him that "favouritism is widespread among émigrés. Of course, it is bad. But how can one criticize friends who are no longer young? If I strongly dislike a book, I refuse to review it."[54] Not only did Pereleshin heap scorn on Soviet poets such as Smeliakov, Evtushenko, and Voznesenskii for their shoddy propagandistic poems, but he also criticized émigré poets, disregarding their established ranks and zealously guarded reputations. His critical observations in generally positive reviews offended poets such as Dmitrii Klenovskii, Boris Nartsissov, Iraida Legkaia, and Lidiia Alekseeva. They left Mary Vezey with a "devastating impression," and made a certain Gratsianskaia call him "a well-known 'retrograde' and 'scoundrel' in the Far East."[55] He soon concluded that the "'literature' of Russia Abroad is truly a swamp where nepotism, pity, and sometimes secret calculations predominate over all other considerations."[56]

He was particularly critical of Igor' Chinnov, whose life had followed a path that Pereleshin's could have: he immigrated to the United States in 1962, became a university professor, enjoyed a steady income, sabbaticals, and a pension and was considered by some to be the best émigré poet. For Pereleshin, he was "a very tiny poet with a mosquito voice," writing "without metre and amusing himself with a cheap game of consonances [...] to hide the absence of thought." Chinnov "managed without pain," the main ingredient of true poetry for Pereleshin. He parodied "an unimaginable nonsense" of Chinnov's experiments in "Cybernakadabra" (*Kibernakadabra*, 12.2.1969) and entitled his review of Chinnov's *Metaphors* (*Metafory*, 1968) "Significant Hints" after Gumilev's comment on significant hints about the contents of an eggshell.[57] When Ivask asked him to withdraw this review, he "reluctantly" tried to do it, but it was too late. Ivask then responded with "On Writings of Valerii Pereleshin," where he chastised Pereleshin for his inability to appreciate other poets, owing to his antiquated views of poetry, and scolded him for "unfair, acrimonious," and "unacceptable" attacks on Terapiano.[58]

Chinnov became a "new phobia": "in the miniature literary world of Harbin and Shanghai we argued, became emotional, but did not quarrel because of differences *in opinion.* Having entered the 'wide' world of Russia Abroad, I am becoming bitterly convinced that the morals here are quite different: some 'pillars' have issued diplomas for the title of a Russian poet, and if someone disagrees with their evaluations, he is boycotted." Ivask "demanded recognition of Chinnov as the best poet of Russia Abroad, otherwise I allegedly could not enter the *Establishment*! I replied: 'Go to hell!'"[59] When Ivask asked him to pipe down and Struve and Rannit asked for apologies, his refusals led to temporary breaks in correspondence. Only later did he grudgingly concede that Chinnov was "one of the best poets of our time."[60]

A fierce row erupted over Iosif Brodsky, seen by Pereleshin as "a typical Soviet poet with an unforgivable cult of carelessness ('write as it comes, just to touch people's hearts')," without "talent and culture." Brodsky's poems were full of "blunders and shortcomings. [...] And this is not *'jalousie de métier'.*" His "unrestrained verbosity" and "incontinence" were noticed in the west only because he was a repressed poet in the USSR. He should have gone to Israel, not to the United States, where "this soap bubble blown out of all proportion settled in a warm spot and willingly accepted a sinecure." Pereleshin gladly kept repeating the nickname someone had given him: "Buterbrodskii" (Sandwich).[61]

Pereleshin's anger found expression in the sarcastic "An 'Image' or a 'Mug'?" (*"Lik" ili "morda"?* 21.8.1972) and then in "'Odysseus to Telemachus'" (*"Odissei – Telemaku,"* 15.11.1972), where he ridiculed a "Yiddish" spelling of Telemachus ending with a *k* instead of the *kh* in Brodsky's poem of the same title. Pereleshin's sonnet asks Phoebe to defend "the Hellenic spirit and Moscow pronunciation" against Brodsky, "an overly familiar Bulat Okudzhava," and "tearful Gennadii Aigi." The émigré press would not publish it, but he sent it to several other people. The indignant Rannit sent him a photocopy from a Soviet dictionary which permitted both spellings, but Pereleshin insisted that Brodsky's poem should have been returned to him "to be translated from Yiddish into Russian." His own sonnet was "not a lampoon, but a sonnet-epigram. [...] Everyone knows that *Telemak* is taken not from Yiddish, but from an ignorant Soviet reference book." Struve demanded an apology, and Pereleshin commented: "the history of Russian poetry is enriched by a new anecdote: Struve quarrelled with Pereleshin when the latter called Brodsky a *graphomaniac.*"[62] In Pereleshin's view, Brodsky "should switch to Yiddish," but would soon start writing in English, just as foreign to him as Russian, because "it is more profitable; a Jew remains a Jew." Brodsky, Okudzhava, and Aigi should "write in their native languages and leave Russian alone," to which Ivask retorted that Pereleshin should then be writing in Polish or Belorussian.[63]

Condemnations of his chauvinistic and anti-Semitic views at first made him want to "hide in my shell, disappear from mirrors, so to speak," but soon he refused "to fall to the ground and bow to Brodsky": "I do not need a Benkendorf [Pushkin's censor]." His "Guardian" (*Opekun*, 5.1.1973), "Friend" (*Drug*, 9.2.1973), and "To Censors" (*Tsensoram*, 9.2.1973) addressed "the *theme* of relations between a poet and 'a guardian of poetic Orthodoxy.'"[64] He "boiled with rage" when Brodsky was awarded an honorary doctorate from Yale University: "Morshen, Chinnov, Ivask, Elagin, and my insignificant and grey person stand three heads *above* Brodsky. […] Yale should have honoured the five abovementioned *true* poets of Russia Abroad. I think that poets on the second tier (Gleb Glinka, Ol'ga Anstei) and even on the third ([Anatolii] Velichkovskii, [Boris] Nartsissov, Iustina Kruzenshtern-Peterets, Larissa Andersen, Lidiia Alekseeva, who is, rather, on the second step, and Nonna Belavina) deserve honorary doctorates before Brodsky."[65] He continued attacking what he saw as the anti-Russian nationalism of the third-wave immigrants and sarcastically predicted that "the Kleins and Co. would get the idea of pushing Brodsky forward for the Nobel Prize."[66]

Brodsky's success reopened old wounds. Pereleshin too could have gained a professorial position without a degree and been published and praised. Once again, he reflected on the injustices of his life: loss of his homeland and social status, the ordeal of being gay in a rigidly bigoted society, unjust deportation, and "double exile: first *from* Russia and then *from* China."[67] Now he was getting old and impoverished, and his Brazilian exile looked permanent.

***Swing*: The Sixth Book of Poetry, 1971**

[…]	
Чуть опадает в бессмысленном сердце хмель,	The moment intoxication recedes in my foolish heart,
Вновь на крылах покаянья могу летать я.	I can fly again on the wings of repentance.
Грех, ты моя удивительная качель,	Sin, you are my astonishing swing,
Благословенье мое и мое проклятье!	My blessing and my damnation!

"Abyss" (*Bezdna*), 15.3.1943

Pereleshin's books were truly his children: he conceived them, gave painful birth to them, sacrificed everything for them, rejoiced in praise of them, and zealously defended them against criticism. His sixth child, *Swing* (*Kachel'*), had already been announced as "in print" in *Southern Home* and now he decided to publish it. Kruzenshtern advised spacing his books over a couple of years, but he replied that in such case publishing everything he wanted "would stretch over fourteen years!"[68]

In October 1970, to cheer him up, his mother gave him her emergency stash of US$100: "I was so touched that I nearly cried (if she had more, she would have given more). I slept on it and got up this morning with a firm resolve to order *Swing*."[69] Nothing was said to "the kindred spirits," as he called Victor and Lidiia, "otherwise, they would eat me alive, gobble me up, and reduce me to dust: 'an unemployed person has no right to publish books, which bring no money, but, on the contrary, take the last he has. One should write in English. One should write like Hemingway. One should write if it brings money' (and if it does not, work as a proofreader or at least as a cleaner)."[70] Publication costs at Possev-Verlag came to nearly DM3,400 for 500 copies; when *Russian Thought* refused to transfer his honorarium, the publishing house agreed to instalments. By the time the book came out, Pereleshin had US$6 in the bank and owed US$300.[71]

Swing, an image from "Abyss" (*Bezdna*, 15.3.1943), "has acquired associations and become the symbol of flying to heaven, to blue sky, to purity, to the incorporeal, and of falling down to earth, to full-bloodedness and physicality," "a symbol of duality of being, of soul and body, of changeability"; "*my* entire life is flying upward to heaven and plunging into dirt," somewhat "akin to Rasputin's: 'If you don't sin, you don't repent'."[72] When some readers argued that in Russian *swing* was a plural noun, the prestigious V.I. Dal's *The Explanatory Dictionary of the Living Russian Language* proved him right, and Ivask sent him Mandelstam's "I was swinging in a distant garden / on a simple wooden swing [*kachel'*]." Pereleshin later published an article on this word.[73]

As in *Southern Home*, the poems were undated because of "the temporal distance between those written in China and the recent works: it seemed as if two different authors were in the book."[74] *Swing*'s forty-four poems consisted of one each from 1934, 1939, 1941, and 1943; nine from 1949; four from 1945; two each from 1946 and 1947; one from 1955, eleven from 1969 and seven from 1970 showed that Brazilian poems had begun to take their place. It also included the long poems "Balaam" (*Valaam*),

"Poem about Universe," and "The Way of the Cross." He considered *Swing* to be "immeasurably superior to *Southern Home*": it had "a single breath, one big theme, and will therefore remain unattainable even for its author to the end of my days." He later observed: "now I certainly would have combined those poems with others which expressed unforgivable doubts and lured with the blackest abysses."[75] Some ten years later, he described it as "the purest, the most sober" book in "To Christian Salatko-Petrishche" (*Khristianu Salatko-Petrishche*, 18.1.1982).

Swing combines an anguished prayer with a challenge to God. The opening "Remorse" (*Raskaianie*, 30.1.1970) says: "by the miracle of amnesia / I learned to live without faith, / without friendship, without Russia, / […] / but where is God's amnesty instead of my oblivion?" In "Pyramid" (*Piramida*, 24.2.1955) the poet pleads to make him "so full of You, / that I would feel to be You!" and in "Mosaic" (*Mozaika*, ca. 1.6.1945) he begs not to be abandoned: "a lamb, who got behind the flock, / I do not follow the crowd, / I go where one should not, / to a wolf's watering place." But the prayers are in vain, and in "Conversation with God" (*Beseda s Bogom*, 13.11.1947) the poet says: "Why do we need Your heavenly Good, / if we can warm ourselves with a brief happiness, / if a fire-bird sometimes drops its feather, / as a light-winged guest in a comfortless house?" Some religious poems, such as "Fishermen" (*Lovtsy*, 1.10.1969), "Prayer" (*Molitva*, 22.8.1969), and "After Sunset" (*Posle zakata*, 9.4.1969), are greatly enhanced by his earlier experimentations with heteroaccentual rhyme, and "Rain" (*Dozhd'*, 24.3.1969), in particular, stands out for its imagery, broken syntax, and exceptional stanzaic structure.

The professor and poet V.F. Markov wrote to him: "A lucid spirit and God are behind your lines, and this spirituality, this lucidity, is luminous, unobtrusive, and even elusive." Petr Lapiken praised it; Professor Struve noted the closeness of "Poem about the Universe" to Gumilev's work; Victor Terras saw a synthesis of Orthodoxy and Catholicism; the poet Strannik, pseudonym of Archbishop Ioann Shakhovskoi, sent "a sweet and sour response," which Pereleshin took as a sign that one "should not write better than the archbishop." An Orthodox nun in France wrote that "the entire monastery read the book and greatly approved it."[76] The Paris poet Ol'ga Mozhaiskaia, however, "severely criticized" it, which Pereleshin attributed to her theosophical beliefs: "a devil reacts in the same way to frankincense."[77]

Irina Odoevtseva's review noted "an almost blasphemous, maniacal assertion of identity and equality with God, which was not a devilish pride, but, on the contrary, a deeply religious state, religious ecstasy. [...] Pereleshin's poetry is deeply tragic in its essence; with an incredible effort he always wants to express what is most important to him, to 'embody himself' truly in images and rhythms, and to reunite with God and the entire universe, but does not succeed in it." She noted "not imitation, but an inner harmony with Gumilev," but felt that "flaunting of formal mastery" in "The Way of the Cross" was "unlikely to touch readers' hearts."[78] He disagreed: "there is the simplest 'Jesus prayer' in the Christian world, but there are also most complex and intricate works, such as crowns of sonnets or acrostics, canons or akathists. [...] The crown of sonnets is written for a sophisticated taste."[79] In his 1978 study of Pereleshin's poetry, Rannit praised *Swing* as "ringing with the silver of neoclassicism and free of any erotic daze."[80]

Sanctuary: The Seventh Book of Poetry, 1972

Стали все врагами грез последних,
кружевных, пленительных обманов.
Лишь у нас устроен заповедник
для больных и раненых туманов.
Им, ненужным, хилым и заблудшим,
опоздавшим века на четыре,
есть ли место в этом наилучшем,
в этом улыбающемся мире?
Разрослись у нас большие сосны,
панцырь их почти непроницаем.
Понапрасну к нам стучатся весны:
мы чужим ворот не открываем!
Наши сосны вырядились в иней,
выпал снег по закоулкам сада.
Мы пасем в прохладе бело-синей
нежное взволнованное стадо.
И напрасно жадным и горячим
стало солнце – не добьется толку!
Все равно ведь мы овечек спрячем
и дорогу загородим волку.

Everyone has become an enemy of last dreams,
of lacelike, captivating deceits.
We alone have created a sanctuary
for ailing and wounded fogs.
For them, unwanted, sickly, and lost,
fallen behind for some four centuries,
is there a place in this best of the best,
in this smiling world?
Tall pines have grown big in our place,
their armour is almost impenetrable.
In vain springs knock to be let in:
we do not open the gates to strangers!
Our pines dressed up in hoar-frost,
snow fell in the nooks of the garden.
In the white-blue coolness
we are tending a tender emotional flock.
And in vain has the sun became greedy
and hot – it will not succeed!
We will certainly hide the lambs
and bar the road to a wolf.

"Sanctuary"(*Zapovednik*), 20.11.1944

At the end of 1971, Rannit recommended Pereleshin to a Mr Talalaev, who wished to sponsor a book of poetry in memory of his parents. Pereleshin, most grateful to Rannit, took his suggestion of "Core"

(*Serdtsevina*) for the title and found "a wonderful epigraph" from Mandelstam's "Staff" (*Posokh*): "My staff, my freedom, / the core of my being," which echoed "core of the world" and "core of history" in Berdiaev's *The Meaning of History* (*Smysl istorii*). He selected "only serious poems, well thought through, in the style of *Southern Home*, with a touch of 'swing,' but without Christian intensity."[81] Two specially written poems, "To Mother" (*Materi*, 14.1.1972) and "Dedication" (*Posviashchenie*, 14.1.1972) were to open the book.

When the sponsor changed his mind, a disappointed Pereleshin reworked the draft into his seventh book. He first wanted to name it *Pendulum* (*Maiatnik*), "swinging forward to our century and even further, and backward to the times of Petrarch and Michelangelo," but he discarded that title for *Sanctuary*, "where one can hide like a snail in its shell. Otherwise, predators would gobble up the defenceless snail."[82] His Shanghai poem "Sanctuary" (*Zapovednik*, 20.11.1944) grew into a book, which "logically follows *Swing*. The latter shows half of the inner world, but there is another half. Cycles and themes move from one state to another. The poems in *Sanctuary* are an important stage for me. If I had not dropped out of literature for almost twenty years, only new poems would have been published at present."[83]

Selection was not easy: "I like *too* many. One poem closes on to another and responds in the second and third like an echo." A few were included "for the sake of my mother's sentimental recollections."[84] In June 1972, he sent it to Possev-Verlag, ordering an extra twenty-five unbound copies on thin paper, to be enclosed, a few pages at a time, in letters to Khaindrova and a few others in the Soviet Union.[85] The cost made the title *Sacrifice* acquire additional meaning: "Now it means precisely sacrifice in the simplest everyday sense. When a poet must choose between publishing a book or buying new clothes and paying for 'daily expenses,' he chooses publication."[86] In January 1973, he and his mother rejoiced at receiving the first copies, and, as before, friends in other countries were ordering copies to sell among friends, "a heroic deed, because I know how hard it is to sell poems."[87]

The frontispiece of the book was his portrait, painted by D.V. Izmailovich in 1967, which presented the poet in profile, in a suit, a tie, and heavy, dark-rimmed glasses.[88] The poems were again undated, and the disparity between the old and new showed: one from 1943, eleven from 1944 (seven from *Island*), two from 1953, one from 1957, one from 1967, four from 1968, eleven from 1969, fifteen from 1970, fifteen from 1971, and six from 1972: a total of sixty-eight.

Sanctuary continues the theme of "Xiangtancheng" (*Siantan'cheng*, 11.10.1948), an imaginary refuge of tall Beijing pines and Shanghai fogs, in *Southern Home*. The poet is no longer searching for the way, but for "a place where one could hide, escape, run away from the world. Let fools 'reflect' and record forever the world's sharp edges and disorderly colours. This is one of my life-long themes."[89] In "Moth" (*Mol'*, 14.2.1971) the poet identifies with a moth drawn to the circle of light falling upon his notebooks. "On My Birthday" (*V den' rozhdeniia*, 18.7.1970) presents life as "an endless night" filled with "empty dense forests," hoots of "sleepless owls," ominous whispers of empty spaces, a tiny firefly on its way through the night, and the realization that door locks are useless. "On the Tower" (*Na bashne*, 7.6.1970) finds the poet, "a hermit and misanthrope," defiantly turning his back on the "noisy and mad epoch" and locking himself in to gaze at the floating clouds. The only true escape is poetry. "Knife-grinder" (*Tochil'shchik*, 26.12.1971) shows the poet practising his art with the same utter precision. In "Upper Reaches" (*Verkhov'ia*, 28.5.1970) creativity, like a river, floods him with rhymes, magical and enchanting in their precision and connotations. The first set, remarkably, is Portuguese, *clan*destino – destino, and the rest Russian, such as *pod*vesnoi – *i* vesnoi, / *nerev*nivoi – *i* nivoi, / *po*kaznoi – *i* kaznoi, / *neschas*tlivoi – *i* slivoi.

The contest for a homeland is now not between Russia and China, but Russia and Brazil. In "Brazilian Spring" (*Brazil'skaia vesna*, 10.5.1971) the poet, in "the sunniest country in the world," raises a glass of Brazilian rum *cachaça* to the old Russian orthography and to northern springs with their ice-breaking and snowdrops. But in "Idyll" (*Idillia*, 25.7.1969) the home is Brazil, and in "Windy Night" (*Vetrenaia noch'*, 21.8.1969), "the quiet voice of Russian Maria / is deprived of its wings by Brazilian Martha," and as a hot, crazy, happy wind is blowing over "the irrelevant map" of Russia, the poet "cuts the Volga by half – / another road to unnecessary Calvary – / and, laughing, moves onto the Dvina / a cup of fragrant coffee."

In contrast to neologisms for Brazil such as "*Travia*" (Land of Grasses) and "*Tsvetia*" (Land of Flowers) in the eulogy "Brazil" (*Braziliia*, 7.1.1972), Russia in "Argument" (*Spor*, 19.1.1972) is called "*Pokloniia*" (Land of Bowing), "*Pozoriia*" (Land of Disgrace), "*Besslaviia*" (Land of No Glory), and "*Terpigoriia*" (Land of Bearing Grief). As the poem says, Russia has seized Estonia, squashed Moldavia, appropriated Belorussia, but has remained an orphan, a girl without a dowry. Russia is a "night leaning like a solid wall / over the precipice of a well" in "Ravnina" (*Plain*, 5.4.1972), a land of wars, gallows, and whips in "Tsar's Heir Aleksei Petrovich" (*Tsesarevich Aleksei Petrovich*, 25.12.1969), a country of "paradises" such as camps in Kolyma and Pot'ma in "Construction" (*Stroika*, 1.4.1970), mute and deaf in "SOS" (*S.O.S.*, 17.1.1972). This depiction reaches its climax in "Russia" (*Rossiia*, 1.6.1957), a remnant of a crown of sonnets, abandoned as "purely descriptive, without dynamics."[90] In this crucial sonnet, which closes *Sanctuary*, Russia is Scythian steppes open to hurricanes, a glacier sliding down to destroy the civilized world, "a conquistador, hypocrite, usurer, / holy prophet – and vile heretic."

The reviewer N. Z-n considered *Sanctuary* to be Pereleshin's "best, because every poem touches an attentive reader with the strength of thought and feeling"; the book was like "a Russian ship, guided by an experienced captain with Gumilev's poems as navigational instruments." Although he did not share Pereleshin's insistence on the importance of rhyme, "Pereleshin's striving to retain traditional rhymes gives excellent results."[91] Ivask started his review by introducing émigré poetry in general and Pereleshin as a poet from China in particular and wrote that his poems had "the cold shine of silver and gold, or the brightness of copper, devoid of warmth. I point this out not as a condemnation. Coldness in art is not worse than heat. [...] Pereleshin's poetics is that of the Acmeists, of the epoch of the first Poet's Workshop. Sometimes he even stands to the right of Gumilev."[92] The Paris poet Tamara Velichkovskaia saw the sanctuary as "his inner world, devoid of people, jealously guarded against the external world, alien and hostile to him"; she noted poems about Brazil and deep nostalgia for Russia and wrote that he was "an experienced poet, who trims and 'sharpens' his poems [...]. Such 'sharpening' is a merit and, at the same time, a danger."[93] In his study of Pereleshin's poetry Rannit described the *leitmotif* of the book as "an escape from the world," "an amplification of the set theme of the first book *On the Way*, the theme of rejection of the world" and defined its key as the sense of "doom."[94]

Poems on a Fan: Anthology of Translations from Chinese Classical Poetry, 1970

君自故乡来
应知故乡事
来日骑窗前
寒梅著花未
王维

Встреча с земляком	Meeting a Fellow-Townsman.
Вы возвратились из родной страны.	You have returned from the native country.
Что происходит там, вы знать должны.	You should know what is happening there.
В тот день, как вы мой миновали дом,	On the day that you passed by my house,
Не расцвела ли слива под окном?	Was the plum by the window blooming?
Ван Вей	Wang Wei, translated in 1947

The appearance of Pereleshin's books of poetry in 1968 and 1971 ran parallel to making another Shanghai dream come true: publishing an anthology of his translations from Chinese classical poetry. On Kruzenshtern's advice, he had applied for a grant from Inter-Language Literary Associates with no success and once again went ahead on his own: "Be what it may. Otherwise, it seems that life is passing in vain. It will, of course, be published at a loss," but "I no longer can write for the desk drawer."[95]

He believed himself to be "one of the first translators of Chinese poetry into Russian" and "very trustworthy": poetic translation required "knowledge of the language of the original, the culture and history of the nation, and, of course, a poetic talent, all of which are present in my humble person." Translations from word-for-word prose renderings and from translations into other languages were "the greatest swindle" and "a game of broken telephone."[96] In 1967, he sent a letter to *Russian Thought*, criticizing N. Tatishchev's translation of a poem by Li Bai, obviously from a French translation. The newspaper did not publish the letter, but *New Russian Word* did, and Pereleshin followed it with an overview article, "Chinese Poetry."[97] In "Translators" (*Perevodchiki*, 23.11.1971) he ridiculed Tatishchev, as well as A.N. Serebrennikova in Tianjin, for not even checking rules for transliterating Chinese names. Arthur Waley was an example "of how not to translate. […] His unrhymed and formless translations convey *only* content, but is poetry really reduced to content?" His point was that "Chinese classical poets used rhyme and there is no ground to distort their concepts and replace their engraved beauty with unstable *vers libre*."[98] Comparison of his translations with those of Soviet translators "was not to their benefit: theirs were ineffectual, trite, with dull interpretations." He rightly guessed that one of the best, A.I. Gitovich, did not know Chinese, though obviously "studied, if not originals, then at least literature about them."[99]

He sent the typescript of *Poems on a Fan* with a third of its cost to Possev-Verlag, and this time *Russian Thought* forwarded his accumulated honorariums to the publisher. Pereleshin told his mother about the submission only when the proofs arrived in December 1969 and added that it was "on favourable terms (which is not quite true). She said: 'It's not that expensive!' It is good that no scolding followed: your clothes are shabby, you should think about clothes, food, and so on. I'll say the same to Victor and Lidiia: favourable terms, on credit. Let this untypical 'lie' be forgiven!"[100]

He was "deliriously happy" on receiving the first copy in March 1970, and he presented it to his mother: "she is *very pleased*: no reproaches," but Victor and Lidiia were "eating me alive." Victor pointed out that he might not sign another contract in Brazil and would return to the United States, taking their mother with him, and what would Pereleshin do then? Lidiia suggested that it should be his last book. After they left, his mother said: "you should not tell them anything and should not give your books as gifts, because they are enemies."[101] The publishers kept 100 copies on commission and sent some for review; the remaining copies were sent to Pereleshin, and he mailed them in batches to friends and acquaintances to be sold privately.[102]

Poems on a Fan opened with a brief introduction to classical Chinese poetry, followed by twenty-four poems and two longer works, the anonymous ballad "Mulan" and Bai Juyi's "Song of Mandoline" (*Pipaxing*), so that "an inexperienced reader would not think that the Chinese had nothing but miniature works."[103] The frontispiece was a portrait of the poet Meng Haoran taken from a negative presented to him by Korostovets in Beijing. The book also contained a secret tribute to his Shanghai lover, Liu Xin, by reproducing a page of Chinese text in his handwriting.[104] The title was taken from "Song of Lament" (*Yuangexing*) by Ban Jieyu, translated on 16 December 1942 and published in *Border* as "Poems on a Fan, Presented to the Han Dynasty Emperor Zheng Di by a Lady of His Court Ban Jieyu." It was "an elegant miniature where a woman poet compares her life to that of a fan: needed when it is hot and thrown away to a distant corner when it gets cold."[105] His choices were works of Li Bai (five poems), Wang Wei (two), Ouyang Xiu (two), and one poem each from Meng Haoran, Zhang Zhi, He Zhizhang, and a few others and included his very first translation, Gai Jiayun's *Yichuange*. Kruzenshtern objected to calling the book of poems which he chose to translate an anthology, but Pereleshin defensively quoted a dictionary definition of an anthology as a collection of selected works by different authors.[106]

For him, "Chinese poetry is an ocean," and in his choices he focused on *shi* and *ci*. *Shi*, poems of four or eight rhymed lines of five or seven characters per line, were composed from the end of the Han dynasty to the end of the Tang dynasty. Pereleshin kept the structure of four to eight lines, occasionally adding a couple of lines, and translated *shi* of five characters per line into iambic pentameter and those of seven characters into iambic hexameter, admitting that "no metre in our sense is possible in the monosyllabic Chinese language."[107] He translated *ci* poems, which evolved during and after the Tang dynasty and had lines ranging from three to nine characters, into "trisyllabic feet and even multi-foot trochee": "every time a poet changes the number of characters in a line, I also try to change the length of the line, ignoring only insignificant variations (from nine to eight characters, etc.)." He "followed rhyme alternation in every poem: in some, four, five, six, seven, and even eight lines (with one rhyme) are rhymed, but some lines are left without a rhyme. *Ci* include up to fifty 'set forms,' each as complex and intricate as our sonnet."[108] In opposition to scholarly quests for "not missing a single detail of the original" and often losing the essence, he aimed not so much at "precision, but at adequacy of impression" in retaining the meaning, structure, and rhyme of each poem.[109] This goal led him to change some titles and details, for example, in Wang Wei's poem presented in the epigraph above, where he supplied the title and changed the original's "patterned window" to "my home" and "winter plum tree" with its connotation of early blooming to simply "plum tree."

Working on *Poems on a Fan* led him to write "Zhao Jun" in November 1970: "it is NOT a translation, but my own poem. Only the last, twelfth part is translated from the Chinese, the song, which Zhao Jun *could* have sung in the silence of a Mongolian night (if this song was written before Zhao Jun)." *The New Review* declined it, and it appeared in the Toronto journal *Contemporary* (*Sovremennik*) only in 1976.[110]

None of the reviewers knew Chinese. The former Harbin poet, Elizaveta Rachinskaia, described the anthology as "the poet's gift of love to China, for many years his second homeland," quoted from some translations, and moved on to praising "The Way of the Cross," but Pereleshin was delighted with this "wide overview of the theme 'China in the poetry' of your humble servant."[111] One anonymous reviewer praised *Poems on a Fan* for "conveying the meaning, the essence, and the music of Chinese poems." Oleg Geliotropov commented that the translator loved China and "its ancient doomed culture," and the Paris poet Olga Emel'ianova declared the translations to be reliable because Pereleshin had lived in China and knew the language. Ivask was "enraptured" by the opportunity to become acquainted with Chinese poetry.[112] Only Lapiken, "an erudite, witty, scholarly sinologist," sent Pereleshin a letter with some compliments and a competent assessment, where he pointed out some mistakes and criticized his reliance on sloppy Chinese anthologies for biographical data given at the back.[113]

Chinese poetry never stopped captivating Pereleshin: "I find so much beauty in it that my head spins. This is a true poetry." He soon started working on his second anthology, "Shadow on a Curtain" (*Ten' na zanaveske*), named after a line from the recently translated Jian Jie's poem "At Dawn." It was to include mostly *ci* poems, and he even contemplated the feat of translating the entire collection *Cixuan*. The second anthology was set aside: the priority was his own poetry.[114] He translated Chinese poems in spurts for the rest of his life: "I love some poems so much that I know them by heart; I often write them on a piece of paper in a restaurant, waiting for lunch to be served." Three years before his death he marked "many translatable miniatures of the Tang dynasty" in Chinese anthologies he owned.[115]

Traces of Chinese poetry are powerfully present in some imagery and structure of Pereleshin's poems: "I always welcome reticence (*nedoskaz*): this is partly the influence of the Chinese classics, who never dotted their 'i's and let readers participate in the creative work. Poems with reticence are far from transrational poetry (*zaum'*); they are justified by the fact that poetic feeling is always to some extent irrational, inexpressible to the end."[116]

Translation of Qu Yuan, *Li Sao*, 1975

己矣哉
国无人
莫我知兮
又何怀乎古都
既莫足与为美政兮
吾将从彭咸之所居
屈原 离骚

Ухожу.
А страна остается без человека.
Я не признан никем.
Но зачем-то люблю я свою страну.
Ею править никто не достоин со мною.
Как Пэн Сянь, и я в быстрине речной
утону.

I am leaving.
And the country remains without a person.
I am not recognized by anyone.
But for some reason I love my country.
No one is worthy of ruling it with me.
Like Peng Xian, I too will drown in the
river rapids.

Qu Yuan, *Li Sao* (translated in 1967)

In 1946 in Shanghai Pereleshin bought a copy of the ancient Chinese masterpiece *Li Sao* by Qu Yuan and "a very poor translation," *The Li Sao Translated into English Verse by Lim Boon King* (Shanghai 1935). He was spellbound: "for the first time / I understood someone else's truth. / The poet, stubborn and persecuted, / transformed me / with his untranslatable long poem / (what if it is possible to translate it?)!"[117]

The title, *Li Sao*, "Overcoming Grief" or "Sorrow of the Rejected," was dear to Pereleshin's heart, and Qu Yuan became "my passion," "a human image very dear to me. He is an aristocrat through and through, connoisseur of subtle aromas, flowers, choices of colours, and an æsthete in the best sense of the word." In this "exceptionally difficult poem in Sichuan dialect […] relations between a king and his minister are presented as relations between two people in love with each other."[118] The long poem was "a magnificent 'political and erotic elegy,' full of allegories and symbols, of an incomparable beauty," "one of the largest pearls of world poetry," and "an astounding literary monument, which will retain its perfection, in spite of ironical chuckles of ill-wishing readers ('somewhat strange relations between the Prince and the poet'), and so on. These 'somewhat strange relations' did not hurt Shakespeare's sonnets and the heroes of *Iliad*."[119]

Pereleshin called himself "a mediocre sinologist," largely self-taught and peaking at some 11,000 characters when working for TASS. By the 1970s he could read modern Chinese "with some effort" and did not know the simplified characters adopted in the mid-1950s.[120] But in his first years in Brazil, "in the loneliness of long evenings / I translated fifteen stanzas / into Russian, in a severe *dol'nik* metre, / as if translating / does not mean reopening old wounds!"[121] In 1967, he looked at the abandoned effort, and "in the course of three consecutive sleepless nights, translated the rest (the poem has ninety-three stanzas). I have not yet revised it critically." He was "pleased that nowhere did I replace Qu Yuan with Pereleshin, I did not defame the great Chinese anywhere, and I did not brand him with Christianity or even Buddhism."[122] In 1968 he learned that it had been translated, "and by whom? By Akhmatova! I trembled, suffered, stopped eating and drinking, and lost weight." When he received a photocopy, "my heart was pounding ferociously and my hands shook as I was opening the parcel, but when I started reading, I calmed down completely: the Soviet translation, done by N.T. Fedorenko and reworked by Anna Akhmatova (wow!), turned out to be below criticism. [...] Poor, poor Akhmatova!" He judged his own translation to be "incomparably more precise, tidier, and better in all respects than hers. [...] The victory is mine on all points." On hearing of Gitovich's translation, he commented: "If Gitovich knows Chinese, he is a competitor, but if he was retelling a word-for-word translation, there is not the slightest danger from that side."[123]

Publication of *Li Sao* had to wait until November 1974, when he ordered 200 copies from Possev-Verlag, with the usual few extras on thin paper for enclosing in letters to the USSR. He "sighed once again for my sad fate," knowing that in the USSR some books had print runs of several hundred thousand copies. *Li Sao* sold for US$5: "I may as well set it at fifty: practically no one will buy it anyway."[124] In February 1975, he and his mother celebrated the arrival of the first copies with ice cream, biscuits, and orange liqueur: "Oh, the serene life of the unemployed in Brazil! [...] Publishing *Li Sao* was possible only thanks to Mum's sacrifices. She is prepared for the two of us to live on her 'pension' (from my brother), so that I can send my meagre earnings to Possev. As you see, I am not alone in guessing my little place in the history of Russian poetry."[125]

In his review Ivask said that, although he could not judge the quality of the translation, it was "an event" in Russian poetry. Lapiken, who knew Chinese, reviewed it at Pereleshin's request. He pointed out some minor mistakes and misprints and highly praised it: translating such a difficult work required "not only knowledge, but also an impeccable exacting taste. [...] From the start of my parallel reading, I was bewitched by the elusive intuitive precision. Let those who are in love with pseudoscience forgive me, but I did not know whether I was reading Chinese or Russian. [...] It is surprising how one could convey a foreign world in a language foreign to one's native tongue without a single unpleasant mistake."[126]

Translating *Daodejing*, 1970s

道可道非常道
名可名非常名
无名天地之始
有名万物之母
道德经

Если Истину произречь,
Суть погибнет, а выйдет речь.
Если имя ты назовешь,
То не имя оно, а ложь.
Ничто – причина Небу и Земле,
И только в них начало всех вещей.
Daodejing (Pereleshin's translation, nos 5 and 6, 1971)

Dao that can be named is not the everlasting Dao,
Name that can be named is not the everlasting Name.
That which has no name is the origin of heaven and earth,
That which has a name is the Mother of all things.
Lao-tzu, 81

Pereleshin first read *Daodejing* in Beijing in a partial translation by Korostovets from an English version. In 1946 his fellow-translator Chen Yi presented him with a copy of the original, and in 1950 another translator, Zheng Lin, gave him his translation into English, entitled *Truth and Nature*.[127] Rereading it in Brazil, he found this major Daoist work "amazing, as deep as Plato. Laozi is not a slightly vulgar, moralist Confucius, but a true philosopher and mystic."[128]

He started working on *Daodejing* in 1971, treating it as "an experiment in poetic translation." He saw it not so much as "a philosophical treatise, but as a *poem*" and disagreed with an attaché at the Taiwan embassy in Brazil, who, on consultation, called it rhythmic prose: "the emphasis should be not on 'prose,' but on 'rhythmic.'" He now saw Zheng Lin's prose translation as "disgusting," because he "managed to expel all poetry and beauty from the book."[129] The work consumed him: "The beauty of the original drives me to a frenzy (I know that my translation, closer to the original than any existing one, is nevertheless a pathetic and helpless attempt in comparison with the divine beauty of the original)."[130] Struggling with Laozi's cryptic style, he even penned an unfinished parody: "Fat will get thin, / Thin will get fat; / Misery will come to toothy birds, / Happiness [a gap in the draft] to peaceful ones. // A hunchback will get straight, / A straight one will lean to one side."

It was finished on 24 February 1971, although some corrections were made later. Instead of the generally accepted order of *Daodejing*'s 180 sections, Pereleshin followed Zheng Lin's order, but supplemented his numbering with the usual order in parentheses.[131] His unrhymed rhythmic sections were at times too interpretive, at times problematic. He used truth (*istina*) for *Dao* and virtue (*dobrodetel'*) for *De*; if the second was acceptable, truth for *Dao* was questionable, especially since it could also mean "the way," a concept crucial in his poetry. It was not a success. Émigré journals and newspapers expressed no interest. It was published only in 2000 in Moscow, well after his death.

9 *From Mount Nebo*

Trip to Europe, 1973

Люблю Дижон – мечту о Карле Смелом,	I love Dijon – a dream about Charles the Brave,
Арль, Авиньон – тоску по старине:	Arles, Avignon – a yearning for antiquity:
Река времен теперь послушна мне	The river of time is now obedient to me
И к дорогим несет меня пределам.	And carries me to the precious borders.
С младенчества я разумом и телом	From infancy with my mind and body
Европы сын и предан ей вполне,	I have been a son of Europe and fully devoted to it,
А пятнышком тускнел на желтизне	But stayed a dim spot, most insignificant,
Ничтожнейшим, непоправимо белым.	Irreparably white, on yellow background.
[…]	

"In France" (*Vo Frantsii*), 6.10.1973

By 1973, Pereleshin had lived in Brazil for twenty years. The United States was closed to him, and dreams of visiting Europe had ended with the loss of his British Council job. Then, out of the blue, a trip to Europe became a possibility. His mother had kept in touch with V.V. Koloshin, her Harbin common-law husband, who, like some other elderly Russians, was accepted in the mid-1950s at a seniors' residence in Belgium. In September 1973 he wrote to her that his life was coming to an end and he wanted her to visit and to have his savings.

The mother and son decided that Pereleshin should go to Belgium and then visit France, hoping that Koloshin's money and his own honorarium from *Russian Thought* would more than cover the expenses: "I dreamt of Europe in school: even then, my spiritual homeland was the

Rome of Caesars, Popes, and the Renaissance. I understood later that our roots lie not only in Rome, but also in the Athens of Socrates and Plato, the Constantinople of ecumenical cathedrals, Egypt, the Athos of the ascetics, and the Palestine of both Testaments."[1] Pereleshin arrived in Belgium on 27 September 1973 and found Koloshin lonely, miserable, "very old (nearly ninety), and unable to recall place names in Harbin." He handed Pereleshin all his modest savings in Belgian francs, calling them rubles. He died in December of that year.[2]

In Paris Pereleshin stayed for a few days with a former Harbin Russian, Nina Fouchier, née Mokrinskaia, who "welcomed me as a relative and showed me some sights";[3] he then travelled to Marseilles to visit Larissa Andersen and her husband, Maurice Chaize, in Yssingeaux. He and Andersen had not seen each other since Shanghai and they talked for hours about old friends, poetry, China, Buddhism, and mysticism. Pereleshin saw "two Larissas. One is Martha, busy with housework, cats, laundry, and cooking, while the other is 'howling like a wolf.' I was with the one I call Maria, anguished and unhappy, a subtle poet. While I was there, Larissa was writing and working on unfinished drafts. She continued when I left, but I am afraid that she will again be choked by daily chores."[4] His acrostic to Andersen, "In Yissengeaux" (*V Issanzho*, 7.10.1973), ended with "Maria is pleasing me with her poems, / but Martha is stuffing me with food!" On 20 October 1973 they went together to Paris to get his money from *Russian Thought* and meet its editor, Princess Z.A. Shakhovskaia. He was invited to an editorial meeting, though some members, Terapiano among them, did not show up. In vain did he hope "to get a job at *Russian Thought*, move to Paris, and escape unemployment with its fetters and humiliations."[5]

He saw "thousand-year-old cathedrals and monasteries, churches and town halls, and became acquainted with each chimera by shaking their paws at the bell tower of the Cathedral of Notre Dame de Paris." He appreciated "a France not for tourists, not 'Tour Eiffel,' but churches unremarkable except for their age and simple houses of volcanic stone," and he was entranced by "the spirit of *antiquity*. I loved the old China for that same thing."[6] He experienced "a strange sense" of unreality, as if "I have fallen out of this world; no letters, no books, no dreams." Paris "remained in my memory like a radiant dream," but left an "indescribable sense of distress and some kind of funereal mood."[7] In "Malicious Joy" (*Zloradstvo*, 9.10.1973) the "mad carousel" takes him to Brussels, Marseilles, and Paris, "but hiding in the briefcase, on guard, / Brazilian cruzeiros gloat maliciously. / As a verdict, as an old anguish, / I will take them out flying over Rio de Janeiro." The trip "was not a loss, but I did not gain anything and returned to the same customary poverty": Koloshin's money covered the ticket, and he and his mother set the rest aside for his next book.[8]

Festival of Poetry in Texas, 1974

Когда-нибудь повалятся в проломы	The trustworthy wall stones will once
Надежные булыжники стены.	Collapse into fissures.
Термитами давно повреждены,	Treasured volumes, long damaged
Рассыплются лелеемые томы.	By termites, will crumble.
А наши сны? Бесплотны, невесомы.	And our dreams? Incorporeal, weightless.
А подвиги? Досмотренные сны.	And heroic deeds? Dreams we saw to their ends.
На перегной пойти обречены	We and our chromosomes
И сами мы, и наши хромосомы.	Are doomed to turn into compost.
Мир – колесо. И сколько ни потей	The world is a wheel. And no matter how you sweat
Для прибыли, для славы, для детей	For profit, for glory, for children,
Обломится и та, и эта спица.	The spokes will break one after another.
Снаружи ночь. Внутри возка темно,	It is night outside. It is dark in the closed carriage,
Спать хочется, но страшно и не спится,	I'm sleepy, but scared, and sleep does not come,
И – черное по черному – окно.	And the window is black on black.

"Black Window"
(*Chernoe okno*), 25.6.1974

A year later Pereleshin went on another trip, this time to the forbidden United States. In 1973, thanks to Iurii Ivask's recommendation, he accepted "with delight" an invitation from the Slavic Department at the University of Texas in Austin to give a two-week seminar on Russian poetry, two poetry readings, and an open lecture on Russian poetry of China. He hoped to go on to New York and Washington, DC, to see Kruzenshtern, poets, professors, and editors, and "develop it into a wide program of public appearances in different cities and universities."[9]

The University of Texas cancelled the seminar, but invited him to the Fourth International Festival of Poetry on 11–13 April 1974. Superstitiously avoiding the thirteenth, he went to the US Consulate on 14 February 1974, writing to Kruzenshtern: "Pray for me." He brought "a suitcase of cuttings" of his published articles, and the consul, Donald J. Yellman, was "*shaken* by my statement that I have been working for *New Russian*

Word for six years." He "*believed* me (that I am 'a victim of slander' and, in his definition, 'a victim of circumstances'). He laughed at suspicions that I was a subversive (after all, I worked for TASS in Shanghai from 1945 to 1948, although only – but is it only? – as a translator from Chinese). I learned from him that an unknown informer reported in 1951 [*sic* – 1950], that I 'had helped Galen or Borodin or Blucher to found the Chinese Communist Party.' I asked the consul: 'Do you know when the Chinese Communist Party was founded?' – 'No, I don't.' – 'But I know: in 1921. How old was I then, or do you need a computer?' – 'Yes, it's true, you were seven ...' Now it has become our *household joke* [Eng.] about *precocious children* [Eng.]." Jokes aside, Pereleshin was appalled: "One could not invent *this*, even if one wanted to. A seven-year-old child, not knowing a word of Chinese, 'helped Blucher-Galen-Borodin to organize the Chinese Communist Party.' This is truly an anecdote, which shows to what extent North Americans are ignorant and gullible."[10]

The consul advised him to apply for a visitor's visa to Austin, Washington, DC, and New York and promised to look into getting "permission not only for a temporary visit, but also for the right of entry." Victor also went to see the consul and was told that had his brother come to the United States half a year earlier or later, he could have stayed: "as it turns out, hysterics of the time (Senator McCarthy plus the Korean War) had cost me almost my entire life."[11] In early March 1974 there was still no answer: "excuses would always be found: 'the quota is closed,' 'your number has not come up yet,' or 'the papers are lost.' [...] And for us, the undeserving ones, 'there is no way.' We are the subversives. We are the Soviet agents." The "agony of waiting" reminded him of Shanghai in the early 1950s, and by the end of March he had lost hope.[12]

On 2 April Victor rushed over with the news that the consulate had phoned to say that Pereleshin had been issued a visa to Austin for fifteen days. The consul showed Pereleshin a telegram from Henry Kissinger's office that a complete "reversion" of the previous exclusion was impossible, because "immigration authorities had received new *derogatory information* [Eng.]. I asked him whether it listed sins like blasphemy, adultery, or something else. He laughed and said that, of course, it was the matter of my 'belonging to the Communist Party.'"[13] Insulted by the strict restrictions on place and time, Pereleshin woke up the next day "with a firm decision to cancel the trip in these conditions of a straitjacket": he would not go "as a person under surveillance." He felt like "a squeezed lemon. Complete devastation. Headache. [...] I'll need a long time to lick my wounds."[14] On getting his letter of cancellation, the

University of Texas phoned the US Consulate in Rio de Janeiro, and the consul, Victor, and his mother talked him into going.[15]

At the festival, the poets Chinua Achebe (Nigeria), Ai (USA), Ana Blandiana (Rumania), Rolf Dieter Brinkman (German Federal Republic), Russell Edson (USA), Angel González (Spain), Valerii Pereleshin (Russia and Brazil), Nanos Valaoritis (Greece, France, USA), and James Welch (USA) gave recitations and exhibited their books. Pereleshin's two recitations, accompanied by English translations, drew a large audience.[16] He entered "a totally different world of intellectual interests, gifted people, and true goodwill" and loved "the university atmosphere and literary meetings and discussions." The two weeks "passed like a wonderful dream," like "the seventh heaven. […] *Now* it is frightening to return home, to poverty and the absence of people. But the kind consul promises to work on my moving here."[17] He hinted to his hosts about a job, but was told that budget cuts made it impossible. In retrospect, he considered the trip "a complete failure," because it did not lead to stimulating friendships or useful contacts. He set aside most of the $2,000 honorarium towards publication of his future books.[18]

On his return, Consul Yellman, who was to be transferred in a couple of years, advised him not to delay applying for immigration, perhaps even as "a defector." Pereleshin refused: "one cannot be an apostate of the ideology one has never believed in."[19] He submitted his previous application, but it was caught up in red tape and came to nothing.

Working on *Poem without a Subject*, 1970s

Когда, над Городом Чудесным
зарозовев, пришла заря
пощекотать лучом воскресным
мозаику календаря,
я не гадал о катастрофе,
но выслушал, смакуя кофе,
как Муза, оседлав карниз,
сердито прошипела вниз:
"За ум берись, бросай лениться:
талантик напрягая свой,
пиши онегинской строфой –
пора у Пушкина учиться.
Буржуй, враждебен ты труду
и пишешь только ерунду."

When, spreading light over
the Marvellous City, the pink dawn rose
to tickle the calendar's mosaic
with a Sunday ray,
I did not foresee a catastrophe,
but listened, enjoying my coffee,
how the Muse, astride the window ledge,
hissed down angrily:
"Come to your senses, stop being lazy:
strain your meagre talent
and write in the Onegin stanza –
it's time to learn from Pushkin.
Bourgeois, you are an enemy of work
and write only rubbish."

Poem without a Subject
(*Poema bez predmeta*),
Canto One, I, 35

Pereleshin began his lengthy autobiographical *Poem without a Subject* (*Poema bez predmeta*) on 2 January 1972, when "the Sun was at eleven degrees of Capricorn where rising Jupiter had been at the moment of my birth. This combination of planets in my sky produces an almost magical action." On that day he was seized by "an irresistible desire to write in the Onegin stanza form and wrote about thirty such stanzas in a couple of days. The concept gradually emerged: it will be (if it will) a *Poem without a Subject*, my own autobiography with hundreds of zigzags, divergences, and digressions."[20]

He emphasized that it had no relation to Akhmatova's *Poem without a Hero* (*Poema bez geroia*), but was an original work, "precisely 'without a subject,' so that it would not have a 'core,' and events of my life would provide only a general background."[21] The idea might have been prompted by Ivask's cycle of septets, *Homo Ludens* (*Igraiushchii chelovek*), defined by the author as "a thanksgiving hymn," which, in a fanciful digressive style with footnotes, spoke of his life and the people he met. Pereleshin responded to it with "Homo Ludens" (*Igraiushchii chelovek*, 16.11.1971), dedicated to Ivask: "You, a magician, are the only one who could / manage such wide vistas." Ivask kept expanding his cycle and in one later septet described Pereleshin as striving for nirvana, but, being a brother to jaguar and puma, he tore his victims apart, like Dionysus.[22]

Both Kruzenshtern and Ivask suggested "inventing – oh, the daring! – a 'Pereleshin stanza,'" but he stayed with Pushkin's stanza in *Eugene Onegin* for its "astonishing *capacity*. Furthermore, its internal subdivisions are three quatrains and a couplet, and all the quatrains [...] have different patterns of rhyming. Altogether they provide an almost inexhaustible wealth of possibilities! It's no joke that I am already deep into the fifth thousand of lines and still see no signs of exhaustibility!"[23] He disagreed with the view that the Onegin stanza is essentially a sonnet, especially that "if poetic forms have *soul*, then the soul of sonnet is quite different from that of the Onegin stanza," with its "predisposition to leaps and jumps, zigzags, digressions, jokes, and sudden moves."[24] He had already experimented with this stanza in a few longer poems, some of which were incorporated in the *Poem*.

He worked on *Poem without a Subject* on and off for four years. Quite early, he saw that "writing this *Poem* according to a plan does not work, and everything disappears. But when I start 'chatting,' all these recollections, thoughts, jokes, and words (and even rhymes) come from nowhere!"[25] In some digressions, he vented his derision of Evtushenko, Voznesenskii, Brodsky, Volin, and a few other poets. In Canto Three, the "pathetic nature of the recollections of that time (1937) was such that I wanted to cry," "to weep rereading stanzas about my grandmother Mariia Petrovna and about the *Pathétique* symphony, the most personal, but also the most important (and the most frightening) matter." Writing Canto Four about his life in Beijing was so painful that it had "almost no digressions and jumps."[26]

From February 1975 he wrote "like a dipsomaniac" and in July "the *Poem* passed its half: I have narrated thirty years of my life, now talking about the events at the end of 1943 and the Friday Circle. The change of location, Shanghai instead of Beijing, unexpectedly helped: I find rhymes rather easily and seldom repeat myself." In December 1975, he "almost wept" over Canto Seven, which detailed the arrests in Harbin in August 1945, but he "laughed to tears" when describing the Carnival in Rio de Janeiro in Canto Eight. The *Poem* "holds me by the throat."[27] He spent the Carnival days in 1976 on the *Poem*, and "suddenly it was finished on the day of the autumn equinox (spring equinox by the northern calendar), on 21 March 1976." He felt "like an orphan: after all, I have worked on it for four years!"[28]

The *Poem* consisted of eight cantos of seventy-five Onegin stanzas each, a total of 8,400 lines, with endnotes in prose. It was "the longest poem in Russian literature, the most candid (without a posture of teaching or prophesy), and the strictest in form. These three superlatives are already *quelque chose* [Fr.]." He did not hesitate to claim that "only Aleksandr Sergeevich Pushkin is stronger than me in Russian versification, but I have outgrown all others."[29]

The *Poem* aimed to present "my entire life and my entire 'philosophy,'" the poet being "a kind of a portable camera for making movies. I promised that the *Poem* would be 'without a subject,' that is, I would write whatever comes into my head."[30] He openly spoke about his gay lovers: "from the point of view of 'Victorian morals,' the *Poem* is indecent in places, but this is not only an *épopée* [Fr.] (a picture of the entire epoch), but also my autobiography." The *Poem* was "Manichean. It denies life, marriage, and procreation, and, on the autobiographical side, contains candid accounts of the so-called unnatural deviation. I know that in the literatures of England and the United States no 'deviation' is an obstacle: quality alone is required. Russian literature has not yet matured to genuine tolerance. I must, however, make a reservation: this 'deviation' has nothing in common with works such as *The Platonic Blow*, where the 'deviation' is presented as *fun* [Eng.]. In *Poem without a Subject* it is not *fun* [Eng.], but a tragedy of an entire life, with all the conclusions that can be drawn about this deviation from the 'norm' of human behaviour."[31]

Unable to self-publish such a large work, he offered it to *The New Review* for serialization, but did not even receive a reply.[32] The professorial "triumvirate" of Ivask, Tjialsma, and Tikos at the University of Massachusetts accepted a copy for its archive with Pereleshin's stipulation that it should be available only to serious literary scholars, "but not, of course, to my enemies (there are such!) and potential blackmailers."[33]

He also circulated several typewritten copies among friends, asking them to preserve the work. Kruzenshtern was appalled at its openness about his lovers, and Struve sent Canto Eight back. His Tianjin friend Leont'ev sent "such an angry response that our correspondence came to an end. It was as if he had flung mud at me"; Pereleshin hid Leont'ev's letter from his mother, who treasured their friendship with the Leont'evs. Such responses "considerably cooled my ardour; it is better to ask first whether *such* a work is needed."[34] Petr Lapiken, on the other hand, wrote: "if you work more on the material, it will turn out to be as *good* as your poetry books. There are astonishingly successful places, but then some trivial gossip ruins it, or some unfortunate data reduce successful lines to a petty, pathetic 'howl.' [...] Work more on your 'rage' at your life." Lapiken also criticized some accounts of historical events, crude digs at other poets, and the occasional wrong stresses. In his view, the endnotes were "a horror."[35] Indeed, though useful in some cases, on the whole they seem out of place. The *Poem* was not published until 1989.

From Mount Nebo: The Eighth Book of Poetry, 1975

Оставь меня, мой спутник, одного,
Пока закат не скрыт грядой туманной:
На лепоту земли обетованной
В последний раз гляжу с горы Нево.
Избрали мы не плен, а сыновство,

И сорок лет пустыней бездыханной
Брели сюда, и насыщались манной,

Ниспосланной от Бога самого.
Влекут меня заветные границы:
И мельницы, и башни, и бойницы,
Но должен я, по Божьему суду,
Остаться здесь. Чужой земному раю,
Бродягою бездомным умираю,
Но в этот край бессмертным я войду!

Leave me alone, my friend,
Until sunset is hidden by a misty ridge:
I am looking for the last time at the beauty
Of the promised land from Mount Nebo.
We have chosen not captivity, but filiation
And for forty years in the lifeless desert
We plodded on to get here, fed by manna
Sent down by God Himself.
I am drawn to the cherished borders,
And to windmills, and towers, and gun-slots,
But I must, by God's judgment,
Remain here. Alien to the earthly paradise,
I am dying as a homeless vagrant,
But immortal I will enter this land!

"From Mount Nebo"
(*S gory Nevo*), 29.5.1972

While Pereleshin was proofreading *Sanctuary,* his heart was already "shifting to the eighth collection," with early titles such as *Gates* (*Vrata*), *Scattering of Nuggets* (*Rossyp'*), *Staff* (*Posokh*), *Repentance* (*Raskaianie*), and, in jest, *Ringing Copper* (*Med' zveniashchaia*) or *Evil Ringing* (*Zlye zvony*).[36] Eventually, he came up with *From Mount Nebo* (*S gory Nevo*) and changed the title of the poem "On the Threshold" (*Na poroge,* 29.5.1972) to "From Mount Nebo." The epigraph to the book explained: "Then the Lord spoke to Moses ... saying: 'Go up this mountain of the Abarim, Mount Nebo, which is in the land of Moab, across Jericho; view the land Canaan, which I give to the children of Israel as a possession. And die on the mountain which you ascend' (Deut. 32:49–50). 'Yet you shall see the land before you, though you shall not go there, into the land' (Deut. 32:52)." As Pereleshin saw it, "I was looking at my Promised Land from afar (from Brazil) and, like Moses, I will die beyond its borders and, like Moses, ascend into it an immortal." Home was "in the still very distant Russia that will come to replace the present system. In that Russia, we will perhaps be truly immortal (posthumously): thus, the thought of 'Mount Nebo.'"[37]

In May 1974, using the honorarium from the Festival of Poetry in Austin, he ordered from Possev-Verlag 500 regular copies of *From Mount Nebo* plus several unbound ones on light paper for letters to the USSR.[38] The order drained him: "Never in my life did I seek and love money. Now, however, I would have been very glad to have it: not for eating and drinking well, not for dressing well, not even for travelling, but for publishing all my collections and larger individual works."[39] As he had done with *Swing,* he concealed the order from Victor and Lidiia: "If they find out, I will not escape abuse," but when it was published, unexpectedly they liked it, and Lidiia bought the earlier collections and paid for *Li Sao* in advance.[40]

Initially, *From Mount Nebo* was to be a book of sonnets, all dated "so that one can judge the development of the sonnet technique."[41] When he showed the draft, subtitled "Sonnets about Russia," to his mother, she "revealed her genius" in advising him not to limit the book to sonnets, but to include other poems on this topic, such as "Three Homelands" (*Tri rodiny,* 27.9.1971). He agreed: "The sonnet is a dry academic form, and it is wrong to restrict a large theme to it." Now the theme, not the genre, influenced his choices. He "arranged poems in 'circles.' First, I establish the *nucleus* of a book, that is, what justifies the title and comprises the main theme. Then I move in circles from the centre to the periphery and include what is 'almost on the theme' and 'partially on the theme.'"[42] Thus, "in the beginning it shows why and how the first homeland has become unacceptable. Then the second and the third homelands are presented in a few strokes, in one or two poems. A certain synthesis is reached at the end: the first homeland does not exist, but its eternal culture and spiritual backbone emerge through the charms of China and Brazil."[43] He included "several mediocre poems, some for thematic considerations, others on Mum's insistence, in particular 'Carousel' (*Karusel'*, 7.4.1944),"[44] which spoke of homesickness and yearning for her "tender hands." The book was dedicated "To My Mother Evgeniia Aleksandrovna Sentianina."

The sixty undated poems in this, his largest book to date, were written, with the exception of "Carousel," in Brazil: one in 1957, one in 1969, five in 1970, eight in 1971, nineteen in 1972, nineteen in 1973, and two in 1974. Thirty-two were sonnets. Thematically, *From Mount Nebo* was "a certain concession to the 'spirit of the times'; it is my most political book. It is contemporary, but not a betrayal of my basic principles, because I am looking at Russia and at myself as if from afar, as if after many decades." For him, "the questions raised in the book are historical, not journalistic. The 'key' is, indeed, the theme of exile." His "Siding" (*Polustanok*, 1.7.1973) echoes a recurrent dream of "wandering as a tramp along the railway ties [...], which attracted me from childhood. Just to go on and on ... and get away to unknown destinations."[45]

The book begins with the same powerful sonnet which had closed *Sanctuary*, but its title "Russia" (*Rossiia*, ca. 1.4.1957) was changed to "USSR" (*SSSR*), because the feminine gender of "Russia" clashed with the masculine gender of epithets such as "usurer," "conquistador," "holy prophet," and "vile heretic." In the rewritten text condemnation and shame were sharpened, particularly in the last two stanzas:

"Russia" in *Sanctuary*	**"USSR" in *From Mount Nebo***
To love you? I will not lie to myself:	Lying to your enemies by habit,
I can no longer love you,	I can no longer lie to myself,
But, connected by mysterious fate	But, sharing with you the disgrace of being Russian,
To you, like to an illness or to a hump,	As a grandfather's illness, as a hump,
Tormented by shame, I, a Trojan myself,	Tormented by shame, I, a Trojan myself,
Would like to destroy this Troy.	Would like to destroy this Troy.

"Shame" (*Styd*, 21.1.1972) continued the theme: "And now, when you are threatening and proud, / I am crying from pain and shame," echoing Nabokov's "Russia," where no one would ever answer "for the torment, tears, and shame" experienced by many émigrés.

The book was "conceived around the pivot 'I and Russia,'" not "Russia and I," and included the other pivots of 'I and China' and 'I and Brazil.'"[46] "Exile" (*Izgoi*, 25.8.1973) asks Russia to remain the source of poetry, but says that "China is love, Brazil is freedom." In "The Hundredth" (*Sotyi*, 25.8.1973), Lake Baikal remained "a fragment of infancy," while the Great Wall of China "sheltered me from storms" and "green-golden" Brazil enticed him from China. "To My Translators" (*Moim perevodchikam*, 26.5.1972) speaks of his love for the Chinese language and its written characters, where "the sound is concealed, but thought revealed, / in places with sharpness, in places with winged wisdom." "Beijing" (*Pekin*, 3.7.1972), the most beautiful poem in the book (quoted as an epigraph to a section of chapter 4, above), is filled with poignant nostalgia for "the light in the window / that used to be yours." In this poem he weaves in a line in Chinese: "Night, spring. Warmth comes from the earth. / This street is *zhi ru fa*: / the poetic line / is singing naturally." "*Zhi ru fa*" is taken from Chu Guangxi's poem "On the Way to Luoyang" and reads, in Pereleshin's translation, "the big road is straight as a hair" (*zhi ru fa*), straight as Chinese hair.[47] In "Destiny" (*Zhrebii*, 24.1.1974), the poet calls himself "Brazil's adopted son," but in "Across the Globe" (*Po globusu*, 1.9.1972) Russia and Brazil merge into "the unknown island Roziliia-Brassiia," and "Return" (*Vozvrashchenie*, 8.11.1973) features Russian-Portuguese neologisms such as *prourubish'* and *prosabiash'*, created on the pattern of the Russian colloquial *provoronish* (to miss, let slip), the root *vorona* (crow) being replaced by *urubu* (Brazilian crow) and *sabia* (a singing bird).

In his review Ivask called Pereleshin "a metaphysical poet," "a master of strict, even the strictest sonnets," who "is not interested in the fashionable experiments of western poets, although he is no stranger to neologisms and paradoxical metaphors." Petr Balakshin, quoting at length from some poems, wrote that Pereleshin was taking a "worthy place in the Russian poetry abroad" with his "wonderful, multifaceted talent."[48]

From Mount Nebo forms a link between his two lives, Chinese and Brazilian. The 1970s were a crucial decade in Pereleshin's life and thus his poetry, for the two were inseparable. His new poems continued the development which started in his Chinese period: the formation of a transnational identity, which embraces and merges three homelands and three languages. Language is the key here. His magical mastery of the Russian language in his poetry and, incidentally, in his letters, is greatly enriched by his knowledge of Chinese and Portuguese; his wonderful and spontaneous embeddings of the two in his Russian poems conjure, like the tip of the iceberg, the depth of his creativity.

At the same time, in the 1970s, a new and crucial development was taking place through the yet unpublished *Poem without a Subject* and many new poems: he started speaking openly and defiantly of the torment over the irreconcilability of religious faith and freedom in human love.

10 The Left-hander

Love by Correspondence, 1971–1974

В отчаянной игре самообмана
Не защитят ни крепости, ни рвы,
И снова я зову тебя на "вы"
За семь морей, за гребни океана.
  На корабле Фернана Магеллана
  Проплыли Вы от пристани Москвы
  Атласами небесной синевы
  С белесыми разводами тумана.
Увенчанный поношенным венком,
Я в диалог вступлю с учеником
Доверчивым, любезным, долгожданным.
  И разговор по свету прогремит:
  Входите же, в одном лице желанном,
  Мой Менексен, мой Лисий, мой Хармид!
	In a desperate game of self-deception
	Neither fortresses, nor moats will protect,
	And again I call thee "you"
	Across seven seas, over crests of the ocean.
	  In Ferdinand Magellan's ship
	  You sailed from the docks of Moscow
	  Along the satins of blue heaven
	  With whitish patterns of fog.
	Crowned with a worn-out wreath,
	I will start a dialogue with a pupil,
	Trusting, amiable, long awaited.
	  And our conversation will thunder in this world:
	  Come in, combined in one desirable person,
	  My Menexenus, my Lysius, my Charmides!

"On Receiving the 'Ocean'"
(*Pri poluchenii "Okeana"*), 11.4.1972

Of several major loves in Pereleshin's life, one stands out as a romantic invention, which had little to do with the actual person involved.

In 1971, a young Muscovite, Evgenii (Zhenia) Vitkovskii, got Pereleshin's address from Lidiia Khaindrova and introduced himself as a reader and researcher of his poetry.[1] Pereleshin answered, and soon, "out of stupidity," Vitkovskii showed some translations and poems sent by Pereleshin to the newspaper *Voice of Homeland* (*Golos rodiny*) and the journal *Homeland* (*Rodina*), published for the so-called dear compatriots by the Committee for Cultural Relations with Compatriots Abroad. Although Pereleshin had "no intention whatsoever of exchanging the lean laurels of a poet abroad for the million-copy 'glory'" of Soviet poets and translators, he sent the committee his books and was even tempted to offer some unpublished works for a fee. Vitkovskii would then present him as poet Aleksandr Kaiurin, while Valerii Pereleshin would remain a Russian poet in Brazil; otherwise his publications in the USSR would deny him access to the émigré press. He strongly emphasized to Vitkovskii that already published works could not be used.[2]

Before long Pereleshin backed away from this precarious venture, but enjoyed Vitkovskii's flattering letters; as "Acrostic" (*Akrostikh*, 20.4.1971) says: "You are like a son, granted by the perfidious / fate on a distant shore. // Oh, I want to find in you a successor / who would serve the radiance of words, / as I do with all my strength." Vitkovskii, a translator from Dutch and a few other languages, sent his own poem "Ocean" (*Okean*), which Pereleshin considered to be influenced by Gumilev and "very good," albeit with many shortcomings. He responded with "On Receiving 'Ocean'" (*Pri poluchenii "Okeana,"* 11.4.1972), quoted in the epigraph to this section, and Vitkovskii started signing some of his letters "Your Menexenus-Lysius-Charmides."[3] Vitkovskii's sonnet "The Last String" (*Posledniaia struna*) expressed great admiration for Pereleshin, who was touched, but upset that Vitkovskii "immediately got scared: what if it appears in *The New Review* or *New Russian Word*. What a 'voice of true Russia' dished up with a political sauce!"[4]

Vitkovskii "set the tone by writing a sonnet about me, and from that time on, I have been writing to Zhenia, about Zhenia, or 'in the presence of Zhenia.'" Pereleshin fell in love with this "person not of flesh, but of spirit, and that's precisely why I 'have taken him on as my son,'" as "my twin brother in spirit; I've been waiting for such a brother all my life."[5] This love fitted the romantic vision of a young man, admirer, disciple, translator, poet, suffering in "a real snake pit. It is almost true that I am his only safety valve, but he might get into serious trouble because of this." He idolized this image: he "understands everything at once. He thanks me for the fact that I *exist*. [...] I have known for a long time that he is *my* pupil. [...] I've already prayed for a 'twin' in Shanghai, but I prayed to *God*. Had I prayed to Anti-God, it would have been clear why my desire has been fulfilled in such a paradoxically incomplete way: a whole chain of abysses separates us, and the worst one is the *age gap* [Eng.]. [...] I don't know if Russian literature has had a piquant page of the Verlaine-Rimbaud type; if not, now there will be Valerii Pereleshin – Evgenii Vitkovskii, but how much more *Victorian*! [Eng.]"[6]

He shared his joy with friends: "I have had many infatuations in my Methuselah life, but they all dragged me down. But this strange person (a poet, a translator of Rainer Maria Rilke and other poets, BUT married and has a son) became my main and inexhaustible source of 'inspiration.' I invented him, [...] I turned him into Ariel, into a being from another world. [...] My Zhenia, of course, is no Ganymede or Antinous, simply a fine young man," but "I love him like my son or even more, because he was chosen by me."[7] Pereleshin felt that "I have *recognized* him almost from his first letter, despite his marriage, parenthood, age (it turned out that he lied: he was not twenty-seven, but twenty-one!), and the unconquerable distance."[8] This "*onlie begetter*" was "a great miracle in my poetic destiny. He should have been angry, offended, and snarling. No such thing: everything is accepted as a ticket to immortality."[9] He started sending Vitkovskii all his poems and compiling an autobibliography for him: "I want *all* my poems to be hidden for some 50–75–100 years, but also copied and circulated, because my *home* is really not in Paris and not in New York, but there. You'll ask: 'Are you chasing immortality?' Why not try?"[10]

No longer a repressed teenager with "no *words*," Pereleshin openly spoke about his "invented love" for a man. During 1971–3 he produced a deluge of poems, mostly sonnets; his crown of sonnets, "Link" (*Zveno*, 18–20.9.1972), was "written with blood" "in one intake of breath in two days." The final line of the magistral, "the synthesis of the crown," came to him first and the rest of the crown stemmed from it: "And again I will shed a part of immortality."[11] As "By the Sea" (*U moria*, 20.9.1972) says: "Today by the morning I've finished the weaving of sonnets / and named the result simply 'Link': / am I not an unnoticeable link in the long chain, / a link passionately in love with a distant link?"

His new crown, "a synthesis of Christianity and Buddhism," speaks of "the inevitability of reincarnations and of gradual purification and refinement in order to return to an initial all-being at the end" for him and his beloved. Vitkovskii's name "grows through" the acrostic magistral, "unique in Russian poetry."[12] His pride knew no bounds: "I am afraid (precisely, afraid) that in a future competition for a Russian crown of sonnets I will have to award the first 'prize' for formal perfection ... to myself. I wrote the magistral with such calculation that any of its lines can begin and end a sonnet, and the caesura is observed rigorously."[13] But "I place 'Link' a step below 'The Way of the Cross': in the latter, the number 'fourteen' was organic and the correlation between the form and idea maximal, but in 'Link' the last line of each sonnet is transferred to the next sonnet, like karma, which is transferred from one reincarnation to another." Here, the structure was "justified by the idea of a cyclic nature, by repeated returns to earth to pay for immortality in instalments."[14]

He was concerned about Vitkovskii's reaction: "perhaps, it is *too much* [Eng.]," but Vitkovskii wrote: "You have immortalized me with it."[15] Iurii Ivask complemented him on "the first crown of sonnets that was not boring to read." Aleksis Rannit suggested "marinating" it, but Pereleshin disagreed: "I might, perhaps, want to rework it at some time, but it is necessary to move a considerable distance away from it. To do so requires many years, but I am almost sixty. It means that *there will be no time.*"[16]

In May 1973, when Lidiia was on a tourist trip to the USSR, she took a taxi and arrived at Vitkovskii's apartment unannounced. It was, as she described, "in one word, a horror": shabby and pitted walls, clothes on the floor, Vitkovskii's wife "just skin and bones" and trembling, and his son quite small for a four-year old. They all seemed to be "just children."[17] Vitkovskii took her to galleries and museums and sent with her gifts for Pereleshin, which included a coin from the Romanov Jubilee of 1913, the year of Pereleshin's birth, and a book of Camões's sonnets in translation, inscribed "Love you very much." Pereleshin stroked and kissed the book, and, "seized by emotional storm, wrote poems every day, sometimes two a day."[18] Lidiia learned that Vitkovskii was not permitted to travel abroad, because, as an epileptic, he had not served in the army. Much as Pereleshin dreamed of Vitkovskii leaving the USSR, he realized that life abroad would be hard and their meeting most likely disappointing.[19]

By September 1973, Vitkovskii's letters were reduced to a trickle. As Pereleshin noted in "A Pain-meter" (*Bolemer*, 18.10.1973) – the title being one of his neologisms – "You are not alone. You have a wife and children: / so remain a source of warmth for them. / My sorrow has almost gone; / like my life, two-thirds of it have decayed." He decided "to let Zhenia go" until the next reincarnation, and this "mystical experience" was "a terrible struggle, a desperate resistance, but the theme of Sacrifice won."[20] When he wrote to Lidiia Khaindrova about it, he got a panicky letter from Vitkovskii, who claimed that, not having heard from Pereleshin, he was "driven into a 'stupor.'" Pereleshin was "overwhelmed with happiness": "Let there be letters. Let there be many letters." Vitkovskii mentioned that three years ago he had decided that, if he was to have a second son, he would be named Valerii, and

Pereleshin understood it as "he has loved me from my first letters" and responded with "To Valerii the Second" (*Valeriiu Vtoromu*, 25.3.1974).[21] Pereleshin's mother did not trust Vitkovskii's devotion, but for Pereleshin his letters "could not be anything but a declaration of love. After all, there is no *purpose*: there can't be any calculation." His love flared up: "I love Zhenia madly, wildly, to delirium. *This* is as strong as life and stronger than death. But I saw our relations only from my side. Today I saw it from his side. And I am choking with happiness."[22] His feelings acquired mystical significance: "A semi-crazy person or the Buddhist in me says that this is a karmic kinship: some time ago we were Siamese twins, and now we wish to be joined in the same way." In lucid moments he was aware that "I have always wanted to invent, to create in my imagination a wonderful image without a single tiny blemish, and I had briefly managed it before. Only now did I succeed in doing it for three years, to the very depth, to the final, darkest bottom."[23]

By mid-1974 the letters had stopped, and he wondered whether Vitkovskii was forbidden to write to "traitors to the homeland" or was "overpowered by it all. I even suspect a certain split in his soul: my 'worship' (if it is worship) flatters him, but there is the conservatism of fate, of daily life (even sex), which bristles against it." He felt "a bitter aftertaste from the 'golden triennial.'" The silence was sobering: "What kind of relations could I have had with a phantom?"[24]

"Betrayal," 1974

Схвати ее в охапку посильней
Наперекор наигранной боязни
И обнажи, и вытяни, и в ней

Всей алчностью, всем бешенством увязни.
Сожми ее, любя и не любя,
Обворожи искусным приворотом,
Чтоб ей отдать и самого себя
Дрожаньем ног и семенем, и потом.

Ты думаешь, блудник и сердцеед,
Мой оскорбить монашеский обычай
Паденьем в грязь и мнимостью побед?

А я и сам, обжорой и добычей,
Живу тобой – и кролик, и удав –
Всего тебя впитав и напитав!

Grab her harder in your hands
Ignoring a feigned fear,
And strip her naked, and stretch, and get stuck
In her with all the greed, all the fury.
Squeeze her, loving and not loving,
Charm her with a skilful bewitching,
In order to give yourself to her
With trembling legs, and sperm, and sweat.
A lecher and heart-throb, do you want
To insult my monastic custom
By falling into filth and by imaginary victories?
But I myself, a glutton and a prey,
Live off you – both rabbit and boa –
Absorbing you and getting you sated!

"Lechers" (*Bludniki*), 17.4.1975

In November 1974 Vitkovskii's mother asked Khaindrova to let Pereleshin know that Vitkovskii had left his family for "a new 'chocolate bon-bon.'" This "betrayal" deeply upset and disgusted Pereleshin: "a disciple with a divine calling could neither marry nor get divorced. It does not matter what happened before. I saw in Zhenia's new marriage a betrayal of his vocation," "a vile act" by "a base philanderer."[25] In crude folk ditties (*chastushki*) and "angry poems" he "'belched out' the pseudo-Ariel theme (I no longer have an heir and follower of my cause!)."[26]

Khaindrova reasoned that Vitkovskii had "a right to personal happiness," but for Pereleshin he stopped being "the Ariel whom I created and lived with for exactly three years." The end felt like "an amputation and great devastation," and he sometimes spoke of "the late E.V. Vitkovskii": "I was wrong about 'the Siamese twins' and invented all the rest," though "for a poet an invention is more tangible than reality." With this "betrayal," "a large period of my life with its circle of themes came to an end, and a new circle has not appeared since."[27]

Heartbroken, he searched for "a replacement among Brazilian youths," for "shards of the disintegrating image of Ariel. One has beautiful fingers, another – lips, the third – eyes, the fourth – smile, and the fifth – voice. I have not succeeded in 'integrating' anything, and the multitude of little wedges does not knock out the big wedge."[28] His "Wedge" (*Klin*, 3.8.1975) used the Russian saying "to knock out one wedge with another," that is, to fight fire with fire. In "To a Bare Acquaintance" (*Edva znakomomu*, 28.10.1974) the poet confesses: "your hair is dark, no match for my grey, / but I want to use us to fight fire with fire: / taking a living stranger to get rid of one dear and no longer living."

In April 1973, even before the "betrayal," he befriended Antônio A., "slim, with shoulder-length hair, rimless glasses, no sign of beard or moustache," "very sweet and totally asexual," "from a very cultured family, clever, bright, and full of goodwill."[29] Antônio helped him to translate Russian poems for a trilingual (Russian, Portuguese, English) anthology "Portugal and Brazil in Russian Poetry," planned, but not published by Ivask. Afterwards, they talked into the early hours: "this Ariel is on the same level as the Muscovite. Spirit communicates with spirit, and the rest does not matter. It is a victory over time: a twenty-year-old enjoys glimpses into metaphysical worlds with a sixty-year old (in a month)." "Brazilian Ariel" (*Brazil'skii Ariel'*, 30.5.1973), dedicated to Antônio, says that "the Brazilian Ariel, sharing / a magic pipe with me, brings / words of heaven to a Caliban pigsty." In the sonnet "In

Brazil" (*V Brazilii*, 30.5.1973), the poet imagines an encounter of his Brazilian and Moscow Ariels: "one is dark-haired with a pale face, / with flashes of lightning behind the eyelashes, / with speech sounding like the call of an *arapong* bird. // The other reproaches us both / for vague nasal diphthongs / and talks plainly in Russian." "Unconquered" (*Nepobezhdennyi*, 17.6.1973) speaks of "the two Ariels and the third one (myself)." When Pereleshin confessed his feelings, Antônio thanked him, but said that he wanted children, though he would have preferred to have them without a woman.[30]

From the second half of the 1970s until the late 1980s, Pereleshin had many passionate infatuations and brief affairs. No longer game to pick up young men at night, he pursued local kiosk or shop assistants, butchers, bakers, cleaners, models in an art school, bus conductors, caretakers, and so on, who were in their late teenage years or early twenties: "I am even glad that I fall in love easily and often. I do not gain 'victories,' there are no 'conquests,' but emotions and thoughts stop only between infatuations."[31] He usually had to pay them, but he was always interested in their lives, tried to befriend and help them, and hoped for some permanency. One young man seemed to be "a reincarnation of Alcibiades, who imposed himself on Socrates to gain wisdom. My Alcibiades asks hundreds of questions and remembers the answers. […] Almost immediately, I became pregnant by him with poems (and not only sonnets)." When he borrowed Cr50 and disappeared, Pereleshin was left so broke that could not even travel to church "to get rid of the scum after this episode," and yet "I got incomparably more from him. I forgive him."[32] Another brief affair produced "A Stream to Narcissus" (*Ruchei – Nartsisu*, 31.10.1975) and "Androgen" (*Androgin*, 4.11.1975), and "thus his existence on 'the little poor earth' is justified (no, but what impudence!)."[33] He amused himself by counting how many sonnets were inspired by each infatuation and "rejoiced in the ability to fall in love at first sight and not despair when it is not a winning ticket. […] It's no joke that I have to imagine entire worlds not to suffocate in emptiness."[34]

Ariel: The Ninth Book of Poetry, 1976

Tutti poeti sono pederasti:	*Tutti poeti sono pederasti*:
Еще валеты юношеской масти,	Still knaves of diamonds, the suit of youth,
Бубновые – и не в числе мужчин,	And not considered men,
Не разумея подлинных причин,	Not understanding the real reasons,

Неблагонравной предаются страсти.	They engage in a disreputable passion.
Они с годами женятся, но сласти	With time they marry, but until old age
Припрятывают ловко до седин	Cleverly hide their pleasures
От зорких глаз дражайших половин	From the vigilant eyes of their precious halves
Tutti poeti.	*Tutti poeti.*
Есть утешенье и в такой напасти.	There is consolation even in such misfortune.
И пусть разъяты их сердца на части,	Although their hearts are split in parts,
Дух эллинский животворит один	The Hellenic spirit alone gives life
Рондо, сонеты, музыку секстин,	To rondeaus, sonnets, music of sestinas,
И благодарны мы нездешней власти,	And we are grateful to unearthly powers,
Tutti poeti.	*Tutti poeti.*

"Poets" (*Poety*), 30.1.1976

In 1973 he began working on two books, the second one of crucial importance in his life: "while Hercules chops off one head of a hydra (*Sanctuary*), it grows two new ones (*From Mount Nebo* and *Ariel*)." *Ariel*, though a "sweetish" title, felt right: it was "a symbol of airiness, spirituality, and heavenly exclusion from the earth's gravity, weight, daily life, and routine. Ariel is also a human being, who, like all human beings, does not escape the power of the flesh."[35] The book was to present "a situation which would have been simply indecent, but for the imaginary nature of the entire 'adventure.'" Its theme was close "to the sonnets of Shakespeare (in our time, when, after all, 'everything is permitted' and there are no forbidden topics, just as there are no forbidden actions) and to Fernando Pessoa."[36]

Vitkovskii's "betrayal" temporarily stopped this work: "I will not forgive him for murdering my book. It now seems incredibly false. And yet, from afar, I see in it such integrity, such 'single breath,' that I will perhaps leave it untouched, at least for a posthumous publication."[37] More sonnets were written "to tear the poetic image of Ariel away from the Calibanic Muscovite. I am parting ways with swinish behaviour. I hope that I will soon forget this entire adventure: it was, after all, invented from the beginning to the end."[38] In January 1975 "the history of 'the affair with the phantom' gradually moved off centre, and the book became more complex with other themes." He was fully aware that it was "the most significant book of all that I have created in my life": its sonnets openly spoke of gay love. *Poem without a Subject*, completed in 1976, was equally candid about being gay: "both stand for the right to *reject* the world."[39]

To test the waters, he sent the draft to several friends. Petr Lapiken, who "has fallen in love with my sonnets, analyses them, savours them, and revels in them," responded with helpful comments and queries. Ivask "expressed his delight with the unusualness of the 'situation,' […] unique not only in Russian poetry, but in the entire world literature." The poet Nora Krouk, "the dearest, great, clever person, and an all-understanding soul, […] warmed my heart" with her appreciation.[40]

Iustina Kruzenshtern, on the other hand, issued "something like an ultimatum": she and her friends, "out of disgust," would not be reading or selling it. His reply to her, "ouch! such an angry letter," was that "there is no 'sickness' in *Ariel* themes. […] I am not judging people on the basis of *my* preferences, but I am being judged on the basis of *their* prejudices, and you are not lagging behind. […] People cannot imagine that the highest may coexist with the lowest under the same roof. Consequently, they have not understood anything in me; after all, *Swing* symbolizes precisely this duality."[41]

At the end of October 1975, haunted by a line from "Link" on fading "into oblivion, into grey-haired indifference," he "woke up with a firm decision to rework 'Link,' initially valid, but now inadequately worked through. […] I made a start and then immediately continued with the final selection of sonnets for *Ariel*."[42] He dreaded "an explosion of public indignation," but Ivask reasoned that homophobes "would read to page ten, see dangerous inclinations, and stop reading," and he wrote an introduction, in which he presented Pereleshin as "one of the most prominent contemporary Russian poets, not only in Russia Abroad, but also in Russia." *Ariel* was his "highest achievement": "It seems that no one in poetry has ever loved phantoms so hopelessly, so blissfully […]. There is madness in Pereleshin's 'love by mail,' but also brightness, power, tension, which are often absent in ordinary 'loves.'" The lower reaches of his eroticism are "dark," and Ariel becomes "a terrifying zoological hybrid or homunculus, but the upper levels strive for nirvana, soar with tenderness, and sing praise to Ariel as worthy of love."[43]

Finally, on 3 December 1975, after "a Gethsemane night," Pereleshin mailed the typescript to the publishers "without the usual enthusiasm and elation; I feel more like 'being sentenced to an execution.'" It seemed akin to "a suicide in progress," though he added, with gallows humour, that "it would be funnier this way." The book left him heavily in debt, but "I do not hesitate at the moment of choosing: I always choose to publish."[44] On receiving the proofs, he "read the sonnets, as if they were written by someone else, and once again they deeply touched me. The point is not in the main theme, but in lateral moves: in resourcefulness, inventiveness, in a word, in *art*." His mother "demanded" that "Wizard" (*Koldun*, 22.12.1974) and "Again to Vadim" (*Opiat' Vadimu*, 5.11.1974) be removed as "malicious and poisonous." "Again to Vadim" tells Vitkovskii's son "to grow up. And to find the father, / to expose the lecherous he-male, / to appear before him, as a new Hiawatha, // and with the truth fight and defeat / the one, who pushed you at one time / into the stream of spittle, sperm, and snot!" Pereleshin refused, but his mother "created a huge storm" and after arguing all night he replaced them.[45]

Pereleshin saw "an incredible coincidence" in the fact that the 153 sonnets he selected for *Ariel* approached Shakespeare's 154: "one should, out of modesty, yield one to Shakespeare," not "my competitor, but my predecessor, whom I admire more than Pushkin did Derzhavin." The number 153 was that of the "*chosen ones*," "perhaps poets, perhaps priests, perhaps 'failures,' who would not give up the primogeniture of spiritual freedom for the mess of potage of external success and prosperity."[46] In "Catchers" (*Lovtsy*, 1.10.1969) fishermen exclaim: "So much fish! Is it not a hundred, / plus half a hundred, plus three?" and in "Catch" (*Ulov*, 6.2.1973) "the male brotherhood" of Gennesaret is guided by the Lord to catch "the silver wealth: / one hundred and fifty-three huge fish."

Ariel was "a lyrical diary written around one theme: 'a passionate love for a phantom.' That's why all the sonnets are fully dated,"[47] from 20 April 1971 to 2 October 1975, tracing the infatuation, acceptance of the beloved's wife and son, jealousy, invented nature of his painful love, dreams of its physical expression, existence of other Ariels, and anger and bitterness over the "betrayal." Ariel is "an invented image, necessary to awaken forces hidden for almost a quarter of a century."[48] "Undefeated" (*Nepobezhdennyi*, 17.6.1973) warns: "Do not be proud: I too am an Ariel!"

The opening "Acrostic" (*Akrostikh*, 20.4.1971) and the magistral of the crown spell "Zhenia Vitkovskii," while another "Acrostic" (*Akrostikh*, 6.3.1975) spells "Ariel or a skirt-chaser" (*Ariel' ili babnik*). He refused Khaindrova's appeal to remove acrostic poems: "must I consider Vitkovskii's career? He can, after all, prove to anyone who is entitled to know that I have not been in Moscow and he has not been in Brazil." If Vitkovskii "out of self-love and cowardice" were to ask personally, Pereleshin would do so "*out of disgust*."[49]

The "monologic dialogue"[50] in the sonnets plays out, in a rather theatricalized way, an imagined love affair between the poet-speaker and the beloved addressee, his "pupil," "brother," "Siamese twin," "son, granted by fate," "successor," "the chosen one," his Menexenus, Lysius, Charmides, Antinous, Ganymede, Alcibiades, Willy Hughes, Bosie. "Confession" (*Priznanie*, 27.9.1972) speaks of Narcissus and Ganymede depicted on vases with "beautiful" inscriptions and ends with: "I like to conceal among the sad iambs / the confession: EUGENES – O EPHEBOS KALOS." The poet and his beloved are opposites: old and young, teacher and disciple, father and son, Socrates and a Greek youth. In the two-sonnet cycle, "Day and Night" (*Den' i noch'*, 20.8.1972), Ariel is "the day," "ardent, enthusiastic," no stranger to boxing, beer taverns, or literary trends, while the poet is "the night," who "has filled the innumerable years / with vigilant quietness" and poems.

Sonnets such as "Phantoms" (*Prizraki*, 17.12.1974), "Death of Invention" (*Smert' vymysla*, 22.12.1974), and "Creator" (*Tvorets*, 14.1.1975) dissect the treacherous image; in the latter "the eyes, and hair, and hands / are transformed into rhymed sounds: / the disjointed, dismembered flesh / swells and strives towards heaven. / But have I, your loving Lord, / promised you a different immortality?" "Fidelity in Infidelity" (*Vernost' v nevernosti*, 26.6.1975) says: "It is not the mortuary, but the brain. And in my brain / you are hacked into composite parts, / where I can barely recognize / my invention, the child of my own passion." The poet's love swings from "the purest adoration to plunges into the darkness of the subconscious [...]. This love was of paradise and of hell. I was dispersing Zhenia to cities and to the world as a communion, but at the same time in my thoughts I submitted myself to sadistic and masochistic actions with him." He agreed with Ivask: "You have brilliantly defined my 'Evgeniad' as something ominous."[51]

There were no reviews by established poets and critics of the émigré press, as if they feared even an indirect association with the book, though some complimented him in letters. Nikolai Morshen found it "the most successful collection *poetically*" and "your highest achievement," Anatolii Velichkovskii admired his poetic mastery, and Igor Chinnov sent "a very tender letter."[52] Ivask as the author of the introduction could not review it. When asked, V.F. Markov, a specialist on Kuzmin, wrote that he found it "difficult" to write about living authors; the poet Ivan Elagin declined; the critic Vladimir Veidle praised this "most mature" book, but refused, because it "did not nourish him poetically."[53] Gleb Struve found *Ariel* too repulsive to take in in one reading. Pereleshin retorted: "as a literary scholar you should not engage in 'moralizing' (?) and advocating copybook 'truths,' but be able to separate wheat from weeds, and poetry from biography. Do you impose the same taboo on most of Kuzmin's poems, on two-thirds of Shakespeare's, on Riurik Ivnev's, on Georgii Adamovich's?" [54] He turned to Lapiken: "you will find the right tone and tolerance towards 'deviations.' You are almost a co-author: all sonnets (except the latest) were 'cleaned up' after your comments." Lapiken held a small private reading in San Francisco and sold three copies, but found the book "insufficiently worked through" and declined.[55] *Russian Language Journal* eventually published an odd review, which said that *Ariel* depicted a desperate affair of the lyrical hero with Russian literature as represented by Evgenii.[56]

Pereleshin, as O.S., reviewed *Ariel* for the São Paulo bulletin *To Friends and Acquaintances* (*Druz'iam i znakomym*), not mentioning the content, but focusing on "creative evolution," on moving "against the trend which marked the twentieth century and might be defined as a decay of form, deterioration of requirements for rhyme, and emergence of 'free,' 'accentual,' or 'purely tonic' poems. The poet's preference is for the sonnet, because it is intended for exploring philosophical questions on a dialectic scheme: thesis – antithesis – synthesis (or acknowledgment that a synthesis is unattainable)."[57]

An excellent review appeared in the English-language journal *Christopher Street* in December 1977. Professor Simon Karlinsky judged *Ariel* to be "a masterpiece," "a major event in contemporary Russian poetry and a breakthrough that is significant for the whole of Western culture," and "its author's finest achievement, crowning a remarkable *oeuvre* that spans four decades." He pointed out: "Pereleshin's poetry before *Ariel* spoke of his love life only in cryptic and ambiguous terms," while *Ariel* was "a full-fledged literary coming out,"

> a narrative sequence of 168 sonnets [counting those in the crown of sonnets, "Link"], which is also the poet's personal diary for a three-year period, a story of one man's love for another told in a sort of epistolary novel in verse, and, finally, a survey of celebrated instances of older men loving younger ones in the Western literary tradition. [...] On one level, then, *Ariel* is an account of the day-to-day lives of two Russian men of two different generations, one of whom lives in Moscow and the other in Rio de Janeiro and who have only their mutual need and a shared literary culture in common. But on another level it is a rich and absorbing philosophical treatise on the nature of love, a study of the ways in which

> love can develop and thrive without the lovers ever experiencing each other's physical presence.

Karlinsky described Pereleshin as "a virtuoso of traditional Russian poetic techniques" and pointed out that "his neoclassical conservative form is a vehicle for an acutely modern sensibility." *Ariel*'s "stylistic and verbal richness and the precision of his language is likely to defeat the best efforts of translators for some time to come." The book, he pointed out, was not reviewed in Russian émigré journals, and Russian bookstores "refused to handle *Ariel*." Russian homophobia "might well cost Valery Pereleshin a loss of a considerable segment of the small following he has so labouriously acquired." Karlinsky supplemented the review with his translations of "Without a Mask" (*Bez maski*, 14.11.1972), "Not for Publication" (*Ne dlia pechati*, 10.9.1973), and "Confession of Love" (*Priznanie v liubvi*, 6.11.1974), and provided Pereleshin's address for those who wanted to buy the book.[58]

Pereleshin started working on his next book, originally entitled *At the Roots of Existence* (*U kornei bytiia*) but changed, on Ivask's suggestion, to *In the Groin of Existence* (*V pakhu bytiia*). It was "to contain everything connected with the 'forbidden' attractions (from about 1934). The poems will be dated (by year). There is no 'growth' here, but changes: probably, a development towards greater shamelessness. Oh well, that's also 'a development'! The 'forbidden nature' of this collection is religious as well. In this sense, it will be 'anti-*Swing*': 'No matter how I argued with you, God ...'"[59] On second thought, Ivask felt that such a title might be unprintable in the Russian press, but for Pereleshin it "sums up the content more precisely than any other. [...] *Ariel* is a lyrical diary of three years; *In the Groin of Existence* is the tragedy of an entire life."[60] He wrote to the appalled Kruzenshtern: "it is difficult to say to what extent the title *In the Groin of Existence* is 'unprintable.' Mum, a principled procreator, feels that it expresses quite precisely the thought of *suppression* and lack of freedom. By someone's whim (whether God's or that of fate) I am kept down precisely in the groin of existence: chained to the question of sex."[61]

By May 1976, *In the Groin of Existence* was compiled, but it kept growing with poems which presented "*not* biography and *not* 'truth,' but a most complex interaction of thoughts and impulses, pluses and minuses, striving for purity and diving into the very cauldron of filth." The book with "the pornographic title," as Kruzenshtern branded it, was not published: "I will never have the money to pay for a 250-page book."[62]

The Left-hander

Воистину, напором полнокровным Духовная прекрасна левшизна, Хоть каторгой карается она Почти по всем законам уголовным. Да только ли? По прописям церковным К безбожию она приравнена За то, что те глотает семена, Что пахарем запасены верховным. Быть батраком земным я не хочу И к шустрому не бегаю врачу, Чтоб излечить проказу головную, А в судный день налево от Христа Усадят нас, а ниже – одесную Правши займут дешевые места.	Verily, by its full-blooded pressure The spiritual left-handedness is beautiful, Although it is punished by hard labour In almost all criminal laws. And is that all? By church interdictions It is equal to godlessness For swallowing the seeds Stocked by the supreme tiller. I do not want to be an earthly labourer And do not run to a hasty doctor To be cured of a mental leprosy. But on the Day of Judgment we will be seated To the left of Christ, and below, to the right, Right-handers will take the cheap seats.

"On Left-handedness"
(*O levshizne*), 23.12.1977

Ariel and the typescript of *Poem without a Subject* "horrified" most of his Russian friends and acquaintances.[63] Many had suspected that he was gay, but had ignored it as long as it was not expressed openly, and now would not buy and distribute *Ariel* as they did his other books. Some did not even acknowledge a gift copy and did not send the customary Christmas card, as his mother "recalled many times with some bitterness and blamed *Ariel*." Kruzenshtern called it "a mixture of Sodom and Black Mass," and he sadly replied: "To read poems *as poems*, regardless of the correctness or delusions of a poet, is also a gift from God. It is not granted to everyone."[64]

It took Pereleshin a long time to reject the instilled and internalized socio-religious judgment of homosexuality as a sin. The first step in this liberation was to regard it as an inborn defect, a flaw. "Pain" (*Bol'*, 28.2.1934) speaks of "a physical ailment," "Another Way" (*Inoi put'*, 7.2.1943) of "a powerless cripple," and "Silence" (*Molchan'e*, 8.7.1949) of "forever exiled" hunchbacks, deaf mutes, and blind people. "Fate" (*Sud'ba*, 7.5.1978), an epigraph in chapter 2, above, plainly says: "from childhood my fate has been fractured, / and with this crack where am I to go?" By the 1970s he had formulated the definition of gay people as "spiritual left-handers," "no less guilty of their 'anomaly' than physical left-handers, colour-blind persons, or hunchbacks." It "emphasizes the fact of not choosing, but of being destined" and expresses "the essence better than all kinds of pejorative terms like the English *queer* and *gay*." He "would not have objected to *homosexual* if it was equivalent to *heterosexual* [Eng.]."[65]

His early "Two Hands" (*Dve ruki*, 24.8.1937) describes his left hand as "an enemy, which stealthily takes vengeance," and in "Mal invicible" (15.3.1940) the hand, cut off as demanded by God, goes for his throat with a dagger. In "Left-hander" (*Levsha*, 11.11.1970) left-handers face difficulties in "learning the complex science / of love from both sides. [...] // Was King David, a hero and genius, / that kind of left-hander?" Another "Left-hander" (*Levsha*, 16.10.1975) concludes: "the way of the world is convenient in the right-handed way, / but I have stayed with my left-handedness!" In "Despair" (*Otchaianie*, 10.1.1980) the poet exclaims: "My Lord! I am created different, / homunculus, left-handed, differently minded, / the verdict for whom has been prejudged for all time."

Left-handed poets have "a different vision of the world. They have freedom from fascist haircuts all in one style, from philistinism, from standard thinking. At one time, my brother called my book *Ariel* pornographic. Alas, he does not know that real pornography is petty journals and petty books, produced not for the minority, but for the *majority* of consumers." The view that gay love is "'dirt,' 'debauchery,' and 'infamy' is less than a step to 'Heil Hitler.'"[66] Marina Tsvetaeva's "Blade" (*Klinok*) said it all: "There are islands, / islands for all kinds of love," although "jeers and condemnation of the majority will remain for a long time. One can ignore them, because it is compensated by the sense of one's 'distinctiveness' and of one's right to make an independent agreement with God without any glance at 'norms.'"[67]

When his dear "mascot," Kruzenshtern, angrily wrote that gay people were "tolerated so far," he asked: "Who precisely does not 'tolerate' us? *You* will not tolerate. [...] We were not asked whether we wanted to be the carriers of an anomaly. If one does not accept the hypothesis of karma, then the guilt in forcing a hump on a hunchback, left-handedness on a left-hander, and colour-blindness on a colour-blind person should be placed on God. None of us want it. We clutch at any straw, so as not to say to God: 'You are the one who made me like this!' But it is impossible *to infect* anyone with an anomaly. Try to infect someone with a physical left-handedness or colour-blindness!"[68] When she advised him to keep his "predilections" private, he answered: "Under the blows of the Judeo-Christian 'morality,' Plato's ideal of loving a young man has become something 'unspoken.' But people *speak*. That same Shakespeare spoke about it with greatness in his sonnets; in Russia, Mikhail Kuzmin spoke brilliantly. Now it is my turn to speak, and the advantage is that at the end of the twentieth century there is no need to hide in the shadows and camouflage it as 'an accidental deviation from the norm.'"[69] As he wrote to her, "you allow the possibility of poetry only when it coincides with the preferences of the overwhelming majority [...] Actually, poetry can be present in the most forbidden and most paradoxical works and be absent from the most well intentioned ones. Statistically, 'left-handers' are more magnanimously gifted (Rozanov wrote well about this in *People of the Lunar Light* (*Liudi lunnogo sveta*): he openly said that 'left-handers' created *the entire culture*)."[70] In vain did he try to point out to her that "out of the five Russian poets abroad, most often published in journals, three are 'left-handers.'" Adamovich "was proud of his left-handedness, less in poems, but constantly in life," and Chinnov was gradually becoming open.[71]

Desperately trying to save his friendship with Kruzenshtern, he even resorted to her term *chukhontsy*, a derogative reference to Finns in old St Petersburg: "Some scholars suggest that this *chukhonstvo* is formed in early childhood, particularly in families where fathers treat children coldly. An unloved boy then guesses that he would have been dearer to his father if he were a girl. To confirm this theory, I confess that in the first years of life I talked about myself in the feminine gender. Other scholars suggest that *chukhonstvo* comes at birth."[72] Her hints that former Harbin and Shanghai Russians who had sent him money were upset by *Ariel* led to the response: "In future let the people who want to help be the ones who see and appreciate only the poetic gift in me and accept me as a literary phenomenon, on my conditions, not on theirs."[73]

In self-defence, he started to call homophobes "rabid he-males and she-females" (*beshenye samtsy i samki*), that is, reproductive animals: "a procreator is given one life and one soul, while a genius has several souls and several lives (remember splendid Oscar: 'For he who lives more lives than one, / more deaths than one must die')."[74] This attitude tied in well with his life-long anti-natalism. In "Immortality" (*Bessmertie*, 25.12.1972), the lot of a "he-male" (*samets*) is to produce children and live through them, while "Lermontov, and Marlowe, and Verlaine / are saved from virgins and matchmakers / by fate and God's mercy" and defiantly remain "rebels, castrates, not fully unfrocked priests." Enlightening his friends was a losing battle, and he burst out in frustration to another homophobic friend: "Rabid he-males and she-females are looking for poems fitting their specificity, and my answer is: 'No way, you shan't fucking have it! Read the poems which fit not your specificity, but *mine*, and try to deny that it is *poetry*!'"[75]

His distressed mother "had a row with me about the 'dirt' of my 'left-handedness.' Adventures of skirt-chasers like Casanova seem to her examples of 'pure' life! Poets who drool and lust after every 'she-female' are justified because 'this is natural.' To sum up, there is no peace for my soul." Only in the last year of her life did she say that, on rereading *Ariel*, she "repented her 'rejection' of that book." His brother, however, remained adamant that gay people "should be destroyed or castrated."[76]

In 1976, the year *Ariel* was published, homophobia was vented in *New Russian Word* after it published Pereleshin's summary of Karlinsky's review of Gordon McVay's *Isadora and Esenin* in the *New York Times Book Review*. Karlinsky, in reference to what the book called Esenin's "latent bisexuality," stated that there was nothing "latent" about Esenin's feelings.[77] Journalist Vladimir Rudinskii declared that Esenin was "a truly Russian, truly national poet" and that "no matter how you look at sexual perversions, with revulsion or condescension, one should not vainly ascribe them to living people, let alone the defenceless dead. [...] Discrediting Esenin is profitable only to those in the west who substitute enmity to Bolshevism with enmity and contempt for Russia and Russians. We, Russian émigrés, must firmly stand on guard of our national literature."[78] When Karlinsky responded that Rudinskii had not read the book or the original review, Rudinskii, having by now done so, defended Esenin as a "clean" Russian heterosexual. Russians customarily kiss, hug, and use terms of endearment, but in the west "sexual obsessions are increasing with the disintegration of religious and moral standards." He did not mince words: "the sin of Sodom was strongly developed in England."[79]

Rudinskii was joined by another homophobe, A. Sergeev (S. Rafal'skii), who protested against attributions of "unnatural sin," "unnatural love," and "sexual perversions" to Esenin: in Russia "the moral level of intelligentsia was always high, and eroticism in literature did not go beyond the set limits," and people "reacted to 'this type of love' with disgust." Sergeev added: "I have an impression that in the west several (or a group of) writers, literary scholars, and historians, for sensation, under the influence of a sick imagination, or for other reasons, or perhaps simply out of 'the love of art,' are trying to ascribe homosexuality or bisexuality (on the basis of shaky suppositions and their own conjectures) to the majority of great and prominent people." In the USSR homosexuals faced five years in prison: "I therefore propose 'to dismiss the case of Esenin S.A., accused according to the article 121 of the Criminal Code, due to the failure of proving the charge.'"[80] Karlinsky then noted Sergeev's "approving mention" of Stalin's Criminal Codex, and asked whether Hitler's laws, by which homosexuals were gassed in camps, indicated the even higher morals of German society of that time.[81]

Pereleshin was incensed by Rudinskii's claim that "genius and homosexuality very rarely appear together in one person." On the contrary, "history testifies that the directly opposite statement is closer to the truth": the percentage of highly gifted people is much higher among homosexuals. Rudinskii "unreservedly said about Arthur Rimbaud: such a *scoundrel* cannot be a good poet! But can another scoundrel, who pursues twelve-year-old girls, likely be a good journalist, critic, and whatever else?"[82]

Some comments in his letters show that he was aware of the gay liberation movement in the United States and of the anti-gay activist Anita Bryant, but his was a lonely anguish and a courageous quest for inner liberation. Even after *Ariel* came out, the struggle against instilled religious precepts is evident in some of his letters which spoke of the duality in his soul. It took time to get rid of the vestiges of shame and pain expressed in "branded by my mutilation" in "Statue" (*Statuia*, 18.12.1972), "plunged down and destroyed" in "Predestination" (*Predopredelenie*, 13.4.1973), "what is the use of a hunchback, left-hander, and albino" in "Autumn" (*Osen'*, 6.3.1977), "narrow-shouldered mongrel" in "From Outside" (*So storony*, 9.6.1977), "left-hander, depraved outcast" in "To Hope" (*Nadezhde*, 17.8.1977), or "semi-involuntary sin" in "More on Fate" (*Eshche o sud'be*,13.11.1979).

In 1980, his review of Sofia Parnok's poetry started with a discussion on the "spiritual left-handedness" of male and female poets, outlining his independently developed view of what would become the queer theory in the 1990s. There was no "norm," "no golden mean," he wrote, but a wide variety of physiques, abilities, predilections, and "anomalies." He cited the names of many Russian gay poets and wrote that "if male poets (Russian, because in the west a greater tolerance has been established for a long time) have to pay during their lives and posthumously for 'spiritual left-handedness,' [...] the position of women who, by a whim of fate, feel indifferent to men and seek happiness in closeness with people of the same sex, is much more difficult." Sophia Parnok was "the only major woman poet in Russia with homoeroticism as the main theme [...]." When Struve commented that he should have written about her poetry and not "the 'peculiarity of her taste,'" Pereleshin asked why scholars compile "Don Juan's list of Pushkin's conquests" instead of analysing his poems.[83]

A few years before his death he reflected: "There was a time when I was almost ashamed of my 'left-handedness,' but then I came to see it not as a defect, but as an advantage: another angle of vision, a lot of free time, orientation towards metaphysics: phantoms and shadows instead of flesh." It was "my innermost core [...]. It comes from genetic depths, from fundamental principles."[84] This new vision came out in his poetry, where, as Karlinsky noted in his review, his neoclassical poetry was combined with an "acutely modern sensibility."

Epilogue to the Affair with the Phantom, 1977–1980

Столетия – игрушки наших муз;	The centuries are toys of our muses;
Бессмертные, друг другом мы воспеты.	Immortal, we sang of each other.
Свинцовые, седые воды Леты	Would leaden, hoary waters of Lethe
Разрушат ли незыблемый союз?	Destroy the stable union?
Напор тяжел, но не прорвется шлюз:	The pressure is heavy, but the locks will endure,
Заклятием положены сонеты:	An invocation produced the sonnets:
Вот я – Шекспир второй Елизаветы,	Here I am, a Shakespeare of Elizabeth the Second,
А ты – другой, прозревший Вилли Хьюз.	And you, a different, enlightened Willy Hughes.
А может быть, ты юноша великий,	Or perhaps you are a great youth,
Божественный, прекрасный, светлоликий	Divine, beautiful, with a luminous face,
Утопленник – умерший, но живой,	A drowned man, dead and yet alive,
Чтоб я глядел за гребни океана	So that I can look beyond the ocean's crests
На мраморный Антиноополь твой	At your marble Antinopoulos
Усталыми глазами Адриана?	With the tired eyes of Hadrian?
	"Parallels" (*Paralleli*), 25.8.1972

The first copies of *Ariel* arrived in 1976 on the same day as a typewritten collection of Vitkovskii's poems, "Kite" (*Vozdushnyi zmei*), sent by Vitkovskii's uncle in Germany. Pereleshin was amazed: "I am right, after all: I am connected to Zhenia from some distant reincarnation, and I recognized it and began to love him almost from the first letter."[85] A year later, as always eagerly looking through the mail, Pereleshin saw an envelope with Soviet stamps: it was "a totally incredible," "tender, warm, and sisterly" letter from Vitkovskii's second wife Nadezhda

(Nadia) Mal'tseva. Addressing him as "the dearest," she wrote that they had obtained a copy of *Ariel*, that they loved him, and that she wished "to be adopted" by him. More letters from her and then from Vitkovskii followed, accompanied by gifts of books, and Pereleshin was touched: "Isn't this a sweet epilogue to the 'affair with the phantom'?"[86]

The renewed correspondence was "a miracle," which revived his image of a "predestined brother" as declared in "Link" and *Ariel*, and he excused Vitkovskii's asking his wife to write first with "Zhenia did not dare." The couple was "simply in love with me, swearing their devotion, offering to send books, and compiling my archive (poems, articles, letters). [...] I am trying to get used to 'being loved': I cannot distrust Nadia and Zhenia." Mal'tseva's letters were "gushing": "she even threatened 'to enter my life not only as a spiritual daughter,'" leaving him to wonder, "how else can one enter my life?"[87] Pereleshin was becoming known in Moscow via Vitkovskii and acquired several correspondents there: "they all call themselves my admirers and not a single one tries 'to show me the true path' towards loving women and children."[88]

In early April 1978, Vitkovskii sent him a five-page letter, "so filled with love and magnanimity that I spent the entire day reading and rereading those pages. [...] What is happening to both of us? Zhenia is in love with me, and I with him." Previously they might have been "too attracted to *my* side of our 'affair,' and Zhenia's complexity started to be felt only last year. I had no doubts that the 'affair' was broken off too early and much has been left undeveloped. Now it is already too late: he pushed me away in 1974 (perhaps under terrible pressure), and from that time I also did not stand in one spot."[89] He closed his eyes to the fact that Vitkovskii's second marriage coincided with the break in correspondence and hungered for assurances: "He is proud that he has become a hero of my myth. [...] I fell in love with him almost from one letter, but he fell in love with me as well. He writes that it is forever. [...] To my direct question of why Ariel loves me, he answered: 'Devil knows.' But the question is, probably, academic."[90]

Once again, "Zhenia has become a living presence: poems (almost all sonnets) are written not only about him, but *always* 'in his presence'." He now lived under the "Ariel Constellation": "I love Zhenia more than before the forced break, I love him *both HIGH AND LOW*." They were "one spirit designed for two. Now I have lost even the slightest desire for new meetings, emotions, and illusions. As before mid-1974, I love only Zhenia, I want him with my spirit, my heart, and with what is left of my body. Again, as then, I wake up with his name. I pray for him. […] I miss him unbearably, but I also enjoy the unbelievable happiness."[91] He wondered whether "with crazy criminal laws in the USSR, his marriage might have been a necessity only as a cover." He "identified me by 'To Lucien Létinous'" and wrote: "'we are not so dim here not to understand.' He forced me to think once again about this entire tangle of relations. I still don't know the last truth about him. Would I know? Would I? Would I?"[92]

In mid-1979 the letters stopped: "the Moscow 'Ariel' is dying almost painlessly. I came to the limit of the pain threshold, and now it is gathering dust."[93] In early 1980, upon learning that Ivask and Morshen had heard from Vitkovskii, Pereleshin wrote to him "in despair": "Without you, the world has become different. I am drying as a poet. […] I am grateful to you for our meeting by mail and for this 'situation,' unique in the history of poetry. […] I love you passionately and tenderly."[94] He received a "somewhat sour" complaint of being forgotten and being told that letters from the USSR presented "a mortal danger" to Pereleshin: "Now, having received my letter, he is convinced that this was not true and called himself a fool. Someone wants my correspondence with Ariel to come to an end." The correspondence revived briefly, but by mid-1981 there were "no signs of life" from "the Moscow Ariel."[95] The epilogue to the affair with the phantom was over, even though in the last years of Pereleshin's life Vitkovskii reappeared for a different reason. By that time Pereleshin had found the last love of his life.

11 New Roads and Great Loss

Family Strife

Я сам еще не знал, чем вышью
лист, ослепленный добела,
когда наперерез двустишью
ночная моль переползла.
   Союзница! Я рад затишью:
   моль улизнула со стола,
   и я юркну проворной мышью
   туда же, в непроглядь угла.
Ведь там, где сумраки ночные
и в бархат кутается звук,
нас не найдут персты тупые
итоги подводящих рук!

I did not know yet how I would
embroider the page blinded white by light,
when a night moth crawled
across two lines of verse.
   My ally! I am glad for the lull:
   the moth slipped away from the desk,
   and I will dart like a nimble mouse
   to the same pitch-dark corner.
For there, in the dusk of the night
and of sounds wrapped in velvet,
the blunt fingers of summing up hands
will not find us!

"Moth" (*Mol'*), 14.2.1971

In the 1970s, Pereleshin's earnings from articles, occasional tuition, and translations were small and irregular, and self-publishing was draining whatever money he and his mother were managing to save. He started selling his stamps to other collectors and various books and materials to universities in the United States; he even approached Bishop Nikandr of the Brazilian-Venezuelan eparchy, his former student at the Harbin Ecclesiastical Seminary, but then changed his mind about serving in the church, fearing obedience, gossip, and stress. In 1972 he was invited to give a few lectures in Portuguese on Russian literature at Anchieta University in São Paulo, but no offer of a teaching position followed.[1] By the mid-1970s, his earnings from émigré newspapers had begun to dwindle: writings of the third-wave immigrants from the USSR were gaining popularity.

It was becoming "unbearable to be supported by Mum (on my brother's money)"; "the importance of money came to me too late. I see now that I should have made an enormous effort to acquire a technical profession. [...] I know, however, that if my life were to begin again, I would most likely have chosen *the same path*."[2] Although he held that "in no way can I conquer the remnants of gentry pride," in 1974 he appealed to the New York Fund for Relief for Russian Writers and Scientists in Exile (the Literary Fund): "how low have I sunk, begging in my old age!" He wrote that he needed "money not for bread, but for publishing books." Andrei Sedykh, the chair of the Literary Fund and editor of *New Russian Word*, replied: "Your life is very sad. All this has inexpressibly distressed me: I had no idea how you lived." The directorate granted him US$25 per month, which over the years increased to $35.[3] This income helped, but did not solve his problems. He kept reiterating: "I will not complain; the gentry does not," but complain he did and most frequently. In 1976, his dire straits compelled Gleb Struve, Iurii Ivask, and V.F. Markov to turn to the Kulaev Educational Fund in San Francisco. The Kulaev family was from Harbin, and Kulaev's wife, a graduate of YMCA, had known Pereleshin from Churaevka. He was allocated US$150 per year, later raised to US$175.[4]

Pereleshin's impoverishment affected family life. At get-togethers or games of bridge lasting well into the night, conversations frequently turned into arguments, his mother taking his side and Lidiia taking Victor's. His brother and sister-in-law were "right in their own way": they provided a rent-free condominium and a monthly allowance for his mother, while he lived with her and spent money on publishing books.[5] Victor, who worked hard at his managerial job on hydroelectric projects and comfortably supported his wife, mother, and brother, resented his brother's leisure, air of intellectual superiority, and constant bragging about his poetry. For him, Pereleshin was simply "a loafer and parasite," who refused to seek unskilled jobs and snobbishly clung to his gentry origin as justification. When Victor said that people should be judged by their achievements, not their ancestry, Pereleshin's view was that his brother had "become plebeian" and "a well-fed North American, a materialist," who had married a woman "of the plebeian class" and criticized him for "a wrong way of life (Russian poems, Russian journals, Russian newspapers, Russian interests). I should have been writing in English [...], because only books in English (but not poetry) bring in a decent income. The only argument is how much one can earn."[6]

When Victor asked Pereleshin to pay maintenance fees and expenses at the condominium, Pereleshin often got behind, dismissing Victor's requests with "what a fuss all this is, and how unnecessary!"[7] Every little thing led to ugly quarrels, depicted by Pereleshin as caused not so much by Victor's insistence on his supporting himself, but by hatred of Pereleshin's views: "If you only knew how they hate me for my culture, poems, *aloofness* [Eng.], pride, gentry prejudice, […], my contempt for trade and profiteering, categorical refusal of *drinks* [Eng.] (because I see what this indulgence leads to), and for my proper Russian."[8] Faced with demands "to earn enough not only to support myself, but also to help Mum," Pereleshin "wanted to throw myself out of the window there and then, just to stop his lectures. […] But my work in this world has not yet been finished." During one quarrel he hinted about a brick falling off a construction site and killing a passer-by.[9] "Brick" (*Kirpich*, 29.2.1972) spoke of a poet, who survived two wars and accidents, faced "a grey-haired old age, a horror / more frightening than a noose or a cross," and now hoped for "the Lord's grace: / praying for a swift brick." At times, in "penultimate despair," he thought of suicide with a note "Do not blame my brother for my death." But "I feel sorry for Mum: it would be worse for her without me."[10]

Sentianina was caught in the middle, both grateful to Victor for his care and supportive of Pereleshin's publications. Her heart ached for her eldest:

> He is a very sweet person in daily life and indifferent to everything except poetry. He is terribly lonely here. You cannot imagine what a swamp it is here in this respect. Victor, and especially his wife Lidiia, are nagging us for laziness, for lethargy, for unwillingness to earn money 'by sweeping streets,' as is done 'in our America.' I am nagging Valerii for various reasons. In life, he is like a child; he knows how to work, but not how to arrange his life well. On the whole, I think, he is almost running away from paid work! But, after all, he and I are publishing books! So many have already been prepared for publication! How would he live if I am gone? Naturally, I am already thinking of this. Without me, he will be completely alone. Everyone who remembers, appreciates, and loves him is far away. In general, all he meets is animosity, envy, and ill will. He is worthy of much. So much has been given to him, probably to his misfortune![11]

In 1976 Victor started building a retirement house in the little town of Muri near Novo Friburgo, planning to sell his large condominium and keep the small one for working as a part-time technical consultant. The new house was "comfortable and spacious," but the future move filled Pereleshin *"with horror"* and he rhymed Muri with *umri,* imperative of the Russian "to die."[12] He saw it as further "unbearable servile dependence on 'the kindred spirits,' helplessness, and transformation into a vegetable (if not an animal)." All his occasional translating jobs, meetings with friends, and "various adventures" were in Rio de Janeiro, a two-hour bus trip away.[13]

At this stressful time, Pereleshin found a new friend, who later played a major role in his life. October is a spring month in Brazil: "the elms are full of birds / (as in the old days in China), / and the same street lamp / is teasing with its glued-on eyelashes. / The Atlantic Ocean / is silvery outside my window," as "Spring Again" (*Opiat' vesna,* 23.9.1977) describes it. One October day in 1977, Pereleshin stood in line in a photocopy shop, "holding an article or poems in Russian and waiting with patient impatience, when someone behind me asked: 'Is this Greek?' – 'No, Russian,' I replied, 'but our alphabet is based on the Greek.' I had a great conversation with this curious thirty-two-year-old [he actually was thirty in 1977] student, handsome, but hardly beautiful; dusky skinned, but not quite a mulatto; shortsighted, like me, and long-sighted (wearing glasses). Within a few minutes he told me about his life, studies, and interests (books, music, painting, sculpture), then walked me home and dropped in."[14]

Pereleshin was drawn to this young Brazilian "with the manners of a Crown Prince," "a semi-mystic and semi-playboy," "modest and completely devoid of ambition." Humberto Marques Passos, born on 2 February 1947, came from a family of landowners near the city of Governador Valadares in Minas Gerais state. He had studied design, film, and art at the State University of New York, but left without a degree; he lived in Rio de Janeiro with his mother and stepfather and supported himself with odd jobs. "Physically and spiritually left-handed," in his childhood he had played with dolls and had relations with male relatives. He felt himself to be "a woman in a man's body" and was "falling in love only with men of the Herculean type. My '*caso*' is different: I fall in love with adolescents of the discus-thrower type."[15]

Pereleshin's mother liked "Humbertik," as she came to call him, and he patiently looked at her souvenirs and mementoes and brought her treats: "Previously, Mum did not understand me and censured me. Only in the last few years, meeting Humberto almost daily, she saw a different side: gentleness, readiness to help, absence of self-promotion, and tolerance for the actions and opinions of others. She came to love *him* sincerely."[16] Humberto introduced them to his mother, who occasionally took Sentianina for walks, and once, when Pereleshin complained about his brother, "dear Dona Emiliana whispered not to despair, because, if Mum were to die and 'the kindred spirits' to throw me out, Humberto would take care of me."[17]

Pereleshin's finances improved after Aleksis Rannit's trip to Brazil for the PEN Club Congress in 1979. Their planned meeting almost fell through because Humberto overslept and did not call Rannit as arranged, but Rannit changed his return flight and rang Pereleshin's doorbell on 24 July, an event "bordering on the miraculous!" Pereleshin's sixty-sixth birthday, 20 July, had just passed and on a stroll to the beach Rannit bought him 500 sheets of paper and a box of carbons, writing on one sheet: "Baroque. Grace. Brazil. Parting,"[18] the words which subsequently concluded Pereleshin's "24 July 1979" (*24-oe iiulia 1979 goda*, 24.7.1979).

On his return home, Rannit wrote to Humberto that Pereleshin was (verbatim from English) "one of the most significant poets from Russia throughout her history and one of the finest poets of the twentieth century," who "not only brought to his new country his sincere and unconditional love for Brazil, its people, language, and culture, but also was able to express that love in artistically and humanly convincing poems, which, notwithstanding the foreign language, actually form an integral part of Brazilian culture." Now that he was old and in poor health, "it falls to Brazilians, and especially Brazilian authorities in welfare or cultural affairs, to return this love to him."[19] Inspired by this appeal, Humberto and his mother helped Pereleshin to apply for a disability pension from the Brazilian Institute of Social Security from September 1979. Initially the pension was Cr$1,137 per month (US$35–$43), but it was gradually increased to Cr$2,100. The same "miserly pension" was soon granted to his mother.[20]

This pension was supplemented by aid from the Literary Fund and from the Kulaev Fund and by irregular contributions from the Harbin Commercial Schools Alumni Association and the Phoenix Chess Club, both in San Francisco. Their generosity made Pereleshin "nearly cry from emotion and shame. […] My God, how humiliating: I am begging money, so to speak, from the entire world!" He could not help recalling the 1950 deportation: "in the United States I would now have been a retired university professor, a pensioner."[21] His occasional earnings included writing for several Russian programs on Radio Vaticana, and he even dreamed of moving to Rome. His recital of "The Way of the

Cross" and some religious poems were broadcast on 27 June 1980 "to prepare Russian listeners for the Polish Pope's visit to Brazil."[22]

On 1 February 1980, Victor temporarily moved his mother and brother to his large condominium and had their furniture and Pereleshin's archive transported to Muri. Aware of his brother's attitude to the move, Victor planned to build an adjacent cottage for them, with a separate entrance, bedrooms upstairs, and a study downstairs. Pereleshin was not appeased: "there will be no Muses, no writing, no friends, no falling in love," and "my agony, the prospect of moving to Muri, has begun; I want to avoid it at all cost, by any means, including the infallible ones."[23] Lidiia was already living in Muri, but Victor still worked in Rio de Janeiro and commuted on weekends. Living with Victor in one condominium worsened their relationship: "we have no life, only torment. Victor does not talk to us and looks at us like a wolf. After work, he watches television and gets drunk. [...] He calls me a 'fool' to my face. [...] He said to Mum without the slightest reason: 'You are a fool, and you are always lying,' and added: 'The best you can do is to get into a coffin.' He hates us. We drag our existence under such pressure that ... it is embarrassing to tell to a lady, but I have become incontinent (always wet!). Mum started to suffocate again, and I to suffer from insomnia. [...] I do not cling to life, but I cannot leave Mum all *alone*. What will happen to her if I can no longer endure?"[24]

His mother tried to mediate, but Victor said that if his brother was not happy with the move, he was free to make his own arrangements. With Humberto's help, Pereleshin looked for an apartment, but could not afford rent, electricity, and other expenses in the better ones, and he feared the cheap ones in distant and unsafe suburbs.[25] He could not see himself moving to "an alms-house of Jesuit fathers, somewhere in São Paulo State, in the middle of a field," or to the Tolstoy Fund Old People's Home, eight hours from Rio de Janeiro. He remembered how miserable V.V. Koloshin had been in the old people's home in Belgium and that the émigré poet V.S. Il'iashenko had shot himself in a home in New York.[26]

At the end of May 1980, while Lidiia was visiting her daughter and grandchildren in the United States, the mother and son were temporarily "exiled" to Muri. The house was comfortable, a housemaid looked after them, poinsettias and hydrangeas were blooming, hummingbirds hovered above aloe flowers, and Victor's boxers enjoyed the grounds. But Pereleshin hated it: electricity was weak, the weather chilly, his typewriter and dictionaries were in Rio de Janeiro, and the stay seemed to last "an eternity and a half."[27] Moreover, "it is not a village where one could meet and observe real masses of people, but a cottage settlement of the rich who want to rest from the 'urban bustle.' Everything is well organized, decorous, and even beautiful (gardens, lawns), but unbearably *boring*. [...] We must leave, but where to? Mum is pitifully attached to things. At her age, she cannot rent an empty apartment with no furniture, dishes, clothes, linen, and trunks."[28]

Back in Rio de Janeiro, "the atmosphere at home has become impossible and most likely we will have to move in a hurry." After one particularly nasty blow-up, Pereleshin went to enquire at a local almshouse, but what he saw sobered him: "Living corpses are lying in beds and do not get up. To reach the toilet they have to crawl through the room of a neighbour, another living corpse. And do you think it costs peanuts? No, they charge Cr$5,000 per month, which includes Brazilian-style meals."[29] He was getting resigned: "Tribulations in looking for an apartment would have cost too much in nervous strain. Thank God that we decided to endure, and everything somehow got settled."[30] His migraines, insomnia, back pain, and arthritis were getting worse, his dentures fitted badly, his hearing was deteriorating, and cataracts were growing in both eyes. He tried to cut down his smoking, but when lines of poetry were coming, he would "turn into a factory smoke-stack, and two packs a day were not enough."[31]

What Pereleshin failed to appreciate was that while he was being forced to move to Muri, his brother was forced to provide for him without any acknowledgment or gratitude. Pereleshin lived without cost in Victor's condominium, where he had a room, meals, and the services of Victor's housemaid, but in his letters he continued to complain about having no money for clothes, public transport, haircuts, paper, postage, cigarettes, sweets, ice cream, and cafes. Not only was Victor's generosity taken for granted, but Pereleshin boasted that his books were published "at a cost of great sacrifices (more Mum's than my own)"[32] and he never faced the plain fact that it was Victor who indirectly and greatly subsidized these books.

Translations

Блажен хромой, припадочный, слепой	Happy the maimed, the halt, the mad, the blind –
И всякий, кто природой искалечен:	All who, stamped separated by curtailing birth,
Любой из них, не связанный с толпой,	Owe no duty's allegiance to mankind

Не должен ей – и ею не замечен.

Но я судьбой унижен не извне,
Не признаком наглядного изъятья,
А изнутри, и все ж укоры мне
Мои же шлют счастливые собратья.
Судьбе видней невидный недочет,

Влекущий боль и холод всенародный,
Но как она себя не узнает

В моей душе, по имени свободной?
И разве я в безумьи и в горбе

Увижу нить не к воле, а к судьбе?

Translated 25.8.1974

Nor stand a valuing in their scheme of
worth!
But I, whom Fate, not Nature, did curtail,
By no exterior voidness being exempt,
Must bear accusing glances where I fail,
Fixed in the general orbit of contempt.
Fate, less than Nature in being kind to
lacking,
Giving the ill, shows not as outer cause,
Making our mock-free will the mirror's
backing
Which Fate's own acts as if in itself shows;
And men, like children, seeing the image
there,
Take place for cause and make our will
Fate bear.

Fernando Pessoa, "Sonnet XXXIV"

Pereleshin had always been interested in languages and translation. In Beijing, having learned some French from Korostovets, he translated a French poem in a short story for *Border* and followed it in Brazil with a few poems by Étienne de la Boétie and Joachim du Bellay.[33] Although opposed to translations from word-for-word renderings, in 1948 he did just that with "Recollection of Emek" (*Vospominanie ob Emeke*), a poem in German by Klara Blum for the Russian-language Jewish journal *Our Life* (*Nasha zhizn'*) in Shanghai.[34]

In Shanghai, he had taken some Spanish lessons and read "Canciones entre el alma y el Esposo," or "El Cántico Espiritual," by San Juan de la Cruz (1542–91).[35] Its search for a path to God and spiritual love was close to Pereleshin's poetic quest, but translating it in 1968 turned out to be "harder than *Li Sao*!" He did not want "to diverge from the original unless necessary" and at times spent a couple of hours on one stanza. His translation was published in the Paris *Le Messager. Vestnik Russkogo khristianskogo dvizheniia* in 1975.[36] He also translated a few poems of Juan Boscán Almogávar, Garcilaso de la Vega, Luis de Góngora y Argote, the Carmelite nun St Teresa of Ávila, and other Spanish poets, the choices revealing thematic similarities in appeals to God, loss of love, and loneliness.

In 1972, he translated "Monument to Horace" from Latin, and in 1977 Aleksis Rannit's "Coda" from the author's word-for-word translation from Estonian. In 1977–9 he worked on poems of the English metaphysical poets and some of Shakespeare's sonnets. Feminine rhymes in

"Sonnet XX" were "clearly not accidental, and I tried hard to translate it only with such rhymes. Of all the 154 sonnets only one has exclusively feminine rhymes, that very same twentieth sonnet."[37] In the 1980s, his translation of Pushkin's "Imitating Arabic" (*Podrazhanie arabskomu*) into English appeared in *The Penguin Book of Homosexual Verse*; the concluding lines in his translation were "We are precisely like a double nut / under a single shell."[38]

These forays aside, the majority of his translations were from Chinese and now increasingly from Portuguese. In 1971 he sought a grant from the Portuguese Ministry of Culture for translating sonnets by Luis de Camões. He was not awarded a grant, but the cultural attaché of the Portuguese embassy, a specialist in the work of Fernando Pessoa, presented him with an anthology of Portuguese poetry, a collection of Pessoa's works, and his own monographs on the bilingual poet.[39] It was a fascinating discovery: Pessoa spoke "covertly ('in a chaste way'), but the tension of thoughts and the disintegration of personality are such that I was overwhelmed for a whole month" by "a certain 'mystical triangle': Shakespeare – Pessoa – I."[40]

In 1974, he "ecstatically" translated Pessoa's thirty-five English sonnets and "visualized a future book" as another "heroic deed" on his part. In the introduction to the unpublished manuscript he commented that Pessoa "often makes mistakes in counting syllables, or uses rhymes with distant euphonic similarity, which the English poet [Shakespeare] never would have done. [...] I strove not for precision, but to adequately convey an impression."[41] When a friend objected that such an approach made the sonnets Pereleshin's, he argued: "we have such a unity of consciousness that we speak the same language (though in two languages)."[42]

In 1976 he worked on Pessoa's English poem "Antinous." Some parts seemed clumsy to him, "but the tension is such that one does want 'to correct mistakes.' It is such a mixture of passion and despair that one shivers. Antinous is already dead, and the poem speaks of Hadrian. There is no action: Hadrian only looks at the body of the drowned young man."[43] Pereleshin was not happy with his "free translation": "I am forced to lose a lot and sometimes lower myself to a pitiful retelling (and the impression is weakened)." Finding the first line "untranslatable," he "somehow rendered" the original "The rain outside was cold in Hadrian's soul" into "Cold rain – and another kind of darkness" (*Kholodnyi dozhd' – i mrak eshche drugoi*).[44] His solution was "'to pretend to be 'a simpleton' and retell the untranslatable with an honest expression on my face. [...] However, the theme of this long poem is indecent, although it was published twice when the Portuguese poet was still alive. The Russian Muse lags behind for at least half a century as far as 'decency' is concerned."[45] In 1981, he and Humberto translated "Antinous" into Portuguese; it had been done previously, but "in an *unrhymed* verse! I will never allow myself to lower the level of the original in translation [...] The smallest admixture of 'one's own' (*otsebiatina*) does not ruin the translation, but lowering the *form* destroys the original once and for all."[46]

Southern Cross: Anthology of Translations from Brazilian Poetry, 1978

Трепет латинского паруса, полыханье мальтийского знака, – нахожу у Тито де Барроса и у Олаво Билака. Влажные джунгли Бразилии, орхидейную теплую прелесть отыскиваю у Сесилии – у несравненной Мейрелес. Мне служит взамен рифмологии португальский словарик тщедушный, но строки смыкаются строгие крепленьем рифмы послушной. "Lirio" – колокол лилии, а "delirio" – бред ностальгии; забрало и бронза – Бразилии, последний выдох – России.	The quiver of Latin sail, flicker of the Maltese sign, I find them in Tito de Barros and Olavo Bilac. The humid jungles of Brazil, The warm charm of orchids, I find them in Cecília – the incomparable Meireles. A puny Portuguese dictionary serves instead of a rhyming dictionary, but strict lines link together secured by the obedient rhyme. "Lirio" – the bell of a lily, and "delirio" – the delirium of nostalgia; the visor and bronze – to Brazil, the last breath – to Russia.

"Quiver of Latin Sail"
(*Trepet latinskogo parusa*), 28.7.1972

Brazilian poetry was "yet another virgin soil (I consider myself to be the first in translating from Chinese: my predecessors and contemporaries certainly achieved nothing). One has to work for the future; sooner or later, Russia will become a normal country, and then both Chinese classical poetry and Brazilian love lyrics would find a certain demand."[47] He wanted his anthology of translations, *Southern Cross* (*Iuzhnyi krest*), to come out in time for the 150th anniversary of Brazilian independence in 1972 and appreciated Ia. Gorbov's "prophetic slip of the tongue" in referring to *Southern Home* as *Southern Cross*.[48]

However, it was not published until 1978, when Victor refused his share for their mother's stay in a hospital and told him to get his teeth fixed, buy new shoes, and have his suits mended. "After a prolonged agony" of indecision, Pereleshin combined this money with a small legacy from E.F. Dubianskaia, their Russian friend in Rio de Janeiro, and, dedicating *Southern Cross* to her memory, had it printed by Posev's offshoot Polyglott-Druck as "a moral debt to my dear Brazil."[49]

The book opened with a foreword, "From the Translator," which introduced Brazilian Portuguese language, literature, and major poets. Although the subtitle was *Anthology of Brazilian Poetry*, "I did not attempt to show the best examples of Brazilian poetry, but collected almost everything that I had translated in a quarter of a century."[50] Such a compilation, as in *Poems on a Fan*, was somewhat accidental in selection and more revealing of Pereleshin's poetic choices.

The first part had poems by fifty-two classical and contemporary poets. The first, "Excerpt," attributed to Tito de Barros, could have been written by Pereleshin himself: "The right hand writes with skill, / the left with heart, pain, soul. / If you have given priority to your feelings, / then do not think, be a left-hander!" There were poems by Joaquim Cardoso, who had taken some Chinese lessons from Pereleshin when he wanted to translate Chinese poetry; João da Cruz e Sousa, the founder of Brazilian Symbolism, who "was black, but his favourite epithet was 'white'";[51] and Manuel Bandeira, whom Pereleshin liked so much at first reading that he "immediately translated the epigraph to *A cinza das horas* (Ash of the Hours). The more I read him, the more I translated."[52] Twenty poems by Bandeira included masterpieces such as "Epigraphe," "Profundamente," "Pneumotorax," "Irene no céu," "Porquinto-da-índia," and "Noite morta." Some poets stood outside the mainstream: a Ukrainian émigré, Wira Wowk (Selianskaia); Zalkind Piatigorskii, a judge born in Rio de Janeiro of Russian Jewish parents; Jesuit Father Afonso Rodrigues from Anchieta University; and his Brazilian Ariel, Antônio Azevedo.[53] The second part consisted of *trovas*, quatrains of serious, ironic, or funny commentary on the nature of love, sorrows, dreams, and poetry. These "philosophical sketches, similar to Persian quatrains," fell in line with *ghazals*, translations of Chinese four-line poems, and his own short poems.[54]

In her review, Iustina Kruzenshtern, who knew Portuguese, pointed out that, though not a true anthology, *Southern Cross* is "the first attempt by a Russian poet abroad to give his compatriots an impression of Brazilian poetry," though, in her opinion, the poems, in particular the sonnets, "in their content and general tone only repeat everything that we had found earlier in other European, particularly French, poets: they have nothing specifically Brazilian." She mentioned a few inconsistencies and mistakes, but complemented Pereleshin for "not only mastering the language, but also imbibing its music, which makes his translations alive and full-blooded."[55] Another reviewer, Boris Nartsissov, noted that Pereleshin was "an experienced translator and thus one can assume that a Russian reader would get a true picture of Brazilian lyrical poetry."[56]

Ivask described the anthology as "a payment of moral debt to the green and golden Brazil for its hospitality." Pereleshin, unlike many émigré poets, loved the countries where he was fated to live and "expanded the borders of Russian poetry, enriching it with new motifs and themes in his poetry and with his translations of Chinese and Brazilian poets"; his translations of *trovas* were "almost a discovery." Ivask concluded: "Some Brazilian modernists are greatly interested in Maiakovsky or nonsensical Aigi and applaud Evtushenko, but it seems that they do not suspect that a great Russian poet, Valerii Pereleshin in Rio de Janeiro, is the true envoy of Russian culture in Brazil."[57]

His Brazilian friend Humberto "enthusiastically campaigned for glorifying *Southern Cross*." Thanks to his efforts, "yesterday was a wonderful day: *Jornal do Brasil* published an interview with me – for the first time in a quarter of a century!" This brief article with Pereleshin's photograph introduced his publications, his views on poetry, and *Southern Cross*.[58]

Mother's Death, 11 October 1980

Еще в шкафу нерозданные платья
Тень запаха знакомого хранят,
И туфельки, построенные в ряд,
Стоят в углу – попарные собратья.
   А ты ушла – в раскрытые объятья
   Спасителя: тебя не возвратят
   Ни ищущий твоей улыбки взгляд,
   Ни жалобы, ни стоны, ни заклятья.
Но почему за пять недель ко мне,
Любимая, ты не пришла во сне:
Забыла ли, что в комнате соседней
   (Тогда – твоей) не удержал я слез,
   А ты с тоской и нежностью последней
   Погладила кружок моих волос?

The dresses, not yet handed round, in the wardrobe
Retain the shadow of a familiar smell,
And the shoes arranged in a row
Stand in the corner like paired brothers.
   But you have left – into the open embrace
   Of the Saviour: neither a glance seeking your smile,
   Nor complaints, moans, and incantations
   Will bring you back.
But why, in these five weeks,
You, my beloved, did not come to me in dreams:
Have you forgotten that in the room next door,
   (Still yours then) I could not restrain my tears,
   And you, with anguish and last tenderness,
   Stroked the circle of my hair?

"In Memory of Mother"
(*Pamiati materi*), 8.11.1980

In February 1980, Pereleshin, enjoying Carnival festivities with friends in a Copacabana cafe, mentioned to Humberto how happy his mother would have been "to breathe the Carnival air." Humberto, who "has a lot of Don Quixote in him and knows it," grabbed Pereleshin, and the two rushed home to get her: there she was playing bridge with herself and gladly joined them. She was "completely charmed" by the whole atmosphere, the heady music of folk instruments, and people dancing with abandon in their spectacular masks and costumes. From their first year in Brazil she "had fallen in love with the Carnival."[59] This one was to be her last.

A severe bout of pneumonia had resulted in hospitalization in 1976, after which she recuperated at Victor and Lidiia's. Lidiia arranged to clean the condominium where she and Pereleshin lived, but it soon reverted to the usual, as Sentianina put it, "constant mess, but still the cosiest place." By the late 1970s, she had grown weak and apathetic, slept a lot, and refused to go out for walks; as she had confided to Kruzenshtern in 1977: "I have fallen apart from my age, illnesses, and a strange spiritual state."[60] By July 1980, when they were living in Victor's condominium, Sentianina was suffering from frequent colds and neuralgia, but resisted treatment: "Today I called a pharmacist to give her a shot of vitamin B12, and what did I get for that! In the mornings, it is hard to wake up my patient, and my heart constricts every time. Recently, after another fight [between brothers], she said: 'How I wish to die!' And this is when she loved life so much!" Pereleshin typically blamed only Victor: "my brother is worried by her condition, which in many ways has been caused by him."[61]

In August, it was clear that she was "*very ill*. I do not dare to look far ahead." By September she was on pain medication. Although forbidden to smoke, she picked out butts from ashtrays, and her doctor said that it no longer mattered. Victor's housemaid, Isabel, dealt with the daily cares: "I would not have been able to cope with this ordeal on my own. What would I have done with cooking, laundry, and ironing if we had stayed in our old apartment or moved to a different one? Now Mum herself is saying that all this was foreseen by Someone." She had lost so much weight that "it is painful to look at her. [...] I am staying in the room next to hers; I recall the past, grieve over the present, and, last of all and only rarely, think of the future." Lidiia consulted doctors, requested more tests, and hired a nurse. By early October the pain was so severe that she begged the doctor to give her poison.[62]

Then, "on the morning of 11 October Mum left us. She had stomach cancer. It was concealed from me, and I believed that it was emphysema. [...]. I was close by all the time, but not next to her, not by her bed. Only on 10 October something pushed me to kneel by the head of her bed and tell her that all my life I have loved and still love her above all. She smiled, put her hand on my head, and said that her only worry was my fate, but Victor and Lidiia had promised to take care of me. That night I had a severe fit of coughing; I read the prayer for the ailing and began to read the Gospel of Matthew. I dozed off at 5 in the morning, and at 7.15 a.m. the nurse woke me up: Mum asked for hot milk, drank half a cup, thanked her, smiled, and left us forever."[63]

Lidiia was in Muri and Victor was at work; both rushed home. On 12 October 1980 E.A. Sentianina was buried in the English Cemetery in the distant suburb of Gamboa. Her sons, Lidiia, Humberto, and about ten former China Russians stood at the graveside. Lidiia had bought adjacent plots for the mother and son, which deeply touched him: "I have not expected such moral sensitivity from her," "she is a real genius in doing that."[64] He sold another part of his stamp collection to pay half the expenses: "For once in my life I wanted to be fully *filial*." Victor would not cash his cheque, but Pereleshin insisted that the payment was not only "a duty, but also a *right*." He sold his land in Vale das Videiras, bought when he was working at the British Council, for Cr$80,000 to pay his share of the dark grey tombstone with an Orthodox cross and inscription: "Eugenia A. Sentianina. 1892 – 1980."[65]

Sixty years before, young and apprehensive, she courageously had left her husband and her homeland and emigrated with her beloved boys to face a life largely filled with hardships and sorrows. She was the most important person in Pereleshin's life and his faithful ally, "encouraging and urging" him in publishing his books, regardless of her own and his sacrifices. She had always stood by him, and he often wished "for her and my lives to end on the same day (e.g., in an airplane crash)." The loss was unbearable: "in my entire long life I did not love anyone as much as Mum," and "all my life I was writing first of all for Mum."[66] His grief was intensified by deep remorse for her suffering over his being a homosexual, becoming a monk, and never making their lives financially comfortable: "I am truly very guilty of many things in relation to Mum. In spite of it all, she loved me. [...] 'Mum, forgive me!' I keep saying, when I go to the cemetery in Gamboa, when I look through her books, manuscripts, and photographs, and when I go to her room, which has so many of her personal things. […] The worst thing is total loneliness, and this is to the very end."[67]

In the first few days he wept continually. Victor and Lidiia had not told him of her cancer, so that he "would not get hysterical […]. Had I known, I would not have left Mum for a moment, but they kept giving me hope and so, instead of sitting with her, I worked on 'Via crucis' in Portuguese (my 'The Way of the Cross')." He did not want to see anyone except Humberto, who came over daily: "he *knows* that there is no death and the parting is temporary."[68] He stooped, walked with difficulty, coughed constantly, could not see well, but would not consult a doctor: "getting treatment would have been somewhat repulsively dishonourable. By the way, in my last conversation with Mum, I promised her not to delay my departure, but suicide does not solve the question: in that case, for example, we may never meet again. I have to endure to the end."[69]

Sorting through her things, he found "a notebook with my poems of the 1930s and 1940s […] and the poems which I had long ago excluded from my lists as failures, or totally forgot about. […] Rereading them, so lovingly copied in Mum's hand, I wept a great deal." He "broke into loud sobs" on seeing issues of *Swallow* (*Lastochka*), a Harbin children's journal, with her contributions. He felt her "presence" in her manuscripts, journals, books, and photographs.[70] Flooded with haunting memories, he kept thinking of death: "The main key to this integral mystery is the Resurrection of Christ. God does not have the dead: everyone is alive. Even my 'deviation' (my partiality towards reincarnation) has somehow straightened out: I want to meet Mum as her son, who lived with her almost all his life, not as an already different 'I,' and to acquire her as a teacher, a sister, a Holy Claire."[71]

On the first anniversary of her death, "step by step, hour by hour, I relived again the unforgettable day of 10 October. In the morning, I rushed around the business section of the city in the belief that the doctor had sent me to get glucose for intravenous feeding. I believed this to such an extent that I did not wonder why I had to get permission from *Saúde Pública* to buy glucose. Later I found out that what I was searching for was a narcotic (which, naturally, is not sold freely) […]. On that day (and for two or three days previously), Mum had not got up: coffee and breakfast were served to her in bed. After running around, I returned home terribly tired. When the nurse gave her an injection, Mum called to me: 'Come sit with me.' But I pleaded tiredness and fell into bed. No one told me anything until the very end. […] I could not sleep: I read a prayer service for the recovery of the ill and then the Bible. Before that, though, I dropped in to see Mum and asked her for forgiveness for all my sins and misdemeanours towards her. On such a day as today I *must* be alone: with my thoughts, my repentance, my pain. […] The first anniversary – my God, a year has passed already! And the wound has not healed. As it should not."[72]

In the second sonnet of a cycle of four, "In Mother's Memory" (*Pamiati materi*, 31.12.1980), an epigraph taken from John 14:2 says, "In my Father's house there are many mansions." The poet tells his mother that he would accept paradise only if they could be next door neighbours in "the promised fatherly home." Otherwise, "I would prefer the earthly bustle, / sickliness and childhood with cod-liver oil, // which, though disliking medicine, / I obediently took from you / and still keep in my weak-sighted memory. // In my youth and in the adult years, / you were my winged Muse, / and now you have left – is it really forever?" The third sonnet, of 14 July 1981, ended with "I look in the window. It is worse than darkness outside. / It is chilly. I feel like crying / about the one fated not to be forgotten." In the fourth sonnet, written on 20 August 1981, the poet severs his acquaintance with a person who "dared to say that I sin against her / whenever I write depraved poems. / She does not need visible gifts. // She is not here. Not in the ground under the cross, / but high in golden space, / where torment has long been forgotten in the light. // She is not here. But through the heavy layer, / I will, in worship, kiss her hands: / she will not give me her hand on the Day of Judgment!" He kept going to the cemetery with masses of "red roses, which she loved so much, and wept to my heart's content. I have no desire to live without Mum: there is no one and nothing to fill the emptiness." With time, the cemetery visits became less frequent: "it is very far, and, the main thing is, *she is not there*."[73]

The second half of the 1970s and the 1980s brought so many losses that he was "afraid to open letters." Poets Dmitrii Klenovskii died in 1976 in Germany and Prince Sumbatov in 1977 in Italy; Harbin poet Elena Nedel'skaia died in 1980 in Sydney, Australia. In 1981 poet Anatolii Velichkovskii died in France, and Harbin Russian A.P. Chernishev, his correspondent and collector of Arsenii Nesmelov's poems, in Sydney. In the same year Pereleshin's old friend, nun Lelia, committed suicide in the United States.[74] On 8 June 1983, his faithful "mascot," Iustina Kruzenshtern, died in California: "so much has been linked to her." Also in 1983, "Murochka" Lapiken, Vladimir Slobodchikov's older brother Lev, and K.M. Karpinskii, who "at one time brightened my hard Beijing years," died in the United States.[75] Rannit died in 1985 in New Haven, Connecticut: "he was, after all, one of the best and completely unselfish friends." In 1986, Struve died in Berkeley, California, and Ivask in Amherst, Massachusetts: "As Ivask wrote to me in a letter of 1 February, which reached me three days after I had written his obituary, he was waiting for the publication of his new book *I Am a Petty Bourgeois* (*Ia meshchanin*)."[76] In the same year, the long-time editor of *The New Review*, Roman Gul', died in New York, and a friend of his China years, Lidiia Khaindrova, died in Krasnodar. In 1987 the poet Ivan Elagin died in Pittsburg and the poet Ekaterina Tauber in France, with both of whom he occasionally corresponded; in 1989 Archbishop Ioann Shakhovskoi, the poet Strannik, died in California.

His deeply beloved mother, friends, poets, correspondents: "our entire life is a bitter chronicle of losses."[77]

Casa dos Artistas, 1983

Я каменная ваза-лотос:
играя с октябрем в снежки,
в заглохший пруд, теперь болото,
свои роняю лепестки.
  Гусей общительную стаю
  я проводил за облака.
  Белею. Зябну. Облетаю
  надбитой роскошью цветка.

I am a lotus-shaped vase made of stone:
having a snow-ball fight with October,
I drop my petals into
a stagnant pond, now a swamp.
  I watch a sociable flock of geese
  disappearing beyond the clouds.
  I am turning white. I shiver. And shed
  the cracked luxury of a flower.

"Lotus-shaped Vase"
(*Vaza-lotus*), 14.1.1972

Their mother's death did not bring about a reconciliation between the brothers. In Victor's view, his brother "sat all day doing nothing" and his gay poetry was "shit." Pereleshin complained that Victor kept calling him an idiot and a cretin: "I must save at least the remnants of my human dignity. These 'titles' can be explained only by my poverty." Lidiia tried to smooth things over, but said that "I am not an interesting person, because I do not want to know anything except poetry, to which Victor added: 'And boys.'"[78]

The situation was difficult for all three. After Sentianina's death, Victor and Lidiia considered moving to California and applied for the US immigration permit for Pereleshin. Kruzenshtern wrote that he was "already *expected* in San Francisco," but Pereleshin feared complete dependence on Victor in the United States and thus restrictions on his freedom and gay life. Furthermore, "I have come to love Brazil and declared it my third and *last* homeland, and, consequently, I do not want to give up Brazilian nationality."[79] Their decision hung over him like "some sword of Damocles." When they opted to stay in Brazil, Pereleshin was told that he would have to move to Muri by May 1981. Victor intended to keep his promise to his mother, but only on certain conditions, which Pereleshin interpreted as not being able to be "the master of my life; others will make decisions for me." He did not want to move "for all the tea in the world. All my life is in Rio de Janeiro," but Victor made it clear that if he did not, there would be no further support.[80] Lidiia felt sorry for him and treated him "even tenderly." She assured him that he and Victor would not have to see each other in Muri, which he understood as meaning "I would sit in an assigned cage, which he could enter at any time with his next expression of displeasure or some other invention."[81]

Yet he could not afford to rent a place in Rio de Janeiro and "cope with food, laundry, and cleaning. Moreover, it is *dangerous* to live alone not only in the distant suburbs such as Bantu, but also in Copacabana or Botafogo." He needed cataract surgery, and his first thought was "Who but Lidiia would want to take care of me?" At times he wished to end it all, but, "as a monk and a priest, I know what suicide is and even 'extenuating circumstances' would not justify it."[82] Victor and Lidiia appealed to Humberto, but he and Pereleshin discovered that boarding houses were "simply businesses aiming to squeeze out as much money as possible and provide as little as possible. In these slightly improved almshouses one cannot have visitors, which is absolutely essential for me, and is not allowed to bring one's own things (desk, bookcase, a few trunks). Only the people, whom, in my opinion, 'it is too early to bury and too late to treat' can vegetate there."[83]

He continued to live in Victor's condominium, though "not for a single day do I give up hope to live on my own." In February 1982, Victor and Lidiia discovered that in their absence he was entertaining young men there: "Just now (almost at midnight), I have received the *second* order to get out of the room, where I live. I don't know where to go." They were furious, but could not bring themselves to kick him out, and they absolutely "forbade me 'to bring boys here' under the threat of the highest measure of punishment." He was told that it was time "to cool down, stop falling in love and amusing myself with illusions. It is, of course, true. However, if you cut off the thorns, the roses will die."[84]

The impasse was resolved in the late January 1983. During a morning coffee with Victor, Pereleshin announced that he would be moving to a retirement home. Victor repeated that he would then have to provide for himself. It was "a calm conversation. I thanked him for everything he had done for Mum and me, for helping us in China and during the thirty years that I have lived here. The main thing is that he got us out of China and made me the gift of my third and final homeland." To their friends, Pereleshin described the move as an "escape from drunkenness and rudeness," while Victor attributed it to their total "incompatibility."[85]

It was Humberto and his mother Dona Emiliana who arranged for Pereleshin to be accepted as an "international poet" at a retirement village, *Casa dos Artistas*, or *Retiro dos Artistas*, in Jacarepaguá, a distant suburb of Rio de Janeiro and a two-hour bus ride from Copacabana. It was similar to Muri in its surroundings, but he was completely on his own. The retirement complex consisted of the main building, various amenities, and many small bungalows, separated by lanes named after famous artists.[86] On 4 February 1983, with Humberto's help, Pereleshin moved to his last home, a "rather primitive, but 'livable'" bungalow of three small rooms, a kitchenette with a gas plate, and a bathroom. One room became his study, furnished with a desk, two wooden trunks from Harbin, and bookshelves; the second served as a bedroom and the third as storage for books and suitcases containing his archive. It was not cheap, but still cheaper than an apartment in Rio de Janeiro. His pension and some of the aid from the Literary Fund in New York, the Kulaev Fund, and friends covered the room and board of three meals a day, and he could have coffee and snacks from his own supplies in his bungalow. The tin-sheet walls made the place hot and stuffy in summer, but at the beginning of 1986, "my decrepit shack with its many holes for *barata* cockroaches and rats was renovated with brick walls" and given a new coat of paint, but inside it remained, as one guest described it, "an unimaginable total mess."[87]

This "Shelter-House" (*Dom-Ubezhishche*), as Pereleshin called it, was "almost an almshouse," but "of a high class in the composition of its residents."[88] They were mostly women, former artists of theatre, ballet, circus, and television: "I feel great tenderness towards them all: these wrinkled faces, eyes without sparkle, hands which had lost their shape, legs swollen or grown thin, crutches, this mournful old age … I try to help everyone, to support, to accompany, or to move a chair closer. I am also nearly seventy."[89] They liked "recalling the distant days of their past, former successes, and long-faded laurels; they quarrel because of their cats or because of 'who said what.'" Being one of them "should have immediately made me an old man, who would live, like others, by reminiscing. […] I am amused and glad that I feel even younger than I should: my age fluctuates (as before) from fourteen to 2,000 years old."[90]

In the circumstances it was a good solution: "I am totally happy here: silence, the wonderful silhouettes of distant mountains, flowers, birds (many doves), and butterflies. I read a lot, write a lot." He often took a bus to Copacabana, and Humberto's visits were "like holidays."[91] He enjoyed feeding doves on his verandah and "cried inconsolably," when many of them, including his favourite Humbertinho (Little Humberto), were shot on the order of the administration.[92] The little dove was mourned in several poems.

On 20 July 1983, Pereleshin turned seventy. He felt that he had lived as "a God's bird," and lines from *Daodejing* often came to him: "Everyone has ground under their feet, / only I have flowing water. / Alone in the power of rearing waves, / in the power of the wind – where would I end?"[93]

Nos odres velhos: Book of Poetry in Portuguese, 1983

Стихи рождались каждый час
без осязаемых усилий,
пока жила в груди у нас
хоть капля воздуха России.
  Не капельку, а целый мех
  мы вынесли на человека:
  хватило воздуха на всех,
  на все края, на все полвека.
Осталось на один прием:
исчерпан воздух забайкальский
и нынче я со словарем
пишу стихи по-португальски.

Poems were born every hour
with no tangible efforts,
as long as in our bosoms
there was a drop of Russian air.
  We took with us not a tiny drop,
  but entire bellows for each person:
  there was enough air for everyone,
  for all regions, for the entire half-century.
Just one intake is left:
the Trans-Baikal air is all used up,
and now with a dictionary
I am writing poems in Portuguese.

"Air" (*Vozdukh*), 21.4.1971

If Pereleshin had stayed in China, he might have written poetry in Chinese, as his Chinese version of "Red Leaves under the Frost" (*Krasnye list'ia pod ineem*, 15.5.1947) indicates. In his new homeland, "had I come twenty years earlier, I could have become a Brazilian poet, writing in Portuguese."[94] "Upper Reaches" (*Verkhov'ia*, 28.5.1970) captures the appearance of "diamond nuggets" of pure rhymes, the first set notably in Portuguese: "*clandestino – destino*." In "Who said, trying to be smart"

(*Kto skazal – ot bol'shogo uma*, 8.4.1972), the poet asks: "Who said that a planet was not home, / that a foreign country was a different continent, / that Portuguese language could not begin / sounding like a native tongue?"

His first Portuguese poems were offerings "to young male acquaintances, but soon the thematic circle expanded: there appeared religious-philosophical and purely lyrical poems, and one sonnet even responded to a social problem."[95] In 1980 "one sonnet came clutching another [...]. Sweet Humberto always helps in polishing them: I make very few mistakes (most often it is in the definite and indefinite articles, as well as prepositions). Might it happen that, instead of conquering Brazil for the Russian Muse, Brazil would conquer a Russian poet?" More and more he felt: "I have become Brazilian, and not only by passport."[96]

His reworking of "The Way of the Cross," "a prayer to the Lord to entrust me with *more* suffering," into Portuguese – "Via cruces. Guirland de sonetos" – was completed "on the eve of Mum's departure." Although he later saw this "parallel work" as "a large failure," at the time it seemed an achievement: "I do not know of a single crown of sonnets in the language of Camões; perhaps they simply do not exist. Obviously, I want to be the author of the *first* crown of sonnets in Portuguese."[97] He mailed it to Prelate Marcos Barboza, the prior of St Benedictine monastery and a poet, but the latter replied that while it had literary merit, "he, Don Marcos, refused to help [with publication], because I was 'an inveterate left-hander.'" Pereleshin sent it, together with *Southern Cross*, to another academician, and on 24 July 1981 he was presented to the Brazilian Academy of Letters as a translator of Brazilian poetry and a Russian poet, "an honour and a privilege, but rather boring."[98]

In the late 1970s and in the 1980s many of his "poems in Portuguese were parallel variants to the Russian ones, but others were new, like the recent "Down with Rhetoric!" (*Abaixo a retórica!* 8.11.1979)."[99] Humberto, "though not a poet, puts his whole heart into my poems: he goes deeply into every stanza, every line, every word, every punctuation mark, and rejoices like a child at every success. I do not know whether the history of literature knows another example of such collaboration." They enjoyed the work: "At times, a word we are searching for comes to both at the same time, and we say it in one voice. Then we wonder: who prompted it?"[100] In June 1982, after working well into the night, Humberto said: "Your Portuguese poems and translations are so good that you should publish them." With the money from the Harbin Commercial Schools Alumni in San Francisco, Pereleshin placed an order for his new book with Edições Achiamé Ltda. The title, *Nos odres velhos* (*In Old Wineskins*), stressed his loyalty to old forms, especially sonnets, while "the 'wine' which I poured into these 'old wineskins' is a vision of the world, unavailable to those who marry and procreate."[101]

Nos odres velhos came out on 23 May 1983, with a fine portrait of Pereleshin by Humberto, who also created the cover illustration of a naked Greek boy serving wine to an older man. The book comprised poems, predominantly sonnets, in chronological order from 5 February 1979 to 22 June 1982, and a small section of translations. Most sonnets spoke of loving young men, making "*Ariel* seem like a soul-saving book."[102] Some were "parallel variants" of Russian poems, such as "O encontro com o passado" (17.5.1980) and "Meeting with the Past" (*Vstrecha s proshlym*, 14.5.1976); "As meninas vizinhas" (15.7.1980) and "Neighbouring Girls" (*Devochki-sosedki*, 9.7.1968); "A Lucien Létinua" (1.8.1980) and "To Lucien Létinous" (*K Lius'enu Letinua*, 4.9.1934); Humberto's favourite, "*O palimpsesto*" (31.10.1979) and "Palimpsest" (8.10.1975); and "Amendoim," written on 21 May 1980 in Portuguese and the day before in Russian. An early, discarded poem "Falam os vermes," became Russian "Worms Speak" (*Govoriat chervi*, 4.10.1967) and was then rewritten in Portuguese on 15 December 1981. Condemning procreation was "the theme of my entire life. [...] I have always been tormented by the unnecessary nature, the meaningless, the aimlessness of being (not the absolute being, of course, but temporary and relative – human life on earth)."[103]

The second part of the book comprised translations of Pessoa's English "Antinous," ten Russian poems largely by émigré and Silver Age poets, and twelve Chinese poems. He was glad that the publisher had placed "Paintings of Portinari" (*Kartiny Portinari*) by the émigré poet Valentina Sinkevich first, to honour the Brazilian painter. His presentation of Tang-dynasty classical poets, all previously translated into Russian, was done in two days' time.[104]

The publisher did not distribute the book or send copies for reviews, and Pereleshin had "no skill in selling my books, but simply presented them to anyone who might pay attention." By September 1983 the sales brought in Cr$60,000 out of the total cost of Cr$250,000.[105] In a "harsh" and "almost hostile" review in *Jornal do Brasil*, "the reviewer, a spiritual twin of Rafal'skii and Rudinskii, tried to show off his wit and did not shy away from sharp remarks." The newspaper *O Estadão de São Paulo*, however, sent a reporter to interview Pereleshin, and an item with his photograph appeared on 23 September 1983; a few provincial newspapers mentioned the book "in a friendly manner." He hoped "gradually to become a literary figure in Brazil."[106]

To Friends and Acquaintances (*Druz'iam i znakomym*) in São Paulo published a review by V.S., written by Pereleshin, although he claimed that the author was a Jesuit of the Eastern Rites. It did not mention the gay themes, but spoke of his devotion to time-tested forms and the new wine, which came from "fermentation of conscious and unconscious strivings, infatuations, and desires, which were suppressed, successfully or not, in real life. [...] The poems are written in the 'key' of the Russian poems of Valerii Pereleshin. They express the same eternal theme of struggle between the seventh heaven and putrid swamps of the earth, and of the poet's favourite symbol of a swing, which at times soars to the clouds, at times falls into muggy dirt. The book presents depths of sensuality, the luxury of 'forbidden' discoveries, and then suddenly a sonnet 'Ave Roma' speaks of another, but most beloved, dream: his wish to visit (and die) in the Eternal City."[107]

Translation of Mikhail Kuzmin's *Alexandrian Songs*, 1986

Когда мне говорят: "Александрия,"
я вижу бледно-багровый закат над зеленым морем,
мохнатые мигающие звезды
и светлые серые глаза под густыми бровями,
которые я вижу и тогда,
когда мне не говорят: "Александрия!"

Quando me dizem "Alexandria,"
vejo o ocaso rubro pálido sobre o mar verde,
as estrelas felpudas cintilantes,
e os olhos cinzentos sob as sobrancelhas densas,
que eu vejo mesmo
quando não me dizem "Alexandria"!

Translated by V. Pereleshin and
Humberto Marques Passos

His next publication was a translation of Mikhail Kuzmin's *Alexandrian Songs* (*Aleksandriiskie pesni*, 1905–6) into Portuguese. He was charmed by Kuzmin's "beautiful clarity," except that "where Kuzmin has 'the merry lightness of a homeless life,' I have a tragedy which resolves itself in loving Nirvana."[108] He and Humberto, both "passionately in love" with Kuzmin's cycle, worked hard and kept "free verse as free, and rhymed as rhymed."[109] In June 1981, they submitted *Cânticos de Alexandria* to a prominent publishing house, Civilização Brasileira. They were almost sure of success: "*such* work could not be refused," and its rejection was "a heavy blow." Humberto sent it to another publishing house, "young and braver," but met with the same result: "no one buys poetry and no one in Brazil knows Kuzmin and Pereleshin."[110]

In December 1983, Pereleshin did what he had always done. With the money from selling some books to the Leiden University Library, he and Humberto, his "accomplice in my sins and transgressions" paid US$700, nearly half of the cost, to Edições Achiamé Ltda: "After all, this is what's important in life."[111] The publisher kept postponing and ignoring Humberto's pleas and Pereleshin's threats to sue. In 1985, Pereleshin joined the Union of Writers, which promised to take up the matter at the Judicial Commission of the Union. It turned out that the publisher owed some Cr$40 million to the printers, which "means that Kuzmin will never be published." In August 1985, Humberto, who owed Pereleshin money from numerous small loans, was able to pay the rest of the money to force publication, but it did not help. It was a total loss.[112]

In 1986, Pereleshin, grateful for cheques from the Harbin Commercial Schools Alumni, submitted the manuscript to another publisher, and *Cânticos de Alexandria* finally came out on 31 July of that year. The cover was enhanced by Luis Ferrera's depiction of Kuzmin's eyes, and the frontispiece was Humberto's drawing of the naked torso of a young man. The title page said: "Traduzidos do russo por Valério Pereliéchin e H. Marques Passos."[113] Encouraged, he and Humberto started translating *Daodejing* into Portuguese; earlier translations, missing from the Central Library, were marked on the catalogue card as "*adaptação*."[114]

Pereleshin was becoming known in Brazil and was invited to be a corresponding member of the *Academia Petropolitana de Letras*: "I joined right away and sent a cheque (very modest); I have made copies of 'Via crucis' and other works 'for the future.' [...] Thus, even along the Brazilian lines I have stopped being a zero."[115] However, no contacts with Brazilian poets followed: "they all are interested in themselves, their publications, and their circles. Russian poetry here is no less exotic than Chinese. Everyone is 'curious,' and that's how far it goes."[116]

Pereleshin's next goal was his second book in Portuguese, *Caçador do sombras* (*Hunter of Shadows*), comprising sonnets and poems on his infatuations with "phantoms and shadows, whom I hunt with no hope of trophies." In 1987, Humberto submitted the typescript to a poetry competition: "I don't think I have a chance: the book is strongly homoerotic and written by a cultural foreigner. I will not be offended. Moreover, rhymed and strictly metrical poems have not been fashionable for a long time. […] In our dear sunny country there are the most incredible variations of love, but it is 'not done' to talk about it."[117] He did not win, and the book was never published.

Publications in the Gay Press

Зарываются корни	Roots are digging themselves
Глубже в тину и слизь,	Deeper into mud and slime,
Чтоб еще непокорней	So that even more rebelliously
Стебли кверху рвались.	Stalks would strive upward.
Даже лист не ложится	Even the leaf does not lay
На оплот водяной:	On the water's bulwark:
К небу – оком сновидца,	Up to the sky with the eye of a dreamer,
К мутной жиже – спиной.	To the murky slush with the back.
И нисходит оттуда,	And from above, where
Где скользят облака,	The clouds glide,
Незапятнанный Будда	An unblemished Buddha
В сердцевину цветка.	Descends into the heart of the flower.
	"Lotus" (*Lotos*), 30.1.1970

In 1977, Pereleshin received a few issues of the San Francisco journal *Gay Sunshine* and a copy of *Orgasms of Light: A Gay Sunshine Anthology* from its editor-publisher, Winston Leyland, who had learned of Pereleshin from Simon Karlinsky. Pereleshin found the anthology "better than the journal, which has almost nothing except descriptions of the sexual act with corresponding pictures, while the anthology has genuine poetry and many works of romanticists (similar to my *Ariel* and other poems)."[118] Later that year, Pereleshin and Humberto welcomed this "very sweet Englishman" to Rio de Janeiro, and Leyland published some of Pereleshin's poems in English translation in *Gay Sunshine*.[119] Prompted by Leyland and Humberto, Pereleshin sent some poems to a Brazilian gay journal, *Lampião* (Street Light), which published "Sacrilege" (*Um sacrilégio*, 25.5.1979) and "Cannibal" (*O cannibal*, 1.6.1979) of "misterioso poeta Perelécihn." It was "the main event of the current year."[120]

On a visit in 1979, Leyland brought *Now the Volcano: An Anthology of Latin American Gay Literature*, in which Pereleshin was represented by "To the One Who Confessed" (*Priznavshemusia*, 15.9.1977), "A Declaration of Love" (*Priznanie v liubvi*, 6.11.1974), "Straight from the Shoulder" (*Splecha*, 28.1.1977), and "Admiration" (*Voskhishchenie*, 11.8.1977) in Karlinsky's translations. Pereleshin loved this "excellent presentation, with notes and information that I was born in Russia, lived in China, and had published nine books and collections of translations." In "To the One Who Confessed" Pereleshin wrote: "Just have a look: *Left-handed Light* [Pereleshin's Russian translation of *Gay Sunshine*], a journal, / with drawings, articles, and interviews, / and here's *Orgasms of Light*, a book of poems. / […] // We're not alone. Believe me, there are millions / who'll follow Leyland in the righteous fight / for our equality, for decent legislation, / for the right to live and be ourselves."[121]

On his visits to Brazil throughout the 1980s, Leyland often met Pereleshin and Humberto and took home more of Pereleshin's Russian and Portuguese poems. The anthology of 1991, *Gay Roots*, included Pereleshin's "Ao jovem de olhos verdes" (To the Green-Eyed Boy, 4.3.1980) in A. Lacey's translation and Pereleshin's article "Pushkin's Gay Poem" in translation.[122]

In 1997, five years after Pereleshin's death, three poems and fifteen sonnets in Karlinsky's and Vitalii Chernetskii's translations honoured him in the anthology *Out of the Blue: Russia's Hidden Gay Literature*. Introducing Pereleshin, Leyland wrote: "During the period 1977–1991 I met him many times in Brazil and found him an engaging, if eccentric, man, fully open to the joys of gay love but retaining many of the formalities of his generation. […] The publication of these poems here is dedicated to the memory of Valery Pereleshin."[123] Pereleshin would have rejoiced at this fine tribute.

12 Growing Recognition

A Home for the Archive, 1983

В России знал я станцию Читу,
На ней депо и верхнюю "площадку,"
Потом Харбин исправил опечатку
В моей судьбе; как будто налету
  Мелькнул Пекин, и эту красоту
  Запомнил я, как час на пересадку
  В пути в Шанхай – к последнему упадку

  Той тихости, что и поныне чту.
Теперь Китай кичится биллионом
Голодных душ, непреходящим стоном
Еще живых, безмолвием могил.
  Он выдержит и этот воздух спертый.
  Трем родинам я честно послужил –
  Не станет ли Голландия четвертой?

In Russia I knew Chita Station,
Its depot and the upper "platform,"
Then Harbin corrected the typo
In my fate; as if in a swift flight
  Beijing passed by, and I retained
  Its beauty as an hour for a transfer
  On the way to Shanghai – to the final
    decline
  Of that stillness which I revere even now.
Now China boasts of a billion
Of hungry souls in endless moans
Of the still living, in the silence of the graves.
  It would endure this stifling air.
  I have honestly served three homelands –
  Would Holland become the fourth?

"Fourth Homeland?"
(*Chetvertaia rodina?*), 16.10.1988

In the 1970s and 1980s, Pereleshin was becoming known from his books and publications in émigré periodicals and anthologies in Europe, Canada, the United States, and Australia. Iurii Ivask, Aleksis Rannit, and Simon Karlinsky wrote articles on his poetry, and he was included in Tamara Pachmuss's *A Russian Cultural Revival: Anthology of Émigré Literature before 1939*, Victor Terras's *A Handbook of Russian Literature*, and Wolfgang Kasack's revised *Lexikon der russischen Literatur ab 1917*. The latter pleased him by mentioning his "passion for young men."

Well aware of how many works and archives of Russian poets of China had been lost, he was concerned that after his death his "books and manuscripts will be swept away, like rubbish" by his brother. He continued to send retyped and signed copies of his poems to several friends in the hope that they would save them, and a few gratefully did so. As early as 1969, he offered some materials to the Bakhmeteff Archive at Columbia University, which bought some, but informed him that generally they only accepted gifts. In the mid-1970s and early 1980s, the impending move to Muri forced him to approach Ivask, Rannit, and various institutions in the United States, but no one wanted to buy his archive or even pay the postage.[1]

A wonderful solution emerged at the end of the 1970s. On a research trip to Moscow, Jan Paul Hinrichs, at the time a student of Slavic languages and literature at Leiden University, had learned about Pereleshin from Evgenii Vitkovskii and written to him. Pereleshin, flattered and grateful for the attention, started sending the young scholar his poems and was delighted when Dr Jan Paul Hinrichs's *Vanuit de verte*, a selection of his poems in Dutch translation with an introduction, came out in several editions.[2] On Hinrichs's initiative, Leiden University expressed interest in Pereleshin's archive, and in December 1983 it was formally agreed that he would donate it to the university, which in return would buy from him some sixty antiquarian books and journal runs for US$756.[3]

Pereleshin was happy that "all these 'papers,' priceless for future historians of Russian literature in exile," would be preserved, while selling his books served "a double purpose: they will not be destroyed or eaten by insects in case of my death, and the money will permit me to publish my second book of Portuguese poems *Caçador do sombras* and Kuzmin's *Cânticos de Alexandria*." He assured Leiden University that its "evaluation of the books and the journals is fair and entirely acceptable," but grumbled to his correspondents that he was paid "the most modest sums" – in his estimate US$10 per book – and his archive was accepted "for free, as a premium." He held back his copies of Arsenii Nesmelov's autographed books of poetry, "hoping to complete negotiations with their sale."[4]

In 1984–5 he started sending some materials to Leiden both by mail, the university reimbursing the postage, and by diplomatic post via J.C.B. Dirkx, the Netherlands consul-general in Rio de Janeiro.[5] The packages held his poems, articles, photographs, and correspondence, including hundreds of letters to his mother, both originals and retyped copies with comments. When Hinrichs noticed gaps in these letters, Pereleshin found more in two trunks, which the consulate-general could not send by diplomatic post. However, the letters to his mother from 2 February 1946 to 26 June 1949, except the one of 19 October 1946, remained missing; they could have been lost, or perhaps he or his mother had destroyed them, because that was the period during which he worked for TASS.[6]

In 1986, the Slavic Department of the Philological Faculty at Leiden University invited Pereleshin for a three-week visit: "I am almost blind and planning to fly to Leiden! [...] I am unwell and walk with difficulty. [...] I should be getting ready not for Leiden, but for a closer place, the cemetery."[7] On 3 May 1986 he was met by Hinrichs in Amsterdam and driven to the International House on one of Leiden's beautiful canals; a vase of tulips and hyacinths welcomed him to his room. On 5 May, he opened an exhibition "A Poet of Three Homelands, Letters, and Documents" (*Dichter met drie vaderlanden. Valerij Perelešin, brieven en documenten*); the posters and the catalogue displayed his portrait by Humberto. He gave one talk on Russian émigré literature in China and another on Nesmelov, was feted by librarians and officials and shown archival collections. Hinrichs took him to Amsterdam, Rotterdam, The Hague, and Gouda; in a bookstore in Maastricht he recited his poems and signed copies of the third edition of *Vanuit de verte*; of the 250 copies only seventeen remained unsold. His poem "Three Homelands" (*Drie vaderlanden*) in Hinrichs's translation was sold as a separate souvenir edition. He was interviewed and photographed for a Dutch newspaper article entitled "A Poet Finds his Fourth Homeland." It was "a total triumph," and he believed that he was "the first Russian poet to visit this hospitable country."[8]

He then flew to Paris, where, after a few days with Nina Fouchier, he was taken by Larissa Andersen to Yissengeaux, where they worked on her second book of poems, *The Blue* (*Sineva*); her first, *Along the Earth Meadows* (*Po zemnym lugam*) had been published in 1940 in Shanghai.[9] René Guerra, a collector and publisher of émigré works, was "exceptionally attentive" and invited him to his place in Issy-les-Moulineaux. On 11–12 June Pereleshin spent a day in Cherbourg with the family of Dr Carl Salatko-Petrishche, "descendants in the tenth or eleventh generation of the Lepel' land-owner Foma (Tomash) Salatko-Petrishche." On 15 June 1986, after this triumphant tour, Humberto met him at the airport in Rio de Janeiro.[10]

Leiden Publications, 1987–1989

Уходил все дальше, все западней	I have been travelling further and further west
мимо зовов и западней.	past summons and ambushes.
От больших и недолгих плаваний,	From voyages long and short,
от мельканья морей и гаваней	from flashes of seas and harbours,
смутный образ тише, бледней	the dim image was descending, getting
опускался на дно несытое.	quieter, paler, to the insatiable bottom.
Становился я сам бедней,	I myself was becoming poorer,
но тоска росла, и под ней	but the anguish grew, and beneath it,
напоследок на склоне дней	at the end, in the evening of life
воскресает почти забытое.	the almost forgotten is rising.

"Outcast" (*Izgoi*), 11.10.1969

In the 1950s and 1960s, not much had been written about Russians in China, except for Petr Balakshin's ground-breaking *Finale in China* (*Final v Kitae*, 1958–9), which upset many émigrés with its honesty.[11] Pereleshin, too, protested to Balakshin: "Neither Semen Kaspe's murder nor other kidnappings for ransom (with the participation of the Japanese gendarmerie) are characteristic of the Russian emigration in Harbin. What is typical are the Polytechnic Institute, the Law Faculty, the Oriental Faculty, the Pedagogical Institute, the Higher Musical School, wonderful libraries, theatres, orchestras, sport organizations, the YMCA, and the Society for the Study of the Manchurian Region with its Museum."[12]

In 1968 Iustina Kruzenshtern's impressionistic recollections, "Churaevka's Nursery (On Far Eastern Poets)" (*Churaevskii pitomnik (O dal'nevostochnykh poetakh)*), appeared in *Resurrection.*[13] Her account made Pereleshin realize "how differently we perceived the same people and events" and prompted him to write "a long tale about Sergin and Granin," which soon developed into "something like a catalogue of Far Eastern writers, poets, and, perhaps, journalists" and then acquired "a novelistic character," somewhat similar to Georgii Ivanov's *Petersburg Winters* (*Peterburgskie zimy*) or Odoevtseva's *On the Shores of the Neva* (*Na beregakh Nevy*).[14] The work engaged him, and he asked Kruzenshtern for "facts, spiced with anecdotes for liveliness," and his mother for recollections: "she knew all these people not as poets, but simply as people, colleagues, and acquaintances."[15]

The title of his account, "Two Sidings" (*Dva polustanka*), subtitled "Memoirs of a Witness and Participant in the Literary Life of the Russian

Emigration in China," came from Nesmelov's *Siding* (*Polustanok*, 1938), where the railway siding on an émigré's journey was Harbin; Pereleshin added Shanghai as the second siding. He started with Harbin and "in five days and nights wrote thirty-five typewritten pages" of "purely personal impressions and observations." In April 1969 he sent it to *New Russian Word* and moved on to write about Shanghai, but neither *New Russian Word* nor *The New Review* was interested.[16] Pereleshin sent typewritten copies to some of his friends, and some twelve years later *Russian Life* in San Francisco started its serialization, but the editors initially mangled the title of the first chapter and then dropped the work as "unkind," ignoring Pereleshin's protests that it had "no sugary pictures and inappropriate raptures."[17]

In 1985 Hinrichs decided to publish this manuscript in Leiden, and Pereleshin retyped the text "like a slave, but blissfully": for the first time in his life he did not have to pay for publication.[18] "Two Sidings" came out in April 1987 as *Russian Poetry and Literary Life in Harbin and Shanghai, 1930–1950: The Memoirs of Valerii Pereleshin*, with Hinrichs's preface, introduction, bibliography, and notes in English. Pereleshin was grateful for Hinrichs's "enormous editorial work," but found the introduction too short and disagreed with some statements. On receiving the first copy, he noted: "modesty not being one of my mortal virtues, I read this little book of mine four times in a row 'from cover to cover,' and keep reading it constantly from 'wherever it opens.'"[19]

In *Two Sidings* Pereleshin described some crucial events of his life, but never mentioned his "left-handedness," even though he rather sloppily revised the 1969 typescript and dated it to 1974–5. There were several inconsistencies and mistakes in dates and facts. *Two Sidings* differed from several rosy memoirs of some Harbin Russians published by this time, but was equally impressionistic and at times self-serving. On the one hand, Pereleshin stated that his goal was "to tell the truth, tell everything" "in this 'novel without lies'"; but on the other hand, he called it "cunning": "I did not promise to write *the truth*: who can remember such distant events? [...] I described our life as I perceived and remembered it."[20] As Karlinsky pointed out in his review, the author was "by no means an impartial chronicler."[21]

His memoirs angered several people, especially Mikhail Volin, whom he presented as a weak poet, poser, braggart, and playboy, who sniffed cocaine and was accountable for Pereleshin's deportation from the United States by failing to exchange his Soviet passport for IRO papers. In the book, Pereleshin often referred to him as "Mifa," mocking his minor speech impediment, but restrained himself from using the derogatory "mishka" (with a small "m"), Mishka Olin, or Mishka Samodovolin (Mishka Self-Satisfied), as he did in letters and some poems.[22] When mutual friends chastised Pereleshin for writing about cocaine, he answered that he had "witnessed 'a great organized snort.' [...] I remember that night with a photographic precision. Judging by the participants, it was a good company: at that time people toyed with cocaine in Paris, in Prague, in China." Not only Volin, but also Granin, the Satovskii-Rzhevskii brothers, the writer Iul'skii, and others snorted cocaine: "all were my friends, and I cannot say anything 'derogatory' about them. Harbin poverty and unsettled life justified any weakness, even alcoholism."[23]

Volin threatened to sue, and Hinrichs's response, as described by Pereleshin, was to let him do that in Australia, in the Netherlands, and in Brazil; it would be an expensive process and the best advertisement for the book.[24] Volin did not take legal action, but wrote to everyone he knew that the memoirs were "total lies, lies, lies!" and fumed to a friend: "Why should we be proud of Pereleshin, an unfrocked monk, a man who boasts of hundreds of lovers, an inmate of three [*sic*] prisons, who hates the normal world and normal people? [...] During his long life Pereleshin 'became adept' at writing poems and some, perhaps, are not bad, but most are filth and lechery!" He also circulated Chinnov's epigram: "It's a hardship to read Salatko's sonnets, / and Petrishche's poems are ever so boring, / the old man Pereleshin / is consoled only by himself and is far from sinless."[25]

Volin's revenge was to write his own memoirs, "Young Churaevka's Tragic End" (*Gibel' Molodoi Churaevki*), in which he alleged that Churaevka had been destroyed by Peterets, Pereleshin, and Lapiken: "Two of these 'devils,' Pereleshin and Lapiken, were homosexuals. [...] In those distant years, well before the 'sexual revolution' of the 1960s and 1970s, homosexuals, especially in Russian society, were regarded with a mixture of surprise and disgust."[26] He described Pereleshin as physically ugly and pathetically in love with Granin, compared him to Dostoevsky's Smerdiakov, and cited anonymous negative recollections. Pereleshin's mother, he claimed, was a gold-digger, who ensnared Sentianin and then tried to do the same with Volin's grandfather. Professor N.M. Christesen of Melbourne University declined to include Volin's memoirs in her series "Russians in Australia," and the incomplete text was published only in 1997, after both enemies were dead, in *The New Review*.[27]

Larissa Andersen accused Pereleshin of "*spitting on ALL* his old friends" and was "stung by my recollection of how Granin disgraced himself by throwing up. But I had to write as a historian, without taking sentiments into account. Granin's escapades after his expulsion and his open persecution of Churaevka and the YMCA led to Churaevka's closure, in which Granin played an ugly role." Andersen had no right to defend him: "I had loved Granin so much that Larissa could not even dream of, and, after all, Granin shot himself because of Larissa." She imagined Churaevka to have been "one family," but "Granin broke away from 'the family' and in the last period of his life flung mud at us all. And mishka [*sic*] never belonged to 'the family.' It was not for nothing that Mary Peterets [Iustina Kruzenshtern] shouted, when I suggested inviting Mishka to the Friday Circle: 'Only over my dead body!' Larissa was present."[28] She wrote to Hinrichs that Pereleshin had turned people into caricatures, that Granin's excesses and Iankovskaia's "lack of culture, skill, and taste" were not true, that Volin "had never been such a melodramatic bore," and that there were mistakes in dates, names, and circumstances. She soberly added, though, that it was "useless to argue about impressions: everyone has his own mirror, which reflects the same things differently."[29]

In preparing *Two Sidings* for publication, Hinrichs asked for a supplementary anthology of Russian poets in China, and Pereleshin was glad to oblige.[30] In 1984, when he and Volin had still been on lukewarm terms, Volin had asked for help in compiling an anthology of Harbin and Shanghai poets, but they soon disagreed: Volin wanted poems written both in China and in the second emigration, while Pereleshin insisted on "one non-negotiable condition: a poem had to be written *in China*."[31] In 1985, Mary Vezey sought a grant for such an anthology, and Pereleshin agreed to be "a *consultative voice*: I will search and offer, but the selection will be yours." As they were compiling the anthology, he suddenly informed her that "my friends in Holland [...] entrusted me with compiling an anthology of poetic samples, so that readers will know all the Far Eastern poets mentioned in my memoirs."[32] He quickly put together a collection of poems, "written exclusively *there* (in China) and *then* (from the beginning of the 1920s to 1955 or 1956)," leaving the selection of his own poems to Hinrichs. Nesmelov was omitted because Guerra was planning to publish, with Pereleshin's help, a collection of Nesmelov's poems under the title of "In the Drowned Submarine" (*V zatonuvshei submarine*).[33]

Two Sidings was published without the anthology, Guerra's book never came out, and Vezey's anthology stalled. In 1988 Pereleshin expanded the draft of the Leiden anthology to ninety-five poems by forty-one poets, with an introduction and notes in the form of "'splotches of life,' including even innocent gossip but not discrediting anyone." Entitled "A Rest on the Way" (*Prival*), it was offered to Ardis Publishers. Their curt refusal angered him: "I guess the Proffers publish exclusively Jews. Well, I don't make it in this respect."[34]

In 1988 Hinrichs wrote that the Slavists Foundation in Leiden might publish what Pereleshin understood to be "a folio 'Valerii Pereleshin, Russian Poet From China'" of several volumes, with poems, translations, letters to his mother and Lidiia Khaindrova, articles, and an autobiography.[35] This proposal was abandoned, but in 1989, with Pereleshin's joyful cooperation, Hinrichs published *A Russian Poet as a Guest in China, 1920–1952* (*Russkii poet v gostiakh u Kitaia, 1920–1952*), a fine collection of 193 poems, which, as the compiler and editor, Hinrichs, explained, were "all the poetry written in China that has ever been included by Pereleshin in a book edition." Pereleshin provided "the latest authorized versions" and "authorized" dates.[36] His wish to reprint his first four books not only came true, but also was amplified by poems of the Chinese period which he had published in later books.

Three Homelands: The Tenth Book of Poetry, 1987

Мы часто плакали: затем ли	We often cried: have foreign
Открылись нам чужие земли,	Countries opened to us
Чтоб в каждой, снова и опять,	So that in each, anew and again,
Частицу сердца потерять?	We would lose a part of our hearts?
Сквозь отуманенные окна	Looking at the birds of passage
На перелетных глядя птиц,	Through fogged windows,
Другие мы нашли волокна	We found other filaments
Взамен растерянных частиц.	To replace the lost particles.
О, вещая судьба изгоя!	Oh, the prophetic fate of an exile!
Он дома здесь, и дома там,	He is at home here and at home there,
А в сердце – с болью пополам –	And in his heart – half mixed with pain –
Густеют сумерки покоя.	The twilight of rest is getting darker.
	"Rest" (*Pokoi*), 21.5.1970

In 1979, on Karlinsky's advice, Russica Publishers in New York expressed an interest in Pereleshin's poems, and he eagerly compiled the provisionally titled *Heart Core / To the Third and Last* (*Serdtsevina /*

Tret'ei i poslednei). The first part comprised selections from his first four books, and the second consisted of poems about Brazil, but "utilitarian considerations" forced him to "castrate" the book by leaving out the "left-handed" poems.[37] Although he submitted the manuscript, Russica did not carry it through to publication, and in 1986 Pereleshin turned this draft into *Three Homelands* (*Tri rodiny*) and paid Guerra's Editions Albatros to publish it. Unexplained delays infuriated him: the "Devil made me get entangled with Albatros: / he gobbled up my money and left me a fool," according to his epigram "Impromptu" (*Eksprompt*, 1.8.1987). He had "lost all hope," when on 8 September 1987 he got a "jubilant" letter from Guerra that seven copies had been mailed to him. He liked its "elegant and wonderfully emblematic cover," which combined St Petersburg's Bronze Horseman, the Southern Cross, and a Chinese dragon.[38] However, the poet and the publisher soon quarrelled so seriously over the delay and typos that Guerra mailed him the entire run and charged postage, though he later returned Pereleshin's cheque "to boast of *his* magnanimity." Guerra had become "a hysterical wench," who "would harm me in every possible way."[39]

Three Homelands kept the original double structure of the draft of *Heart Core / To the Third and Last*. Sixty-two poems in the first part were taken from his first four books, while the theme of Brazil dominated in sixty-one previously published and unpublished poems in the second part, dedicated to "Humberto Marques Passos and all my Brazilian friends." His love for Brazil is eloquently expressed in poems such as "Idyll" (*Idilliia*, 25.7.1969), "Windy Night" (*Vetrenaia noch'*, 21.8.1969), and "Brazil" (*Braziliia*, 7.1.1972). In "Brazilian Spring" (*Brazil'skaia vesna*, 10.5.1971), however, the poet raises a glass of *cachaça* to the old Russian alphabet and ice-breaking northern springs, and in "The Quiver of Latin Sail" (*Trepet latinskogo parusa*, 28.7.1972) he gives his "last breath to Russia." "Not a Monument" (*Ne pamiatnik*, 16.4.1972) confesses his love for the Russian Muse, enticed by him to Brazil: "But my companion is ready to revenge herself: / she will run away north, and by the Moscow River / she will not say a kind word about me, / neither in a list of names nor in a footnote." The two countries merge into a Brazilian-Russian forest in "Dream" (*Son*, 3.1.1970) and the undiscovered island Rozilia-Brassia in "Across the Globe" (*Po globusu*, 1.9.1972).

Out of the Depths Have I Cried: The Eleventh Book of Poetry, 1987

Не в алтаре – люблю Тебя в себе,	Not in the altar, I love Thee in myself,
В презрении к питательным наукам,	In the contempt for nourishing sciences,
В растерянном прищуре близоруком,	In the perplexed near-sighted squinting,
В невидности, в порочной худобе, –	In plain looks, in depraved thinness –
В бездетности, в безженности, в горбе,	In being childless, unmarried, a hunchback,
В пристрастии к разрывам и разлукам,	In predilection for breaks and partings,
К несбыточным, пригрезившимся мукам:	In unrealized, day-dream torments:
Люблю Тебя во всей моей судьбе.	I love Thee in my entire fate.
Смесь горькая, но в тесто этой смеси	It is a bitter mixture, but into its dough
Ты не вмешал ни жадности, ни спеси,	Thou did not mix in greediness, arrogance,
Ни помыслов о прибыльном добре –	And designs for profitable goods –
Тех нескольких непрошенных молекул,	Those few unbidden molecules,
С которыми, проснувшись на заре,	Which would have made me wake up at dawn,
Клевал бы я зерно да кукарекал!	Peck at grains and crow!

"Thanksgiving" (*Blagodarenie*), 21.5.1975

In the "Afterword" to *Three Homelands* Pereleshin wrote that publishing poems about his "three homelands (inherited Russia, blessedly acquired China and Brazil) did not satisfy my inner hunger. What remained untouched is my belief in God and Church, but here too deep doubts, rebellion, despair, and bitter feelings of abandonment by God are inevitable."[40] This "inner hunger" led to a collection of religious poems: nine from Harbin books, twenty-seven from *Swing*, and forty-six published and unpublished poems, a total of eighty-two. The book concluded with "The Way of the Cross" and "Poem about the World Creation." Owing to Guerra's delay, this eleventh book, paid for by Pereleshin and published by New England Publishing in Holyoke, Massachusetts, came out before the tenth.[41]

The title, *Out of the Depths Have I Cried* (*Iz glubiny vozzvakh*), printed, on his insistence, in the Old Church Slavonic script, was taken from Psalm 129 (Psalm 130:1 in the English Bible): "De profundis clamavi ad te Domine" (Out of the depths have I cried unto thee, O Lord). Pereleshin's introduction explained that these words from "the psalm of repentance [...] were coming as a sigh from the grieving and humble heart of the ardent and frivolous Benvenuto Cellini, the sophisticated master of paradox Oscar Wilde, and innumerable thinkers, poets, painters and ordinary people, wounded by sharp corners of reality and forced to turn to the metaphysical world."[42]

Like *Three Homelands*, this book was largely a summarizing selection of previously published poems. As Mary Vezey said in her brief review, it "reads like a prayer."[43] It traces some of his religious thoughts from the earliest "Eternal Rome" [*Vechnyi Rim*, 1932–3] and "The Way of the Cross" [*Krestnyi put'*, 1945] to the mid-1980s. The poems reflect his conflict between accepting and rejecting God, who had abandoned him in his struggles, and his refusal to accept divisions between the Orthodox and the Roman Catholic Churches: "the Catholic Church (i.e., simply Church, because the Church is one) has always understood that NOT ALL monks and priests are holy, but argued that a monk would sin and then come to his senses." In his view, "Sts Ignatius, Torquemada, and Anchieta are *honest* and *righteus* people, no comparison to Calvin, Luther, and Feofan Prokopovich. My saints are St Francis of Assisi, St Serafim of Sarov, St Sergii of Radonezh, St Teresa the Great, St John of the Cross, St Thérèse of Lisieux, St Bernadette, but NOT Holy Prince Vladimir, whom I place on the same level as the emperors Constantine and Justinian."[44]

This "Christian," as he called it, collection is somewhat misleading in softening his defiance of God and excluding his appreciation of Buddhism. As he wrote in one letter, "we created a God who 'ordered' us to do various stupid things. It means that we should create a different God," who would not "shut the mouth of a questioner with 'It's God's will!'" The Buddhist karma was "*the best* of all existing answers to the question of the inequality of souls and the inequality of fates."[45] He also did not include poems on his principled stand against natalism; for him, the church's insistence on "the perpetuation of suffering by producing children is the greatest crime."[46] Equally absent from the collection are the poems which "make it obvious that the tragedy of my life became the basis for my Manichean world view and for my hatred towards human striving to deceive death by procreation, even though it suits death well: 'mortal children' ensure its triumph (and ensure a steady supply of meat for maggots). [...] 'Left-handers' in my meaning of the word are no more 'deprived by the nature' than physical left-handers. Hostility towards them is exclusively a demonstration of the majority's tyranny over the minority, although it would seem that the 10 per cent of men who refuse to multiply help a little in slowing down the indecent growth of the population on earth. They should not be persecuted and condemned, but awarded medals and even titles of counts and marquises for life. Their existence is beneficial to humanity *as a whole*."[47]

International Festival of Poetry in Rotterdam, 1989

Последний ушел собеседник,
надвинулась ночь, как ледник.
Я в мой ухожу заповедник –
в гарем непрочитанных книг.
  Сиамский престолонаследник,
  кого изберу, окружен,
  из тысячи девственных жен?

My last companion is gone,
the night like a glacier moved closer.
I am going into my sanctuary,
into my harem of unread books.
  An Heir to the throne of Siam,
  whom would I choose, surrounded
  by a thousand of virginal wives?

"Late Evening"
(*Pozdnii vecher*), 29.1.1969

An invitation to the Poetry International Festival in Rotterdam, to take place on 17–24 June 1989, which included the travel and hotel expenses, was "a miracle," which could not be missed even in view of his greatly deteriorating health.[48] He eagerly attended this grand affair, packed with readings, meetings, workshops, receptions, interviews, and celebratory dinners. Individual brochures introduced each poet, and Pereleshin's contained a fine selection of sixteen poems.[49] He was "welcomed with all possible indulgence and care," but became upset that he was limited to reciting only his short "Late Evening" (*Pozdnii vecher*, 29.1.1969) rather than his choices of "Under the Full Moon" (*V polnolunie*, 14.10.1943) and "From Afar" (*Izdaleka*, 19.5.1953).[50]

Hinrichs devoted considerable time to him, and the festival director Martin Mooy, "the soul of the Festival," and other Dutch Slavists were most attentive.[51] The Soviet poets Evgenii Rein, Bella Akhmadulina, Aleksei Parshchikov, and Tat'iana Shcherbina took him out for a drink, but ignored him after Brodsky's arrival, who "contrived *not* to become acquainted with me. The piss of fame obviously had rushed to his head."[52] Pereleshin's acrimony flared up with new force. Brodsky's 1987 Nobel Prize was "motivated not by literary, but nationalist considerations, and the committee's axiom is that only a Jew is worthy of representing *Russian* poetry. I dare to disagree with this 'axiom.' In the twentieth century we had Khodasevich,

Akhmatova, Georgii and Viacheslav Ivanov, Kuzmin, Baron Shteiger, Lidiia Alekseeva, Adamovich, Ladinskii, Smolenskii, dozens of others, and, finally, Nesmelov. But only 'those from Odessa' and no one else are thrust upon us. I have never liked Pasternak or Brodsky. Brodsky, in particular, shoves his Jewishness upon us ('Abraham and Isaac' [the actual title "Isaak and Avraam"] of twenty-two poems, each on one letter of the Jewish [Hebrew] alphabet)."[53]

For Pereleshin the festival was a time of pride and of great frustration: not only was he hard of hearing and semi-blind, but he also grew weak and incontinent, especially after unaccustomed drinking with other poets: "all ten days in Rotterdam I was very ill [...]. At times I simply could not walk, kept falling, and wanted most of all to lie down on a footpath and not get up at all. However, I had enough strength to recite my tiny 'Late Evening' from the stage of the De Doelen Theatre, to give an interview for the press and the radio, and to meet with the representatives of the television company."[54]

The Hotel Central complained to the organizers about his incontinence, and he was moved to a nursing home and lent a wheelchair. A Dutch poet, Hannie Groen, one of the festival's hosts, was asked to look after him. As she recalled, "there was something in his figure (in a wheelchair) that was joyful. Although he was deaf, felt ill, and could not see much, he was far from pitiful or pathetic. No, he was, as I saw it, happy."[55] Indeed, "were it not for my illness and the wheelchair, in which the kindest Ioganna [Hannie Groen] wheeled me around, it would have been truly great." A doctor recommended an extended treatment, and the Dutch minister of culture was persuaded to offer free hospitalization, but all Pereleshin wanted was to go home. On his departure, Hannie Groen loaded him with clothes and underwear, and a doctor sent a report translated into Portuguese for Pereleshin's doctor in Brazil.[56]

He returned home on the evening of 27 June and "with difficulty and help from two volunteers pushed my way through the June festivities at Casa dos Artistas to my shelter." He was "full of impressions, but, unfortunately, ill": "in our old age we are supposed to have the same illnesses that pestered us in childhood. This is true about my uremia. Doctors order me to drink more fluids and I do; they order me to walk more and I do. Nevertheless, I understand that things are coming to an end. Well? It's time to end it all."[57]

Poem without a Subject, 1989

Ты старомодница – кружево, накидка, муфта с собачкой, а лезешь в месиво, в луживо? Вернись и туфель не пачкай: ведь сырость, уже предзимняя, чадит по кружным дорогам! Но некогда Полигимния – дурной пример недотрогам, хотя под ногами брызгами урчали моча и пена, ходила взглянуть хоть издали на вшивого Диогена.	You are old-fashioned: lace, cape, a muff with a little snout, but why do you get into mush and puddles? Come back and don't muddy your shoes: already the dampness of the coming winter is misting the surrounding roads! But a long time ago, Polyhymnia, a bad example for touch-me-nots, in spite of the rumbling piss and foam splashing under her feet, went to look, at least from afar, at the lice-ridden Diogenes. "My Muse" (*Moia Muza*), 30.7.1973

In 1977–8, his lengthy *Poem without a Subject* unexpectedly found a publisher in the Toronto journal *Contemporary* (*Sovremennik*), which began its serialization on the insistence of a new editorial board member, A.G. Guidoni, against the objections of several old-timers. When Guidoni became the editor, rumours of his sinister KGB past caused members of the old board leave the journal.[58] As a result, *The New Review* and *New Russian Word* asked their contributors not to publish in *Contemporary*. Many agreed, but compliance with the boycott would have had dire financial consequences for Pereleshin: "I cannot manage without a journalist's mess of pottage: thus, farewell, the primogeniture of a poet!" He appealed to the editors "from the depths of despair," explaining that the serialization of *Poem* in *Contemporary* was "the matter of my entire life." Sedykh, the editor of *New Russian Word*, withdrew the ultimatum in his case: "this is a *man* for you. He is more intelligent and *kinder* and has a greater respect for Russian literature than many others." *The New Review* also gave in: "both editors turned out to be the most worthy persons, not fanatics, not stubborn, but precisely *human beings*."[59]

The *Poem* was not well received. Boris Nartsissov objected to offensive references to Roerich and himself in Canto One and demanded that the serialization stop. Irina Odoevtseva accused Pereleshin of libel for writing that her late husband, Georgii Ivanov, had stolen the 1923 translation of Coleridge's *Christabel* from Gumilev and M.L. Lozinskii.[60]

Guidoni urged Pereleshin to respond, and after the initial refusal "to blow this up into a petty scandal," he wrote "Don't Argue with Fools," pointing out that *Christabel*'s cover said that it was translated by Georgii Ivanov while the "Afterword" ambiguously referred to "poetic editing" by Gumilev and Lozinskii. He offered to rewrite the offending lines, but refused to apologize.[61]

K. Pomerantsev in an article "And He Covered Up His Little Talent with a Great Disgrace" judged this "long and boring" work to be notable only for its "libellous and hooligan attacks" on Georgii Ivanov and Evgenii Evtushenko. The directorate of the Union of Russian Writers and Journalists in Paris censured Pereleshin for "lies, malicious, unscrupulous, and senseless. [...] By this act Mr Pereleshin placed himself once and forever outside the Russian émigré community." Kruzenshtern, while seeing the work as his "De Profundis," criticized his portrayals of some poets, Volin in particular.[62] M. Sergeev wrote that *Poem* parodied Pushkin's *Eugene Onegin*, at times successfully, at times displaying "serious graphomania with an ox-like patience and versificatory diarrhea." Moreover, "in his perceptive observation, I am 'not a p[ederast], but an o[nanist].'"[63]

Contemporary soon became "inwardly alien" to him for Guidoni's crude attacks on the editors of *The New Review* and *New Russian Word*, Zionist statements, promotion of Ukrainian and Belorussian separatists, and proposal of a Nobel Prize for the Ukrainian writer Ulas Samchuk. Pereleshin's belief in "total independence and self-determination of nations" did not extend to the Ukraine and Belorussia, 'the younger brothers" and "organic parts of the Russian Empire"; nor did he see "Ukrainian speech or Belorussian dialect as languages: both are artificial."[64] He also was offended by the interview with a third-wave immigrant writer, Eduard Limonov, who claimed that "Russian literature abroad had not created anything particularly significant or extraordinary, with the exception of the endlessly mentioned and remembered Nabokov and those who left Russia as fully formed writers."[65] Pereleshin decided to sever his ties with *Contemporary* as soon as the serialization was completed, but publication of the last two cantos was postponed to allow space for Guidoni's own novel.[66] The journal folded at the end of 1980 amid nasty allegations, and his hope for a complete serialization died with it.

In August 1987, Pereleshin received "an unbelievable, fantastic, regal letter" from Karlinsky, who offered to publish *Poem without a Subject*. Pereleshin, who "did not even dare to think of *such* thing and naturally went crazy with joy," wrote back: "Let God make this 'miracle' happen."[67] Pereleshin had always greatly admired Karlinsky, who "*never acts against his conscience*, does not hold back or pretend that he 'has not found a maiden whose beauty is worthy of me.'"[68] Karlinsky went ahead "at his own expense and that of other 'admirers' (the term he introduced)" for the final cost of US$6,000 from New England Publishers: "verily, God himself has sent you to me, and I am eternally grateful to Him and to you. *Poem without a Subject* is the major work of my entire life. When it is published, I will have the right to say my '*Nunc dimittis*.'"[69]

Pereleshin did some minor rewriting and braced himself: "And so, Valerii, squeak, moan, groan, but sit down at your 'Masha' (his affectionate name for his typewriter, from *mashinka*) and retype the entire text. It's all right: a big goal justifies even bigger efforts and sacrifices." He resisted the temptation to compose Canto Nine about his new books, his mother's death, the deaths of so many friends, and other events of his life.[70] Then, to his despair, the retyped copy was lost in the mail, and his beloved "Masha" was stolen from his bungalow. Only in February 1988 was he able to send a copy of an earlier, now corrected draft to the publishers, "dreaming day and night of an elegant book, *Poem without a Subject*, even though I know that our 'highly moral' press will try not to notice it, as happened with *Ariel*, and there will not be a single review."[71]

The *Poem* with Karlinsky's analytical introduction came out in September 1989, and Pereleshin wrote to him: "I love your publication of *Poem without a Subject* very much and constantly caress it. [...] Thank you once again."[72] His joy was ruined, however, by numerous typographical errors and a few missing lines, and he furiously demanded that pages of errata be included at the end of each copy.[73] He was further angered that his request for gift copies for some sixty people was refused by the "mercenary publishers." His *Two Sidings* was selling for US$25, *A Russian Poet as a Guest in China* for $60, and *Poem without a Subject* for $30, all of which he saw as pure "robbery: everyone who takes some trouble is profiting, while the author is skinned alive." He complained to Karlinsky: "if the unscrupulous comrade Levin [at New England Publishing] thinks that he will force me to buy my own book, he is mistaken: ON NO ACCOUNT will I pay for the stolen book. [...] The publication financially belongs to you, but, from the point of view of the author's right, it belongs to me." Pereleshin received three more copies and offered to reimburse Karlinsky for postage in sending gift copies to some friends.[74]

Breach of Promise

Живу – и признателен Богу,
что небо дождит не всегда
и высушит ветер дорогу,
когда я поеду – туда.
  К червям собираясь на травлю,
  успею животик наесть.
  А русские книги оставлю
  соседу, какой он ни есть.

I am alive – and grateful to God
that it is not always raining
and the wind will dry the road
when I will be going – there.
  Preparing for being hunted by worms,
  I'll have time to fatten my tummy.
  And I'll leave my Russian books
  to a neighbour, whoever he is.

"I am alive …" (*Zhivu …*),
14.11.1986

As the consul-general of the Netherlands, J.C.B. Dirkx, reported in 1985, Pereleshin had decided to hold on to the rest of the correspondence and five photo albums for a while, though he assured the consul that all would gradually be sent to Leiden University Library. Moreover, Humberto and the director of Casa dos Artistas would be instructed to hand over his archive to the consulate-general in the event of his death.[75] He continued to mail materials to Leiden University Library, but in 1987 considered leaving his remaining archive to various close friends or to Karlinsky, all the while assuring Hinrichs that he had no intention whatsoever of breaking up the archive and it would in its entirety go to Leiden. This promise was strongly reiterated in 1988, and in 1989 he gave Hinrichs the address of his executor, A.B. Kirilloff, to be contacted when he died to make arrangements for the rest of the archive.[76]

Publication of *Two Sidings* in 1987 led to the first crack in his relations with Hinrichs and Leiden. Pereleshin had always paid for publication of all his books, was magnanimous in sending copies to many people, and was totally ignorant of the realities of commercial publishing. Furthermore, he did not know that Hinrichs had financed the publication. When his "rather extensive" list of gift copies was cut down and he had "to buy the book 'from myself' (not quite so, but sounds impressive)" for gifts, he threatened "to write an ode 'In Praise of Thrift,' but I am afraid that it will turn out to be a satire ON STINGINESS. I often swear to myself in Chinese, referring to someone's ancestors with Dutch surnames down to the ninety-ninth generation."[77]

When *A Russian Poet as a Guest in China* came out in 1989, he gratefully mailed his collection of Nesmelov's books to the Leiden University Library, even though previously he had hoped to sell it "to one of the best libraries or to a collector like Thomas Whitney," imagining its price to be US$12,000.[78] The uniqueness of this collection lay not only in its rarity, but also in its inscriptions. Nesmelov had opened his first three Harbin books, *Bloody Reflection* (*Krovavyi otblesk, 1928*), *Without Russia* (*Bez Rossii*, 1931), and *Across the Ocean* (*Cherez okean*, 1934), at their title pages and inscribed all three at once, using one word (in Russian) for each title page, so that the inscription could be read only when the books were joined together: "To Dear [*Dorogomu*] – Valerii – Pereleshin / – from – Arsenii – Nesmelov / 29 – March – 1936." Each of the next three books, *Archpriest's Wife* (*Protopopitsa*, 1939), *Siding* (*Polustanok*, 1938), and *White Flotilla* (*Belaia flotilia*, 1942), was separately inscribed to Pereleshin.

When he was sent one "author's copy" of A *Russian Poet as a Guest in China*, he claimed that he was "swindled out" of the precious Nesmelov books. On receiving three more copies, he "offered no thanks: I consider the book to be my property, and thanking for it would mean recognizing the rights of the highway-robbers to a part of my soul." He became even angrier when he learned that he would have to pay for the book to be sent to some sixty-five people on his gift list. Hinrichs explained that gift copies were sent only to important institutions and reviewers, but for Pereleshin the exclusion of his friends from the list was "repulsive."[79]

In letters, he started referring to the "greedy and unscrupulous Dutch" as "Scots," who were rumoured to be overly stingy. He suspected Hinrichs of "shark-like greed" and of being responsible for several typos in *A Russian Poet as a Guest in China*, which in fact had been proofread by Pereleshin himself. He further raged to Hinrichs that an author alone was the owner of a book he had written, and he now forbade any further publication of materials from his archive at Leiden; they had no right to enrich themselves at his expense.[80] Seeing himself as a victim of robbery, he asked for the return of all originals of his letters to his mother, Khaindrova, Ivask, Struve, Adamovich, Baturin, Ladinskii, Anita Gincenberg, and others.[81] Hinrichs and the Leiden University Library reminded him that he had donated his archive to the library, but he was beyond reason: "Can I prove that I DID NOT donate it? To whom? Where? In Brazil or in Holland? In return for all six of Nesmelov's books with autographs, for all the letters and diaries, for all unpublished articles these *sv.* (not 'saints' [*sviatye*], but a different word) issued me ONE copy of *A Russian Poet as a Guest in China*."[82]

He also wanted them to return his small gold crucifix, allegedly lent for an exhibition at the Rotterdam Festival, although there had been no such exhibition and his monastic cross presented earlier to Hinrichs was neither small nor gold.[83] His anger knew no bounds: "on the whole, the Dutch robbed me […]. All that's left is to complain to God, but I will avenge it and have already started with the sonnet "Little Cross" (*Krestik*, 15.11.1989), which I *will dedicate* to the main thief." He declared his poem "The Fourth Homeland?" (*Chetvertaia rodina?* 16.10.1988) to be "obsolete" and swore that "on every convenient occasion I will tell *urbi et orbi* of the greediness and shamelessness of many of its nationals."[84]

When Hinrichs later sent a copy of *Verbannte muze*, his essays on Russian émigré poets with "twelve very tender pages about me," which were "extremely flattering because I am judged to be in the first tier," he warmly thanked the author, but did not calm down. Hinrichs tried "to remain on good terms, but he is mistaken: I will not say even a simple 'thank you' to him. A swindler remains a swindler."[85] He continued to rage, at length and vehemently, that he "had simple-heartedly entrusted almost everything to the Leiden University Library, but the Dutch are the most greedy and stingy people on earth (the Scots are maligned in vain)."[86] Finally, Hinrichs simply stopped answering Pereleshin's insulting statements about the Dutch nation in general and himself in particular.[87]

The Leiden University and Hinrichs had not only fulfilled all the conditions on which the archive was accepted, but also had invited him to Leiden and had had two of his books published. In return, Pereleshin dishonourably reneged on the agreement and kept slandering Hinrichs and Leiden University to his friends and correspondents.

Approaches from the Soviet Union

В две тысячи сороковом году
(Прости просчет на три-четыре года)
В моей стране затеплится свобода,
И я туда, раскопанный, приду.
До той поры в одном твоем роду
Я затаюсь. Меня не тронет мода
И пощадит журнальная погода:
Ведь мертвые живут не на виду.
Тогда твой внук уложит в предисловье

Читу, Харбин, ученье, нездоровье,
Моих друзей – и деда своего.
Отверженный, заранее утешен,
Грядущее предвижу торжество:
Московский том "Валерий Перелешин."

In the year two thousand and forty
(Forgive the error of three-four years)
Freedom will glimmer in my country,
And, excavated, I will get there.
Until then I will lie low only
In your clan. Fashion will not touch me,
And journalistic trends will spare me:
After all, the dead live in seclusion.
Then your grandson will fit into the preface
Chita, Harbin, my studies, poor health,
My friends – and his grandfather.
An outcast, I am consoled in advance
As I foresee a future triumph:
The Moscow volume "Valerii Pereleshin."

"In the Year 2040" (*V 2040 godu*),
23.5.1973

Pereleshin, like some other émigré writers, thought that "the home of a Russian poet is in the future Russia" and hoped that "my collections, tapes, and typescripts will reach Russia and readers far and wide."[88] In the mid-1980s a few poems by China Russians occasionally appeared in the Soviet *Fatherland* (*Otchizna*) and *Voice of Homeland* (*Golos rodiny*). With the beginning of *perestroika* and *glasnost'*, the mainstream Soviet literary journals *Banner* (*Znamia*), *New World* (*Novyi mir*), and *October* (*Oktiabr'*) published some of Nesmelov's poems, and a former Harbin Russian, E. Indrikson, was not ashamed to state that Nesmelov was among the first to return, when in fact he was arrested by SMERSH in 1945 and died in prison. As Pereleshin observed, they were "resurrecting the dead, but feared the living."[89]

Pereleshin's name appeared in the Soviet press in 1987 in a letter to the weekly *Little Flame* (*Ogonek*), where an "obviously pseudonymous Kostolomov (Bone-breaker)" complained that a library had denied his request for émigré publications, including Pereleshin's *On the Way*.[90] Pereleshin wrote to Slobodchikov in Moscow that his poems could be published in the Soviet Union, but "on one condition: no 'corrections.'" Pointing out an omitted stanza in a Nesmelov's poem in *Voice of Homeland*, he naively threatened "to complain, create scandals, and write to Pope John Paul, the Jesuit Fathers, and the nearest police officer."[91]

In 1988, Vitkovskii published Pereleshin's translation of Juan Boscán Almogáver's sonnet in *Moscow Literatus* (*Moskovskii literator*) with a comment that Pereleshin "had turned up" in Harbin in 1920, published books of poetry, and had a "totally fantastic fate." He sent Pereleshin only a handwritten copy of the article, but this "first swallow" delighted him: "This is a greater victory than trips to Leiden and Rotterdam. After all, my real reader is *in Russia*."[92] Vitkovskii blamed his silence on unnamed reasons and alcoholism caused by fear and signed his letters "Your E." or "A." for Ariel. His proposal to have thirty of Pereleshin's poems published in the literary journal *October* (*Oktiabr'*) made Pereleshin's head "spin." He did not see it as "'a betrayal' of my convictions. I did not change, but 'the homeland' has come up to me without any demands."[93]

Nothing was published in *October*, but in the same year a selection of poems by Harbin poets in *Voice of Homeland* reprinted Pereleshin's "Gallipoli Soldiers" (*Gallipoliitsy*, 24.3.1935) and "Nostalgia" (*Nostal'giia*, 19.9.1943), and in 1989 the same newspaper presented a selection of his poems, which included a few celebrating Brazil and the religious "Corcovado" (*Korkovado*, 1.7.1953).[94] In September 1989 *New World*

(*Novyi mir*) published "Tribute to the Living" (*Dan' zhivym*), a selection of poems by Igor' Chinnov, Nikolai Morshen, and Pereleshin, with Vitkovskii's introduction.[95] In an interview in a Soviet newspaper, entitled "Guardian of the Icon Lamp" (*Storozh u lampadki*) Vitkovskii claimed to be the "guardian" of the so-called Russian Poetry Abroad and said that his favourite poets were Georgii Ivanov, Vladislav Khodasevich, Don Aminado, and a few others, but he mentioned Pereleshin only in the context of rekindling his interest in the field.[96]

Other Soviet journals were now asking for poems and translations: "The slogan *carpe diem* remains in force. A clump of fur can be got even from the mad dogs of the Moscow press. Especially since they publish in millions of copies." The possibilities were exciting: "just now and only now, by the will of God, I have truly 'conquered' even the impregnable Russia," and "the wish for the split into Soviet and émigré literature to end and for a single Russian literature to live and flourish is coming true."[97] He was flattered that the Central Library of Theatre Workers in Moscow asked him for his archive: "even Moscow is bowing to the ground to me!" But he did not want his archive to end up in the USSR: "they guard only the interests of the 'dear party.'"[98]

Recitals of émigré poetry became fashionable in Moscow, and Vitkovskii sent Pereleshin an invitation to an evening of his poetry on 15 February 1989. Various notables recited his poems, including "Poem of the World Creation" (*Poema o mirozdanii*), allegedly to "a *standing ovation* [Eng.]." Another recitation was held in the Literary Museum on 19 April 1989.[99] On hearing of a devastating earthquake in Armenia, Pereleshin sent a few of his religious sonnets and "Funereal Canon" (*Zaupokoinyi kanon*, 17.10.1970) to *Literary Armenia* (*Literaturnaia Armeniia*) and asked that the royalties go to the victims.[100] Fragments from *Two Sidings* and a few poems appeared in *Literary Study* (*Literaturnaia ucheba*), and his four poems published in *Little Flame* were accompanied by his portrait by Humberto with the latter's initials removed. *Little Flame* introduced him as "the best Russian poet of the Southern Hemisphere," a dubious compliment, as he was the only one living there, and quoted him as saying that "it is time to forget the strife and internal wars which lost their meaning a long time ago."[101] Pravda Publishing House sent him a money order for a little over US$200 for various publications in periodicals – not much, but "important, flattering, and pleasant."[102]

Pereleshin's life "suddenly became filled with meaning; as long as I, in my seventies, remain relatively healthy, there is no time to get bored. Zhenia (Vitkovskii) has a multitude of different plans, but what upsets me is that, having made one plan, he forgets it in a day and is full of other plans!"[103] He was right: the plans were just that – plans. In 1989, Sovremennik Publishing House announced publication in 1991 of a book by "Pereleshin V." entitled *Southern Home: Poems 1933–1989* (*Iuzhnyi dom. Stikhotvoreniia 1933–1989*), in a run of 50,000 copies. His prediction of a Moscow volume in the sonnet "In the Year 2040" (*V 2040-om godu*, 23.5.1973) "turned out to be pessimistic, I was late by almost half a century."[104] Vitkovskii was "to monitor the royalties, which would be quite large. Yesterday I sent him a power of attorney notarized in the local consulate-general of the USSR. [...] I think that if my POOR health will allow, in June–August 1990 I will visit Moscow, St Petersburg, the Crimea, and the Caucasus." Some money was to be sent to Anita Gincenberg in Latvia.[105] He had heard that a visit of the elderly émigré writer Nina Berberova to the Soviet Union "turned into a real triumph," and, believing Vitkovskii that "I am now possibly the most famous and favourite Russian poet," he expected "to be properly invited and go, in spite of my illnesses and the terrible age of seventy-six," but "only as an honoured guest."[106] His poems continued to appear in *The New Review* in New York and in the annual *Meetings* (*Vstrechi*) in Philadelphia, but he sadly commented that, after all, he "had rejoiced more when a poem of my Chinese period appeared at the top of the first page of the dear, unforgettable *Border*" in Harbin.[107]

Interest in émigré literature grew, and he started receiving many letters: "only now does Russia realize the cultural treasures that have been lost during the years of tyranny: 'We come to you, émigrés, with an outstretched hand and beg for alms.'"[108] In 1989, a "passionate admirer," Iu.V. Linnik, wrote from Petrozavodsk about his radio talk on Pereleshin and his plans for a "Museum of Russian Culture Abroad" and begged him "for photographs, autographs, and drafts for exhibits." His letters were "truly of a man in love." He wanted to publish Pereleshin's poems and an anthology of crowns of sonnets, where "The Way of the Cross," "a work of a genius," would take "a place of honour."[109] Linnik even planned to visit Pereleshin in 1990 in order to interview him for "an already prepared large book" and "to take a part of my archive with many photographs, facsimiles, and a copy of my album of autographs of the Far Eastern poets and prose writers." He would "spend ten days in my cave. It seems a long time, but there will be so many conversations that the *fortnight* [Eng.] will fly like one moment. I have prepared many documents (copies) for him, photographs (only to see), and even books."[110]

In 1990, in honour of his eightieth birthday in 1993, a Moscow publisher was proposing to bring out a "Selected Works" of some 21,000 lines, to be followed by a reprint of *Two Sidings* and a collection of his translations: "Now my only dream is to see, while still alive and not on an astral level, 'the Moscow volume: Valerii Pereleshin.' Relative immortality almost never comes immediately."[111] He saw his rift with Leiden as "providential: I am truly 'returning to the first homeland,' where I have already become one of the most favourite poets," and he wondered whether "to entrust all my remaining masterpieces to Russia."[112] At times, however, he sobered up: "Moscow cannot have any claims on publications abroad, although in some sense I 'have appointed an executioner to be my heir.' There cannot be any 'return' (one way): let *them* return to us what they took away."[113]

The second half of the 1980s, when Pereleshin was in his mid-seventies, could have been a time of triumph and pride in his impressive publishing record, in finding an appreciative home for his archive, visiting Leiden University as a guest of honour, and in the prestige of participating in the International Festival of Poetry. Not one of the former Russian poets of China who lived abroad in much better financial circumstances and faced no personal anguish over their identity, had achieved that much. However, he was too embittered by homophobia, injustices, and hardships, and too self-centred. Traumatized from his youth by bigoted society, he became just as intolerant of divergent views and positions as his mentors at the Theological Faculty who had waged war on other religions, sects, and "deviations." In his judgments and attacks on Volin, Terapiano, Chinnov, Evtushenko, Brodsky, and now Hinrichs he easily lowered himself to ridicule, crudeness, and racist slurs. As sometimes happens in old age, these aspects of his personality hardened and began to corrode him.

13 Last Love, Last Books, Last Years

Humberto

От вечности мы связаны в клубок
И, встретившись, друг друга опознали:
Изгнанники, из межпланетной дали

Пришедшие на неизвестный срок.
Шесть полных лет. Немало было склок,

Не раз, не два мы братство разрывали,

Но без тебя я выжил бы едва ли

Такой, как был – упрям и одинок.

Но и к тебе я прислан по указу,
Чтоб соскребать с души твоей заразу,
Обратно звать к воскресшему Христу,
К источникам Господней благодати:
Нечистый сам, прославить чистоту,
Сломив греха постыдные печати.

From eternity we are entwined in a skein
And, having met, we recognized each other:
We are exiles, coming from an interplanetary expanse
For an unknown period of time.
Full six years. There have been many spats,
And several times we have broken the brotherhood,
But it is unlikely that I would have survived
Without you, the way I am, obstinate and lonely.
But I have also been sent to you by a decree
To scrape away infection from your soul,
To call you back to resurrected Christ,
To sources of Lord's grace:
Impure myself, to glorify the purity,
Having broken shameful brands of sin.

"From Eternity" (*Ot vechnosti*), 13.10.1986

In Harbin, at their first meeting in the poetic circle Churaevka, Georgii Granin asked Pereleshin whether he was in love: "in his simple world view, a poet must be constantly in love." If it seemed somewhat funny then, in his seventies he saw a certain wisdom in seeing love as a source of inspiration.[1] His poems and letters continued to speak of many affairs, but more and more often partners required payment. "In

Defiance" (*Naperekor*, 1.12.1980) was inspired by "music of the young boy's body," but when the youth disappeared, Pereleshin commented: "I should have given more money (I have no idea of market prices)." "Sonnets to a Model" (*Sonety naturshchiku*, 13.4.1982 and 16.4.1982) speaks of a "luminous Ephebe," an eighteen-year-old male model in Humberto's art class, whom Pereleshin paid for a brief "steady relationship (something like a legal marriage)." The sonnet "To Leisurely Fabio" (*Medlitel'nomu Fabio*, 24.11.1986) says to a labourer at Casa dos Artistas: "So I, your voluntary captive, am waiting, / although you'll come only because of the money; / otherwise, I would not find one equal to you."[2] Aging and lonely, he sadly reflected that "in my entire life, only two men, both Chinese, truly loved me. Brazilians 'love' while it is useful and leave without a glance when there is nothing to expect or take. Is it painful? Of course, it is. But they feed the Muse, and when the Muse 'talks it out,' it is no longer painful."[3]

Humberto remained a good and caring friend, often visited Pereleshin after his mother's death, forced him to go out, and took him to *La Traviata*, where Pereleshin wept quietly throughout the opera, "not for the heroine, but for my pain."[4] When Humberto's mother permanently moved to Governador Valadares, he rented a small apartment, but at times had problems with paying the rent. Pereleshin, himself short of money, helped out in return for having a key and staying overnight on trips to Rio de Janeiro. The two sometimes shared casual lovers.[5] Pereleshin greatly valued Humberto's "culture, knowledge of languages, love of art, and wonderful manners," encouraged his interest in sculpting, and often accompanied him to open-air art markets: "it would be great if Humberto could sell his most original works: crucifixions, removal from the cross, madonnas, angels, and saints." He chatted with artists and craftsmen and enjoyed glimpses of "simply a beautiful face, setting one's heart on fire." He befriended one artist, a deaf mute, "but how *luminous*!"[6]

In March 1981, to distract Pereleshin from grieving, Humberto took him to his family's *fazenda* (plantation) near Governador Valadares: "For ten days I lived in an earthly paradise among trees in bloom, plantations, birds, and butterflies. I was driven in cars, in a truck, and once even on a tractor. I became acquainted with cows, an ox, horses, piglets, and guinea pigs." He enjoyed reading and writing "on the veranda over the Rio Doce, flooded with sunlight during the day and with liquid lunar silver at night." His "one-day (but unforgettable) affair" with a hired cowboy produced passionate sonnets such as "At the Farm by the Rio Doce" ([*Na ferme u Rio Doche*, 9.3.1981), "No Letter!" (*Net pis'ma!* 11.6.1981), and "Stork" (*Aist*, 4.7.1981).[7]

What Pereleshin did not foresee was falling in love with Humberto, neither beautiful, nor as young (now in his thirties) as his usual infatuations, though "astonishingly *boyish* [Eng.], sometimes looking like a teenager, light-footed and agile."[8] This last love of his life crept up imperceptibly: "When Mum left for the better world, Humberto became the meaning of my life." Only once, in April 1984, did "my friend come to me at night, and now I love him not only as a colleague and friend, but I am also in love with him as a lover." Pereleshin felt that it was "fate, his and mine," and marvelled at "what force pushed us towards each other on the day when we first met in the photocopy shop." Humberto became "*my life* and continues to be. I am exaggerating: poems are my life first of all, but all poems come via the beloved. Poems and he are one and the same thing."[9]

His love was not reciprocated. With brutal honesty Humberto told him that he was "old and quite unattractive." Pereleshin tried to be "simply friends in the noblest and purest sense of the word," but anguish and its poetic expression were in the making: "Oh, if only he were mine! After all, I do deserve it."[10] In spite of the tensions, they took trips together, Pereleshin paying all expenses; his failing eyesight prevented him from travelling alone, while "in his company I would even climb Mount Everest." They visited the seaside towns Mangaratiba and Paratý, appreciating their seventeenth-century architecture, and in historical São João del Rey and Congonhas do Campo they viewed "statues of twelve prophets in front of one of the churches and stupendous sculptures depicting the stations on the road to Calvary." They saw works of the sculptor Aleijadinho (the Little Cripple), born Antônio Francisco Lisboa (1738–1814), which displayed "blasphemy of his endless torment / and the impersonal coldness of fate," as Pereleshin wrote in "Aleijadinho" (*Aleizhadin'o*, 27.3.1970).[11]

Now he "lived only for seeing him," but Humberto, a member of the Brazilian Spiritualist Federation (*Federacão Espírit a Brazileira*), spent most of his free time at meetings, where people spoke in tongues, induced convulsions and vomiting, received messages from spirits, and studied healing passes. He wished to become a medium and agonized at being "defiled by lust and therefore unworthy of transmitting the powers of good," to which Pereleshin retorted: "Do you think that other spiritualists, successfully married, do not perform similar unworthy acts with their women?"[12]

When they first met, Humberto had lent him books on spiritualism, including a collection of poems "dictated from beyond the grave," and Pereleshin even translated one poem and wrote an article about these "psychograms."[13] But once in love, he developed "an unconditional hostility to spiritualism" as "the basest African Umbanda, a primitive animism. These 'Christian spiritualists' are seized by fits of hatred towards the cross, Christians of the Church, and churches. In China, I was friendly with Buddhists, Taoists, and pagans, but they were not apostates. These 'Christian spiritualists,' were *baptized* and left the Church, like Julian the Apostate." He swore at every page of Allan Kardeck's works, "enraged by the anti-Christian direction of 'Kardeck's teachings,' where Jesus Christ is allegedly the same person as Kardeck."[14]

Pereleshin, who always resisted control over his life and at times described himself as an atheist, Buddhist, and Manichean, became set on "returning Humberto to Christ." Suddenly Christianity mattered. If for Humberto spiritualism was the best thing in his life, for Pereleshin "the best thing is poetry, and the second is the joy of serving an Orthodox liturgy."[15] Humberto's dedication filled him "not only with contempt, but also with direct hatred" for spiritualists, whom he blamed for Humberto's dropping out of university, having no profession or skills, and living largely on handouts from his mother and successful siblings.[16]

They started having frequent rows, instigated by Pereleshin, about spiritualism and about Humberto's trips to prisons with "a gang of spiritualists" to "visit condemned recidivists, preach reincarnation to them, and sing feeble songs."[17] Pereleshin once agreed to attend a spiritualist meeting, but when Humberto went into convulsions, Pereleshin quickly made a sign of the cross over his back and Humberto failed to summon spirits, "which is what I wanted to prove."[18] Once, however, when Pereleshin had a bad cold, Humberto made passes over him, and "I felt the breeze from the rapid movements of his fingers. When he finished, I ran into the bathroom and had such a fit of vomiting that it seemed as if my stomach would fall out. When I returned, Humberto smiled and said: 'Well, now your catarrh is gone!' It turned out to be true. From that time, I have had lighter or heavier colds, but in general I am well."[19]

He helplessly lavished gifts on his beloved: an expensive set of pencils, paints, and brushes, a new watch when the old one was stolen, Chinese souvenirs, and presents for his family. He gladly lent him money: "in my long life I have not loved anyone so much, except Mum, and now I have no one close except Humberto."[20] Humberto was "irrepressibly attracted to men, young and beautiful of course, and too often his attempts 'to find a partner' land him in bad situations." He once fell in love with a twenty-year-old rower, married and a father, and watched him from afar: "we all need our 'Ariels' and our love for phantoms [...]. It is better and safer than frequent visits to a sauna." Pereleshin became so jealous and quarrelsome that Humberto eventually forbade him to stay overnight, and Pereleshin had to sit on a bus for two hours to get home to Jacarepaguá.[21] The more Humberto limited their contact to working on Portuguese translations, the more Pereleshin's longing grew: "I understand him, commiserate with him, help him as much as I can, and pray for him. [...] I am glad that, in spite of his passion for anonymity, I have introduced him into Russian poetry."[22]

On Humberto's fortieth birthday on 2 February 1987 Pereleshin took him on a trip to Paratý, where he became "tempted ... how shall I put it in a more sophisticated way? ... by the desire to embrace him, kiss him, and so on. At 11:00 at night Humberto jumped up, went to the bathroom, shaved, and left. He spent some time on the square and then dozed off in some corner of our hotel. He returned at 3:00 a.m. and immediately fell into a deep sleep. Later he said that he had had to run away, because he felt that I was enveloping him with desire. He cannot take me: I am old and unattractive."[23] It did not matter: "I have had many infatuations and adventures, but I love only Humberto, unattractive, balding, and unavailable [...]. I write many sonnets and poems about him. He avoids my displays of passion and gets angry, but I simply cannot live without our meetings and passionate arguments, even quarrels."[24] In vain did he seek consolation with young men. Once, "singed by the beauty of a fifteen-year-old youth" in a local shop, he failed to entice him, and Humberto remarked that he should have "put the money down; there is no need for declarations of love and poems."[25]

Love for his "embodied Ariel, an ideal friend (and lover, had he wanted to)," consumed him: "I would have hanged myself long ago from loneliness, ennui, and the sense of meaningless existence, if it were not for Humberto, who is like me in many ways, equally lonely and equally passionate (he is even more insatiable and receptive to infections and various illnesses). The main thing is that he *understands* everything. [...] He is more of a cross than a blessing, but this cross is given to me personally, and I am resurrected through this cross, at least in the best poems."[26] As it had once been with Vitkovskii, Pereleshin believed that he and Humberto "are connected by karma, and no matter how much we argue and quarrel, some mystical chain ties me to him"; "in another reincarnation there will be no such *age gap* [Eng.], *inshallah*, and we will be spouses or brothers. Now I have *only him*: he is the focus of the entire life of a lonely old man."[27] His continuing attempts to "save" Humberto led to further estrangement, and after one particularly vicious quarrel Pereleshin felt that "*it may be a good riddance* [Eng.]." It was easier said than done: "I cannot part with Humberto."[28]

In 1986–7, Humberto's arms became covered with blisters and lesions, which he attributed to an infection caught from parasitic worms on the beach or in a sauna. Expensive ointments helped, but further outbreaks left most of his body covered with sores, abscesses, and scars. He imagined that "absolutely everyone, even children, could immediately see that he was *gay* [Eng.]," and he prayed in a Catholic church "to be taken away from this earth soon and given a different fate in the next reincarnation."[29] It became a "*perpetuum mobile* of saunas, infections, treatments, cures, and again sauna, infections, treatments," leading to suspicions of skin cancer or even AIDS. Pereleshin was familiar with the symptoms of AIDS and knew that he could not become infected without close contact, but still he ardently wished to be intimate with Humberto.[30]

Pereleshin felt "terrible pity for him," but at times stooped to repugnant judgments: the illness was "an educational punishment for renouncing Christ. Humberto had studied in the Ecclesiastical Seminary of the Jesuit Fathers, served in a church, and then had exchanged Christ for African demons and hopeless fatalism and become a weak-willed rag, a porter, a steward, and a 'librarian' for a band of necromants, submitting to the power of witches."[31] Humberto naturally started "moving further and further away (I am old and very unattractive, while he is an 'aesthete' of the sauna and worms, with insatiable lust which leads to hellish torment). My experience does not mean anything to him, although I have been through the same agony of being outcast, despised, and hounded."[32] By the end of 1987 their rare meetings ended in fierce rows. Pereleshin poured out his "bitter sorrow and disappointments" in poems and letters, deriding Humberto as "a Mediterranean type: egotist to the marrow of his bones. In his language, love is only sex, and sex is a synonym for love. [...] My misfortune is that I have fallen in love with him *totally* and not excluding sex at all. But he does not want that from me, though he will take it from any person younger than me. [...] What can I give him? If I had a car, if I lived in a luxurious apartment ..."[33]

As always, love and suffering fuelled his poems: "Thoughts of 'Roberto' [as Pereleshin called him in his poems] attack me incessantly. […] What a strange fate for a Russian poet in foreign Brazil: prayers and laurels come from him (from 'Robertik'), but he will not read a single line inspired by him."[34] It was hard to write after the estrangement: "I was writing *to him* and *about him*. […] I concede that I loved Humberto not only as a friend, but what I miss now is precisely a friend, a person who understood everything, who was created the same, and has filled the emptiness, which has become unbearable from the day of Mum's death. […] I was never bored in his company, even though from the first day of our acquaintance I have hated necromancy, spiritualism, an almost open hatred of the Church, Wednesday gatherings (thirteen witches and three old or ageing loafers), the probable orgies, trances, ventriloquism, and so on."[35]

Humberto remained the subject of painful post-mortems: "It is now clear that the person who seemed to be my friend was not a friend. He has never loved anyone in his forty-one years. That is, he loved *his own* pleasure (in sauna he went through five or six lovers at one 'visit'), but never remembered anyone, never became attached to anyone. […] Not only do I not love him, but also I deeply despise him. I don't want to see him and do not seek meetings. Recently, I have left (twice) with the porter [at his apartment] eighteen Brazilian stamps for his collection. No word of gratitude followed. There will be no more gifts. That's enough. For eight years I breathed only him. I received, it's true, much inspiration."[36]

Two Last Books, 1987–1988

Всю жизнь искал я спутника и брата,	All my life I was searching for a companion and brother,
А попадал на записных "правшей,"	But came across inveterate "right-handers,"
На бабников и подлых торгашей,	Skirt-chasers, and vile hucksters,
Поставщиков нормального разврата.	Suppliers of normal depravity.
И, наконец, нашел аристократа,	And, finally, I found an aristocrat,
Прелестного от пяток до ушей,	Charming from his ears to heels,
Но даже он прогнал меня взашей,	But even he booted me out,
И до сих пор свербит моя утрата.	And my loss is still aching.
Не двадцать пять ему, а сорок лет,	He is not twenty-five, but forty,
Но все равно: такого больше нет	But it doesn't matter: there is no magician,
Кудесника, врача и духовидца.	Healer, and clairvoyant equal to him.
Вчера другой мне встретился *rapaz*,	Yesterday I met another *rapaz* [youth],
Но сразу же велел остановиться:	But he immediately ordered me to stop:
"Эй, дедушка, видать, и ты туда ж?"	"Hey, grandpa, looks like you as well?"

"Searches" (*Poiski*), 3.10.1987

Inspiration from this love created his last two books. The twelfth, with a cumbersome title *Two – and Again Alone?* (*Dvoe – i snova odin?*), presented "a history of my love for Humberto." The question in the title was "for self-consolation, because nothing will happen anymore."[37] He ordered the book in February 1987 from New England Publishing, and the publisher persuaded him to print 600 copies. The slim book had twenty-seven poems, some in cycles of two or three sonnets or triolets, fully dated and written from 1979 to 1987, peaking at fourteen in 1986.

They read like excerpts from desperate letters to a lost lover, with revealing titles such as "Daydreams" (*Mechty*, 30.9.1978), "Despair" (*Otchaianie*, 10.1.1980), "Not without Bitterness" (*Ne bez gorechi*, 14.10.1985), "We Are Different" (*My raznye*, 12.10.1985), "In Irritation" (*V razdrazhenii*, 29.11.1985), "The Break" (*Razryv*, 21.1.1986), "On Jealousy" (*O revnosti*, 23.3.1986), "Towards Forgetting" (*K zabveniiu*, 27.9.1986), and "More on the Loss" (*Eshche o potere*, 9.10.1986). If he had once criticized Mary Vezey for "women's poems," defined by him as written for and to a beloved man, that is precisely what he wrote now: all poems were "about or to Humberto," with theatricalization similar to that in *Ariel*.[38] Pereleshin translated them into English prose for Humberto, but during one bitter quarrel Humberto tore them up.[39]

In the poems, the poet Valerii, described in "Despair" (*Otchaianie*, 10.1.1980) as a "homunculus, left-hander, with an alien mind, / whose sentence has been determined long ago," speaks to or about Roberto, "a transparent pseudonym."[40] In the cycle "We Are Different" (*My raznye*, 12.10.1985), the first sonnet states: "We are different. We are opposites. / We argue hotly about everything," but the second disagrees: "We are the same. We rave about beauty / [...] / We admire a crowd of suntanned athletes, / the movements of their legs and the muscles of their shoulders." In "To a Sculptor" (*Vaiateliu*, 4.10.1985) both seek delight in God and in a beautiful male athlete. The sonnet "Twins" (*Bliznetsy*, 13.3.1986) echoes *Ariel*: "we are – fortunately – Siamese twins, / we are connected not by a decrepit umbilical cord, / but by souls – by an invisible heart core, / and, though different, we both are monks." "Not without Bitterness" (*Ne bez gorechi*, 14.10.1985) declares: "I love you, and it is no secret at all / that I have the same fracture as you, / that I often lose my head from languor, / from lust, and there is no escape."

The painful break is presented as caused not by the beloved's rejection, but by the poet's rejection of spiritualism. He bitterly accuses Roberto of serving Satan and letting spiritualism turn him into a nonentity by the age of forty. An impotent anger leads to a further "lowering" of style which has begun in the 1970s: in "We Are Different" (*My raznye*, 12.10.1985) the poet says: "You have succeeded / only in the art of vomiting"; "In Irritation" (*V razdrazhenii*, 29.11.1985) asks what "bitches" reduced Roberto to "a he-dog"; "Memento Visionem" (29.7.1986) depicts Roberto having sex in a sauna; "Other Friends" (*Inykh druzei*, 27.9.1986) speaks of his preference for "group sex and eczema." Life answered the question *Two – and Again Alone?*: "yes, alas, alone, alone, alone – more alone that ever before."[41] In September 1987 he had some twenty pages of poems for what he first called "No. 12-A," or "a *sequel* to the twelfth (to avoid the 'unlucky' thirteen),"[42] but then, as explained in the introductory "From the Author," he decided that "it is customary to fear the number thirteen. But I am rather proud of it: I have published thirteen books, which means that I have not lived my life in vain. Thus, let the book be the thirteenth, a twin sister of the twelfth, so that, if I stay alive, the next one, the fourteenth, will be not a small notebook, but a full-scale 'Exile into Flesh' (*Izgnanie v plot'*)."[43]

The title of this thirteenth book was *In Pursuit* (*Vdogonku*), even though "I would not catch up to him. It is my own fault: I have fallen in love too hotly, even though in the eight years 'there had been nothing between us' except jealousy, and I have no right to be jealous." Humberto remained "the most charming person that fate has sent me. Lately, we meet very seldom, but ... poems to him or connected with him keep appearing one after another. [...] It is easy – and impossible – to replace him with some seventeen-year-old procreator. Humberto had a magnetic force, and it has been my task for many years to reach his 'inner depths,' while new encounters *do not* promise *anything*."[44]

When he learned that there was a surplus of over US$2,000 after the publisher had printed his two previous books, he ordered 200 copies of *In Pursuit* in October 1987: "even that would be too much for selling from Brazil." Not hearing back, he "grew cold" and even hoped that the order would be declined: "three books in a year has bled or thinned me out."[45] The book, the last published by him, came out in July 1988, including as a frontispiece his portrait by D.V. Izmailovich, the same as in *Sanctuary*. It opened with an epigraph from a Chinnov poem: "Ah! Poisoned by filth, / towards the end I will sing / of that which most likely / will be forbidden in paradise."[46]

The thirty-three poems in the book, fully dated from May 1978 to October 1987, were even more "autobiographic and 'Robertographic,'" "a direct continuation and development of the themes in *Two –and Again Alone?* There is some karmic predestination in this metaphysical interconnection."[47] Chronologically overlapping with those in the twelfth book, the poems were largely addressed to his lost love, again called "Roberto" as a precaution against the unlikely possibility that Humberto might stop the publication: "the 'hero' would remain just as mysterious as Mr W.H. and even more mysterious than my Moscow Ariel."[48]

The opening, "Fate" (*Sud'ba*, 7.5.1978), the poetic epigraph for one of the sections in chapter 2, above), is crucial to Pereleshin's vision of his and Humberto's lives: "from childhood my fate was fractured, / and what am I to do with the crack?" Many poems voice agonizing jealousy, accusations, warnings, worries over Roberto's skin ulcers, and rage at spiritualists; a few speak of a lifelong search for love, recall childhood games, and offer helpless prayers. Pereleshin saw the book as an exorcism: "with this book I have finally freed myself from the dark charms of a certain apostate."[49] Yet he still grieved over Humberto, who was "getting more and more distant and sinking deeper and deeper into necromancy and godlessness. I cannot accept his departure. I have made it a rule to keep praying: '*Saint Antoine de Padoue, faites-moi trouver ce que j'ai perdu*' [Fr.]. The prayer helps."[50] Many years before, in "Evening" (*Vecher*, 16.12.1953) the poet said: "But, perhaps, in my Gethsemane evening, / when, fallen, I will drop into a semi-sleep, // Antoine of Padua will descend here: / after all, he, as people say, / rewards us hundredfold for the pain of losses."

He was dismayed when New England Publishing mailed the entire runs of the eleventh, twelfth, and thirteenth books to him: "Why, instead of the agreed sales in the USA, were all copies sent to Brazil, where there is no one not only to sell, but even to present books of Russian poems?" The publisher obviously "wanted to be free of distributing books, corresponding with small booksellers, making reports, and so on."[51] Then, after the quarrel with Guerra, he had to deal with the entire run of *Three Homelands* as well, and "the abundance of emotions is such that I feel like a paranoiac or a newly-wed: so much to do, and I don't know where to start." The wardrobe in his bungalow could not accommodate the books, and they were stacked "everywhere: on the floor, on the veranda, on the wardrobe, on the bookshelf."[52]

Victor mailed back the "pornographic" twelfth book with "an indignant letter," but Pereleshin "simply laughed: it was not easy for me to 'find myself' in the philistine milieu of the Russian emigration, but I turned out to be strong and won." He recalled Victor and Lidiia's reaction to *Ariel*: "For them, poems are not works of art, but 'confessions,' photographs." Mary Vezey's response is obvious from Pereleshin's reply: "I considered you to be 'initiated,' that is, capable of appreciating the structure of poems, particularly of sonnets, their unique nature, and ingenuity in the choice of words ... But your attention got frozen on 'bitch' and 'he-dog'. Shame!"[53]

The books were ignored in the émigré press, but *The New Review* forwarded an unpublished and unsolicited review with no return address, but with Australian stamps. P. Aleksandrov, likely Volin, wrote that "Pereleshin has never concealed his unnatural tendencies. Struggling with 'impure flesh' in his youth, he became a monk, but not for long. Back in China, still in a cassock, he openly had 'affairs' with Chinese youths, and in Brazil, in the years of 'the sexual revolution,' he openly boasted of hundreds of lovers." His *Two – and Again Alone?* was "a return to the bosom of homosexuality," and the reviewer felt sick while reading "this semi-intelligible and absolutely filthy nonsense," wanted to wash his hands afterwards, and stated that "Russian poetry, with the exception of Mikhail Kuzmin, never had a place for the theme of homosexual love, but now Pereleshin has more than compensated for that" with this "example of psychopathological creativity." Pereleshin's Soviet passport and deportation from the United States were mentioned.[54] Although Pereleshin stated that the gentry did not respond to anonymous attacks that had no return address, he drafted a rumbling rebuttal disputing statements about his Soviet passport, deportation, and not being noticed as a poet in China, and he deplored the reviewer's rabid homophobia.[55]

Early in 1989 he received an anonymous letter, with a return address care of A. Savin in Sydney, Australia, "on the same topic: how immoral it is not to want to procreate! The arguments are those of a seminary: a man and a woman are called to fill the earth (and overfill? After all, the earth has been full for a long time). What the Creator wants from humanity is not the totalitarian monotony of communists or fascists, but a most diverse flourishing of all thoughts, wishes, and the most contradictory creations of art."[56] Pereleshin again suspected Volin and did not bother to reply.

He continued to desperately miss Humberto, "my only ray of light; there is none any more, the window is shut," and spoke of his grief and anger in letters: Humberto "had thousands of lovers, but did not love any and did not even remember them. He loved and loves only his orgasm. He is a monster, and quite a pathetic one. I did not even have that from him."[57] Accidentally bumping into Humberto early in

1988, he was most distressed to see ulcerous sores covering most of his body: "it is better not to see him in order not to soften. Isn't it time 'to end it'?"[58]

The estrangement condemned him to utter loneliness. In March 1988, he met "a charming sixteen-year-old, Andre, and five sonnets in Portuguese appeared in one evening. The next day, I presented them to my new despot, but there was no response. He probably recoiled inwardly. It is, nevertheless, a consolation: if I can write in Portuguese for Andre, I will be writing in Russian in the near future." Pathetically, he sought young lovers, paying them for visits and inviting them for trips to holiday places; he even offered to pay for dental work for a beautiful youth.[59]

In 1991, already quite ill and helpless, Pereleshin heard from an acquaintance that Humberto had died of AIDS.[60]

New Wine in Old Wineskins, 1970s–1980s

Есть музыка в усталости осенней
И тишина в палитре хризантем.

Есть россыпи поэту нужных тем

В роскошестве сосчитанных мгновений.
От мудрости прощальных наблюдений
Со стороны – и явно низачем –
Юнеет мой стареющий гарем
И тленное становится нетленней.
И попросту снимается вопрос:
Зачем горбун, левша и альбинос

Среди прямых, правшей и ясноглазых?

Подведены итоги бытия,
И с похвалой отмечены в приказах
Платон, Верлен, Рембо, Кузмин и я.

There is music in the autumnal weariness
And silence in the palette of chrysanthemums.
There are gold fields of themes sought by the poet
In the luxury of counted moments.
From wisdom of last observations
From aside – and obviously for nothing –
My aging harem is getting younger
And mortal becomes more immortal.
And the question simply becomes void:
Among the upright, right-handed, and clear-eyed
What are a hunchback, a left-hander, an albino for?
The summation of lives is finished,
And honours are granted in edicts
For Plato, Verlaine, Rimbaud, Kuzmin, and me.

"Autumn" (*Osen'*), 6.3.1977

On returning to poetry in 1967, Pereleshin largely led "some kind of illusory life, only in poetry," and sometimes wondered whether his "fertility holds the danger of exhaustion, of 'self-devouring,' and rehashing of themes. I calm myself with the fact that my poetic life had an almost twenty-year break, and in those long years poetic work continued subconsciously. When underground waters have sprung from the ground, the small stream has quickly turned into a powerful torrent."[61] Some people questioned this large output, but he held that "one should write all the time. A pianist or a violinist must practice constantly. [...] Why does a poet have the right to neglect his craft?" Then, "the best will be remembered, the average will somehow get stuck, and the worst will be forgotten."[62]

Pereleshin rejected the notion that "a further development 'ahead' (?) requires the destruction of rhyme and metre. It makes me personally 'want to vomit irresistibly' towards *vers libre* and similar cacophony." If in his earlier poems of the Chinese period he allowed himself approximate, imprecise rhymes, his Brazilian period is marked by steady progression towards greater and greater precision: "I discovered an inexhaustible wealth of rhymes and consonances (for internal echoing of consonants) in the Russian language."[63] Rannit noted: "Pereleshin's poetics in its development is a ship sailing against the wind and current. The trend of the century is a decline of symmetrical centralized form (namely, fluctuating metres, approximate rhymes flowing into assonances, fashion for blank and even free verse), but Pereleshin did not follow this trend."[64]

The 1970s–1980s became dominated by his "infatuation," if not obsession, with sonnets.[65] In "Prayer" (*Molitva*, 26.1.1974) he prayed to be burdened and consumed by "sonnet-sons" and "daydream-daughters"; "One of the Lightnings" (*Odna iz molnii*, 27.11.1977) says: "Home, homeland? Promises are mocked: / long ago have I become a homeless fugitive, / but I knew how to be a husband and father / and mother: I reared sonnets." He prided himself on mastering the form: "there is no sonnet writer in Russian poetry equal to me. Perhaps it is an unforgivable conceit, but I am convinced that this is so."[66] Sonnets answered something in his soul, a deep-rooted need for complete mastery and perfection within the confinement of metrical semantics. The sonnet was "an amazing form: one can write about anything," but "must have a conflict of ideas: thesis in the first quatrain, antithesis in the second, 'tense struggle' in the tercet, and finally an almost unexpected conclusion." They "could be saturated with African passions, the most ardent and the most irrational." He wrote many "religious, philosophical, almost descriptive, satirical, and epigrammatic sonnets. The deeper I get into a sonnet, the more inexhaustible I find its possibilities."[67]

Very few sonnets were written in China, his first being "Ars Longa" (7.12.1935), and only ten in the first years in Brazil. When he surpassed his "youthful incontinence" with 135 poems in 1969, only three of them were sonnets. During 1970 he produced 144 poems (three sonnets) and 155 poems (six sonnets) in 1971. Then"an incredible poetic creativity" of 214 poems (102 sonnets) followed in 1972, and 175 poems (124 sonnets) "rushed out of me like a stream" in 1973.[68] Another 184 poems (113 sonnets) were written in 1974, and the flow subsided with 85 poems (61 sonnets) in 1975. He produced 32 poems (27 sonnets) in 1976, 83 poems (68 sonnets) in 1977, 91 poems (76 sonnets) in 1978, and 84 poems (56 sonnets) in 1979. He wrote so much that it was "getting hard to give titles. [...] The title is part of the poem, and sometimes one can give an unexpected turn to the whole theme with it."[69]

Sonnets ruled. Most were Italian or Petrarchan (4-4-3-3), but he also wrote some English or Shakespearean sonnets (4-4-4-2), which he considered to be "an easier English form."[70] Believing that Pushkin always used caesura in his iambic pentameter, he "accepted it as an axiom: caesura is compulsory in a sonnet. You will find lines without caesura in my early sonnets, but not anymore. [...] My precision is increasing throughout my entire life."[71] He had reworked his early sonnets to have an obligatory caesura. His experiments included reverse sonnets (3-3-4-4), sonnets of one long sentence, sonnets in iambic pentameter or with feminine rhymes, a sonnet built on only two rhymes, and "Brittle Sonnet" (*Lomkii sonnet*, 23.2.1977) with a feminine caesura after the fifth syllable.

Pereleshin believed that "as a verse maker, a craftsman, I 'have attained the highest power.' But the torment begins right here. My own past 'records' are forcing me to stay at their level, and this becomes almost impossible." In 1980, he reiterated that "it is unlikely that anyone in the twentieth century, as well as in the nineteenth, is equal to me in poetic mastery ('I should be ashamed of boasting')."[72] Perhaps he should, but his boasting contains a large element of truth. To quote Aleksis Rannit, Pereleshin "reached limits of the *mastery*. [...] He is one of the masters who have learned their craft so well that they can let themselves not think of it and even break its basic rules. No matter what his place in the literary history of the second half of the twentieth century is, he is guaranteed recognition as one of the best Russian sonnetists."[73]

The title of his book of Portuguese poems, *Nos odres velhos* (*In Old Wineskins*), stands as the quintessence of his Russian and Portuguese poetry. It emphasizes his unwavering devotion to neoclassical mastery of metre and rhyme, even in the experiments of 1968–71, and the new wine, lavishly poured into these old wineskins, tasted of the "acutely modern sensibility."[74] He was a man of his time. His poetry embraced a wide range of modernist concerns: self-reflection, search for identity and for the right to be what he was, challenge to religious dogmas, and a tragic view of the world. He saw gay love, like all love, as a source of great happiness and great misery, as well as freedom from the biological "duty" of reproduction.[75]

In the 1970s, the religious torment of his Chinese period gradually gave way to an inner freedom, at times expressed in images of the lotus and of Cinderella, "one of the symbols of the soul, Psyche. She is imprisoned bodily in dust, ashes, dirt, but 'all the beauty is within.' [...] A beautiful pure soul is praying for liberation from the slavery of material body, for a miracle, so that she can rise, like a lotus, above the muddy swamp."[76]

Although he claimed to observe the world "with the indifference of radar," as he put it in "Radar" (*Radar,* 6.1.1970), poems such as "Idyll" (*Idillia,* 25.7.1969), "In the Beginning" (*V nachale,* 18.2.1970), "Atomic Bomb" (*Atomnaia bomba,* 23.7.1970) expressed an anxiety over potential nuclear war, while "Entomologist" (*Entomolog,* 12.11.1970), "Song of Creation" (*Pesn' tvoreniia,* 12.11.1970), and " Slaughterhouse" (*Boinia,* 16.3.1971), spoke of ecological concerns. He was fond of his occasional epigrams, but "so far none have been published (will they be ever published?)." He wanted them to "find a place in my literary legacy. They show what the poet accepts and what he rejects, what angers him, what puts him in a merry mood."[77]

From the mid-1970s, he favoured *nedoskaz* (reticence) and glimpses into a "super-rational and (more often) subconscious world. [...] 'A voice of dark depths' has started to sound distinctly in poems of nostalgia, exile, refusal to accept the world, and escape."[78] In the 1980s, a new development arose from his sense that "although colloquial language cannot predominate over the literary – as poetry is, nevertheless, part of literature – I personally like 'lowering' the inevitably elevated style of even philosophical, religious, and metaphysical poems, giving them concreteness, substance, and tangibility."[79] He turned against "'poeticisms' (ready-made 'beautiful' clichés), though how far I still am from Khodasevich, who openly said that he 'loves *prose* in poems.' [...] Now I take upon myself an obligation to *lower* the style, to break an abstract composition with concrete, visual, even if crude, details." He came to admire "the prison stink" and "smell of urine and eternity" in Iurii Ivask's poems.[80] In the last painful years of his relations with Humberto, he freely used in his poems words such as "bitches," "lust," "vomit," "stink," "pederast," "feces," "group sex," "male organ," and explicit descriptions of sex.

The output of the 1980s, however, was no match for the abundance of the 1970s. He wrote 220 poems, peaking with 55 in 1987, the year of his break with Humberto. His thematic range narrowed to obsession with Humberto and frequent infatuations with adolescents and young men. He felt his age: "Mirror" (*Zerkalo*, 3.12.1981) describes the poet as "a helpless, unskilled, / depraved vile old man." Some of the late poems speak of deep loneliness, insomnia, and nostalgia for beloved China; in "Christmas Poem" (*Rozhdestvenskoe*, 31.8.1988) the poet "is now praying for a drop of warmth / from human hands – a heavenly mercy."

The Last Years

[...]
Я в Бразилии жизнь доживаю, но мой невпопад,
Мой печальный закат угасает в нечаянном блеске.
  Как поэт я замечен в когда-то враждебной Москве
  (Возмещенье суждений бессудных и дерзких заглавий)
  И с бразильцами многими дружен: стоит во главе
  Девятнадцатилетний услужливый беленький Флавий.
Возвращается ветер? Бесследно потерян Китай:
Тан Дун-тянь, Бай Цзи-чжан и Лю Син – в океане иголки.
Твой поэт одинок. Если хочется, перечитай
Или перелистай уцелевшие письма на полке.

[...]
I am coming to the end of my life in Brazil, but my being misfit,
My sad sunset is dying in an unexpected brilliance.
  As a poet I am noticed in previously hostile Moscow
  (A compensation for unproved judgments and insolent titles),
  And many Brazilians are my friends: ahead of all is
  Nineteen-year-old obliging blond Flavio.

Is the wind returning? China is lost without a trace.
Tang Dongtian, Bai Jizhang, and Liu Xin are needles in the ocean.
Your poet is lonely. If you want, reread
Or leaf through the surviving letters on your shelf.

"To Each of Many"
(*Kazhdomu iz mnogikh*),
21.4.1990

By July 1988 his compilation of left-handed poems, *Exile into Flesh*, had over 200 pages; it would have been his fourteenth book. He also hoped to publish his second book of Portuguese poems, *Caçador do sombras* (Hunter of Shadows), translations of Chinese classical poems, *Daodejing*, Pessoa's sonnets, and "Antinous." He felt that "while my allotted time in God's hands has not run out, let's live as if there is no end to time!"[81] He was proud of his capacity for work: "Poets usually stop at my age (only Fet wrote to the end, to his suicide), and many stop even earlier (Khodasevich wrote until about forty-five). I will say about myself (without superfluous and always insincere modesty) that, in spite of stagnating in total isolation from the Russian milieu and even from the living Russian speech, at times I feel unprecedented inspiration."[82]

There were no regrets. In 1990 he wrote that being a left-hander "is my innermost lining. […] This passion comes from genetic depths, from primary bases. Ignorant medical specialists are trying to 'cure' us, thus proving only their own lack of talent. Were Michelangelo, Bramante, Benvenuto Cellini 'sick'? Is the entire purpose of a human being reduced to an obligation to continue the clan and to aid the overpopulation of the much too crowded world? […] I *can* produce babies, but for whom and why? […] What would Kuzmin and Baron Shteiger be without 'this very thing'? What would I have been? This unwillingness 'to be like everyone' (is it really everyone? is it?), which is the best thing in my soul and my fate, appeared in early adolescence."[83]

While his heart remained full of creativity and passion, his health worsened. In 1984 his doctor put him on a strict diet and forbade him to smoke. That did not last long, and by 1987 he had fits of coughing, knowing that "I am committing suicide, smoking a pack of cigarettes a day (this is progress; earlier I smoked two packs)." Excessively high blood pressure forced him to quit again, but he felt "tense and restless," "painfully" yearning for a cigarette. On the way back from the Rotterdam Festival, a delay in Amsterdam "pushed me towards the counter selling Dutch cigarettes," and he started smoking again.[84]

Unsteady on his feet, he walked with a cane, and it was an ordeal to travel by bus to Rio de Janeiro to see a doctor, to wait in hospitals for appointments and tests, and to get back home: "at times I am tempted to let it all go to … very far, but my doctor is warning me that if I will not follow the treatment, I might become totally paralyzed." His "old weak point" was uremia, which "had tormented me in my childhood" and kept "poisoning my existence." In May 1988, while walking to his bank in Copacabana, he fell down several times and lost control of his bladder: "I crawled to the doctor's apartment all wet. It was very repulsive."[85]

His hearing aid broke in September 1988, but he did not bother to buy a new one. Victor paid for cataract surgery on one eye, but the doctors refused to do the other because of his diplopia, and Pereleshin now read with a magnifying glass. His bungalow grew even more unkempt, dirty, and smelled of tobacco, and his clothes grew old and shabby. Only his books and materials were kept in some order.[86] In 1989 Victor and his wife decided to move permanently to Santa Rosa, California. Although the brothers had had little contact or affection, Pereleshin felt he was "being left in total loneliness … with my illnesses, though with all my books," but "I always know 'in my heart' that if I need real help, Victor would not pour cold water over me."[87]

In January 1989, his pursuit of young men led the administration at Casa dos Artistas to ask him to leave: "they, of course, found reasons, the largest card 'being an Ariel.' The procreators cannot and/or simply do not want to allow it." The expulsion was "pure hypocrisy: I am being thrown out for the thing that has been flourishing here for years." In panic, he thought of moving to the Netherlands or even to the Soviet Union, where the return of the elderly Irina Odoevtseva was regarded as some kind of propagandistic victory.[88] He could not afford to rent an apartment, and even if he did, he could not live on his own: "what's left for me is 'to commit suicide' or find myself on the street with all my possessions and books." He sought help, not from Victor, but from Simon Karlinsky: "Not only my future, but also my life depends on this. […] If you cannot help, I will have 'to take my life,' as they used to say in the old days." Karlinsky immediately sent US$2,500: "I have not dared to expect anything like this. […] My brothers will not let me drown."[89] The administration relented: "it is awkward to throw an old man of seventy-five out on the street. The earlier 'sentence' was announced verbally and not confirmed by a letter." He sent the cheque back to Karlinsky "with the greatest gratitude for your life-giving response" and ended one of his letters with a phrase reserved for special friends: "Yours for the rest of this life and after."[90]

The threat of expulsion did not stop his pursuits, but his young lovers sometimes stole things and were "always unscrupulous, and I keep getting the impression that 'a friend' looked *only* for money." In March 1990 he "fell head over heels in love" with a twenty-three-year-old man, who took tender care of his wife in a wheelchair: "he is precisely *St Francis of Assisi*." Then there was another "passionately beloved," whom Pereleshin kept inviting to visit, to go to the theatre, or to take a trip to Paratý," but the young man did not keep his promises. On reflection, "all my life I have been chasing shadows."[91]

Death of the Poet

Quando eu morrer, os meus nobres colegas,
digno papel de necrologistas,
Enganados por muitas falsas pistas,

Perseguirão a minha sombra às cegas.

– "Foste um herege (será que ainda o negas?),
Mas, apesar dos preceitos budistas,

Adoravas os corpos dos banhistas,

Freqüentavas as suspeitas bodegas."
Faráo o resumo o *primus inter pares*:
"As alcovas tomava por altars,

Mas no soneto a todos excedeu.
Ergo, merece o maricão danado
Que o nome seu esteja mencionado
Ao pé da página no livro meu."

When I am dead, my dear colleagues, I trust,
worthy necrologists – that's their profession –
will blindly chase my phantom through the dust,
misled by my false clues, and their obsessions.
"Heretic, own your acts' impiety!
Despite your Buddhist principles, your choice
was to adore bodies of beachcombing boys
and frequent bars outside society!"
Finally the chief of those who never falter will say:
"He mistook the bedroom for an altar.
But he was king of the art of the sonnet:
that cannot be denied. So the blasted queen
deserves mention. A footnote will appear
in my next book, bearing his name upon it."

"Um Immortal" (An Immortal, 11.10.1979)[92]

In October 1989, Pereleshin wrote to a friend: "On the whole and in general I am very tired [*A v obshchem i tselom ia ochen' ustal*]," commenting, ever a poet, that it was "almost a tetrameter: a poetic line in a four-syllable anapest. *Daodejing* ends with the same conclusion." His life was "coming to an end. Poems no longer come, and it's time to stop, to finish at some point."[93] In early 1990, he noted: "there are days when I simply cannot walk. Yesterday in the centre of the city I felt so ill that a kind lady had to help me cross the street. This happens frequently." He was no longer permitted to leave Casa dos Artistas without an escort and had to pay a resident nurse to accompany him on a bus or in a taxi.[94]

In early 1991 he had a minor stroke and was moved to the hospital at Casa dos Artistas. He had difficulty in reading and writing. When his concerned friend Georgii Volkoff sent a letter that required his signature on delivery, the card came back signed by someone else. Volkoff then received an unfinished letter in wobbly, barely legible handwriting, dated 1990, although it was April 1991.[95] By July 1992 Pereleshin could barely recognize visitors. A friend found him very weak and incontinent.

He "hungrily devoured the biscuits" which she had brought, but when she offered to take him out to sit in the sun, he refused.[96]

At the end of October 1992, Pereleshin fell and broke his hip. He was operated on, but nothing could be done for his arteriosclerosis and increasing Parkinson's disease. He developed pneumonia and died at 11:50 p.m. on 6 November 1992. The cause of death was "Insuficiência respiratóia aguda, Pneumonia bacteriana, P.O. fratura de femur." His trustee, A.B. Kirilloff, gave the date of his death as 7 November 1992.[97] The prediction of dying on the 7th had almost come true.

On 9 November 1992, the funeral service was held by an Anglican priest in a non-denominational chapel at the English cemetery, attended by A.B. Kirilloff, acquaintance V.V. Bakich, and Victor's secretary.[98] He was buried in the same grave as his beloved mother. The inscription reads: "Valery Pereleshin 1913–1992."

Pereleshin's will originally left everything to Humberto, who, after one stormy fight in 1986, sent him a registered letter refusing to be his heir and asked a notary public to annul the will, but was told that only Pereleshin could do so. His refusal infuriated Pereleshin: "God be his judge. God save me from fanatics and egotists."[99] By 1988 he no longer wanted this "real devil" to be his heir and dreamed of "plunging an aspen stake into Humberto's grave." He appointed A.B. Kirilloff to be the trustee and asked for small sums to be distributed among employees at Casa dos Artistas, but not a penny to "Antichrist Humberto": he "had already received 'his' share of my inheritance."[100] As noted earlier, Pereleshin did not honour his agreement with the Leiden University Library, but on 30 January 1990 wrote to Kirilloff that, owing to "the shark-like greed of the Dutch publisher" and "dishonesty" of the Dutch, he was planning to leave the remaining archive to Iu.V. Linnik: "present-day Russia hungers for free Russian culture, in particular for the spiritual wealth it was deprived of for over seventy years."[101]

In the absence of a will, Victor was the heir. He did not attend the funeral, but came to Rio de Janeiro later to deal with legal and financial matters and take home some family papers, documents, and stamp collections. He asked Kirilloff to trash the unsold copies of *Two – and Again Alone?* and *In Pursuit*. At the time Victor said that he would sell the stamp collections to publish a selection of Pereleshin's poems in the United States.[102] Lidiia died on 28 November 2000, and Victor on 3 November 2006, leaving his considerable estate to various institutions and individuals, but not a penny for publishing his brother's works. In his last years, Victor was not always lucid, and many of his possessions and family materials had disappeared, most likely disposed of by his mercenary and unscrupulous caregivers, one of whom even tried to marry him.[103]

The fate of Pereleshin's remaining archive is most unfortunate. He no longer wanted his archive to go to Russia and was too ill to send it to Leiden or make other arrangments. However, the Soviet consul, A. Jebit, having learned about it from a certain A.G. Lermontov, visited Pereleshin to persuade him to leave his materials to Russia. It was standard practice for Soviet consuls and officials to prey on elderly émigrés and grab their archives, art treasures, and possessions. Both Lermontov and the consul saw that Pereleshin showed no reaction whatsoever to this request, obviously in no state to give a coherent answer. Jebit, however, later alleged that Pereleshin "confirmed his agreement to transfer the archive to Russia, thanked me for the fruit, and, bidding goodbye, dragged himself back to the ward, supported by a nurse."[104] On learning of Pereleshin's death, both Jan Paul Hinrichs and J.J.M. van Gent of the Leiden University Library wrote to Victor and to Kirilloff, pointing out that Pereleshin had explicitly promised that after his death the remaining archive would be deposited in Leiden. Victor, indifferent to the archive, let the remaining materials to be sent to the USSR by the Soviet consul. The document concerning the transfer of the materials was signed on 8 January 1993 by A. Kirilloff, Victor Salatko, and A. Jebit.[105]

As a result, the bulk of his archive is preserved in the Leiden University Library, while some materials are in the Institute of World Literature in Moscow and others in collections of his friends. Pereleshin did not bequeath copyright of his works to any individual or institution and reiterated on several occasions that anyone was welcome to publish his poetry.[106]

In the early 1980s he wrote: "If I had a chance to choose my life again (in another reincarnation), I would have chosen the same path, the same cross, and the same happiness."[107] As one of his best poems says, "on the day that I die, I will for sure return to China," and we may hope that he has returned to his beloved Celestial Kingdom, taking with him the poetic, passionate, contradictory, and complex world of the unique phenomenon that was Valerii Pereleshin.

What he left us is his poetry.

Abbreviations

Sources in the endnotes are indicated with the aid of these abbreviations.

BPL	Archive of Valerii Pereleshin, Leiden University Library, Leiden. Detailed information is in "Valerij Perelešin (1913-1992). Catalogue of his Papers and Books in Leiden University Library" by Jan Paul Hinrichs. Leiden: Leiden University Library, 1997
BSO	Journal *Biulleten' Soiuza okonchivshikh uchebnye zavedeniia KhSML*, Sydney
DOD	Journal *Druz'iam ot druzei*, Sydney
DP	*Dva polustanka*, memoirs of Valerii Pereleshin
KhKU	Journal *Kharbinskie kommercheskie uchilishcha Kit. Vost. zhel. dor.*, San Francisco
KhN	Journal *Khleb nebesnyi*, Harbin
KhV	Newspaper *Kharbinskoe vremia*, Harbin
NRS	Newspaper *Novoe russkoe slovo*, New York
NZh	Journal *Novyi zhurnal*, New York
OB	Olga Bakich
PBP	*Poema bez predmeta*, by Valerii Pereleshin
RLJ	*Russian Language Journal*, Ann Arbor
RM	Newspaper *Russkaia mysl'*, Paris
RZh	Newspaper *Russkaia zhizn'*, San Francisco
US/INS	Files on V.F. Salatko-Petrishche, US Department of Homeland Security, US Citizenship and Immigration Services, United States Department of Justice, Immigration and Naturalization Service

TH	*Russian Literary and Ecclesiastical Life in Manchuria and China from 1920 to 1952: Unpublished Memoirs of Valerij Perelešin.* Edited by Thomas Hauth. The Hague: Leuxenhoff, 1996.
VP	Valerii Pereleshin
VFSP	Valerii Frantsevich Salatko-Petrishche
VSP	Valerii Salatko-Petrishche

The following are abbreviations for references to Pereleshin's letters to various people. When quotations from his letters are given in the text, the notes indicate the first few words of the quotation.

To AG	Letters to Anita Gincenberg
To AR	Letters to Aleksis Rannit
To EAS	Letters to E.A. Sentianina
To EG	Letters to E.A. Genkel'
To EV	Letters to Evgenii Vitkovskii
To GS	Letters to Gleb Struve
To ID	Letters to Ingrid Drizul'
To ISF	Letters to Ioann Shakhovskoi
To IV	Letters to Iurii Ivask
To JPH	Letters to Jan Paul Hinrichs
To KP	Letters to Iu.V. Kruzenshtern-Peterets
To LK	Letters to Lidiia Khaindrova
To MV	Letters to Mary Custis Vezey
To NF	Letters to Nina Fouchier, née Mokrinskaia
To NK	Letters to Nora Krouk
To OB	Letters to Olga Bakich
To PB	Letters to Petr Balakshin
To PL	Letters to Petr Lapiken
To SK	Letters to Simon Karlinsky
To VAS	Letters to Vladimir Slobodchikov
To VL	Letters to Vadim Leonard (Leont'ev)
To VS	Letters to Valentina Sinkevich

Notes

Preface

1 To IV.13.6.1968 ("in my opinion").
2 To AR.11.10.1971 ("it is best").
3 VP, "Valerii Salatko-Petrishche" ("I will not omit").
4 To NF.16.10.1967; To EAS.19.10.1942; To EAS.16.7.1943; To NF.19.6.1987; Victor Salatko to A.A. Jebit, 16.8.1998.

1. Russian Childhood

1 VP, "O rode Salatko-Petrishche" ("Grandpa").
2 To KP.4.4.1972 ("any of these").
3 Elizaveta Adal'bertovna Salatko-Petrishche; VP, "O rode Salatko-Petrishche" ("a mine collapsed"); *PBP*, Canto One, XIII–XVI, 41–3, 73n11.
4 "Attestat"; Passport of Erazm Frantsevich Salatko-Petrishche; E.F. Salatko-Petrishche, death notice; VP, "O rode Salatko-Petrishche"; *PBP*, Canto One, XX–XXI, 45; To OB.26.4.1980; F.E. Salatko-Petrishche, registration form and "Avtobiograficheskie svedeniia" for the Bureau for the Affairs of Russian Émigrés, 18.6.1935, and F.E. Salatko-Petrishche, registration form for the Bureau for the Affairs of Russian Émigrés, January 1936.
5 To KP.4.7.1974 ("a theme").
6 VP, "Valerii Pereleshin," typescript, 1970s; EAS, "Pol'sha u russkogo poeta"; To AR.14.1.1972 [*sic* – 1971]; F.E. Salatko-Petrishche, registration form for the Bureau for the Affairs of Russian Émigrés, January 1936; To AG.1.5.1967; To OB.26.4.1989.
7 VP, "Biograficheskie svedeniia" ("Belorussian converts"); To AG.10.2.1967 ("the first mention"); To MV.31.12.1968; To Ktorova, A. 7.11.1972 ("Polish-Belorussian"); To GS.7.3.1972; To KP.2.12.1971.

8 *PBP*, Canto One, XI, 40; To LK.16.3.1940 ("inborn attraction"); To AR.17.1.1980 ("can it be"); To EAS.14.12.1940.
9 To EAS.27.1.1940 ("commiserating"); To EAS.29.1.1941, comment; To AG.10.2.1967.
10 To GS.17.10.1976 ("all Russian culture"); To KP.24.3.1972.
11 To KP.10.3.1982; To KP.4.4.1972; drawing of the coat of arms; To GS.26.10.1977.
12 VP, "Priamye i bokovye predki Valeriia Pereleshina."
13 Papers related to emigration procedures; VP, "Priamye i bokovye predki Valeriia Pereleshina"; EAS to P.P. Balakshin, 23.2.1976 ("wherever we lived").
14 VP, "Priamye i bokovye predki Valeriia Pereleshina"; papers related to emigration procedures; school certificates of EAS; VP, "Eshche ob udareniiakh v sobstvennykh imenakh"; *Sankt-Peterburgskie Vysshie Zhenskie (Bestuzhevskie) kursy*, 9-19; EAS, "S nasizhennykh mest."
15 To EAS.6.9.1943, comment ("preferred my father"); To KP.10.3.1974; papers related to emigration procedures; EAS, "S nasizhennykh mest."
16 To MV.31.12.1968; *Pravoslavnaia tserkov'*, 174.
17 To ID.15.7.1990 ("my favourite"); To AR.14.9.1971 ("did you notice").
18 VSP, "Zagadochnoe chislo."
19 To ID.15.7.1990 ("it would be"); Certidão de óbito, 9 novembro 1992.
20 VSP, "Iapontsy v Kharbine," typescript ("one of the best"); Rannit, "Kitai Valeriia Pereleshina," *RM*, 22.6.1972 ("mother's grand").
21 VP, "Valerii Pereleshin ("the first conscious").
22 VP, "Valerii Salatko-Petrishche" ("complex fates").
23 Passport of E.A. Sentianina; Victor Salatko to OB, ca. 2005.
24 VSP, "Iapontsy v Kharbine" ("while we are"); Passport of E.A. Sentianina.
25 VSP, "Petr Ivanovich Krechetov," typescript ("the lash of hunger"); *PBP*, Canto One, XXIII, 46; To VAS.14.12.1988.
26 To KP.12.7.1967 ("memories of"); To IV.14.2.1979 ("I had no childhood").
27 To LK.10.12.1940 ("Mum left").

2. Harbin: On the Way to Becoming a Poet

1 To NK.21.12.1986 ("it was in").
2 VSP, "Semidesiatiletie Kharbina"; To EAS.5.7.1942, comment; *PBP*, Canto One, XXV, 47.
3 M.S. Rokotov to VP.27.5.1971; KP to VP.19.12.1979; To JPH.4.4.1984, as quoted in the Introduction, *DP*, 9.
4 Victor Salatko to OB, undated letter ca. 2004; V.E. Sentianin to EAS.16.2.1922 and 5.5.1922 ; V.E. Sentianin to EAS.3.2.1922 and undated card.

5 V.E. Sentianin to EAS.17.5.1922 ; V.E. Sentianin to EAS, undated letter after 17.6.1922 ; Passport of E.A. Sentianina; Marriage certificate of E.A. and V.E. Sentianin.
6 To JPH.4.4.1984, as quoted in the Introduction, *DP*, 9; VSP, "Semidesiatiletie Kharbina"; To GS.8.10.1968.
7 Victor Salatko to N. Gracheva-Mel'nikova, 23.3.late 1970s ; VSP, "Semidesiatiletie Kharbina" ("a member of the Russian"); To IV.14.5.1975 ("wonderful stepfather"); VFSP, "Russkie na Dal'nem Vostoke"; To SK.10.7.1988; Rannit, "Kitai Valeriia Pereleshina."
8 V.E. Sentianin. Udostoverenie; Ternavskii, *Ves' Kharbin na 1926 g.*, "Spisok domovladel'tsev," 99; "Otryvok iz vospominanii o Turgeneve" ("literally all Harbin").
9 Volin, "Gibel' Molodoi Churaevki," 222; To EAS.5.10.1942; To EAS.4.10.1943; To EAS.6.10.1944; *PBP*, Canto Two, LXXII, 115; To PL.14.2.1975 ("a rather cultured"); To OB.21.7.1988 ; To MV.13.2.1985 ("its sonorous").
10 Ternavskii, *Ves' Kharbin na 1926 g.* lists a number of people with the surname of Salatko-Petrishche; F.E. Salatko-Petrishche, registration and "Avtobiograficheskie svedeniia."
11 To GS.19.8.1969 ("much bitterness"); VP, "Valerii Salatko-Petrishche" ("the roots"); To LK.10.12.1940 ("was right"); To IV.14.5.1975 ("my childhood"); To LK.10.12.1940 ("tyrant," "terrible character"); To EAS.12.8.1936, comment ("cold man").
12 To GS.19.8.1969; visiting card, "Valerii Aleksandrovich Pereleshin"; *Churaevka* 4/10 (November 1933); To GS.2.11.1967.
13 To EAS.12.8.1936, comment ("with the passing"); To EAS.12.8.1936, comment ("my shortage"); *PBP*, Canto Two, XIV–XV, 86.
14 VP, "Priamye i bokovye predki Valeriia Pereleshina"; family correspondence, comment; A.M. Naam to VP, comment; VSP, "Kharbin and Pomgol"; M. Dobrinina to OB.19.9.2006; M. Dobrinina to OB.1.10.2006.
15 "Kitaiskaia Vostochnaia zheleznaia doroga. Prikaz no. 53."
16 VP, "Pamiati Khauard Li Kheiga" ("without hesitation").
17 "Kak sozdavalas' Gimnaziia KhSML"; To EAS.6.9.1925, comment; To SK.15.8.1988; N.P. Avtonomov, "Khristianskii soiuz molodykh liudei."
18 VP, "Pamiati Khauard Li Kheiga" ("we never").
19 School report; To GS.24.10.1978; To KP.23.5.1968; *PBP*, Canto One, XXXVI, 53; Z.P. Popova to OB.4.9.2003; V.V. Mouhanoff to OB, March 2005; V.A. Slobodchikov to OB, undated letter, ca. 10.12.2005; N.P. Avtonomov to VP.5.3.1968 ; To KP.20.3.1968 ("hated crowds").
20 *PBP*, Canto One, XXXVI, 53.
21 VSP, "Pochtovaia marka i reklama"; To LK.6.2.1938 ("a passionate stamp").

22 Early poems, comments.
23 To OB.26.9.1987 ("delightful"); To EAS.29.1.1940, comment; To EAS.24.9.1943, comment ("before my invention").
24 VP, "Priamye i bokovye predki Valeriia Pereleshina"; To EAS.24.9.1943, comment ("grew more").
25 VSP, "Staraia orfografiia na Dal'nem Vostoke" ("the *fait accompli*").
26 To PL.15.10.1971; VSP, "Staraia orfografiia na Dal'nem Vostoke" ("totally devastated"); *Pis'ma zapreshchennykh liudei*, 16–17.
27 OB, "Russian Education in Harbin"; *PBP*, Canto Two, XVI, 87, and Canto One, XXII, 46; VP, "Valerii Salatko-Petrishche" ("without the slightest").
28 VP, "Valerii Salatko-Petrishche" ("Roman Law"); *PBP*, Canto Two, XVII–XXII, 87–90; *DP*, 68.
29 Volin, "Russkie poety v Kitae," 340–1.
30 To OB.29.12.1987 ("the Russian emigration").
31 To EAS.16.7.1936; To EAS.26.9.1925, comment; To EAS.17.9.1939; *DP*, 77 (Pereleshin dates it to 1936, but it was on 20 August 1935); VP, "Valerii Salatko-Petrishche"; To IV.19.7.1974 ("discovered Chinese"); *PBP*, Canto Two, LI, 104; Rannit, "Kitai Valeriia Pereleshina."
32 Koretskii, "Epopeia russkogo emigranta (bez geroiki)," 127–9.
33 To EAS.27.8.1936, comment ("studied it"); To OB.29.8.1989 ("fault-finding"); To KP.24.3.1972 ("instilled in me").
34 *DP*, 29.
35 "Young Reader Page," *Rupor*, 22.10.1927, 12.11.1927, 3.12.1927; VP, "Kak ia 'nachinalsia'" ("summoned the courage").
36 VP, as René, "Papinu-Sibiriaku"; VP, "Kak ia 'nachinalsia'" (Pereleshin mistakenly calls the poet Vania-Sibiriak; Papin-Sibiriak was an early pseudonym of a young poet, Nikolai Svin'in, who soon took another pseudonym, Nikolai Svetlov); *DP*, 30.
37 VP, "Valerii Salatko-Petrishche" ("sensed being"); To KP.20.4.1976 ("you can"); To VS.23.4.1990, second letter of that date ("immediately given").
38 To OB.17.5.1988 ("many of my"); To KP.13.10.1972.
39 VP, "Posleslovie," in *Tri rodiny*, 159 ("stealing from"); *DP*, 30; VP, as Avrelii, "O iunykh poetakh" and "O nashikh poetakh."
40 *DP*, 30; VP's comment on the typescript of the poem "*Pomniu Rossiiu!*" ("one day").
41 *DP*, 30–1.
42 M.S. Rokotov to VP, undated postcard received on 11.7.1977 ("an elegant"); M.S. Rokotov to VP, 13.10.1967 ("youthful, but"); *DP*, 31; Volin, "Gibel' molodoi Churaevki," 220; V. Iankovskaia to V.A. Slobodchikov, 3.11.1993.

43 VP, "Laskovyi redaktor. Pamiati M.S. Rokotova (Bibinova)" ("devastatingly bad"); this first poem in *Rubezh* was published in issue 24/229, 11.6.1932, and VP's comment about Abramov is on a typewritten copy of the poem sent to OB.
44 VP, "Laskovyi redaktor. Pamiati M.S. Rokotova (Bibinova)"; *DP*, 31–2.
45 Kreyd and Bakich, *Russkaia poeziia Kitaia*, 704–9.
46 Rachinskaia, "Zamolknuvshie golosa"; To MV.10.6.1988 ("to Mum and me").
47 Kruzenshtern-Peterets, "Vospominaniia," 43.
48 Achair, "Po stranam rasseianiia," in *Pervaia*, 70; VP, "Konets Alekseia Achaira" ("long-winded"); *PBP*, Canto One, XXXVI–XXXVII, 53.
49 *DP*, 33–4; Slobodchikov, *O sud'be izgnannikov pechal'noi*, 135, 137; V.A. Slobodchikov, "Kharbinskaia Churaevka"; Achair, "Nash kruzhok"; Luganov, "Sem' let Churaevki."
50 Achair, "Nash kruzhok"; Luganov, "Sem' let Churaevki"; "Molodaia Churaevka," *Rupor*, 25.9.1927.
51 Avtonomov, "Khristianskii soiuz molodykh liudei," *KhKU* 9 (1969), 43–8; "Pamiati F.A. Kheig," *DOD* 7 (1969), 3–4; "Spetsial'nyi vypusk Molodaia Churaevka"; Achair, "Tvorcheskaia molodezh'."
52 N.A. Slobodchikov, "Kharbinskaia Churaevka."
53 Kruzenshtern-Peterets, "Churaevskii pitomnik," 67; Slobodchikov, *O sud'be izgnannikov pechal'noi*, 142–3; *DP*, 44.
54 "Lidiia Khaindrova," 5; *DP*, 39; VP, "Valerii Salatko-Petrishche" ("for generalities").
55 VP, "Valerii Salatko-Petrishche ("baptism by fire"); *DP*, 39.
56 *DP*, 39–40; VP, "Valerii Salatko-Petrishche" ("something unforeseeable").
57 V.A. Slobodchikov to OB, undated, ca. 10.12.2005.
58 Ivask, "Valerii Pereleshin o poezii"; Granin, "Bol'shie korabli"; Slobodchikov, *O sud'be izgnannikov pechal'noi*, 147–9.
59 To GS.29.3.1968; To IV.25.12.1968; To LK.6.3.1939; *DP*, 27, 43.
60 *DP*, 40, 42.
61 Granin, "Bol'shie korabli."
62 Anastigmat, "O churaevskikh lirikakh," as quoted in VP, "A chto obo mne pisali polveka tomu nazad" ("modifiers of time").
63 Loginov, "Grechnevaia kasha," as quoted in VP, "A chto obo mne pisali polveka tomu nazad," 2; VP, "Blizhe k Zapadu!" ("our cultural capital").
64 Adamovich, *Poslednie novosti*, quoted with Pereleshin's comment in *DP*, 64.
65 Shchegolev, "Ot zamyslov moikh nepodkreplennykh," *Chisla* 9 (1933); VP's comment on the typescript of "Illness" that it was accepted, but not published in *Chisla*; Iu.T., "*Churaevka*," 234; VP, as Sigma, "Churaevka v 'Chislakh'" ("brilliant *Numbers*"); *DP*, 65–6.

66 Kruzenshtern-Peterets, "Churaevskii pitomnik," 63; *DP*, 40–1.

67 Both *DP*, 40, and Slobodchikov, *O sud'be izgnannikov pechal'noi*, 160, give the name of the new group as "Poets' Circle" (*Krug poetov*), while Kruzenshtern-Peterets, in "Churaevskii pitomnik," 63, calls it "Poets' Workshop" (*Tsekh poetov*); *DP*, 44; Slobodchikov, *O sud'be izgnannikov pechal'noi*, 161; Shtern, "Vernyi drug russkoi molodezhi"; Kruzenshtern-Peterets, "Churaevskii pitomnik," 63; Achair, "Pered nachalom." In his memoirs and letters to OB on 5.10.2002, 11.2.2003, and 10.12.2005, Slobodchikov alleged that Peterets hated and persecuted Achair and forced all members to sign his declaration of a new workshop, written by his lover Kruzenshtern. However, at the time, she was already in Shanghai and had no ties with Peterets until he moved there later.

68 Kruzenshtern-Peterets, "Churaevskii pitomnik," 52–3; Slobodchikov, *O sud'be izgnannikov pechal'noi*, 156–7.

69 *DP*, 34; Kruzenshtern-Peterets, "Churaevskii pitomnik," 67.

70 Slobodchikov, *O sud'be izgnannikov pechal'noi*, 155–6; *DP*, 41–2.

71 *DP*, 42.

72 Slobodchikov, *O sud'be izgnannikov pechal'noi*, 157; *DP*, 61.

73 *DP*, 61–2.

74 *DP*, 67; "Zhizn' poeta G.I. Granina spasena"; "Tragediia poeta Granina"; "Ne vynesla dusha poeta."

75 Comment on a typewritten copy of the poem ("repulsive"). In Pereleshin's autobibliography, the dating of these poems is wrong. The first is dated 28 February 1932, but he joined Churaevka and met Granin in October 1932 and the poem was published in the Shanghai journal *Parus* 11 (February 1933). The second poem is dated 28 December 1933, but had already been published in *Rubezh* 4/261 (21 January 1933).

76 *DP*, 34.

77 Slobodchikov, *O sud'be izgnannikov pechal'noi*, 144.

78 VP, "Kharbinskie literatory" ("so gloomy"); *DP*, 51–2.

79 *DP*, 68; VP, "O literaturnoi studii" ("to read poems").

80 *DP*, 67–8.

81 Slobodchikov, *O sud'be izgnannikov pechal'noi*, 163.

82 *DP*, 68–9.

83 "Dvoinoe samoubiistvo v gostinitse 'Nankin'"; Vladimir, "Demon samoubiistva," 34–5.

84 Slobodchikov, *O sud'be izgnannikov pechal'noi*, 169–70; *DP*, 70 (lines from the suicide notes are quoted from memory by Pereleshin and differ from the texts published in newspapers).

85 *DP*, 68–9.

86 To KP.19.3.1969 ("a typical martyr").
87 To KP.19.3.1969 ("by no means"); DP, 71–3; To GS.27.7.1978 ("I will be laughing"); L. Andersen to KP, undated.
88 Slobodchikov, *O sud'be izgnannikov pechal'noi*, 159; *DP*, 43; To GS.27.11.1973; Volin, "Russkie poety Kitaia," 342–3.
89 "Evening of Russian Culture"; *DP*, 49–50.
90 Lukin, *V mire symvolov*; To GS.2.11.1976; "KhSML – pora na pokoi! Okruzhnoe poslanie arkhiiereev osuzhdaet KhSML," *Nash put'*, 22 November 1934, as quoted in Dubaev, *Kharbinskaia taina Rerikha*, 111 (for more on the attacks see 125–36, 152, 154–6).
91 Gryzov, "Bog, rodina i chestnost'."
92 To IV.5.10.1978 ("a vile invention").
93 Slobodchikov, *O sud'be izgnannikov pechal'noi*, 170.
94 *DP*, 74, 76; To LK.6.2.1938 ("a transitional step").
95 VP, "A chto obo mne pisali polveka nazad."
96 Lingva, "Chudim i bormochem."
97 Kablukov, "Literaturnye mertvetsy,' 19–20.
98 V. Khodasevich's review in *Vozrozhdenie* (May 1935), A. Ladinskii's review in *Poslednie novosti* (27 July 1935), and M. Tsetlin's review in *Sovremennye zapiski* 58 (1935), as quoted in VP, "A chto obo mne pisali polveka tomu nazad."
99 To GS.8.10.1968 ("absolutely awful").
100 To AR.1.10.1971 ("a piece of my").
101 To ISF.27.11.1972.

3. Harbin: The Poet as a Monk

1 To EG.17.4.1937, comment; To EAS.26.9.1925, comment ("wanted me"; wrongly dates their meeting to 1936).
2 To KP.23.10.1979 ("mistaken (!)"); To EAS.26.9.1925, comment ("get straight").
3 To EAS.12.8.1936, comment; To GS.24.9.1974.
4 To EAS.16.7.1936, with note from E.A. Genkel' at the end.
5 *PBP*, Canto Two, XXXIII, 95.
6 To KP.23.10.1979 ("understood everything"); *PBP*, Canto Two, XXXVI, 97, XXXVIII, 98.
7 To EG.7.4.1937 ("if I could").
8 To LK.6.2.1938 comment ("the amorous Dairen"); To LK.5.10.1938 ("the old woman"); To LK.7.6.1939 ("understands absolutely"); To LK.7.2.1939 ("as a most evil").

9 *PBP*, Canto Two, XXXIV, 96, XXXI, 94; To EAS.26.9.1925, comment ("this was my"); To OB.19.9.1987 ("advising me").
10 To LK.6.8.1939 ("catastrophically impoverished"); VSP, "Kharbin i Pomgol," typescript ("included embezzlers").
11 VP, "Valerii Salatko-Petrishche" ("a mortgaged house"); various papers from Russia and China; *DP*, 74; To EAS.25.4.1940, comment ("heavily mortgaged").
12 To EAS.20.8.1936, comment.
13 To EAS.12.8.1936 ("no matter how").
14 To EG.7.4.1937 ("I lost"); To EAG.7.4.1937 ("vile job").
15 *DP*, 77.
16 To EAS.27.10.1942, comment; To LK.8.2.1939; *PBP*, Canto Three, I–IX, 121–5, 159n3; To LK.8.2.1939.
17 *PBP*, Canto Three, XXII–XXVI, XXX–XXXIII, 131–4, 136–7, 159n6.
18 VP, "Valerii Salatko-Petrishche" ("the futility").
19 *PBP*, Canto Three, XIX, 130, XX, 131.
20 Booklets "MCMXXXIII," "MCMXXXIV," and "MCMXXXIV-II."
21 VP, "Vechnyi Rim," *KhV*, 30 July 1933, and *Feniks* 10 (November 1935).
22 *DP*, 54.
23 "Mariia Kareeva," typescript ("prompted"), where Pereleshin mentions seven of Kareeva's poems, but in fact ten were written; To GS.30.12.1974 ("all Tsvetaeva").
24 To GS.30.12.1974 ("an utter horror"); To EAS.1.11.1942 ("to throw"); To EAS.2.1.1943 ("I do not consider").
25 To LK.8.8.1938 ("very suitable").
26 To EAS.2.8.1936; Hinrichs, "Valerij Perelešin's Poetry from his Chinese Years," xxii, xxxiv n8,
27 VP, "Levan Khaindrava,"("immediately"); *DP*, 32–3.
28 Khaindrova to P. Balakshin, 23.8.1937.
29 The poem "*Gallipoliitsy*" was listed twice; the second listing should be "*Nastavlenie*" (44).
30 VP, "Ot avtora," *Iz glubiny vozzvakh*, 7.
31 Hinrichs, "Valerij Perelešin's Poetry from his Chinese Years," xxii, xxxiv n7; Pereleshin's notes on a typewritten text of *V puti*, sent to Hinrichs in 1983 ("the first open"); Ivask Archive, Box 5, f. 19, comment ("storm").
32 Hinrichs, "Valerij Perelešin's Poetry from his Chinese Years," xxii, xxxiv n7; Pereleshin's notes on a typewritten text of *V puti*, sent to Hinrichs in 1983 ("camouflage"); Pereleshin's notes on typescripts of poems about Nezhin.
33 To LK.6.2.1938 ("it has a thematic").

34 Inscription in a copy of *V puti* sent to A.P. Chernishev ("many poems"); Ivask, "Valerii Pereleshin o poezii" ("one of my first").
35 All reviews are quoted in part in VP, "A chto obo mne pisali polveka tomu nazad"; Adamovich, "Literaturnye zametki."
36 Rannit, "O poezii i poetike Valeriia Pereleshina," 83.
37 VP, "Valerii Pereleshin" 1970s ("Verlaine and Lucien").
38 "Otkrytie Instituta Sviatogo Vladimira v g. Kharbine"; "Deportatsiia iz predelov Man'chzhu-di-go"; "Postrizhenie v monashestvo i vozvedenie v san ieromonakha professora V.G. Pavlovskogo, nyne ieromonakha Vasiliia"; "Otchet o sostoianii Bogoslovskogo Fakul'teta Instituta Sv. Vladimira za 1939 g."
39 To IV.18.12.1972 ("Larissa Andersen").
40 V. Gur'ev, "Bogoslovskii Fakul'tet Instituta Sv. Vladimira."
41 *PBP*, Canto Three, XXXIV, 138; To AR.11.8.1971.
42 News item; "Kratkie biograficheskie svedeniia ob o. Arkhimandrite Iuvenalii"; "Ocherk vozniknoveniia i ustroeniia Kazansko-Bogoroditskogo Muzhskogo Monastyria v Kharbine"; "Prestol'nyi prazdnik i 15-letie Kazansko-Bogoroditskogo Muzhskogo Monastyria."
43 I.P. Pasynkov to OB.11.9.2004; To GS.19.8.1969 ("responded to"); To LK.6.2.1938 ("on the whole"); *DP*, 89; To EAS.20.11.1944, comment.
44 VP, "Valerii Salatko-Petrishche."
45 To IV.17.10.1978 ("I spent three"); I.P. Pasynkov to OB.11.9.2004; To LK.17.5.1938 ("immediately felt").
46 To LK.17.5.1938 ("personal freedom").
47 To LK.8.2.1939 ("the entire"); *DP*, 90; To LK.16.2.1939 ("real madman").
48 VP, "Igumen Varsonofii" ("exceptionally warm").
49 Ibid. ("many call").
50 To EAS.15-17.4.1940, comment ("possessed"); VP, "Igumen Varsonofii" ("did it become").
51 *DP*, 89–90; To LK.1.9.1938 ("your reflection").
52 To LK.12.9.1938 ("anything unorthodox").
53 *DP*, 90; To LK.7.10.1939, letter and comment ("kept attacking"); To LK.19.5.1939 ("of course, I have"); To LK.17.5.1938 ("for Mum").
54 "Uspekh vechera poetov"; AG to VP, ca. 1944, comment to the second letter of that year.
55 *DP*, 90; To LK.12.9.1938 ("'Eternal Rome'"); *PBP*, Canto Seven, XXIX, 377.
56 To EAS.26.9.1925, comment ("entering a world").
57 To LK.6.2.1938 ("would a black").
58 LK to PB, 6.2.1939 ; To LK.8.2.1939 ("rejoiced"); To LK.7.2.1939 ("the inner aspect").

59 To AG.26.6.1945 ("one of the evil"); To LK.16.3.1939 ("an unbearable atmosphere"); VP, "Valerii Salatko-Petrishche" ("the place which"); LK to PB, 16.2.1939.
60 *DP*, 90; To LK.20.4.1939; To LK.6.8.1939.
61 To LK.7.10.1939 ("not a single").
62 Meng and Sylvester, "Valerii Pereleshin at the International Poetry Festival," 5; VP, "Stikhi Kamilly Al'bertovny Khorvat" ("drawn by the desire").
63 To LK.19.8.1939; To LK.4.9.1939.
64 To LK.6.8.1939 ("mad with anger").
65 VP, "Valerii Pereleshin" [MS] ("it was a terribly").
66 To LK.19.5.1939 ("old poems").
67 To LK.28.6.1938 ("caused, according").
68 Ivask, 'Valerii Pereleshin o poezii" ("a year in a monastery").
69 Nesmelov, "Stikhi odnoi temy"; To LK.7.10.1939 ("he is right").

4. Beijing: "Wonderful, Beloved City"

1 *DP*, 83; To EAS.25.9.1939; *PBP*, Canto Four, V, 167; *PBP*, Canto Four, II, 166.
2 VSP, "Chetyre goda Rossiiskoi dukhovnoi missii v Kitae"; M.K., *Bei-guan'*, 14; Ipatova, "Rossiiskaia dukhovnaia missiia v Kitae," 316, map facing 353; *Bei-guan'. Kratkaia istoriia Rossiiskoi dukhovnoi missii v Kitae.*
3 VP, "Chetyre goda Rossiiskoi dukhovnoi missii v Kitae"; Pozdniaev, *Pravoslavie v Kitae*, 49; M.I.M., "Rossiiskaia Dukhovnaia missiia v Kitae (kratkii istoricheskii ocherk)," 22; Ipatova, "Prazdnovanie 250-letiia Rossiiskoi dukhovnoi missii v Kitae (1935 g.)," 74–84.
4 To EAS.25.9.1939 ("a real Chinese"); VSP, "Chetyre goda Rossiiskoi dukhovnoi missii v Kitae" ("its heart").
5 Pekinets, "Otkrytie Rossiiskogo doma v Pekine"; Balakshin, *Final v Kitae*, 2: 238–9; US/INS, transcript of questioning Pereleshin, 26.5.1950, D571 ("he very often").
6 VP, "Igumen Varsonofii" ("as a relative"); To LK.7.10.1939 ("exceptionally charming").
7 *DP*, 90.
8 *DP*, 89; To LK.26.9.1939 ("here I will"); To LK.12.11.1939 ("fed a bare").
9 To EAS.29.12.1939 ("hard and thankless"); To EAS.10.3.1941, note added on 17.3.1941 ("soundly criticized").
10 VP, "Chetyre goda Rossiiskoi dukhovnoi missii v Kitae"; To EAS.6–7.4.1940 ("a great joyous").
11 To EAS.22.11.1939 ("yesterday we").
12 *DP*, 94; To EAS.17.11.1939; To EAS.18.12.1939; To EAS.29.1.1940.

13 To LK.26.9.1939 ("found a multitude"); To EAS.12.3.1940 ("the entire correspondence"); To EAS.3.1.1940.
14 To EAS.16.3.1940; To EAS.2.1.1940; To EAS.25.3.1940 ("a slanderer").
15 To EAS.10.4.1940 ("amazingly sophisticated"); To LK.18.4.1940 ("without a shade"); To EAS.16.3.1940, postscript of 17.3.1940 ("he has an inspired").
16 To EAS.10.4.1940 ("a wonderful branch"); To EAS.24.1.1941; VP, "Arkhimandrite Nafanail (Porshnev)" ("which forever").
17 *DP*, 91–2; VP, "Stikhi Kamilly Al'bertovny Khorvat"; VP, "Baronessa Ol'ga Vladimirovna Stal'-Gol'shtein."
18 To EAS.7.12.1939 ("the sweetest old").
19 *DP*, 92; VP, "Dmitrii Petrovich Panteleev," typescript ("totally and forever"); To EAS.17.11.1939 ("everything shows").
20 To EAS.17.11.1939 ("for a long time").
21 *DP*, 91–2; To EAS.24.3.1941.
22 To EAS.28.1.1940, comment ("for his quietness"); VP, "Orden 'Vozrozhdeniia Azii.'"
23 *DP*, 91–2; To EAS.27.9.1940.
24 DP, 91; To LK.12.11.1939; To EAS.22.11.1939; To EAS.1.12.1939; To EAS.27.12.1939; To EAS.12.3.1940.
25 Korostovets to VP.13.7.1971 ("I knew that").
26 To EAS.5.5.1941 ("for her sake").
27 To EAS.16.1.1941 ("joyful and"); *DP*, 93.
28 *DP*, 92–3; To EAS.11.6.1941; To GS.20.7.1972 ("to know opportunities"); To IV.27.4.1977.
29 To EAS.30.3.1940 ("I am rushing"); To LK.3.4.1940 ("now life").
30 To EAS.2.1.1940 ("strong sympathy").
31 To EAS.10.4.1940; To LK.18.4.1940 ("to absorb more"); To EAS.11.5.1940 ("a model priest").
32 To EAS.20.4.1940 ("to be greeted"); To EAS.20.4.1940; To EAS.7.5.1940.
33 To EAS.1.5.1940 ("a good look"); To EAS.20.4.1940 ("a stone mass").
34 To EAS.7.5.1940 ("such dates"); To EAS.24.5.1940 ("in Beiguan").
35 To EAS.5.5.1940 ("very happy").
36 VSP, "Pis'mo iz Brazilii" (1983); To EAS.7.12.1939 ("almost untranslatable"); To LK.3.3.1939 ("taking advantage"); To LK.20.4.1939.
37 To EAS.16.12.1939 ("the content"); To EAS.19.12.1939; To EAS.11.1.1940 ("distracted the reader"); To EV.20.4.1971.
38 *S.T. Kol'ridzh*; *DP*, 113, where he writes that he learned of Gumilev's translation "only last year," that is, in the late 1960s to mid-1970s, which contradicts the information in To EAS.21.6.1944 ("in vain, because"); To GS.17.2.1969; To GS.5.9.1970 ("very intrigued"); To GS.9.4.1973.

39 To LK.27.12.1939 ("did not pursue").
40 To EAS.18.3.1940.
41 To LK.6.2.1938 ("neurasthenic").
42 Victor Salatko to A.A. Jebit, ca. 1999.
43 To EAS.19.12.1939, comment ("for an insignificant"); To EAS.3.5.1943.
44 Salatko, excerpt from a letter, 38; "Torzhestvennyi akt v Politekhnicheskom institute"; "Nagrady inzh"; *Haerbin gongye daxue*, 68; Salatko, "Razocharovannye dali," 1.11.1994.
45 Salatko, "Razocharovannye dali," 2.11.1994.
46 To EAS.23.2.1940; To EAS.15.4.1940; Salatko, "Razocharovannye dali," *RZh*, 2.11.1994.
47 Salatko, "Razocharovannye dali," 2.11.1994.
48 To EAS.10.4.1940 ("the miracle"); To EAS.1.5.1940 ("with tears"); To EAS.12.4.1940 ("was forced").
49 To EAS.11.5.1940 ("painful and nervous"); Salatko, "Razocharovannye dali," 5.11.1944; To EAS.27.12.1943 ("I often think"); To GS.11.5.1976.
50 To LK.2.7.1940 ("after the storms"); To EAS.7.5.1940; To LK.13.9.1940 ("the old city").
51 To EAS.7.10.1940; To EAS.14.12.1940 ("possible future"); To LK.9.11.1940 ("monastery life").
52 To EAS.8.3.1941; To EAS.21.4.1941; To EAS.11.6.1942; To EAS.3.2.1941 ("in the monastery").
53 To EAS.28.5.1941 ("fed up").
54 To EAS.24.9.1942 ("with a passion"); To LK.27.12.1939 ("ample Chinese"); To EAS.13.12.1939; To EAS.19.12.1939; To EAS.2.1.1940; To EAS.11.1.1940; To EAS.15.1.1940.
55 To OB.29.8.1989 ("would not come"), where he gives the date of the translation as 18 November 1936, an obvious mistake, as the letter To LK.7.2.1939 and the date in *Dobryi ulei* show. In 1968, sending a copy of *Dobryi ulei* to A.P. Chernishev, Pereleshin corrected the name of the author from Li Bai to Gai Jiayun and changed the last line: the dreams were "about the dear guest from a distant land."
56 Serebrennikovy, *Tsvety kitaiskoi poezii*, 3, 140, 128; VP, "Ot perevodchika," in *Stikhi na veere*, iv–v.
57 To EAS.1.5.1940; To LK.3.4.1940; *DP*, 111.
58 VP, "Mulan," *Rubezh* 1/770, 30.12.1942 – 1.1.1943; *DP*, 111.
59 Fu, "Projecting Ambivalence," especially 93–8; *DP*, 111.
60 To EAS.15.1.1941 ("the matters of"); To EAS.24.1.1941 ("thank God"); *PBP*, Canto Five, XLI, 235.
61 To EAS.2.6.1941, comment; To EAS.29.4.1945 ("fate joined"); To EAS.22.2.1945 ("we lived").

62 To EAS.11.6.1941 ("both women"); To EAS.11.6.1941 ("forbade Mariia Pavlovna").
63 To EAS.29.4.1945, comment; To LK.24.7.1941 ("I have been").
64 To LK.27.12.1941; To EAS.27.4.1944.
65 To OB.6.2.1988 ("new glorious").
66 To EAS.14.12.1940, comment; VP, "Poezdka na Chol"; "Prazdnik russkoi poezii"; To EAS.5.3.1941; To EAS.24.3.1941; To EAS.27.3.1941.
67 "Vostochno-aziatskii konkurs russkikh poetov i pisatelei."
68 VP, "Poezdka na Chol" ("I have a foggy"); "Kul'turnyi prazdnik emigratsii"
69 *U rodnykh rubezhei* 2 (1943), 5.
70 "Parad poetov *Rubezha*"; To EAS.8.12.1942; To EAS.15.3.1943 ("I doubt").
71 VP, "Poezdka na Chol" (Pereleshin wrongly places Chol settlements on the east line).
72 To EAS.19.10.1945, comment; VP, "Poezdka na Chol" ("across Xing'an").
73 To AG.1.5.1967 ("conducted the liturgy"); To OB.26.4.1989; To EAS.21.7.1944 ("I fear that"); Meng and Sylvester, "Valerii Pereleshin at the International Poetry Festival in Austin, Texas (April 1974)," 3; A.M. Naam to VP. 11.11.1953; Salatko, excerpt from a letter, 39.
74 To EAS.18.5.1942 ("I was sure"); *PBP*, Canto Six, IX, 267.
75 To LK.2.7.1940 ("the immediate goal").
76 To LK.31.1.1941 ("thanks to recent"); To LK.1.4.1941 ("the greatest event"); To EAS.8.2.1941 ("pleasantly surprised").
77 To LK.3.9.1940; To LK.24.7.1941; To EAS.8.4.1941; To EAS.5.5.1941 ("I will always").
78 To LK.31.1.1941 ("central"); To EAS.14.9 (*sic* – 10).1940 ("perhaps it is"); comment on *Zvezda nad morem* in a typescript copy ("faith in the final"); To LK.31.1.1941.
79 To GS.13.7.1970; To AR.14.9.1971 ("the star could").
80 To LK.31.1.1941 ("it is best").
81 Translated into English by Jeanny Lam.
82 VP, "A chto obo mne pisali polveka tomu nazad?" quoting Savskii, "Mudraia muza"; N.R., "Valerii Pereleshin. *Zvezda nad morem*"; Iul'skii, "Zvezda nad morem."
83 To EAS.1.12.1939; To EAS.17.1.1940 ("to devote myself"); To EAS.18.5.1942; To EAS.28.2.1941
84 To EAS.11.6.1942; To EAS.20.6.1942; To EAS.10.8.1942; To EAS.20-21.9.1942; To LK.31.3.1939; To EAS.22.5.1942.
85 VP, as Ieromonakh German, "Filosofiia stradaniia"; To AG.14.6.1967 ("at the time").
86 To EAS.5.5.1943; "Khronika"; VP, as Ieromonakh German, "Uchenie knigi Iova o stradanii"; VP, as Ieromonakh German, "Novozavetnoe

uchenie o stradanii," *KhN*, 9 (1943), 8–13; VP, as Ieromonakh German, "Zabluzhdeniia Dostoevskogo."

87 To EAS.5.5.1943 ("yet another"); To EAS.11.5.1943 ("we had wine").

88 To EAS.23.6.1942, comment ("heresy seekers"); To EAS.27.8.1942, comment ("stole"); To LK.7.10.1939, comment ("one of the evil"); To LK.8.2.1939, comment ("evil force"); To LK.8.2.1939; To EAS.27.8.1942, comment; To AG.1.5.1967.

89 As quoted and summarized in Kostiuchik, "Otvet dotsenta Bogoslovskogo fakul'teta Instituta sv. Vladimira v Kharbine I.I. Kostiuchika na 'Otzyv o rabote ieromonakha Germana na temu 'Filosofiia stradaniia,' sostavlennyi professorom K.I. Zaitsevym 12 dekabria 1943 goda."

90 To EAS.27.8.1942, comment ("enraged, threatened"); Kostiuchik, "Otvet dotsenta Bogoslovskogo fakul'teta Instituta sv. Vladimira v Kharbine I.I. Kostiuchika na 'Otzyv o rabote ieromonakha Germana na temu 'Filosofiia stradaniia,' sostavlennyi professorom K.I. Zaitsevym 12 dekabria 1943 goda."

91 To EAS.21.9.1944; To EAS.9.12.1944 ("how wretched"); To EAS.27.11.1944 ("it will be").

92 To EAS.26.4.1942; To EAS.11.5.1942 ("a regular Beijing").

93 To EAS.11.5.1942 ("it is nerves").

94 Dobrinin to OB.19.9.2006; To EAS.18.11.1942, comment ("horror"); To EAS.29.1.1941 ("lived in her").

95 To EAS.13.1.1943; To EAS.19.1.1943; To EAS.5.3.1943.

96 To EAS.23.6.1942; To EAS.10.1.1941 ("your knight").

97 To EAS.24.8.1943; To EAS.16.5.1943; To OB.19.2.1988 ("was not a 'marriage'"); To EAS.6.9.1943 ("endlessly glad").

98 VP, "Perelozhenie ostankov E.V. Kniazia Igoria Konstantinovicha v novyi grob" ("dark figures"); VP, as Vl. Nezhdanov, "Iz pekinskikh vospominanii."

99 To EAS.21.12.1942, the letter, dated 21 December, but written over several days and describing the events of 21–3 December ("the death of"); VP, "Arkhimandrit Nafanail (Porshnev)," with the handwritten comment in the typescript in Bakhmeteff Archive ("finishing this").

100 To EAS.21.12.1942, comment ("there were"); VP, "Arkhimandrit Nafanail (Porshnev)" ("berries"); To EAS.21.12.1942 ("merciless persecution"); To EAS.23.6.1942, comment; To EAS.1.7.1942.

101 To EAS.19.1.1943 ("planned every").

102 To EAS.15.6.1943; To EAS.24.9.1943; To EAS.24.9.1943 ("relations became").

103 To EAS.9.12.1943 ("a real attack"); To EAS.14.10.1943 ("the greatest evil"); To ISF.15.9.1974 ("in the way").

104 To EAS.24.11.1942, comment; To EAS.9.2.1943; To EAS.16.5.1943 ("bite people's"); To EAS.3.2.1943 ("to the point"); To EAS.4.4.1943.
105 To PL.23.7.1975 ("played into"); To ISF.15.9.1974 ("a very bad monk").
106 To EAS.2.9.1943 ("to move").
107 To EAS.24.10.1943; To EAS.9.12.1943 ("the mission head grabbed").
108 To EAS.31.10.1943 ("tomorrow").
109 To EAS.29.4.1945 ("grateful memories").
110 To EAS.24.8.1943 ("until better"); To EAS.2.10.1943.
111 To EAS.16-17.5.1944 ("eternally"); To GS.2.9.1967 ("a heroic deed"); To GS.2.9.1969; To EAS.27.6.1944; To EAS.4.4.1944 ("the cost of two").
112 To EAS.19.10.1942; To EAS.15.3.1943 ("life sacrificed").
113 *PBP*, Canto Five, XXIV, 227.
114 Ivask, "Valerii Pereleshin o poezii."
115 To EAS.10–11.2.1944.
116 To EAS.24.9.1943.
117 VP, "A chto obo mne pisali polveka tomu nazad?" quoting from Khaindrova's review in *Shanghaiskaia zaria* written under the pseudonym Eristavi.
118 VP, "A chto obo mne pisali polveka tomu nazad?"; To EAS.21.7.1944 ("intelligent and fair").
119 To EAS.16–17.5.1944 ("it excited"); To AR.6.3.1973 ("felt such desire").

5. Shanghai: Fogs and Chimeras

1 *PBP*, Canto Five, XLII–XLV, 236–7; *DP*, 89.
2 VP, "Valerii Salatko-Petrishche" ("starving and freezing").
3 To EAS.24.11.1943 ("hated it"); To EAS.4.11.1943 ("unkind and unattractive"); To EAS.30.1.1944 ("the sky is always"); To EAS.1.9.1944; To EAS.21.7.1944 ("totally motionless").
4 To EAS.7.12.1943, comment; To EAS.27.12.1943 ("came daily").
5 Comment on a copy sent to OB indicated Bishop Dimitrii Voznesenskii in particular.
6 VP, "Valerii Salatko-Petrishche" ("always smiling"); To EAS.24.1.1944 ("one cannot").
7 To GS.2.11.1967; To EAS.10.3.1944; To EAS.24.1.1944 ("burdensome"); To EAS.7.12.1943; To EAS.1.2.1944 ("finding loopholes"); To EAS.16-17.5.1944 ("in a compact").
8 To EAS.16-20.11.1943 ("I still don't").
9 To EAS.10.3.1944; To EAS.21.6.1944; To EAS.2.8.1944 ("a two-faced"); To EAS.5.7.1944 ("actively hiding").
10 To EAS.28.3.1945 ("my heart is").

11 To EAS.27.12.1943 ("I pray for"); To EAS.22.2.1945 ("you are my greatest"); To EAS.1.9.1944.
12 Zhiganov, *Russkie v Shankhae*, unpaginated introduction; Vershinin, "Puti samopoznaniia," 10. Both sources give the number of Shanghai Russians as about 25,000.
13 To EAS.1.2.1944; To EAS.16-17.5.1944; To EAS.24.11.1943; To EAS.7.12.1943; To EAS.29.5.1944 ("made more"); To EAS.27.6.1944.
14 *L.I. Khaindrova: serdtse poeta*, 388–90; *Na Vostoke*, 10; To EAS.2.8.1944; To EAS.21.9.1944.
15 To EAS.4.11.1943; To EAS.10-11.2.1944; To EAS.27.6.1944, comment ("the Gumilev couple"); To EAS.9.12.1944; To GS.21.1.1973 ("behaved like"); To OB.1.8.1987; VP, "Poetessa Ol'ga Tel'toft."
16 To EAS.27.7.1944; To EAS.29.5.1944; *DP*, 125; Kruzenshtern-Peterets, "Artist otoshel tantsuia"; To KP.13.9.1970 ("devoutly pray").
17 To EAS.16-17.5.1944; To EAS.6.2.1945.
18 *DP*, 94–5.
19 Slobodchikov to OB.5.10.2002; Somova, "Ponedel'nik, chetverg, piatnitsa," 4; To EAS.20.12.1944; To EAS.10–12.1.1945 ("the expression"); To EAS.26.12.1944, comment ("a monk, but even"); To EAS.24.7.1945 ("cumbersome thing").
20 AG to VP, ca. October 1944; AG to VP, ca. October 1944, VP's comment ("a great heart").
21 AG to VP, second letter of 1944; AG to VP.24.6.1945.
22 To EAS.19.3.1945; To EAS.15.4.1945 ("previously I loved").
23 To EAS.28.3.1945 ("for some reason").
24 To EAS.9.5.1945, addition to the letter ("I did not know").
25 To EAS.16-17.5.1944 ("another little"); To EAS.29.6.1944 ("I am exhausted"); To EAS.21.6.1944; To EAS.29.6.1944; To EAS.21.7.1944.
26 To EAS.20.11.1944 ("unfortunate infatuations"); To EAS.8.4.1945 ("a fine adventure").
27 To EAS.9.5.1945, addition to the letter ("sinful joys").
28 Somova, "Vozvrashchenie," 2; To LK.5.10.1938 ("they are not").
29 Carey, *The War Years in Shanghai*, 85; personal information from several Shanghai Russians.
30 Krouk, "Nam ulybalas' Kvan-in'," 163; *DP*, 101–2; To GS.26.3.1970 ("the choice"); To EAS.4.11.1943; To EAS.16-18.11.1943; To EAS.29.6.1944.
31 Slobodchikov to OB.24.7.2002.
32 Somova, "Vozvrashchenie," 2; Carey, *The War Years in Shanghai*, 84–5; Nikiforov, "Vozvrashchenie, ili Put' na Rodinu," 11.
33 To EAS.6.10.1944; Archive of Shanghai Tuesday Circle.
34 Kruzenshtern-Peterets, "Vospominaniia," *Rossiiane v Azii* 7, 141.

35 N.Z., "Velichaishii muzykant sovremennosti," 20.
36 "Ot Gofmana do Pauliusa," 7; Medi, "Khristianstvo i gitlerism," 6; OB, "Segodniashnii vzgliad na *Segodnia*," 210–28.
37 "Kriticheskie tseli *Segodnia*," 2.
38 Tsvetaev, "Koniushni shankhaiskogo Parnasa."
39 Vershinin, "Bez mysli o tvorchestve," 16; "Vne literatury," 11, 21–3; Val', "Iz mestnykh literaturnykh nravov i obychaev"; Parro, "Buria v literaturnoi chashke chaia," 13–20.
40 VP, "Valerii Salatko-Petrishche" ("God himself").
41 Slobodchikov to OB.24.7.2002; Slobodchikov to OB.14.1.2002; To GS.20.12.1971 ("green youth").
42 VP's comment to his letters to LK; To EAS.11.4.1945, comment ("unfailingly and silently").
43 Somova, "Ponedel'nik, chetverg, piatnitsa," 4.
44 *DP*, 106; To GS.9.10.1969 ("merciless criticism").
45 OB, "Ostrov sredi bushuiushchego moria."
46 Kruzenshtern-Peterets, "Vospominaniia," *Rossiiane v Azii* 7, 148.
47 To EAS.5.8.1944; To EAS.1.9.1944.
48 VP, "Valerii Salatko-Petrishche" ("escaped into"); *DP*, 101, 103, 104.
49 To AG.15.3.1967 ("my poems were").
50 To EAS.6.10.1944; To EAS.20.10.1944; To KP.5.3.1967; VP, "'Solov'inyi sad' Aleksandra Bloka"; To EAS.10.3.1944); Shchegolev, typescript.
51 To EAS.16-17.5.1944; To EAS.29.10.1944; To AG.29.4.1969; To AG.18.6.1969 ("to find a trace").
52 To EAS.21.7.1944 ("émigré cocktail"); To EAS.10.3.1944; To EAS.10.3.1944 ("maniac"); To EAS.28.10.1944 ("the wolf pit").
53 Khaindrova, "Kak sozdavalas' Piatnitsa"; To EAS.20.10.1944; To EAS.20.11.1944; To EAS.27.11.1944; Kruzenshtern-Peterets, "Vospominaniia," *Rossiiane v Azii* 7, 148; To EAS.9.12.1944, a note to the letter of that day ("everyone was"); To EAS.20.12.1944.
54 To KP.15.8.1967 ("most enlightened"); To VAS.30.11.1968 ("one of the most"); To EAS.20.12.1944; To EAS.21.2.1945 ("more gloomily").
55 Korostovets to VP, 24.6.1969; *DP*, 108, where Pereleshin recalls this incident almost verbatim from Korostovets's letter without mentioning the source.
56 To EAS.24.1.1944 ("a cosmogonic poem"); To EAS.16-17.5.1944 ("very sweet person").
57 To VL.11.4.1954 ("an example of"); To EAS.29.5.1944 ("I have stocked").
58 To EAS.16-17.5.1944 ("singing, silvery"); To EAS.29.5.1944 ("I have never"); US/INS, Letter to G. Volkoff, 2.8.1946, D112 ("a work as unearthly").

59 To EAS.19.6.1944; To EAS.16-17.5.1944 ("a book of"); Peterets, typescript; To EAS.27.6.1944 ("subjected it"); To AR.6.11.1972 ("some ten years").
60 To EAS.27.7.1944; To EAS.27.12.1943 ("in snatches"); To EAS.16-17.5.1944; To EAS.3.3.1945 ("burned all candles").
61 To EAS.2.8.1944; To EAS.23-25.10.1944 ("merrily").
62 To EAS.20.12.1944 ("unheard of"); To EAS.9.12.1944 ("there is nothing"); To EAS.6.2.1945 ("I dropped by").
63 To EAS.28.3.1945; To EAS.18.1.1945 ("repulsive cold"); To EAS.18.1.1945 ("you are absolutely").
64 To EAS.17.1.1945 ("treacherous and"); To EAS.8.4.1945 ("I often see"); To EAS.21.2.1945 ("my joy").
65 To EAS.17.1.1945 ("almost agreed"); To EAS.21.2.1945 ("the Lord saved"); To EAS.22.2.1945 ("it was necessary"); To EAS.29.4.1945 ("fate acted").
66 *PBP*, Canto Five, XLIX, 239.
67 To EAS.30.1.1944; To EAS.5.7.1944 ("with all her good").
68 To EAS.2.8.1944 ("divorced"); To EAS.29.8.1944 ("adopted an unbearably")
69 Somova, "Ponedel'nik, chetverg, piatnitsa," 4; To EAS.29.4.1945 ("patron"); To EAS.1.9.1944 ("Mrs Korostovets").
70 To EAS.29.4.1945 ("decisively and"); To EAS.29.4.1945 ("breaking the agreement").
71 To EAS.15.4.1945 ("nasty character"); To EAS.29.4.1945 ("hit her").
72 To EAS.15.4.1945 ("everyone is").
73 To EAS.17.11.1939, comment; To EAS.11.4.1945 ("another repulsive").
74 To EAS.18.5.1945; To EAS.21.6.1945 ("the stinking cesspool").
75 To EAS.4.6.1945 ("that lunatic").
76 To EAS.4.6.1945; To EAS.21.6.1945 ("I would not"); To EAS.18.6.1945 ("I no longer").
77 To EAS.7.7.1945 ("almost three").
78 To EAS.22.12.1944 ("most fruitful"); To EAS.13.10.1944; "Iuzhnyi dom," manuscript; To EAS.21.2.1945 ("liked the title").
79 To EAS.17.1.1945; To EAS.21.6.1945; To EAS.1.8.1945 ("the price of paper"); To EAS.27.10.1945; To EAS.27.1.1946.
80 To EAS.9.5.1945 ("the end of the war"); To EAS.21.8.1945 ("a pathetic provincial").
81 To EAS.8.8.1945, addendum of 13.8.1945 ("Harbin, Hailar"); To EAS.8.8.1945, addendum of 13.8.1945 ("the war will").
82 To EAS.8.8.1945, addendum of 13.8.1945 ("I take my notebook").
83 Carey, *The War Years in Shanghai*, 215, 228; To EAS.3.9.1945; To EAS.19.10.1946; To GS.11.5.1976.

84 To EAS.8.8.1945 ("exceptional elegance").
85 To ID.15.7.1990 ("except for").
86 To AG.26.10.1966 ("a religious work"); To KP.16.3.1970 ("a Latin heresy").
87 To KP.7.5.1967 ("it is written"); To AG.25.7.1967; To AR.29.11.1971 ("hints at justifying"); To OB.23.4.1988 ("the highest achievement").
88 Balakshin, *Final v Kitae*, 2: 257–8; Somova, "Orkestru Lundstrema – 60 let," 5.
89 To EAS.6.10.1944; To EAS.28.10.1944; To EAS.27.11.1944; To EAS.9.5.1945, addendum ("probably join"); To EAS.27.10.1945 ("paid so much").
90 To EAS.7.9.1949 ("'fatal step'").
91 US/INS, D567 ("I remained"); VP to US State Department, Immigration Office, 29.10.1968 ("very reluctantly").
92 PBP, Canto Six, XLVII, 286; *DP*, 114; Kruzenshtern-Peterets, "V krasnom Shankhae."
93 To EAS.1.8.1945 ("a vast publishing"); VFSP, "Smysl 'kul'turnoi revoliutsii' v Kitae," 128; To EAS.27.1.1946 ("a humongous amount").
94 *PBP*, Canto Six, XLIII, 284; To ISF.15.9.1974; To EAS.18.6.1945; *PBP*, Canto Six, XLIII, 284; To GS.2.11.1967 ("the best TASS translator"); US/INS, VP to G. Volkoff, 2.8.1946, D111 ("privileged conditions").
95 To GS.26.6.1969 ("a 'sinologist' like"); *DP*, 112.
96 To GS.17.11.1972 ("hopelessly weak"); To KP.14.8.1970; *DP*, 112; V.A. Slobodchikov to OB.24.7.2002.
97 *DP*, 111–12.
98 To GS.22.8.1971; To GS.21.11.1972 ("of astonishing beauty"); To EAS.19.10.1946 ("almost happy").
99 To EAS.3.9.1945; To EAS.15.4.1945 ("now adult"); To EAS.8-13.8.1945 ("joy").
100 To OB.29.8.1989; *PBP*, Canto Six, XXXI, XXXII, 278–9; To EAS.19.10.1946 ("a significant part").
101 To PL.23.7.1975 ("to serve liturgy"): *PBP*, Canto Six, XXXI, XXXII, 279.
102 VP, "Moi posviashcheniia" ("visited"); *PBP*, Canto Six, LI–LVII, 288–90; To IV.19.7.1974.
103 To IV.24.7.1968.
104 VP, "Moi posviashcheniia" ("a most honest"); *PBP*, Canto Six, LXVII, 296, 308nn65–7; VP, "Valerii Salatko-Petrishche" ("pernicious books").
105 *PBP*, Canto Seven, IV, 315, VI, 216; VP, "Moi posviashcheniia," states that Liu Xin was imprisoned for two months.
106 To EAS.28.3.1945 ("belonging to")
107 To EAS.9.5.1945, addendum ("a step towards"); To EAS.4.6.1945 ("I am a passionate"); To EAS.29.4.1945 ("during the Lent").

108 To EAS.19.3.1945 ("alarming telegram"); To EAS.28.3.1945, comment ("of great contempt").
109 To EAS.19.3.1945; To EAS.16.7.1945 ("cowardice again"); To EAS.19.3.1945 ("most of all I fear").
110 VP to Father Gur'ev, 23.4.1945, typescript; To EAS.22.4.1945.
111 To EAS.16.7.1945 ("if some lever").
112 To EAS.16.7.1945 ("my poems are").
113 To KP.2.7.1967 ("pecked for").
114 To EAS.1.8.1945 ("I have a copy").
115 Balakshin, *Final v Kitae* 2: 240–2; To AG.15.3.1967 ("to preserve the Beijing"); Pozdniaev, *Pravoslavie v Kitae*, 88–9.
116 Balakshin, *Final v Kitae*, 2: 242–52; Pozdniaev, *Pravoslavie v Kitae*, 92–103.
117 Pozdniaev, *Pravoslavie v Kitae*, 103.
118 Kirilloff to OB.23.12.2004; Kirillov, "Kitaiskaia avtonomnaia pravoslavnaia tserkov'," 17.
119 To KP.9.5.1967 ("both were dear").
120 To PL.23.7.1975 ("left a letter"); US/INS, D591.
121 To GS.5.9.1981 ("I attempted to").
122 To KP.9.5.1967 ("one day, on Avenue").
123 To EAS.27.8.1942, comment; To AG.15.3.1967 ("utmost black-hundred").
124 To KP.9.5.1967 ("formally I am"); To ISF.18.11.1974 ("canonical leave"); US/INS, D111, VP to G. Volkoff, 2.8.1946 ("in the street"); handwritten notes; To EAS.x.1.1944.
125 VP, "I eto obmanuvshee siian'e!" ("stood in the central"). The line comes from Georgii Adamovich's poem "Nu, vot i koncheno teper'."
126 VFSP, "Russkie na Dal'nem Vostoke" ("the best collection").
127 Shchegolev, "Predislovie," *Ostrov*, 13; To GS.13.2.1970 ("unacceptable to"); OB, "Ostrov sredi bushuiushchego moria," 174–215.
128 Kruzenshtern-Peterets, "Vospominaniia," *Rossiiane v Azii* 7, 145–6; *DP*, 109; To EAS.27.1.1946; To GS.26.4.1973; To KP.17.5.1968; V.A. Slobodchikov to OB.24.7.2002; *PBP*, Canto Six, LX, 293; To KP.15.4.1972.
129 *DP*, 122–3; *PBP*, Canto Six, LXV, 295; Nikiforov, "Vozvrashchenie ili Put' na Rodinu," 10–11; Somova, "Vozvrashchenie," 2.
130 Somova, "Vozvrashchenie," 2; US/INS, 29.5.1950, D579–580.
131 Puliaevskaia, "Odisseia nashego detstva" 1–2; Puliaevskaia, "Moe shankhaiskoe detstvo," 10; Puliaevskaia, "Moi otets" 4; Balakshin, *Final v Kitae*, 2: 285–8; Zaitsev, "Put' na Rodinu," 3; Somova, "Vozvrashchenie," 3.
132 Balakshin, *Final v Kitae*, 2: 288–9; Nikiforov, "Vozvrashchenie ili Put' na Rodinu," 6, 11.

133 Somova, "Vozvrashchenie"; Tsepilov, "Posokh Vladyki Ioanna (Maksimovicha)"; Somova, "Orkestru Lundstrema – 60 let"; Zaitsev, "Put' na Rodinu"; Balakshin, *Final v Kitae*, 2: 289–91.

134 Kruzenshtern-Peterets, "Otkrytoe pis'mo Natalii Il'inoi"; To GS.24.5.1974.

135 US/INS, D117, VP to Dr James Saint-Clair Sobell, 22.6.1948; US/INS, D113, VP to G. Volkoff, 1.11.1948; US/INS, D116–117, VP to Dr Sobell, 22.6.1948; US/INS, D34–36, Dr G. Volkoff to Dr H. Keenlyside, Deputy Minister of Mines and Resources, 2.6.1949; US/INS, D37–38, Dr G.Volkoff to John H. McGowan of 30.6.1950.

136 US/INS, D113, VP to G. Volkoff, 1.11.1948 ("liquidate my").

137 To EAS.2.6.1941, comment; To KP.18.9.1968; To OB.6.2.1988; From VP to US State Department, Immigration Office, 29.10.1968 ("mere coincidence"); To KP.18.9.1968; To EAS.2.6.1941, comment; US/INS, D592 ("very lonely").

138 VP, "Pamiati Mitropolita Viktora" ("the late Metropolitan").

139 US/INS, D114, VP to G. Volkoff, 10.3.1949; US/INS, D570, transcript of questioning, 26.5.1950; US/INS, D577 ("underpaid"); To KP.5.9.1970.

140 Moravskii, "Ostrov Tubabao," 266–9.

141 *DP*, 114; To KP.21.11.1979 ("dishonest actions").

142 US/INS, D667–668, VP, "A Sworn Statement" ("why did I not").

143 US/INS, D573, transcript of questioning VP, 29.5.1950; US/INS, D668, "A Sworn Statement."

144 To V.V. Koloshin, 26.2.1949.

145 US/INS, D114–115, VP to G. Volkoff, 10.3.1949; To EAS.7.9.1949 ("friends are very").

146 *DP*, 124, where he wrongly dates the Chinese Communist takeover of Shanghai to 25 May 1948; the correct date is 25 May 1949.

147 US/INS, D114, VP to G. Volkoff, 10.3.1949; To AG.7.2.1950 ("there is no one").

148 To AG.7.2.1950 ("descending into").

6. The Long Farewell

1 US/INS, 26.5.1950, D568, transcript of questioning on 29.5.1950; US/INS, D678, D587; *PBP*, Canto Seven, XXIII, 324, 353n30; Hinrichs, "Introduction," *DP*, 12.

2 EAS, Diary.

3 VP, "Valerii Salatko-Petrishche"; To EAS.21.8.1949 ("exceptionally faithful").

4 *PBP*, Canto Seven, XXV, 325, XXVI–LXX, 325–48.

5 VP, "'Drug moei materi,'' typescript; US/INS, D469; *PBP*, Canto Seven, LXXIV, 350, Canto Eight, II, 364.

6 *DP*, 115.
7 Saranin, *Child of Kulaks*, 154–5.
8 US/INS, File A-7491208, 24.8.1950; US/INS, D711-12, Operations Memorandum to Rio de Janeiro, 15.3.1974.
9 US/INS, File No. A-7491208, 22.6.1950.
10 To ISF.15.9.1974 ("hundreds of most"); To KP.7.7.1967 ("focusing on").
11 US/INS, D586, 29.5.1950 ("a translator's work").
12 US/INS, D575, 29.5.1950, D584.
13 *DP*, 115.
14 *PBP*, Canto Eight, XXIV, XXVI, 375, 376.
15 US/INS, D514-15.
16 US/INS, D527-9, 6.6.1950.
17 US/INS, D153-61, 23.6.1950.
18 US/INS, D147-8, 30.6.1950, D152, D148.
19 *DP*, 115; *PBP*, Canto Seven, XXIX, 377.
20 *DP*, 115.
21 *DP*, 115; To KP.7.7.1967; To PL.23.7.1975; *PBP*, Canto Eight, XL–XLI, 383.
22 To PL.23.7.1975 ("tried to convince"); To KP.7.7.1967 ("her main argument"); *PBP*, Canto Eight, XL, 383, 404n37.
23 *PBP*, Canto Eight, XL, 383; To PL.23.7.1975; AG to VP, undated, ca. July 1954, comment; US/INS, D564, Victor F. Salatko, letter.
24 *DP*, 115; US/INS, D31-8, 108.
25 US/INS, D643-4, 29.8.1950.
26 *DP*, 118–19; *PBP*, Canto Seven, XXX, 378, XXXII, 379, XXXV–XXXVII, 380–1; Saranin, *Child of Kulaks*, 155.
27 To KP.7.7.1967 ("a lion in captivity"); To PL.23.7.1975 ("the best consolation"); *DP*, 117–18; *PBP*, Canto Seven, XXXIX, 382; To GS.30.12.1981 ("this replacement").
28 US/INS, D663-675, "A Sworn Statement," D678; To IV.16.3.1974 ("never and under"); To PL.23.7.1975 ("their upbringing").
29 US/INS, D695; *DP*, 119; *PBP*, Canto Seven, XLII, 384.
30 *DP*, 120.
31 *PBP*, Canto Seven, LXXII, 349; To PL.23.7.1975 ("how I hate").
32 *PBP*, Canto Seven, XLIII, 384, 405n42; EAS to Lidiia Salatko, 4.8.1951.
33 VP to J.P. Hinrichs, 10.10.1983, as quoted in Hinrichs, "Introduction," *DP*, 12; To VS.23.4.1990 second letter ("it was with"); Interview with VL, November 2005.
34 Tang Dongtian to VP.19.10.1951; Tang Dongtian to VP.6.3.1952; To IV.19.7.1974 ("affinity of souls"); To VS.11.8.1990; VP's comments on "Kedr i ptitsa" ("no dynamics").

35 To ID.6.3.1981 ("truly"); VP, "Valerii Salatko-Petrishche" ("unselfishly"); To VS.21.3.1990 ("whom I loved").
36 To NK, undated, ca. March 1966 ("tried to adapt"); To GS.23.5.1978 ("Mum and I saw"); *DP*, 127.
37 Papers relating to emigration procedures.
38 To KP.17.5.1968; To VL.12.3.1976 ("dear home").
39 Interview with VL, November 2005; To AR.18.8.1971; Kirilloff to OB.26.2.2003; To EAS.2.6.1941, comment.
40 To NK ca. March 1966; To AR.18.8.1971; papers related to emigration procedures.
41 VP's comment on "Pis'ma k materi" ("sending me"); To OB.29.12.1987; To OB.20.12.1987.
42 *DP*, 116; To MM.19.11.1988; papers related to emigration procedures; To VL.30.10.1952; To VS.23.4.1990 second letter; To GS.27.8.1970 ("such things").
43 To VL.16.12.1952; To IV.25.12.1968; To IV.14.1.1974.
44 To IV.24.1.1974; To VL.16.12.1952 ("spent a wonderful"); *DP*, 120.
45 *DP*, 127–8.
46 *DP*, 116.
47 Editor's foreword, *Russkii poet v gostiakh u Kitaia*, xvi.
48 These figures are based on the bibliography of Pereleshin's poems compiled by OB.
49 Hinrichs, "Introduction," to *DP*, 14; To OB.1.8.1987 ("my themes were").
50 EAS, "Kharbinskie pisateli i poety," pt 2 (1940) ("somewhat academic"); mother and son worked together on this two-part survey, and he wrote the entry about himself; To EAS.22.2.1945 ("perfect harmony").
51 Rannit, "O poezii i poetike Valeriia Pereleshina – shest' pervykh sbornikov poeta," 94.
52 Ivask Archive, Box 5, f. 19, comment on the poem ("could not have").
53 Rannit, "Kitai poeta Valeriia Pereleshina."
54 To PL.4.8.1975, second letter ("if it were").
55 To GS.9.10.1968 ("one of my favourite").
56 To KP.7.3.1969 ("proud that").
57 To VL.19.9.1968 ("a shelter for").
58 Translation of "From Afar" by Jeanny Lam; To IV.13.6.1968 ("there was no").
59 To KP.12.5.1976 ('even now"); To VL.5.5.1954 ("completely indifferent").

7. *Cidade maravilhosa*

1 To MV.20.12.1967 ("out of all"); To VAS.20.1.1967; To AR.8.6.1971 ("paradise"); AG to VP.2.4.1954, quoting him ("I love, love").

2 To VL.3.3.1957 ("drunk with samba").
3 To VL.2.2.1958 ("I like almost").
4 VP, as Sigma, "Russkie v Brazilii"; To AR.8.6.1971 ("a single Russian"); To GS.30.11.1967 ("mainly terrible"); To VAS.16.4.1967; VP, as Sigma, "Russkaia pravoslavnaia tserkov' v Brazilii"; Lirika, "Russkaia Paskha v Rio-de-Zhaneiro."
5 To KP.9.5.1967 ("terrible backwoods"); To AG.25.7.1967 ("a cultural backyard"); To PL.5.10.1971 ("a real Dead-End"); To AR.30.6.1971 ("here I am").
6 To KP.23.5.1968; To VL.10.3.1953.
7 EAS, Diary.
8 To VL.10.3.1953; To VS.23.4.1990 ("it is enough").
9 To VL.11.8.1953; Sigma, "Russkie v Brazilii," *RM*.8.2.1968; To VL.11.8.1953 ("all my education").
10 To VL.22.12.1953 ("on the day"); EAS, Diary.
11 To VL.3.10.1954 ("fired, and left"); To VL.3.10.1954; EAS, Diary.
12 To VL.22.12.1953 ("our beloved city"); To VL.14.2.1954.
13 To VL.14.2.1954; To AG.24.4.1966 ("a six-storey house"); To AG.10.2.1967 ("climbing up"); To KP.5.8.1967; To VL.5.5.1954 ("a wonderful day").
14 To VL.22.12.1953; To VL.21.6.1954; To VL.20.8.1954 ("hated office"); To VL.10.3.1955; To VL.27.11.1954; To VAS.20.1.1967; To IV.7.4.1971; To VL.20.8.1954; To VL.3.3.1957 ("his wife's influence"). To VL.21.6.1954 ("very frugally"); To VL.20.8.1954; To VL.21.7.1954; To VL.14.1.1955;
15 To VL.13.10.1957 ("no work, money").
16 AG to VP.6.2.1954.
17 AG to VP.2.4.1954, comment; To AG.3.5.1955 ("cousins"); To AG.1.5.1967 ("I personally would").
18 AG to VP.13.9.1959.
19 To AG.28.6.1970.
20 To VL.11.4.1954 ("I have always").
21 To VL.21.7.1954 ("the soul ascends").
22 To VL.14.4.1956 ("small joys"); To NK, undated, ca. March 1966 ("for planned conquests").
23 To VL.20.8.1954 ("many astonishing"); To VL.21.6.1954 ("Chinese shadows").
24 To AR.14.9.1971 ("its theme").
25 To VL.28.12.1953; To KP.12.1.1969 ("best for philosophical"); To GS.7.6.1969; To KP.5.6.1970; To AR.3.8.1971, first letter of that date; To GS.2.4.1971.
26 To VL.14.2.1954; To VL.5.5.1954; To VL.16.1.1960 ("will never be"); To VL.30.1.1955; To M.K. Karpovich, 29.1.1955; *NZh* to VP, 9.7.1955, unsigned carbon copy.

27 To VL.21.7.1954 ("my cross has"); To VL.25.9.1956 ("written by someone").
28 To VL.25.9.1956 ("my intimate"); To AG.26.10.1966 ("ashamed that").
29 To VL.2.2.1958 ("distress and"); To VL.12.2.1958 ("I have only one").
30 Kirilloff to OB.23.10.2002; To VL.23.9.1958; To VL.13.2.1960.
31 To VL.2.7.1958 ("very monotonous"); To EV.27.5.1971; To AG.1.5.1967; To EAS.24.7.1945; To VL.25.9.1956 ("the only thing").
32 To AG.13.10.1966; To AG.8.12.1966; To KP.7.5.1967 ("the only musical").
33 To NK, ca. March 1966; To VL.13.2.1960.
34 To VL.13.2.1960; To VL, Christmas/New Year card, ca. December 1962.
35 To VAS.16.4.1967; To KP.7.5.1967; To AG.9.7.1960 ("estranged us"); To AG.26.10.1966 ("the psychology of"); To AR.2.8.1971.
36 To AG.23.6.1963; To VL, Christmas card, ca. December 1963 ("in spite of the limping"); To AG.1.9.1965; To KP.11.6.1974; To AG.23.6.1963; To AG.20.9.1963; To VL, Christmas card, ca. December 1963 ("Cyclops' glasses").
37 To AG.20.9.1963; To AG.19.10.1963.
38 To AG.22.8.1967 ("one does not").
39 Lopez to OB.28.1.2008.
40 To NK.23.8.1966; To AG.14.6.1967 ("agony"); To KP.12.7.1967 ("but when I imagine").
41 To KP.15.7.1967; To AG.25.7.1967; To KP.2.7.1967; To KP.23.7.1967; To KP.25.11.1974.
42 To AG.26.10.1966 ("Victor, after all"); To KP.17.11.1967 ("I have no job").
43 To IV.4.2.1968.
44 EAS to PB.23.2.1976; To VAS.13.12.1968 ("it is half past").
45 To AR.11.8.1971 ("it is easy to lose").
46 To KP.10.4.1972; To KP.20.3.1972; Bakich to OB.30.8.2002.
47 To AG.30.12.1966 and postscript to 1.1.1967.
48 *PBP*, Canto Seven, XVII–XVIII, 321–2.
49 To VL.5.5.1954; To MV.29.8.1983 ("an ardent temper").
50 *DP*, 128, with a typographical mistake: she contacted him not in 1957, but in 1967, as the typescript of the memoirs and their letters confirm; To KP.17.4.1967; To KP.17.4.1967 ("to burden her").
51 KP to VP, ca. 1967.
52 To KP.2.7.1967 ("your letters").
53 To KP.7.5.1967 ("grew mouldy"); To KP.9.5.1967 ("endless attention"); To KP.12.7.1967 ("you cannot").
54 KP to VP.1.7.1967 ("I am glad"); KP to VP.18.5.1967.
55 To KP.25.6.1967 ("did not go"); KP to VP, 2.5.1967.
56 To KP.28.1.1970 ("life itself"); To KP.7.5.1976 ("write often"); To MV.20.12.1967; To KP.15.12.1967 ("without you").

57 To AG.14.6.1967; To KP.11.5.1968 ("I would have"); To AG.14.6.1967 ("your sonnets"); "The Way of the Cross" was also published as a supplement to *Druz'iam i znakomym*.
58 To GS.29.12.1969 ("very warm"); Gorbov, "Valerii Pereleshin: *Zhertva*."
59 To KP.17.12.1967 ("it became a").
60 To KP.5.8.1967 ("bohemian lifestyle"); To KP.15.10.1967 ("in a state called").
61 EAS to KP.23.5.1968.
62 To KP.11.5.1968; To IV.28.4.1972 ("abstention").
63 To VL.15.5.1968 ("without this blow").
64 To NK, ca. March 1966 ("two almost"); To KP.17.4.1967 ("compilation of all").
65 To NK.24.4.1966 ("a very lyrical work").
66 To IV.8.5.1968; To KP.26.2.1970; To GS.8.12.1974 ("quite archaic"); To OB.26.4.1989 ("now I would").
67 To KP.25.3.1969 ("the influence of Chinese").
68 To KP.29.5.1967 ("terribly outdated"); To KP.25.6.1967 ("a subconscious").
69 GS.29.9.1970; To MV.10.5.1971; To EAS.29.2.1940; To EAS.16.12.1943; To AG.10.2.1968 ("Good Dog"); To KP.23.2.1970 ("Bom cachorro"); comment on a copy of "Bom Cachorro" ("this mythical beast"); another comment on "Bom Cachorro" in a copy in Leiden University Archive ("one of my extra-literary"); To KP.12.2.1970 ("my projection").
70 To GS.13.12.1972 ("was shifting"); To GS.13.7.1970; To KP.5.2.1969 ("moved forward"); To GS.11.8.1969 ("with all my present").
71 VP, "Upadok formy v poezii"; VP, "Poeziia i stikhi"; VP, "Russkaia rifma."
72 To KP.9.1.1970 ("today there").
73 Markov, "V zashchitu raznoudarnoi rifmy (Informativnyi obzor)"; To GS.16.2.1969; VP, "Zritel'nyi element rifmy."
74 To KP.12.7.1979 ("particularly modernist").
75 To IV.17.6.1972; To AR.18.8.1971 ("to let thoughts").
76 VP's 1983 comment on the typewritten copy of "Southern Winter" (*Iuzhnaia zima*, 23.6.1969) ("worse than").

8. Resurrection of the Poet

1 Kirilloff, "In Memoriam – Valerii Pereleshin – Ieromonakh German"; Kirilloff to OB.23.12.2004; To KP.11.1.1968.
2 To KP.2.7.1967 ("obligated"); To KP.23.7.1967 ("it will be difficult"); To IV, undated note ca. 1968 ("rather old").
3 Application for Immigration to the USA from Brazil, 30.7.1967 ("to reverse"), Biographical Statement, ca. 1968 ("had worked for"); Statement, 29.10.1968 ("an outspoken, militant"); To KP.7.7.1967; Letter

from Maria J. von Kruzenshtern-Peterets' to the Secretary of State, 11.10.1968; To KP.11.8.1967 ("he knows").

4 To GS.2.11.1967 ("a vicious circle"); To KP.26.8.1967; Application for Immigration to the USA from Brazil, curriculum vitae; List of universities and some responses, Ivask Archive, Box 5, f.15; To KP.19.8.1967; KP.29.8.1967; To KP.7.7.1967; To ISF.20.1.1968; To KP.4.9.1967; To KP.10.12.1967; To ISF.20.1.1968.

5 To AG.16.6.1968; To KP.9.6.1968.

6 To KP.19.11.1968; To KP.27.4.1969; To IV.7.4.1971 ("almost as much").

7 To KP.7.5.1967; To KP.5.6.1967; To KP.21.12.1968 ("a dollar per immortal").

8 To KP.22.10.1968; To KP.25.3.1969; To IV.31.7.1968 ("I can work").

9 To KP.28.4.1968; To IV.8.5.1968 ("a dream of"); To IV.8.5.1968; To KP.23.5.1968; To KP.23.5.1968.

10 To ISF.27.11.1972 ("your word"); To IV.27.11.1972 ("all kinds of"); To KP.3.4.1973.

11 Application for Immigration to the USA from Brazil, 30.7.1967 ("I must refer"), Statement, 29.10.1968 ("early in 1951"); To ISF.20.1.1968; To ISF.15.9.1974; To AG.14.6.1967; To AR.18.8.1971; *DP,* 114, 127.

12 To KP.3.2.1968; To KP.20.2.1968; To KP.18.5.1968; To IV.15.5.1968; To KP.11.2.1968; To KP.23.2.1968.

13 To VL.6.7.1968 ("atrocious exploitation"); To KP.8.7.1968; To AG.26.7.1968.

14 To AR.30.6.1971 ("should write"); To IV.7.7.1968 ("poets never").

15 To KP.17.6.1968; To AG.16.7.1968; VSP, "Russkii iazyk v Brazil'skoi Morskoi akademii," 9; To AG.16.7.1968 ("one of the pillars"); To VL.15.8.1968; To GS.7.6.1969; To KP.29.8.1969.

16 VP, "Otpoved' piati," typescript.

17 To GS.29.10.1969; To GS.3.6.1970; To GS.23.9.1969; To GS.4.4.1973 ("I am not a democrat").

18 To GS.3.3.1971 ("what an enormous").

19 To VL.15.5.1968; To KP.15.12.1967.

20 To VL.27.1.1971 ("an inner conviction"); To KP.11.2.1968; To KP.3.2.1968 ("perhaps that's true").

21 To KP.29.5.1967.

22 To KP.27.8.1968; To KP.23.7.1967; To KP.23.7.1967; To GS.2.11.1967; To GS.16.11.1967; To GS.7.6.1969; To GS.7.6.1969; To GS.2.11.1967; To KP.20.2.1968 ; To KP.28.4.1968 ("day and night").

23 To KP.23.7.1968 ("I have immediately"); To KP.29.9.1968 ("enraptured").

24 Gorbov, "Literaturnye zametki," 139, 142.

25 To AG.7.2.1950 ("a sin and a crime").

26 Rokotov to VP 16.7.1968.

27 Z-n, "Piataia kniga Valeriia Pereleshina"; Mozhaiskaia, "Svirel' luny"; Gorbov, "Literaturnye zametki,"139, 142.
28 Karlinskii, "*Iuzhnyi dom* Valeriia Pereleshina."
29 Terapiano, "Novye knigi."
30 To GS.30.9.1968 ("an imitator of"); To AG.4.10.1968 ("terribly sloppy"); To KP.22.9.1968 ("*burro*").
31 Kruzenshtern-Peterets, "Pis'mo v gazety"; Kruzenshtern-Peterets, "O predvziatosti"; Karlinskii, "*Iuzhnyi dom* Valeriia Pereleshina"; Kruzenshtern-Peterets, "Pis'mo v redaktsiiu. Ne travlia, a polemika"; Terapiano, "Po povodu pis'ma v redaktsiiu Iu. Kruzenshtern-Peterets"; Odoevtseva, "Vyiasnenie odnogo nedorazumeniia"; Adamovich, "Vpechatleniia i nedoumeniia."
32 To GS.29.10.1969; VP, "Dva Parizha"; To GS.20.11.1969; Iu.T., "*Churaevka*, literaturnaia gazeta. Nomera 3-4-6-7-8"; Sigma, "*Churaevka* v *Chislakh*."
33 To GS.28.12.1969; To KP.9.1.1970; Terapiano, "Vynuzhdennyi otvet."
34 To KP.18.3.1969; To PB.1.9.1975; "Pervyi den' poezii"; "Vtoroi den' poezii"; To GS.9.6.1971.
35 To GS.20.11.1969 ("boring"); To PB.18.9.1975 ("Blevotskaia-Bledovskaia-Blefskaia"); Vl. Kaiurin, "Pis'mo v redaktsiiu. O trekh volkvakh."
36 VP, "Durnaia mistika"; To GS.19.12.1969 ("startled the snake-pit").
37 To KP.11.12.1969 ("to defend myself"); To PB.17.11.1975 ("spiritual leprosy").
38 To KP.23.11.1969 ("gutter dwellers"); Ivask Archive, Box 5, f.16.
39 Mitskevich, "O preemstvennosti v russkoi lirike"; To AR.12.11.1971 ("I snarled"); VP, "Pis'mo v redaktsiiu"; Mitskevich, "K opredeleniiu epigonstva."
40 Rannit, "O poezii i poetike Valeriia Pereleshina," 90.
41 To IV.6.8.1973, second letter ("Brazilian hermit/recluse"); To GS.30.3.1969 ("substituted"); To GS.27.12.1974 ("cameleiro"); To SK.23.7.1988.
42 To MV.18.11.1969 ("as before, that is, rather").
43 To IV.7.11.1972 ("*most trusted friend*"); To GS.2.10.1975 ("looking very").
44 To AG.25.8.1972 ("truly borrowed"); To AR.18.8.1971 ("a spiritual impregnation").
45 To KP.23.9.1972 ("for the next book").
46 Ivask, "Valerii Pereleshin o poezii"; IV to Andrei Sedykh, 8.4.1975; To VAS.5.1.1975; To KP.25.8.1974.
47 Struve, *Russkaia literatura v izgnanii*, 370.
48 To GS.2.9.1967 ("not quite flattering"); To GS.25.9.1968.
49 To EV.3.8.1971 (quoting from from Rannit's letter: "what particularly").
50 To MV.9.6.1971; To AR.2.9.1971 ("the appearance of"); To AR.24.8.1971 ("in your hands").

51 To AR.14.9.1971; To AR.1.10.1971; Rannit, "Kitai poeta Pereleshina"; To AR.5.7.1972 ("head spin"); To AR.27.6.1972 ("endlessly grateful"); Rannit, "Braziliia V. Pereleshina"; To AR.17.5.1974 ("splendid, brilliant").
52 Rannit, "O poezii i poetike Valeriia Pereleshina"; To AR.30.10.1976 ("the best gift"); To MV.27.9.1978; To AR.26.9.1978; Rannit, "Valerii Pereleshin posle *Kacheli*"; To AR.14.6.1979 ("for the first time").
53 To MV.9.6.1971 ("face-to-face"); To IV.13.6.1968 ("speak totally").
54 IV to VP.22.6.1968.
55 VP, "Predosennie dni"; VP, "Zaletnaia dusha"; VP, "*Shakhmaty* – ne o shakhmatakh!"; VP, "Liudiam nuzhny i svechi i slezy"; VP, "M. Vizi, *Golubaia trava*"; Ivask, "O pisaniiakh Valeriia Pereleshina"; Nartsissov, "Pis'mo v redaktsii"; To MV.10.10.1972; To MV.10.5.1971; To MV.12.12.1973; To MV.10.5.1971 ("a well-known retrograde").
56 To GS.9.1.1974 ("'literature' of").
57 To GS.3.6.1970; To KP.29.12.1970 ("a very tiny poet"); To GS.7.8.1969 ("without metre"); To KP.23.2.1969 ("an unimaginable nonsense"); VP, "Mnogoznachitel'nye nameki"; To KP.27.7.1970.
58 To IV.11.4.1970; To VL.10.4.1970 ("reluctantly"); To KP.16.3.1970; To KP.31.3.1970; Ivask, "O pisaniiakh Valeriia Pereleshina."
59 To GS.16.6.1970 ("new phobia"); To GS.27.5.1970; To GS.8.1.1972 ("in the miniature literary").
60 To AG.25.8.1972; To GS.25.1.1973; To AG.30.12.1972; To GS.25.7.1976 ("one of the best").
61 To GS.25.7.1969 ("a typical Soviet"); To MV.20.5.1988 ("blunders and"); To GS.13.9.1969 ("unrestrained verbosity"); To IV.17.8.1972 ("incontinence"); To IV.18.1.1974 ("this soap bubble"); To GS.16.7.1973 ("Buterbrodskii").
62 To KP.29.11.1972; To IV.2.12.1972; To GS.16.11.1972 ("to be translated"); To IV.18.12.1972 ("not a lampoon"); To AR.6.3.1972 ("the history of").
63 To IV.10.5.1978 ("should switch"); To AR.10.10.1978; To AR.30.11.1972 ("write in their native"); To IV.30.4.1978.
64 To GS.17.12.1972 ("hide in"); To IV.18.12.1972 ("to fall to the ground"); To GS.25.2.1973 ("I do not need"); To GS.28.2.1973 ("the *theme* of the relations"); To KP.21.8.1973.
65 To GS.10.10.1978 ("boiled with rage"); To AR.7.11.1978 ("Morshen, Chinnov"); To IV.12.11.1978.
66 To GS.15.4.1973 ("Kleins and Co.").
67 To IV.18.1.1974 ("double exile").
68 To GS.11.12.1968 ("would stretch").
69 To VL.25.10.1970 ("I was so touched").

70 To KP.28.2.1971 ("the kindred spirits"); To IV.7.4.1971 ("otherwise, they").
71 To AR.18.10.1971; To KP.31.10.1970; To AR.30.6.1971.
72 VP, "'Kachel' ili tol'ko 'Kacheli'" ("has acquired"); To VL.9.3.1971 ("a symbol of duality"); To IV.4.2.1968 ("akin to Rasputin's").
73 To GS.11.11.1971; To AR.9.11.1971; AR.29.10.1971 (Mandelstam's 1908 poem "To read only children's books"); VP, "'Kachel' ili tol'ko 'Kacheli.'"
74 To VL.16.1.1972 ("the temporal distance").
75 To KP.3.1976 ("immeasurably higher"); To IV.5.12.1973 ("a single breath"); To VL.18.4.1975 ("now I certainly").
76 Markov to VP as quoted in To AR.27.6.1972 ("a lucid spirit"); To AR.30.6.1971; To AR.18.10.1971; To ISF.27.11.1972; To PL.18.11.1971 ("a sweet and sour"); To KP.26.5.1971 ("the entire monastery").
77 To MV.9.6.1971 ("severely criticized").
78 Odoevtseva, "Valerii Pereleshin: *Kachel'*."
79 To GS.19.10.1971 ("there is the simplest").
80 Rannit, "Valerii Pereleshin posle *Kacheli*," 115.
81 To AR.14.1.1972, first letter of that date; To AG.24.1.1972; To AR.10.12.1971, note on a page with VP's poems; To AR.14.4.1972 ("core of the world"); To AR.14.1.1971 [*sic* – 1972], second letter of that date ("only serious poems").
82 To AR.21.5.1972 ("swinging forward"); To AR.9.5.1972 ("where one can").
83 To IV.17.10.1972 ("logically follows").
84 To AR.2.5.1972 ("I like *too* many"); To AR.10.6.1972 ("for the sake").
85 To AR.30.6.1972; To MV.22.3.1973.
86 To AR.20.9.1972; To MV.10.10.1972 ("now it means").
87 To MV.29.4.1975 ("a heroic deed").
88 VP, "Russkie khudozhniki v Brazilii"; VP, "Zamechatel'nyi russkii khudozhnik."
89 To AG.12.3.1973 ("a place where").
90 To KP.15.7.1967 ("purely descriptive").
91 Z-n, "Novyi sbornik Valeriia Pereleshina."
92 Ivask, "*Zapovednik* Valeriia Pereleshina."
93 Velichkovskaia, "O novom sbornike stikhov V. Pereleshina."
94 Rannit, "Valerii Pereleshin posle *Kacheli*," 116-17.
95 To KP.3.4.1969; To GS.5.5.1969; To GS.7.6.1969; To VL.27.8.1969 ("be what it"); To KP.12.11.1969 ("I no longer can").
96 To KP.7.3.1969 ("one of the first"); KP.2.2.1973 ("very trustworthy"); To GS.25.6.1975 ("knowledge of"); To IV.30.4.1978 ("the greatest swindle"); To GS.10.7.1969; To GS.26.3.1970; To KP.12.7.1969 ("game of broken").
97 Tatishchev, "Derev'ia, kamni, slova"; VP, "Pis'mo v redaktsiiu po povodu stat'i 'Derev'ia, kamni, slova'"; VP, "Kitaiskaia poeziia."

98 To KP.27.7.1970 ("of how not to"); To GS.4.11.1971 ("Chinese classical").
99 To KP.13.11.1972 ("was not to"); To GS.25.6.1969; To GS.10.7.1969; To GS.9.9.1974 ("studied if").
100 To KP.28.11.1969; To KP.5.6.1970; To VL.3.2.1970; To KP.23.2.1970 ("on favourable terms").
101 To KP.6.3.1970 ("deliriously happy"); To KP.3.3.1970 ("she is *very pleased*"); To KP.6.3.1970 ("eating me alive"); To KP.27.4.1970 ("you should not").
102 To GS.31.3.1970.
103 To KP.11.9.1968 ("an inexperienced reader").
104 To EAS.15.2.1941, note added on 17.2.1941; Chinese texts of *Stikhi na veere*.
105 VP, "Stikhi na veere" ("an elegant miniature").
106 To KP.6.4.1970.
107 To OB.5.5.1987 ("Chinese poetry"); To GS.25.9.1969 ("no metre in").
108 To KP.18.3.1969 ("trisyllabic foot"); To GS.25.9.1969 ("every time"); To GS.25.9.1969 ("followed rhyme").
109 To AR.16.7.1971 ("not missing a single"); To KP.23.7.1970 ("precision").
110 To GS.5.12.1970; To AR.16.7.1971 ("it is NOT a translation"); To IV.4.1.1971; To AR.16.7.1971.
111 Rachinskaia, "Dan' poetu"; To KP.30.6.1970 ("wide overview").
112 "Knizhnaia polka"; Geliotropov, "*Stikhi na veere*"; Emel'ianova, "*Stikhi na veere*"; To KP.13.4.1970 ("enrapture").
113 VP's comment to letters from P.P. Lapiken ("an erudite, witty"); To PL.12.1.1972.
114 To KP.15.4.1969 ("I find so"); To KP.11.9.1968; To GS.10.8.1968; To KP.18.3.1969.
115 To NK.11.6.1974 ("I love some poems"); To VS.11.10.1989 ("many translatable").
116 To MV.9.6.1971 ("I always welcome").
117 To GS.25.6.1975 ("a very poor"); *PBP*, Canto Six, LXV, 295.
118 To PL.3.7.1975 ("my passion"); To IV.14.6.1975 ("a human image"); *DP*, 113.
119 VP, "Ot perevodchika," *Li Sao*, 3 ("a magnificent 'political'"); To GS.25.6.1975 ("one of the largest"); To KP.1.7.1971 ("an astounding literary").
120 To GS.24.5.1971 ("a mediocre sinologist"); To SK.16.8.1989; To AR.2.8.1971 ("with some effort"); To GS.19.4.1976.
121 *PBP*, Canto Six, LXV, 295.
122 To AG.10.11.1967 ("in the course of"); To IV.14.6.1975 ("pleased that nowhere").
123 To GS.29.3.1968; To GS.9.4.1973 ("and by whom?"); *DP*, 113-14; To KP.1.5.1968 ("incomparably more"); To GS.9.4.1973 ("if Gitovich").
124 To GS.13.11.1974, first letter of that date; To PB.3.1.1975; To GS.25.2.1975; To VAS.8.1.1969 ("sighed once again"); To MV.28.1.1975 ("I may as well").

125 To PL.25.2.1975 ("oh, the serene life").
126 Ivask, "Tsiui Iuan', *Li Sao*"; To PL.17.12.1974; Lapiken, "Tsiui Iuan'. *Li Sao*."
127 To EAS.15.11.1939; To VL.27.1.1971; To VL.5.5.1954.
128 To VL.21.6.1954 ("amazing, as deep").
129 To MV.10.6.1988 ("an experiment"); To EV.21.3.1971 ("a philosophical treatise"); To AR.20.10.1971 ("the emphasis should"); To KP.6.10.1981 ("disgusting").
130 To GS.6.2.1971 ("the beauty of").
131 VP, "Ot perevodchika," *Daodejing*, 234; To AG.9.11.1966.

9. *From Mount Nebo*

1 To GS.31.10.1973; To KP.23.9.1973; VSP, "Luchshe pozdno, chem nikogda?" ("I dreamt").
2 To KP.29.9.1979; VSP, "Luchshe pozdno, chem nikogda?" 24; To OB.19.2.1988 ("very old"); "Skorbnaia stranitsa."
3 To KP.20.9.1974; VSP, "Luchshe pozdno, chem nikogda?" 24 ("welcomed me").
4 To NK.15.12.1973 ("two Larissas").
5 To GS.14.11.1973; To GS.22.11.1973 ("to get a job").
6 VSP, "Luchshe pozdno, chem nikogda?" 24; To GS.22.11.1973 ("thousand-year-old"); To KP.9.10.1973 ("France not for"); To IV.19.11.1973 ("the spirit of *antiquity*").
7 To IV.5.10.1973 ("a strange sense"); To NF.14.7.1975 ("remained in my memory"); To GS.22.11.1973 ("indescribable state").
8 To GS.31.10.1973; To AR.8.1.1974; To KP.19.11.1973 ("was not a loss").
9 IV to Professor William Edgerton, 27.7.1973; To IV.6.6.1973 ("with delight"); To KP.20.6.1973 ("develop it").
10 To KP.12.2.1974 ("pray for me"); To KP.21.2.1974 ("a suitcase of cuttings"); To IV.15.2.1974 ("*shaken* by my statement"); To ISF.28.6.1974 ("believed me"); To KP.20.9.1974 ("one cannot invent").
11 To KP.12.2.1974, postscript 16.2.1974 ("permission not only"); To IV.12.3.1974 ("as it turns out"); To KP.10.3.1974.
12 To IV.28.2.1973 ("excuses would"); To VL.14.3.1974 ("agony of waiting"); To KP.30.3.1974.
13 To KP.3.4.1974; To VL.15.7.1974 ("reversion").
14 To KP.3.4.1974, postscript of 4.4.1974 ("with a firm decision"); To MV.10.1.1975 ("as a person under"); To D.J. Yellman, 4.4.1974; To KP.3.4.1974, postscript 4.4.1974 ("a squeezed lemon").
15 To IV.4.4.1974; To MV.10.1.1975; To IV.23.4.1974.

16 "Fourth International Poetry Festival at the University of Texas," "Some Notes on the Poets," and "A Minimal Anthology"; VP, "Prazdnik poezii"; To KP.23.4.1974.
17 To GS.23.4.1974 ("a totally different"); To ISF.28.4.1974 ("the university atmosphere"); To KP.23.4.1974 ("passed like"); To NK.10.6.1974 ("the seventh heaven").
18 To ISF.24.10.1974; To KP.23.4.1974; To GS.21.4.1975 ("a complete failure").
19 To ISF.28.6.1974); To IV.14.8.1974 ("one cannot be").
20 To IV.10.1.1973 ("the Sun was").
21 To GS.22.2.1978; To KP.25.3.1975; To IV.27.3.1975 ("precisely 'without a subject'").
22 Ivask, "Igraiushchii chelovek," nos 240, 241, and 242; Ivask, *Igraiushchii chelovek*, septet to Pereleshin, 75.
23 To KP.25.3.1975; To GS.3.2.1975 ("inventing – oh, the daring!"); To IV.27.3.1975 ("astonishing capacity").
24 To GS.6.2.1975 ("if poetic forms").
25 To VL.11.11.1975 ("writing this Poem")
26 To IV.13.7.1974 ("pathetic"); To GS.19.9.1973 ("to weep rereading"); To KP.25.3.1975 ("almost no digressions").
27 To PL.14.2.1975 ("like a dipsomaniac"); To GS.4.3.1976 ("almost wept"); To VL.12.3.1976 ("holds me").
28 To GS.4.3.1976; To PB.26.3.1976 ("suddenly it was").
29 To VL.17.2.1976 ("the longest poem"); To KP.25.3.1975 ("only Aleksandr Sergeevich").
30 To VL.11.2.1976 ("my entire life"); To IV.3.8.1974 ("a kind of a portable").
31 To KP.3.6.1976 ("from the point"); To L. Tikos, 21.4.1976 ("Manichean").
32 To KP.22.5.1978; To KP.29.8.1979.
33 To L. Tikos, 21.4.1976; To AR.30.10.1976 ("triumvirate"); To L. Tikos, 21.4.1976 ("but not, of course").
34 To KP.3.6.1976; To VL.11.11.1975; To GS.11.5.1976; To KP 30.3.1979 ("such an angry response"); To GS.30.3.1976 ("considerably cooled").
35 PL to VP.5.4.1976; PL to VP.10.12.1978 ("a horror").
36 To AG.30.10.1972 ("shifting to the eighth"); To KP.1.9.1972.
37 To NK.10.10.1973 ("I was looking"); To ISF.27.11.1972 ("in the still").
38 To NK.10.6.1974; To PB.3.1.1975; To VAS.31.10.1974.
39 To NK.15.12.1973 ("never in my life").
40 To ISF.24.10.1974 ("if they find out"); To VL.18.2.1975.
41 To KP.13.9.1972; To KP.13.10.1972 ("so that one"); To GS.25.9.1972.
42 To KP.15.1.1974 ("revealed her genius"); To IV.13.7.1974 ("arranged poems").

43 To IV.6.1.1975 ("in the beginning").
44 To GS.28.10.1974 ("several mediocre").
45 To PL.14.3.1975 ("a certain concession"); To NK.3.5.1975 ("the questions raised"); To IV.21.7.1973 ("wandering as").
46 To IV.13.7.1974 ("conceived around").
47 VP, "Odno kitaiskoe stikhotvorenie."
48 To PL.14.2.1975; Ivask, "Valerii Pereleshin. *S gory Nebo*"; Balakshin, "*S gory Nebo*."

10. The Left-hander

1 KP.8.3.1972; EV to VP, 17.2.1971.
2 To GS.15.5.1971 ("out of stupidity"); To EV.20.5.1971; To GS.15.5.1971 ("no intention"); To EV.20.4.1971; To EV.21.3.1971; To EV.20.5.1971.
3 To KP.12.4.1972 ("very good"); To AG.26.2.1977.
4 To GS.18.12.1974 ("immediately got").
5 To NK.15.12.1973 ("set the tone"); To MV.6.2.1973 ("person not of"); To NK.10.10.1973 ("my twin").
6 To KP.23.9.1972 ("a real snake pit"); To IV.19.9.1972, postscript ("understands everything").
7 To NK.15.12.1973 ("I have had many"); To AG.5.2.1973 ("I love him").
8 To GS.3.12.1974 ("I have *recognized*").
9 To NK.15.12.1973 ("*onlie begetter*"); To IV.21.7.1973 ("a great miracle").
10 To MV.14.1.1973 ("I want *all*"); To PL.10.4.1973.
11 To GP.13.10.1972 ("written with"); To AG.26.12.1972 ("in one intake"); To GP.13.10.1972 ("a synthesis").
12 To ISF.27.11.1972 ("a synthesis of Christianity"); To AG.5.2.1973 ("inevitability of"); To AR.6.11.1972 ("grows through"); To KP.23.9.1976 ("unique in Russian").
13 To GS.25.1.1973 ("I am afraid").
14 To MV.6.2.1973 ("justified by the idea").
15 To GS.19.1.1973 ("perhaps, it is"); To PL.14.2.1975 ("you have immortalized").
16 To KP.29.12.1972 ("the first crown"); To AR.17.11.1972 ("marinating").
17 To IV.1.7.1973 ("in one word"); To KP.4.7.1973 ("just skin and bones"); To NK.28.8.1974 ("just children").
18 To KP.3.7.1973; To IV.1.7.1973 ("love you"); To KP.4.7.1973 ("seized by").
19 To GS.9.9.1974; To KP.3.7.1973; To GS.9.9.1974.
20 To IV.20.8.1973 ("to let Zhenia"); To NK.15.12.1973 ("mystical experience").
21 To NK.8.3.1974; To KP.21.2.1974 ("driven into a stupor"); To KP.1.3.1974 ("overwhelmed"); To IV.24.3.1974, postscript 26.3.1974 ("he has loved").

22 To IV.19.2.1974; To IV.27.2.1974 ("could not be"); IV.15.2.1974 ("I love Zhenia").
23 To NK.8.3.1971 ("a semi-crazy person"); To IV.13.9.1974, second letter ("I have always").
24 To NK.8.3.1974 ("traitors to"); To NK.10.6.1974 ("overpowered"); To NK.28.8.1974 ("a bitter aftertaste"); To GS.29.10.1974 ("what kind").
25 To GS.6.11.1974 ("a new 'chocolate bon-bon'"); To GS.13.11.1974, second letter ("a betrayal"); To KP.26.12.1974; To IV.22.9.1977 ("a disciple"); To KP.6.11.1974 ("base philanderer").
26 To KP.8.3.1975 ("angry poems").
27 To GS.18.12.1974 ("a right to personal"); To KP.4.2.1975 ("an amputation and"); To GS.10.8.1976 ("the late E.V. Vitkovskii"); To GS.19.2.1975 ("I was wrong"); To NK.3.5.1975 ("for a poet invention"); To GS.9.10.1976 ("a large period").
28 To AG.26.2.1977 ("a replacement"); To GS.11.8.1975 ("shards of").
29 To IV.30.5.1973, first letter of that date ("slim, with shoulder-length"); To KP.20.6.1973 ("very sweet"); To GS.1.6.1973 ("from a very cultured").
30 To KP.20.6.1973; To IV.13.6.1973, second letter of that date ("this Ariel is"); To KP.6.3.1973 ("the two Ariels"); To IV.30.5.1973, second letter of that date.
31 To KP.8.8.1976 ("I am even glad").
32 To IV.19.2.1977 ("a reincarnation of"); To IV.24.2.1977; To IV.20.3.1977 ("to get rid of"); To IV.13.3.1977 ("I got").
33 To IV.3.2.1976; To IV.31.10.1975; To IV.19.11.1975 ("thus his existence").
34 To AG.10.4.1977; To IV.31.12.1977 ("rejoiced in").
35 To GS.22.6.1973 ("while Hercules"); To IV.9.1.1974 ("sweetish"); VP, as O.S., "*Ariel*' Valeriia Pereleshina," 2.
36 To PL.9.3.1975 ("a situation which"); To NK.3.5.1975 ("of the sonnets of Shakespeare").
37 To GS.6.11.1974 ("I will not forgive").
38 To KP.19.11.1974 ("to tear the poetic").
39 To KP.22.1.1975; To IV.14.7.1975 ("the history of"); To PL.17.12.1974 ("the most significant"); To IV.12.5.1977 ("both stand for").
40 To NK.3.5.1975 ("has fallen in love"); To PL.9.3.1975 ("expressed his delight"); To NK.8.3.1974 ("the dearest, great").
41 To GS.19.11.1974 ("something like"); To MV.8.12.1983 ("out of disgust"); To KP.19.11.1974 ("ouch! such an angry").
42 To IV.31.10.1975 ("woke up with").
43 To VL.27.12.1975 ("an explosion of public"); Ivask, 'Ob avtore," *Ariel*, 3–7.
44 To IV.3.12.1975 ("a Gethsemane night"); To IV.2.12.1975 ("without the usual"); To GS.21.9.1976 ("a suicide in progress"); To KP.11.2.1976; IV to VP.30.10.1976; To KP.4.9.1976 ("I do not hesitate").

45 To GS.14.6.1976 ("read the sonnets"); To KP.16.6.1976; To IV.6.6.1976, note dated 16.6.1976 ("malicious and poisonous"); To AG.26.2.1977; To GS.25.6.1976.
46 To GS.2.10.1974 ("an incredible coincidence"); To IV.22.7.1978 ("not my competitor"); PL.16.1.1975 ("*chosen ones*"); VP, as O.S., "*Ariel'* Valeriia Pereleshina," 2.
47 To MV.26.4.1977 ("a lyrical diary").
48 To GS.4.9.1974 ("an invented image").
49 To PL.9.3.1975 ("must I consider").
50 To GS.16.12.1974 ("monologic dialogue").
51 To AG.26.2.1977 ("the purest adoration"); To IV.13.9.1974 ("you have brilliantly").
52 To AR.27.12.1979 ("the most successful"); To KP.4.12.1979 ("your highest"); To AR.27.12.1979; To KP.17.12.1976 ("a very tender letter").
53 To IV.26.6.1976 ("difficult"); To IV.15.3.1978; To PL.25.9.1979; To IV.31.3.1979, comment on a page with poems ("most mature").
54 To KP.23.9.1976; To GS.9.10.1976; To GS.21.1.1978 ("as a literary scholar").
55 To PL.19.2.1976 ("you will find"); To PL.31.10.1976; To IV.30.12.1978 ("insufficiently worked").
56 Lifshits-Losev, "Valerii Pereleshin. *Ariel'*."
57 To KP.27.11.1976; VP, as O.S., "*Ariel'* Valeriia Pereleshina," 2; To AR.9.2.1977.
58 Karlinsky, "A Hidden Masterpiece," 38, 41, 38.
59 To IV.28.10.1975 (*At the Roots of Existence*); To GS.21.2.1976 (*In the Groin of Existence*); To GS.17.12.1975 ("to contain").
60 To IV.9.7.1978 ("sums up the content"); To VL.27.12.1975 ("*Ariel* is a lyrical").
61 To KP.8.12.1979 ("it is difficult").
62 To VAS.17.5.1976; To PL.4.8.1975 second letter of that date ("*not* biography"); To KP.12.11.1979 ("the pornographic title").
63 To VAS.17.5.1976 ("horrified").
64 To MV.31.3.1978 ("recalled many"); To KP.4.12.1979 ("a mixture of Sodom").
65 To GS.27.8.1981 ("spiritual left-handers"); To GS.5.9.1981 ("emphasizes the point"); To GS.3.3.1978 ("would not have").
66 To ID.6.3.1981 ("a different vision").
67 To PL.4.8.1975, second letter ("jeers and condemnation").
68 To KP.21.11.1979 ("tolerated so far").
69 To VL.17.2.1976 ("predilections"); To KP.7.4.1976; To VL.17.2.1976 ("under the blows").
70 To KP.12.11.1979 ("you allow").
71 To KP.23.10.1979 ("out of the five Russian poets").
72 To KP.8.12.1979 ("some scholars").

73 To KP.7.10.1980 ("in future").
74 To IV.30.3.1977 ("a procreator is given").
75 To VL.17.2.1976 ("rabid he-males").
76 To KP.23.10.1979 ("had a row"); To KP.27.2.1980, second letter ("repented her"); To ID.6.3.1981 ("should be destroyed").
77 Karlinsky, "Esenin," 3, 38; VP, "Pobol'she by takikh statei!"
78 Rudinskii, "Napraslina na Esenina"; Karlinskii, "Pis'mo v redaktsiiu."
79 Karlinskii, "Pis'mo v redaktsiiu"; Rudinskii, "Esenin – kak on byl."
80 Sergeev, "Nezdorovaia sensatsiia."
81 Karlinskii, "Pis'mo v redaktsiiu."
82 Rudinskii, "Esenin – kak on byl"; To GS.17.9.1976 ("history testifies").
83 VP, "Sofiia Parnok," 206–7; To KP.7.10.1981 (quoting "the 'peculiarity of her taste'"); To GS.5.9.1981 ("Don Juan's list").
84 To OB.19.9.1987 ("there was a time"); To VS.23.4.1990 ("my innermost core").
85 To KP.11.8.1976 ("I am right").
86 To GS.3.9.1977 ("totally incredible"); To KP.19.8.1977 ("tender, warm"); To GS.3.9.1977 ("isn't this a sweet");
87 To IV.2.9.1977 ("a miracle"); To IV.18.8.1977 ("simply in love"); To KP.30.9.1977 ("gushing").
88 To KP.7.10.1980 ("they all call").
89 To IV.2.4.1978 ("so filled with"); To IV.14.4.1978 ("too attracted").
90 To KP.19.5.1978 ("he is proud"); To IV.9.7.1978 ("to my direct").
91 To AR.26.9.1978 ("Zhenia has"); To IV.27.5.1978 ("Ariel Constellation"); To IV.30.5.1978 ("I love Zhenia"); To IV.27.5.1978 ("one spirit designed").
92 To IV.18.6.1979 ("with crazy"); To MV.27.9.1978 ("identified me").
93 To KP.8.12.1979 ; To IV.10.10.1979 ("the Moscow 'Ariel'").
94 To EV.22.2.1980 ("without you").
95 To IV.21.2.1980; To IV.23.3.1980 ("somewhat sour"); To KP.27.3.1980 ("a mortal danger"); To KP.12.6.1981 ("no signs of life").

11. New Roads and Great Loss

1 To AR.27.7.1971; To ISF.28.6.1974; To IV.9.5.1972; To AR.3.6.1972; To AR.4.5.1972.
2 To KP.6.11.1974 ("unbearable to be"); To IV.7.11.1972; To IV.22.12.1974; To AR.20.2.1972; To VL.9.3.1971 ("the importance of money").
3 To GS.6.11.1974 ("in no way can"); To GS.3.12.1974 ("how low have"); To IV.22.12.1974 ("money not for"); A. Sedykh to VP, 1.12.1974; To MV.13.2.1985.

4 To IV.28.4.1976 ("I will not complain"); GS to the Kulaev Fund, 27.4.1976; IV to the Kulaev Fund; Kulaev to Ivask, 25.4.1976; To IV.6.9.1976; To KP.23.10.1979.
5 To ISF.24.10.1974 ("right in their own").
6 To AR.21-27.11.1971; To AR.11.8.1971 ("become plebeian"); To IV.2.10.1972 ("a well-fed North"); To MV.16.9.1987 ("of the plebeian class"); To KP.29.9.1979 ("a wrong way").
7 To AR.28.2.1972; To PB.3.1.1975; To AR.28.2.1972 ("what a fuss").
8 To IV.7.4.1971 ("if you only knew").
9 To KP.25.11.1974 ("to earn enough"); To AR.28.2.1972.
10 To ISF.24.10.1974 ("penultimate despair"); To IV.3.8.1977 ("do not blame").
11 EAS to PB.23.2.1976 ("he is a very sweet").
12 Bakich to OB.3.8.2002; To IV.17.8.1976; To IV.24.10.1977 ("comfortable spacious"); To IV.13.3.1977 ("with horror"); To KP.10.9.1979.
13 To KP.24.2.1975 ("unbearable servile"); To IV.24.2.1977 ("various adventures").
14 To OB.1.8.1987 ("holding an article") and similar descriptions in "V chem ne priniato priznavat'sia," in To NK.28.2.1986, To MV.15.2.1987, and in VP, "Zagrobnaia poeziia." Pereleshin dated this meeting to 1978 in VP, "Em vez de um prefàcio" (*Nos odres velhos*, 7), in VP, "V chem ne priniato priznavat'sia," and in some letters, including To OB.1.8.1987. However, his letters To IV.5.11.1977 and To IV.19.11.1977 already mention Humberto, and a note in a typescript of "Peacocks" (*Pavliny*, 9.10.1977] states that it was written after a conversation with Humberto.
15 To NF.28.2.1986 ("with the manners"); To IV.10.10.1979 ("semi-mystic"); To MV.8.7.1986 ("modest and completely"); To GS.6.3.1981; To GS.25.8.1979 ("physically and spiritually"); VP, "V chem ne priniato priznavat'sia" ("woman in a man's"); VP, "Zagrobnaia poeziia"; To AR.12.8.1979 ("falling in love").
16 To IV.5.11.1978; To MV.23.9.1986 ("Humbertik"); To IV.11.5.1979; To NF.7.5.1985; To ID.6.3.1981 ("previously Mum").
17 To IV.11.5.1979 ("dear Dona Emiliana").
18 To AR.22-23.7.1979); To IV.24.7.1979 ("bordering on").
19 AR to H. Marques Passos, 24.8.1979 ("one of the most"); From H. Marques Passos to AR.30.9.1979.
20 To AR.30.8.1979; To IV.31.8.1979; To GS.22.11.1979; To KP.5.11.1979 ("miserly pension").
21 To IV.23.9.1979; To AR.30.8.1979; To IV.31.8.1979; To KP.5.11.1979; To IV.23.9.1979; To KP.26.8.1979 ("nearly cry"); MV.18.10.1979 ("in the United States").

22 To MV.26.3.1980; To GS.1.6.1980; To KP.16.9.1980; To AR.15.6.1980 ("to prepare Russian"); "Programma peredach Radio Vaticana na russkom iazyke za mesiats noiabr' 1980."
23 To GS.18.1.1980; To KP.11.10.1979 ("there will be"); To AR.14.8.1979 ("my agony"); To IV.14.12.1979; To GS.18.1.1980; To KP.27.1.1980.
24 To KP.9.2.1980 ("we have no life").
25 To KP.27.2.1980; To MV.26.3.1980; To IV.31.8.1979; To KP.21.11.1979.
26 To IV.31.8.1979 ("an alms-house of Jesuit"); To IV.23.9.1979; To KP.25.9.1979 .
27 To AR.15.6.1980 ("exiled"); To IV.27.6.1980; To IV.5.6.1980; To AR.15.6.1980; To IV.16.7.1980 ("an eternity and").
28 To IV.16.7.1980 ("it is not a village").
29 To MV.14.7.1980 ("the atmosphere"); To KP.26.7.1980 ("living corpses").
30 To KP.13.9.1980 ("tribulations in").
31 To KP.28.8.1970; GS.25.11.1980; To GS.18.1.1980; To GS.22.11.1973 ("turn into a factory").
32 To KP.24.2.1975 ("at a cost of").
33 To EAS.12.10.1942.
34 Comment on the typescript.
35 To NK.21.12.1986; To GS.6.9.1973; GS.6.9.1973.
36 To GS.1.2.1968 ("harder than"); VP, comment on the typescript of the translation of "El Cántico Esperitual" ("to diverge from").
37 To AR.27.12.1979 ("clearly not accidental").
38 Coote, *The Penguin Book of Homosexual Verse*, 198.
39 To GS.15.5.1971; To VL.16.5.1971; To VL.16.5.1971; To KP.26.5.1971.
40 NF.28.8.1974 ("covertly"); To NF.28.8.1974 ("a certain 'mystical").
41 To KP.12.8.1974 ("ecstatically"); To NK.28.8.1974 ("visualized a future"); To PL.16.2.1975 ("heroic deed"); preface to the typescript of "English Sonnets of Fernando Pessoa" ("often makes").
42 To VL.1.11.1974 ("we have such").
43 To GS.6.8.1974 ("but the tension").
44 To GS.25.6.1976 ("free translation"); To KP.16.6.1976 ("I am forced").
45 To GS.14.6.1976 ('to pretend to be").
46 To GS.25.7.1981 ("in an *unrhymed* verse"); To ID.15.7.1981.
47 To VL.28.12.1953; To VL.14.2.1954 ("yet another").
48 To KP.29.9.1968; To AR.20.2.1972; Gorbov, "Literaturnye zametki," 142, 143; To VL.9.10.1968 ("prophetic slip").
49 To IV.24.2.1977; To KP.18.4.1978; To GS.10.11.1977 ("after a prolonged"); To IV.6.2.1977 ("a moral debt").
50 To IV.10.5.1978 ("I did not attempt").

51 To KP.7.11.1967; To KP.28.12.1967; VP, "Pamiati druga"; VP, "Chernyi poet belizny"; To VAS.30.11.1968 ("was black").
52 To KP.27.4.1969 ("immediately translated").
53 To AR.19.6.1972; VP, "Ot perevodchika," in *Iuzhnyi krest*, 16.
54 VP, "Zalkind Piatigorskii"; VP, "Ot perevodchika," in *Iuzhnyi krest*, 16.
55 Kruzenshtern-Peterets, "*Iuzhnyi krest*."
56 Nartsissov, "Valerii Pereleshin. *Iuzhnyi krest*."
57 Ivask, "Valerii Pereleshin. *Iuzhnyi krest*."
58 To IV.18.7.1978 ("enthusiastically campaigned"); Vivian Wyler, "Quando traduzir pode ser também um ato de gratidão"; To KP.9.9.1979 ("yesterday was").
59 To GS.22.2.1980; To IV.21.2.1980 ("has a lot of"); EAS to P.P. Balakshin, 17.12.1967 (*sic* – 1976).
60 To PL.13.9.1976; To GS.17.9.1976; To GS.30.9.1976; To IV.26.9.1976; To KP.17.4.1979; EAS to KP, 1977 Christmas card.
61 To IV.23.7.1980 ("today I called"); To IV.29.7.1980 ("my brother").
62 To GS.25.8.1980 ("*very ill*"); To OB.2.10.1989; To KP.16.9.1980 ("I would not"); To KP.7.10.1980 ("it is painful"); To KP.16.9.1980; To GS.8.10.1980; To KP.12.10.1980.
63 To GS.15.10.1980 ("on the morning"); To KP.12.10.1980.
64 To KP.12.10.1980; To KP.12.10.1980; To IV.16.10.1980 ("I have not expected"); To NF.5.11.1980 ("she is a real genius").
65 To ID.7.1.1981; To KP.1.12.1980 ("for once in my"); To KP.11.1.1981; To IV.8.1.1981 ("a duty, but"); To KP.14.12.1980.
66 To ISF.18.11.1974 ("encouraging"); To AG.1.5.1967 ("for her and my lives"); To MV.16.2.1987 ("in my entire long"); To ID.29.10.1980 ("all my life").
67 To KP.11.11.1980 ("I am truly").
68 To NF.5.11.1980; To GS.16.10.1980; To KP.12.10.1980 ("would not get"); To KP.12.10.1980; To IV.16.10.1980 ("he knows").
69 To ID.29.10.1980; To IV.16.10.1980 ("treatment would").
70 To ID.19.11.1980 ("a notebook"); To IV.16.10.1980 ("broke into loud"); To KP.11.1.1981 ("presence").
71 To MV.23.4.1981 ("the main key").
72 To KP.10.10.1981 ("step by step").
73 To KP.12.2.1981 ("red roses"); To KP.4.8.1981 ("it is very far").
74 4 To ID.29.5.1981 ("afraid to open").
75 To IV.1.7.1983; To MV.26.10.1983 ("at one time"); To NF.10.12.1983.
76 To IV.8.3.1985 ("he was after all'"); VP, "Iurii Ivask."
77 To KP.4.8.1981 ("our entire life").

78 To ID.24.3.1981 ("sat all day"); To KP.11.1.1981; To ID.7.1.1981 ("I must save"); To IV.8.1.1981 ("I am not").
79 To KP.11.1.1981; To IV.19.11.1980; To GS.6.3.1981 ("already expected").
80 To KP.4.8.1981; To GS.8.7.1981 ("some sword"); To ID.5.4.1981; To ID.20.1.1981 ("the master of"); To KP.7.10.1981 ("for all the tea"); To ID.24.3.1981.
81 To GS.3.5.1981 ("even tenderly"); To ID.24.3.1981 ("I would sit").
82 To KP.25.3.1981 ("cope with food"); To ID.5.4.1981 ("who but Lidiia"); To ID.24.3.1981 ("as a monk").
83 To KP.25.3.1981 ("simply businesses").
84 KP.29.12.1981 ("not for a single"); To KP.15.2.1982 ("just now"); To KP.24.4.1982 ("forbade me"); To MV.17.4.1982 ("to cool down").
85 Bakich to OB.3.8.2002; To IV.18.2.1983 ("a calm conversation"); To NF.11.8.1983 ("escape from").
86 To MV.16.2.1987; To NF.11.8.1983 ("international poet"); VSP, "Vtoroe pis'mo iz Brazilii."
87 To MV.29.9.1983; To OB.28.3.1989; To IV.18.2.1983 ("rather primitive"); To VAS.28.9.1983; To JPH.2.2.1986 ("my decrepit shack"); Bakich to OB.3.8.2002 ("an unimaginable").
88 To NF.11.8.1983 ("Shelter-House"); GS.21.3.1983 ("almost an almshouse"); Bakich to OB.3.8.2002.
89 To GS.9.7.1983 ("I feel great").
90 To GS.12.11.1983 ("recalling the distant"); To VS.28.9.1983 ("should have").
91 To NF.10.12.1983 ("I am totally happy"); To GS.9.7.1983; To NF.11.8.1983 ("like holidays").
92 To NF.26.10.1984; To GS.6.12.1984; To IV.26.10.1985 ("cried inconsolably").
93 VSP, "Pis'mo iz Brazilii," 18 (1983):10 ("a God's bird"); *Daodejing*, s. 170.
94 To AR.27.12.1971; To KP.25.8.1972; To AR.21–27.12.1971 ("had I come").
95 VP, "Valerii Salatko-Petrishche" ("to young male").
96 To GS.12.3.1980 ("one sonnet came"); To Iastrebov, 1985 ("I have become").
97 To ID.29.10.1980 ("a prayer to the Lord"); To KP.16.9.1980 ("Via cruces"); To GS.8.10.1980 ("a parallel work"); "Via cruces. Guirland de sonetos," comment ("a large failure").
98 To KP.12.11.1980; To IV.21.1.1981 ("he, Don Marcos"); To GS.25.7.1981; To KP.4.8.1981 ("an honour and").
99 To NF.4.12.1979 ("poems in Portuguese"); To GS.1.6.1980.
100 VSP, "Pis'mo iz Brazilii," *DOD* 18 (1983): 10 ("though not a poet"); To KP.19.5.1982 ("at times the word").
101 To KP.10.6.1982 ("your Portuguese"); To KP.19.5.1982; To GS.9.6.1982; To VS.25.10.1983 ("the 'wine' which").

102 To KP.10.6.1982 ("*Ariel* seem").
103 To VL.13.2.1960 ("the theme of").
104 V. Sinkevich, "Kartiny Portinari," *Perekrestki* 4 (1980): 28; To GS.30.9.1983; To VS.25.10.1983.
105 To NF.11.8.1983; VSP, "Vtoroe pis'mo iz Brazilii" ("no skill in selling"); To VAS.23.9.1983.
106 To IV.1.7.1983 ("harsh") To VS.25.10.1983 ("harsh"); To GS.9.7.1983 ("the reviewer"); To GS.30.9.1983; "A língua portuguesa nos versos de um poeta russo"; To MV.26.10.1983; To GS.12.11.1983 ("gradually to become").
107 V.S., "Valerii Pereleshin – brazil'skii poet"; VS, "Valerii Pereleshin v Gollandii".
108 To IV.6.11.1970 ("beautiful clarity"); To IV.28.1.1980 ("where Kuzmin has").
109 To GS.19.5.1981; To ID.22.5.1981 ("passionately in love"); To NK.21.12.1986 ("free verse as free").
110 To KP.1.7.1981; To ID.15.7.1981 ("almost sure of"); To GS.25.7.1981; To GS.25.7.1981 ("young and braver"); To KP.16.9.1981 ("no one buys").
111 To MV.8.12.1983; To MV.29.5.1984 ("accomplice in"); To NF.10.12.1983 ("after all, this"); To MV.16.12.1983.
112 To MV.29.6.1984; To GS.6.12.1984; To IV.8.3.1985; VP, "Valerii Pereleshin v Gollandii"; To MV.27.8.1985.
113 To MV.12.4.1986; To MV.8.7.1986; To NK.2.9.1986.
114 To GS.5.9.1981; To KP.16.9.1981; To KP.6.10.1981; To NF.19.6.1987; To SK.11.9.1987; To MV.16.9.1987;
115 To VAS.24.3.1989 ("I joined right away").
116 To VS.23.4.1990 ("they all are").
117 To VS.5.12.1983 ("phantoms and shadows"); To SK.25.8.1987; To SK.21.8.1987 ("I don't think").
118 To IV.30.7.1977 ("better than"); To IV.8.12.1979.
119 To IV.30.7.1977; To PL.14.9.1977 ("very sweet Englishman"); To GS.17.1.1978.
120 NF.4.12.1979; "O misterioso poeta Pereléchin" *Lampião*, October 1979; To NK.27.12.1979 ("the main event").
121 To AR.4.10.1979 ("excellent presentation"); translation by S. Karlinsky.
122 Leyland, *Gay Roots*, 648–9.
123 To GS.2.1.1982; Moss, *Out of the Blue*, 183.

12. Growing Recognition

1 To AR.8.2.1972 ("books and manuscripts"); To GS.11.8.1975; To GS.3.10.1969; To KP.12.10.1980; To GS.10.11.1980; To GS.26.10.1983; To KP.30.4.1981; To OB.29.12.1987.

2 To GS.22.5.1979; To GS.30.9.1983; Hinrichs, *Vanuit de verte: gedichten*; To VAS.28.9.1983.
3 J.R. de Groot, Librarian of Bibliotheek der Rijksuniversiteit te Leiden, to VFSP, 8.12.1983; VFSP to J.R. de Groot, 26.12.1983; A.J.M. Linmans, Deputy Librarian of Leiden University Library, to VFSP, 13.1.1984; Invoice of 6.4.1984 submitted by VFSP.
4 To MV.8.12.1983 ("all these 'papers'"); To GS.12.11.1983 ("a double purpose"); From VP to J.R. de Groot, 26.12.1983 ("evaluation"); To MV.26.10.1983 ("the most modest"); To OB.21.9.1987.
5 To MV.29.5.1984; To MV.17.12.1984; VFSP, excerpt from letter (1984); VFSP, "Kotoroe-to pis'mo iz Brazilii,"
6 To JPH.23.10.1987; To OB.30.10.1987; To NK.21.12.1986; To NF.19.6.1987; Hinrichs, *Valerij Perelešin. Catalogue of His Papers and Books in Leiden University Library*, 55.
7 To MV.12.4.1986 ("I am almost"); To NK.2.9.1986.
8 To NF.6.5.1986; VP, "Po priglasheniiu ot universiteta (i bez)," 15; Mokrinskaia, "Poslednie dni russkogo poeta"; Hinrichs, *Dichter met drie vaderlanden*; To NF.6.5.1986; To MV.8.7.1986; To MV.23.9.1986; To OB.19.2.1988; To NF.7.5.1986; To MV.8.7.1986 ("a total triumph"); To OB.31.10.1986 ("the first Russian").
9 To NF.7.5.1986; VP, "Po priglasheniiu ot universiteta (i bez)," 16–17; To OB.31.10.1986.
10 Mokrinskaia, "Poslednie dni russkogo poeta"; To NK.2.9.1986 ("exceptionally attentive"); To NF.7.2.1982 ("descendants"); To MV.8.7.1986.
11 Balakshin, "Emigratsiia i vetka sireni," an insert in *Final v Kitae*, vol. 2.
12 To PB.14.7.1975 ("neither Semen").
13 Kruzenshtern-Peterets, "Churaevskii pitomnik."
14 To KP.20.2.1969 ("how differently"); To KP.30.3.1969 ("a long tale"); To GS.9.10.1968 ("something like"); To KP.20.2.1969 ("a novelistic character").
15 To KP.6.9.1968 ("facts, spiced"); To KP.20.2.1969 ("she knew all"); KP.23.2.1969.
16 To AG.10.5.1969; To VL.28.4.1969 ("in five days and"); To KP.11.6.1969 ("purely personal"); To GS.7.6.1969; To KP.26.9.1969.
17 VP, "Dva polustanka, Vospominaniia svidetelia i uchastnika literaturnoi zhizni na Dal'nem Vostoke"; To MV.9.5.1984; To MV.29.5.1984 ("unkind").
18 To MV.14.2.1985 ("like a slave"); To MV.23.9.1986.
19 To OB.5.5.1987; To SK.21.8.1987 ("enormous editorial"); To SK.21.4.1987 ("modesty not"); To OB.5.5.1987.

20 To MV.26.2.1985 ("to tell the truth"); To NK.28.4.1987 ("in this novel"); To NF.23.5.1987 ("cunning").
21 Karlinsky, "Memoirs of Harbin."
22 *DP*, 45, 51–2, 96–9, 114; To VAS.20.1.1967; To KP.17.4.1967; To OB.5.5.1987; To NF.23.5.1987; To NK.25.7.1987; To VAS.21.12.1987; To NF.3.2.1989; To VAS.27.7.1989.
23 To NK.25.7.1987 ("witnessed a 'great"); To NK.20.4.1987 ("all were my").
24 To OB.5.5.1987; To NK.28.4.1987; To NF.23.5.1987.
25 Volin to L. and M. Yastrebov, 30.11.1988.
26 Volin, "Gibel' Molodoi Churaevki," 221.
27 Professor N.M. Christesen in conversation with OB; Volin, "Gibel' molodoi Churaevki," 221–34.
28 To NF.19.11.1987 ("spitting on"); To NF.29.8.1987 ("stung by my"); To OB.24.12.1987 ("I had loved Granin"); To NF.29.8.1987 ("one family").
29 Andersen, L. *Odna na mostu*, 368–77.
30 To KP.31.10.1986; VFSP, "Kotoroe-to pis'mo iz Brazilii," 14.
31 To MV.29.5.1984; To MV.4.1.1985; To MV.24.3.1985 ("one non-negotiable").
32 To MV.24.7.1985 ("a consultative voice"); To MV.17.8.1985; To MV.19.10.1985 ("my friends in Holland").
33 To OB.31.10.1986 ("written exclusively"); VFSP, "Kotoroe-to pis'mo iz Brazilii," 14; To NF.16.4.1986; To OB.24.12.1987.
34 To OB.25.3.1988 ("'splotches of life'"); To OB.10.3.1988; From Ardis to OB, 18.5.1988; To ID.7.6.1988 ("I guess, the Proffers"). Pereleshin did not know that Carl Proffer had died in 1984 and he used the plural for the husband and wife publishing team.
35 To ID.7.6.1988; To OB.1.7.1988 ("a folio 'Valerii Pereleshin'").
36 Hinrichs, editor's foreword to *Russkii poet v gostiakh u Kitaia*, xvi, xix, n12.
37 To KP.8.12.1979; To KP.21.11.1979 ("utilitarian considerations"); To KP.21.11.1979; To NK.27.12.1979.
38 To NF.27.7.1987 (13 June 1986); To NF.29.8.1987 ("lost all hope"); To OB.9.9.1987; To SK.11.9.1987 ("jubilant"); To OB.19.19.1987 ("elegant and").
39 To NF.19.11.1987; To NF.11.12.1987; To OB.29.12.1987; To NF.24.2.1988 ("to boast of his"); To OB.29.12.1987 ("a hysterical wench"); To OB.25.1.1988 ("would harm").
40 VP, "Posleslovie," in *Tri rodiny*, 160.
41 To MV.16.2.1987.
42 VP, "Ot avtora," in *Iz glubiny vozzvakh*, 7.
43 Vizi, "*Iz glubiny vozzvakh.*"
44 To AG.22.8.1967 ("Catholic church"); To KP.31.8.1974 ("St Ignatsius").
45 Inscription on a copy to Nina Fouchier, 11.11.1987 ("Christian"); To AG.22.8.1967 ("we created"); To IV.27.4.1977 ("shut the mouth").

46 To AG.16.3.1966 ("perpetuation of suffering").
47 To KP.23.10.1979 ("make it obvious").
48 To OB.2.11.1988 ("a miracle").
49 To OB.20.5.1989.
50 To MV.29.6.1989 ("welcomed with"); To NF.17.7.1989; To VS.23.4.1990.
51 To MV.29.6.1989; To OB.16.8.1989 ("the soul of the Festival").
52 To MV.29.6.1989; To OB.12.7.1989 ("contrived *not* to").
53 To MM.20.11.1988; To VS.23.4.1990 second letter ("motivated not").
54 To SK.16.8.1989 ("all ten days"); To MV.29.6.1989.
55 To NF.17.7.1989; Hannie Groen to OB.20.8.2004, email; Hannie Groen to OB.7.9.2004, email.
56 To NF.17.7.1989 ("were it not for").
57 To OB.12.6.1989 ("with difficulty"); To SK.16.8.1989; To OB.12.7.1989 ("full of impressions"); To JPH.2.7.1989 ("in our old age").
58 To MV.26.4.1977; To KP.4.11.1977; To IV.18.1.1978; To KP.29.10.1978; Panin, "Otkrytoe pis'mo Alekseiu Kosachevu."
59 To GS.17.1.1978; To KP.9.10.1978 ("from the depth"); To GS.4.10.1978 ("the matter of my"); To IV.16.10.1978 ("this is a *man*"); To GS.24.10.1978 ("both editors").
60 *PBP*, Canto One, IV, 37 and 73n6, and LVI, 63; "Khronikal'naia zametka"; To GS.31.1.1978; *PBP*, Canto One, XLIII, 56, and 74n22; To GS.13.3.1978.
61 To GS.3.4.1978 ("to blow this up"); VP, "I ne osparivai gluptsa"; To GS.21.6.1978.
62 Pomerantsev, "I malyi svoi talant pokryl bol'shim pozorom"; "Iz redaktorskoi pochty"; To KP.11.10.1979 ("De Profundis"); To GS.5.10.1979 ("De Profundis").
63 Sergeev, "Periodika"; To GS.25.10.1979; To GS.13.10.1979 ("not a p[ederast]").
64 "Zametka redaktora"; To GS.5.10.1979 ("inwardly alien"); To AR.14.6.1979 ("Zionist declarations"); To GS.27.6.1978); Tetenov and Skuratov letters to the editor; "Po sledam gazetnykh publikatsii"; "Nashi interv'iu. Beseda s ukrainskim pisatelem Ulasom Samchukum"; To AR.5.2.1972 ("total independence"); To KP.22.6.1974 ("younger brothers"); To IV.12.4.1980 ("organic parts"); To KP.24.3.1972 ("Ukrainian speech"); "K literaturnoi obshchestvennosti"; To GS.8.10.1980; To GS.25.8.1980.
65 "Nashi interv'iu," 151; To GS.25.8.1980.
66 To KP.12.11.1980.
67 To SK.21.8.1987 ("unbelievable, fantastic"); To OB.1.9.1987 ("did not even"); To KP.17.12.1976.
68 To KP.21.11.1979 ("*never acts*")
69 To SK.30.9.1987; To VAS.21.12.1987 ("at his own expense"); To MV.26.7.1988; To SK.12.2.1988 ("verily, God himself").

70 To SK.30.9.1987 ("and so, Valerii"); To OB.11.11.1987; To SK.19.11.1987.
71 To OB.6.2.1988; To SK.12.2.1988; To SK.25.12.1988 ("dreaming day and night").
72 To SK.10.6.1990 ("I love your publication").
73 To SK.10.2.1990; To OB.29.8.1989.
74 To OB.2.10.1989; To VS.11.10.1989 ("mercenary publishers"); To VS.19.11.1989 ("robbery: everyone"); To SK.1.5.1990 ("if the unscrupulous"); To SK.21.5.1990.
75 J.C.B. Dirkx to Van Gent, 14.5.1985.
76 To SK.4.10.1987; To OB.20.10.1987; To JPH.3.11.1987; To JPH.6.1.1988; JPH to A.B. Kirilloff, 26.11.1992.
77 To OB.5.5.1987; To NF.23.5.1987 ("a rather extensive"); To MV.27.6.1987 ("to write an ode").
78 To OB.29.8.1989; To JPH.23.9.1988.
79 To A.B. Kirilloff, 30.1.1990 ("author's copy"); To VS.11.10.1989 ("swindled out"); To OB.2.1.1990; To VS.10.1.1990; To JPH.25.7.1989; To OB.11.1.1990 ("offered no thanks"); To OB.2.10.1989 ("repulsive").
80 To SK.2.2.1990 ("greedy and unscrupulous"); To OB.2.1.1989 [*sic* – 1990] ("Scots"); To A.B. Kirilloff, 30.1.1990 ("shark-like greed"); To OB.2.10.1989; To JPH.18.11.1989.
81 To JPH.19.1.1990; To JPH.18.11.1989.
82 To OB.2.2.1990 ("can I prove").
83 To OB.11.1.1990 ("my small gold"); To JPH.8.12.1989; To A.B. Kirilloff, 30.1.1990.
84 To VS.19.11.1989 ("on the whole"); To SK.2.2.1990 ("obsolete").
85 Hinrichs, *Verbannte muse* (1990); Hinrichs, *Verbannte muse* (1992); To VS.9.6.1990 ("twelve very tender"); To VAS.8.6.1990 ("extremely flattering"); To VS.10.1.1990 ("tried to remain").
86 To ID.15.7.1990 ("had simple-heartedly").
87 To JPH.19.6.1990.
88 To KP.29.7.1973 ("the home of a Russian"); To MV.17.4.1982 ("my collections").
89 "Strochki, zateriannye na chuzhbine"; "Arsenii Nesmelov"; Arsenii Nesmelov, "Vtoroi Moskovskii"; Arsenii Nesmelov, "Vozvrashchenie," 76–86; Arsenii Nesmelov, "Iz literaturnogo nalslediia"; "A. Nesmelov"; Arsenii Nesmelov, "V etot den'"; To OB.13.1.1988 ("resurrecting the dead").
90 To VAS.2.9.1988 ("obviously pseudonymous"); M. Kostolomov, letter to the editor.
91 To VAS.2.9.1988 ("on one condition'"); To VAS.25.6.1988 ("to complain"); To VAS.21.12.1987. The last stanza of Nesmelov's poem "Episode"

(*Epizod*) from *White Flotilla* (*Belaia flotiliia*, 1942) was omitted in *Golos rodiny* 7 (1987).

92 Vitkovskii, "Iz pis'ma Evgeniia Vitkovskogo ot 29 avgusta 1988 g."; Vitkovskii, soobshcheniia o publikatsii; To OB.10.9.1988; To VAS.14.12.1988 ("first swallow"); To OB.2.11.1988 ("this is a greater").
93 Vitkovskii to VP.2.10.1988; To MV.25.12.1989 ("spin"); To OB.20.12.1988 ("'a betrayal'").
94 "O Rodine – izdaleka"; "Slyshu sneg i pushkinskie iamby"; To OB.5.2.1989.
95 Vitkovskii, "Dan' zhivym."
96 "Storozh u lampadki"; VAS to VP.1.11.1989.
97 To OB.19-30.1.1989; To NK.3.2.1989 ("the slogan"); To MV.25.12.1988 ("just now").
98 To OB.13.1.1988; To ID.16.7.1988 ("even Moscow"); To OB.6.2.1988 ("they guard only").
99 To OB.20.12.1988; To NK.15.1.1989; To OB.19-30.1.1989; To OB.3.3.1989 ("a standing ovation"); To OB.26.4.1989.
100 To OB.3.3.1989; To OB.28.3.1989; To SK.16.8.1989; "Valerii Perelishin [*sic*] "; To NK.22.8.1989.
101 "V. Pereleshin"; "Valerii Pereleshin" (1989); EV to VP.2.10.1988; To NK.22.8.1989 ("it is time to"); To NK.15.1.1989.
102 VFSP, excerpt from a letter (1990): 38; To OB.2.1.1990 ("important, flattering").
103 To OB.26.4.1989 ("suddenly became").
104 *Novye knigi SSSR*; *Plan vypuska literatury izdatel'stva Sovremennik*, 16; VFSP, "Pis'mo iz Brazilii" (1989); To OB.2.1.1990; To OB.11.1.1990 ("turned into").
105 To OB.3.3.1989; To OB.29.8.1989 ("to monitor"); To NF.7.9.1989; To OB.2.10.1989.
106 To OB.11.1.1990 ("turned out to be"); To OB.11.1.1990 ("I am now"); To OB.2.1.1990 ("to be properly invited"); To NK.27.5.1990 ("only as an honoured").
107 To VAS.28.12.1988 ("had rejoiced"); To VAS.14.1.1989.
108 To VAS.14.12.1988; To SK.10.2.1990 ("only now does").
109 To OB.28.1.1990 ("passionate admirer"); To SK.2.2.1990 ("for photographs"); To OB.2.1.1990; To ID.15.7.1990; To VS.19.11.1989 ("truly of a man"); To OB.11.1.1990; To VS.11.8.1990.
110 To ID.15.7.1990 ("an already"); VP, excerpt from a letter, 1990, 39 ("to take a part"); To VS.11.8.1990 ("spend ten days").
111 To SK.11.4.1990; VP, excerpt from a letter, 1990, 38 ("now my only dream").
112 To OB.2.10.1989 ("providential"); To VAS.26.11.1989 ("to entrust my").
113 To OB.31.3.1990 ("Moscow cannot").

13. Last Love, Last Books, Last Years

1 *DP*, 34; To JPH.23.9.1988.
2 To IV.5.12.1980 ("I should have"); To MV.17.4.1982; To NF.10.12.1983 ("steady relationship").
3 To ID.6.3.1981 ("in my entire life").
4 To IV.19.11.1980 ("not for the heroine").
5 To IV.18.9.1984; To MV.29.5.1984; To NF.19.6.1987.
6 To MV.27.6.1987 ("culture, knowledge"); To KP.24.4.1982 ("it would be great"); To KP.19.5.1982; To GS.9.6.1982 ("simply a beautiful face").
7 To GS.6.3.1981 ("for ten days"); To GS.31.10.1981 ("on the veranda"); To OB.1.8.1981 ("one-day"); To ID.23.7.1981; To MV.27.8.1985; To NF.28.2.1986.
8 To NF. ca. June 1987 ("astonishingly *boyish*").
9 To OB.1.8.1987 ("when Mum left"); To JPH.1.5.1984, unmailed postcard in Ivask Archive ("my friend come"); To MV.8.5.1984; To MV.23.9.1986; To NF, ca. June 1987; To OB.19.10.1987 ("*my life* and continues").
10 To MV.19.2.1987 ("old and quite"); To ID.6.3.1981 ("simply friends"); To MV.9.5.1984 ("oh, if only he").
11 To IV.18.9.1984; To MV.13.12.1985 ("in his company"); To MV.4.1.1986 ("statues of the twelve"); To NF.4.1986. Aleijadinho is believed to have suffered from leprosy.
12 To IV.18.9.1984 ("lived only"); To MV.24.1.1985 ("defiled by lust").
13 VP, "V chem ne priniato priznavat'sia"; VP, "Zagrobnaia poeziia."
14 To GS.30.12.1981 ("an unconditional hostility"); To ID.20.2.1981 ("the basest"); To GS.31.10.1981 ("swearing at every"); To GS.28.11.1981 ("enraged by the").
15 To MV.16.2.1987 ("returning Humberto"); To NK.2.9.1986 ("the best thing").
16 To NK.2.9.1986; To MV.16.2.1987; To SK.4.10.1987; To NK.2.9.1986 ("not only with").
17 To NF.10.12.1983 ("a gang of spiritualists"); To MV.13.12.1985 ("visit condemned").
18 To OB.1.8.1987 ("which is what").
19 To OB.1.8.1987 ("I felt the breeze").
20 To MV.8.7.1986; To NK.21.12.1986; MV.16.2.1987 ("in my long life").
21 To NF, undated second page of letter, ca. June 1987 ("irrepressibly attracted"); To MV.27.6.1987; To MV.8.7.1986; To OB.1.9.1987 ("we all need"); To MV.8.7.1986; To OB.26.9.1987.
22 To MV.16.9.1987 ("I understand").
23 To OB.9.2.1987; To MV.6.3.1987; To MV.16.2.1987 ("tempted").

24 To OB.9.2.1987 ("I have had").
25 To OB.19.9.1987 ("singed by the beauty").
26 To OB.20.10.1987 ("embodied Ariel"); To NF.13.11.1987 ("I would have").
27 To MV.16.9.1987 ("are connected"); To OB.1.9.1987 ("in another reincarnation").
28 To OB.7.9.1987 ("*it may be a good*").
29 To MV.27.6.1987; To OB.1.9.1987; To OB.1.8.1987 ("absolutely everyone"); To MV.27.6.1987 ("to be taken away").
30 To OB.19.10.1987 ("*perpetuum mobile*"); To JPH.11.12.1987.
31 To OB.19.10.1987 ("a terrible pity"); To OB.19.9.1987 ("an educational punishment").
32 To OB.19.9.1987 ("moving further").
33 To SK.19.11.1987; To OB.13.1.1988 ("bitter sorrow").
34 To SK.4.10.1987 ("thoughts of 'Roberto'").
35 To OB.19.2.1988 ("I was writing *to him*").
36 To MV.20.5.1988 ("it is now clear").
37 To MV.6.3.1987 ("a history of"); To OB.1.8.1987; To OB.19.9.1987 ("for self-consolation").
38 VP, "M. Vizi" ("women's poems"); To MV.19.2.1987 ("about or to Humberto").
39 To OB.1.8.1987.
40 To ID.4.9.1988 ("a transparent pseudonym").
41 To MV.21.4.1988 ("yes, alas, alone").
42 To OB.1.9.1987 ("No. 12-A"); To OB.19.9.1987; To OB.26.9.1987; To MV.18.10.1987.
43 "Ot avtora," *In Pursuit*, 7.
44 To SK.30.9.1987 ("I would not catch"); To OB.26.9.1987 ("the most charming").
45 To OB.13.1.1988; To OB.25.3.1988 ("even that would"); To OB.25.1.1988 ("grew cold"); To OB.10.3.1988; To OB.21.1.1988 ("three books").
46 Chinnov, "Giatsintom, lefkoem," in *Kompozitsiia*.
47 To SK.4.10.1987 ("autobiographic and").
48 To SK.4.10.1987 ("the 'hero' would").
49 To ID.11.7.1988 ("with this book").
50 To NF.13.11.1987 ("getting more").
51 To SK.24.12.1987 ("why, instead of"): To OB.25.1.1988 ("wanted to be free").
52 To SK.30.9.1987 ("the abundance"); To SK.24.12.1987; To OB.29.12.1987 ("everywhere").
53 To MV.16.9.1987 ("pornographic"); To NF.15.11.1987 ("an indignant letter"); To OB.19.10.1987 ("simply laughed"); To NF.15.11.1987 ("for them, poems"); To MV.18.10.1987 ("I considered").

54 Aleksandrov, review, typescript sent to *NZh*; Aleksandrov, "*Dvoe i snova odin?*" typeset text, from Sydney newspaper *Edinenie*; it is not possible to verify if it was published.
55 Untitled typescript of a rebuttal to P. Aleksandrov's review.
56 To NK.3.2.1989 ("on the same topic").
57 To OB.13.3.1988 ("my only ray"); To ID, ca. 1988 ("had thousands").
58 To OB.19.2.1988; To OB.10.3.1988 ("it is better not"); To OB.20.12.1988.
59 To OB.25.3.1988 ("a charming sixteen-year-old"); To SK.2.2.1988; To SK.15.3.1990; To SK.21.5.1990.
60 V. Salatko to A.A. Jebit, 16.8.1998.
61 To NF.26.6.1973 ("some kind of"); To KP.26.12.1974 ("fertility holds").
62 To GS.16.11.1972 ("one should write"); To GS.9.3.1973 ("the best will be").
63 To VL.22.3.1972 ("a further development"); To KP.29.12.1972 ("I discovered").
64 Rannit, "O poezii i poetike Valeriia Pereleshina," 94.
65 Comment on the draft of "V nachale sotvorikh" (11.7.1972) ("infatuation").
66 To KP.25.3.1975 ("there is no sonnet").
67 To KP.26.7.1972 ("an amazing form"); To KP.15.6.1970 ("must have"); To GS.10.1.1973 ("could be saturated"); To GS.22.12.1972 ("religious, philosophical").
68 To GS.26.12.1971 ("youthful"); To GS.30.12.1972 ("an incredible poetic"); To NF.26.2.1974 ("rushed out").
69 Figures are based on the bibliography of Pereleshin's poems compiled by OB; To MV.14.1.1973 ("getting hard").
70 To AG.26.12.1972 ("an easier English").
71 To AR.7.8.1971 ("accepted it").
72 To NK.15.12.1973 ("as a verse maker"); To MV.26.3.1980 ("it is unlikely").
73 Rannit, "Valerii Pereleshin posle *Kacheli*," 121.
74 Karlinsky, "A Hidden Masterpiece," 38, 41.
75 VP, "Posleslovie," in *Tri rodiny*, 159–60.
76 To KP.16.12.1970 ("one of the symbols").
77 To GS.27.8.1970 ("so far have not"); To AR.19.7.1972 ("find a place").
78 VP, "Posleslovie," in *Tri rodiny*, 159–60.
79 To MV.26.3.1980 ("although colloquial language").
80 To MV.21.2.1980 ("'poeticisms'"); To GS.12.3.1980 ("prison stink").
81 To OB.1.7.1988 ("Exile into Flesh"); To MV.6.7.1988; VFSP, excerpt from a letter (1988) ("while my allotted").
82 To OB.31.10.1986 ("poets usually").
83 To VAS.23.4.1990 ("is my innermost").
84 To NF.23.5.1987 ("I am committing"); To SK.23.4.1988; To NK.15.1.1989 ("tense and restless"); To VAS.27.7.1989 ("pushed me"); To NK.22.8.1989.

85 To MV.8.7.1986; To MV.16.2.1987; To OB.12.9.1987; To MV.6.7.1988 ("at times I am"); To ID.11.7.1988 ("old weak point"); To VAS.2.9.1988; To VAS.14.12.1988 ("had tormented"); To MV.29.6.1989 ("poisoning my existence"); To ID.7.6.1988; To SK.1.6.1988; To VAS.2.9.1988 ("I crawled").
86 To OB.16.4.1989; To NF.7.9.1989; To VAS.26.11.1989; To VS.4.7.1990; To OB.28.1.1990; To OB.29.5.1990; Jebit (Zhebit), "Literaturnoe nasledie 'sen'ora Valerio,'" 109.
87 To VAS.26.11.1989; To NF.7.9.1989 ; To NF.17.7.1989 ("being left").
88 To NF.4.1.1989; To SK.4.1.1989 ("they, of course"); To NF.4.1.1989.
89 To NF.4.1.1989 ("what is left"); To SK.4.1.1989 ("not only my"); To OB.5.2.1989; To SK.1.2.1989 ("I have not dared").
90 To NF.4.1.1989 ("it is awkward"); To SK.1.2.1989 ("with the greatest"); To SK.17.2.1989 ("yours for the rest").
91 To VS.23.4.1990 ("always unscrupulous"); To VS.21.3.1990 ("fell head over"); To VS.21.3.1990 ("passionately beloved"); To VS.23.4.1990, second letter of that date; To VS.17.5.1990 ("all my life").
92 Translated from Portuguese by Edward A. Lacey, *The Collected Poems and Translations of Edward A. Lacey*, 581–2.
93 To OB.2.10.1989 ("on the whole"); To MV.10.6.1988 ("was coming").
94 To OB.31.3.1990 ("there are days"); To VS.9.6.1990; To SK.10.6.1990.
95 To Volkoff, 3.3.1990 (*sic* – 3.4.1991).
96 Bakich to OB.30.8.2002 ("hungrily devoured").
97 Kirilloff to JPH, 27.1.1993; "Certidão de óbito," 9.7.1992; Kirilloff to OB.23.6.2004.
98 Bakich to OB.30.8.2002.
99 To MV.11.12.1985; To NK.21.12.1986 ("God be his judge"); To NF.5.7.1986; MV.23.9.1986; To OB.1.8.1987; To SK.4.10.1987.
100 To SK.1.6.1988 ("real devil"); To SK.29.8.1988 ("plunging an aspen"); To JPH.2.8.1988; To JPH.7.8.1988; To JPH.12.8.1988; To ID.4.9.1988 ("had already").
101 To Kirilloff, 30.1.1990 ("the shark-like greed").
102 V. Salatko to Kirilloff, 9.1.1993 and 25.1.1993; Kirilloff to OB.8.7.2005.
103 V. Salatko, excerpt from a letter, *BSO* 17 (2000), 37.
104 Kirilloff to Lidiia Salatko, 20.10.1992; Jebit (Zhebit), "Literaturnoe nasledie 'sen'ora Valerio,'" 108.
105 JPH to V. Salatko, 24.6.1993; J.J.M. Gent to Kirilloff, 4.3.1993; Ata de transferência parcial de herança literária.
106 VSP, excerpt from a letter, *DOD* 19 (1983), 50; To OB.28.3.1989; To VS.25.10.1983.
107 VP, "Valerii Salatko-Petrishche" ("if I had a chance").

Bibliography

This is a selection of materials relevant to this book; a complete list of everything related to Pereleshin, his life, his poetry, relatives, friends, and acquaintances would be much longer.

I. Works by Valerii Pereleshin

Books of Poetry Published by Valerii Pereleshin

V puti. Stikhi, 1932–1937. Harbin: E.A. Sentianina, 26 October 1937.
Dobryi ulei. Vtoraia kniga stikhotvorenii. Harbin: Valerii Pereleshin (Monakh German), 5 September 1939.
Zvezda nad morem. Tret'ia kniga stikhotvorenii. Harbin: Valerii Pereleshin (Ieromonakh German), 8 September 1941.
Zhertva. Chetvertaia kniga stikhotvorenii. Harbin: E.S. Kaufman, 20 May 1944.
Iuzhnyi dom. Piataia kniga stikhotvorenii. Munich: I. Baschkirzew Buchdruckerei, izdanie avtora, 1968.
Kachel'. Shestaia kniga stikhotvorenii. Frankfurt: Possev-Verlag, by Author, 1971.
Zapovednik. Sed'maia kniga stikhotvorenii. Frankfurt: Possev-Verlag, by V. Pereleshin, 1972.
S gory Nevo. Vos'maia kniga stikhotvorenii. Frankfurt: Possev-Verlag, by V. Pereleshin, 1975.
Ariel'. Deviataia kniga stikhotvorenii. Frankfurt: Possev-Verlag, by V. Pereleshin, 1976.
Nos odres velhos. Poesias. Rio de Janeiro: Achiamé, 1983.

Tri rodiny. Desiataia kniga stikhotvorenii. Paris: Editions Albatros, by V. Pereleshin, 1987.

Iz glubiny vozzvakh … Odinnadtsatyi sbornik stikhotvorenii. Holyoke, MA: New England Publishing, 1987.

Dvoe – i snova odin? Dvenadtsatyi sbornik stikhotvorenii. Holyoke, MA: New England Publishing, 1987.

Vdogonku. Trinadtsatyi sbornik stikhotvorenii. Holyoke, MA: New England Publishing, 1987.

Translations Published by Valerii Pereleshin

S.T. Kol'ridzh. Skazanie starogo moriaka. Perevod Valeriia Pereleshina. Harbin: Valerii Pereleshin (Ieromonakh German), 1940.

Stikhi na veere. Antologiia kitaiskoi klassicheskoi poezii. Frankfurt: Possev-Verlag, 1970.

Tsiui Iuan'. Li Sao. Poema v stikhotvornom perevode Valeriia Pereleshina s kitaiskogo originala. Frankfurt: Possev-Verlag, by V. Pereleshin, 1975.

Iuzhnyi krest. Antologiia brazil'skoi poezii. Frankfurt: Polyglott-Druck GmbH, by V. Pereleshin, 1978.

Mikhail Kuzmin. Cânticos de Alexandria. Traduzidos do russo por Valério Pereliéchin e H. Marques Passos. Rio de Janeiro: Ānima produções artístas e culturais ltda, 1986.

Works Published by Others

Vanuit de verte. Leiden: De Lantaarn, April 1985. 2nd ed., April 1986. 3rd ed., August 1986.

Drie vaderland. Mastricht: Huit clos, 1986.

Dva polustanka. Published as *Russian Poetry and Literary Life in Harbin and Shanghai, 1930–1950: The Memoirs of Valerii Pereleshin.* Edited in Russian with an introduction by Jan Paul Hinrichs. Amsterdam: Rodopi, 1987.

Russkii poet v gostiakh u Kitaia, 1920–1952. Sbornik stikhotvorenii. Edited and with an introduction and notes by Jan Paul Hinrichs. In the series Émigré Literature in the Twentieth Century: Studies and Texts. Ed. Jan Paul Hinrichs. Vol. 4. The Hague: Leuxenhoff Publishing, 1989.

Poema bez predmeta. Pod redaktsiei Semena Karlinskogo. Holyoke: New England Publishing, 1989.

Russian Literary and Ecclesiastical Life in Manchuria and China from 1920 to 1952: Unpublished Memoirs of Valerij Perelešin. Edited in Russian with an introduction and notes by Thomas Hauth. In the series Émigré Literature in the Twentieth Century: Studies and Texts. Ed. Jan Paul Hinrichs. Vol. 6. The Hague: Leuxenhoff Publishing, 1996.

Dao de tszin. Poema. Perevel s kitaiskogo Valerii Pereleshin. Moscow: Vremia, 2000. Posthumous publication of *Daodejing.*

II. Pereleshin's Collected Works in Olga Bakich Collection

Poems in Russian

This collection contains, in chronological order, Pereleshin's poems in Russian, published and unpublished, typewritten and handwritten, some in several versions and with insightful commentary by Pereleshin, which he sent over the years to Olga Bakich and to other correspondents who later entrusted them to her. It also includes the following material.

1. Photocopies of poems from Leiden University Archive: "Early Poems," BPL 3260/1; "Siniaia ptitsa" and "Vechnyi Rim," BPL 3260/2; "Dve korolevy," BPL 3260/3; "Greshnye dumy" and "Priniatie tainy," BPL 3260/4; "MCMXXXIII," BPL 3260/5; "MCMXXXIV," BPL 3260/6; "MCMXXXIV-II," BPL 3260/7; Variant version of "Dve korolevy," BPL 3260/8; "Various Poems," BPL 3260/9; poems by "Mariia Kareeva," BPL 3260/10; "Transcripts in the Hand of Iurii Volkov," 3260/11; "Poems from Shanghai," BPL 3261/5; "Iuzhnyi dom," and some poems for "Rosa Mystica," BPL 3261/17.
2. Poems and translations published in the following émigré periodicals and anthologies. Harbin: in the newspapers *Rupor, Kharbinskoe vremia,* and *Gun-bao;* the journals *Molodaia Churaevka, Churaevka, Luch Azii,* and *Rubezh;* and the anthologies *Semero, Gumilevskii sbornik, U rodnykh rubezhei,* and *Priboi.* Shanghai: in the journals *Parus* and *Feniks,* and the anthology *Ostrov.* Paris: in the anthology *Iakor',* the newspaper *Russkaia mysl',* and the journals *Vozrozhdenie* and *Le Messager. Vestnik Russkogo Khristianskogo dvizheniia.* Ann Arbor: in the journal *Russian Literary Triquarterly.* New York: in the newspaper *Novoe russkoe slovo* and the journal *Novyi zhurnal.* Philadelphia: in the journal *Perekrestki (Vstrechi).* San Francisco: in the newspaper *Russkaia zhizn',* the journals *Kharbinskie kommercheskie uchilishcha Kit. Vost. zhel. dor.* and *Gay Sunshine,* and the anthologies *Now the Volcano, Gay Roots,* and *Out of the Blue.* Toronto: in the journal *Sovremennik.* Munich: in the anthology *Outside of Russia* and the journal *Kontinent.*

Sydney: in the journals *Druz'iam ot druzei* and *Biulleten' Soiuza okonchivshikh uchebnye zavedeniia KhSML.*

Poems in Other Languages

The collection also contains Pereleshin's published and unpublished poems in Portuguese and in English and one poem in Chinese.

TRANSLATIONS

The collection includes poetic translations of Chinese classics and some modern poets with the originals of each poem and commentary, as well as a photocopy of Chinese texts, some of which were included in *Stikhi na veere*, BPL 3265/1.

Translations of Brazilian and Portuguese poets, including those of Fernando Pessoa.

Translations of Russian and Chinese poems into Portuguese, including Pereleshin's Russian "Krestnyi put'" into Portuguese as "Via cruces: Guirland de sonetos," BPL 3261/33

Translations of English, French, Latin, German, and Estonian poems.

TYPESCRIPTS

Dva polustanka. Two typescripts by Pereleshin, one of 61 pp. and another of 80 pp. OB Collection.

Iuzhnyi dom. Manuscript. BPL 3261/17.

Kedr i ptitsa. Typescript. BPL 3261/24.

Li Sao. Poema Tsiui Iuania v stikhotvornom perevode s originala. Typescript.

Poema bez predmeta. Two typescripts with Pereleshin's comments. OB Collection.

"U dobrogo drakona." Incomplete anthology of Russian poetry in China, compiled by Valerii Pereleshin and Mary Custis Vezey, typewritten by Pereleshin with his handwritten notations and comments and with some poems added in typescript by Mary Custis Vezey. OB Collection.

III. Pereleshin's Theological Thesis

Ieromonakh German. "Filosofiia stradaniia. Kandidatskoe sochinenie ieromonakha Germana Salatko-Petrishche. MCMXII." Unpublished master's thesis for the degree of Candidate of Theology, submitted to Theological Faculty of the Institute of St Vladimir, Harbin. BPL 3261/3.

IV. Autobibliographies and Bibliographies

Autobibliographies

"Valerii Pereleshin. Polnaia bibliografiia stikhotvorenii i poem, za iskliucheniem detskikh i nenapechatannykh iunosheskikh." Typescript compiled by Pereleshin up to 2 February 1988, complete, but with wrong pagination: 1–45, 51–4, and 65–81. OB Collection.

"Escritos em Português." Typescript of his poems in Portuguese compiled by Pereleshin, 6 pp. OB Collection.

"Valerii Pereleshin. Autobibliography of translations from Chinese." Typescript by Pereleshin, 6 pp. OB Collection.

"Valerii Pereleshin. Autobibliography of Translations from Portuguese." Typescript by Pereleshin, 6 pp. OB Collection.

"Valerii Pereleshin. Autobibliography of Translations from Spanish, French, Latin, German, Estonian, English." Typescript by Pereleshin, 2 pp. OB Collection.

Bibliographies Compiled by OB

Pereleshin's poems in Russian in alphabetical order by title and the first line, including juvenilia; the same in chronological order.

Pereleshin's translations from Chinese into Russian in alphabetical order by author; the same in chronological order.

Pereleshin's poems in Portuguese in alphabetical order by author; the same in chronological order.

Translations from Portuguese into Russian in alphabetical order by author; the same in chronological order.

Translations from other languages.

V. Selected Articles by Pereleshin

Published Articles

This list includes articles consulted for this work and is not all-inclusive; the complete bibliography contains some 400 published articles and reviews. Although some of Pereleshin's typescripts were published in *TH*, the originals were used in all cases.

"A chto obo mne pisali polveka tomu nazad." Typescript, BPL 3261/38. OB Collection. Published in *TH*, 1–42.

"Afro-brazil'skie kul'ty," as Sigma. *RM*, 26 September 1968.
"*Ariel'* Valeriia Pereleshina," as O.S. *Druz'iam i znakomym* 133 (November 1976), 2-4.
"Arkhimandrit Nafanail (Porshnev)." Typescript. BPL 3261/17 . Also in Bakhmeteff Archive, Butler Library, Columbia University. Published in TH, 90–6.
"'Aut-aut' Ibsena," as Ieromonakh German. *KhN* 1 (1943), 18–37.
"Baronessa Ol'ga Vladimirovna Stal'-Gol'shtein." Typescript. BPL 3261/40 [18]. Also in Bakhmeteff Archive, Butler Library, Columbia University. Published in TH, 64–5.
"Blizhe k Zapadu!" *Churaevka* 6 (May 1934).
"Chernyi poet belizny." *NRS*, 11 August 1973.
"Chetyre goda Rossiiskoi dukhovnoi missii v Kitae," as V.F. Salatko-Petrishche. *NRS*, 28 September1969.
"Churaevka v *Chislakh*," as Sigma. *Churaevka* 7 (October 1934). Quoted in full in *DP*, 65–6.
"Dmitrii Petrovich Panteleev." Typescript. BPL 3261 [9]. Published in *TH*, 78–81.
"Durnaia mistika," *Grani* 73 (1969): 208–12.
"Dva Parizha." *NRS*, 9 November 1969.
"Dva polustanka. Vospominaniia svidetelia i uchastnika literaturnoi zhizni na Dal'nem Vostoke," *RZh*, 4 February 1984.
"Eshche ob udareniiakh v sobstvennykh imenakh." *NRS*, 16 December 1977.
[Excerpt from a letter], as V.F. Salatko-Petrishche. *DOD* 19 (1983): 50.
[Excerpt from a letter], as V.F. Salatko-Petrishche. *BSO* 2 (1984): 42.
[Excerpt from a letter], as V.F. Salatko-Petrishche. *BSO* 4 (1987): 34.
[Excerpt from a letter], as V.F. Salatko-Petrishche. *BSO* 5 (1988): 26.
[Excerpt from a letter], as V.F. Salatko-Petrishche. *BSO* 7 (1990): 38–9.
"Fernando Pessoa. *Lirika*. Moscow: Khudozhestvennaia literatura, 1978," *RLJ* 33, no. 114 (1979): 217–21.
"I eto obmanuvshee siian'e!" Typescript. Published in *TH*, where the source is listed as BPL 3261/40, f. 47, but it is not listed in the BPL catalogue. A typescript is also in Bakhmeteff Archive, Butler Library, Columbia University.
"I ne osparivai gluptsa." *Sovremennik* 39–40 (1978): 216–18.
"Igumen Varsonofii." Typescript. BPL 3261/40 [13]. Published in TH, 87–9.
"Iurii Ivask." *NZh* 163 (1986), 292–5.
"Iz pekinskikh vospominanii," as Vl. Nezhdanov. *RM*, 24 April 1969.
"'Kachel' ili tol'ko 'Kacheli.'" *NRS*, 10 February 1972.
"Kharbinskie literatory." *NRS*, 19 April 1970.
"Kitaiskaia poeziia." *NRS*, 26 May 1968.
"Konets Alekseia Achaira." *NRS*, 10 December 1972.

"Kotoroe-to pis'mo iz Brazilii," as V.F. Salatko-Petrishche. *BSO* 3 (1986): 13.
"Levan Khaindrava." *NRS*, 6 May 1973.
"Liudiam nuzhny i svechi i slezy." *Grani* 72 (1969): 224–6.
"Luchshe pozdno, chem nikogda," as V.F. Salatko-Petrishche. *DOD* 14 (1978): 23–4.
"M. Vizi. *Golubaia trava*." *NZh* 114 (1974): 248–9.
"Mnogoznachitel'nye nameki. Poeziia I. Chinnova." *NRS*, 15 March 1970.
"Novozavetnoe uchenie o stradanii," as Ieromonakh German. *KhN* 9 (1943): 8–13.
"Novyi God v Brazilii," as Sigma. *RM*, 25 January 1968.
"O iunykh poetakh" and "O nashikh poetakh," as Avrelii. *Rupor*, March 1932.
"O khristianskom vospitanii detei," as Inok German. *Kitaiskii blagovestnik* 9–10 (September–October 1939): [16–19].
"O metricheskoi inversii." *NRS*, 31 October 1971.
"Odno kitaiskoe stikhotvorenie." *NRS*, 19 October 1969.
"Orden vozrozhdeniia Azii." Typescript. BPL 3261/40 [20]. Bakhmeteff Archive, Butler Library, Columbia University. Published in TH, 71.
"Pamiati druga." *NRS*, 21 November 1978.
"Pamiati Khaurd Li Kheiga." *RM*, 13 May 1976. Reprinted in *DOD* 14 (1978): 20–1.
"Pamiati Mitropolita Viktora." *Novaia zaria*, 10.3.1967, and *Druz'iam i znakomym* 23 (March 1967).
"Pamiatnik Goratsiia." *Sovremennik* 33–4 (1977): 144–53.
"Papinu-Sibiriaku," as René. *Rupor*, 7 March 1929.
"Po priglasheniiu ot universiteta (i bez)." *BSO* 3 (1986): 15–17.
"Perelozhenie ostankov E.V. Kniazia Igoria Konstantinovicha v novyi grob." Dated 6.11.1942 and sent in letter To EAS.4.11.1942, for publication in a Harbin newspaper and signed Ieromonakh German; the name of the newspaper has not been found.
"Pis'mo iz Brazilii," as V.F. Salatko-Petrishche. *BSO* 18 (1983): 9–11.
"Pis'mo iz Brazilii," as V.F. Salatko-Petrishche. *BSO* 6 (1989): 22.
"Pis'mo v redaktsiiu. O trekh volkhvakh," as Vl. Kaiurin. *NRS*, 1 September 1969.
"Pis'mo v redaktsiiu." *RLJ* 90 (February 1971): 32–3.
"Pis'mo v redaktsiiu po povodu stat'i 'Derev'ia, kamni, slova.'" *NRS*, 10.3.1968.
"Pobol'she by takikh statei!" *NRS*, 9 July 1976.
"Pochtovaia marka i reklama," as V.F. Salatko-Petrishche. *NRS*, 23 March 1972.
"Poetessa Ol'ga Tel'toft." Typescript. BPL 3261/40 [6] and Bakhmeteff Archive, Butler Library, Columbia University. Published in TH, 87–9.

"Poezdka na Chol." Typescript. BPL 3261/40 [14]. Published in TH, 82–6.
"Prazdnik poezii." *NRS*, 3 May 1974.
"Predosennie dni." *NRS*, 7 September 1969.
"Redchaishie varianty chetyrekhstopnogo iamba." *NRS*, 30 May 1971.
Review of *Iuzhnyi krest. Literaturno-khudozhestvennyi sbornik gruppy russkikh pisatelei i zhurnalistov v Argentine*, unsigned. *Vestnik Brazilii* 4, 1 November 1953. BPL 3262/4 [4].
"Rio de Zhaneiro. Pervye vpechatleniia." *Vestnik Brazilii* 1, 11 October 1953, and 2, 18 October 1953. BPL 3262/4 [1], [2].
"Rozhdestvo v Pekinskoi missii," as Ieromonakh German. *Zaria*, 7.1.1942.
"Russkie khudozhniki v Brazilii." *RM*, 13 March 1969.
"Russkaia pravoslavnaia tserkov' v Brazilii," as Sigma. *RM*, 14 March 1968.
"Russkie na Dal'nem Vostoke," as V.F. Salatko-Petrishche. *NRS*, 15 March 1970.
"Russkie poety-perevodchiki na Dal'nem Vostoke." *RLJ* 87 (February 1970): 6–9.
"Russkie v Brazilii," as Sigma. *RM*, 8 February 1968.
"Russkii iazyk v Brazil'skoi Morskoi Akademii," as V.F. Salatko-Petrishche *DOD* 7 (1969): 9.
"Semidesiatiletie Kharbina," as V.F. Salatko-Petrishche. *NRS*, 14 February 1974.
"Smysl kul'turnoi revoliutsii v Kitae," as V.F. Salatko-Petrishche. *Vozrozhdenie* 189 (1967): 124–9.
"*Shakhmaty* – ne o shakhmatakh!" *RZh*, 6 August 1975.
"Sofiia Parnok. *Sbornik stikhotvorenii*." *RLJ* 119 (1980): 206–8.
"'Solov'inyi sad' Aleksandra Bloka." *Grani* 68 (1968): 132–6.
"Stikhi Kamilly Al'bertovny Khorvat," *NRS*, 15 October 1972.
"Stikhi o lotose." *NRS*, 2 July 1972.
"Stikhi na veere." *NRS*, 15 February 1970.
"Tserkovnaia zhizn' v Rio de Zhaneiro," unsigned. *Vestnik Brazilii* 3, 25 October 1953. BPL 3262/4 [3].
"Uchenie knigi Iova o stradanii," as Ieromonakh German. *KhN* 7 (1943): 9–12.
"Upadok formy v poezii." *NRS*, 5 October 1969.
"Valerii Pereleshin – brazil'skii poet," as V.S. *Druz'iam i znakomym* 180 (November 1983).
"Valerii Pereleshin v Gollandii." *DOD* 22 (May 1985): 43.
"Vtoroe pis'mo iz Brazilii," as V.F. Salatko-Petrishche. *BSO* 1 (1984): 7.
"Vystavka skul'ptury v Muzee iziashchnykh iskusstv v Rio de Zhaneiro," as VS. *Vestnik Brazilii* 1 (1953).
"Zabluzhdeniia Dostoevskogo," as Ieromonakh German. *KhN* 10 (1943): 21–4.
"Zagadochnoe chislo," as V.F. Salatko-Petrishche. *RM*, 29 February 1968.
"Zagrobnaia poeziia." *NRS*, 14 May 1978.

"Zaletnaia dusha." *Grani* 78 (1970): 241–7.
"Zalkind Piatigorskii." *NRS*, 18 April 1976.
"Zamechatel'nyi russkii khudozhnik." *NRS*, 17 April 1977.
"Zhizn' Rossiiskoi Dukhovnoi missii v Pekine," as Vl. Nezhdanov. *Zaria*, 26 January 1941.
"Zloupotreblenie pirrikhiem." *NRS*, 29 August 1971.
"Zritel'nyi element rifmy." *NRS*, 4 July 1971.

Unpublished Articles

"Arsenii Nesmelov (k dvadtsat' piatoi godovshchine gibeli poeta)." Typescript. Bancroft Library, University of California, Berkeley, and Bakhmeteff Archive, Butler Library, Columbia University.
"Drug moei materi." Typescript. Bakhmeteff Archive, Butler Library, Columbia University.
"Formal'naia kritika obraza." Typescript. BPL 3261/41 [2].
Handwritten notes. BPL 3261/36.
"Iapontsy v Kharbine." Typescript. Bakhmeteff Archive, Butler Library, Columbia University.
"Kharbin i Pomgol." Typescript. Bakhmeteff Archive, Butler Library, Columbia University.
"Laskovyi redaktor. Pamiati M.S. Rokotova (Bibinova)." Typescript. OB Collection.
"Moi posviashcheniia." Typescript. Bakhmeteff Archive, Butler Library, Columbia University.
"O literaturnoi studii. Vmesto otcheta." Typescript. BPL 3261/6.
"Otpoved' piati." Typescript. OB Collection.
"Petr Ivanovich Krechetov." Typescript. Bakhmeteff Archive, Butler Library, Columbia University.
"Poeziia i stikhi." Typescript, early 1970s. BPL 3261/41 [11] and Aleksis Rannit Papers, Beinecke Rare Books and Manuscript Library, Yale University.
"Russkaia poeziia v Kitae. Opyt bibliografii." Typescript, 1.12.1968. OB Collection.
"Russkaia rifma." Typescript, ca. 1974. BPL 3261/41 [1].
"Staraia orfografiia na Dal'nem Vostoke." Typescript. Bakhmeteff Archive, Butler Library, Columbia University.
Untitled article on Antonin Ladinskii and his poem "Kairskii sapozhnik." Iurii Ivask Papers. Amherst Center for Russian Culture.
Untitled typescript of a rebuttal to P. Aleksandrov's review of *Dvoe i snova odin?* BPL 3261/41 [6].

VI. Autobiographical and Biographical Materials

Autobiographical Writings by Valerii Pereleshin

O.S. [VP]. "Poet Valerii Pereleshin." *Druz'iam i znakomym* 47 (March 1969). OB Collection.

VP. "Biograficheskie svedeniia." Typescript, with handwritten comments, ca. 1977. OB Collection.

VP. "Kak ia 'nachinalsia.'" Typescript. BPL 3261/40 [3] and OB Collection.

VP. "O rode Salatko-Petrishche." Typescript. OB Collection.

VP. "Priamye i bokovye predki Valeriia Pereleshina. S kotomkoi i posokhom." Typescript. BPL 3261/40 [2] and Bakhmeteff Archive, Butler Library, Columbia University.

VP. "V chem ne priniato priznavat'sia." Typescript. 16 August 1988. BPL 3261/40 [4] and OB Collection.

VP. "Valerii Pereleshin." Manuscript of a short unfinished biography ca. 1970s. BPL 3261/36.

VP. "Valerii Pereleshin." Typescript. 1970s. OB Collection.

VP. "Valerii Pereleshin." Typescript. Iurii Ivask Papers. Amherst Center for Russian Culture. Amherst, MA.

VP. "Valerii Pereleshin v Gollandii i vo Frantsii." Manuscript. OB Collection.

VP. "Valerii Salatko-Petrishche." Typescript. 21 June 1981.Written for *DOD*, but not published. OB Collection.

Biographical Materials

Archive of Shanghai Tuesday Circle. OB Collection.

Ata de transferência parcial de herança literária, 8 January 1993 (an official document written after VP's death and signed by A. Kirilloff, Victor Salatko, and Soviet Consul A. Jebit on transferring his remaining archive to Moscow). Rio de Janeiro. OB Collection.

"Attestat" [Certificate] of Erazm Ioann Kazimir Frantsevich Salatko-Petrishche. Photocopy. OB Collection.

Certidão de óbito, 11 October 1980. Estado do Rio de Janeiro. (Death certificate of E.A. Sentianina). OB Collection.

Certidão de óbito, 9 novembro 1992. Cartório do registro civil da segunda zona judiciária, Estado do Rio de Janeiro (Death certificate of V.F. Salatko-Petrishche). OB Collection.

Diploma of Viktor Frantsevich Salatko from Electromechanical Faculty of Harbin Polytechnic, 27 December 1937. OB Collection.

Drawing of the coat of arms of the Salatko-Petrishche family. BPL 3265/14 [11].
E.A. Sentianina at a fancy dress ball. Photograph in "E.A. Sentianina in Manchuria and China." BPL 3266/8.
E.F. Salatko-Petrishche. Death notice. *KhV*, 4 March 1938.
F.E. Salatko-Petrishche. Registration form and "Avtobiograficheskie svedeniia, 8 June 1935." Bureau for the Affairs of Russian Émigrés in Manchukuo. Photocopy. OB Collection.
F.E. Salatko-Petrishche. Registration form, January 1936. Bureau for the Affairs of Russian Émigrés in Manchukuo. Photocopy. OB Collection.
V.F. Salatko-Petrishche (Valerii Frantsevich). Registration form and "Kratkaia biografiia," ca. 1935. Bureau for the Affairs of Russian Émigrés in Manchukuo. Photocopy. OB Collection.
V.F. Salatko-Petrishche (Viktor Frantsevich). Registration form, 8 September 1939. Assessment by Gryzov and by anonymous informer "x-275" on his character and political views. Bureau for the Affairs of Russian Émigrés in Manchukuo. Photocopy. OB Collection.
"Elizaveta Adal'bertovna Salatko-Petrishche." Photograph and comment. BPL 3266/12.
High School Diploma of V.F. Salatko-Petrishche. Harbin Young Men's Christian Association. 18 June 1930. OB Collection.
Family correspondence and comment. BPL 3267/17.
"Fourth International Poetry Festival at the University of Texas, Austin, April 11, 12, 13, 1974." Program, "Some Notes on the Poets" and "A Minimal Anthology: Poems by Poets visiting UT, Austin, April 11–13, 1974." OB Collection.
Kostiuchik, I.I. "Otvet dotsenta Bogoslovskogo fakul'teta Instituta Sv. Vladimira v Kharbine I.I. Kostiuchika na 'Otzyv o rabote ieromonakha Germana na temu 'Filosofiia stradaniia,' sostavlennyi professorom K.I. Zaitsevym 12 dekabria 1943 g.'" Typescript. OB Collection.
"Kul'turnyi prazdnik emigratsii." *Foto-novosti* 154, 1 April 1942. Includes a photograph of VP accepting the award for the best poem at the Second East Asian Competition of Poets and Writers. OB Collection.
Legal documents concerning the loan taken by E.A. Sentianina. OB Collection.
Marriage certificate of E.A. Sentianina and V.E. Sentianin. Harbin, 1922. OB Collection.
Materials on International Festival of Poetry, Rotterdam, 17–24 June 1989. OB Collection.
"Otryvok iz vospominanii o Turgeneve." Comment on a typescript. Bakhmeteff Archive, Butler Library, Columbia University.

Papers related to emigration procedures. BPL 3267/2.
Passport of E.A. Sentianina. BPL 3267/5.
Passport of Erazm Frantsevich Salatko-Petrishche. BPL 3267/6.
Programma peredach Radio Vaticana na russkom iazyke za mesiats noiabr' 1980. BPL 3264/18 [14].
Sentianina, E.A. Diary. BPL 2367/8.
Sentianina, E.A. "Po iuznym moriam v Braziliiu." Typescript with Pereleshin's introduction. BPL 3261/49, and Hoover Institution on War, Revolution, and Peace, Stanford University.
Sentianina, E.A. "S nasizhennykh mest." Typescript. Includes her biography written by Pereleshin. Hoover Institution on War, Revolution, and Peace, Stanford University.
School certificates of E.A. Sentianina. BPL 3267/12.
School report of V. Salatko-Petrishche. BPL 3267/1.
Various papers from Russia and China. BPL 3267/15 [3].
V.E. Sentianin. "Udostoverenie." 11 November 1927. Hoover Institution on War, Revolution, and Peace, Stanford University.
Visiting card of "Valerii Aleksandrovich Pereleshin." P.V. Shkurkin Far East Archive.

VII. Materials on Immigration to the United States and Deportation, 1950 and 1967–1968

Application for Immigration to the United States from Brazil and letter from V.F. Salatko-Petrishche, 30 July 1967.
Application for alien employment certification, ca. 1968.
Biographical statement. Typescript, ca. 1968.
Letter from from Maria J. von Krusenstern-Peterets to the Secretary of State. Signed and notarized in Washington, DC, 11 October 1968.
Statement by V.F. Salatko-Petrishche to the US State Department Immigration Office. Secured with a red ribbon and a seal, sworn and signed by Salatko-Petrishche and US Vice-Consul in Rio de Janeiro, Richard M. Bash, 29 October 1968.
US Department of Homeland Security, US Citizenship and Immigration Services, United States Department of Justice, Immigration and Naturalization Service. Files on V.F. Salatko-Petryshche released under the Freedom of Information Act in 2006–2008.
V.F. Salatko-Petryshche. Curriculum vitae. 1968.
All of the above are in OB Collection.

VIII. Letters

Letters from Valerii Pereleshin

To Bakich, M.A. 1968. OB Collection.

To OB [Bakich, O.] 1986–91. Includes many inserts and materials. OB Collection.

To Bakich, V.V. 1967. OB Collection.

To Balakshin, P.P. 1974–6. Bancroft Archive, University of California, Berkeley.

To Chernishev, A.A. 1971. OB Collection.

To Chernishev, T.L. 1982. OB Collection.

To Chinnov, I. 1980–7. In *Pis'ma zapreshchennykh liudei. Literatura i zhizn' emigratsii 1950–1980-e gody. Po materialam arkhiva I.V. Chinnova*. Moscow: IMLI RAN, 2003.

To Davies, R. 1986–8. Brotherton Collection, Special Collections, Leeds University Library.

To Drizul', I. 1980–90. BPL 3257 (4) and 1988, OB Collection.

To Fouchier (Mokrinskaia), N. 1967–90. OB Collection.

To Franz Erazmovich Salatko-Petrishche. BPL 3257 [14].

To Genkel', E.A. BPL 3257 [5].

To Gincenberg, A. 1950–77. BPL 3257 [6].

To Gur'ev, Father. 23 April 1945. Draft in BPL 3261/15 [6].

To Hinrichs, J.P. 1979–90. J.P. Hinrichs Collection.

To Iastrebov, M. and L. 1987, 1989. OB Collection. One letter to M. Iastrebov is published in *DOD* 23 (December 1985).

To Ivask, Iu. 1967–85. Iurii Ivask Papers. Amherst Center for Russian Culture, Amherst, MA.

To Karlinsky, S. 1987–90. Simon Karlinsky Collection.

To Karpovich, M.K. and response from *NZh*, 1955. *NZh* Archive. Amherst Center for Russian Culture, Amherst, MA.

To Khaindrova, L. 1931–41. BPL 3257; BPL 3261/2; and Bakhmeteff Archive, Butler Library, Columbia University. Excerpts from some letters not held in the above archives are partly quoted in L. Dzemeshkevich, *Don Kikhot kharbinskii*. 232–68. Omsk: s.n., 2001.

To Kirilloff, A.B. 30 January 1990. Photocopy. OB Collection.

To Koloshin, V.V. 1946–9. BPL 3257 [8].

To Krouk, N. 1966–90. BPL 3257 [9] and OB Collection.

To Kruzenshtern-Peterets, Iu.V. 1967–83. OB Collection.

To Ktorova, A. 1972–3, 1975. In Alla Ktorova, "Tri pis'ma Valeriia Pereleshina." *NZh* 216 (1999): 147–54; 219 (2000): 181–2.

To Lapiken, P.P. 1971–9. P.V. Shkurkin Far East Archive. Correspondence includes a typewritten copy of a draft of *Ariel'* with Lapiken's handwritten comments. Partially published in Olga Bakich, "Valerii Pereleshin. Pis'ma k P.P. Lapikenu." *NZh* 233 (2003): 63–98; 234 (2004): 168–208.

To Leiden University Library and invoice, 6 April 1984.

To Leonard (Leont'ev), V.A. 1952–76. OB Collection.

To Mel'nikova, M.M. 1988–9. OB Collection.

To Panin, G.G. 1970–4. Gennadii Panin Papers. Beinecke Rare Books and Manuscript Library, Yale University.

To Rannit, A. 1971–80. Aleksis Rannit Papers. Beinecke Rare Books and Manuscript Library, Yale University.

To Salatko, V. and L. 1989–1900. OB Collection.

To Salatko-Petrishche, F.E. 1920. BPL 3257 [14].

To Sentianina, E.A. 1936–49, 1958, 1960–76. BPL 3258; BPL 3261/1; letter ca. 1925. Hoover Institution on War, Revolution, and Peace, Stanford University.

To Shakhovskoi, Ioann, of San Francisco 1968, 1972–4. Amherst Center for Russian Culture, Amherst, MA. Partially published in E.A. Gollerbakh, "K istorii russkoi zarubezhnoi literatury. Materialy iz arkhiva arkhiepiskopa Ioanna San-Frantsisskogo (D.A. Shakhovskogo)." *Ezhekvartal'nik russkoi filologii i kul'tury* (St Petersburg) 2/2 (1996): 295–320.

To Sinkevich, V.A. 1981–90. OB Collection.

To Slobodchikov, V.A. 1967–89. Photocopies. OB Collection.

To Struve, G.P. 1967–85. Hoover Institution on War, Revolution, and Peace, Stanford University.

To Struve, M.S. 1985–9. OB Collection.

To Tikos, L. 1976. Iurii Ivask Archive, Amherst Center for Russian Culture. Amherst, MA.

To Veidle [Weidle], V.V. 1973–4, 1979. Bakhmeteff Archive, Butler Library, Columbia University.

To Vezey, M. 1967–9. OB Collection.

To Vitkovskii, E.V. 1971. As retyped by Vladislav Rezvyi.

To Volkoff, G. 1944, 1971–91. BPL 3462.

To Yellman, D.J. 4.4.1974. Kept in the file Anschuetz, C., BPL 3256 [7].

Letters to Valerii Pereleshin

From Avtonomov, N.P. 1968. Bakhmeteff Archive, Butler Library, Columbia University.

From Balakshin, P.P. 1974–6. Bancroft Library, University of California, Berkeley.

From Genkel', E.A. to Salatko-Petrishche family. BPL 3256 [57].

From Gincenberg, A. 1944–59, Bakhmeteff Archive, Butler Library, Columbia University; and 1944–81, BPL 3256 [60]
From De Groot, J.R., Librarian, Biliotheek der Rijksuniversitet te Leiden. 8 December 1983. Leiden University Library.
From Ivask, Iu. A few letters in Iurii Ivask Papers, Amherst Center for Russian Culture, Amherst, MA.
From Krouk, N. 1990. OB Collection.
From Korostovets, M.P. 1968–72. Bakhmeteff Archive, Butler Library, Columbia University.
From Kruzenshtern-Peterets, Iu.V. 1967–82. BPL 3256 [91].
From Ladinskii, A. 1935. BPL 3256 [94].
From Lapiken, P.P. 1970–9, and comment. BPL 3256 [95],
From Linmans, A.J.M. Deputy Librarian of Leiden University Library, 13 January 1984. Leiden University Library.
From Mozhaiskaia, O.N. [Emel'ianova]. 1968–73. Bakhmeteff Archive, Butler Library, Columbia University.
From Naam, A.M. 1953–69. Includes VP's comments. BPL 3256 [119].
From Naam, E.Z. 1950. Includes VP's comments. BPL 3256 [120]
From Rokotov (Bibinov), M.S. 1967–82. Retyped with commentary by VP. OB Collection.
From Tang Dongtian 1950–5. BPL 3256 [192].
Unsigned carbon copy of a letter from *Novyi zhurnal* to VP. 9 July 1955. *NZh* Archive. Amherst Center for Russian Culture, Amherst, MA.
From Vitkovskii, E.V. 1970–80. BPL 3256 [210]. A few letters are in Iurii Ivask Papers, Amherst Center for Russian Culture, Amherst, MA. Two more letters, one as "Iz pis'ma Evgeniia Vitkovskogo or 29 avgusta 1988 g.," retyped by VP, and another of 2 October 1988 are in OB Collection.
From Xing Cai. 1952. BPL 3256 [192].

Correspondence between Other People Relevant to Pereleshin

Andersen, L. to Nora Krouk. 1965, 1977, 1983, 1997. OB Collection.
Andersen, L. to Iu.V. Kruzenshtern-Peterets. 1957, 1958, 1968, 1972, 1977. OB Collection.
Ardis Publishers to OB. 18 May 1988. OB Collection.
Bakich, V.V., to OB. 1998–2002. OB Collection.
Balakshin, P.P., to L. Khaindrova. 1974–7. Bancroft Library, University of California, Berkeley.
Balakshin, P.P., to E.A. Sentianina. 1976–7. Bancroft Library, University of California, Berkeley.

Carrol, N., to OB. 2007. Letters and email and notes taken during an interview in autumn. OB Collection.

Dirkx, J.C.B., to Van Gent, Librarian of Leiden University Library. 14 May 1985. Leiden University Library.

Dobrinina, M., to OB. 2006. Email and letters. OB Collection.

Geary, A., to OB. 2007. Telephone interviews; letter of 30 October. OB Collection.

Gent, J.J.M., to A.B. Kirilloff. 4 March 1993. OB Collection.

Groen, H. (Hannie Schram-Hekkert), to OB. 2004. Emails and letters. OB Collection.

Hinrichs, J.P., to OB. 2003–2013. Emails. OB Collection.

Hinrichs, J.P., to A.B. Kirilloff. 26 November 1992. OB Collection.

Hinrichs, J.P., to Victor Salatko. 24 June 1993. OB Collection.

Iankovskaia, V., to V.A. Slobodchikov. 3 November 1993. OB Collection.

Ivask, Iu., to the Kulaev Fund. 1976. Iurii Ivask Papers. Amherst Center for Russian Culture, Amherst, MA.

Ivask, Iu., to Andrei Sedykh. Iurii Ivask Papers. Amherst Center for Russian Culture, Amherst, Mass.

Ivask, Iu., to Professor William Edgerton. Iurii Ivask Papers. Amherst Center for Russian Culture, Amherst, Mass.

Jebit [Zhebit], A., to OB. 2004. OB Collection.

Khaindrova, L., to P.P. Balakshin, 1937–9, 1974–8. Bancroft Library, University of California, Berkeley.

Khionin, A.P., to P.V. Shkurkin, 14 December 1930. P.V. Shkurkin Far East Archive.

Kirilloff, A.B., to OB, 2002–9. OB Collection.

Kirilloff, A.B., to J.P. Hinrichs. 1992–3. OB Collection.

Kirilloff, A.B., to A. Jebit [Zhebit]. 3 October 1995. OB Collection.

Kirilloff, A.B., to Lidia Salatko. 30 October 1992. OB Collection.

Ktorova, Alla, to OB. 24 March 2004. Includes notes taken during telephone conversations in March and July. OB Collection.

Kulaev, V.I., to Iurii Ivask. 1976. Iurii Ivask Papers. Amherst Center for Russian Culture, Amherst, MA.

Leonard (Leont'ev), V.A., to OB. 2002–6. Includes notes taken during interviews in 2002, 2003, and 2005. OB Collection.

Leyland, Winston, to OB. 2003–7. Emails and interviews. OB Collection.

Lopez, Venusto Casto Francisco, to OB. 2006–8. OB Collection.

Marques Passos, Humberto, to A. Rannit. 30 September 1979. Aleksis Rannit Papers. Beinecke Rare Books and Manuscript Library, Yale University.

Mikhaillov, Z., to OB. 2005. OB Collection.

Mouhanoff, M.V., to OB. 2005. OB Collection.

Pasynkov, I.P., to OB. 2004. OB Collection.

Popova, Zinaida, to OB. 2003. OB Collection.
Rannit, A., to Humberto Marques Passos, 24 August 1979. Aleksis Rannit Papers. Beinecke Rare Books and Manuscript Library, Yale University, and BPL 3256 [140].
Rezvyi, Vladislav, to OB. Email. 2006. OB Collection.
Rokotov (Bibinov), M.S., to Iu.V. Kruzenshtern-Peterets. 1975. OB Collection.
Salatko, Victor , to editors. *BSO* 11 (1994): 38; 17 (2000): 37.
Salatko, Victor, to OB. 2004–5. OB Collection.
Salatko, Victor, to N. Gracheva-Mel'nikova. Ca. late 1970s. OB Collection.
Salatko, Victor , to A.A. Jebit [Zhebit]. 16 August 1988. OB Collection.
Salatko, Victor to A.B. Kirilloff, 9 January and 25 January 1993. OB Collection.
Salatko-Petrishche, Maria Petrovna. Letters: BPL 3257/15, BPL 3259/15. Photographs: BPL 3266/7 [4], BPL 3266/13.
Sentianin, V.E., to E.A. Sentianina. Ca. 1922. Sentianin Family File. Hoover Institution on War, Revolution, and Peace, Stanford University. 1925. BPL 3259 [16], BPL 3259 [17].
Sentianina, E.A., to P.P. Balakshin. 1976. Bancroft Library, University of California, Berkeley.
Sentianina, E.A., to Iu.V. Kruzenshtern-Peterets. 1967. OB Collection.
Sentianina, E.A., to B.I. Iukhnovich. 1957–8. OB Collection.
Sentianina, E.A., to Lidia Salatko. 1951. OB Collection.
Sentianina, E.A., to Iu.K. Terapiano. 1973–6. Hoover Institution on War, Revolution, and Peace, Stanford University.
Shmidt, O., to OB. 2006. OB Collection.
Slobodchikov, V.A., to OB. 2001–6. OB Collection.
Vitkovskii, E., to OB. 2006. Email. OB Collection.
Volin, M., to L. and M. Iastrebov. 30 November 1988. OB Collection.
Volkoff, G.M., to OB. 1989–91. OB Collection.

IX. Secondary Sources

"A lingua portuguesa nos versos de um poeta russo." *O Estado de São Paulo*, 23 September 1983.
Achair, Aleksei. "Nash kruzhok." *Churaevka*, Harbin, 3/9 (28 March 1933).
Achair, Aleksei. "Pered nachalom." *Churaevka*, Harbin, 4/10 (November 1933).
Achair, Aleksei. *Pervaia*. Harbin: Meditat, 1925.
Achair, Aleksei. "Tvorcheskaia molodezh'." *Molodaia Churaevka*, Harbin, 3 (18 July 1932).
Adamovich, G. "Literaturnye zametki." *Poslednie novosti*. Paris, 24 February 1938. Quoted in VP, "A chto obo mne pisali polveka tomu nazad."

Adamovich, G. Review. *Poslednie novosti*. Paris, April 1934. Quoted in *Dva polustanka*, 64.

Adamovich, G. "Vpechatleniia i nedoumeniia." *NRS*, 24 August 1969.

Aleksandrov, P. "*Dvoe – i shova odin*?" Typeset text, allegedly from *Edinenie*, Sydney, with a handwritten notation at the bottom: 'Petr Vas. Aleksandrov. Melbourne." BPL 3264/23.

Anastigmat [Arsenii Nesmelov]. "O churaevskikh lirikakh. Po stranitsam gazety Churaevki." *Rupor*, Harbin, 1934. Quoted in VP, "A chto obo mne pisali polveka tomu nazad."

Andersen, Larissa. *Po zemnym lugam*. Shanghai: Sovremennaia zhenshchina, 1940.

Andersen, Larissa. *Odna na mostu*. Moscow: Russkii put', 2006.

Archive of the Tuesday Circle, Shanghai. OB Collection.

Avtonomov, N.P. "Khristianskii soiuz molodykh liudei." *KhKU*, San Francisco, 9 (1969): 43–8.

Bakich, Olga. "Russian Education in Harbin, 1898–1962." *Transactions of the Association of Russian-American Scholars in the USA* 26 (1994): 269–94.

Bakich, Olga. "Het vierde vaderland van Valeri Peresjin." In *Bronnen van kennis. Wetenschap, kunst en cultuur in de collecties van de Leidse Universiteitsbibliotheek*. 249–54. Ed. Paul Hoftijzer, Kasper van Ommen, Geert Warnar, Jan Just Witkam. Leiden: Scaliger Instituut, Universiteit Leiden, 2006.

Bakich, Olga. "Ostrov sredi bushuiushchego moria." *NZh* 239 (2005): 174–215.

Bakich, Olga. "Segodniashnii vzgliad na *Segodnia*." *NZh* 237 (2004): 174–200.

Bakich, Olga. "Venok na mogilu poeta (Valerii Pereleshin: 1913–1992)." *Transactions of the Association of Russian-American Scholars in the USA* 26 (1994): 414–18.

Balakshin, P. "Emigratsiia i vetka sireni." An article inserted in the second volume of *Final v Kitae*.

Balakshin, P. *Final v Kitae. Vozniknovenie, razvitie i ischeznovenie Beloi Emigratsii na Dal'nem Vostoke*. 2 vols. San-Francisco: Sirius, 1958–9.

Balakshin, P. "*S gory Nevo*. Vos'maia kniga stikhotvorenii Valeriia Pereleshina." *RZh*, 9 May 1975.

Barber, Noel. *The Fall of Shanghai. The Communist Take-Over in 1949*. London: Macmillan, 1979.

Beaudoin, Luc. "Reflections in the Mirror: Iconographic Homoeroticism in Russian Silver Age Poetics." *Rereading Russian Poetry*. 161–82. Ed. S. Sandler. New Haven: Yale University Press, 1999.

Bei-guan'. Kratkaia istoriia Rossiiskoi dukhovnoi missii v Kitae. Moscow/St Petersburg: Al'ians-Arkheo, 2006.

Berberova, N. *Chaikovskii*. Berlin: Petropolis, 1936.

"Beseda s Eduardom Limonovym." *Sovremennik*, 45–6 (1980): 151–9.
B.G. "Zarubezhnaia zhizn'. Pamiati poeta Valeriia Pereleshina." *Nasha strana*. Buenos Aires, 10 April 1993.
Brazil. New York: Knopf Guide, ca. 2005.
Buzuev, O.A. *Tvorchestvo Valeriia Pereleshina*. Komsomol'sk-na-Amure, 2003.
Carey, Arch. *The War Years in Shanghai*. New York: Vantage Press, 1967.
Chinnov, Igor'. *Kompozitsiia*. Paris: Rifma, 1972.
Chernetsky, Vitaly. "Displacement, Desire, Identity and the 'Diasporic Momentum': Two Slavic Writers in Latin America." *Intertexts* 7/ 1 (2003): 49–69.
Chinese texts of *Stikhi na veere*. BPL 3256/1/
Chinnov, Igor'. *Sobranie sochinenii v dvukh tomakh*. Moscow: Soglasie, 2002.
Coote, Stephen, ed. *The Penguin Book of Homosexual Verse*. London: Allen Lane, 1983.
"De doelen Rotterdam 17-19 t/m 24 Juni. Dichters uit de hele wereld nieuwe Russische poëzie. Valeri Perelesjin, Brazilië." Vertaling: Jan Paul Hinrichs, 1989.
"Deportatsiia iz predelov Man'chzhu-di-go." *Luch Azii*, Harbin, 12 (1935): 44.
Dmitriev, Viktor. "Smutnye vospominaniia Ledy." *NZh* 183 (1991): 128–49.
Dubaev, M.L. *Kharbinskaia taina Rerikha*. Moscow: Sfera, 2001.
"Dvoinoe samoubiistvo v gostinitse 'Nankin.'" *Russkoe slovo*, Harbin, 6 December 1934.
Emel'ianova, O. [O. Mozhaiskaia]. "*Stikhi na veere*." *Grani* 79 (1971): 245–7.
Evdokimov, Valentin. "'Chertrovy kacheli' i sed'moe nebo (Zhizn' i tvorchestvo Valeriia Pereleshina)." *Le Messager. Vestnik russkogo khristianskogo dvizheniia*, Paris 139 (1983): 173–93.
[Evening of Russian Culture]. *Rupor*, Harbin, 4 June 1934.
Ezhedel'nyi biulleten' Novye knigi SSSR, no. 25, 1990. BPL 3264/20 [6].
[Farewell Address to N.P. Avtonomov]. *KhKU*, 2 (1956).
Fotiev, K. "O poezii Valeriia Pereleshina." *NRS*, 22 April 1973.
Fu, Poshek. "Projecting Ambivalence. Chinese Cinema in Semi-Occupied Shanghai." In *Wartime Shanghai*. 86–109. Ed. Wen-hsin Yeh. London: Routledge, 1998.
Geliotropov, Oleg. "*Stikhi na veere*." *RM*, 21 January 1971.
Gorbov, Ia.N. "Valerii Pereleshin. *Zhertva*." *Vozrozhdenie* 191 (1967): 144–9.
Gorbov, Ia.N. "Literaturnye zametki (Valerii Pereleshin, "*Iuzhnyi dom*" – Sergei Lenskii, "Na chuzhbine" – "Russkii invalid," no. 161)." *Vozrozhdenie* 201 (1968): 139–43.
Granin, Georgii. "Bol'shie korabli." *Churaevka*, Harbin, 5 (30 July 1932).

Gryzov, Aleksei (Aleksei Achair). "Bog, rodina i chestnost'." *Churaevka,* Harbin, 10/4 (14 November 1933).

Gumilevskii sbornik. Harbin, 1937.

Gur'ev, V. "Bogoslovskii Fakul'tet Instituta Sv. Vladimira." *KhN,* Harbin, 11 (1939): 55–6.

Haerbin gongye daxue. Tongxuelu, 1920–1944. Harbin: n.p.

Hinrichs, Jan Paul. *Dichter met drie vaderlanden. Valerij Perelešin, brieven en documenten.* Leiden: Universiteitsbibliotheek, 1986.

Hinrichs, Jan Paul. "Valerij Perelešin's Poetry from his Chinese Years." In *Russkii poet v gostiakh u Kitaia, 1920–1952.* The Hague: Leuxenhoff Publishing, 1989, xxi–xxxv.

Hinrichs, Jan Paul. *Valerij Perelešin (1813–1992). Catalogue of His Papers and Books in Leiden University Library.* Leiden: Leiden University Library, 1997.

Hinrichs, Jan Paul. *Vanuit de verte: Gedichten.* Leiden: Stichting de Lantaarn, 1985.

Hinrichs, Jan Paul. *Verbannte muse. Vijftien essays over schrijvers van de Russische emigratie.* Leiden: Slavische Stichting, 1990.

Hinrichs, Jan Paul. *Verbannte muse. Zehn Essays über russische Lyriker der Emigration.*Munich: Otto Sagner, 1992.

Iablonskaia-Zakhova, Alina. "Vospominaniia o poete Valerii Pereleshine." *Na sopkakh Man'chzhurii* 37 (November 1996). Also interview with Alina Iablonskaia-Zakhova in Prague in 1995.

Iakor'. Paris, 1936.

Ipatova, A.S. "Prazdnovanie 250-letiia Rossiiskoi dukhovnoi missii v Kitae (1935 g.)." In *Pravoslavie na Dal'nem Vostoke.* 74–84. St Petersburg: Andreev i synov'ia, 1993.

Ipatova, A.S. "Rossiiskaia dukhovnaia missiia v Kitae: vek dvadtsatyi." In *Istoriia Rossiiskoi dukhovnoi missii v Kitae. Sbornik statei.* 281–317. Moscow: Izdatel'stvo Sviato-Vladimirskogo bratstva, 1997.

Iu.T. [Iu. Terapiano?]. "*Churaevka,* literaturnaia gazeta, nomera 3-4-6-7-8." *Chisla* 10 (1934): 233–46.

Iul'skii, Boris. "Zvezda nad morem." *Luch Azii* 89, no. 1 (1941). Quoted in VP, "A chto obo mne pisali polveka tomu nazad."

Ivask, Iurii. *Konstantin Leont'ev. Zhizn' i tvorchestvo.* Bern: P. Lang, 1974.

Ivask, Iurii. *Igraiushchii chelovek. Homo ludens.* Paris, New York: Tret'ia volna, 1988. The early version was published in *Vozrozhdenie* 240 (January-February 1973): 7–36; 241 (May 1973): 7–14; 242 (August 1973): 7–19.

Ivask, Iurii. "O pisaniiakh Valeriia Pereleshina." *NRS,* 24 May 1970.

Ivask, Iurii. "Ob avtore," *Ariel',* 3–7.

Ivask, Iurii. "Tsiui Iuan', *Li Sao.*" *NZh* 121 (1975): 297–8.

Ivask, Iurii. "Valerii Pereleshin." In *Handbook of Russian Literature*. Ed. Victor Terras. New Haven: Yale University Press, 1985.

Ivask, Iurii. "Valerii Pereleshin. *Iuzhnyi krest*. Antologiia brazil'skoi poezii." *RLJ* 32/113 (1978): 232–4.

Ivask, Iurii. "Valerii Pereleshin. *S gory Nevo. Vos'maia kniga stikhotvorenii.*" *NZh* 121 (1975): 298–300.

Ivask, Iurii. "Valerii Pereleshin." Typescript, 1975. Iurii Ivask Papers. Amherst Center for Russian Culture, Amherst, MA.

Ivask, Iurii. "Valerii Pereleshin o poezii." *NRS*, 27 July 1975.

Ivask, Iurii. "*Zapovednik* Valeriia Pereleshina." *NRS*, 18 March 1973.

"Iz redaktorskoi pochty. Georgii Ivanov." *RM*, 22 June 1978.

Izluchiny. Harbin: izd. M.N. Volodchenko, 1935.

Johnston, Tess, and Deke Erh. *God and Country. Western Religious Architecture in Old China*. Hong Kong: Old China Hand Press, 1996.

"K literaturnoi obshchestvennosti." *Sovremennik* 45–46 (1980): 283.

Kablukov, L. "Literaturnye mertvetsy." *Natsiia* 6 (June 1935).

"Kak sozdavalas' Gimnaziia KhSML." *Kharbinskii soiuz molodykh liudei* 2/14 (1928): 16–17.

Karlinskii, S. "Pis'mo v redaktsiiu. V zashchitu gomoseksualizma." *NRS*, 1 December 1976.

Karlinskii, S. "Pis'mo v redaktsiiu. Napraslina na Esenina." *NRS*, 30 September 1976.

Karlinskii, S. "*Iuzhnyi dom* Valeriia Pereleshina." *NRS*, 9 February 1969.

Karlinsky, Simon. "Esenin." *New York Times Book Review*, 9 May 1976.

Karlinsky, Simon. "A Hidden Masterpiece: Valerii Pereleshin's *Ariel*." *Christopher Street* 2, no. 6 (December 1977): 37–42.

Karlinsky, Simon. "Memoirs of Harbin." *Slavic Review* 48, no. 2 (1989): 284–90.

Kazak, Wolfgang. *Entsiklopedicheskii slovar' russkoi literatury s 1917 goda*. Trans. from German by Elena Wargaftik and Igor' Burikhin. London: Overseas Publications Interchange, 1988.

Khaindrova, Lidiia. "Kak sozdavalas' Piatnitsa." Typescript. OB Collection.

Khaindrova, Lidiia. *Stupeni. Stikhi, 1931–1939*. Harbin: Zaria, 1939.

"Khronika," *KhN* 6 (June 1943): 43–4.

"Khronikal'naia zametka." *Sovremennik* 37–38 (1978): 236.

Kirilloff [Kirillov], A.B. "In Memoriam – Valerii Pereleshin – Ieromonakh German." Typescript. OB Collection.

Kirilloff [Kirillov], A. "Kitaiskaia avtonomnaia pravoslavnaia tserkov'." *Russkie v Kitae* 25 (2001).

Kirilloff [Kirillov], Aleksandr. "In Memoriam. Valerii Pereleshin – Ieromonakh German." *Druz'iam i znakomym* 201 (May 1993).

Kirilloff [Kirillov], Aleksandr. "Pamiati Valeriia Pereleshina, ieromonakha Germana." *Edinenie*, Sydney, 25 June 1993.

Kirilloff [Kirillov], Aleksandr. "Valerii Pereleshin: Ieromonakh German." *RZh*, 25 February 1993.

"Knizhnaia polka." *RZh*, 7 August 1970.

"Kitaiskaia Vostochnaia zheleznaia doroga. Prikaz no. 53." *KhKU* 2 (1956): 49.

Koreneva, O. "Nasha zhizn' v Sidnee." *BSO*, 9 (1992): 3.

Koretskii, A.P. "Epopeia russkogo emigranta (bez geroiki)." *Rossiiane v Azii*, Toronto, 3 (1996): 111–68.

Kostolomov, M. Letter to the editor. *Ogonek* 44 (1987).

"Kratkie biograficheskie svedeniia ob o. Arkhimandrite Iuvenalii." *KhN* 2 (1935): 20–2.

"Kriticheskie tseli *Segodnia*." *Segodnia* 34, 1 October 1943, 2–4.

Krouk, Nora. "Nam ulybalas' Kvan-in'. Litsa skvoz' vremia." *Rossiiane v Azii*, Toronto, 7 (2000): 151–97.

Kruzenshtern-Peterets, Iu. "Artist otoshel tantsuia." *NRS*, 4 October 1970.

Kruzenshtern-Peterets, Iu. "Churaevskii pitomnik (O dal'nevostochnykh poetakh)." *Vozrozhdenie* 204 (December 1986): 45–70.

Kruzenshtern-Peterets, Iu. "*Iuzhnyi krest*." *RZh*, 27 April 1978.

Kruzenshtern-Peterets, Iu. "Mistika poezii." *NRS*, 9 September 1973.

Kruzenshtern-Peterets, Iu. "O predvziatosti." *NRS*, 7 September 1969.

Kruzenshtern-Peterets, Iu. "Otkrytoe pis'mo Natalii Il'inoi." *RZh*, 12 October 1957.

Kruzenshtern-Peterets, Iu. "Pis'mo v gazetu." *RM*, 3 October 1968.

Kruzenshtern-Peterets, Iu. "Pis'mo v redaktsiiu. Ne travlia, a polemika." *NRS*, 24 November 1969.

Kruzenshtern-Peterets, Iu.V. "Vospominaniia." *Rossiiane v Azii*, Toronto, 5 (1998): 25–83; 6 (1999): 29–104; 7 (2000): 93–149.

L.Iu. Khaindrova: serdtse poeta. Kaluga: Poligraf-Inform, 2003.

Lapiken, P.P. "Tsiui Iuan'. *Li Sao*." *NZh* 121 (1975): 285–9.

Lao-tzu: 'My Words are very easy to understand.' Lectures on Tao Teh Ching by Man-jan Cheng. Richmond, Calif.: North Atlantic Books, 1981.

Leont'ev, V. [Leonard]. "Valerii Frantsevich Salatko-Petrishche." *DOD* 52 (June 2000): 40–4.

Leyland, Winston, ed. *Gay Roots. Twenty Years of Gay Sunshine. An Anthology of Gay History, Sex, Politics, and Culture.* San Francisco: Gay Sunshine Press, 1991.

Leyland, Winston, ed. *Now the Volcano. An Anthology of Latin American Gay Literature.* San Francisco: Gay Sunshine Press, 1979.

"Lidiia Khaindrova." *Segodnia* 33, 15 September 1943 , 5–6, 25–6.
Lifshits-Losev, L. "Valerii Pereleshin. *Ariel'. Deviataia kniga stikhotvorenii.*" *RLJ* 32/111 (1978), 218–19.
Lilly, Ian K. *The Dynamics of Russian Verse*. Nottingham: Astra Press, 1995.
Lingva [Loginov, V.]. "Chudim i bormochem." *Gun-bao*, 5 May 1935.
Lingva [Loginov, V.]. "Grechnevaia kasha." *Gun-bao*, 24 May 1934. Quoted in VP, "A chto obo mne pisali polveka tomu nazad."
Linnik, Iurii. "Valerii Pereleshin." *NZh* 189 (1992): 227–56.
Lirika, V. "Russkaia Paskha v Rio-de-Zhaneiro." *NRS*, 12 May 1981.
Luganov, K. "Sem' let Churaevki." *Rubezh*, Harbin, 12/269, 18 March 1933.
Lukin, Iu.N. *V mire simvolov. K poznaniiu masonstva*. Harbin: 1936.
Malmstead, John, and Nikolay Bogomolov. *Mikhail Kuzmin: A Life in Art*. Cambridge, MA: Harvard University Press, 1999.
"Man'chzhuriskii konkurs poetov, organizovannyi Molodoi Churaevkoi." *Rubezh*, Harbin, 23/124, 31 May 1930.
Markov, V.F. "V zashchitu raznoudarnoi rifmy (Informativnyi obzor)." In *Russian Poetics*. 235–61. Ed. T. Eekman and D.S. Worth. UCLA Slavic Studies. Vol. 4. Columbus, OH: Slavica, 1982.
McVay, Gordon. *Esenin. A Life*. Ann Arbor, MI: Ardis, ca. 1976.
Medi, Nikolai. "Khristianstvo i gitlerism." *Segodnia* [22], 29 March 1943, 5–7, 23–4.
Meng, Li. *Queshide yihuan. Zai Hua Eguo qiaomin wenxue*. Beijing: Beijing University Press, 2007.
Meng, Li [Li Meng]. "Yige Eqiao shirende Zhongguo 'ai.'" *Wangxiang. Panorama* 2, no. 10 (October 2000): 79–92.
Meng, Li [Li Meng]. "Valerii Pereleshin i ego Kitai." *Problemy Dal'nego vostoka* 3 (2007): 135–52.
Meng Li [Li Meng]. "Russian Émigré Literature in China: A Missing Link." PhD diss., University of Chicago, 2004.
Meng, Li [Li Meng], and Richard D. Sylvester. "Valerii Pereleshin at the International Poetry Festival in Austin, Texas (April 1974)." *Toronto Slavic Quarterly* 14 (2005): 1–55.
M.I.M. "Rossiiskaia dukhovnaia missiia v Kitae (kratkii istoricheskii ocherk)." *Kitaiskii blagovestnik*, Beijing, November 1946, 20–5.
Mitskevich, Denis. "K opredeleniiu epigonstva." *RLJ* 90 (February 1971): 33–42.
Mitskevich, Denis. "O preemstvennosti v russkoi lirike." *RLJ* 87 (February 1970): 57–63.
M.K. [M.V. Kolobov]. *Bei-guan'. Rossiiskaia dukhovnaia missiia v Kitae*. Tianjin: Ideal Press, 1939.
"Molodaia Churaevka." *Rupor*, 25 September 1927.

"Molodoi bogoslov V. Salatko-Petrishche priniat poslushnikom v monastyr'." *KhV*, 25 December 1937.

Mokrinskaia, Nina (Fouchier). "Poslednie dni russkogo poeta." *RZh*, 11 February 1995.

Moravskii, N.V. "Ostrov Tubabao. 1949–1951." *Rossiiane v Azii*, ,Toronto, 4 (1994): 265–303.

Moss, Kevin, ed. *Out of the Blue. Russia's Hidden Gay Literature*. San Francisco: Gay Sunshine Press, 1997.

Mozhaiskaia, O. "Svirel' luny." *Grani* 71 (1969): 205–8.

My zhili togda na planete drugoi. Antologiia poezii russkogo zarubezh'ia, 1920–1990. 4 vols. Moscow: Moskovskii rabochii, 1995.

N.P. "Russkaia poeticheskaia i literaturnaia zhizn' v Kharbine i Shankhae." *RZh*, 23 May 1987.

N.R. [N. Reznikova]. "Knizhnye novinki." *Rubezh*, Harbin, 25/438, 13 June 1936.

N.R. [N. Reznikova]. "Valerii Pereleshin. *Zvezda nad morem*." *Rubezh*, Harbin, 44/717, 30 November 1941. Quoted in VP, "A chto obo mne pisali polveka tomu nazad."

N.Z. [N. Shchegolev]. "Velichaishii muzykant sovremennosti." *Segodnia* 23, 15 April 1943, 18–19.

Na Vostoke. Kaluga: izd-vo N. Bochkarevoi, 2000.

Nagel', V.S. *Pesni s Vostoka*. Adelaide, 1989.

"Nagrady inzh. V.F. Salatko-Petrishche i Liu I-tian'." *KhV*, 29 December 1937.

Nartsissov, Boris. "Pis'mo v redaktsiiu." *RZh*, 30 August 1975.

Nartsissov, Boris. "Valerii Pereleshin. *Iuzhnyi krest*, Antologiia brazil'skoi poezii." *NZh* 138 (1980): 237–8.

"Nashi interv'iu. Beseda s ukrainskim pisatelem Ulasom Samchukom. Beseda s belorusskim pisatelem Kastusei Akuloi." *Sovremennik* 35–36 (1977): 240–50.

"Ne vynesla dusha poeta." *KhV*, 4 April 1933.

Nesmelov, A. *Belaia flotiliia*. Harbin: 1942.

Nesmelov, A. "Iz literaturnogo proshlogo." *Oktiabr'*, 11 (1988), 144–9.

Nesmelov, A. "Stikhi odnoi temy." *Zaria*, 1 October 1939.

Nesmelov, A. "V etot den'." *Novyi mir*, 4 (1991), 135–46.

Nesmelov, A. "Vozvrashchenie." *Znamia*, 9 (1988), 76–86.

Nesmelov, A. "Vtoroi Moskovskii." *Golos rodiny*, 30 (1988).

News item. *Nash put'*, 8 July 1937.

Nikiforov, M.I. "Vozvrashchenie, ili Put' na Rodinu." *Russkie v Kitae* 19 (1999): 8–11.

Novye knigi SSSR, 25 (1990), 19.

"O misterioso poeta Pereléchin." *Lampião*, October 1979.

"O Rodine – izdaleka." *Golos rodiny* 51, December 1988.

"Ocherk vozniknoveniia i ustroeniia Kazansko-Bogoroditskogo Muzhskogo Monastyria v Kharbine." Supplement to *KhN* 11 (November 1934): 4.

"Ocherk vozniknoveniia i ustroeniia Kazansko-Bogoroditskogo Muzhskogo Monastyria v Kharbine." Supplement to *KhN* 7 (1939).

Odoevtseva, Irina. "Iz redaktorskoi pochty. Georgii Ivanov." *RM*, 22 June 1978.

Odoevtseva, Irina. "Valerii Pereleshin: *Kachel'*." *RM*, 7 November 1971.

Odoevtseva, Irina. "Vyiasnenie odnogo nedorazumeniia," *NRS*, 22 October 1969.

Ostrov. Sbornik stikhotvorenii. Shanghai: Drakon, 1946. [The copy in OB Collection belonged to Iu.V. Kruzenshtern-Peterets who pasted many unpublished poems by the members of the Friday Circle and their autographs.]

"Ot Gofmana do Pauliusa." *Segodnia* 23, 13 April 1943, 7–8, 27–9.

"Ot redaktsii." *KhN* 1 (1936).

"Otchet o sostoianii Bogoslovskogo Fakul'teta Instituta Sv. Vladimira za 1939 g." *KhN* 2 (1940): 33.

"Otkrytie Instituta Sviatogo Vladimira v g. Kharbine." *KhN* 11 (1934): 21–2.

"Otkrytie Instituta Sviatogo Vladimira v g. Kharbine." *Zaria*, 23 September and 8 October 1934.

Pachmuss, Temira, ed. and trans. *A Russian Cultural Revival. A Critical Anthology of Émigré Literature before 1939.* Knoxville: University of Tennessee Press, 1981.

Panin, Dm. "Otkrytoe pis'mo Alekseiu Kosachevu." *Sovremennik* 42 (1979): 151–3.

"Pamiati F.A. Kheig." *DOD* 7 (1969) 3–4.

"Parad poetov *Rubezha*." *Rubezh*, Harbin, 44/768, 30 November 1942.

Parro, K. [N. Peterets]. "Buria v literaturnoi chashke chaia." *Segodnia* 33, 15 September 1943, 13–20.

Pekinets. "Otkrytie Rossiiskogo doma v Pekine." *Vozrozhdenie Azii*, Tianjin, 14 December 1937.

"Pervyi den' poezii." *Vozrozhdenie* 228 (January 1971): 34–52; "Vtoroi den' poezii." 229 (February 1971): 38–51.

Peterets, N. Untitled typescript with comments on VP's "Angely." OB Collection.

Pis'ma zapreshchennykh liudei. Literatura i zhizn' emigratsii, 1950–1980-e gody. Po materialam arkhiva I.V. Chinnova. Moscow: IMLI RAN, 2003.

Plan vypuska literatury izdatel'stva Sovremennik, Moskva, 1991. Publisher's catalogue. Moscow: 1990, p. 16. BPL 3264/20 [10].

"Po sledam gazetnykh publikatsii." *Sovremennik* 37–38 (1978): 230–3.

Pomerantsev, K. "I malyi svoi talent pokryl bol'shim pozorom." *RM*, 8 June 1978.

"Postrizhenie v monashestvo i vozvedenie v san ieromonakha professora V.G. Pavlovskogo, nyne ieromonakha Sv. Vladimira." *KhN* 3 (1935): 34–6.

Pozdniaev, D. *Pravoslavie v Kitae.* Moscow: Izdatel'stvo Sviato-Vladimirskogo bratstva, 1998.

Pravlenie soiuza russkikh pisatelei i zhurnalistov v Parizhe. "Iz redaktorskoi pochty." *RM*, 22 June 1978.

Pravoslavnaia tserkov'. Kiev-Moscow: Monolit-Evrolints-Traditsiia, 2002.

"Prazdnik russkoi poezii." *Luch Azii* 79/3 (March 1941): 41–4.

"Prestol'nyi prazdnik i 15-letie Kazansko-Bogoroditskogo Muzhskogo Monastyria." *KhN* 7 (July 1939): 55.

Programma peredach Radio Vaticana na russkom iazyke za mesiats noiabr' 1980.

Puliaevskaia, Z. "Moe shankhaiskoe detstvo." *Russkie v Kitae* 11 (1998): 9–10.

Puliaevskaia, Z. "Moi otets." Supplement to *Russkie v Kitae* 17 (1999): 4.

Puliaevskaia, Z. "Odisseia nashego detstva (Otpravka detei iz Shankhaia)." *Russkie v Kitae* 5 (1996): 1–2.

Rachinskaia, E. "Dan' poetu." *NRS*, 21 June 1970, and *Edinenie*, Sydney, 8 May 1970.

Rachinskaia, E. "Zamolknuvshie golosa." Typescript. OB Collection.

Rannit, Aleksis. "Braziliia V. Pereleshina." *NRS*, 5 May 1974.

Rannit, Aleksis. "Kitai poeta Pereleshina." *RM*, 22 June 1972.

Rannit, Aleksis. "O poezii i poetike Valeriia Pereleshina – shest' pervykh sbornikov poeta (1937–1971)." *RLJ* 30/106 (1976): 79–104.

Rannit, Aleksis. "Valerii Pereleshin posle *Kacheli*." *RLJ* 32/113 (1978): 115–22.

Rudinskii, Vladimir. "Esenin – kak on byl." *NRS*, 31 October 1976.

Rudinskii, Vladimir. "Napraslina na Esenina." *NRS*, 29 August 1976.

Russkaia poeziia Kitaia. Compiled and edited by Vadim Kreyd and Olga Bakich. Moscow: Vremia, 2001.

Salatko, Victor. Excerpt from a letter. *BSO* 11 (1994): 38–9.

Salatko, Victor. [Excerpt from a letter]. *BSO* 17 (2000), 37.

Salatko, V.F. "Razocharovannye dali." *RZh*, 1, 2, 3, 4, 5, 8, and 9 November 1994.

Samarin, Vladimir. "Vozdukh Rossii." *NRS*, 23 January 1972.

Sankt-Peterburgskie Vysshie Zhenskie (Bestuzhevskie) kursy (1878–1918 gg.). Leningrad: Leningradskii universitet, 1965. 2nd rev. ed. 1973.

S.T. Kol'ridzh. Poema o starom moriake. Perevod i predislovie N. Gumileva. Petrograd: Vsemirnaia literatura, 1919.

Saranin, Alex. *Child of Kulaks*. Brisbane: University of Queensland Press, 1997.

Savskii, G. [G. Satovskii-Rzhevskii]. "Mudraia muza." *Zaria*. Quoted in VP, "A chto obo mne pisali polveka tomu nazad."

Scherr, Barry P. *Russian Poetry: Meter, Rhythm and Rhyme*. Berkeley: University of California Press, 1986.

Segodnia. Shanghai. Complete set of issues from March 1943 to 1 November 1943. Includes handwritten comments by Iu.V. Kruzenshtern-Peterets. OB Collection.

Semero. Harbin: Molodaia Churaevka, KhSML, 1931.
Sentianina, E.A. "Kharbinskie pisateli i poety." Co-written with Valerii Pereleshin. *Rubezh*, Harbin, 24/645, 8 June 1940; 25/646, 15 June 1940.
Sentianina, E.A. "Na pamiat'." *RZh*, 7 August 1981.
Sentianina, E.A. "Po iuzhnym moriam v Braziliiu." Typescript. BPL 3261/49.
Sentianina, E.A. "Pol'sha u russkogo poeta." *RM*, 4 October 1973.
Serebrennikovy, A.N. and I.I. *Tsvety kitaiskoi poezii*. Tianjin, 1938.
Sergeev, A. [S. Rafal'skii]. "Nezdorovaia sensatsiia." *NRS*, 6 November 1976.
Sergeev, A. [S. Rafal'skii]. "Periodika." *RM*, 19 August 1978.
Shchegolev, Nikolai. Typescript of a talk at the Friday Circle. OB Collection.
Shiliaev, E.P. "Pamiati brata, Andreia Shiliaeva, - russkogo l'va iz Kharbina." *Rossiiane v Azii*, Toronto, 5 (1998): 107–25.
Shtern, O. [Dm. Satovskii-Rzevskii]. "Vernyi drug russkoi molodezhi." *Rupor*, 8 October 1933.
Sinkevich, V. "Kartiny Portinari." *Perekrestki*, Philadelphia, 4 (1980): 28.
Sinkevich, V. "Valerii Pereleshin." *Vstrechi*, Philadelphia, (1993): 5–7.
"Skorbnaia stranitsa." *Politekhnik*, Sydney, 7 (1975): 126–126A.
Slobodchikov, N.A. "Kharbinskaia Churaevka." Typescript. OB Collection.
Slobodchikov, V.A. *O sud'be izgnannikov pechal'noi*. Moscow: Tsentrpoligraf, 2005.
"Slyshu sneg i pushkinskie iamby." *Golos rodiny* 3, January 1989.
Sodruzhestvo. Iz sovremennoi poezii Russkogo Zarubezh'ia. Washington, DC: Victor Kamkin, 1966.
Solov'eva, T.M. "Lirika Valeriia Pereleshina. Problematika i poetika. Avtoreferat dissertatsii." Moscow, 2002.
Somova, M.L. "Orkestru Lundstrema – 60 let." *Russkie v Kitae* 1 (1995): 5.
Somova, M.L. "Ponedel'nik, chetverg, piatnitsa." *Russkie v Kitae* 3 (1996): 2–4.
Somova, M.L. "Vozvrashchenie." *Russkie v Kitae* 5 (1996): 2–3.
"Spetsial'nyi vypusk Molodaia Churaevka." *KhSML zhurnal* 1 (January 1928).
Spravochnaia knizhka po lichnomu sostavu sluzhashchikh Kitaiskoi Vostochnoi zheleznoi dorogi na 1-e ianvaria 1917 goda. Harbin: KVzhd, 1917.
Stepanov, E. "Bukva zakona." *NRS*, 18 October 1954.
Stepanov, S.F. Typescript of his translations of Chinese poetry. OB Collection.
"Storozh u lampadki." *Moskovskii komsomolets*, 10 September 1989.
Straat, Kerk. "Valerii Pereleshin. Dva polustanka." Literary Supplement no. 3/4. *RM*, 5 June 1987.
"Strochki, zateriannye na chuzhbine." Introduction by Erast Indrikson. *Otchizna* 11 (November 1986): 56.
Struve, Gleb. *Russkaia literatura v izgnanii*. New York: Chekhov Publishing House, 1956.

Sutherland, Fraser, ed. *The Collected Poems and Translations of Edward A. Lacey*. Toronto: Colombo, 2000.
Tatishchev, Nik. "Derev'ia, kamni, slova." *RM*, 14 and 21 December 1967.
Terapiano, Iu. "Novye knigi." *RM*, 15 August 1968.
Terapiano, Iu. "Po povody pis'ma v redaktsiiu Iu. Kruzenshtern-Peterets." *RM*, 21 November 1968.
Terapiano, Iu. "Vynuzhdennyi otvet." *NRS*, 7 December 1969.
Ternavskii, S.T. *Ves' Kharbin na 1926 g*. Harbin: 1925.
Terras, Victor. *Handbook of Russian Literature*. New Haven: Yale University Press, ca. 1985.
Tetenov, M. Letter to the editor, and M. Skuratov, Letter to the editor. *Sovremennik* 35–36 (1977): 251–5.
Tjalsma, H.W., ed. *Outside of Russia: Anthology of Poetry Written by Russian Poets in Emigration, 1917–1975*. Russian title: *Vne Rossii. Antologiia emigrantskoi poezii*. Munich: Wilhelm Fink Verlag, 1979.
"Torzhestvennyi akt v Politekhnicheskom institute." *KhV*, 28 December 1937.
"Tragediia poeta Granina." *Zaria*, 4 April 1933.
Troitskaia, S. *Kharbinskaia eparkhiia, ee khramy i dukhovenstvo*. 2nd rev. ed. Brisbane: Author, 2005.
Tsepilov, N. "Posokh Vladyki Ioanna (Maksimovicha)." *Russkie v Kitae* 13 (1998): 18.
Tsvetaev, Valentin [N. Peterets]. "Koniushni shakhaiskogo Parnasa." *Novosti dnia*, Shanghai, February 1935.
U rodnykh rubezhei, Harbin, 2 (1943) (1942 on the cover). Harbin.
"Uspekh vechera poetov." *Zaria*, 28 May 1939.
"Valerii Pereleshin. "'... Slyshu sneg i pushkinskie iamby'." *Golos Rodiny* 3, January 1989.
"Valerii Pereleshin." *Ogonek* 29 (July 1989): 15.
"Valerii Perelishin [*sic*]. Poeziia." *Literaturnaia Armeniia*, May 1989, 64–6.
Val'. "Iz mestnykh literaturnykh nravov i obychaev." *Vecherniaia zaria*, Shanghai, 23 August 1943.
Velichkovskaia, Tamara. "O novom sbornike stikhov V. Pereleshina." *RM*, 21 June 1973.
Vernut'sia v Rossiiu stikhami. Compiled and edited by V. Kreyd. Moscow: Respublika, 1995.
Vershinin, Boris [N. Shchegolev]. "Bez mysli o tvorchestve." *Segodnia* [22], 29 March (1943): 16–19.
Vershinin, Boris [N. Shchegolev]. "Puti samopoznaniia." *Segodnia* 26 (1 June 1943): 9–12.
Vitkovskii, E. "Dan' zhivym." *Novyi mir* 9 (September 1989): 57–67.

Vitkovskii, E. "V. Pereleshin," and "Dva polustanka (fragment)." *Literaturnaia ucheba* 6 (November-December 1989): 110–24.

Vitkovskii, E. (Ariel). "Pamiati ushedshikh. 'V den' konchiny moei.' Pamiati Valeriia Pereleshina." *NZh* 190–1 (1993): 447–50.

Vitkovskii, E.V. [Soobshcheniia o publikatsii]. *Moskovskii literator* 25–26, 17 June 1988.

Vizi, M. [Mary Vezey]. "*Iz glubiny vozzvakh …*" *RZh*, 19 July 1987.

Vladimir, Ieromonakh. "Demon samoubiistva." *Katolicheskii vestnik*, Harbin, 2 (1935): 34–43.

"Vne literatury." *Segodnia* 30, 1 August 1943, 11, 21–3.

Vonk, Roland. "Russische dichter Valeri Perelesjin slijt zijn laatse dagen in Rio de Janeiro." *Leeuwarder Courant*, 16 June 1989.

Volin, Mikhail. "Russkie poety v Kitae." *Kontinent* 34 (1982): 337–57.

Volin, Mikhail. "Gibel' molodoi Churaevki." *NZh* 209 (1997): 216–40.

"Vostochno-aziatskii konkurs russkikh poetov i pisatelei." *Luch Azii* 91/3 (1942): 27–33.

Wachtel, Mikhael. *The Development of Russian Verse. Meter and Its Meanings.* Cambridge: Cambridge University Press, 1998.

Warner, Michael. *Fear of a Queer Planet: Queer Politics and Social Theory.* Minneapolis: University of Minnesota Press, 1993.

Woods, Gregory. *A History of Gay Literature. The Male Tradition.* New Haven: Yale University Press, 1998.

Wyler, Vivian. "Quando traduzir pode ser também um ato de gratidão." *Jornal do Brasil*, 8 September 1979.

Z-n, V. [Zavalishin, V.]. "Novyi sbornik Valeriia Pereleshina." *NRS*, 4 March 1973.

Z-n, V. [Zavalishin, V.]. "Piataia kniga Valeriia Pereleshina." *NRS*, 11 January 1969.

Zaitsev, Georgii. "Put' na Rodinu." *Russkie v Kitae* 5 (1996): 3.

"Zametka redaktora. Nemnogo o klounade i printsipakh." *Sovremennik* 43–44 (1979) 208–12.

Zeeler, V.F. "Spravedlivo li?" *RM*, 20 October 1954.

Zhebit [Jebit], A. "Literaturnoe nasledie 'sen'ora Valerio.' Brazil'skii arkhiv 'sen'ora Valerio.'" *Nashe nasledie* 46 (1998): 108–13.

Zhiganov, D. *Russkie v Shankhae.* Album. Shanghai: Author. Several unpaginated editions, 1936–9.

"Zhizn' poeta G.I. Granina spasena." *Rupor*, 4 April 1933.

Index

www.ingramcontent.com/pod-product-compliance
Lightning Source LLC
LaVergne TN
LVHW040153080826
844660LV00014B/950/J
9781442648920